Urban Economics
A Global Perspective

D0148088

Urban Economics
A Global Perspective

Paul N. Balchin

Reader in Urban Economics
University of Greenwich

David Isaac

Professor of Real Estate Development
University of Greenwich

Jean Chen

Lecturer in Financial Management
University of Surrey

palgrave

© Paul N. Balchin, David Isaac and Jean Chen 2000

All rights reserved. No reproduction, copy or transmission of this publication may be made without written permission.

No paragraph of this publication may be reproduced, copied or transmitted save with written permission or in accordance with the provisions of the Copyright, Designs and Patents Act 1988, or under the terms of any licence permitting limited copying issued by the Copyright Licensing Agency, 90 Tottenham Court Road, London W1P 0LP.

Any person who does any unauthorised act in relation to this publication may be liable to criminal prosecution and civil claims for damages.

The authors have asserted their rights to be identified as the authors of this work in accordance with the Copyright, Designs and Patents Act 1988

First published 2000 by
PALGRAVE
Houndmills, Basingstoke, Hampshire RG21 6XS and
175 Fifth Avenue, New York, N.Y. 10010
Companies and representatives throughout the world

PALGRAVE is the new global academic imprint of
St. Martin's Press LLC Scholarly and Reference Division and
Palgrave Publishers Ltd (formerly Macmillan Press Ltd.)

ISBN 0–333–77128–1

This book is printed on paper suitable for recycling and made from fully managed and sustained forest sources.

A catalogue record for this book is available from the British Library.

10 9 8 7 6 5 4 3 2 1
09 08 07 06 05 04 03 02 01 00

Printed in Great Britain by
Creative Print & Design (Wales), Ebbw Vale

330.91732
B1744

Contents

v

List of Figures

List of Tables

xi

List of Boxes

List of Abbreviations

ACCs	Advanced capitalist countries
AFID	Agency for International Development
AFTRP	*L'Agence Foncière et Technique de la Région Parisienne*
AQSs	Air quality standards
ASH	Aided self-help
BICC	Bank of Industrial Commerce and Credit
BP	British Petroleum
CBA	Cost–benefit analysis
CBD	Central Business District
CCP	Comprehensive Community Programme
CDPs	Community Development Projects
CEC	Commission of the European Community
CED	Community Economic Development
CFCs	Chlorofluorocarbons
CMSAs	Consolidated metropolitan statistical areas
CO_2	Carbon dioxide
COMECON	Council for Mutual Economic Assistance
CPO	Compulsory purchase order
CSHA	Commonwealth State Housing Agreement
CVM	Contingent valuation methods
DETR	Department of the Environment, Transport and the Regions
DLGs	Derelict land grants
DoE	Department of the Environment
EBDR	European Bank for Reconstruction and Development
EC	European Community
ECU	European currency unit
EQSs	Environmental quality standards
ERDF	European Regional Development Fund
EU	European Union
EUV	Existing use value
EZs	Enterprise zones
FDI	Foreign direct investment
FRG	Federal Republic of Germany
FRI	Full repairing and insuring (lease)
FTZs	Free trade zones
FURs	Functional urban regions

GATT	General Agreement on Tariffs and Trade
GDP	Gross domestic product
GDV	Gross development value
GLC	Greater London Council
GNP	Gross national product
HIP	Housing investment programmes
HIPC	Heavily Indebted Poor Country Initiative
HK	Hong Kong
HMCs	Housing management companies
HMPI	Her Majesty's Inspectorate of Pollution
HSBC	Hong Kong & Shanghai Banking Corporation
IBM	International Business Machines
IDC(s)	Industrial development certificate(s)
ILO	International Labour Office
IROs	Integrated regional offices
JVs	Joint ventures
LEBs	Local enterprise boards
LDC	Land Development Corporation
LIT	Local income tax
LST	Local sales tax
LVT	Land value taxation
MIR	Mortgage Interest Relief
MSC	Multimedia Super Corridor
MTR	Mass transit railway
NAFTA	North American Free Trade Agreement
NATO	North Atlantic Treaty Organization
NAV	Net annual value
NCDP	National Community Development Project
NICs	Newly-industrializing countries
NO_x	Nitrogen oxides
NRA	National Rivers Authority
NUDSP	National Urban Development Strategy Project
ODPs	Office development permits
OECD	Organization for Economic Co-operation and Development
PCUP	Presidential Commission on Urban Poor
PHARE	*Pologne et Hongrie Assistance pour le Réstructuration Économique*
PRC	People's Republic of China
PSBS	Private sector partnership schemes
RDG(s)	Regional development grant(s)
RICS	Royal Institution of Chartered Surveyors
RMB	Renminbi
RSA	Regional selective assistance

RTB	Right to buy
SEZ(s)	Special Economic Zone(s)
SME	Small and medium-sized enterprises
SO$_2$	Sulphur dioxide
SOC	Social opportunity cost
SOE(s)	State-owned enterprise(s)
SRB	Single regeneration budget
STP	Social rate of time preference
SVR	Site-value rating
TEV	Total economic value
TNCs	Transnational corporations
TSM	Transportation system management
UAR	United Arab Emirates
UDAG(s)	Urban development action grant(s)
UDCs	Urban development corporations
UHRU	Urban Housing Renewal Unit
UK	United Kingdom
UN	United Nations
UNDP	United Nations Development Programme
UPA	Urban Priority Areas
URGs	Urban regeneration grants
US(A)	United States (of America)
USAID	United States Agency for International Aid
VAT	Value added tax
WCED	World Commission on Environment and Development
WHO	World Health Organization
ZACs	*Zones d'Aménagement Concerté*
ZADs	*Zones d'Aménagement Déféré*

Preface

Urban Economics has developed as a separate discipline since it evolved from neo-classical economics in the early twentieth century. It has subsequently absorbed many aspects of Keynesian and Marxian economics, but it also uses data, information and theory derived from studies in demography, sociology, geography, real estate development and investment, urban planning and environmental studies in order to shed light on economic processes and to assist in the formulation of urban economic theory.

Increasingly, it is recognized that urban economics – like mainstream economics – can only be studied or applied effectively within a global context. National boundaries are no defence against the adverse effects of world economic trends anymore than they are a safeguard against the spread of pollution, but neither are periods of economic growth nor an enhanced environment always confined to one nation state at a time.

The purpose of this book is thus to provide a key text on urban economics in a global context, and as such it should be essential reading for students on university degree courses on Development Economics, Environmental Studies, Geography, Real Estate Development and Investment, Urban Planning and Urban Sociology.

The book has been published at a time when the role of the city in the global economy is again attracting attention, after a long period in which – in developed countries at least – attention has been focused on the drift of population and economic activity from the urban core to the suburbs or the countryside.

It was not that long ago that – in reviewing urban development from its origins to the first half of the twentieth century – Lewis Mumford (1938), in *Culture of Cities*, concluded 'that the great city is doomed . . . that Megalopolis, the giant multi-million city, represented a station on the way to necropolis' (Hall, 1998: 6). But at the end of the century, Sir Peter Hall convincingly argued that 'we are as far as ever from seeing the destruction of the giant city. On the contrary: rechristened the Global City, it disproportionately attracts the organizations that command and control the new global economy, as well as the specialist service agencies that minister to them' (Hall, 1998: 7). Hall – in his explanation of the growth of large cities – reminds us that: Athens (*the fountainhead*) introduced our notion of civilization between 500 and 400 BC, while – much later – Florence, London, Vienna, Paris and Berlin witnessed the flourishing of the arts and sciences; Manchester (*the first industrial city*) was the crucible of the Industrial

Revolution between 1760 and 1830, with major innovations in industrial processes taking place in such cities as Glasgow, Berlin, Detroit, San Francisco, Palo/Berkeley and Tokyo–Kanagawa over the following century and a half; Los Angeles (*the dream factory*) and Memphis facilitated the marriage of art and technology in the twentieth century; and the establishment and maintenance of urban order were responsible – in their quite different socio-political ways – for the survival and growth of Rome (*the imperial city*), London, Paris, New York, Los Angeles and Stockholm.

Within a global context, the 'command and control' functions of urban development were recognized as early as the Industrial Revolution and have subsequently had a considerable impact on large cities, not only in economically-developed countries but also in the developing world – an impact that is increasing in magnitude with the ascendency and consolidation of the free market throughout much of the global economy. Marx and Engels – in *The Communist Manifesto* – foresaw and predicted the fundamental economic attributes of globalization that we observe at present. One of their most relevant passages states that 'The need of a constantly expanding market for its products chases the bougeoisie over the whole surface of the globe. It must nestle everywhere, settle everywhere, establish connexions everywhere . . . All old established national industries have been destroyed . . . [and] . . . in place of the old wants, satisfied by the productions of the country, we find new ones, requiring for their satisfaction the products of distant lands' (Marx and Engels, 1848; 1985 edition: 83–4).

Arguably, the contemporary urban world is far more complex. Urbanization and urban growth are indeed changing the location of economic activity, but in different ways and in different places. There are not only wide variations in the proportion of national or regional populations living in towns and cities, but also in the way in which – over the years – economic, social and political forces have helped to shape and reshape the global built-environment. At the beginning of the new millennium, the environment has become centre stage, but while the causes of environmental affliction vary from country to country, solutions need to be applied on a global scale if sustained development – and not least urban development – are to be attained.

In reflecting on this scenario, the subject matter of this book is compartmentalized in each chapter into a consideration of urban economic factors relating to advanced capitalist countries; countries in political and economic transition; and countries that are newly-industrializing or developing. Overall, the book attempts to analyze the interrelationships between demographic and economic change, consequential changes in urban land use, development and planning, and the economics of the environment. Chapter 1 provides an introductory examination of urbanization. Chapter 2 deals with urban growth. Chapter 3 sets out to distinguish between different patterns of urban structure. Chapter 4 considers housing provision, housing need, tenure, and the condition and location of housing. Chapter 5 seeks to explain the location of non-residential urban land uses. Chapter 6 examines the processes of urban development. Chapter 7 explores the attributes of property development. Chapter 8 analyzes the principles of property investment. Chapter 9 discusses the economics of urban planning and the role of land and property taxation. Chapter 10 focuses on the environment, urban congestion and transportation, and Chapter 11 concludes by considering the possible direction and consequences of urbanization and urban growth in the early years of the twenty-first century.

In writing this book, we were continually aware of being overtaken by demographic, economic, political and social events. Urban economics – particularly when related to global development – is often plagued by major differences in public policy and by the difficulties of accessing and interpreting comparable data. However, every effort has been made to ensure that legislative and statistical detail is – as far as possible – accurate at the time of going to press.

We must acknowledge a debt we owe to Christopher Glennie of Macmillan Press for his kind encouragement and advice throughout the production of this book, Bill Perry for painstakingly co-editing the transcript and Gregory Bull for contributing a substantial part of Chapter 10, as well as for some of the content of other chapters. Thanks are also due to present and past colleagues who have advised or inspired us in the production of this book, and we are particularly grateful to Sue Brimacombe and Pauline Newell who helped to type and collate much of the material used in this book, and to Sue Lee, Peter Stevens and Angela Alwright who produced many of the drawings. Finally we would like to thank our respective families for the continual patience they showed throughout the preparation of this book.

Paul Balchin
David Isaac
Jean Chen

REFERENCES

Hall, P. (1998) *Cities in Civilization*, London: Weidenfeld & Nicolson.
Marx, K. and Engels, F. (1848; 1985 edition) *The Communist Manifesto*, Harmonsworth: Penguin.
Mumford, L. (1938) *The Culture of Cities*, New York: Harcourt, Brace.

1

Introduction

URBANIZATION

An increasing proportion of the rapidly growing world population is attempting to satisfy its economic and social needs in an urban context. The enormous migration of people into towns and cities is producing a distinct possibility of an uncontrollable urban explosion – an unprecedented increase in population, greater demands on the urban infrastructure, higher levels of pollution and a decrease in the non-material (and in some cases material) standard of living.

There are five major forces determining the pace of urbanization throughout the world: economic growth and development; technological change; a rapid growth in the total population; a large-scale movement of people from rural areas to cities; and, in some countries, a net outward movement of population from cities to towns and villages. Despite recessions in recent years, the world production of goods and services continues to increase. As a result of improvements in telecommunications, transportation and the supply of power, production becomes *more* rather than less concentrated in those locations, and offers the greatest comparative advantages. These tend to be increasingly large metropolitan-centred market areas, or 'world cities'. This trend is compounded by the simultaneous growth of large, often transnational, companies which, with their increasing market dominance and internal and external economies of scale, form an interdependent relationship with areas of large population and high purchasing power.

Economic growth since the Industrial Revolution of the eighteenth and nineteenth centuries has had a direct effect upon mortality. An improved food supply, better living conditions and medical advances have all led to a decline in death rates – in Britain, for example, from 30 per 1,000 of the population in 1750 to 11 per 1,000 in 1995. While birth rates in industrial countries have also been declining – in Britain from 35 to 12 per 1,000 between 1750 and 1995 – the rate of fertility has remained very high in many developing countries, often in excess of 4 per woman of child-bearing age. Recently the population of the world has been growing by about 1.9 per cent per annum, a rate of increase unparalleled in history. Although it took from palaeolithic times to 1850 for the world population to reach 1,000 million, by 1925 this number had doubled and by 1962 it had trebled. By the 1980s, the world population exceeded 5,000 million and by 1999 it had increased to 6,000 million.

Small settlements are incapable, however, of evolving into major cities solely through the process of natural population increase – the migration of people from the countryside is an equally or more important determinant of growth. Apart from the economic 'pull' of towns there is also the 'push' effect of agricultural change such as land-reform or the application of capital-intensive farming. In global terms there has thus been a decrease in the ratio of the rural population to the total population, and a reciprocal increase in the relative size of the urban population. By the year 2000 more than 50 per cent of the world's population of 6 billion lived in urban areas, compared to only 15 per cent in 1900 and 2 per cent in 1700. However, country by country, the level of urbanization varies considerably, for example from 100 per cent in Singapore or 97 per cent in Belgium in 1996, to as little as 6 per cent in Rwanda. As a global phenomenon, urbanization became a major feature of the late twentieth century. Every year, an average of 312 million more people were added to the world's towns and cities than to its rural areas (Clark, 1996). The urban population as a proportion of the world's population is set to rise to even higher levels in the new millennium, particularly in the poorer countries of the world where urban population growth was running at about 3 per cent per annum at the end of the twentieth century, greatly ahead of employment opportunities in the formal sectors of economy, particularly manufacturing (Dickenson *et al.*, 1996: 194).

Historically and geographically, it was evident that low levels of economic development and the failure to generate sufficiently large surplus products imposed a limit on the number of people that could be sustained in urban places. However, 'this constraint was broken irrevocably and irreversibly when industrialisation raised levels of economic output to unprecedented levels' (Clark, 1996: 59) and provided the conditions for self-perpetuating urbanization.

In examining the relationship between economic development and levels of urbanization, it is important to distinguish between the effects of indigenous growth on urbanization – focusing on the 'stages' model of economic growth, and the consequences of nationally or internationally diffused growth as set out in the interdependency theory.

THE STAGES OF ECONOMIC GROWTH AND LEVELS OF URBANIZATION

The process of urbanization follows very broadly the same time-sequence as the process of economic growth. Rostow's (1960) *The Stages of Eco-*

nomic Growth defined and analyzed five stages of economic growth. Accordingly, in a 'traditional society', long-lived economic and social systems and customs are associated with low output per head and the absence of a 'surplus' – a 'quantity of material resources and product that is appropriated for one segment of society at the expense of others' (Potter and Lloyd-Evans, 1998: 34). This stage tends to be replaced eventually by the establishment of the pre-conditions for 'take-off' in which the economy becomes capable of exploiting the products of modern science and technology and yielding a surplus. 'Take-off' is reached when surpluses – in the form of profit – generate investment and technological improvements, and ensure that growth yields even larger surpluses and becomes virtually self-sustaining and the normal condition of the economy. This in turn will stimulate a 'drive to maturity', at which stage steady growth provides the background for the development of import-substituting and export industries, and the economy is increasingly able to absorb and apply the fruits of modern technology. The fifth stage occurs when a country reaches an 'age of high mass consumption' and an affluent population enjoys an abundance of durable consumer goods and services.

However, with regard to urbanization, the principal disparities – with notable exceptions – are: between the advanced capitalist countries – with high levels of urbanization; countries in political and economic transition – with moderate levels of urbanization; and newly-industrializing and developing countries – with low levels of urbanization. Globally, distinctive 'push' and 'pull' factors result in disparities in the rate of rural–urban migration and consequential levels of urbanization – producing, on a world-wide scale, a positive relationship between economic development (as indicated by GDP per capita) and urbanization (figure 1.1).

The advanced capitalist countries (ACCs)

When the ACCs were experiencing economic 'take-off', the dominant 'push factor' in rural–urban migration was the reduced demand for rural labour as a consequence of increasing agricultural productivity, while the dominant 'pull factor' was industrial development in existing or newly-established urban locations. Initially, urbanization proceeded gradually, but this was followed by a period of accelerated growth as the drive towards economic 'maturity' gathered pace. However soon after levels of urbanization reached 50 per cent, the growth curve began to flatten out as countries entered an 'age of high mass consumption' – a time in which urban populations reached 75 per cent of the total (Potter and Lloyd-Evans, 1998). During the nineteenth and early twentieth centuries – and for the first and last time – industrialization and urbanization thus occurred simultaneously.

Table 1.1 shows that, among the ACCs during the 1990s, a very small proportion of the working population was employed in agriculture and an

Table 1.1 Population, economic indicators and urbanization, selected countries, 1996

	Fertility rate (per woman)	Birth rate per 1,000 pop.	Death rate per 1,000 pop.	Average annual growth in pop. 1990–2000	Structure of employment (per cent)		
					Agriculture	Industry	Services
Advanced capitalist countries							
Belgium	1.6	11.2	11	0.30	3	31	66
Netherlands	1.6	11.9	9	0.60	4	22	74
United Kingdom	1.7	12.0	11	0.14	2	27	78
Germany	1.3	9.3	11	0.41	3	35	72
New Zealand	2.0	15.4	8	1.13	9	25	66
Denmark	1.8	13.0	12	0.26	4	27	69
Australia	1.9	14.3	7	1.10	5	23	72
Sweden	1.8	11.9	11	0.39	3	26	71
Japan	1.5	10.3	8	0.24	5	33	62
Canada	1.6	11.9	7	0.99	4	23	73
United States	2.0	13.8	9	0.90	3	24	73
Spain	1.2	9.7	9	0.14	9	30	61
Norway	1.9	13.4	11	0.39	5	23	72
France	1.6	11.6	9	0.41	5	27	68
Italy	1.2	9.1	10	0.03	7	41	52
Greece	1.4	10.0	10	0.36	20	23	57
Finland	1.8	12.0	10	0.38	7	27	66
Switzerland	1.5	10.9	9	0.81	4	28	68
Ireland	1.8	13.0	9	0.20	11	27	62
Austria	1.4	10.3	10	0.73	6	29	65
Portugal	1.5	11.2	11	−0.09	12	31	57
Average	1.6	10.7	10	0.40	6	28	66
Countries in political and economic transition							
Russia Federation	1.4	9.6	14	−0.15	16	34	50
Bulgaria	1.5	10.3	13	−0.49	14	50	36
Czech Republic	1.4	10.7	12	−0.11	6	42	58
Hungary	1.4	10.2	15	−0.55	13	35	52
Poland	1.7	11.9	11	0.16	22	32	46
Slovakia	1.5	11.7	11	0.22	9	37	54
Romania	1.4	11.0	11	−0.31	38	32	30
Average	1.5	10.8	12	−0.13	17	37	46

Origins of GDP 1995 (per cent)				GDP per capita (US$)	Average annual growth in real GDP 1990–96	Urban population (per cent)
Agriculture	Industry	Manufacturing	Services			
1.3	30.7	22.9	68.0	26,440	1.2	97
3.3	28.2	n.a.	68.5	25,850	2.2	89
1.8	26.5	21.3	71.7	19,810	1.6	89
1.0	32.3	n.a.	66.7	28,860	2.8	87
8.0	25.0	18.5	67.0	15,850	3.3	86
4.1	28.6	19.6	67.3	32,250	2.2	85
8.4	23.5	17.1	68.1	20,370	3.7	85
2.2	27.0	21.6	70.8	25,770	0.6	83
1.9	38.0	24.7	60.1	41,080	1.4	78
2.6	30.5	21.3	66.9	19,200	1.9	77
1.7	22.9	17.4	75.4	27,590	2.4	76
3.7	33.5	n.a.	62.8	14,200	1.3	76
2.2	30.0	n.a.	67.8	34,780	3.9	73
2.5	23.5	n.a.	74.0	26,290	1.1	73
3.4	33.2	n.a.	63.4	19,930	1.0	67
11.2	25.3	n.a.	63.5	11,440	1.6	65
5.0	33.1	25.1	61.9	23,230	0.3	61
2.6	32.1	n.a.	65.3	43,420	−0.3	61
8.0	38.0	n.a.	54.0	17,450	6.1	58
2.1	35.2	n.a.	62.7	27,940	1.6	56
4.1	36.1	n.a.	59.8	10,290	1.4	36
3.9	30.2	20.9	65.9	24,383	2.0	74
6.4	37.9	n.a.	55.7	2,410	−9.0	76
11.7	32.6	n.a.	55.7	1,190	−3.5	71
5.0	40.6	n.a.	54.4	4,770	−1.0	65
7.2	31.8	n.a.	61.0	4,441	−0.4	65
6.0	32.4	n.a.	61.6	3,230	3.2	65
5.2	31.0	n.a.	63.8	3,400	−1.0	59
19.1	42.2	n.a.	38.7	1,600	0	55
11.2	35.5	n.a.	53.3	3,006	−2.1	65

continued

Table 1.1 continued

	Fertility rate (per woman)	Birth rate per 1,000 pop.	Death rate per 1,000 pop.	Average annual growth in pop. 1990–2000	Structure of employment (per cent)		
					Agriculture	Industry	Services
Newly-industrializing and developing countries							
Singapore	1.8	15.7	5	1.73	0	30	70
Hong Kong	1.3	10.6	6	1.11	0	26	74
Venezuela	3.0	24.9	5	2.15	13	24	63
Argentina	2.6	19.9	8	1.30	2	25	73
Chile	2.4	29.9	6	1.50	16	26	58
South Korea	1.7	15.0	6	0.90	12	32	36
Saudi Arabia	5.9	34.3	4	3.00	5	26	69
Brazil	2.2	19.6	7	1.34	26	20	54
Taiwan	1.8	15.1	6	1.14	10	37	53
Mexico	2.8	24.6	5	1.73	22	18	60
Iraq	5.3	36.4	9	2.46	n.a.	n.a.	n.a.
Colombia	2.7	23.4	6	1.77	n.a.	n.a.	n.a.
Peru	3.0	24.9	7	1.74	36	18	46
Turkey	2.5	21.9	7	1.59	46	22	32
Iran	4.8	34.0	6	2.55	39	23	38
Algeria	3.8	29.2	6	2.37	2	25	73
Malaysia	3.2	25.2	5	2.21	19	32	49
Philippines	3.6	28.4	6	2.11	42	17	41
South Africa	3.8	29.7	8	2.22	11	25	64
Morocco	3.1	25.3	7	1.87	4	36	60
Egypt	3.4	26.1	7	1.91	34	22	44
Cameroon	5.3	39.3	12	2.76	70	9	21
Côte d'Ivoire	5.1	37.2	14	2.60	60	10	30
Nigeria	6.0	42.3	14	2.92	43	7	50
Indonesia	2.6	23.1	8	1.51	44	18	38
Pakistan	5.0	36.1	8	2.70	44	18	38
Zimbabwe	4.7	37.1	14	2.32	68	8	24
China	1.8	16.2	7	1.00	48	21	31
Kenya	4.9	36.9	11	2.57	80	7	13
India	3.1	25.2	9	1.69	64	16	20
Thailand	1.7	16.7	6	0.85	53	n.a.	n.a.
Bangladesh	3.1	26.8	10	1.57	63	10	27
'Four Tigers'*	1.7	14.1	6	1.22	6	31	63
Other newly-industrializing and developing countries	3.6	28.4	8	2.01	37	18	45

* Singapore, Hong Kong, South Korea and Taiwan.

Source: Economist (1998).

Origins of GDP 1996 (per cent)				GDP per capita (US$)	Average annual growth in real GDP 1990–96	Urban population (per cent)
Agriculture	Industry	Manufacturing	Services			
0.2	35.5	26.0	64.3	27,480	8.7	100
0.1	15.4	7.2	84.5	24,760	5.9	95
5.5	40.8	16.2	53.7	3,020	1.9	93
7.2	35.2	24.3	57.6	8,380	4.9	88
7.1	35.9	17.8	57.0	4,860	7.2	84
6.4	44.1	30.0	49.5	10,660	7.3	81
6.3	53.4	9.4	40.3	7,240	1.7	80
10.7	42.0	28.3	47.3	4,410	2.9	78
3.3	35.8	28.2	60.9	12,880	6.6	75
5.4	26.3	19.6	68.3	3,690	1.8	75
5.1	72.9	11.6	22.0	1,095	4.2	75
20.6	29.1	19.2	50.3	2,140	4.5	73
12.9	37.1	23.3	50.0	2,420	1.3	72
17.6	29.3	n.a.	53.1	2,870	3.6	69
25.2	34.4	n.a.	40.4	1,302	4.2	59
10.3	67.1	n.a.	22.6	1,520	0.6	56
12.8	46.2	34.3	41.0	4,360	8.7	54
21.4	31.8	22.6	46.8	1,160	2.9	54
4.7	34.9	23.8	60.3	3,130	1.2	51
20.4	30.5	16.9	49.1	1,290	2.1	48
16.6	33.8	n.a.	49.6	1,080	3.7	45
33.5	21.1	10.2	45.4	610	−1.0	45
30.7	19.4	13.4	49.9	660	2.4	44
37.3	19.6	6.5	43.1	240	2.6	39
16.3	41.6	24.6	42.1	1,080	7.7	35
24.8	26.4	18.1	48.8	480	4.6	35
17.5	22.2	17.9	60.3	610	1.3	32
19.9	48.6	n.a.	31.5	750	12.3	30
30.3	n.a.	10.4	59.3	320	1.9	28
28.8	29.2	n.a.	41.2	380	5.8	27
11.8	38.6	29.3	49.6	3,020	8.3	20
29.8	15.2	9.3	55.0	260	4.3	18
2.5	32.7	22.9	64.8	18,984	7.1	88
17.5	35.8	18.5	47.7	2,228	3.9	54

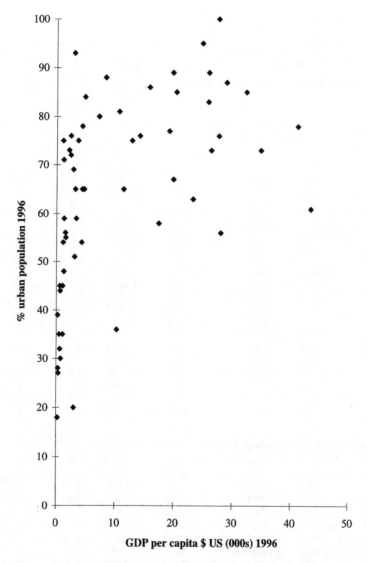

Figure 1.1 *The relationship between economic development and urbanization on a worldwide scale*

even smaller proportion of GDP was derived from that sector. The working population was predominantly employed in service activities and the GDP was overwhelmingly derived from this sector (industry, and particularly manufacturing, performing a proportionately more important role in the nineteenth and early twentieth centuries). Low fertility rates, low birth rates and even lower death rates accounted for a slow average annual growth in population. These countries thus enjoyed a high GDP per capita (despite a relatively modest rate of growth in the real GDP per capita per annum) and sustained a high level of urbanization.

Countries in political and economic transition

Although the countries currently in the process of transition – the nations of East Central Europe and the Russian Federation – experienced industrialization and urbanization in broadly the same way as the ACCs, albeit later in the nineteenth century or in the early twentieth century, land reform and agricultural changes – which occurred subsequently under socialist governments – failed to generate large-scale migration to the towns and cities, while simultaneously industrialization was proceeding at a rapid pace. With birth rates falling ahead of death rates, both population growth and urbanization often lagged seriously behind industrialization in many regions of the Eastern bloc.

Table 1.1 shows that in the 1990s, countries in transition still had a significantly higher proportion of their working population employed in agriculture, and the agricultural sector accounted for a much larger proportion of the GDP. Although the service sector was dominant in terms of employment and output, industry (including manufacturing) played a more important role than in the ACCs. Marginally lower fertility rates and birth rates (but higher death rates) resulted in a decrease in population, a decrease in the annual rate of growth in real GDP and a comparatively lower level of urbanization.

Newly-industrializing and developing countries

In the newly-industrializing and developing countries, rural–urban migration – as is normally the case – was the outcome of a combination of push and pull factors. The former comprised the commercialization of agriculture, the consequential squeezing-out of subsistence agriculture, a high incidence of drought and famine, and the prevalence of wars and disease, while the latter included the development of import-substituting industries and the superior health-care facilities of urban areas (Potter and Lloyd-Evans, 1998).

It was not surprising that industrialization took place mainly in the primary gateway cities – for example, in the principal ports – where infrastructure and markets were comparatively well developed. With birth rates remaining high and with a big reduction in death rates, the urban population has been growing at a very rapid rate, often in excess of 6 per cent per annum and frequently by more than 10 per cent (Potter and Lloyd-

Evans, 1998). In contrast to the more developed areas of the world during the heyday of their Industrial Revolution, urbanization in the less developed world is often running dramatically ahead of industrialization and is occurring at an unprecedented rate (Potter and Lloyd-Evans, 1998). Clearly, 'the simple association which previously held between cities, industry and modernization has broken down' (Potter, 1992: 5).

The newly-industrializing countries (NICs) are far from being an homogeneous group. Some are rapidly 'maturing' economies and are almost indistinguishable from countries of the developed world (and, in terms of urban design and architecture, their cities might appear to be even ahead of those in the developed world); others – the 'contemporary' NICs – are consolidating their economic gains, while a third group – the 'emerging' NICs – still retain many of the features of developing countries.

The 'maturing' newly-industrializing economies of Singapore, the Special Administrative Region of Hong Kong, South Korea and Taiwan (the 'Four Tigers'), together with Chile and Argentina, are clearly on the threshold of absorbing all the attributes of advanced capitalism and experiencing an 'age of high mass-consumption'. Table 1.1 reveals that (like the ACCs) they have a very small proportion of their workforce employed in agriculture, and the sector makes only a minor contribution to the GDP. The service sector is the principal employer and the largest contributor to the GDP (with industry, and particularly manufacturing, producing a smaller share of the GDP than it achieved in the 1960s–1970s). However, in contrast to the ACCs, these countries experienced fairly high birth rates and a rapid rate of increase in population in the 1990s, substantial annual rates of growth in real GDP, high GDPs per capita and high levels of urbanization.

Table 1.1 shows that among the 'contemporary' NICs (such as Brazil, Mexico, Colombia, Turkey, Malaysia, Philippines, Indonesia, Thailand and India), agriculture is the largest or second largest employer and contributor to the GDP, and the export of goods is very evident in 'the drive to maturity'. Fertility rates and birth rates are high, as are death rates, but population growth is rapid. However, although the rate of growth of the real GDP per annum is high, the GDP per capita and level of urbanization are still relatively low. China, however, although having many of the attributes of contemporary NICs, has low fertility and birth rates, low population growth and a comparatively low GDP per capita. Despite its rapid economic growth, China still has a low level of urbanization.

'Emerging' NICs, such as Vietnam, are undoubtedly at the 'take-off' stage and are 'beginning to implement economic measures leading to an increase in industrial output and have the requisite foundations for becoming NICs' (Chang and Spinelli, 1998: 264). However, there is a need to ensure that industrialization gathers pace in parallel with urbanization. In postwar

Vietnam, there was a massive decline in urban population in an attempt by communist elites to eliminate the power and influence of the urban bourgeoisie or petty bourgeoise. It therefore remains to be seen what effects economic growth will have on the level of urbanization.

Although the 'developing' countries of, for example, Cameroon, Côte d'Ivoire, Nigeria, Zimbabwe and Kenya all aim to secure the pre-conditions for 'take-off', economic potential has been constrained by a very large agricultural sector both in terms of employment and its contribution to the GDP, by small industrial and service sectors, and by international debt. Despite high fertility rates and birth rates, high death rates act as a brake on rapid population increase, and there are only low rates of economic growth, very low GDPs per capita and a comparatively low level of urbanization (see table 1.1).

In each of the major economic regions of the world, there is a clear, but distinctive, relationship between population increase, the extent to which levels of urbanization have risen and GNP per capita. This is examined below for each of the main economic regions in turn.

The Advanced Capitalist Regions

The European Union

The European Union has experienced the slowest population growth of any of the world's regions in recent years, for example – between 1975 and 1990 – the population increased by as little as 0.5 per cent per annum, diminishing to 0.3 per cent per annum between 1990 and 2000 (table 1.2). Consequently, the level of urbanization rose only moderately, from 70 per cent in 1975 to an estimated 79 per cent in 2000, although the latter percentage masks disparities throughout the EU. Whereas it was estimated that the level of urbanization in Belgium, Luxembourg and the United Kingdom was in excess of 90 per cent by 2000, in Portugal it was as low as 38 per cent. There was also only a moderate positive relationship between the level of urbanization and GNP per capita.

North America

Compared with the growth of population in the European Union, population growth in North America has been relatively rapid – although it has been diminishing in recent years. In the United States, the average annual rate of increase was 0.97 per cent between 1975 and 1990, falling very marginally to 0.96 per cent between 1990 and 2000, and in Canada an increase of 1.20 per cent between 1975 and 1990 diminished to 1.10 per

Table 1.2 European Union: total and urban populations, urban change
and gross national products per capita

	Total population 2000* (millions)	Population growth (per cent) per annum		Urban percentage		Change in urban percentage 1975–2000*	GNP per capita 1998 (US$)
		1975–1990	1990–2000*	1975	2000*		
Belgium	10.2	0.1	0.3	94.9	97.4	2.5	25,380
Luxembourg	0.4	–	–	73.7	91.1	–17.4	–
United Kingdom	59.0	0.1	0.3	88.7	90.0	1.3	21,400
Netherlands	15.9	0.6	0.6	88.4	89.5	1.1	24,760
Germany	81.7	0.1	0.3	81.2	87.7	6.5	25,850
Denmark	5.2	0.1	0.1	81.8	85.8	3.0	33,260
Sweden	8.9	0.3	0.5	82.7	83.4	0.7	25,260
Spain	39.8	0.7	0.2	69.6	77.7	8.1	14,080
France	58.3	0.5	0.4	73.0	73.5	0.5	24,940
Greece	10.6	0.8	0.3	55.3	67.8	12.5	11,650
Italy	59.0	0.2	0.0	65.6	67.1	1.5	20,250
Finland	5.2	0.4	0.4	58.3	65.1	6.8	24,110
Ireland	3.6	0.7	0.3	53.6	58.7	5.1	18,340
Austria	8.1	2.0	1.0	53.2	56.4	3.2	26,850
Portugal	9.8	0.6	–0.1	27.7	38.1	10.4	10,690
European Union	375.7	0.5	0.3	69.8	75.3	5.5	21,916

* Estimates.

Source: HABITAT (1996); World Bank (1999).

BOX 1.1: URBANIZATION IN WESTERN EUROPE

With the lowest fertility rates and birth rates among the regions of the world, it can be expected that the level of urbanization in the countries of Western Europe in recent years has been determined largely by immigration – particularly from the former Democratic Republic of Germany and many other parts of East Central Europe to Western Germany or Austria (HABITAT, 1996). In addition, there were labour migrants from North Africa to Mediterranean Europe, and refugees from Asian countries such as Sri Lanka, India, Pakistan, Bangladesh, Iran, Iraq and Afghanistan. Within Western Europe, there has also been cross-border migration by skilled labour and by the retired. In 1990, there were between 15 and 20 million people who were foreigners in their country of abode.

Nevertheless, contrary to what might have been expected, there was no clear flow of migrants from the periphery of Western Europe to its core in, for example, the London–Paris–Frankfurt triangle. Rather, 'areas of migration gain and migration loss were widely scattered across the map' (HABITAT, 1996: 57). Whereas there was a net outflow of population from the heavily-urbanized and industrialized areas centred on London, Paris, Brussels and Copenhagen (and also from the less-developed low-income rural areas of southern Europe, Ireland and Scandinavia), there was a net inflow of population and an increase in urbanization in the Randstad of Holland, around London and Copenhagen, in the 'sunbelt' areas of southern England, Germany, France and Portugal, and in the hinterlands of the larger urban centres of Mediterranean Europe, Scandinavia and Ireland. Despite these flows, net inter-regional migration in Western Europe in the 1990s was far lower than that in the 1960s–1970s and had less of an impact on the level of urbanization – stabilizing the proportion of the total population living in urban areas.

cent per annum between 1990 and 2000 (table 1.3). However, the level of urbanization rose only modestly in the two countries, from an annual average of 74 to 77 per cent in the United States over the two periods, and from 76 to 77 per cent in Canada. However, there was no apparent relationship between urbanization and GNP per capita, since – with broadly similar levels of urbanization – the per capita GNP of the United States was almost 50 per cent higher than that of Canada in 1998.

Although Australia, New Zealand and Japan are also part of the advanced capitalist world, it is now customary to consider these countries as part of the Asia Pacific region (see pages 21, 27–9).

Table 1.3 United States and Canada: total and urban populations, urban change and gross national products per capita

	Total population 2000* (millions)	Population growth (per cent) per annum		Urban percentage		Change in urban percentage 1975– 2000*	GNP per capita 1998 (US$)
		1975– 1990	1990– 2000*	1975	2000*		
United States	275.1	0.97	0.96	73.7	77.5	3.1	29,340
Canada	31.0	1.20	1.10	75.6	77.1	1.6	20,020
North America	306.1	1.09	1.03	74.7	77.3	2.6	24,680

* Estimates.

Source: HABITAT (1996); World Bank (1999).

BOX 1.2: URBANIZATION IN THE UNITED STATES AND CANADA

In recent years, both the United States and Canada had marginally higher fertility rates and birth rates (and lower death rates) than Western Europe, and a more rapid rate of population growth. Nevertheless, like Western Europe, migration – rather than the natural increase in population – was the principal demographic determinant of urbanization. Migration – together with economic and technological development – created massive metropolitan complexes in formerly peripheral areas, established new and dispersed forms of urban agglomeration, and redefined long-standing patterns of dominance and interdependence among cities, and between cities and their suburbs (HABITAT, 1996). Whereas in 1950 – except for California – the most populous states (New York, Pennsylvania, Illinois and Ohio) were all in the North East and Great Lakes Region, in 1990 – except for New York – the most populous states (California, Texas and Florida) were in the west and south. At an urban level, disparities in internal net migration resulted. Whereas, for example, the population of Chicago (Illinois) decreased by 11 per cent in the 1980s, the population of Tampa (Florida) increased by 25 per cent (HABITAT, 1996).

In Canada, in the 1980s, the net flow of migrants was essentially towards provincial capitals and the federal capital – Ottawa-Hull (which increased its population by 9.4 per cent during the decade), while agricultural and resource-based communities declined, particularly in the east and northern regions – the population of the mining centre of Sudbury, for example, decreasing by 9.8 per cent during the same period.

Levels of urbanization were also influenced by immigration. In the USA, immigrants tended to settle – at least initially – in the gateway cities of New York, Miami, Los Angeles and San Francisco, and in the border towns of Texas and the south west, whereas in Canada around 75 per cent of all recent immigrants have settled in Toronto, Montreal and Vancouver (HABITAT, 1996).

Regions in Political and Economic Transition

East Central Europe

Although this region experienced population decline during the latter decade of the twentieth century (by an estimated average of 0.1 per cent per annum between 1990 and 2000), its level of urbanization rose substantially – by 12.8 per cent – between 1975 and 2000 (table 1.4), although

Table 1.4 East Central Europe: total and urban populations, urban change and gross national products per capita

	Total population (millions) 2000*	Population growth (per cent) per annum		Urban percentage		Change in urban percentage 1975– 2000*	GNP per capita 1998 ($US)
		1975– 1990	1900– 2000*	1975	2000*		
Bulgaria	8.6	0.2	–0.47	57.5	73.4	15.9	1,230
Hungary	9.9	–0.1	–0.42	52.8	67.3	14.5	4,510
Poland	38.8	0.2	0.17	55.4	67.1	11.7	3,900
Czech Republic	10.4	0.2	0.04	57.8	66.4	8.6	5,040
Slovakia	5.5	0.7	0.40	46.3	61.2	14.9	3,700
Romania	22.6	0.6	–0.26	46.2	57.8	11.6	1,390
East Central Europe	95.8	0.3	–0.1	52.7	65.5	12.8	3,295

* Estimates.

Source: Carter (1995); HABITAT (1996); World Bank (1999).

urbanization was not as high as in the EU. The rate of increase in urbanization between 1975 and 2000 was particularly marked in Bulgaria, Hungary and Slovakia, but even in the least urbanized country, Romania, the population was mainly urban rather than rural at the end of the twentieth century. In contrast to most other regions, there was only a weak positive correlation between the level of urbanization and GNP per capita – possibly a reflection of the diverse ways in which the economic, social, cultural and political attributes of the individual countries of the region interacted with each other.

BOX 1.3: URBANIZATION IN EAST CENTRAL EUROPE

The process of urbanization in East Central Europe during the latter half of the twentieth century has been interpreted in three contrasting ways. First, French and Hamilton (1979), and virtually all urban geographers – in claiming that there were essential differences between the processes of capitalist and socialist urbanization – suggested that whereas in capitalist countries urbanization is market-led, in socialist countries urbanization is – in large part – derived from 'the collective ownership of land and urban infrastructure, from

continued

the centrally planned provision of development funds, and from comprehensive strategies for the development of the national settlement network'
(Enyedi, 1996: 101). French and Hamilton argued that – under socialism, and
in cities such as Prague, Budapest and Warsaw – it was implicit that solutions
would be found to such problems as urban residential segregation, urban
sprawl and so forth, but there is little evidence that these aims were achieved
(see Enyedi, 1996).

Second, it was suggested – for example by Enyedi (1996) – that rather
than representing a new model of modern urbanization, 'East Central European socialist countries [merely] replicated the stages of a more generally
applicable global process of [industrial based] urban development' (Enyedi,
1996: 102). Enyedi explained that East Central Europe, after passing through
the stages of economic 'take-off' and 'the drive to maturity', experienced the
phenomenon of 'under-urbanization' from the 1950s to around 1990 in
which there was a 'failure of investment in urban housing and services to keep
pace with the creation of urban jobs . . . [resulting] in large sections of the
blue-collar working class living in rural settlements and commuting to work'
(Harloe, 1996: 14–15). However, in the new millennium, the liberalization of
the economy (and possibly membership of the European Union) should ensure
that the region gradually catches up with Western Europe, the pace of economic growth and urbanization runs broadly in parallel and that 'an age of
mass-consumption' eventually materializes.

Third, in contrast, it is argued by Szelenyi (1996) that, although socialist
cities in the region undoubtedly achieved industrialization with less urban
population growth and less spatial concentration of population than in capitalist cities at similar stages of growth, post-socialist East Central Europe may
soon experience forms of peripheral urbanization typical of cities in newly
industrializing or developing countries. In these countries, the growth of rural
unemployment might result in mass migration to urban areas, and a consequential transition from 'under-urbanization' to 'over-urbanization' – a process
probably delayed until the conclusion of post-socialist transformation (see
Harloe, 1996; Szelenyi, 1996). It could thus be concluded that although East
Central Europe is being incorporated into the global economy, it is possibly
a cause for concern – within the region – that this will be at the periphery
rather than at the core.

The former Soviet Union

Table 1.5 shows that the population of the former Soviet Union increased
very slowly towards the end of the twentieth century – diminishing from an
average annual increase of 1.2 per cent between 1975 and 1990 to an
annual rate of increase of only 0.6 per cent between 1990 and 2000.
However, within a fairly stable total population, there was a very dramatic

Table 1.5 The former Soviet Union: total and urban populations, urban change and gross national products per capita

	Total population 2000* (millions)	Population growth (per cent) per annum		Urban percentage		Change in urban percentage 1959–2000*	GNP per capita 1998 (US$)
		1975–1990	1990–2000*	1959	2000*		
Russian Federation	145.6	0.7	-0.2	52.4	77.9	25.5	2,300
Lithuania	3.7	0.8	-0.1	38.6	75.0	36.4	2,440
Belarus	10.1	0.6	-0.1	30.8	74.7	43.9	2,200
Estonia	1.5	0.6	-0.5	56.5	74.6	18.1	3,390
Latvia	2.5	0.5	-0.8	56.1	74.6	18.5	2,430
Ukraine	51.0	0.4	-0.1	45.7	72.8	27.1	850
Armenia	3.8	1.1	1.3	50.0	70.3	20.3	480
Kazakhstan	17.7	1.1	0.6	43.7	62.1	18.4	1,310
Georgia	5.5	0.7	0.2	42.4	61.1	18.7	930
Azerbaijan	8.0	1.5	1.1	47.8	57.7	9.9	490
Moldava	4.5	0.9	0.3	22.3	55.6	33.3	410
Turkmenistan	3.5	2.5	2.2	46.2	45.8	-0.4	550 (1996)
Kyrgyzstan	4.6	1.9	1.7	33.7	40.5	6.8	350
Tajikstan	7.0	2.9	2.8	32.6	33.1	0.5	350
Former Soviet Union	265.2	1.2	0.6	47.9	62.6	14.7	1,320

*Estimates.

Source: HABITAT (1996); Economist (1998); World Bank (1999).

increase in urbanization, with the proportion of the population living in towns and cities increasing from 47.9 to 62.6 per cent between 1975 and 2000. During the last twenty five years of the twentieth century, of which fifteen were under communism, there was a strong positive relationship between those states that had experienced high levels of urbanization and enjoyed comparatively large GNPs per capita (the Russian Federation, Lithuania, Belarus, Estonia and Latvia), and those that had remained largely rural and had relatively low GDPs per capita (Turkmenistan, Kyrgyzstan and Tajikstan).

Newly-Industrializing and Developing Regions

Latin America and the Caribbean

From 1920 to 1970, Latin America and the Caribbean had the most rapid population growth of any of the regions of the world and, although this rate of growth subsequently decelerated, the region's population totalled 522 million by 2000 – nearly treble its size in 1960. In the late twentieth century, the region as a whole consolidated its transformation from being predominantly rural to predominantly urban – the level of urbanization rising from 59.9 per cent in 1975 to 67.5 in 2000. Table 1.6 shows that the degree of urbanization was greatest in Venezuela, Uruguay, Argentina and Chile – where their respective urban populations each exceeded 80 per cent, while the pace of transformation was particularly dramatic in Bolivia, the Dominican Republic and Brazil. Very broadly, there was a positive relationship between the level of urbanization and the GNP per capita (figure 1.2 and table 1.6).

Sub-Saharan Africa

By the 1970s, the population of Africa began to grow more quickly than that of Latin America and the Caribbean. Table 1.7 shows that the population of sub-Saharan Africa increased by an annual average of 2.9 per cent between 1975 and 1990, and the increase diminished only very marginally to 2.8 per cent between 1990 and 2000 – the fastest rate of growth of any of the world's regions during this period. It was within this context that the level of urbanization rose dramatically by 12.4 per cent between 1975 and 2000, exceeding that of all other newly-industrializing and developing regions – except the Arab world. However, there was little relationship between the size of the GNP per capita and the degree of urbanization.

Table 1.6 Selected Latin American and Caribbean countries: total and urban populations, urban change and gross national products per capita

	Total population 2000* (millions)	Population growth (per cent) per annum		Urban percentage		Change in urban percentage 1975–2000*	GNP per capita 1998 (US$)
		1975–1990	1990–2000*	1975	2000*		
Venezuela	24.2	2.8	2.2	77.8	94.5	16.8	3,500
Uruguay	3.3	0.6	0.6	83.1	91.3	8.2	6,180
Argentina	36.6	1.5	1.2	80.7	89.4	8.7	8,970
Chile	15.3	1.6	1.5	78.4	84.7	6.3	4,810
Brazil	174.8	2.1	1.6	61.2	81.2	20.0	4,570
Cuba	11.4	0.9	0.7	64.2	78.1	13.9	163 (1996)*
Mexico	102.4	2.1	1.9	62.8	77.7	14.9	3,970
Puerto Rico	3.8	1.1	0.8	62.8	75.5	12.7	818 (1996)*
Colombia	37.8	2.0	1.6	60.7	75.2	14.5	2,600
Peru	28.1	2.4	1.9	61.5	74.5	13.0	2,460
Trinidad & Tobago	1.4	1.3	1.1	63.0	74.4	11.4	4,430
Dominican Republic	8.5	2.3	1.8	45.3	68.1	22.8	1,770
Nicaragua	5.2	2.8	3.4	50.3	65.9	15.6	760*
Bolivia	8.3	2.2	2.4	41.5	65.2	23.7	1,000
Ecuador	12.6	2.6	2.1	42.4	61.9	19.5	1,530
Paraguay	5.6	3.2	2.6	39.0	56.4	17.4	1,760
Jamaica	2.5	1.1	0.7	44.1	56.2	12.1	1,680
Panama	2.9	2.2	1.8	48.7	55.3	6.6	3,080
Costa Rica	3.8	2.9	2.2	41.3	52.7	11.4	2,780
El Salvador	6.4	1.6	2.2	40.4	46.8	6.4	1,850
Honduras	6.5	3.2	2.9	32.1	47.3	15.2	730
Guatemala	12.2	2.8	2.8	36.7	44.1	7.4	1,640
Haiti	8.0	1.8	2.1	21.7	34.9	13.2	410
Latin America & Caribbean	521.6	2.0	1.8	53.9	67.5	10.6	2,672

* Estimates.

Source: HABITAT (1996); Economist (1998); World Bank (1999).

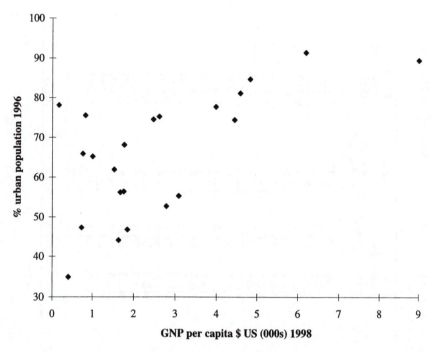

Figure 1.2 *The relationship between economic development and urbanization in Latin America and the Caribbean*

BOX 1.4: URBANIZATION IN LATIN AMERICA AND THE CARIBBEAN

From 1950 to 2000, Latin America and the Caribbean evolved from being a predominantly rural region to one where all countries with a population in excess of 1 million had a level of urbanization of more than 50 per cent. The transformation was particularly notable in Brazil, Mexico, Venezuela, Colombia, Peru, the Dominican Republic and Puerto Rico; in Brazil, Mexico, the Dominican Republic and Colombia this was particularly attributable to rapid economic growth and the growth in manufacturing (HABITAT, 1996).

In this region, there are essentially three levels of urbanization. The most urbanized countries are Argentina, Uruguay, Chile and Venezuela, where around 80 per cent of the population live in urban areas. In the nineteenth and early twentieth centuries, most immigrants had little choice but to settle in cities, since land-owning interests severely limited rural settlement. Although the three 'Southern Cone' countries of Argentina, Chile and Uruguay have been among the most urbanized in the world for almost a century, the slow rate of urbanization in the cone for at least the last fifty years has been attributable to the lowest rates of economic growth and manufacturing growth in Latin America.

In contrast, the moderately urbanized countries of Brazil, Mexico, Colombia, Ecuador and the Dominican Republic experienced rapid industrial development and urbanization throughout the second half of the twentieth century, while with slower rates of economic development Cuba, Bolivia, Peru, Nicaragua, Jamaica and Trinidad & Tobago similarly had levels of urbanization of between 50 and 80 per cent of the total population.

The least urbanized countries of the region – Paraguay, Haiti, Costa Rica, El Salvador, Guatemala and Honduras – had less than 50 per cent of their population living in urban areas, commensurate with their low levels of development.

It is remarkable 'that the region's most urbanized countries in 1950 are still the most urbanized, while the least urbanised have remained the same' (HABITAT, 1996: 43), but there was a tendency for the spatial distribution of the most urbanized areas to change because of disproportionately high levels of economic growth in, for example, south-east Brazil and areas centred on Guadalajara and Monterrey in Mexico (HABITAT, 1996).

The Arab World

Table 1.8 shows that the population of this region increased dramatically by an average of 3.43 per cent per annum between 1975 and 1990, but declined marginally to 2.45 per cent per annum between 1990 and 2000. The level of urbanization also rose substantially during the last quarter of the twentieth century, and in proportionate terms exceeded that of both sub-Saharan Africa and most of Asia. Broadly, there was a positive relationship between the level of urbanization and the GNP per capita – in part attributable to a rapid increase in urbanization in the oil-rich states of Kuwait, Libya and Saudi Arabia.

Asia Pacific

The population of this region increased by an average of 1.8 per cent per annum between 1975 and 1990, and again between 1990 and 2000. By the beginning of the new millennium the region contained over half of the world's population. There was also a substantial rise in the level of urbanization, from 40.4 to 51.1 per cent of the total population between 1975 and 2000 (table 1.9). This latter figure, however, disguises the very wide range in the level of urbanization across the continent, ranging – in 2000 – from only around 17 per cent in Nepal and 21 per cent in Bangladesh

Table 1.7 Sub-Saharan Africa: total and urban populations, urban change and gross national products per capita

	Total population 2000* (millions)	Population growth (per cent) per annum		Urban percentage		Change in urban percentage 1975–2000*	GNP per capita 1998 (US$)
		1975–1990	1990–2000*	1975	2000*		
Congo, Rep.	2.9	2.9	2.9	34.9	63.3	28.4	680
Zambia	10.8	3.5	2.8	34.8	59.9	25.1	330
Mauritania	2.6	2.5	2.5	20.3	59.0	38.7	410
Gabon	1.5	3.9	2.8	30.6	53.8	23.2	400 (1996)*
South Africa	46.2	2.5	2.2	48.0	53.1	5.1	2,880
Cameroon	15.2	2.8	2.8	26.9	49.3	22.4	610
Liberia	3.6	3.1	3.3	30.4	48.1	17.7	–
Côte d'Ivoire	16.8	3.8	3.4	32.1	47.0	14.9	700
Senegal	9.5	2.8	2.6	34.2	45.1	10.9	530
Namibia	1.8	2.7	2.6	20.6	42.9	22.3	1,940
Nigeria	128.8	2.8	2.9	23.4	42.3	18.9	300
Mauritius	1.2	1.1	1.1	43.4	41.7	-1.7	10,899
Central African Rep.	3.7	2.4	2.4	33.7	41.6	7.9	300
Sierra Leone	5.1	2.1	2.4	21.1	40.2	19.1	140
Mozambique	19.0	2.0	2.9	8.6	41.1	32.5	210
Ghana	20.2	2.8	3.0	30.1	39.2	9.1	390
Burkina Faso	11.7	2.5	2.6	6.4	37.5	31.1	240
Angola	13.1	2.7	3.2	17.8	36.2	18.5	340
Zimbabwe	12.5	3.2	2.3	19.6	36.0	16.4	610
Benin	6.3	2.8	3.1	20.5	33.9	13.4	380

Togo	4.8	2.9	3.1	16.3	33.7	17.4	330
Guinea	7.8	2.2	3.0	16.3	33.6	17.3	540
Botswana	1.7	3.5	3.0	12.0	33.3	21.3	3,600
Kenya	32.6	3.6	3.2	12.9	31.8	18.9	330
Congo, Dem. Rep.	51.1	3.2	3.1	30.0	31.1	1.1	110
Madagascar	17.3	3.2	3.2	16.1	30.8	14.7	260
Mali	12.6	2.7	3.1	16.2	30.4	14.2	250
Tanzania	34.1	3.2	2.9	10.1	28.2	18.1	210
Somalia	10.8	3.1	2.2	21.3	27.9	6.6	–
Lesotho	2.3	2.8	2.7	10.8	27.1	16.3	570
Chad	7.3	2.1	2.7	15.6	22.8	7.2	230
Niger	10.8	3.2	3.4	10.6	19.2	8.6	190
Eritrea	4.0	2.6	2.7	12.2	19.0	6.8	200
Malawi	12.1	3.9	2.6	7.7	15.6	7.9	200
Ethiopia	63.8	2.6	3.0	9.5	14.9	5.4	100
Uganda	24.6	3.2	3.2	8.3	14.2	5.9	320
Burundi	7.3	2.7	2.9	3.2	9.1	5.9	230
Rwanda	9.0	3.1	2.6	z4.0	6.7	2.7	250
Sub-Saharan Africa	629.4	2.9	2.8	20.4	32.8	12.4	1,087

* Estimates.

Source: HABITAT (1996); *Economist* (1998); World Bank (1999).

BOX 1.5: URBANIZATION IN SUB-SAHARAN AFRICA

Most cities in sub-Saharan Africa were established only in colonial times, for example Johannesburg in 1886, Harare in 1890, Abijdan in 1891 and Nairobi in 1899, while 'colonial regimes and the economic activities which they promoted raised the level of migratory activity [from rural to urban areas] to a much higher level' (HABITAT, 1996: 87). With the development of cash economies, and with goods and services being exchangeable for wages, African labour not only migrated to plantations and mines in search of employment, but also to towns and cities – urban areas receiving perhaps one-quarter of all migrants (HABITAT, 1996). Among the major cities, average population growth rates of 5 to 7 per cent were common in the 1950s–1960s.

Urbanization thus became a major cause of concern in sub-Saharan Africa in the 1960s–1970s. In Tanzania, for example, the government – by means of its Second Five Year Plan 1969–74 – attempted to reduce rural–urban differences and the pull of Dar es Salaam (the country's largest city) through a process of *ujamaa*: the concentration of scattered rural populations in viable settlements to facilitate the provision of essential services such as health care, education and basic utilities. However – by 1974 – a policy of voluntary 'villagization' gave way to one of persuasion or coercion as a means of hastening the developmemt of new settlements, but this approach was rejected in 1978 because of the severity of the problems associated with its enforcement. It was consequently superseded – in the country's Fourth Five Year Plan 1981/82–1985/86 – by a policy which favoured industrial development and further urbanization (Potter and Lloyd-Evans, 1998).

In the 1980s and 1990s, Tanzania subsequently experienced many of the problems associated with rapid urbanization elsewhere in Africa – for example, city governments throughout much of the continent were unable to provide suitably serviced land and infrastructure for urban development in the face of escalating rural–urban migration. An ensuing 'urban crisis' was marked, first, by a decrease in the level of formal employment – particularly in manufacturing, administration and the large-scale service sector such as banking and tourism; secondly by a rapid rise in the informal sector which it was estimated employed around 60 per cent of the urban labour force even in the mid-1970s; thirdly by a deterioration in both the quality and distribution of basic services such as water supply and sewerage, refuse collection, road maintenance and improvement, public transport, schools and medical care; and, finally, by a decline in the quality of the built environment (HABITAT, 1996).

Compounding these problems, it is predicted that urbanization in sub-Saharan Africa will increase – at a more rapid rate than in any other region of the world – from around 30 per cent in the late 1990s to about 48 per cent by the year 2020 (HABITAT, 1996), and – like most other developing regions – the social as well as the economic costs of over-urbanization might rise before they fall.

Table 1.8 The Arab World: total and urban populations, urban change and gross national products per capita

	Total population 2000* (millions)	Population growth (per cent) per annum		Urban percentage		Change in urban percentage 1975-2000*	GNP per capitat 1998 (US$)
		1975-1990	1990-2000*	1975	2000*		
Kuwait	1.8	5.0	-1.6	83.1	97.7	14.6	9,361*
Libyan Arab Jamahiriya	6.4	4.1	3.4	61.0	88.4	27.4	–
Saudi Arabia	21.3	5.3	2.8	58.7	81.8	23.1	7,240 (1996)
Iraq	23.8	3.3	2.7	61.4	77.1	15.7	1,095 (1996)
Jordan	6.4	3.3	4.1	55.3	74.4	19.1	1,520
Tunisia	9.7	2.4	1.8	49.9	59.9	10.0	2,050
Algeria	31.2	3.0	2.2	40.3	59.7	19.4	1,550
Syrian Arab Republic	17.3	3.4	3.4	45.1	54.9	9.8	1,020
Morocco	29.7	2.3	2.0	37.7	50.9	13.2	1,250
Egypt	69.1	2.5	2.1	43.5	46.4	2.9	1,290
Yemen	17.1	3.2	4.1	16.4	38.4	22.0	300
Arab World	233.8	3.4	2.5	50.2	63.4	13.2	2,698

* Estimates.

Source: HABITAT (1996); Economist (1998); World Bank (1999).

BOX 1.6: URBANIZATION IN THE ARAB WORLD

By the end of the twentieth century, it was clear that the countries of the Arab World could be classified into five distinctive types, with very different levels of urbanization (see Abu-Lughod, 1996). First, there were the 'nouveau riche' states dependent on oil exploitation and linked to the world economy. These comprise Libya, Saudi Arabia, Bahrain, Qatar, Kuwait, the United Arab Emirates (UAE) and Oman. In these countries, there has been a very rapid rate of population increase and, as an outcome, very rapid rates of urbanization up to levels approaching 90 per cent in Bahrain, Kuwait, Qatar and the UAE. Growth was very largely due to a high rate of immigration, and, in many of the cities of the region, immigrants constituted up to 85–90 per cent of their populations. Cities in the region had become essentially sites for consumption rather than centres of production, with as much as 75 per cent of employment being concentrated in the service sector (Abu-Lughod, 1996). Because of inhospitable terrain, cities inevitably provided the principal or only locations for settlement.

Second, there were the 'diversified land-based agricultural states with some oil production' – specifically Algeria and Iraq. Although both states were economically halfway between the dependent oil-rich states on the one hand, and the impoverished and dependent countries such as Egypt on the other, and gradually developed their economies during the 1970s and 1980s, they were disadvantaged from the outset by an over-concentration of population in their respective capitals of Algiers and Bagdad, and – in Algeria – by the effects of protest movements from dissidents in the 1990s, and – in Iraq – by the effects of the eight year war with Iran in the 1980s and the Gulf War in 1990–91 (see Abu-Lughod, 1996).

The third type of economy comprised the 'heartland confrontation states' of Egypt, Syria, Palestine, Lebanon and (to an extent) Jordan. All are more urbanized than most other states in the region, while urban growth has recently been at about 4–5 per annum largely because of natural increase rather than in-migration. Often disrupted by war, their economies are weak and much dependent on outside funds. Consequently, capital cities are dominant in the urban economy, much investment from abroad is associated with land speculation and (in some cases) excessive development of luxury flats rather than the provision of productive facilities, while – within a severely inflated economy – an underfunded public sector disadvantages the inadequately-housed poor.

The fourth type consisted of the 'neo-colonial' economies of Morocco and Tunisia which, in effect, exchanged political dependence in the 1960s for economic dependence – based on the 'export' of labour and the provision of tourist services on the one hand, and the import of manufactured goods on the other, while the urban hierarchy imposed by the French colonisers on the indigenous pattern of towns and cities was retained. Whereas the new urban elite often inherited the better housing or created a demand for expensive new villas and apartments, and funds were also found to preserve some of the precious historic quarters of cities such as Tunis or Fez, this was 'more with an eye towards the tourist trade than to creating a healthy environment and viable livelihoods for the poor who crowd into these districts' (Abu-Lughod, 1996: 195), while squatter settlements absorbed an increasing flow of migrants from rural areas.

Finally, there were the economically marginal countries of the 'Fourth World' – Sudan and Yemen. These are not only outside the international economy but have very low levels of urbanization. With stagnating agriculture and little industrialization, the development of viable urban economies has proved difficult, and there is a tendency for 'urban degregation to outstrip urban improvements' (Abu-Lughod, 1996: 194).

to as much as 98 per cent in Hong Kong and 100 per cent in Singapore. In general, there was a positive relationship between the level of urbanization and GNP per capita (figure 1.3).

Very broadly, the countries and regions of Asia Pacific can be divided into three groups, according to their level of urbanization (see table 1.9):

- Singapore, Hong Kong and the Republic of Korea (together with the advanced capitalist countries of New Zealand, Australia and Japan), where each economy – in terms of population – is predominantly urban, with agriculture contributing to less than 10 per cent of their GDPs in 1996, but with services accounting for well over a half.
- The 'Asean 4' (Malaysia, Philippines, Indonesia and Thailand) and Pakistan, where – except for Thailand – between 30 and 50 per cent of the population are urban, and where the contribution of agriculture to the GDP declined dramatically between 1960 and 1990 in contrast to a marked growth in industrial and service activity.
- China and all the countries of southern Asia Pacific (except Pakistan), whose populations are predominantly rural and agriculture accounts for the largest share of the GDP. However, it is probable that in the early years of the twenty-first century, China will graduate to the second group of countries because of its rapid rate of economic development and urbanization.

Clearly, because of the wide spatial diversity of both China and India, aggregate national statistics can be misleading. The attributes of both the first and second group of countries exist – to a varying degree – in the

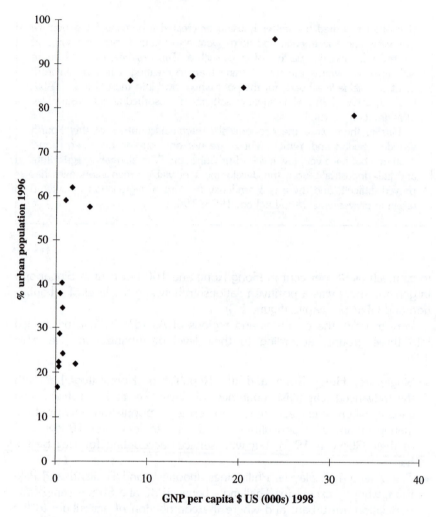

Figure 1.3 *The relationship between economic development and urbanization in Asia Pacific*

provinces or states of the two mega-states. It should also be borne in mind that since the population of China and India both exceeded 1.0 billion by 2000, the comparatively low level of urbanization in the two countries (respectively 34.5 and 28.6 per cent) represents very large urban populations in absolute terms. As with other major regions of the world, there is a moderate positive correlation between the level of urbanization and GDP per capita.

Table 1.9 Asian Pacific countries: total and urban populations, urban change and gross national products per capita

	Total population 2000*	Population growth (per cent) per annum		Urban percentage		Change in urban percentage 1950–2000*	Gross national product per capita 1998 (US$)
		1975–1990	1990–2000*	1975	2000*		
Singapore	3.0	1.2	0.9	100.0	100.0	0	30,060
Hong Kong	6.0	1.7	0.5	89.7	95.7	6.0	23,670
New Zealand	3.8	0.6	1.1	82.8	87.2	4.4	14,700
Republic of Korea	47.1	1.3	1.0	48.0	86.2	38.2	7,960
Australia	19.2	1.3	1.3	85.9	84.7	-1.2	20,300
Japan	126.5	0.7	0.2	75.7	78.4	2.7	32,380
Dem. People's Rep. of Korea	26.0	1.8	1.8	56.5	63.1	6.6	–
Iran	74.6	3.8	2.4	45.8	61.9	16.1	1,770
Philippines	74.6	2.3	2.1	35.6	59.0	23.4	1,050
Malaysia	22.3	2.5	2.2	37.7	57.5	19.8	3,660
Indonesia	212.7	2.0	1.5	19.4	40.3	20.9	680
Pakistan	161.8	3.3	2.8	26.4	37.9	11.5	480
China	1,284.6	1.5	1.1	17.3	34.5	17.2	750
India	1,022.0	2.1	1.8	21.3	28.6	7.3	430
Myanmar (Burma)	51.5	2.1	2.1	23.9	28.4	4.5	–
Sri Lanka	19.5	1.6	1.2	22.0	24.2	2.2	810
Vietnam	82.6	2.2	2.2	18.8	22.3	3.5	330
Afghanistan	26.7	-0.2	5.7	13.3	22.1	8.8	–
Thailand†	61.9	2.0	1.1	15.1	21.9	6.8	2,200
Bangladesh	134.4	2.3	2.2	9.3	21.3	12.0	350
Nepal	24.8	2.6	2.6	5.0	16.7	11.7	210
Asia Pacific	3,485.6	1.8	1.8	40.4	51.1	10.7	8,618

* Estimates.
† The apparent discrepancy between a low level of urbanization and a comparatively high per capita income in Thailand may be attributable to the definition of urban areas used in Thailand which excludes many settlements that would be classified as 'urban' in other countries.

Source: HABITAT (1996); World Bank (1999).

BOX 1.7: URBANIZATION IN INDONESIA

Despite being the world's fourth most populous nation, Indonesia has for long been regarded as one of the least urbanized and least industrialized countries in the world with the majority of its population living in rural areas and employed in agriculture. However, by the mid-1990s, this view was no longer valid since 35 per cent of the population was urban (compared with less than 10 per cent in 1945), and less than half of the nation's workforce was employed in agriculture (Hugo, 1996). In the provinces of Jakarta, Yogyakarta and West Java, the respective levels of urbanization in 1990 were as high as 100, 44 and 35 per cent, whereas in Sumatra provincial urbanization ranged from 12.4 to 36 per cent, and in Kalimantan it ranged from 18 to 49 per cent. In the smaller islands, however, levels of urbanization were as low as 8–11 per cent (Hugo, 1996). There was clearly a broad positive relationship between economic development and levels of urbanization in Indonesia's provinces.

Although economic development in the 1970s and early 1980s was, in no small part, dependent on oil export income, oil revenues subsequently became less and less important since manufacturing production increased from 10 per cent of the GDP in 1970 to 21 per cent in 1992, and industrial production as a whole escalated from 19 to 40 per cent during the same period – in contrast to agricultural production which decreased from 45 to 19 per cent of the GDP. The rapid expansion in manufacturing industry was generated by a marked change in public policy, whereby the promotion of exports and private investment superseded a policy of import-substitution, high import tariffs and controls on the distribution of capital (Schwarz, 1990; Hugo, 1996).

Apart from stimulating growth and influencing the pattern of employment, this major shift in policy had a major impact on the level and spatial pattern of urbanization. From 1971 to 1990, employment increased almost three times as fast in urban areas than in rural areas, while the proportion of the workforce living in cities increased from around 17 per cent in 1971 to 27 per cent in 1990 (Hugo, 1996).

BOX 1.8: URBANIZATION IN CHINA

Since the Communist revolution, China has experienced three contrasting periods of urbanization (see Chen and Parish, 1996). In the 1950s, urbanization proceeded at a rapid pace despite attempts to introduce a system of communes in the countryside. A dramatic fall in agricultural production and living standards resulted in large-scale migration from rural areas to the towns and cities – not dissimilar to that experienced by most developing countries at an initial stage of industrialization.

During the 1960s and 1970s, it was official policy to contain or reduce the level of urbanization – largely by ensuring that highly subsidized housing, food, state-sector jobs and associated benefits (such as medical care and disability and pension payments) were allocated only to households registered as resident (the 'entitled' population), whereas most recent migrants from the countryside would have been 'non-entitled'. Although anti-urbanization may have stemmed from an entrenched view that a peasant society was 'superior' to an urban society, it was also a reaction to the high cost of providing heavily subsidized urban living standards (Chen and Parish, 1996). To compensate for slow or zero urban growth, China – like the Soviet Union hitherto – increased the proportion of the urban population at work (mainly by increasing the number of women in the urban labour force), and sharply increased capital intensity in industrial production. As a result, industrialization outpaced urbanization – output soaring by 10 per cent per annum with the level of urbanization, at best, remaining constant.

The 1980s and 1990s witnessed a relaxation of administrative controls, and the level of urbanization rose. The urban population grew by 3.8 per cent per annum, comparable to that of 21 other developing countries that averaged over 3 per cent per annum (Findley, 1993), and although the level of urbanization in 1995 reached only 30 per cent of the total population, in absolute terms China had a larger urban population than any other country (499 million), equivalent to one in six of the world's total urban population.

From a period of under-urbanization or zero-urban growth in the preceding two decades, China's towns and cities moved into a state of near-equilibrium since production and urban population increased broadly in parallel. However, to ensure that there was not a progression to over-urbanization, the size of the entitled population was kept in check, and the development of non-agricultural employment in rural areas was encouraged. Even so, continuing rural–urban migration resulted in the unentitled population amounting to as much as one-third of the total urban population by 1993 (Chen and Parish, 1996).

BOX 1.9: URBANIZATION IN INDIA

The level of urbanization in India rose comparatively slowly in the latter half of the twentieth century – from around 18 per cent in 1951 to about 26 per cent in 1991. With an urban population in the latter year of 279 million,

continued

India was second only to China in having the largest urban system in the world (Clark, 1996). However, between 1981 and 1991, the rate of urban population growth began to diminish – from 3.86 to 3.15 per cent per annum, notwithstanding any reduction in the rate of increase in the total population. This might suggest that either rural development programmes in the 1980s had been very successful, or that insufficient jobs, particularly in manufacturing, had been created in urban areas, possibly because of too little infrastructure investment, and that consequently the attraction of towns and cities to would-be in-migrants had been reduced (Mohan, 1996). Almost by default, India was able to curb – if only marginally – the general trend towards over-urbanization.

There were significant disparities in levels of urbanization across India. Whereas the poorest states of Bihar and Orissa in the east had urbanization levels of respectively 13.2 and 13.4 per cent in 1991 – comparable to the least-developed countries in the world, the more developed states of Gujarat and Maharashtra in the west had urbanization levels of 41.0 and 38.7 per cent – comparable to the level of urbanization in many middle-income countries (Mohan, 1996).

It might be assumed that the more-developed states of India would have enjoyed faster rates of economic growth and urbanization than those experienced by the less-developed states, but the converse is true, for example Bihar and Orissa are among a number of least-developed states that, since 1950, have recorded the highest rates of urbanization, while the rate of urban growth in the more developed states has been comparatively modest. However, on a decade-by-decade basis, variations in levels of urbanization in the 1980s were less than variations in the 1950s, 1960s and 1970s, on account of the slowing-down in the rate of urbanization nationally.

From the above analysis, it is very evident that – in proportionate terms – both population increase and urbanization have been on a significantly greater scale in those regions with low GNPs per capita such as sub-Saharan Africa and the Arab world, than in the richer regions of the world such as the European Union and North America (table 1.10). However, it is of note that regions in a state of political and economic transition (specifically East Central Europe and the former Soviet Union) have, paradoxically, a low rate or negative rate of population increase, but a marked increase in urbanization. However, there are wide variations in these indicators in most of the world's regions, for example there are major differences in population growth, urbanization and per capita GNP across the Asia Pacific region (for example, between Singapore or Hong Kong on the one hand, and Vietnam or Bangladesh on the other hand), and between the European and Central Asian states of the former Soviet Union (see tables 1.5 and 1.9).

Table 1.10 Population increase, increased urbanization and gross national product: a comparison of economic regions

| Region | Population (000s) 2000* | Population increase | | Urban population (per cent) | | Growth in urbanization (per cent) 1975–2000* | GNP per capita 1998 (US$) |
		1975–1990	1900–2000*	1975	2000*		
North America	306.1	1.1	1.0	74.7	77.3	2.6	24,680
European Union	375.7	0.5	0.3	69.8	75.3	5.5	21,916
Asia Pacific	3,485.6	1.8	1.8	40.4	51.1	10.7	8,618
East Central Europe	95.8	0.3	–0.1	52.7	65.5	12.8	3,295
Arab World	233.8	3.4	2.5	50.2	63.4	13.2	2,698
Latin America & Caribbean	521.6	2.0	1.8	53.9	67.8	10.6	2,672
Former Soviet Union	265.2	1.2	0.6	47.9	62.6	14.7	1,320
Sub-Saharan Africa	629.4	2.9	2.8	20.4	32.8	12.4	1,087

* Estimates.

Source: HABITAT (1996); World Bank (1999).

THE INTERDEPENDENCY THEORY OF GLOBAL URBAN DEVELOPMENT

Whereas Rostow's (1960) approach focused on the economic development of individual countries, the interdependency theory of urban development is concerned essentially with the economic and corporate relations between countries and how these lead to disparities in levels of urbanization. It is evident that the accumulation of surpluses at a national level and rising levels of urbanization (during the 'take-off' and 'drive to maturity' stages of economic development) firstly led to a spread of urbanization to adjacent areas with similar economic and social systems – creating a core region of industrial growth, and secondly to the imposition of urbanization in dependent territories tightly linked to the core. From this basic premise, it has been argued that the drive for ever-higher levels of output and profit occurred sequentially in the context of mercantilism, industrial and monopoly capitalism and transnational capitalism (see Castells, 1977; Goldfrank, 1979; Clark, 1996), and that the world became divided into increasingly larger spheres of association and exchange, culminating in the emergence of a single integrated capitalist world economy (see Chase-Dunn, 1989; Taylor, 1993; Clark, 1996).

The Stages of Urban Development

Under *mercantilism* and *early colonialism*, the foundations for urban development at the core were established in Western Europe from the fifteenth to the eighteenth centuries. Balance of trade surpluses were considered essential for the accumulation of wealth, but although wealth may have originated in rural areas or abroad, its consumption was largely confined to towns and cities where good communications, trading opportunities and sources of finance were centred. Not only was a well-developed urban pattern established at the core, with London, Paris, Lisbon, Amsterdam, Rome, Madrid and Naples being – in descending order – the largest cities in the world, but an embryonic urban framework emerged at the periphery (see Taaffe et al., 1963; Vance, 1970; Friedmann, 1972; Clark, 1996).

From the late eighteenth to the late nineteenth centuries, *industrial capitalism* became the dominant mode of production and exchange in the Western world. Wealth was now created by manufacturing industry rather than by trade alone. Substantial supplies of labour and industrial capital were required in order to make standard products, and overseas trade was required on a large scale to ensure that large inputs of imported raw materials could be paid for by the export of manufactured goods. Levels of urbanization in the core areas escalated, for example in Britain – the first country to embrace industrial capitalism – the urban population soared by 946 per cent between 1801 and 1891 compared with a national increase of 'only' 326 per cent, its urban population increasing consequently from 26 per cent of the total in 1801 to more than 50 per cent by 1861 – higher than that of any other country (Carter and Lewis, 1991; Clark, 1996).

By 1890, industrialization had not only spread across much of Europe but also throughout parts of the USA and Canada, Russia and Japan – the largest cities in the world now being London, New York, Paris, Berlin, Chicago, Philadelphia and Tokyo. In peripheral areas, urbanization was associated with the export of food and raw materials, for example Buenos Aires (mutton, wool and cereals), São Paulo (coffee), Accra (jute) and Calcutta (jute) (Gilbert and Gugler, 1992). Urbanization was thus closely linked to the market and urban system of the colonial power rather than to the network of rural towns and villages locally.

By the end of the nineteenth century, industrial capitalism was superseded by *monopoly capitalism* – a much larger-scale process whereby manufacturers progressed from producing a narrow range of basic products (such as iron and steel or textiles) to the production of a wide range of goods and services, while – often under conditions of imperialism – many independent firms formed themselves into monopolistic corporations to exploit more effectively the raw materials and markets of the periphery (Clark, 1996). At the core, the rate of economic growth speeded up, countries were approaching an 'age of high mass consumption', and levels of urbanization were reaching new heights, but at the periphery urban development had hardly begun (Clark, 1996).

From around 1950 onwards, urban development became a global phenomenon. The production of goods and service, the use of brand names and expanding patterns of trade became global in extent; monopoly capitalism was replaced by *transnational corporate capitalism*; and rapid urbanization occurred in many of the world's peripheral areas, although it did not exceed 20 per cent in China, India, Indonesia, Bangladesh and Pakistan until 1990 (Clark, 1996). Both the economic performance of countries and levels of urbanization became increasingly dependent on the role of transnational corporations such as Royal Dutch Shell, Exon, BP, Ford, General Motors and IBM. Whereas under industrial and monopoly capitalism, the periphery supplied raw materials while the core was concerned with manufacture or processing, now the periphery often uses its cheap labour to produce low-cost manufactured goods for consumption worldwide while the dominant core specializes in research, development, design, administration and control.

Although the periphery continued to generate low GDPs per capita, dominant core states enjoyed higher and higher per capita GDPs. This was facilitated by the consolidation of a global system of finance, directed and controlled by a small number of cities in the core economies, for example, of the twenty world's largest banks in 1996, seven had their headquarters in either Tokyo (Tokyo-Mitsubishi, Fuji, Dai-Ichi-Kangyo, Sakura and Industrial Bank of Japan) or in Osaka (Sumitomo and Sanwa), four were based in New York (Chase Manhattan, Citicorp, Bank America Corp. and Nations Bank) and two had their head offices in London (HSBC Holdings and National Westminster) (*Economist*, 1998).

On a global scale, urbanization is *either* a direct result of transnational corporate capitalism whereby foreign investment is concentrated in cities across the periphery, for example in São Paulo (Brazil), Santiago (Chile), Lagos (Nigeria), Abidjan (Côte d'Ivoire), Jakarta (Indonesia) and Bangkok (Thailand), where manufacturing attracts in-migrants from subsistence or semi-subsistence agriculture, *or* an indirect outcome of structural adjustments to the economy of peripheral areas such as a switch from subsistence to commercial agriculture and the subsequent migration of surplus labour into the towns and cities. In both circumstances, post-colonial governments have stimulated urban growth by discriminatory public expenditure on infrastructure and services in cities rather than in rural areas, while higher wage rates and better employment protection in the cities (often the result of trade union pressure) attract migrant labour from rural areas (see Clark, 1996).

In much of Africa and Asia, urbanization is taking place in countries with the lowest level of economic development and is on a scale far larger than was the case at the core in the nineteenth century. Whereas at the core, the processes of urbanization ran in parallel with indigenous industrialization, at the periphery 'over-urbanization' is endemic. There is a marked tendency for in-migration to be on such a scale that urban populations increase at a greater rate than urban job opportunities. 'The result is a high level of unemployment or underemployment, acute housing shortages, a large urban homeless population, and the growth of shanty towns' (Szelenyi, 1996: 294). Since there is normally a lack of basic welfare services, a large proportion of in-migrants (up to 1 billion people in cities in the developing world) have little choice but to join the 'informal economy' – which provides jobs such as street vending, hawking, shoe cleaning, drug-peddling and prostitution for people who otherwise would have no means of economic support, while others in a similar plight might find casual employment as mechanics, carpenters, barbers and personal servants (Clark, 1996: 94).

The interdependency theory is, arguably, not without its weaknesses. It might be suggested that, since urbanization in the newly-industrializing and developing countries is lagging so far behind that in the developed world, it should not be assumed to be part of the same process, yet a century or more might be the necessary time-span for interdependency to work. It might also be argued that interdependency theory is irrelevant to many developing countries where urbanization took place, not under capitalism, but under conditions of religious or military governance or feudalism – such as in the ancient civilizations of Egypt, Mesopotania, India, China, Mexico and Peru. It might also have been irrelevant in the socialist countries of the Eastern bloc before the late 1980s–early 1990s, and in China where urbanization has been a consequence of domestic and social circumstances. Whereas, from the 1960s to the mid-1970s, the level of urbanization in China remained broadly unchanged because of an industrial strategy which focused on job creation in the communes of the countryside, the consequential growth of population in the countryside together with the economic reforms which were introduced in 1979 created a vast surplus of labour which could not be absorbed by the already over-extended rural economy (Clark, 1996: 92). In China, the level of urbanization is thus rapidly increasing as a necessary consequence of the adjustment from a controlled rural economy to a liberal service-based urban economy, rather than as an incipient result of transnational corporate capitalism.

GLOBALIZATION AND URBAN ECONOMICS

Except for averting a catastrophic war or famine, there are few challenges and problems that appear so daunting and intractable as the problems of urban areas. To many, the city has seemed synonymous with civilization, with the height of humankind's achievement in the arts and sciences, in technology and in administration. To others, not least since industrialization, the city has offered insecurity, poverty, disease and misery – both in the developed world and in newly-industrializing and developing countries. Yet, while economic processes may have brought distress to millions, economics as a discipline has helped to solve many of the problems of the human condition.

Despite the recent interest shown in urban economics, particularly in the USA, the discipline is still in its infancy. This is because conventional economic analysis cannot easily be applied to an urban situation. The market is absent for many products, especially those associated with the urban infrastructure, there are many externalities, and investment decisions are usually undertaken without reference to the urban structure in general and to external scale economies and diseconomies in particular. With the emergence of a global economy, it is even more difficult to allocate resources optimally, either in terms of location or between the public and private sectors.

Where there are markets, these often function imperfectly. In respect of urban land, for example, there tends to be a scarcity of sites for certain uses (such as affordable housing) and an availability of sites for other uses (such as retail development), while – for a variety of reasons, such as speculation and the desire to remain in possession of a site for business purposes or because of its residential utility value – transactions might not occur even when market prices are offered. Since the urban real estate market thus involves heterogeneous buildings, sites and locations, it is quite unlike the stock market or a commodity market. It is not highly organized, there is no central buying or selling place, and it consists of an aggregate of a vast number of deals, large and small. The market functions – however imperfectly – with the involvement of the various professions concerned with land and buildings who attempt to bring together buyers and sellers, generally within a fairly local context.

The complexity of urban life invariably provides an obstacle to the application of economic analysis. There is no satisfactory resource allocation model (with a manageable set of variables) which can determine the optimal combination of land, labour and capital in an urban economy – an economy which changes both over time and in its spatial manifestation. Yet economic analysis can and must be applied to the many problems relating to the urban arena. Within the context of urbanization on a global scale, an understanding of urban growth and spatial structure, housing, the location of urban land uses, urban development, property and investment, and urban planning and the urban environment might help to provide the economist with the opportunity to apply his or her special powers of analysis and to investigate – in specific contexts – the productive and distributive processes of urbanized society. These issues will be addressed, in turn, in the subsequent chapters of this book.

REFERENCES

Abu-Lughod, J. (1996) 'Urbanization in the Arab world and the international system', in Gugler, J. (ed.), *The Urban Transformation of the Developing World*, Oxford: Oxford University Press.

Carter, F.W. (1995) 'East Europe: population distribution, urban change, housing and environmental problems', background paper prepared for the *Global Report on Human Settlements*.

Carter, H. and Lewis, C.R. (1991) *An Urban Geography of England and Wales in the Nineteenth Century*, London: Edward Arnold.

Castells, M. (1977) *The Urban Question: A Marxist Approach*, London: Edward Arnold.

Chang, S.S. and Spinelli, J.G. (1998) 'Newly industrializing countries: a discussion of terms', in Gonzales, A. and Norwine, J. (eds), *The New Third World*, 2nd edn, Oxford: Westview Press.

Chase-Dunn, C. (1989) *Global Formation: Structures of World Economy*, London: Blackwell.

Chen, X. and Parish, W.L. (1996) 'Urbanization in China: reassessing an evolving model', in Gugler, J. (ed.), *The Urban Transformation of the Developing World*, Oxford: Oxford University Press.

Clark, D. (1996) *Urban World/Global City*, London: Routledge.

Dickenson, J., Gould, B., Clarke, C., Mather, D., Prothero, M., Siddle, D., Smith, C. and Thomas-Hope, E. (1996) *Geography and the Third World*, 2nd edn, London: Routledge.

Economist, The (1998) *World in Figures*, London: Profile Books.

Enyedi (1996) 'Urbanization under socialism', in Andrusz, G., Harloe, M. and Szelenyi, I. (eds), *Cities after Socialism*, Oxford: Blackwell.

Findley, S.E. (1993) 'The third world city: development policies and issues', in Kasarda, J.D. and Parnell, A.M. (eds), *Third World Cities*, London: Sage.

French, R.A. and Hamilton, F.E.I. (eds) (1979) *The Socialist City: Spatial Structure and Urban Policy*, Chichester: Wiley.

Friedmann, J.P. (1972) 'The spatial organisation of power in the development of urban systems', *Development and Change*, 17: 69–74.

Gilbert, A. and Gugler, J. (1992) *Cities, Poverty and Development*, Oxford: Oxford University Press.

Goldfrank, W.L. (1979) *The World System of Capitalism Past and Present*, Beverly Hills CA: Sage.

HABITAT (1996) *An Urbanizing World: Global Report on Human Settlements*, Oxford: United Nations Centre for Urban Settlements and Oxford University Press.

Harloe, M. (1996) 'Cities in transition', in Andrusz, G., Harloe, M. and Szelenyi, I. (eds), *Cities after Socialism*, Oxford: Blackwell.

Hugo, G. (1996) 'Urbanization in Indonesia: city and countryside linked', in Gugler, G. (ed.), *The Urban Transformation of the Developing World*, Oxford: Oxford University Press.

Mohan, R. (1996) 'Urbanization in India: patterns and emerging policy issues', in Gugler, J. (ed.), *The Urban Transformation of the Developing World*, Oxford: Oxford University Press.

Potter, R.B. (1992) *Urbanisation in the Third World*, Oxford: Oxford University Press.

Potter, R.B. and Lloyd-Evans, S. (1998) *The City in the Developing World*, Harlow: Longman.

Rostow, W.W. (1960) *The Stages of Economic Growth: A Non-Communist Manifesto*, London: Cambridge University Press.

Schwarz (1990) 'A miracle comes home', *Far East Economic Review*, 19 April: 40–4.

Szelenyi, I. (1996) 'Cities under socialism – and after', in Andrusz, G., Harloe, M. and Szelenyi, I. (eds), *Cities after Socialism*, Oxford: Blackwell.

Taaffe, E.J., Morrill, R.L. and Gould, P.R. (1963) 'Transport expansion in underdeveloped countries: a comparative analysis', *Geographical Review*, 53: 503–29.

Taylor, P.J. (1993) *Political Geography: World Economy, Nation-State and Locality*, London: Longman.

Vance, J.E. (1970) *The Merchant's World: The Geography of Wholesaling*, Englewood Cliffs NJ: Prentice Hall.

World Bank (1999) *Entering the 21st Century: World Development Report 1999/2000*, New York: World Bank and Oxford University Press.

2
Urban Growth

INTRODUCTION

Urban economics is in its infancy and therefore – as yet – cannot be expected to produce entirely satisfactory models of urban growth. The complexity and diversity of economic forces, processes of urban growth, administrative systems, social and cultural influences and inadequate data sometimes lead economists to misinterpret demographic data and equate urbanization (i.e. a relative increase in the total population living in towns and cities) with urban growth (i.e. an absolute increase in urban population).

Clearly the population of an urban area will increase if there is a natural increase in its population (an excess of births over deaths) and/or if there is a net in-migration from rural areas. The two causes of population increase will be related since, if the in-migrants are mainly young adults of both sexes, it can be expected that the natural increase in population will rise. Also, in most developing countries, net in-migration has for long exceeded natural increase – for example, accounting for 54 per cent of urban growth between 1975 and 1990 (Findley, 1993); a high proportion of in-migration is temporary (for example, up to 70 per cent in West Africa and South East Asia) and therefore natural increase is a major component of urban growth (Clark, 1996).

Between 1985 and 1995, the urban population of the world increased by 730 million. But whereas urban population in China increased by 226 million, in India by 87 million, in Brazil by 32 million, in Indonesia by 26 million, and in Nigeria by 22 million (Clark, 1996), there was virtually no increase in urban population in north-west Europe and the north-eastern United States because of high levels of out-migration and low rates of natural increase. In the developing world, the population of towns and cities increased at an average annual rate of 45 million during the last two decades of the twentieth century, whereas in the developed world the urban population increased by only 7 million per annum (Potter and Lloyd-Evans, 1998). In the developing countries – during the 1990s – the annual rate of growth of cities such as Dhaka was as high as 7 per cent, Bangalore 5.7

Table 2.1 The growth in the number of urban agglomerations with 8 million or more persons, 1970–2000

	1970	1990	2000
Developed countries	New York	Tokyo	Tokyo
	London	New York	New York
	Tokyo	Los Angeles	Los Angeles
	Los Angeles	Moscow	Moscow
	Paris	Osaka	Osaka
		Paris	Paris
Newly-industrializing countries	Mexico City	Mexico City	Mexico City
	Buenos Aires	São Paulo	São Paulo
	São Paulo	Buenos Aires	Buenos Aires
		Seoul	Seoul
		Rio de Janeiro	Rio de Janeiro
			Istanbul
			Lima
Developing countries	Shanghai	Shanghai	Shanghai
	Beijing	Calcutta	Calcutta
		Bombay	Bombay
		Beijing	Beijing
		Tianjin	Jakarta
		Jakarta	Dehli
		Cairo	Lagos
		Dehli	Tianjin
		Manila	Dhaka
			Cairo
			Manila
			Karachi
			Bangkok
			Tehran
			Bangalore

Source: United Nations (1991) *World Urbanization Prospects*, Table 11.

per cent, Lagos 5.6 per cent, Dehli 6 per cent, Jakarta 4.4 per cent, Karachi 4.4 per cent and Bangkok 4.1 per cent (Clark, 1996).

In the developing world, it was clear that an increasing number of cities were growing to an enormous size, while the number and size of large cities in the developed world remained almost constant. Table 2.1 shows that, whereas in 1970 the number of mega-cities or urban agglomerations with eight million or more persons amounted to only five both in the developed world and the newly-industrializing and developing countries, by 2000 (according to United Nations forecasts) the number would increase to only six in the developed world but to as many as 22 in the newly-industrializing and developing countries (Clark, 1996).

BOX 2.1: URBAN GROWTH IN WESTERN EUROPE

In Western Europe, the current pattern of urban areas has evolved gradually over the last two and a half thousand years. Cities have evolved from very small settlements at varying speeds, but urban development in most countries has been particularly rapid since the eighteenth and nineteenth centuries, or more specifically since the Industrial Revolution. It has been suggested that – at the top of the urban hierarchy – four levels of cities of 'European importance' have emerged in recent years (see Kunzmann and Wegener, 1991). In first rank order are Paris and London, the only two global cities in the European Union (EU) which, in terms of population (respectively 10.7 and 10.5 million in the mid-1990s) compare with, say, New York, Tokyo, Mexico City, Cairo or Bombay.

Of second rank importance are the conurbations of Rhine-Ruhr (Bonn/Cologne/Düsseldorf–Dortmund/Essen/Duisburg), Copenhagen/Malmö, Manchester, Leeds, Liverpool and the Randstad (Amsterdam/Rotterdam) with populations ranging from 2 million to 9.2 million. Of similar European importance are a number of large free-standing cities ('Eurometropoles') such as Athens, Barcelona, Berlin, Birmingham, Brussels, Hamburg, Madrid, Milan, Munich, Rome, Vienna and Zürich – all of which perform essential economic, financial or political and cultural functions on a European scale. With the probable enlargement of the EU in the first decade of the new millennium, certain cities in East Central Europe could be added to this list, such as Budapest, Prague and Warsaw.

The third rank of cities comprise some national capitals such as Dublin and Lisbon (with populations of respectively 1 million and 1.3 million), and other cities of European importance such as Glasgow, Naples, Palermo, Strasbourg, Stuttgart and Turin – although their functions are more national rather than continental. Kunzmann and Wegener (1991) suggest that below this level, various urban hierarchies follow (see Christaller, 1933), depending on national definitions of central places (in, for example, Germany, Austria, the Netherlands and Denmark), and that as Europe becomes increasingly integrated these hierarchies will be superseded by a single urban hierarchy throughout the EU. Clearly, the spatial dimension of the urban economy is not static, but dependent upon the processes of urban growth.

An alternative but not dissimilar approach to classifying cities and their

continued

Figure 2.1 *Major cities in Western Europe, 1990*

functions involves an examination of the dominant characteristics of their regions rather than their population size and hinterlands. It is suggested that core cities are the economic centres of 'functional urban regions' (FURs) defined in terms of concentrations of employment and a commuting hinterland comprising all those areas from which more people commute to the core than to some other city (see Cheshire and Hay, 1988). In Western Europe, the principal FURs are centred on global cities (for example, London and Paris), growing high-tech/service centres (such as Bristol, Reading and Munich), declining industrial cities (Metz, Oberhausen, Mons, Sheffield) and port cities (Liverpool, Genoa, Marseille). Other FURs include growing cities without modern industrialization, company towns, new towns, monofunctional satellites, small towns, rural centres and 'rurban' belts, tourism and cultural centres, and border and gateway cities. It is recognised that the function of cities, employment patterns and commuting vary over time, and that this will be both a cause and an effect of urban growth.

There has also been quite a substantial change in the location of large cities. Whereas in the early 1920s, there were 24 cities in the world with more than 1 million inhabitants and their average latitude was 44°30', in the 1980s there were as many as 198 such cities but they were located at an average latitude of 34°07' – markedly closer to the equator (Potter and Lloyd-Evans, 1998).

BOX 2.2: URBAN GROWTH IN THE UNITED STATES AND CANADA

In the second half of the twentieth century, the United States and Canada contained some of the world's most rapidly growing cities, all of which were relatively new and malleable in comparison to cities in other advanced capitalist countries, and – in contrast to Western Europe – with rates of urban growth affected substantially by the migration of people, firms and jobs, often over very great distances (HABITAT, 1996). This was associated with major changes in the relative importance of different cities. While the gateway ports of New York, Boston, Philadelphia and Baltimore, and the larger industrial cities of Chicago, Detroit, Cleveland, Buffalo and Pittsburg all declined in their relative economic importance, the new urban hierarchies in the south and on the west coast experienced rapid economic growth (HABITAT, 1996).

Population growth, a rising GDP associated with technological change, and changes in the spatial division of labour led to the creation of new metropolitan complexes, often in formerly peripheral regions. Between 1950 and 1990, the number of metropolitan statistical areas (MSAs) therefore increased from 169 to 284 – their population rising correspondingly from 85 million to 193 million, or from 45 to 78 per cent of the total USA population. Many of the newer MSAs are merged into consolidated metropolitan statistical areas (CMSAs) embracing the larger urban agglomerations; for example, the CMSAs of New York–New Jersey–Connecticut (with a population of 19.3 million in 1990), Los Angeles–Riverside–Anaheim (with over 14.5 million), Chicago (with 8.2 million) and Washington–Baltimore (with 6.7 million) (HABITAT, 1996).

In contrast to Europe, Latin America, North Africa and Asia, most large metropolitan areas in the USA are of recent origin, for example Miami,

continued

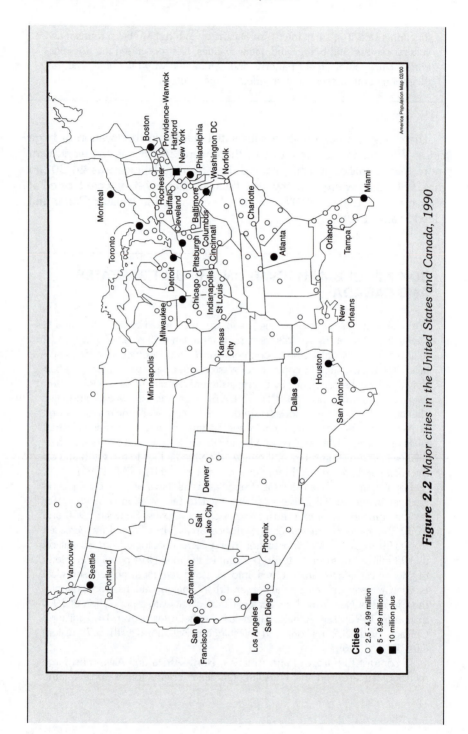

Figure 2.2 *Major cities in the United States and Canada, 1990*

Seattle, Phoenix (with populations of 2 to 4 million in 1990) were not even founded in 1850, while Los Angeles, San Diego and Houston had but a few thousand inhabitants in the mid-nineteenth century. In recent years, however, their growth rates have been among the fastest in the world.

In Canada, metropolitan areas have grown comparatively slowly because growth started from a lower base (there were only 28 urban centres with populations of over 100,000 in 1991), the country's resources are widely dispersed, and the relatively low density of the total population militates against rapid urban growth. It was therefore only in the 1960s that Canada's population became largely metropolitan (at least a decade after the USA). Thus, whereas there were no metropoltan areas with more than 1 million inhabitants before 1930, by 1991 Toronto, Montreal and Vancouver had populations of respectively 3.9, 3.2 and 1.6 million (HABITAT, 1996).

The spatial manifestation of growth has been dominated by 'bi-coastal' urban development – from Seattle to San Diego in the west, and from Maine to Miami in the east. Commercial and residential locations along both the Pacific and Atlantic coasts are particularly accessible to national and international urban systems. However, across the USA, rates of urban growth have been very variable during the last two decades of the twentieth century. The fastest growing urban areas were the smaller metropolitan areas – which grew by 46.9 per cent in the 1980s. Most were in Florida, Arizona, Nevada and on Vancouver Island or on the lower mainland, and their economies were often based on retirement services and recreation. The second fastest growing group comprised cities concerned primarily with public administration at a national, state or provincial level or with defence. Growth rates averaged 17.5 per cent during the 1980s. Cities in the third fastest growing group were the 'control and management centres' of the financial and service sectors of the economy. In the USA, metropolitan areas in this group grew by 14.5 per cent. A fourth group includes manufacturing cities, but these grew by only 1.5 per cent on average, while urban areas involved in mining and resource-based activities declined by 2 per cent on average over the 1980s (HABITAT, 1996). Very broadly, there were similar patterns of growth in Canada. Last, there are a group of urban areas whose growth is dependent on government policy, for example Silicon Valley in San José, Software Valley near Salt Lake City, San Diego (as a military location), Dallas and Atlanta (as regional service centres in growing regions) and – in Canada – Kanata near Ottawa (as a centre for expanding high-tech industries).

CAUSES OF URBAN GROWTH

Prior to a consideration of urban growth, it is important to appreciate that cities have – since their early origins – been inextricably associated with the generation of a 'surplus' (see Childe, 1950; Harvey, 1973). In this context, a surplus can be defined both 'as a quantity of material resources and product that is appropriated for one segment of society at the expense of others . . . [and as] . . . an amount of material product that is set aside to provide for improvements in human welfare' (Potter and Lloyd-Evans, 1998: 34). If it is accepted that urban growth increases the size of the GDP per capita, investment should be directed at either the most profitable opportunities in order to maximize urban growth, or at socially or communally oriented needs within the urban arena, or both.

The principal problem in directing investment at urban growth, is that the processes of growth are both highly complex and vary not only within a single country but also globally. Hoselitz (1955) suggested that urban growth could be 'generative' or 'parasitic'. It is probable that in most developed countries, urban growth is generative in that it stimulates economic growth and creates a 'surplus' in the wider urban region, whereas in developing countries growth was parasitic at the colonial stage in their development (i.e. surpluses were extracted from surrounding regions) but is now largely generative (see Potter and Lloyd-Evans, 1998).

With regard to the generative process, explanations of urban growth in the developed world are provided by the central place, urban base and Keynesian theories, and in less developed countries by the modernization theory, but in the context of the parasitic process an explanation of growth is offered by the dependency theory.

Central Place Theory

Christaller (1933) hypothesized that the distribution of centralized services accounts for the spacing, size and functional pattern of urban centres. On the assumption that urban settlements locate on a uniform plane, centralized service centres would be distributed regularly within a systematic pattern. Market areas or spheres of influence would take the form of a hexagonal mesh. This would avoid either certain areas not being served, or other areas being served by overlapping hinterlands – consequences of a pattern of circular market areas. The main function of each town would be to supply goods and services to the countryside – town and country being interdependent.

A hierarchy of centres would evolve. Towns with the lowest level of specialization would be evenly spaced and surrounded by their hexagonally-shaped market areas. For each group of six towns there would be a larger city with more specialized functions which would be located an equal distance from other cities with the same degree of specialization. Such cities would have larger hexagonal hinterlands for their own specialized services. Even larger and more specialized settlements would have larger market areas and be situated at an equal distance from each other. Christaller

Table 2.2 *The urban hierarchy in South Germany (after Christaller)*

Market centre	Distance apart (km)	Population	Tributary area size (km^2)	Population
Market hamlet (*Marktort*)	7	800	45	2,700
Township centre (*Amstort*)	12	1,500	135	8,100
County seat (*Kresstadt*)	21	3,500	400	24,000
District centre (*Bezirksstadt*)	36	9,000	1,200	75,000
Small state capital (*Gausstadt*)	62	27,000	3,600	225,000
Provincial head capital (*Provinzhauptstadt*)	108	90,000	10,800	675,000
Regional capital city (*Landeshauptstadt*)	186	300,000	32,000	2,025,000

Source: E. L. Ullman, *American Journal of Sociology*, 46 (1941) 857.

believed that the lowest-ranked centres were likely to be located 7 km apart. Settlements of the next highest rank would serve three times the area and three times the population. Thus they would be situated 12 km apart ($\sqrt{3} \times$ 7). Similarly, the market areas of centres of the next rank would again be three times larger (table 2.2, figure 2.3). Since the number of settlements of successively lower rank follows a geometric progression (1, 3, 9, 27, ...) the pattern is referred to as a $k = 3$ hierarchy. Towns within the hierarchy would grow as a result of an increase in the production of goods and services to satisfy an increased demand from a growing population within their zones of influence, but generally they would remain within their rank and the rule of three would persist.

Christaller recognised that the hierarchy would be modified by long-distance trade, by transport routes and by administrative functions. Towns influenced by these factors would have larger populations than their local market would imply, and would be part of a $k = 4$ or even $k = 7$ hierarchy. Settlement would tend generally to be clustered along main routes and be larger at route junctions. Large-scale manufacturing industry would also have an agglomerating influence, increasing population out of proportion to the size of the immediate service hinterland.

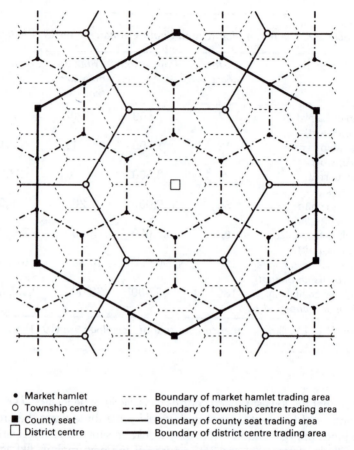

• Market hamlet	- - - - Boundary of market hamlet trading area
○ Township centre	— · — · Boundary of township centre trading area
■ County seat	——— Boundary of county seat trading area
□ District centre	■■■ Boundary of district centre trading area

Figure 2.3 *Christaller's theory of the arrangement of central places*

The central place theory is criticised as it is dependent upon the evolution of settlement on a uniform plane – Christaller largely ignored variable topography. The influence of manufacturing industry both past and present and below a large scale is also discounted, the production of goods and services for distribution to other areas is not considered, local specialization is ignored, and it is not appreciated that growth generates the internal needs of cities (for example, schools, hospitals, and general service and manufactured requirements). Neither the growth of industrial suburbs nor of outlying business districts fits in with the central place theory, and there is no consideration of the effect upon the size of towns of a large in-migration of labour.

But the central place theory is useful in that it stresses the relevance of the market area to the size of a town's population, and it introduces

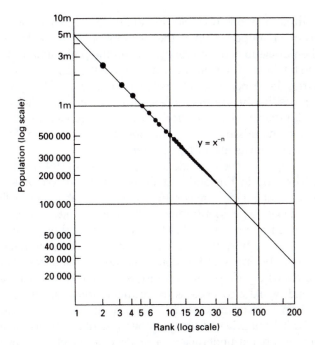

Figure 2.4 *The rank–size rule: the hypothetical population of cities in relation to their ranking*

the idea of the urban hierarchy. It has led to the introduction of the 'rank–size rule' which states that the population of a given urban area tends to be equal to the population of the largest city divided by the rank of the population size into which the given urban area falls, the population of settlements thus being arranged according to the series $1, \frac{1}{2}, \frac{1}{3}, \frac{1}{4}, \ldots$ $1/n$. If plotted on a graph this produces the result exhibited in figure 2.4.

Whereas the central place theory was idealistic, not being derived from empirical information, the rank–size rule is based on the study of actual population data. Yet generally the rank–size rule is in accord with the central place theory. Both imply that there are very few large cities, and where Christaller's urban hierarchy would produce a stepped arrangement of population sizes and the rank–size rule shows a smooth progression of settlements through the ranks, this divergence is largely illusory. Christaller's theory is most relevant to small rural areas and to the lower ranks of the hierarchy, whereas the rank–size rule is particularly relevant to a large area – possibly a whole country. Because of regional variations in the degree of industrialization, the development of transport services and administrative structures, a series of stepped hierarchies merge together to produce a relatively smooth population curve blurring the edges of individual hierarchical systems. The rule depends upon the assumption of a stable relationship between the populations of central places and the population of the market areas served by them. The principal weakness of the rank–size rule is that in most countries the largest city is larger than the rule would suggest.

Central place theory and the rank–size rule provide an efficient basis for administering urban regions and for allocating resources. Investment decisions must take the urban hierarchy or rank–size into account if the desired private or social returns are to be realised.

Based on empirical studies made in 1938, Smailes (1944) suggested that the urban hierarchy in England and Wales comprised six ranks of settlement: that is, major cities, major towns, towns, sub-towns, villages and hamlets. To qualify as a fourth-rank, 'fully-fledged' town, an urban settlement would need to possess at least three banks, a Woolworth's store, a secondary school, a hospital, a cinema and a weekly newspaper. Settlements which did not possess this complete range of services were categorized as sub-towns or villages. In contrast, a city would have all the services of a town and would also possess department stores, specialized hospital services and an evening newspaper. A major city would in addition have the regional offices of private firms and government departments; and when the research was being undertaken, a major city would also have its daily morning newspaper and a civic university. But Smailes was not prepared to identify market areas and recognized that the location and spacing of urban settlements showed no hexagonal pattern.

Smith (1978) using a much larger number of indicators of urban rank than Smailes had used in his 1938 classification, showed that the urban hierarchy in England and Wales had remained very stable. Of the 606 urban centres, only 138 rose in rank, and 78 declined over the period 1938–78. Change occurred mainly among the lower-order centres, especially in the north, but the south and east were particularly stable because of the dominance of London. In research funded by the Royal Institution of Chartered Surveyors and the Economic and Social Research Council (Schiller, 1985), it was also shown that the hierarchy of shopping centres in Britain had changed little over the period 1961–84.

In the United States, central place theory has been further developed. Berry and Garrison (1958) suggested that the concepts of 'range' and 'threshold' control the distribution of central places. The range of a good or service is the distance over which people are prepared to travel to obtain that product, and the threshold is the minimum amount of purchasing power necessary to support the supply of a good or service from a central place. The range of a product is limited at the upper level by the degree of competition from other central places supplying the same product, and at the lower level by the threshold necessary to permit it to function. As more specialized products require a larger threshold they usually need a more extensive range, therefore it is logical for an urban hierarchy to evolve based on the degree of specialization of central places.

The central place theory and considerations of urban rank have been generally concerned with towns as service centres. But Pred (1966) argued that (at least in the United States) the rate of development of a city is related functionally to the diversification of its manufacturing sector, and that city size depends largely on the number or extent or its overlapping hinterlands.

Urban Base Theory

Unlike the central place theory, which was concerned with the distribution of products from an urban centre to its hinterland, the urban base theory involves a consideration of demand from anywhere outside the boundaries of the settlement.

The more a city specializes, the more it destroys its self-sufficiency. Urban growth will thus depend upon the urban area's ability to export goods and services to pay for its imported needs. The production of goods and services for export is known as a 'basic' activity and the output of products for distribution solely to the urban area itself is referred to as a 'non-basic' activity. According to the theory, the growth of an urban area depends upon the ratio of basic to non-basic activities – the higher the ratio, the greater the rate of growth. Non-basic industries will be dependent upon the basic sector, employees in the latter providing much of the demand for the products of the former.

The theory assumes that once the underlying economic, technological and social structure of a country has stabilised, the basic–non-basic ratio of an urban area and the ratios of these activities (separately or combined) to the total population remain constant. If there is an injection of basic employment into the town, eventually non-basic employment will have to increase to meet the higher local demand for goods and services, and the total dependent population will also increase. Thus any temporary instability resulting from an initial increase in basic employment will be eliminated through an upward adjustment in both non-basic employment and total population (table 2.3). The extent of the overall change will therefore be at a multiple of the initial injection of basic employment.

The urban base theory also suggests that if an urban area loses some basic employment, less non-basic employment will be required and the town's population will decline at a multiple of the initial withdrawal of basic employment.

Many criticisms have been expressed regarding the validity of the theory. There is unlikely to be a constant basic–non-basic ratio for an urban area

Table 2.3 The basic–non-basic equilibrium

	Number	I Initial equilibrium ratio to basic employment	Number	II Disequilibrium ratio to basic employment	Number	III Eventual equilibrium ratio to basic employment
Basic employees	10,000	1.0	12,500	1.0	12,500	1.0
Non-basic employees	15,000	1.5	15,000	1.2	18,750	1.5
Total employees	25,000	2.5	27,500	2.2	31,250	2.5
Total population	50,000	5.0	55,000	4.4	62,500	5.0

even if the overall underlying conditions remain fairly stable. Total non-basic activity increases in relative importance as urban areas increase in size, and individual basic and non-basic activities may experience economies of scale (and possibly eventual diseconomies) thereby altering ratios. Undue importance is attached to basic employment; non-basic employment may sometimes be more important in determining economic activity in an urban area, and while the theory argues that non-basic employment is dependent upon basic employment, the reverse is often true. Well-developed non-basic activities will attract basic industry, which will be dependent upon the non-basic activities' ability to supply goods and services, capital, ancillary labour and developable land. The theory only suggests what might happen if there is a change in basic activity; it gives no indication of what future changes may be anticipated in an urban area. But a major weakness is that it ignores the importance of imports. If all the increase in export earnings of basic activities was spent on imported goods and services there would be no increase in demand for the products of non-basic industries. Any application of the urban base theory (or one where non-basic activities were assumed to be dominant) would involve the difficult problem of first defining and then identifying basic and non-basic activities and employment, since industries, institutions, firms and employees may not demarcate between production for the local market and production for export.

Nevertheless, although the numerical aspects of the theory are unrefined, in many urban areas (especially in medium-sized and small towns) changes in overall economic activity and in population depend largely upon changes in basic activity. The theory also shows that there is a multiplier effect following initial injections (or withdrawals) of activity. In general it

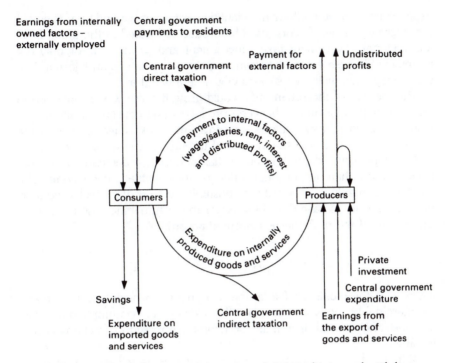

Figure 2.5 *Money flows circulating around, injected into and withdrawn from an urban area*

should be assumed that there is interdependence between basic and non-basic activities, and that the multiplier of each activity is different and varies over time and over different population and income levels.

Keynesian Model

Whereas the urban base theory concentrated upon urban employment, additions to the level of employment and multiplier effects upon the total population, the flow of money theory is essentially concerned with the economic growth of an urban area expressed in monetary terms. It involves the assessment of the effect upon total income of the circular flow of money between producers and consumers, export earnings and import expenditure, investment and savings and public spending and taxation (figure 2.5).

This approach, developed with regard to the national economy by Keynes (1936) in the 1930s, identifies money inflows as export earnings, the earnings of externally-employed factors, and national government expenditure; money outflows are identified as import expenditure, payment for externally-owned factors (used by producers located in the urban area) and national government taxes. Investment and saving may or may not be retained for use within the town, but net investment is an injection into the money flow, while net savings would be a withdrawal.

The income of the urban area would grow if there was an increase in the circular flow of money between producers and consumers, money inflows exceeded money outflows, and investment exceeded savings. If the opposite trends occurred the income of the urban area would decline.

A multiplier would result in any initial increase (or decrease) in income having a more than proportionate effect on the eventual urban income. The greater the marginal propensity to consume (MPC) or the smaller the marginal propensity to save (MPS) the larger the eventual increase in income. The extent of the multiplier is measured accordingly:

$$K = \frac{1}{1 - \text{MPC}} \qquad \text{or} \qquad K = \frac{1}{\text{MPS}}$$

where K is the multiplier. (Note: the marginal propensity to consume and the marginal propensity to save are the additions to consumption and savings resulting from an increment of income expressed as fractions of that income.)

Although the money flow theory of growth is as relevant to an urban area as it is to a national economy, its weakness is that data at a local level are largely unavailable and that even if information were to hand the theory would not predict when a change in variables would occur. But like the urban base theory it suggests that there is a causal relationship between the export activities of an urban area and its rate of growth, and that basic and non-basic activities are mutually dependent. While the urban base theory is primarily concerned with employment and assumes that incomes within the urban area will increase at some proportion to an increase in population, the money flow theory is mainly concerned with income. If increased, urban income might or might not be associated with a subsequent increase in population but it would probably have an effect, possibly substantial, on the built environment.

BOX 2.3: URBAN GROWTH IN EAST CENTRAL EUROPE AND THE FORMER SOVIET UNION

In East Central Europe, government policies promoted large-scale inter-regional migration and the growth of large towns and cities – during the

1960s, 1970s and 1980s – to provide the workforce for major plants and enterprises. Nevertheless, a considerable proportion of the region's urban population continued to live in small urban centres with fewer than 100,000 inhabitants, while only one-quarter of the region's population lived in cities of more than 100,000 – in contrast to a half in the European Union (HABITAT, 1996). Very large cities within the region – those with populations of more than 1 million – declined in most countries since it was a priority of planning policy to control the growth of major cities such as Budapest (because of its popularity) and develop lower rank centres in the urban hierarchy, for example by means of establishing new towns to accommodate the population associated with a new industrial development.

The promotion of urban growth in the former Soviet Union was similar to that undertaken in East Central Europe although on a considerably larger scale. Between 1959 and 1989, industrial development policy had a major impact on migration and urban development. In this period, and associated with investment in oil and natural gas production, several of the republic's most rapidly growing cities were in the Volga–Ural regions, while, to the west, the modernization of metallurgical industries (including iron and steel) was associated with urban development – the Kursk region benefiting from a higher standard of infrastructure provision than in the east, and proximity to the markets of East Central Europe (through COMECON) and Western Europe (HABITAT, 1996). Whereas 33 of the Soviet Union's fastest growing cities were in these regions between 1979 and 1989, only two were in the older industrial regions closer to Moscow. Conversely, of the 36 cities with the slowest rates of urban growth (or negative growth), two-thirds were in the Kuznetsk basin, the Donbas coalfield or the Central Region.

Urban growth in the latter part of the twentieth century soon led to the proliferation of large cities. Whereas in 1959, only 49 per cent of the Soviet Union's urban population lived in cities of more than 100,000 inhabitants, by 1989 the proportion had increased to 61 per cent. This was markedly higher than in East Central Europe, where only 22 per cent lived in urban areas of this size (HABITAT, 1996). Clearly, official policy – which had aimed at controlling the growth of large cities since the 1930s – was not working. Undoubtedly, large cities had the best infrastructure and largest supply of skilled labour, and, unlike cities in the capitalist world, they did not necessarily have higher costs than smaller cities. By the 1970s, optimum city size was no longer of any relevance to Soviet planners. Large urban agglomerations had emerged in the Soviet Union – centred, for example, on Moscow, the Donetsk mining centre, the Kuzbass coalfield, the central Dnepr region, and the metallurgical and mining cities of the Urals (HABITAT, 1996).

With the transition from socialist planning to a market economy in the late twentieth and early twentieth centuries, it will be interesting to monitor urban

continued

growth in both East Central Europe and the former Soviet Union in order to discover whether the processes of growth in the two regions gradually converge with those of the advanced capitalist states, or diverge from these processes by assuming many of the attributes of urban growth in the newly-industrializing or developing world.

Dependency Theory

Applicable to developing countries, as well as to the developed world, dependency theory maintains that – under *laissez-faire* – cities grow parasitically by exploiting and holding back their surrounding regions. Myrdal (1957) suggested that economic growth follows the principle *of cumulative causation*, whereby – once established in a city – economic development promotes further local development – the *spread effect*, but this is only at the expense of surrounding areas or other areas elsewhere – the *backwash effect*. This trend has become more apparent in recent years, since industrial plants, often owned by transnational corporations, tend to be concentrated in the larger urban areas and provide few spread effects to surrounding areas. The same is increasingly true of service activity – including retailing and entertainment.

With regard to developing countries, in particular, dependency theory is very much based on the contention that in relative terms the poor countries of the world are getting poorer and poorer, not so much because of their separation from advanced capitalist countries, but because of their closer association. Frank (1967) suggests that this is attributable to the developing countries joining the global economic system at the bottom and being held in a dependent position by cities in the capitalist world such as London, New York and Paris. According to Frank, a chain of dependency stretched from these 'metropoles' down to the 'satellite' cities in the developing world and beyond to the backward rural areas, and the more these countries were associated with the 'metropoles', the more they were held back (see Potter and Lloyd-Evans, 1998).

BOX 2.4: URBAN GROWTH IN LATIN AMERICA AND THE CARIBBEAN

Before 1980, the population growth of Latin America and the Caribbean was second only to Africa, and the region contained some of the world's fastest growing large cities. Over the long term (1900–90), the rate of urban growth

Cities
○ 1 - 3.99 million
● 4 - 9.99 million
■ 10 million plus

S. Am Population Map 02/00

Figure 2.6 *Major cities in Latin America, 1990*

has been dramatic. The number of cities in the region containing more than 1 million or more inhabitants increased from zero to 36, the total number of inhabitants in these cities grew from 15 million to 300 million, and the number of cities in the region that were among the world's largest 20 cities doubled from two to four (HABITAT, 1996).

As a result of urban growth, Mexico City and São Paulo have become the largest and second largest cities in the region – the former city having an estimated population of 31 million by 2000, and the latter having an estimated

continued

population of 25.8 million in the same year (HABITAT, 1996). Buenos Aires, Rio de Janeiro, Lima and Bogota are some way behind – all having reached populations of between 5 and 10 million. In addition, many new cities have been created away from centres of economic power, for example Belo Horizonte, Porto Alegre, Curitiba and Campinas in Brazil, with populations of between 1 and 5 milllion, and Guadalajara and Monterrey in Mexico, with populations approaching 5 million.

In recent years, however, rates of increase in the total and urban populations have slowed down owing to lower fertility, less immigration and slower economic growth. Whereas in 1980, the populations of São Paulo, Mexico City, Buenos Aires and Rio de Janeiro amounted in turn to 10.6, 20.0, 36.0 and 7.4 per cent of their national populations, by 1990–91 their respective populations had fallen to 10.5, 18.5, 34.5 and 6.5 per cent (HABITAT, 1996).

Modernization Theory

As an alternative to dependency theory, modernization theory suggests that urban growth is primarily generative rather than parasitic. It is based on the observation that since developing countries are characterized by a traditional, indigenous and underdeveloped sector on the one hand, and an innovating, westernized and modern sector on the other, growth eventually trickles down to poorer regions – even though economic activity and wealth are initially concentrated or polarized in cities (see Hirschman, 1958). In his interpretion of development pole theory Boudeville (1966) suggests that this is an inevitable and spontaneous process, an outcome of *laissez faire* (see Potter, 1992; Potter and Lloyd-Evans, 1998). Under *laissez-faire* conditions, cities would thus perform a generative role in economic development and provide the location for import-substituting industries whose products would be distributed through the city's hinterland, while new towns or growth poles would be required within the backward regions as centres of new development – facilitating the dispersal of economic activity and wealth over wider areas.

Since the modernization theory implies that growth occurs in an hierarchical sequence from the largest urban places to the smallest, Hudson (1969) argued that the trickling-down process could be applied to the central place system, whereas Rostow (1960) saw cities as 'engines of growth' for a country as a whole, implying that as the country progressed through its various stages of economic growth until it reached an age of high mass consumption, the manifestations of growth would filter down from the largest to smallest urban areas.

BOX 2.5: URBAN GROWTH IN SUB-SAHARAN AFRICA

In the 1970s, the population of sub-Saharan Africa began to grow more rapidly than that of Latin America and the Caribbean – with national populations trebling between 1950 and 1990, but this rate of growth was small when compared to a tenfold increase in the population of most African cities over the same period. By 1990, the population of Lagos had increased to more than 10 million, and the population of Kinshasa was approaching 5 million, while 22 other cities had populations that had risen rapidly to between 750,000 and 2.49 million (HABITAT, 1996: 84).

By the 1980s–1990s, however, rates of urban growth began to diminish

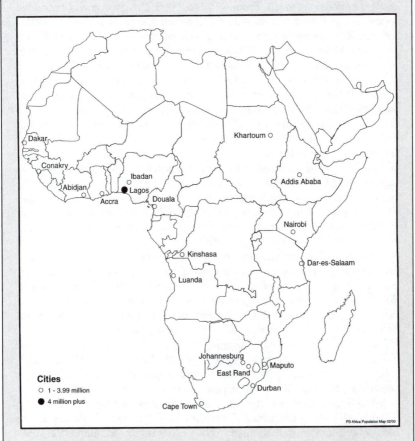

Figure 2.7 *Major cities in sub-Saharan Africa, 1990*

continued

as natural increase superseded rural–urban migration as the principal determinant of population increase, while the growth of the largest cities lagged behind that of medium-sized cities such as Dakar, Abijdan, Nairobi and Harare.

BOX 2.6: URBAN GROWTH IN INDONESIA

The urban population of Indonesia increased by more than twentyfold from 1920 to 1996, rising from 2.9 million to 70.2 million. In the second half of the century, following independence in 1949, there have been three contrasting periods of growth. From 1949 to 1969, the government promoted industrial development in an attempt to reduce a dependency on imports – industrialization stimulating the rapid growth of cities in the 1950s. However, war with Malaysia in the 1960s and the breakdown in the Indonesian economy in the early-1960s depressed the rate of urban growth. An oil boom from the late-1960s to the mid-1980s revived the economy, and an increase in real GDP by an average of 6.3 per cent per annum throughout the period was associated with a simultaneous average annual increase of 4 per cent throughout much of the period (World Bank, 1984; NUDSP, 1985; Hugo, 1996). Faced with a slump in oil prices in the mid-1980s and the fear of a breakdown in the Indonesian economy, the government introduced a policy of liberalization by terminating its import-substitution strategies and encouraging foreign investment and the expansion of exports, particularly from the manufacturing sector. The transformation of the economy went hand-in-hand with a doubling of the urban population from 32.8 in 1980 to 70.2 million in 1996 – West Java alone increasing its population from 5.8 to 12.2 million over the same period (see Hugo, 1996).

Apart from dramatic increases in urban population, Indonesia's urban areas have expanded spatially – particularly along major transport routes extending out from the major cities (Firman, 1991; McGee, 1991). In densely-settled Java, this has led to an overlap of urban and rural populations; also in areas around Jakarta (the capital) and Surabaja and, for example, between Jakarta and Bandung, and Yogyakarta and Semarang (see Hugo, 1996).

With a population rapidly approaching 15 million, Jakarta became the world's 19th largest city in the early 1990s (United Nations, 1993), and it was estimated that by 2000 the metropolitan region of Jakarta would have a population of about 30 million – larger than Los Angeles, rendering it the seventh largest mega-city in the world (Douglass, 1988; Hugo, 1996). Although Jakarta is undoubtedly a primate city, the level of primacy is not high when compared with many other countries (it accommodates only around 20 per cent of the total urban population), but it is substantial when compared to other countries of similar size. Primacy is undoubtedly an

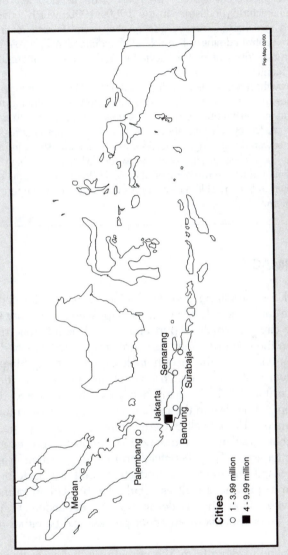

Figure 2.8 Major cities in Indonesia, 1990

continued

outcome of the economy retaining many of the attributes of the 'dependent' colonial period, for example continuing to export raw materials and importing processed goods, but it is also the result of the development of export-oriented manufacturing industries in the 1980s–1990s which tended to be concentrated in Jakarta. Primacy also resulted from Jakarta retaining and extending its central administrative role after independence, a role strengthened by the development of transportation and communications in recent years which centred on the capital.

Urban growth, however, is not without its price. Although Indonesia's burgeoning cities are – for economic and social reasons – continuing to attract in-migrants in increasing numbers, the advantages of urban growth have been increasingly eroded by 'chronic shortages of housing; limited accessibility to fresh water, sewerage, garbage collection, and other infrastructural services; unacceptably high levels of air, noise and water pollution; and high levels of unemployment and underemployment' (Hugo, 1996: 173). Clearly, solutions to these growth-related problems – as a priority – will need to be found in the new millennium.

URBAN PRIMACY

In many newly-industrializing and developing countries, the central place theory and the rank–size rule are entirely inapplicable. One city in particular, a *primate* city – normally a port and located peripherally rather than centrally within the country – may have grown to a position of dominance over all other urban areas, the most notable examples being Singapore and Hong Kong (when it was a crown colony) and numerous cities in sub-Saharan Africa (table 2.4). In many newly-industrializing and developing countries, people either live in the primate city or in a considerable number of small settlements. Primate cities were centres of colonial or post-colonial control, and major outlets for the export of products from economically-dependent hinterlands. They benefited from the transition from a subsistence to a capitalist mode of production, and the lack of effective competition from provincial centres (Clark, 1996). 'Urban primacy' does not conflict with either the modernization or dependency theories of urban growth. It could derive from either process and be either generative or parasitic.

In the short and medium term, the primate city increases its dominance since it becomes more and more a focus of internal and international trade. Since primate cities are invariably national capitals, they are centres of decision-making and opinion-forming. They are thus able to dominate their countries both economically and politically. They are centres of communication systems (television and telecom), they often have the only

Table 2.4 Primate cities in selected countries, 1991

Country	Largest city	Population in largest city	
		Urban population (per cent)	Total population (per cent)
Singapore	Singapore	100	100
Hong Kong	Hong Kong	100	94
Guinea	Conakry	89	23
Mauritania	Nouakchott	83	39
Costa Rica	San José	77	36
Congo	Brazzaville	68	28
Angola	Luanda	61	17
Thailand	Bangkok	57	13
Gabon	Libreville	57	26
Liberia	Monrovia	57	26
Haiti	Port au Prince	56	16
Togo	Lomé	55	14

Source: World Bank (1991).

international airport in their respective countries, and are the link-points between the domestic and global economies.

Although primate cities became more integrated with the global urban economy than with their domestic urban system, with economic development the degree of primacy decreases as the population becomes more evenly spread across other urban areas, although one city tends to retain its dominance (Clark, 1996). However, there is little empirical evidence to suggest 'that there is a single trend from urban primacy to a rank–size pattern at the national scale' (Potter and Lloyd-Evans, 1998: 62).

It must not be assumed, however, that at a national level there is a high degree of primacy in all newly-industrializing or developing countries, for example it is absent in Brazil (where Rio de Janeiro and São Paulo are both mega-cities), in China (where Shanghai, Tianjin, Beijing and now Hong Kong are all among the world's largest agglomerations), in India (where Calcutta, Bombay, Madras and Dehli are of broadly equal economic importance) and in Turkey (where Ankara and Istanbul compete for dominance). Within these countries, there is instead a high degree of primacy at the regional level.

Urban primacy, however, also exists within the advanced capitalist world. In Australia, for example, state capitals contain a high proportion of the

Table 2.5 Urban primacy in Australia in the 1990s			
State	*Percentage of national population*	*Capital*	*Percentage of state population*
South Australia	8.0	Adelaide	73.5
Western Australia	9.6	Perth	72.8
Victoria	24.9	Melbourne	71.5
New South Wales	33.9	Sydney	61.7
Queensland	18.2	Brisbane	45.5
Northern Territory	0.9	Darwin	45.5
Tasmania	2.6	Hobart	31.2

Note: In addition to the above states, the Australian Capital Territory contains only 1.6 per cent of the national population but its principal urban area – Canberra – contains 99.9 per cent of its population.

Source: Australian Bureau of Statistics (1997).

population of their respective states (table 2.5) – a legacy of their colonial past when the principal (or only) port town became a centre of administration, a conduit for trade and a focus for railway development, all of which were facilitated by a lack of physical barriers to easy communications with the rest of the colony. In New Zealand, by contrast, the complex mountainous landscape of its two islands impeded communication and led to the development of a number of comparatively small towns – each within self-contained regions – although Auckland's share of the country's total population had grown from less than 15 per cent of the total population in the 1920s to almost 30 per cent of the country's population by the 1990s (Robinson *et al.*, 2000). Even in the older developed world, urban primacy is evident, for example in France (in the case of Paris), Austria (Vienna), Denmark (Copenhagen) and Greece (Athens), although its formulative factors are different from those in the less developed world – more a reflection of continental political history than an outcome of colonialism.

BOX 2.7: URBAN GROWTH IN CHINA

In the 1950s, it was the aim of official policy to divert resources from large coastal cities – such as Shanghai – to the interior to facilitate production rather

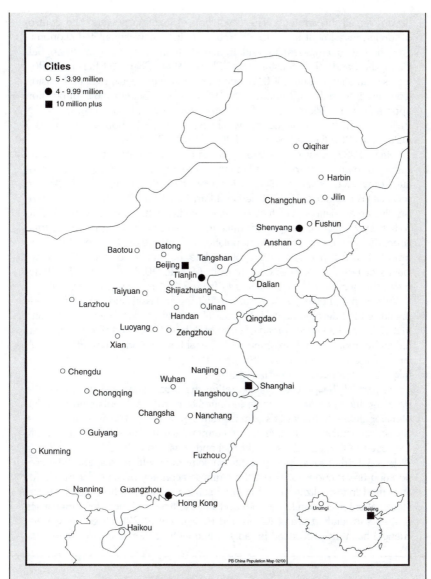

Cities

○ 5 - 3.99 million
● 4 - 9.99 million
■ 10 million plus

○ Qiqihar

○ Harbin

Changchun ○   ○ Jilin

Shenyang ● ○ Fushun

Anshan ○

Baotou ○   Datong ○   Tangshan ○
Beijing ■   Tianjin ●
Taiyuan ○   Shijiazhuang   Dalian
Lanzhou ○   ○ Jinan
Handan ○   Qingdao
Luoyang ○   ○ Zengzhou
Xian ○

Chengdu ○   Nanjing ○
Wuhan ○   Shanghai ■
Chongqing ○   Hangshou ○
Changsha ○   ○ Nanchang
Guiyang ○
Kunming ○   Fuzhou ○

Nanning ○   Guangzhou ●
○   Hong Kong
Haikou ○

Urumqi ○   Beijing ■

PB China Population Map 02/00

Figure 2.9 *Major cities in China, 1990*

than consumption, to enhance security and to promote regional equality (Chen and Parish, 1996). By the late 1970s, therefore, there was more of an even balance between small, medium and large cities than hitherto (Parish, 1990). However, since 1978 policies have been employed that, to an extent,

continued

have reversed this strategy. The devolution of taxation powers, and control of foreign investment funds to a number of cities, have stimulated economic growth, low unemployment and in-migration in, for example, Shanghai, Guangzhou and other coastal areas (Chen, 1994; Chen and Parish, 1996). It was estimated that by 2000, Shanghai's population would reach 24 million (compared to only 5.8 million in 1950), while Guangzhou's population approached 5 million. Apart from Shanghai, the only other mega-city is Beijing – which as state capital would have grown in population to 20.9 million by 2000 (United Nations, 1985; HABITAT, 1996).

Since 1982, however, central government has granted 'town' and 'city' status to many semi-rural settlements – giving them varying degrees of autonomy in handling foreign investment, collecting taxes and dispensing revenue (Yeh and Xu, 1990; Chen and Parish, 1996). The number of administrative areas, defined as cities, consequently increased from 239 in 1982 to 570 in 1993. During this period, since most new cities were small rather than large, the number of cities with populations of more than 1 million decreased from 8.4 to 5.8 per cent of the total, while the number of cities with populations of less than 200,000 grew from 50.6 to 60.2 per cent. Simultaneously, the number of towns increased from 2,664 to more than 15,000.

Although it should not be assumed that the reclassification of urban areas prejudiced the development of the coastal cities, it needs to be borne in mind that China had an even spread of cities of different sizes and a complex urban hierarchy prior to the development of coastal foreign trade cities after the collapse of the pre-1911 empire (Skinner, 1977). It is this pattern that the state might be attempting to re-establish.

As part of the process of integrating the urban and rural economy, the state also incorporated an increasing number of rural authorities on the edge of major cities into the latter's administrative framework. The average Chinese city consequently became increasingly semi-rural with a workforce fairly evenly employed in the agricultural, industrial and service sectors.

By conferring town or city status on semi-rural settlements, and by incorporating urban and rural areas, the Chinese economy became decentralized, and 'rural industrialization has created subcontracting relationships between industrial enterprises in large cities and small villages and township enterprises in their surrounding areas' (Chen and Parish, 1996: 72). Urban growth (or change) has thus proceeded broadly in line with economic development.

BOX 2.8: URBAN GROWTH IN INDIA

Throughout the twentieth century, most urban growth in India arose more from the enlargement of existing towns and cities, rather than from the establishment of new towns. Whereas the urban population increased eightfold –

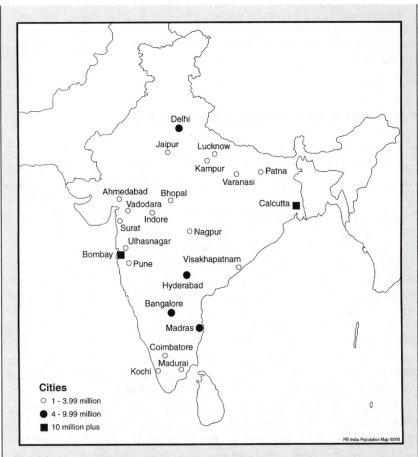

Figure 2.10 *Major cities in India, 1990*

from 25.6 million in 1901 to 212.9 million in 1991, the number of urban areas only doubled – from 1,811 to 3,609 in the same period (Mohan, 1996). Certain cities, however, grew substantially. Between 1950 and 2000, it is estimated that the population of Bombay would have increased from 3 million to 16.8 million, the city rising in rank from the 14th to the 8th largest city in the world, while the population of Calcutta would have increased from 4.6 to 16.4 million, the city rising in rank from 10th to 9th place (United Nations, 1985).

In every region and sub-region of India, there is an age-old hierachy of settlements which has remained stable for a considerable period of time – the number and spatial network of urban areas reflecting the demand for cen-

continued

tralized services from their hinterlands. However, in areas where there are comparatively few urban settlements, a number of new towns could be developed and, provided agricultural surpluses are adequate, could generate both population increase and economic growth.

SIZE, URBAN GROWTH AND OPTIMALITY

It must not be assumed that urban growth can be related immediately to an increase in welfare. Although large urban areas might enjoy economies of scale and benefit from access to services, they might also be disadvantaged by a poor environment and a higher cost of living. Even if the GDP per capita rises in parallel with urban growth, this could be attributed more to higher incomes being realised beyond the boundaries of the urban areas rather than to the economic performance of cities.

While small- to medium-sized urban areas accommodate most of the world's urban population, and provide economic and social links between town and country, on a global scale there was a total of 270 cities in 1990 with more than 1 million inhabitants, while 10 per cent of the world's urban population lived in 20 agglomerations of 8 million or more, of which the largest were Mexico City (20 million), Tokyo (18 million), São Paulo (17.4 million) and New York (16 million) (Clark, 1996). In 1995, China alone had 28 cities with populations of more than 2 million, and 46 cities with populations of between 1 and 2 million (Clark, 1996).

However, although more and more urban areas have become megacities, an examination of optimal city-size theory might suggest that the costs of growth are sometimes greater than the benefits. The benefits of large city size for consumers lie in a greater choice and range of goods and services created by the demands of a large urban population. This follows directly from central place theory. For producers the benefits are essentially twofold. First, agglomeration economies are either derived from firms in different or similar industries locating close together (i.e. *localization economies*); or stem from proximity to many different economic factors (i.e. *urbanization economies*). With localization economies, there is evidence that productivity 'rises with city size, so much that a typical firm will see its productivity climb 5 or 10 per cent if city size and the scale of local industry double' (World Bank, 1999: 126; see also Shukla, 1996; Henderson, 1998; Henderson *et al.*, 1998). In contrast, urbanization economies can be generated when either older, well-established industries concentrate in smaller, more specialized cities where congestion costs are low, or where new dynamic industries 'locate in large urban centres and benefit from the cross-fertilization provided by diverse factors' (World Bank, 1999: 127). Where there is a diversified economic base – as is normally the case in an agglomeration – both labour and consumers are less vulnerable to economic fluctuation, since 'employment can flow from one sector to another, keeping average unemployment low' – (World Bank, 1999: 127; see also Lucas, 1998), while consumers can benefit from a variety of services and shopping and entertainment opportunities. Secondly, internal economies of scale can be obtained by firms operating with larger factories and workforces, and more specialized equipment. Internal and agglomeration economies have the effect of reducing unit production costs and can therefore be expected to result in higher levels of output (and earnings) per worker.

Optimal city-size theory defines the non-monetary as well as the monetary costs and benefits of urban size and examines these in a welfare economic framework. Such considerations are important and may have far-reaching implications for urban and regional planning. The theory may help determine, for example, whether the size of the largest cities should be controlled and, at the other end of the scale, whether there exists some minimum urban size. Unfortunately, many of the non-monetary costs and benefits relating to city size – such as congestion, pollution and crime – are difficult to measure precisely and even more difficult to evaluate monetarily, in common with other costs and benefits. Nevertheless, some attempt should be made if such factors are likely to have important effects on welfare.

The cost of increasing city size involves, first, the direct costs to the public sector in providing urban services and infrastructure. These are generally assumed to form a 'U' shape with average costs initially falling as urban size increases, remaining fairly flat for a while, but eventually rising for large cities. Although various studies suggest that average costs fall and rise at different rates for different activities, the overall view for a wide range of countries is that public expenditure per capita rises significantly in the largest cities, often caused by the rising costs of public works, transport, staff, public security and social services. For example, in one study of local authority expenditure (per capita) in eight European countries it was found that when compared to the (national) average for towns of around 15,000–50,000 inhabitants, expenditure in larger towns was between 5 per cent and 213 per cent higher, and for the largest cities expenditure was between 49 per cent and 484 per cent higher (Commission of the European Communities, 1975). To some extent such estimates for large cities may be unduly high, since large centres provide high-level services for smaller centres nearby, as well as for their own populations. But overall, it is unlikely that differences in service structure between urban areas could explain away easily such sizeable disparities in per capita expenditure – especially notable in the largest urban conurbations.

One social cost related to urban size concerns the time and cost involved in the journey to work. In 1940 the Barlow Report on the distribution of industry in Britain condemned the economic and social consequences of excessive travel to work, in particular concerning the London conurbation. More recent figures from the Department of Transport confirm that average distance and travel time to the urban centre tend to be higher for London and the major conurbations, in contrast to smaller urban areas and rural areas.

For many years it has been recognized that social costs relate to urban size and include most notably the time and cost involved in commuting, the costs of atmospheric pollution (through emissions of sulphur dioxide, nitrogen dioxide and particulate concentrations), and the cost of crime (and especially serious crime) – all of which increase with city size (Hoch, 1972; Vanhove and Klassen, 1980; McLintock and Avison, 1968).

One of the undoubted complexities in assessing how social costs vary with city size is that low-income, central-city residents may suffer disproportionately more from the social ills of pollution, crime and congestion than do other groups. High-income residents may find they are more easily able to escape these problems by relocating to the suburbs, and may continue to benefit disproportionately more from the cultural facilities of the big city. As a result, it can be argued that cities optimally sized for the middle class are often too big from the point of view of those on lower incomes (Cox, 1979). The latter are seen as benefiting relatively little from central-city amenities and suffering relatively greatly from the social problems generated by big cities. One implication of this argument is that it becomes difficult – if not impossible – to distinguish optimality from distributional considerations in determining the 'optimal' city size. What is optimal for one social class may well be too large for another.

In practice, given the difficulties of placing monetary values on social costs and benefits, most studies on city size have restricted themselves to examining only a few of the indicators discussed so far. Cost data are generally based on local authority expenditure, while measures of urban benefits have tended to rely on earnings (as a proxy for output per worker). Concerning the latter, most studies show that average benefits tend to rise with increasing city size (Fuchs, 1959; Alonso, 1971; Hoch, 1972, 1987). As Richardson (1978) points out, this relationship still holds true when incomes are corrected for the higher cost of living associated with large cities. Such costs rise with city size because of higher land values and urban rents. These in turn push up housing costs and consumer costs in retailing and so on. According to Hoch (1976), cost-of-living differences explain between a half to two-thirds of the wages differential between city sizes (in

Table 2.6 Gross domestic product (GDP) per head by county at factor cost and household disposable income (GDP per head UK = 100)

GDP per head (UK = 100)		County/Metropolitan area	Household disposable income per head 1994 (UK = 100)
1977	*1993*		
98	91	Tyne & Wear	85
111	89	Cleveland	86
110	98	West Midlands	88
100	92	Greater Manchester	90
94	76	Merseyside	87
141	145	Greater London	120

Source: CSO Regional Accounts 2, *Economic Trends*, HMSO (various).

United States' cities). However, the various unpriced costs mentioned above are not reflected in any cost-of-living index, and could well help to offset the benefits of large cities.

In a broad sense, therefore, higher incomes must reflect both the productivity gains as well as the inconveniences of big cities. In support of this view, Porrell (1982) has shown that employees are found to trade off a range of disamenities against higher wages, and amenities against lower wages. After accounting for cost-of-living and amenity–disamenity effects Hoch (1987) suggests that influences on migration will emerge if wage rates in an urban area are more or less than expected. Following this line of reasoning, if output or income per worker is observed to decline in cities relative to elsewhere – reflecting a relative decline of urban productivity – we would expect to observe a rise in net out-migration (or fall in net in-migration). Table 2.6 shows UK national accounts estimates at county level, where these appear to match closely the major metropolitan areas. Gross domestic product (GDP) per head clearly declined relative to the rest of the UK in all major metropolitan areas shown, apart from Greater London, over the 1980s–early 1990s. Perhaps more significant, however, is the fact that most such areas now appear to have levels of output per head not only below the national average, but in some cases below that of surrounding areas. For example, in the West Midlands region in 1994, Warwickshire achieved a level of GDP per head similar to that given in table 2.6 for the West Midlands metropolitan area. However in 1994, GDP per head in Warwickshire had been considerably lower in relative terms, only achieving an index of 75 against an index of 98 for the metropolitan area. Furthermore,

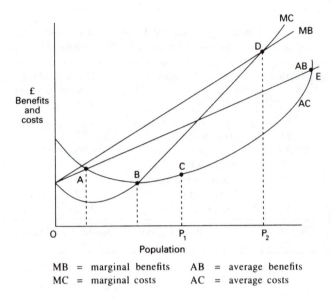

MB = marginal benefits   AB = average benefits
MC = marginal costs   AC = average costs

Figure 2.11 *The benefits and costs of city size (adapted from Alonso, 1971)*

in 1994 Warwickshire achieved a level of household disposable income of about the national average, whereas in the metropolitan area disposable income was more than 10 per cent lower.

Finally, one suggestion has been to use land values as an index of net urban benefits (Richardson, 1978). This approach assumes that all benefits and costs – even those of a non-monetary nature – are fully internalized in the land market and therefore capitalized in higher or lower urban land values. Unfortunately there is little agreement on the extent to which external effects such as pollution and congestion are fully internalized. Walker (1981), for example, argues that the land market accounts only very imperfectly for the costs of urban living, and he suggests that imperfect knowledge and ignorance of external effects tend to inflate land values, rendering them a false index of net urban benefits.

From the preceding discussion, it should be clear that the measurement of costs and benefits associated with city size presents considerable problems. Nevertheless, a useful generalization is given in figure 2.11. The average benefits (AB) curve is shown rising fairly steadily as population increases, although it is possible that urban diseconomies at larger city sizes could eventually cause average benefits to decline.

The results from a number of studies suggest that the average cost (AC) curve might be expected to reach a minimum point at a population size somewhere between 100,000 and 500,000 inhabitants (Vanhove and Klassen, 1980). After this point the average (or unit) cost would rise.

Several population sizes are of significance and deserve some discussion. The first occurs at point A where AC = AB; this is the *minimum efficient city size* below which the unit cost of providing urban infrastructure and services exceeds the average benefit (AC > AB). Point B corresponds to the least-cost city size (minimum AC), but this is clearly not an optimum since no account is taken of average benefits rising with population size. Point C – population size P_1 – is the optimal city size from the point of view of the city's residents. It corresponds to the point where the distance between the AB and AC curves is greatest (and the slopes of these curves are the same), that is, where net benefits per capita are highest (maximum AB – AC). Any further increase in population size beyond this point would clearly reduce the level of net benefit (AB – AC) for existing inhabitants.

Point D (P_2) represents the optimal city size from the view of maximum social welfare. This can be seen from the fact that below P_2 the marginal cost (MC) of adding another inhabitant is less than the marginal benefit (MB) to society (MC < MB); hence by expanding city size up to the point where MC = MB, the total (net) benefits are maximized. In practice, however, cities elsewhere in the urban system may be well below this optimum size, so that expanding these smaller cities would increase total welfare by more than if expansion were limited to only a few centres of population P_2. One recent study has suggested that the optimum city size may be below 0.5 million population (Bergovic, 1991), if so, it seems likely – for many countries – that expansion of a larger number of smaller centres would generally be preferable to allowing over-concentration of national resources in capital cities.

A final possibility – and one that strengthens the case for planning – is to consider what might happen if no efforts were made to control expansion of the city and further in-migration beyond P_2. Then, the population would probably increase up to point E (where AC = AB). Pressure for expansion would indeed be great since new entrants in reality tend to face average costs and benefits rather than marginal costs and benefits, as assumed in the previous case. On the cost side, this occurs because, in practice, charges and taxes for urban services are averaged over *all* service users and cannot distinguish between new (high-cost) and existing (low-cost) residents (or firms). Also, new residents (or firms) do not face the rising marginal external costs (of congestion, pollution, noise and so on) inflicted on other city residents. In the absence of control there may therefore be a tendency for cities to grow well beyond an optimum size (P_1 or P_2).

In practice, optimal city-size theory has received some criticism. One objection is that many urban costs and benefits may be specific to particular conurbations and related to factors such as density, industrial structure or road layout rather than city size itself. Some research has shown, for example, that polycentric as opposed to monocentric cities are less prone to problems of congestion (Gordon *et al.*, 1987). Urban economic structure may also influence optimal city size; research has suggested that the optimum from the point of view of business services, for example, may well be larger than the optimum for manufacturing or construction (Bergovic, 1991).

Furthermore, the theory tells us nothing about the desirable spatial distribution of the population in the context of the national urban hierarchy, and it sits uneasily with other theories (such as central place theory) which do. From the point of view of planning, the loss of (net) benefits of urban size might be outweighed by the benefits of greater spatial accessibility if a more dispersed pattern of smaller urban settlements is considered. On the latter point, if, as previously suggested, the average cost curve is rather flat around the least-cost city size (point B), it is probably that there would exist a broad range of city sizes over which net benefits per capita (AB – AC) are fairly similar (compare net benefits at B with those at C and D in figure 2.11).

Given that average costs appear to rise substantially in the largest conurbations there would seem to be a strong case for encouraging a settlement structure of medium-sized towns and cities rather than one involving only a few large cities. While productivity may well be higher in large cities, as we have seen, the evidence is not so compelling as to suggest that any loss from encouraging smaller urban sizes would be at all substantial. Perhaps a few major capital cities with significant international functions (for example, London, Tokyo and New York) may have to remain very large in order to carry out effectively their world roles. For others, particularly the burgeoning mega-cities of the developing world, there must remain a question mark over their economic and social viability. Indeed, the recent experience of declining cities in many developed countries may perhaps be taken as evidence to suggest that the agglomeration economies which existed in the past, are now much less significant.

REFERENCES

Alonso, W. (1971) 'The economics of urban size', *Regional Science Association Papers*, 26.

Australian Bureau of Statistics (ABS) (1997) *Australian Social Trends*, Canberra: ABS.

Bergovic, B. (1991) 'The economic approach to optimal city size', *Progress in Planning*, 31.

Berry, B.L.J. and Garrison, W.L. (1958) 'Recent developments in central place theory', *Papers and Proceedings of the Regional Science Association*, 4.

Boudeville, J.R. (1966) *Problems of Regional Economic Planning*, Edinburgh: Edinburgh University Press.

Chen, X. (1994) 'New spatial division of labour and commodity chains in Greater South China Economic Region', in Gereffi, G. and Korzeniewicz, M. (eds), *Commodity Chains and Global Competition*, Westport CT: Greenwood Press.

Chen, X. and Parish, W.L. (1996) 'Urbanization in China: reassessing an evolving model', in Gugler, J. (ed.), *The Urban Transformation of the Developing World*, Oxford: Oxford University Press.

Cheshire, P. and Hay, D. (1988) *Urban Problems in Europe*, London: Allen and Unwin.

Childe, V.G. (1950) 'The urban revolution', *Town Planning Review*, 21: 3–17.

Christaller, W. (1933) *Die Zentralen Orte in Suddeutschland*, Jena: Fischer.

Clark, D. (1996) *Urban World/Global City*, London: Routledge.

Commission of the European Communities (1975) *Le Coût des Concentrations Urbaines et la Dépopulation Rurale dans la CEE*, Working Paper, Brussels: European Commission.

Cox, K.R. (1979) *Location and Public Problems*, Oxford: Blackwell.

Douglass, M. (1988) *Urbanization and National Urban Development Strategies in Asia: Indonesia, Korea and Thailand*, University of Hawaii, Department of Urban and Regional Planning, Paper No. 9.

Findley, S.E. (1993) 'The third world city: development policies and issues', in Kasarda, J.D. and Parnell, A.M. (eds), *Third World Cities*, London: Sage.

Firman, T. (1991) 'Penataan Koridor Antar Kota' [Managing intercity corridors], *Kompas*, 11 January.

Frank, A.G. (1967) *Capitalism and Underdevelopment in Latin America*, New York: Monthly Review Press.

Fuchs, V.R. (1959) *Differentials in Hourly Earnings by Region and City Size*, Washington DC: National Bureau of Economic Research.

Gordon, P., Kumar, A. and Richardson, H.W. (1987) 'Congestion, changing metropolitan city structure and city size', mimeo, School of Urban and Regional Planning, University of Southern California.

HABITAT (1996) *An Urbanizing World: Global Report on Human Settlements 1996*, Oxford: United Nations Centre for Human Settlements and Oxford University Press.

Harvey, D.W. (1973) *Social Justice and the City*, London: Edward Arnold.

Henderson, J.V. (1998) *Urban Development Theory, Fact and Illusion*, New York: Oxford University Press.

Henderson, J.V. *et al.* (1998) 'Externalities, Location and Industrial Concentration in a Tiger Economy', Department of Economics, Brown University [Processed].

Hirschman, A.D. (1958) *The Strategy of Economic Development*, New Haven CT: Yale UP.

Hoch, I. (1972) 'Urban scale and environmental quality', in Ridker, R.G. (ed.), *Population, Resources and the Environment*, Research Report III, Washington DC: US Commission on Population Growth and the American Future.

Hoch, I. (1976) 'City size effects, trends and policies', *Science*, 193.

Hoch, I. (1987) 'City size and US urban policy', *Urban Studies*, 24.

Hoselitz, B.F. (1955) 'Generative and parasitic cities', *Economic Development and Cultural Change*, 3.

Hudson, J.C. (1969) 'Diffusion in a central place system', *Geographical Analysis*, 1: 45–58.

Hugo, G. (1996) 'Urbanization in Indonesia: city and countryside linked', in Gugler, G. (ed.), *The Urban Transformation of the Developing World*, Oxford: Oxford University Press.

Keynes, J.M. (1936) *The General Theory of Employment, Interest and Money*, London: Macmillan.

Kunzmann, K.R. and Wegener, M. (1991) 'Pattern of urbanisation in Western Europe 1960–1990', *Berichte aus dem Institut für Raumplanning*, 28, Dortmund: Universität Dortmund.

Lucas, R. (1998) 'Internal migration and urbanization: recent contributions and new evidence', background paper for *World Development Report 1999/2000*, Washington DC: World Bank.

McGee, T.G. (1991) 'The Emergence of Desa Kota Regions in Asia: Expanding an Hypothesis', in Ginsburg, N., Koppel, B. and McGee, T.G. (eds), *The Extended Metropolis: Settlement Transition in Asia*, Honolulu: University of Hawaii Press.

McLintock, F. and Avison, N. (1968) *Crime in England and Wales*, London: Heinemann.

Mohan, R. (1996) 'Urbanization in India: patterns and emerging issues', in Gugler, J. (ed.), *The Urban Transformation of the Developing World*, Oxford: Oxford University Press.

Myrdal, G. (1957) *Economic Theory and Undeveloped Areas*, London: Duckworth.

NUDSP (1985) *NUDs Final Report*, Jakarta: National Urban Development Strategy Project, Directorate of City and Regional Planning, Department of Public Works.

Parish, W.L. (1990) 'What model now?', in Kwok, R. *et al.* (eds), *Chinese Urban Reform*, 78–106.

Porrell, F.W. (1982) 'Intermetropolitan migration and quality of life', *Journal of Regional Science*, 22.

Potter, R. (1992) *Urbanisation in the Third World*, Oxford: Oxford University Press.

Potter, R.B. and Lloyd-Evans, S. (1998) *The City in the Developing World*, Harlow: Longman.

Pred, A.R. (1966) *The Spatial Dynamics of US Urban–Industrial Growth 1800–1914*, Cambridge MA: MIT Press.

Richardson, H.W. (1978) *Regional and Urban Economics*, Harmondsworth: Penguin.

Robinson, G.M., Loughan, R.J. and Tranter, P.J. (2000) *Australia and New Zealand*, London: Edward Arnold.

Rostow, W.W. (1960) *The Stages of Economic Growth: A Non-Communist Manifesto*, London: Cambridge University Press.

Schiller, R. (1985) 'A ranking of centres using multiple branch numbers', *Estates Gazette*, 23 March.

Shukla, V. (1996) *Urbanization and Economic Growth*, Delhi: Himalaya Publishing House.

Skinner, G.W. (1977) *The City in Late Imperial China*, Stanford CA: Stanford University Press.

Smailes, A.E. (1944) 'The urban hierarchy in England and Wales', *Geography*, 29.

Smith, R.D.P. (1978) 'The changing urban hierarchy', *Regional Studies*, 2.

United Nations (1985) *Demographic Year Book*, New York: United Nations.

United Nations (1993) *World Urbanization Prospects: The 1992 Revision*, New York: United Nations.

Vanhove, N. and Klassen, L.H. (1980) *Regional Policy: A European Approach*, Farnborough: Saxon House.

Walker, B. (1981) *Welfare Economics and Urban Problems*, London: Hutchinson.

World Bank (1984) 'Economic and social development: an overview of regional differentials and related processes', main report from *Indonesia: Selected Aspects of Spatial Development*, Report No. 4776-IND, World Bank: Country Programs Department, East Asia and the Pacific Regional Office.

World Bank (1991) *World Development Report, 1991*, New York: World Bank.

World Bank (1999) *Entering the 21st Century: World Development Report 1999/2000*, New York: World Bank and Oxford University Press.

Yeh, A.G. and Xu, X. (1990) 'Changes in city size and regional distribution, 1953–1986', in Kwok, R. *et al.* (eds), *Chinese Urban Reform*, 45–61.

3

The Spatial Structure of Urban Areas

INTRODUCTION

The ability of activities to compete for sites depends upon whether they have the means to benefit from accessibility and complementarity within the urban framework. But economic conditions, population, other land uses both public and private, and the size of the urban area continually change, subjecting the urban land market to forces of perpetual adjustment.

The underlying influences upon urban growth are both national and regional. At a national level the size and rate of growth of the gross national product (GNP) *per capita* determine the quantity and quality of urban land use activity. Yet the less industrialized the country, the greater the potential rate of urbanization, while countries with high GNP *per capita* may witness a decline in their city centres and an increased rate of suburbanization and decentralization. Nationally, non-economic forces reinforce economic factors. Population growth and migration to urban areas tend ultimately to increase living standards and to lower death-rates. Technological development similarly raises real incomes and affects the urban land use pattern. For example, improved construction techniques allow the development of taller buildings and new production methods might necessitate larger buildings on the periphery of cities. Government intervention, even where it is minimal, imposes a national influence over urban growth. But if the government is concerned with such issues as the nationalization of development land, the taxing of increased values and strategic planning rather than with merely controlling, say, public health or building standards, the degree of influence is substantial and the economic consequences immense.

Regional or local economic, social and political factors may result in some cities growing more rapidly than others. An area may be endowed with expanding industries and, because of greater job opportunities and other attractions, there may be a net inward migration of population. Conversely, other areas may be disadvantaged by declining industries, an outdated infrastructure and an outward migration of population. The structure of local government and the impact of its policies may or may not be favourable to the growth or improvement of the urban area.

Urban Rent – Land Values – Density

Urban growth alters not only the pattern of land use and land values, but also the intensity of site use. As the supply of land in an urban area is fixed in the short term, this will create scarcity. Commercial users will double-up and may operate less efficiently, households may have to live in shared dwellings. Only in the medium and long term will business and residential development extend the city outwards. In the meantime, rising rents will increase the degree of competition for sites within the existing built-up area.

The medium- and long-term supply of land is elastic provided that there is an absence of constraints such as green belt controls and use-restrictions, and assuming the availability of transport. With the extension of the radius of the urban area the supply of land increases in geometric proportions, and if the demand for sites is relatively inelastic any increase in demand should cause site values and rents to fall. But it would be wrong to assume that outward-decreasing site values and rents are due to higher transport costs, and that higher values and rents inward are due to a saving in transport costs. Urban rent is determined by productivity (or profitability), which is highest at the place of maximum accessibility, that is, the central business district. Even if general accessibility begins to diminish when congestion in the centre increases to severe levels, values and rents may continue to rise if sites benefit from some form of special accessibility. In the same location within the urban area, large sites may be more valuable than small ones, as economies of scale can be realised even if the site has many uses.

Land value gradients vary from city to city, and because of higher incomes and internal and external scale economics, peaks are generally higher in larger cities. But the rate of fall in value is not the same for every use. Competition among commercial users in the central business district produces a very steep slope, but further out the slope becomes gentler as competition diminishes. The residential gradient is very gentle as values may be adversely affected in the inner areas of cities because of small sites. The gradient may be flattened out by decentralization and the diffusion of journey destinations. Smaller peaks may be found at suburban route foci and especially in outlying business districts.

Values continually change because of changes in general and special accessibility. Planning controls, especially those concerning residential and commercial densities, may modify the gradient, and green belts might create local areas of scarcity and so raise values. Rating differences between local authorities also affect gradients. Where there is an absence of industry (for example, in high-income residential areas) a high rate poundage could depress residential values, but this might be more than offset by the appreciating effect of amenity.

There is, of course, a general reduction in population density with the increase in the radial distance from the inner areas of cities (although the central business district may have an almost complete absence of a residential population). In the case of older cities, where employment and housing evolved centrally, the density gradient can be quite steep, whereas in cities of recent origin there is a greater dispersal of commercial, industrial and residential use and the gradient may flatten out and comprise numerous outer peaks. If the public transport system is highly developed in the inner areas of cities and if there are social customs such as workers returning home for lunch, gradients will be very steep. Although gradients of the daytime population density or of net residential densities may produce smoother slopes, it is probable that the gradient of gross population density is a preferable measure of urban structure.

Accessibility and Demand

Profitability and utility are largely determined by accessibility. The greater the accessibility of a location (and the lower the net economic cost of movement in terms of distance, time and convenience), the greater the comparative advantage and the greater the demand for property at that location.

In the case of business use, general accessibility refers to nearness to transport facilities (rail termini, bus stations, motorways), labour, customers, and service facilities such as banks and post offices. Special accessibility exists when complementary uses are in close proximity to each other, for example in London lawyers are close to the Law Courts, stockbrokers are near the Stock Exchange, commercial and merchant banking is located adjacently, and the wholesale and retail clothing industry is situated in the Oxford Street area. (Special 'inaccessibility' is desirable when there are incompatible uses, for instance noxious heavy industry and new high-income housing, or take-away food shops and retailers of luxury merchandise.) The importance of accessibility to residential land is illustrated when the utility of particular sites depends upon monetary factors such as schools, shops, public and private open space, and travelling costs to work and upon non-monetary considerations such as peace and quiet (or the reverse), compatible neighbours, fresh air and other less tangible amenities.

The greater the accessibility (general or special) and the greater the relevance of accessibility to the user of land, the higher the value of the land in question. Therefore the pattern of accessibility creates a pattern of urban land use which will be concomitant with the pattern of land values. In addition there is a relationship between accessibility, land uses and values, and the intensity of utilization. As demand is greatest for those sites with the highest degree of accessibility, it is more feasible to develop those sites intensively. Users able to put the site to its most productive use would be prepared to pay the highest price or rent to acquire the developed property.

The relationship between accessibility, land uses and land values was first set out in Heinrich von Thünen's theory of rural land use. In 1826, in the light of empirical evidence, von Thünen (1826) postulated that around a 'central town', rural land of constant fertility assumed different forms, land use diminishing intensively in inverse relationship to increased distance from the town. The land use pattern from the centre outwards would comprise the following concentric belts: horticulture and dairying, silviculture, intensive arable rotation, arable with long ley, three-field arable and ranching (figure 3.1). Although in part influenced by practicality (for example, milk could not be transported great distances to the market prior to refrigeration, therefore dairying would be close to the town), land in greatest demand would be that land as near as possible to the market because of low transport costs. The highest rent would be gained for this advantage and the highest value output per hectare would accrue. In the outer belt there would be little demand for land because of high transport costs, rents would be low and the value of extensive production would be correspondingly low.

The overall land use pattern might be modified by the existence of a navigable river. In contrast to fairly high transport costs over land, costs of river transport are low, especially for bulky commodities. The river would have the effect of extending the different land uses almost parallel along its course. A further modification might occur if a small city with its own production zones was located within the land use pattern of the main settlement.

Although the von Thünen model has been criticised because it assumed unlikely conditions such as production taking place around an isolated market and soil being of constant fertility, it nevertheless established a distance–cost relationship which has recently become the basis of urban location theory.

THE URBAN LAND USE PATTERN

As with rural land, there are, of course, wide differences in the land use patterns of different urban areas. Varying topographical features have an effect on land use; so do climatic conditions, past and present social and religious customs, legislation and legal decisions, demand for goods and services (including varying consumer preferences), and the policy of local and central government in the supply of public utilities and social services. These

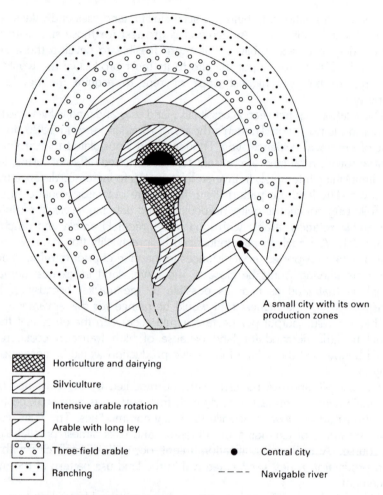

A small city with its own
production zones

⌗	Horticulture and dairying	
⫽	Silviculture	
▨	Intensive arable rotation	
⫽	Arable with long ley	
o o o	Three-field arable	● Central city
∴	Ranching	- - - - Navigable river

Figure 3.1 *Von Thünen's model of agricultural land use*

variations provide different frameworks within which competition between
the existing and potential land users decides the pattern of land use in any
urban area. Within these frameworks and subject to the imperfections of
the market, the forces of demand and supply provide the means by which
land is developed up to its highest and best use. It is as a result of this
process that a general pattern of land use has evolved in most urban areas,
which in advanced capitalist countries comprise the following areal components: the central business district, the zone of transition, the suburban
area and the rural–urban fringe.

The Central Business District

Having the maximum overall accessibility to most parts of the urban area, the central business district is the focus of intra-city transport routes. Competition for sites among commercial users raises land values and the intensity of development to a peak. Population increase and economic growth increase densities within the central business district, development usually being vertical rather than horizontal. The central business district becomes a decreasing proportion of the expanding urban area. If a number of urban areas merge into a conurbation, the central business district with the greatest comparative advantage in terms of accessibility will become the most intensively developed centre at the expense of the other centres.

Within the larger central business districts the shopping area is usually separated from the main office area, although office users will produce a demand for more localized retail services. A separate entertainment area may emerge, but the dispersed siting of cinemas, theatres and concert halls may make it difficult to delineate its boundaries.

The central business district merges almost unnoticed into the surrounding transitional zone, but usually its boundaries are marked by public transport (especially rail) termini, reflecting the general absence of the lateral growth of the central business district since the nineteenth century.

The Zone of Transition

In most industrial nations over the last hundred years an area of mixed use has developed around the central business district. This consisted of warehousing and light manufacturing (serving the commercial activities of the central business area) interspersed with transport facilities and residential land. Housing initially would have been for the middle and higher income groups, but generally it has become decayed and dilapidated, largely because of its conversion into multiple occupancy low-income dwellings. There are also areas of local authority and charitable trust housing, much of which is old and in need of renewal. Almost alone, London has some transitional areas (such as Belgravia and South Kensington) which have retained their status as high-income enclaves.

The transitional zone is generally beset with many social and economic problems, for example mass deprivation (including homelessness, disease and delinquency). Land might be continually blighted because of the slow pace at which planning proposals are implemented, and many landlords (both private and public) may forgo rents, keeping their properties empty pending redevelopment. The maintenance or improvement of dwellings may be impeded by rent regulation and vagaries in public policy concerning housing rehabilitation. The zone of transition is often referred to as 'the twilight zone'.

Yet new development within the zone does take place. To some extent the market enables land to be developed to its highest and best use as commercial development takes place along the radial routes towards the suburbs or in areas specifically designated for publicly-assisted regeneration.

The Suburban Area

The predominant use in this area is moderate or low density residential land. Housing is segregated by socio-economic class or ethnically, and there is clustering close to railway stations and the main road foci – the area being dependent upon easy access to the employment opportunities and the general attractions of the central part of the city.

Although there is a scattering of schools, churches, public houses and medical facilities, shops tend to be more concentrated into parades and neighbourhood shopping centres. Where office development takes place on a sufficiently large scale, shopping and other commercial and social facilities may have been developed comprehensively to form an 'outlying business district'.

Since the expansion of motor transport and electricity supply, manufacturing industry has been attracted to suburban locations. Sites adjacent to major routes are particularly favoured, making it easy to distribute goods not only to the urban area but also to the regional or national market. Manufacturers also benefit from relatively low-cost sites convenient for further development.

Interspersed with other uses, there are generally extensive areas devoted to golf courses, race tracks, parks, cemeteries, allotments and public open space.

The Rural–Urban Fringe

As the density of the suburban area becomes less, and the built-up parts become largely residential, public open space is replaced by market gardens or farmland. There may also be extensive 'green belt' areas for the purpose of constraining urban expansion. The rural–urban fringe is mainly a commuter belt, its high-income adventitious population now usually outnumbering those engaged in horticulture and agriculture.

THEORIES OF URBAN STRUCTURE

Although the attributes of the physical structure and population of cities are heterogeneous, the city is a unit of social behaviour. It is also an aggregate of smaller homogeneous areas, all focusing on the central business district. The spatial structure of a city is a product of centripetal forces of attraction and congestion, centrifugal forces of dispersion and decongestion, and forces of areal differentiation. Many theories of spatial structure and urban growth are unsatisfactory because they fail to take into account sufficiently suburbanization, decentralization, the development of sub-centres, greater flexibility of location, improvements in technology and transportation, and the effects of central and local government policies. It tends to be the more complicated theories which have lost their credibility, and ironically it is the earliest and simplest ones which are still valid, however loosely.

Ecological Theories of Urban Development

Influenced by ecology, which studies the relationship between living organisms and their physical environment, Park and Burgess (1925) suggested that human beings compete for scarce resources such as land and raw materials with the aim of establishing spatially-disparate urban environments to satisfy their different economic and social needs. As in ecology, the boundaries between such environments are continually changing – largely as an outcome of demographic and economic centripetal forces of attraction, centrifugal forces of dispersal and the forces of spatial differention; and by means of the economically and politically-strong acquiring land at the expense of the weak. From this basic premise, a number of ecological theories of urban land use emerged throughout the twentieth century – most notably the concentric zone, sector and multiple nuclei theories of respectively Burgess, Hoyt, and Harris and Ullman.

Concentric zone theory

This emerged from a study of Chicago by Burgess (1906) and was essentially an application to urban land use of von Thünen's earlier theory relating to rural land around a city (see page 83). It was suggested that any city extends radially from its centre to form concentric zones and that as distance from the centre increased there would be a reduction in accessibility, rents and densities. Land use would assume the following forms from the centre outwards: the central business district, a zone of transition, an area of factories and low-income housing, an area of higher-income housing and a commuter zone (figure 3.2). There would also be declining proportions of recent immigrants, delinquency rates, poverty and disease as distance increased from the centre.

The concentric zone theory allows for underlying conditions to change continually. Natural population increase, in-migration, economic growth

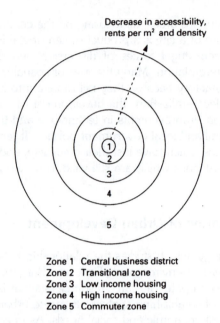

Decrease in accessibility,
rents per m² and density

Zone 1 Central business district
Zone 2 Transitional zone
Zone 3 Low income housing
Zone 4 High income housing
Zone 5 Commuter zone

Figure 3.2 *The concentric zone theory*

and income expansion will all result in each zone within the urban area 'invading' the next zone outwards. But there may not be a simple transformation in land use outwards. As the central business district expands, the locational advantages of central sites might diminish, the transitional zone (awaiting redevelopment) might become more and more a twilight area, and as suburban populations increase, new outlying business districts may evolve. There are further effects upon the spatial structure as traffic flows become more complex in response to decentralization.

Many criticisms can be made of the theory. Land uses within many parts of the urban area are heterogeneous – shops, offices, factories and housing may all be located close to each other, although they may have potentially different site and locational requirements; and there may be many possible locations for different activities which do not all conform with the idealized model. Accessibility may be a relatively unimportant consideration for many uses, especially housing, and commercial users may find it disadvantageous to agglomerate if there is an opportunity to corner an undeveloped market. Decentralized shopping centres and offices may further distort the pattern, and the central business district might experience a decrease in rents and density following the reduction in its acces-

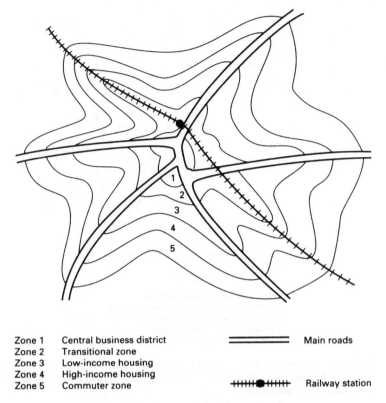

Zone 1	Central business district
Zone 2	Transitional zone
Zone 3	Low-income housing
Zone 4	High-income housing
Zone 5	Commuter zone

Main roads

Railway station

Figure 3.3 *The axial development theory*

sibility through congestion. The concentric zone model also ignores physical features, takes little account of industrial and railway use, and disregards the effect of radial routeways upon land values and uses. It is more likely that a star-shaped pattern of land use will emerge, travel time rather than transport costs often being more important as a determinant of use. An axial development model (figure 3.3) modifies the concentric zone pattern, taking into account the effect of transport routes. The assumption of a single focal point remains, though maximum accessibility need no longer be found at a central location.

However, even in its modified form, the concentric zone theory is little more than descriptive, showing *how*, rather than *why*, urban growth takes place. It is deterministic and assumes that social groups have to accord with a specific urban structure. Its greatest weakness is that it assumes a free or perfect market, it ignores imperfections (such as locational inertia, sub-optimal use and long leases) and takes no account of planning controls. It

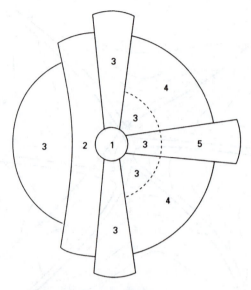

Sector 1 Central business district
Sector 2 Manufacturing and warehousing
Sector 3 Low-income housing
Sector 4 Middle-income housing
Sector 5 High-income housing

Note: The diagram assumes a prevailing wind from the east. The manufacturing sector is thus located to the west of the high-income housing sector. In the United Kingdom the reverse conditions usually apply.

Figure 3.4 *The sector theory*

disregards the purchasing of sites for future development, with current use being retained at a sub-optimal value. But the pattern of urban land use is not wholly irrational and is not subject to an incomprehensible welter of paradoxes and anomalies. The concentric zone theory is illuminating; it shows that, in general, accessibility, rents and densities diminish with increased distance from the central business district, and that the process of invasion is responsible for changing land use.

Sector theory

This theory, as presented by Hoyt (1939), propounds that growth along a particular transport route takes the form of land use already prevailing and that each sector of relatively homogeneous use extends outwards from the centre (figure 3.4). Compatible land uses would lie adjacent to each other (for example, warehousing and light manufacturing, and low-income housing) and incompatible uses will be repelled (for instance, high-income housing, and warehousing and light industry). Residential uses will tend to be segregated in terms of income and social position, and will expand in different directions in different parts of the city. As with the concentric zone theory there is a process of invasion as economic and population growth takes place. When the inner areas are abandoned by high-income households they are infilled (usually at a higher density) by lower-income households.

The criticisms of the theory are broadly the same as those made of the concentric zone theory, and so are the merits. But while recognizing the relationship between accessibility, land use and values, and densities, Hoyt believed that the interdependence of these variables expresses itself differently in terms of the spatial structure of the city.

In considering theories of urban growth it has been assumed so far that zones or sectors 'invade' each other, generally outwards, low-income housing moving into the high-income housing area, and the latter expanding into the commuter belt. But with increased costs of commuter travelling the inner areas of cities have again attracted higher-income households – invasion and 'gentrification' taking place inwards. If, simultaneously, the central business district expands outwards, the area of low-income housing will be squeezed between two invading forces. Increased occupancy of the remaining low-income dwellings, migration to country towns or homelessness will consequently be compounded.

Multiple-nuclei theory

Unlike the theories of urban growth considered so far, which have all assumed that cities grow from one central point, the multiple-nuclei theory produced by Harris and Ullman (1951) in the United States is based on the assumption that urban growth takes place around several distinct nuclei. The nuclei could include the first urban settlement (probably a market town), a nearby village, a factory, a mine, a railway terminal or waterside facility. Ultimately they would be integrated into one urban area largely agglomerated by residential use and intra-city transportation. The original nuclei would help to determine current use, for example the market town might become the central business district, the village an outlying business district, the factory site might evolve into an area of wholesaling and light manufacture, and the mine or waterside facility could become an area of heavy industry (figure 3.5).

Within the urban area, compatible uses are attracted to each other – for example, low-income residential land would be close to wholesaling and light manufacturing and near-heavy industry, and the medium- and high-income residential areas would surround the outlying business district. Incompatible uses would remain far apart – for example, high-income housing and heavy manufacturing. The number of nuclei would generally

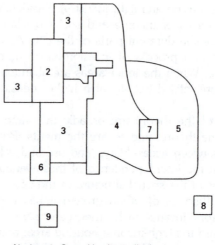

Nucleus 1   Central business district
Nucleus 2   Wholesale and light manufacturing
Nucleus 3   Low-income residential
Nucleus 4   Middle-income residential
Nucleus 5   High-income residential
Nucleus 6   Heavy manufacturing
Nucleus 7   Outlying business district
Nucleus 8   Residential suburb
Nucleus 9   Industrial suburb

Notes: (i) The diagram assumes a prevailing wind from the east.
(ii) It is assumed that land use boundaries coincide with the main traffic routes of a 'grid-iron' street pattern.
Neither of these conditions is applicable to cities in the United Kingdom.

Figure 3.5 *The multiple-nuclei theory*

be greater in large urban areas than in small cities and there would be a greater degree of specialization within each nucleus.

The multiple-nuclei model related initially to cities within the United States where grid-iron road patterns separated land uses geometrically. But less regular route patterns and use boundaries in other countries do not invalidate the basic principles of the theory.

Theories of urban spatial structure are as much descriptive as analytical. They explain how cities change their form, and very rarely will a single theory be adequate for this task. The concentric zone theory, while recognizing that the transitional zone experiences deterioration prior to eventual redevelopment, ignores the same trend occurring elsewhere – for example, on the rural–urban fringe. None of the theories explains satisfactorily the significance of sub-centres to urban growth, and none pays sufficient attention to agglomeration; most ignore the important changes that occur within the central business district and which affect the urban area as a whole; and, perhaps more importantly, all fail to consider the process of decentralization.

While the above theories of urban structure are particularly relevant to North America and to much of Europe, they are less relevant to urban areas in Australia and New Zealand. In contrast to the United States and the United Kingdom, where there are fairly discrete zones or sectors of specific types of housing and socio-economic class, Australian and New Zealand cities are characterized by separate single-storey houses, large expanses of open space, a comparative lack of social polarization and relatively few areas of slum housing (except in Sydney). These differences in Australasia were attributable – in the early years of the twentieth century – to a fully employed and high-wage workforce, an abundance of cheap land and good public transport, the latter producing a star-shaped pattern of urban land use. Such influences were compounded in the late twentieth century by a substantial increase in car-ownership, reduced reliance on public transport and more extensive urban sprawl – consolidating the areas between and beyond the largely discontinued radial tram and train routes (Robinson *et al.*, 2000). Apart from residential development in the urban periphery (much of it being in the form of public-sector housing estates), the outer suburbs have also attracted manufacturing, retailing and other services (Robinson *et al.*, 2000).

However, whereas in the United States and the United Kingdom the poor and ethnic minorities have increasingly concentrated in inner city areas, in Australasia the inner cities have become increasingly attractive to the affluent particularly since the 1970s – a reversal of US (and UK) experience (Babcock, 1997). However, there has also been a significant increase in social polarization. With higher levels of unemployment and below-average wage increases since the 1970s, low-income households (with children) have become increasingly concentrated in public-sector housing estates in the outer suburbs, while there has been an increase in the proportion of low-income single-person households accommodated in the private rented sector in some of the less affluent inner city areas (Babcock, 1997).

BOX 3.1: URBAN LAND USE IN WESTERN EUROPE

For centuries, market forces have determined the use of land and land rents in Western Europe – interrupted from time to time by major wars and tempered in the twentieth century by planning legislation and practice. With

continued

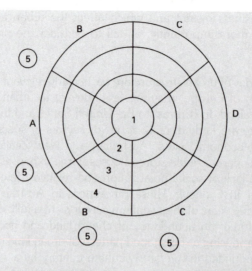

Zone 1	Central business district
Zone 2	Transitional zone
Zone 3A	Large old houses
Zone 3B	Large bye-law houses
Zone 3C and D	Small terrace houses
Zone 4	Post-1918 residential areas, with post-1945 housing on the periphery
Zone 5	Commuter 'villages'

Sector A	Middle-class
Sector B	Lower middle class
Sector C	Working class (main areas of municipal housing)
Sector D	Industry and lower working class

Figure 3.6 *The structure of a hypothetical British city*

population and economic growth, the evolving pattern of land use is either concentric or sectoral, or a mixture of the two, while residential areas tend to be highly segregated according to household income. In general, land values per m² diminish outwards from the centre to the periphery, inversely in relation to maximum accessibility.

One of the first analyses of urban structure in Western Europe, by Jones (1960), revealed that within Belfast there was a juxtaposition of sectors in the west and zones in the east, separated by the River Lagan.

From a study of Nottingham, Sheffield and Huddersfield, Mann (1963) subsequently produced a hybrid model of a hypothetical British city – an urban area large enough to have distinct internal differentiation, but not too large to exhibit the complexities of a conurbation. The main additional feature is the existence of commuter villages separated from the built-up area of the city (figure 3.6).

Based on more detailed quantitative analysis of a number of British cities, Robson (1975) showed how – in relation to social, housing and physical data and information – land uses arrange themselves in a mixed concentric and

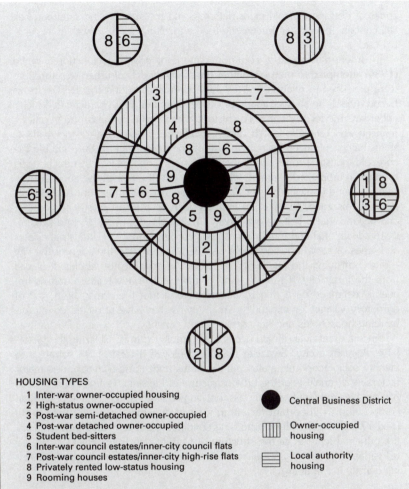

HOUSING TYPES

1 Inter-war owner-occupied housing
2 High-status owner-occupied
3 Post-war semi-detached owner-occupied
4 Post-war detached owner-occupied
5 Student bed-sitters
6 Inter-war council estates/inner-city council flats
7 Post-war council estates/inner-city high-rise flats
8 Privately rented low-status housing
9 Rooming houses

● Central Business District

▥ Owner-occupied housing

▤ Local authority housing

Figure 3.7 *The structure of an archetypal British city – as indicated by detailed quantitative analysis (adapted from Robson, 1975)*

sectoral form, with the age of housing concentrically patterned and socio-economic groups sectorally organized (figure 3.7).

In an attempt to produce a model of the ecological structure of a typical West European city based on her research in Vienna, Lichtenberger (1972) – like Mann – recognized a mix of sectors and concentric zones, and suggested that European cities differed from their North American counterparts since, in the former, the city core is often a high-status residential area as well as a location for offices and retailing; the inner city contains mixed

continued

zones of housing and old industrial uses; and the surrounding suburban belt still contains pockets of intensively used agricultural land, as well as residential use.

In order to illustrate a common pattern of economic functions, White (1984) attempted to merge together the many models of urban structure that were produced in relation to West European cities during the 1970s. In his hybrid model, he showed many of the features that had characterized Lichtenberger's model of Vienna. The historic core is not only the centre of offices, retailing and recreation, it is also a middle-class residential district with its status being enhanced by reurbanization and gentrification. Surrounding the core, old industrial zones are in the process of being replaced by new housing to meet 'reurbanizer' demand, while housing in the rest of the zone of transition is being gentrified – squeezing-out low-income/immigrant households. Beyond this zone, there is an inner residential zone of inter-war housing, and beyond that a belt of low-density, middle-class housing in close proximity to educational and employment nodes on the periphery. Industrial estates and areas of social housing might also be found around the edge of the city – often satisfying the needs of low-income/immigrant households displaced from the inner city. The outer limit of the contiguously built-up area is frequently delimited by a ring road, and beyond that there may be a ring of dormitory villages or expanding small towns that have attracted counterurbanizing households and new service employment.

Since a great deal of data needs to be employed in considering the factorial ecology of a city, Sweetser (1965) employed a total of 93 variables to identify socio-economic status, family status and home-ownership as major factors in an analysis of the urban structure of Helsinki; Robson (1969) used 89 variables to identify social class, housing conditions, tenure and household composition as important factors in a study of Sunderland; Herbert (1970) used 77 variables to identify housing conditions, ethnicity and high status as the principal features of the structure of Cardiff; and Friedrichs (1977) used 60 variables to identify social rank, the attributes of urbanization and building density in Hamburg.

Models of urban structure became increasingly sophisticated with the introduction of social area analysis and factorial ecology. While social area analysis – undertaken, for example, by Shevsky and Bell (1955) – suffered from utilizing only a few pre-selected social characteristics such as social rank, family type and ethnicity to illustrate urban structure, factorial ecology analysis employs a much wider range of indicators to measure the factors that might be important to urban life.

It might be asked whether or not factorial ecology makes the concentric zone, sector and multiple-nuclei theories (and others derived from them) obsolete. Berry and Rees (1969) thought not. They suggested that if certain indicators of socio-economic status were the principal or only determinant

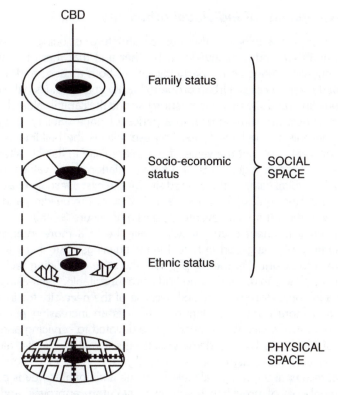

Figure 3.8 *Spatial components of urban structure (adapted from Murdie, 1969)*

of physical space, cities would tend to divide themselves into sectors; if characteristics of family type operated alone, different demands for space could cause households to arrange themselves in concentric zones; and if aspects of ethnicity were the only major factor in the determination of structure, minorities would tend to be segregated in ethnic communities throughout different parts of the city. However, if – over time – commercial uses and new technology increasingly compete for urban land, new business districts and industrial suburbs would be developed away from more central locations, as suggested in the multiple-nuclei theory. In reality, however, no single social characteristic operates in isolation. Instead, as Murdie (1969) and Macionis and Parrillo (1998) point out, most manifestations of family status, socio-economic status and ethnicity influence each other and produce a complex pattern of social space, and this in turn forms a causal relationship with the pattern of physical space (figure 3.8) – making it unlikely that any single model of urban structure can adequately explain the full range of historical and cross-cultural urban life.

The development of individual urban sites

Whichever of the ecological theories of structure is being considered, it is assumed that land uses invade each other and that there is a varying pace of renewal. Changing property values are both a cause and a consequence of these processes. Urban property has two basic values – the capital value of buildings and sites in their *existing use* and the capital value of cleared sites in their *best alternative use*. In a period of price stability, the capital value of the building and site in existing use falls as the building becomes obsolete or wears out, but the value of the cleared site in its best alternative use remains constant (figure 3.9(a)). During inflation, both values increase although the capital value of the cleared site for the best alternative use would probably rise more quickly than the capital value of the building and site in existing use – the latter value eventually declining (figure 3.9(b)).

When redevelopment occurs it will usually be to a more intensive use and, assuming planning consent, to higher buildings. But there are economic limits to height. On the supply side, the state of building technology could mean that sub-ground conditions are unsuitable. Increasing costs occur as additional storeys are added because of the necessity for increased hoisting and more costly foundations. There is an increasing percentage of unremunerative space which needs to be devoted to servicing and maintenance of buildings. On the demand side, there may be limits, although penthouses command high values. Basically, the developer may go on adding storeys until the marginal yield from the additional storey is equal to the marginal cost of providing it subject to statutory approvals and structural considerations. Beyond this point, further storeys would be unprofitable. For housing developers, terraces of narrow-fronted housing achieve

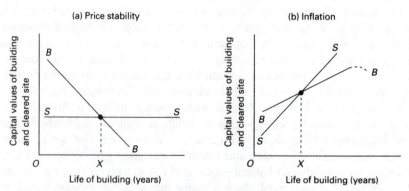

Note: *BB* = capital value of building and site in existing use
      SS = capital value of cleared site in its best alternative use

Figure 3.9 *The maximum economic life of a building*

higher density and lower site costs. Stone (1970) contends that the real costs of providing and maintaining dwellings rise more rapidly than the requirement for land falls; hence the real costs per hectare of land saved increase with the number of storeys. Frequently, the use of high-density development is advocated as a means of housing more people nearer the centre of the city and nearer their work; however, additional space must be made available for local shopping and other facilities, and this increases the amount of land required and hence reduces the numbers that can be housed near the centre.

In figure 3.9 redevelopment should take place after X years, *ceteris paribus*. But because of the durability of buildings (and often because of their architectural merit or historic interest) redevelopment might not take place until the buildings are structurally unsound. In other cases inaccurate valuation of the cleared site or building (or both) may create inertia. The multiplicity of interests, properties being retained by their existing owners for non-monetary reasons, and the length of leases and legal rights of tenants, may also inhibit the redevelopment of a site. The continued use of the building after X years therefore implies that the land is being used inefficiently or sub-optimally, although it must be recognized that non-economic or indirect influences may be important.

On the rural–urban fringe, the direct value of agricultural or horticultural activities may be considerably less than the capital value of sites. Again, redevelopment may be restricted through planning controls – not least by green-belt restrictions. In both urban and rural areas when the capital values of buildings fall below the capital values of cleared sites, the possibility of the nationalization of development land and the taxation of increased values might deter development – sub-optimal use consequently resulting.

The micro-economic aspects of the change (or lack of change) in the use of individual sites is consistent with macro-economic explanations of the urban structure and the theories of urban growth. Firey (1951) argued that although accessibility and the capital value of sites diminish outwards from the centre of the city, the rate of fall in site value is not the same for each use. There is a greater rate of decline of those uses most dependent on accessibility, namely the commercial uses of the centre. Where the site value of one use becomes less than that of another, change to the higher value will occur eventually. In figure 3.10 commercial use will replace residential use when the distance from the city centre becomes less than X km. Any remaining residential sites within the central area will probably be redeveloped as commercial properties.

Firey's hypothesis of site value is related to Alonso's theory of rent (see pages 192–6). Both approaches help to clarify the rationale of the numerous models of urban structure discussed earlier in this chapter, and the theories of urban growth offer explanations of why the underlying deter-

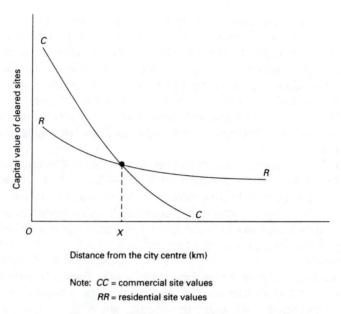

Note: *CC* = commercial site values
      RR = residential site values

Figure 3.10 *Site values of competing uses*

minants of the capital values of cleared sites and buildings fluctuate – the values reflecting the levels of economic activity, technological application and government policy.

The Urban Political Economy Paradigm

By the end of the 1960s, theories of urban ecology were being increasingly questioned. It seemed that some other paradigm was necessary to explain urban change at a time of high unemployment in the older industrial regions, an increased rate of migration from regions of decline to regions of growth, large-scale out-migration to the suburbs and the intensifying fiscal problems of so many cities (Macionis and Parrillo, 1998). A political economy of location – based on the ideas of Marx – thus emerged in the 1970s–1980s. Lefebvre, Harvey and Castells, in particular, attempted to explain the unevenness of urban development in terms of the relationship between capital, labour, profit, wages, class exploitation and inequality.

Lefebvre (1970, 1991) suggests, *first* that there are two circuits of investment capital: the 'primary circuit' within manufacturing industry (whereby resources are hired in order to produce consumer and producer goods), and the 'secondary circuit' in real estate (where property is purchased in anticipation of an increase in value and/or with the intention of developing it for industrial, commercial or residential purposes) – the prime purpose of each circuit being to generate a profit and to reinvest this in further projects. *Second*, that urban space is closely linked to behaviour since people (in concert with planners and developers) construct their surroundings to meet particular needs and objectives – similar behaviour organizing space in a similar way, as, for example, in the suburban areas of the United States, Canada and Australia. *Third*, that there is a distinction between 'abstract space' (which is of concern to business firms, investors and government when considering the development of property, profit and location) and 'social space' (which is the environment in which people live, work and play). Lefebvre suggests that – in attempting to realize spatial needs – there is an inherent conflict between business, investors and the government on the one hand, and local people on the other hand – analogous to the class conflict discussed by Marx. 'These three ideas of Lefebvre – two circuits of capital, space as a component of social organization, and the role of government in managing space – were highly influential in charting the course others would take' (Macionis and Parrillo, 1998: 199).

Dividing Baltimore into a number of different socio-economic areas from the core to the outer suburbs, Harvey (1973) uses Lefebvre's hypothesis in a Marxist analysis to show how the capitalist real estate system directly shapes many of the city's problems concerning social inequality. Harvey reveals that the secondary circuit of capital varies in its investment arrangements from place to place – banks showing no interest in lending to the inner city poor, while West Baltimore – more than other poor areas in the city – benefited from government renewal programmes. He suggests, however, that public urban renewal projects might essentially be aimed at restoring an area's profitability in order to attract finance and commercial capital once again, rather than at benefiting the poor.

Castells (1977, 1983) – in examining welfare capitalism – goes beyond the traditional conflict between capital and labour, and focuses on how the provision of 'worker subsidies' (in such areas as housing, education, mass transportation, health and welfare) represents an effort to 'extend' capitalism, and – through a dependency culture – gives rise to new urban struggles and conflicts unknown in Marx's time (see Macionis and Parrillio, 1998). Clearly such conflicts have a spatial dimension, for example when local government needs to determine the location of public projects such as a housing scheme, a school or a mass transit route.

In considering industrial growth in suburban locations, Castells introduced the concept of the 'mode of development' – the key element of which is the development of new forms and sources of information. Derived from Marx's 'mode of production' – which tied producers to labour or material locations, the 'mode of development' enables corporations to choose a much more flexible range of locations. Castells found that emerging high-tech businesses tend to locate disproportionately in suburban rather than inner-city locations in order to take advantage of low-cost land (to enable the development of large-batch production facilities), access to inter-city highways, and proximity to research and design centres and defence establishments (see Macionis and Parrillo, 1998).

Scott (1980, 1988), however, offers a non-Marxist analysis of the relationship between a city's well-being and the globalization of the economy. He suggests that whereas over the course of the twentieth century until about 1970, companies formed themselves into horizontally-integrated oligopolies and maintained their headquarters in the major cities, during the latter part of the century they vertically disintegrated by unloading many of their production processes to locations abroad where labour and energy costs were lowest. While a few cities such as New York, London and Tokyo consequently consolidated their position as the command and control centres of the global economy and are also important locations for finance and specialized service firms, thousands of jobs were lost by plant closures in the older industrial cities, and the viability of local retailing and other consumer services was severely reduced. Attempts to compensate for this loss by developing local job opportunities in business services were rarely successful.

Developing Lefebvre's concepts of 'abstract space' and 'social space', Logan and Molotch (1987) suggest that financial, business and property interests pressure city government to create – in its widest sense – a 'good business climate' to attract investment and development, with the aim of promoting urban growth and maximizing profits. In contrast, local residents may oppose growth, preferring instead to protect the 'character' of their neighbourhood by preserving its older buildings, limiting traffic flow, and maintaining its parks and other open spaces (see Macionis and Parrillo, 1998). Logan and Molotch clearly recognize that whereas the advantages of urban growth are increased economic activity, more jobs and a wider tax-base, the disadvantages include higher rents, greater traffic congestion, an infrastructure less able to handle an increased population, environmental degradation and more crime.

In the view of Macionis and Parrillo (1998: 204), 'urban political economy presents an alternative to what its proponents see as the biased approach of the older ecological model: an assumption that profit making and capitalism are the natural forces that shape cities'. In short, it explains how a city's form and growth result, not from natural processes, but from capitalism and its *raison d'être* – the realization of profits; how urban land use and social arrangements reflect conflicts over the distribution of resources; how government plays an important role in urban life; and how urban growth is an outcome of economic restructuring (see Macionis and Parrillo, 1998).

However, the political economy paradigm fails to shed very much light on how the spatial development of land uses in capitalist cities might have been instrumental in raising the standard of living of the city as a whole, or on the weaknesses of socialist cities historically in meeting the needs of most of their inhabitants. As Hall (1984) implies, a dialogue might emerge that focuses on the comparative merits and demerits of the ecological and political economy approaches and ultimately produces a more sophisticated understanding of urban land use. It is possible that whereas there may be a continuing need to rely on ecological models to explain – in physical terms – *how* patterns of urban land use evolve, it may also be necessary to employ the political economy paradigm to explain – in economic and political terms – *why* the urban land use pattern assumes the form it takes.

Urban Land Use in Countries in Political and Economic Transition

Under socialism, the state ownership of land along with central planning meant that urban development was subject to much greater control than under capitalism. It was hoped that this would help promote the efficient operation of the economy, facilitate the provision of a wide range of social services as a means of collective consumption, and guarantee a high quality of life for the urban population (Smith, 1996). As a high priority, the public provision of housing was intended 'to ensure satisfactory and relatively egalitarian living standards for all' and cheap public transport was developed 'to ensure convenient access to work, leisure and other sources of need satisfaction leisure' (Smith, 1996: 72).

Clearly, neither socialism nor its cities could have been built overnight. Smith (1996) drew attention to the distinction between partially changed cities and new cities. Examples of the former were the large and long-established national capitals of Moscow, Budapest, Prague and Warsaw, where socialist planning, to an extent, replaced the previous urban fabric – depending on the amount of war damage and the availability of resources allocated for development. The new cities, on the other hand, were developed in relation to mineral extraction or industrial production and were 'the purest version of the planned socialist city with its stark functionality' (Smith, 1996: 73).

BOX 3.2: URBAN LAND USE IN EAST CENTRAL EUROPE

Until the early-1990s, land use and rents in the larger cities of East Central Europe and the former Soviet Union had not been determined by the interplay of market forces for generations. Planners had allocated urban land uses and determined the development of urban sites in ways that were normally impossible in the West, while – in contrast to advanced capitalist cities – there was little socio-spatial segregation in areas of residential land use. However, urban change throughout the region can only be understood within a historic context, and this varies from country to country.

Because of relatively little damage during the second world war, the development of the built environment of Prague – under socialism, from the late-1940s to 1989 – modified rather than replaced the pre-existing capitalist structure (Smith, 1996). In the 1930s, it was evident that the proletariat increasingly sought housing on the periphery, the wealthier strata of society were out-migrating from the centre and the industrial areas of the intermediate zone to newly developed enclaves, while the city centre accommodated the bourgeoisie and skilled working classes (Mateju *et al.*, 1979). However, from the late-1940s to the late-1950s, geographical differences in the distribution of the housing stock were evened out, and the proportion of manual workers living in the inner zones increased from around 25 per cent in 1930 to 40 per cent in 1961 (Musil, 1987; Smith, 1996). But in the 1960s–1970s, large-scale housing development took place on the periphery to accommodate the growing workforce and to decongest the centre to facilitate the renewal of inner areas (Smith, 1996).

Despite fairly successful attempts to socially homogenize residential space (for example, in the new outer suburbs where housing of uniform quality was allocated largely on the basis of need), some areas still retained their high status, while older people tended to live in poor and overcrowded housing. During the 1980s, there was a tendency for housing to be differentiated within both the old and new areas of the city. Better-quality housing was increasingly dispersed (unlike that of capitalist cities), and on the periphery, residential estates comprised both state and co-operative housing (Smith, 1996). During the transition to capitalism, only time will tell whether programmes of privatization will further modify the residential land use pattern of Prague.

In the late-1940s, and in contrast to Prague, Budapest suffered from a legacy of immense war-time damage. Initial attempts to restrict the growth of Budapest led to substantial housing shortages, and resulted in plans being produced in the late-1950s to build 250,000 houses in the city, of which 80 per cent would be funded by the government. But, because of financial constraints on public investment, 30 to 40 per cent of housing needs were met by private sector development. Consequently, extensive public-sector high-

rise estates were developed in the 1960s–1970 between the edge of the continuously built-up area and outlying suburban settlements; high-quality single-
family and multi-family blocks remained within the traditional residential
estates surrounding the central area; while the most dilipidated housing was
found in the run-down area between the centre of the city and the estates
(Smith, 1996).

It has been suggested that the development of public sector housing estates
has led to the growing polarization of society (see Hegedus and Tosics, 1983),
but this is a view questioned by Sillance (1985) and Ladányi (1989) who consider that a patchwork of socio-economic differentiation has emerged rather
than clearly demarcated homogeneous zones (see Smith, 1996). In the cities
of Pecs and Szeged, however, Szelényi (1983) found marked inequalities
in the provision of housing – compounding other inequalities resulting from
occupational status. Unlike Prague, programmes of privatization have been
in place since the 1980s, and intensified in the 1990s – with possibly dramatic effects on the distribution of wealth and patterns of residential use during
the process of transition.

Warsaw suffered from even more war damage than Budapest, and thus
there were dramatic changes in the spatial structure of the city in the
post-war period. In 1931, and in contrast to more advanced capitalist cities,
there was a clear decline in the socio-economic status of households from the
central city to the peripheral zone – a phenomenon explained by the failure
of wealthier people to migrate outwards and suburbanize (Weclawowicz,
1979). By 1970, however, Warsaw's spatial structure was a mosaic differentiated by a wide range of socio-economic variables. Its pattern reflected socio-
economic position and a selective housing policy after an extensive period of
post-war reconstruction. However, between 1978 and 1988, there was evidence of a substantial increase in social disparity (Weclawowicz, 1991) – possibly as a result of housing shortages and political and social transformation
(Smith, 1996). An alternative explanation of disparity was offered by Dangschat and Blasius (1987), who suggested that the level of educational attain-
ment was the principal consideration in the determination of access to a
differentiated housing stock. Taking into account housing shortages, it is not
surprising that the Polish government was slow to introduce programmes of
privatization at the onset of transition. This was clearly 'conducive to a per-
petuation of the existing differences in the socio-spatial structure' – at least
as far as housing was concerned (Smith, 1996: 87).

There is a view, however, that – because of a broadly historic and
physical legacy – the cities of East Central Europe and the former
Soviet Union remained fundamentally the same as the capitalist cities
of Western Europe throughout the period of socialism. But it has also
been suggested that whereas there were certain similarities between
capitalist and socialist patterns of urban land use, there were also marked

differences. French and Hamilton (1979) attempted to illustrate this by suggesting that the socialist city of the Soviet bloc comprised several distinct zones:

(1) a historic core – pre-1800;
(2) a CBD;
(3) former upper- and middle-class housing;
(4) a zone of socialist renewal where industry, warehousing and former working-class housing was subject to clearance and redevelopment;
(5) socialist housing of the 1950s;
(6) integrated socialist neighbourhoods and other residential districts of the 1960s, 1970s and 1980s;
(7) open or planned 'isolation belts';
(8) industrial zones; and
(9) open countryside, forest and hills – including tourist complexes.

Although concentric zone patterns were clearly evident (figure 3.11), these tended to overlay a more sectoral distribution of functional zones associated with radial transportation arteries, historic traditions and site qualities. The principal distinction, however, is between the pre-socialist inner zones and the more extensive socialist outer zones, and whereas the latter zones are characterized by their planned uniformity, the preservation of the historic core often necessitates the construction of a new city centre on its edge.

The degree to which the cities of the former Eastern bloc could be described as socialist depended greatly on the scale of neighbourhood or *mikroraion* development. Accommodating between 5,000 and 15,000 people, *mikroraion* consisted of blocks of flats and associated services, and became the basic building block of the Soviet city – before being adopted by other socialist countries. On a broader spatial scale, each neighbourhood became part of a hierarchy of micro-districts – headed by larger complexes of 30,000–50,000 inhabitants (Smith, 1996).

BOX 3.3: URBAN LAND USE IN THE FORMER SOVIET UNION

In contrast to the cities of East Central Europe, the influence of socialism on Moscow and other Soviet cities can be traced back to 1917 rather than to the aftermath of the Second World War. The introduction of *mikroraion* in the inter-war period was intended to ensure that all households had equal access to the urban infrastructure and the provision of services. However, with regard to services, this was not the case. The quality of services varied from district to district, and these services were more accessible to workers in favoured enterprises than in others; there were time-lags between the construction of housing and the provision of local services; and some services were located centrally to satisfy the needs of a city-wide population. Generally, the inner districts of Moscow were at an advantage in being close to the hub of the city's transportation system which ensured accessibility to a large population and thus the provision of more specialized services.

Housing tenure in the Soviet Union was of two types: a very small private sector of poor standard and confined to the periphery of towns and cities (accounting for no more than one-quarter of the total stock), and a large socialized sector – subdivided into governmental, industrial or ministerial, and co-operative housing. In Moscow in 1989, three-quarters of the stock was owned by the city government, and 16 per cent by industrial or ministerial owners (Smith, 1996). It was evident, however, that there was a strong positive correlation between the spatial distribution of high status households and the most spacious housing (Hamilton, 1993), and also between the spatial distribution of these households and people's perceptions of the prestige of residential areas (Siderov, 1992). Although the inner areas of Moscow accommodated a variety of social groups, the outer areas of the city were differentiated by wedges of disparate environmental quality and social status. Some of these contained a relatively high proportion of co-operative housing and households with comparatively high status occupations who were willing to trade off access to city-centre services for new housing and a pleasant environment on the edge of Moscow. Other outer sectors contained large areas of state housing, occupied by people of lower occupational status, but in conditions more environmentally favourable than in the inner city (Smith, 1996). The effect of urban planning, however, was that population density increased as distance from the city centre increased – in contrast to most cities in the advanced capitalist world. Nevertheless, in terms of land use, French (1987) suggests that Moscow contains elements of both the concentric zone and sector models of urban spatial structure. The Burgess model is exemplified by the concentration of central area functions and the surrounding system of ring roads which tend to differentiate land use, whereas the Hoyt model is compatible with the sectoral development of industry, the outward movement of different social groups and the provision of green wedges.

Smith (1996) suggests that in other large Soviet cities, socio-economic and environmental differentiation is largely concentric. From the city centre outwards, there are inner high-status areas of comparatively good housing – occupied disproportionately by professional groups; inner low-status areas of old and deteriorating housing – occupied by service workers and artisans, and environmentally affected by industrial and commercial development; outer areas of relatively high status, with high proportions of co-operative flats, and accommodating white collared workers; outer areas of low status with

continued

predominantly state housing accommodating manual workers and in-migrants, and suffering environmentally from the proximity of industry; and suburban enclaves of private housing of poor quality. Clearly, accessibility to the city centre and the provision of services diminish outwards. It was also evident that family size was negatively linked to socio-economic status and increased outwards towards the periphery (Bater, 1986).

Although rent and land values were largely irrelevant in explaining the distribution of socio-economic groups in socialist countries (French and Hamilton, 1979), it is sometimes argued that the degree of social segregation and inequality in Eastern bloc cities was, to an extent, as endemic as in capitalist cities. Dangschat (1987), for example, found 'surprisingly high' segregation of social groups in Warsaw in respect of household size, age and education, and it was also apparent that – as in capitalist cities – there was some ethnic segregation in the socialist cities of East Central Europe and the Soviet Union (Smith, 1996). To these examples of social differentiation can be added (less conspicuously) segregation by income, and marked 'differences in local levels of service provision and in general environmental quality' (Smith, 1996: 97). However, other observers took a different view, suggesting that urban inequality under socialism was less than under capitalism, but where it did exist it could best be described as patchy – a conclusion reached by Weclawowicz (1979, 1981) in his studies of Warsaw and other Polish cities. Harloe (1996) was in no doubt that in socialist cities 'socio-economic segregation was far more limited than in comparable capitalist cities' (Harloe, 1996: 13), and was confident that the unequal access to urban services, which Smith describes, is now being altered in the transition. However, only time will tell whether the patterns of social distributions achieved in the socialist cities of the former Soviet bloc until the final decade of the twentieth century will aid or hinder them as they rapidly embrace capitalism.

Urban Land Use in Newly-Industrializing and Developing Countries

Cities in newly-industrializing and developing countries have either originated very rapidly from their pre-industrial beginnings, or remain quintessentially pre-industrial (Dickenson *et al.*, 1996). Sjoberg (1960) suggested that pre-industrial cities differed substantially from the Burgess model. Although the pre-industrial city lacked a CBD (in contrast to cities of the developed world), the central area had pre-eminence over the periphery, since – instead of offices and shops – its focus was religious or government

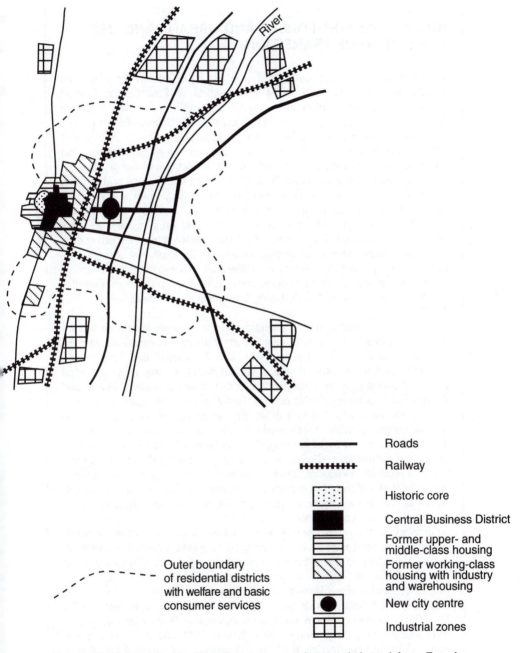

River

	Roads
	Railway
	Historic core
	Central Business District
	Former upper- and middle-class housing
	Former working-class housing with industry and warehousing
	New city centre
	Industrial zones

Outer boundary
of residential districts
with welfare and basic
consumer services

Figure 3.11 *Model of an East European socialist city (adapted from French and Hamilton, 1979)*

BOX 3.4: MARKET FORCES AND URBAN LAND USE IN A PERIOD OF TRANSITION

Market forces will undoubtedly determine the future pattern of residential density, land use and land prices in the cities of East Central Europe and the former Soviet Union. In Moscow, for example, residential population densities – under socialism – tended to increase with distance from the core since they were determined by planned allocations, whereas in capitalist cities – such as Paris – densities were, and are, determined mainly by market forces that recognize either the benefits of central location or the demand for them, and thus decline outwards (figure 3.12(a)). In the absence of a market, the land price gradient in socialist cities tended to be flat, whereas in capitalist cities it often slopes steeply as distance from the city centre increases. During the 1990s, however, there was evidence that land price gradients in, for example, Moscow and Krakow began to slope downward from the urban core – Krakow having the steeper gradient because of its somewhat earlier adoption of market pricing. As market forces take hold, economic activity is increasingly concentrated in the urban core, and – as well as land prices – densities are diminishing outward (World Bank, 1999; see also Bertaud and Renaud, 1997).

Possibly the most dramatic changes in urban morphology in a former socialist city are to be seen in east Berlin. With its incorporation into the Federal Republic of Germany in 1990, and the introduction of a private market in land, a new pattern of land use has quickly emerged. In the central areas, office and other commercial developments have proceeded apace, and non-profitable or less-profitable non-residential uses have been forced to move out. On the periphery, the lack of effective planning has led to a proliferation of shopping malls, car-dealerships and other extensive uses (Harloe, 1996). In the case of social housing, the transfer of accommodation from the state to municipalities and co-operatives soon led to a rapid increase in rents – with a probable outflow of better-off tenants, residualization of the remainder and deterioration in the condition of estates. As elsewhere in the capitalist world, this in turn might result in gentrification and the displacement of remaining low-income tenants (Harloe, 1996).

In Warsaw, there has likewise been a substantial amount of office development in the city centre in recent years (very largely for international lessees), for example the $20,000\,m^2$ Sienna centre close to the central square and the $23,000\,m^2$ Warsaw Towers in the burgeoning CBD. But, as in east Berlin, decentralization – along Western lines – is much in evidence. A large-scale scheme at the Mokotow business park near the airport was completed by the late-1990s, and out-of-town retail developments at Reduta and Targowek were scheduled for completion by 2000 (Kellett, 1999). Similarly, in response to the demand from foreign banking and finance, both central and decentralized office development were undertaken in the 1990s in Katowice – the centre of the Silesian industrial heartland (Kellett, 1999).

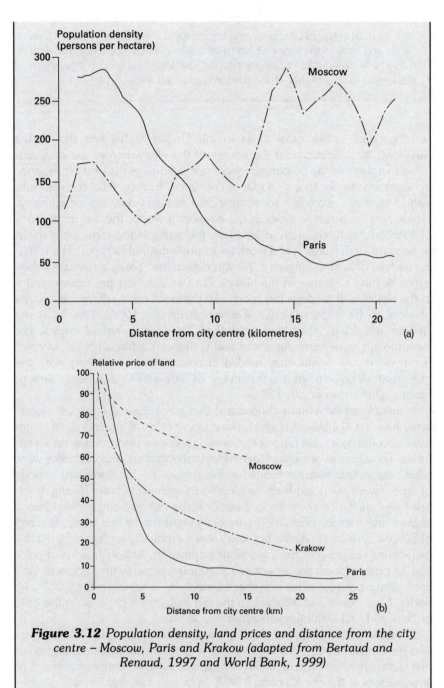

Figure 3.12 *Population density, land prices and distance from the city centre – Moscow, Paris and Krakow (adapted from Bertaud and Renaud, 1997 and World Bank, 1999)*

continued

> With market forces thus becoming the principal determinant of urban land values and uses in the former Eastern bloc, the political economy paradigm might have become just as relevant to the analysis of urban development in this region as it is to that of the advanced capitalist world.

buildings and, unlike most cities in the United States and the United Kingdom, it accommodated the homes of the elite whereas the disadvantaged members of the community were relegated to peripheral settlements. In intermediate locations, social areas were further differentiated into distinct quarters according to occupational status, family ties or ethnicity. However, in contrast to cities in the developed world, there is an absence of functional differentiation in land use, for example the same plots might be used for both housing and work (as in pre-industrial Europe). The resulting pattern of land use (figure 3.13) was determined partly by cultural values which defined residence in the historic core as the most prestigious, and – in the absence of modern transport – by the need for dwellings and places of work to be juxtapositioned (Dickenson et al., 1996). Clearly, many African and Asian cities have pre-colonial and pre-industrial origins, but even though most Latin American and Caribbean settlements are of comparatively recent origin, they tended in colonial times to incorporate the pre-industrial patterns of urban land use of sixteenth to eighteenth century Europe (Dickenson et al., 1996).

It should not be assumed, however, that pre-industrial cities will necessarily become like Western cities, since many cities of pre-industrial origin were affected by a wide range of colonial influences, often over several centuries. Through the process of 'dependent urbanization', colonial cities were reliant on industrialization located in Europe, and – for significant periods of time – were restricted from developing indigenous industry. Being developed essentially for commercial functions, the colonial city evolved into a distinct urban form, containing palaces, administrative buildings, churches of European design and elite housing areas – ethnically segregated from the high-density housing of the indigenous population. Although areas of colonial (or post-colonial) settlement are often interspersed with traditional land uses, some colonial cities are characterized by a separate European city having been developed adjacent to the old indigenous city – as in the case of New and Old Dehli (Dickenson et al., 1996).

In recent years, industrial development, modern transport and congestion have distorted the urban morphology of both pre-industrial and colonial cities, threatening community structures and the economic survival of large sectors of the city (Chokor, 1989). In many newly-industrializing countries, the traditional desire to reside as close as possible to the centre is being gradually replaced by suburbanization, with the elite – in particular –

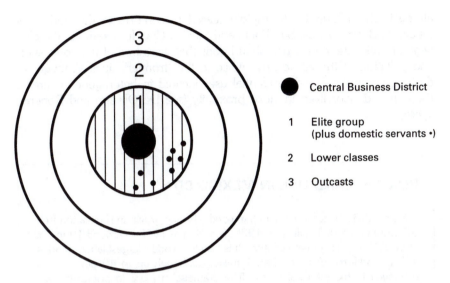

Figure 3.13 *The pre-industrial city (adapted from Sjoberg, 1960)*

moving out to high-income enclaves on the outer fringe of cities. It has been suggested, however, that while cities in Latin America are assuming the economic and social attributes of cities in the developed world, African and Asian cities are more likely to retain their traditional pre-industrial urban structures into the forseeable future (see Horvath, 1969; McGee, 1971). However, this is by no means certain.

Given the dramatic rate of growth in urbanization and industrialization in Latin America in recent years (see pages 20–21), cities in this region might seem destined to experience the same processes of urban growth and assume the same patterns of land use as cities in the developed world. However, it could be argued that because, historically, Latin American cities have been significantly different from those in the developed world in terms of their economic and demographic structure, it is unlikely that convergence will occur until well into the new millennium (see Ward, 1993). Until the mid-twentieth century, the normal pattern of land use in the older and less dynamic cities of Latin America was broadly pre-industrial and concentric. In the centre, a *zocalo* (colonial plaza) was surrounded by ecclesiastical buildings, major government offices and commercial establishments, and the mansions of the elite; and this zone was in turn surrounded by an area of declining social importance with mixed housing and business uses accommodating artisans. On the periphery, there were often extensive areas of squatter settlement, housing the poorest inhabitants of the city employed largely in the informal economy (see De Oliveira and Roberts, 1998). However, the pattern of land use in those cities that were industrializing in the 1920s–1930s rapidly ceased to conform to the traditional model. In Buenos Aires, São Paulo and Mexico City, for example, the elite began to relocate in new neighbourhoods that were free of the congestion and pollution of the city centre, while in the 'frontier' cities although industrial, commercial and residential uses located in heterogeneous areas, the rich and poor lived in close proximity (see De Oliveira and Roberts, 1998).

BOX 3.5: LAND USE IN MEXICO CITY

Mexico City is the largest city in the world – having grown in population from 370,000 in 1900, 1 million in 1930, 5 million in 1960 to around 19 million at the end of the twentieth century. It is also the world's largest labour market, with a workforce of more than 7 million, although up to 40 per cent are employed in the informal sector. The dramatic increase in population and employment generated substantial spatial growth, mainly through the development of low-income neighbourhoods – *colonias proletarias* – to the east and south (immediately after the 1917 Mexican Revolution), to the south (in the 1920s) and to the west (in the 1930s).

The spatial development of Mexico City since the 1950s is indicated in figure 3.14. The city is characterized by: a commercial sector which extends

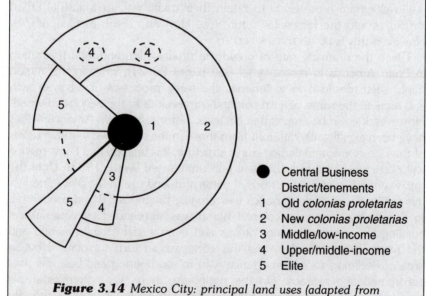

●	Central Business District/tenements
1	Old *colonias proletarias*
2	New *colonias proletarias*
3	Middle/low-income
4	Upper/middle-income
5	Elite

Figure 3.14 *Mexico City: principal land uses (adapted from Dickenson et al., 1996)*

westwards from the CBD – containing Western-style amenities and the residences of many of the city's elite; a westward extension of the sector developed in the 1970s – to accommodate some of the elite who were escaping from the congestion, pollution and crime of the central area; a middle-class wedge in the south-west of the city – where status increased with distance from the centre; a number of upper middle-class satellites developed in the north-west and north of the city; and expanding *colonias prolatarias* around most of the periphery – encroaching extensively into the surrounding countryside (see Potter and Lloyd-Evans, 1998).

Because the majority of the working population has received less than the minimum wage in recent years (Dickenson *et al.*, 1996), the problem of low-income housing provision is not easily resolved. Housing need, however, is met in a number of ways and in different locations within the city. In the centre, tenements (*vecindades*) are located in overcrowded purpose-built apartments or in dilapidated colonial buildings; and in the low-income neighbourhoods (*colonias proletarias*), housing is provided either on illegally subdivided sites (*fraccionamientos clandestinos*) where the developer lacks the legal title to the land or fails to obtain planning permission, or in squatter settlements (*colonias paracaidistas*). The poor also found shelter in shack yards (*cuidades perdidas*) on privately owned plots scattered across the city, or in government-funded projects (*cuidades perdidas*) intended for households in need, but with cost levels beyond the earning capacity of the lowest one-third of income earners (Dickenson *et al.*, 1996).

Urban development in Latin America in the latter third of the twentieth century was substantially influenced by macroeconomic conditions. Until the late 1990s, Latin American cities did not experience the same investment boom and slump conditions that cities in most developed countries had; a higher proportion of their working population was employed in industry and a lower proportion in services than in cities in developed countries; and whereas, among the elite, patterns of wealth and consumption have been converging, there has been a divergence in incomes and wealth across society as a whole (Armstrong and McGee, 1985).

Although Latin American cities still display characteristics of their colonial and pre-industrial past, traditional patterns of land use have now been overlaid by modern industrial development and transport infrastructure, compressed by the inflow of millions of migrants, and stretched by the land use demands of the emerging middle classes and the elite (Potter and Lloyd-Evans, 1998). Latin American cities are consequently changing their structure (figure 3.15). In many, according to Griffin and Ford (1980), a prominant sector of high rent land has emerged in the Hoytian sense –

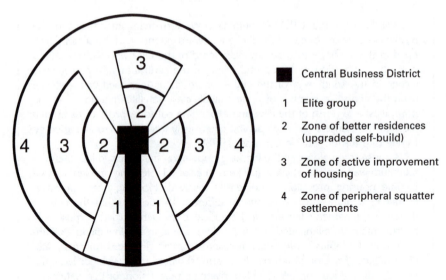

Figure 3.15 *Latin American city structure (adapted from Griffin and Ford, 1980)*

extending radially from the CBD, and containing prestigious offices, hotels, restaurants, theatres, private hospitals and leisure facilities, as well as a substantial proportion of high-income housing. But in cities such as Santiago, Lima, Quito, Bogota, Caracas and Port of Spain, the elite have deserted the core altogether, and moved out to high-income enclaves on the outer urban fringe (see Amato, 1970, 1971; Morris, 1978; Conway, 1981; Potter, 1993; Potter and O'Flaherty, 1995). Apart from the high rent sector, the pattern of land use in Griffin and Ford's (1980) model is largely concentric, comprising a series of zones characterized by the opposite socio-economic attributes from those found in developed countries – i.e. household incomes and the condition and value of housing diminish outward. In the inner zone, former areas of elite housing have filtered down to middle-income groups and are reasonably well served in terms of electricity, sanitation and transportation. However, there are also older – formerly colonial – residences around the central plaza that have suffered from a lack of repair and maintenance. In the intermediate zone, a variety of housing types of modest quality accommodate poorer households – who move in and out of the zone according to their life-cycle and status. This is also a zone of commercial and informal economic activity.

On the periphery, there is often large-scale industrial and environmentally polluting activity, frequently interspersed with extensive squatter settlements (see Potter and Lloyd-Evans, 1998). Here the poor are really poor.

In Buenos Aires, for example – in one area of peripheral settlement – 60 per cent of the population of 276,000 had incomes of less than US$ 160 per month in 1999, and in the periphery as a whole around 40 per cent of squatter dwellings lacked sewage connections and 30 per cent relied on increasingly contaminated well water (Hall, 1999). However, because of low wages, housing is very rarely built for the poor, and in Buenos Aires – as in many other Latin American cities – it satisfies only a very small proportion of low-income need (De Oliveira and Roberts, 1998). Whereas in the USA and elsewhere in the developed world, 'the poor are trapped in the central cities, in Buenos Aires they are trapped in the suburbs' (Hall, 1999: 299).

Griffin and Ford's analysis however has been subject to criticism since it implies that the desire of the elite to suburbanize contributed to a deterioration in the quality of the city centre; whereas in many large Latin American cities, elites suburbanized because of high-density conditions, traffic congestion, pollution and high crime rates in the centre (Ward, 1990; Gilbert and Varley, 1991). Griffin and Ford also emphasize the extent to which residential areas are segregated on the basis of income and wealth. While this may be generally true throughout Latin America, and undoubtedly became more evident in, for example, Santiago during the 1970s–1980s, in Montevideo and Bogota polarization was partially reversed in the 1980s as a result of the economic crisis that affected most income groups, and in Rio de Janeiro and São Paulo the occupation of space became more socially and economically mixed as middle-class housing was built in poor areas (see De Oliveira and Roberts, 1998). Similarly, it cannot be assumed that settlements of the poor will always be confined to the periphery – they are sometimes located close to the centre, for example on hillsides in Rio de Janeiro and in ravines in Guatemala City. Finally, there is also little evidence that – in contrast to cities in the developed world – suburbanization has contributed to the demise of the inner city, which although in need of renewal in some cases, still retains its vitality and importance (see Potter and Lloyd-Evans, 1998).

Over a shorter time than in Latin America and the Caribbean, many African cities have been much affected by European settlement. Research has shown that they normally contain an indigenous core surrounded by concentric zones of residential land use – accommodating the indigenous population at high density close to the centre, mixed ethnic groups at moderate densities in intermediate locations, and elite colonial or post-colonial groups close to the periphery (see United Nations, 1973). Beyond, shanty towns are scattered around the edge of the periphery, together with industry and large-scale institutions (figure 3.16). Whereas in the east and south of the continent segregation was maintained through legislation, in West Africa – where there were smaller numbers of European settlers – divisions

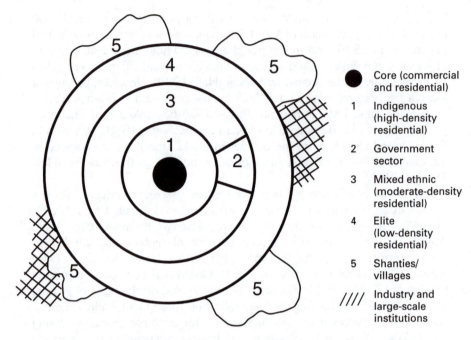

Figure 3.16 *Sub-Saharan city structure (after United Nations, 1973)*

were less formal (Potter and Lloyd-Evans, 1998). In South Africa, however, apartheid led to the forced relocation of the black population from the inner city to townships on the periphery, and segregated access to urban amenities and services through much of the second half of the twentieth century. The end of apartheid has provided an opportunity to restructure the city and redistribute wealth and incomes in a more equitable way than in the past.

In terms of urban structure, there is a clear distinction between the cities of South East Asia, China and Southern Asia. In colonial times, urban areas such as Singapore, Hong Kong and Jakarta were essentially developed as trading ports with central cores comprising local bazaars and densely developed commercial uses, separate 'Western' and 'non-Western' sectors, and very mixed land uses (Potter and Lloyd-Evans, 1998). By the end of the twentieth century, this pattern remained broadly intact but in a restructured guise. Within the typical South East Asian city (figure 3.17) there is now a Western-style CBD, distinct commercial segments that have been developed along ethnic lines (Chinese, Indian, European etc.), and zones of squatter settlements and industry are located on the periphery – the latter expanding into rural areas and merging imperceptibly with village settlements and

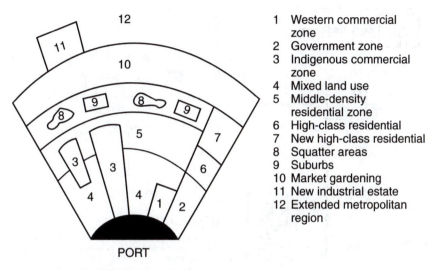

1	Western commercial zone
2	Government zone
3	Indigenous commercial zone
4	Mixed land use
5	Middle-density residential zone
6	High-class residential
7	New high-class residential
8	Squatter areas
9	Suburbs
10	Market gardening
11	New industrial estate
12	Extended metropolitan region

PORT

Figure 3.17 *South East Asian city (adapted from McGee, 1967)*

agricultural areas (McGee, 1967; McGee and Greenberg, 1992). In most cities in the region, residential zones are mixed in terms of traditional and modern housing, although there is some locational differentiation in terms of ethnicity, for example there is a distinct 'Chinatown' in Jakarta, while there is a general tendency for the elite to suburbanize, as in other newly-industrializing regions – a process aided by the development of rapid mass transit systems (Potter and Lloyd-Evans, 1998). By the end of the twentieth century, many cities in the region had become major centres of growth and development (Dwyer, 1995), with Singapore, for example, becoming a global city. Yet despite rapid technological change, the majority of the population live and work in indigenous buildings, in areas disadvantaged by the lack of modern infrastructure.

In five stages, the basic form and structure of the archetypical Chinese city has evolved over three thousand years (see Gaubatz, 1998). Initially, cities were rectangular, walled settlements with grid-iron street patterns and established essentially for administrative and military purposes. However, by the sixth century AD – during the Tang Dynasty – new settlements were established primarily for economic reasons, while existing cities assumed commercial functions and expanded beyond their walls. During the Treaty Port era (1842–1949) and partly-overlapping Republic era (1911–49), there was a further period of urban growth since coastal cities expanded in terms of industrial production, trade, population and physical extent, while city walls were modified to permit the development of transport infrastructure. From 1949 to 1978, the Maoist city became superimposed on the

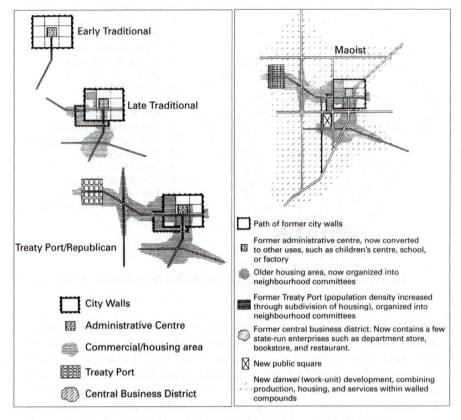

Figure 3.18 *The evolution of the archetypal Chinese city*
(after Gaubatz, 1998)

form and structure of cities inherited from previous eras. Cities were transformed from centres of consumption to centres of production – where retail districts were eliminated and 'large scale factories and adjacent workers' housing and service facilities were constructed in concentrated areas . . . surrounding the traditional urban core' (Gaubatz, 1998: 256). Such concentrations of mixed land use – referred to as *danwei* (similar in concept to the Soviet *mikroraion*) – thus effectively eliminated the need for specialized districts. Since 1978, however, large cities – particularly in coastal locations – have attempted to assume a world role with as many trading links with external markets as with the domestic hinterland (Gaubatz, 1999). With the emergence of a market economy, and aided by the upgrading of the road and rail infrastructure, housing development – to satisfy different segments of the market – soon became spatially separated from industrial

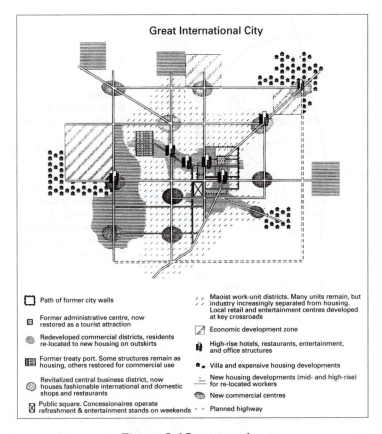

Great International City

☐ Path of former city walls	Maoist work-unit districts. Many units remain, but industry increasingly separated from housing. Local retail and entertainment centres developed at key crossroads
⊡ Former administrative centre, now restored as a tourist attraction	▨ Economic development zone
≋ Redeveloped commercial districts, residents re-located to new housing on outskirts	▯ High-rise hotels, restaurants, entertainment, and office structures
▦ Former treaty port. Some structures remain as housing, others restored for commercial use	▲▲ Villa and expensive housing developments
⊘ Revitalized central business district, now houses fashionable international and domestic shops and restaurants	New housing developments (mid- and high-rise) for re-located workers
⊠ Public square. Concessionaires operate refreshment & entertainment stands on weekends	New commercial centres
	= = Planned highway

Figure 3.18 continued

development, specialized commercial and business districts were re-established and industrial development zones were designated in an attempt to attract foreign and domestic investment (Gaubatz, 1995a, 1995b, 1999). Chinese cities today thus not only represent a layered amalgam of urban forms (figure 3.18) reflecting very different determinants of growth at different periods of history, but an accelerated rate of change in both economic and physical terms.

In Southern Asia, cities such as Dehli, Kolkata (Calcutta), Mumbai (Bombay) and Chennai (Madras) expanded during colonial times as administrative centres or as ports. When built as ports they invariably contained a walled fort, an administrative area, a Western-styled CBD and adjacent – though segregated – residential areas, where Europeans were accommodated in low-density and well-serviced neighbourhoods, while the

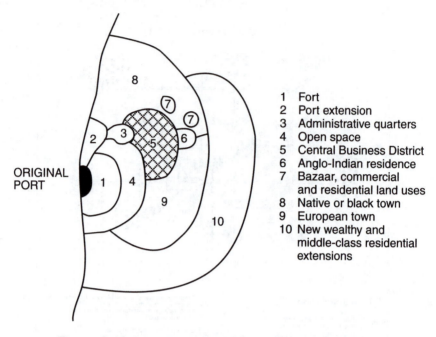

1 Fort
2 Port extension
3 Administrative quarters
4 Open space
5 Central Business District
6 Anglo-Indian residence
7 Bazaar, commercial
   and residential land uses
8 Native or black town
9 European town
10 New wealthy and
   middle-class residential
   extensions

Figure 3.19 *South Asian colonial city (adapted from Brunn and Williams, 1983)*

indigenous population lived at high density in ill-planned streets (Potter and Lloyd-Evans, 1998). Since these cities did not experience a socialist revolution after India gained independence in 1947, the colonial structure is still evident in many modern cities in much of the sub-continent (figure 3.19).

Although the cities of Latin America, sub-Saharan Africa and much of Asia are converging with those of the developed world in terms of modern CBDs, architectural design, transport developments, popular culture and the consumption patterns of the elite, they are still socially segregated in terms of access to wealth, employment, urban services and adequate shelter. 'If nothing else, the existence of . . . massive squatter settlements surrounding such cities, make them distinct urban forms in their own right' (Potter and Lloyd-Evans, 1998: 137). However, as the cities of the developing world reach economic maturity and eventually enter an age of high mass-consumption (see Rostow, 1960), models of pre-industrial and contemporary urban structure – which are essentially ecological – may need to be superseded by the political economy paradigm to promote a better understanding of urban structure.

REFERENCES

Amato, P. (1970) 'Elitism and settlement patterns in the Latin American city', *Journal of the Institute of American Planners*, 36: 96–105.

Amato, P. (1971) 'A comparison of population densities, land values and socio-economic class in four Latin American cities', *Land Economics*, 46: 447–55.

Armstrong, W. and McGee, T.G. (1985) *Theories of Accumulation: Studies in Asian and Latin American Urbanisation*, London: Methuen.

Babcock, B. (1997) 'Recently observed polarising tendencies and Australian cities', *Australian Geographical Studies*, 35: 61–73.

Bater, J.H. (1986) 'Some recent perspectives on the Soviet city', *Urban Geography*, 7: 93–102.

Berry, B.J.L. and Rees, P.H. (1969) 'The factoral ecology of Calcutta', *American Journal of Sociology*, 74: 445–91.

Bertaud, A. and Renaud, B. (1997) 'Socialist cities without land markets', *Journal of Urban Economics*, 41: 137–51.

Brunn, S.D. and Williams, J.F. (1983) *Cities of the World: World Regional Urban Development*, New York: Harper & Row.

Burgess, E.W. (1906) 'The growth of the city', in Park, R.E. and Burgess, E.W. (1925), *The City*, Chicago IL: University of Chicago Press.

Castells (1977) *The Urban Question: A Marxist Approach*, London: Edward Arnold.

Castells (1983) *The City and the Grass Roots*, Berkeley CA: University of California Press.

Chokor, B.A. (1989) 'Motorway development and the conservation of traditional third world cities', *Cities*, 6: 4, 317–24.

Conway, D. (1981) 'Fact or opinion on uncontrolled peripheral settlement in Trinidad: or how different conclusions arise from the same data', *Ekistics*, 286: 37–43.

Dangschat, J. (1987) 'Sociospatial disparities in a "socialist" city: the case of Warsaw at the end of the 1970s', *International Journal of Urban and Regional Research*, 11: 1, 37–60.

Dangschat, J. and Blasius, J. (1987) 'Social and spatial disparities in Warsaw in 1978: an application of correspondence analysis to a "socialist" city', *Urban Studies*, 24: 173–91.

De Oliveira, O. and Roberts, B. (1998) 'Urban development and social inequality in Latin America', in Gugler, J. (ed.), *The Urban Transformation of the Developing World*, Oxford: Oxford University Press.

Dickenson, J., Gould, B., Clarke, C., Mather, S., Prothero, M., Siddle, D., Smith, C. and Thomas-Hope, E. (1996) *Geography and the Third World*, 2nd edn, London: Routledge.

Dwyer, D.J. (1995) 'Urbanization', in Dwyer, D.J. (ed.), *South East Asian Development*, 2nd edn, Harlow: Longman.

Firey, W. (1951) 'Ecological considerations in planning for urban fringes', in Hatt, P.K. and Reiss, A.J. (eds), *Cities and Society*, New York: Free Press.

French, R.A. (1987) 'Changing spatial patterns in Soviet cities – planning or pragmatism?', *Urban Geography*, 8: 309–20.

French, R.A. and Hamilton, F.E.I. (eds) (1979) *The Socialist City: Spatial Structure and Urban Policy*, Chichester: John Wiley.

Friedrichs, J. (1977) *Stadtanalyse*, Hamburg: Rowohlt.

Gaubatz, P. (1995a) 'Changing Beijing', *Geographical Review*, 85: 1, 79–96.

Gaubatz, P. (1995b) 'Urban transformation in post-Mao China: impacts of the reform era on China's urban form', in Davis, D. *et al.* (eds), *Urban Space in Contemporary China*, Cambridge: Cambridge University Press.

Gaubatz, P. (1998) 'Understanding Chinese urban form: contexts for interpreting continuity and change', *Built Environment*, 24: 4.

Gaubatz, P. (1999) 'China's urban transformation: patterns and processes of morphological change in Beijing, Shanghai and Guangzhou', *Urban Studies*, 39: 9.

Gilbert, A. and Varley, A. (1991) *Landlord and Tenant: Housing the Urban Poor in Mexico*, London: Routledge.

Griffin, E. and Ford, L. (1980) 'A model of Latin American City Structure', *Geographical Review*, 70: 397–422.

Hall, P. (1984) 'Geography', in Rodwin, L. and Hollister, R.M. (eds), *Cities of the Mind*, New York: Plenum.

Hall, P. (1999) 'Buenos Aires – city of extremes', *Town and Country Planning*, 68: 10.

Hamilton, E. (1993) 'Social areas under state socialism: the case of Moscow', in Soloman, S. (ed.), *Beyond Sovietology: essays on politics and history*, New York: M.E. Sharp, 192–225.

Harloe, M. (1996) 'Cities in transition', in Andrusz, G., Harloe, M. and Szelenyi, I. (eds), *Cities after Socialism*, Blackwell: Oxford.

Harris, C.D. and Ullman, E.L. (1951) 'The nature of cities', in Hatt, P.K. and Reiss, A.J. (eds), *Cities and Society*, New York: Free Press.

Harvey, D.W. (1973) *Social Justice and the City*, London: Edward Arnold.

Hedegus, J. and Tosics, I. (1983) 'Housing classes and housing policy: some changes in the Budapest housing market', *International Journal of Urban and Regional Research*, 7(4).

Herbert, D.T. (1970) 'Principal components analysis and urban social structure', in Carter, H. and Davies, W. (eds), *Urban Essays: Studies in the Geography of Wales*, London: Longman, 79–100.

Horvath, R.J. (1969) 'In search of a theory of urbanisation: notes on the colonial city', *East Lakes Geographer*, 5: 69–82.

Hoyt, H. (1939) *The Structure and Growth of Residential Neighbourhoods in American Cities*, Washington DC: Federal Housing Administration.

Jones, E. (1960) *Towns and Cities*, Oxford: Oxford University Press.

Kellett, J. (1999) 'Poland's scramble for modernisation', *Chartered Surveyor Monthly*, June.

Ladányi, J. (1989) 'Changing patterns of residential segregation in Budapest', *International Journal of Urban and Regional Research*, 13: 1, 55–72.

Lefebvre, H. (1970) *La Revolution Urbaine*, Paris: Gallimard.

Lefebvre, H. (1991) *The Production of Space*, Oxford: Blackwell.

Lichtenberger, E. (1972) 'Die Europaische Stadt – wesen modelle Probleme', *Raumforsch. Raumond*, 16: 3–25.

Logan, J. and Molotch, H. (1987) *Urban Fortunes: The Political Economy of Place*, Berkeley CA: University of California Press.

Macionis, J.J. and Parrillo, V.N. (1998) *Cities and Urban Life*, Upper Saddle River NJ: Prentice Hall.

Mann, P.H. (1963) *An Approach to Urban Sociology*, London: Routledge & Kegan Paul.

Mateju, P., Vecernik, J. and Jerabek, H. (1979) 'Social structure, spatial structure and problems of urban research: the example of Prague', *International Journal of Urban and Regional Research*, 3: 2, 181–200.

McGee, T.G. (1967) *The Southeast Asian City*, London: Bell.

McGee, T.G. (1971) *The Urbanization Process in the Third World: Explorations in Search of a Theory*, London: Bell.

McGee, T.G. and Greenberg, C. (1992) 'The emergence of extended metropolitan regions in ASEAN', *Economic Bulletin*, 1: 6, 5–12.

Morris, A.S. (1978) 'Urban growth patterns in Latin America with illustrations from Caracas', *Urban Studies*, 15: 299–312.

Murdie, R.A. (1969) 'Factoral analysis of metropolitan Toronto, 1951–1961', *Research Paper 116*, Chicago IL: Department of Geography, University of Chicago.

Musil, J. (1987) 'Housing policy and the sociospatial structure of cities in a socialist country: the example of Prague', *International Journal of Urban and Regional Research*, 11: 10, 27–37.

Park, R.E. and Burgess, E.W. (1925) *The City*, Chicago IL: University of Chicago Press.

Potter, R.B. (1993) 'Urbanization and development in the Caribbean and trends in global convergence–divergence', *Geographical Journal*, 159: 1–21.

Potter, R.B. and Lloyd-Evans, S. (1998) *The City in the Developing World*, Harlow: Longman.

Potter, R.B. and O'Flaherty, P. (1995) 'An analysis of housing conditions in Trinidad and Tobago', *Social and Economic Studies*, 44: 165–83.

Robinson, G.M., Loughran, R.J. and Tranter, P.J. (2000) *Australia and New Zealand: Economy, Society and Environment*, London: Edward Arnold.

Robson, B. (1969) *Urban Analysis*, London: Cambridge University Press.

Robson, B. (1975) *Urban Social Analysis*, Oxford: Oxford University Press.

Rostow, W.W. (1960) *The Stages of Economic Growth: A Non-Communist Manifesto*, London: Cambridge University Press.

Scott, A.J. (1980) *The Urban Land Nexus and the State*, London: Pion.

Scott, A.J. (1988) *Metropolis*, Berkeley CA: University of California Press.

Shevsky, E. and Bell, W. (1955) *Social Area Analysis*, Stanford CA: Stanford University Press.

Siderov, D.A. (1992) 'Variations in the perceived level of prestige of residential areas in the former USSR', *Urban Geography*, 13.

Sillance, J.A.A. (1985) 'The housing market of the Budapest urban region 1949–1983', *Urban Studies*, 22: 141–9.

Sjoberg, G. (1960) *The Preindustrial City: Past and Present*, New York: Free Press.

Smith, D. (1996) 'The socialist city', in Andrusz, G., Harloe, M. and Szelenyi, I. (eds), *Cities after Socialism*, Oxford: Blackwell.

Stone, P.A. (1970) 'Urban Development in Britain: Standards, Costs and Resources, 1964–2004', *Population Trends and Housing*, 1, Cambridge: National Institute for Economic and Social Research, Cambridge University Press.

Sweetser, F. (1965) 'Factor structure as ecological structure in Helsinki and Boston', *Acta Sociologica*, 26: 205–25.

Szelényi, I. (1983) *Urban Inequalities under State Socialism*, Oxford: Oxford University Press.

United Nations (1973) *Urban Land Policies and Land-Use Control Measures, Vol. 1, Africa*, New York: United Nations.

von Thünen, H. (1826) *Der Isolierte Staat*, English translation by Wartenberg, C.M. (1968) *Von Thünen's Isolated State*, Oxford: Pergamon.

Ward, P.M. (1990) *Mexico City. The Production and Reproduction of an Urban Environment*, London: Belhaven.

Ward, P.M. (1993) 'The Latin American inner city: difference of degree or kind?', *Environment and Planning A*, 25: 1131–60.

Weclawowicz, G. (1979) 'The structure of socio-economic space of Warsaw 1931 and 1970: a study in factoral ecology', in French, R.A. and Hamilton, F.E.I. (eds), *The Socialist City: Spatial Structure and Urban Policy*, Chichester: John Wiley, 387–423.

Weclawowicz, G. (1981) 'Towards a theory of intra-urban structures of Polish cities', *Geographia Polonica*, 44: 179–200.

Weclawowicz, G. (1991) *The Socio-spatial Differentiation in the Urban Region of Warsaw*, Warsaw: Institution of Geography and Spatial Organisation, PAN.

White, P. (1984) *The West European City: A Social Geography*, Harlow: Longman.

World Bank (1999) *Entering the 21st Century: World Development Report 1999/2000*, New York: World Bank and Oxford University Press.

4

Housing

INTRODUCTION

Housing is one of humankind's most essential material needs, yet in no country in the world is the need for housing in complete equilibrium with its supply. At this point it should be recognized that 'need' is not necessarily the same as 'demand': the former is an essential requirement, the latter is the quantity or an attribute of a product that can be afforded at a price. According to Burns and Grebler (1977), there are four principal forms of disequilibria:

(1) static disequilibrium which 'refers to the overall disparity between the number of dwellings in a geographical unit such as a country and the number of households' (Doling, 1997: 9);
(2) dynamic disequilibrium which quantifies the extent to which shortages or surpluses of supply in relation to need are changing over time;
(3) spatial disequilibrium which indicates shortages or surpluses within different parts of a country, region or urban area;
(4) qualitative disequilibrium 'which denotes that some households may be living in accommodation that falls short of a standard that would be acceptable to society at large' (Doling, 1997: 9), for example in relation to its size, condition and amenities such as a fresh water system, an internal WC and adequate heating arrangements.

In all developed countries of the world, governments attempt to reduce or eliminate disequilibria either by intervening in parts of the housing market for the first time or by remedying the weaknesses of existing policies or both. However, in newly-industrializing and developing countries, quantitative and qualitative deficiencies in housing supply are exacerbated by rapid population growth and rural–urban migration on an enormous scale – resulting in overcrowding, squalor and life-threatening insanitary conditions that stagger the imagination. Estimates by the World Bank indicate that for every unit of permanent housing built in low-income developing countries, nine new households are formed. Land development issues regarding land-use planning and control remain largely unaddressed. According to researchers, many cities have master plans in place which prescribe – in some detail – the directions for future growth, yet plans, by and large, languish in metropolitan offices and stand little chance of being implemented. The degree of government intervention in urban land development is, however, varied. In Bangkok and metropolitan Manila, there appear to have been virtually no effective measures taken to either influence or control urban land development, whereas in Singapore urban land development decision-making has been highly centralized and effective, not least in respect of housing provision.

Housing Paradigms

Among advanced capitalist countries, there are three over-arching housing paradigms (Doling, 1997):

(1) The West European paradigm

During the Industrial Revolution in the nineteenth century, and increasingly under free market conditions, rapid urbanization and housing development were associated with outbreaks of typhoid and cholera. The need for improved sanitary conditions prompted governments to impose regulations concerning environmental health and housing. In the late nineteenth century, housing also became an economic issue since a large proportion of the population could not afford the market price for adequate housing. Non-profit alternatives to the free market were therefore introduced, with governments facilitating the development of public housing.

After both the First and Second World Wars, governments imposed rent controls and security of tenure in the private rental sector, while undertaking large-scale programmes of subsidized social housing development. In recent years, however, governments have increasingly retreated from their role in providing affordable rented housing, leaving it once again to the free market to satisfy general housing needs, particularly within the owner-occupied sector. Across Western Europe, there are of course variations in this paradigm. Some countries, for example the Netherlands, still retain a large social rental sector, others such as Switzerland and Germany maintain a viable private rental sector, while Spain and Greece have witnessed significant developments in policy only in the latter part of the twentieth century.

Many of the more recent attributes of the West European paradigm are

---

BOX 4.1: THE STAGES OF HOUSING POLICY IN WESTERN EUROPE SINCE THE SECOND WORLD WAR

In Western Europe since the Second World War, there have been four stages in the development of housing policy:

- The first stage was characterized by a high degree of government involvement – mainly through the use of object subsidies – in order to eradicate large-scale housing shortages during the post-war period.
- The second stage, commencing in the late 1950s, witnessed a concentration on housing quality through the adoption of large-scale programmes of slum clearance and redevelopment and a subsequent shift of emphasis to housing rehabilitation and subject subsidies after the 1973 oil crisis heralded cuts in state expenditure.
- The third stage, beginning in the late 1970s, saw major cuts in public expenditure, new housebuilding in the social sector being superseded by renovation, the introduction of privatization schemes, the abolition or relaxation of rent control, and – increasingly – the replacement of object subsidies by subject subsidies, benefiting those already reasonably well housed at the expense of those inadequately accommodated or homeless.
- The fourth stage, emerging in the 1990s, necessitates the introduction of programmes to reduce shortages of affordable housing for the less-well-off and the 'socially excluded'.

Clearly, the different stages of policy development did not coincide in all countries, while some countries experienced more than one stage concurrently (see Boelhouwer, 1991).

---

shared with Australia and New Zealand – particularly the diminishing role of the public sector in the provision of affordable housing.

(2) The USA

Historically, both federal and state governments have generally failed to develop a public housing sector – in contrast to Europe (and to some extent Australasia), although there is currently a very small stock of welfare housing for households in greatest need, as determined by means-testing. Throughout the twentieth century, housing policy has been strongly oriented towards the private sector. Since 1913, house buyers have been able to claim relief from federal income tax and local property tax on mortgage interest, while tax policy provided incentives to private landlords to maintain the condition of private rented housing. During the 1980s, house-building in the public sector decreased substantially, and rents soared as the federal government became even less involved in meeting housing need.

(3) Japan

The housing needs of a rapidly growing urban population have been met largely by the private sector. A total of 34 million private dwellings were built between 1945 and 1985, 85 per cent of the total. At the same time rent controls encourage private landlords to sell off their properties to tenants – the sector decreasing from 75 per cent of the housing stock in 1941 to 24 per cent in 1990. Governments have seen the need, however, to build low rent housing for those on incomes below specified levels – 2.6 million dwellings being built by local authorities with Treasury subsidies (1945–85).

In addition, in *East Central Europe* and the *former Soviet Union*, housing is in a state of transition. Within this region, prior to the establishment of Communist governments in the first half of the twentieth century, urban housing was mainly privately rented whereas rural housing tended to be owned largely by peasant farmers. Under socialism, state and co-operative rented housing was developed on an extensive scale in urban areas, while the private rented sector was largely taken into state ownership. With political change in the 1990s, however, the public-rented sector has been increasingly privatized – with former tenants being encouraged to buy their homes with the assistance of substantial discounts (for example, in Hungary and Poland), or with past owners being able to claim their former properties ('restitution'), for example in the Czech Republic (see Balchin, 1996). The expansion of the owner-occupied and private-rented sectors in urban areas, however, is as yet constrained by the under-development of a housing finance market and housing subsidies geared to the private sector.

In most *newly-industrializing countries* and in all *developing countries*, there is an altogether separate paradigm. The majority of people are unable to purchase houses that have been professionally surveyed or built (Potter, 1992). At least half of all city dwellers in these countries live in sub-standard informal housing, for example 90 per cent in Addis Ababa, 70 per cent in Casablanca, 61 per cent in Caracas, and 60 per cent in Bogota and Mexico City in recent years (Potter and Lloyd-Evans, 1998), while vast numbers are so poor that they sleep in the streets, for example in Kolkata (Calcutta), Mumbai (Bombay) and Dehli. Altogether 1 million people in the world either live illegally in squatter settlements on land that they do not own and where planning permission has not been acquired, or legally in shanty towns (where they own or rent their homes). Self-build housing in both squatter settlements and shanty towns is normally in very poor condition and lacks water, taps and flush toilets – while residents need to collect water from standpipes.

Housing Policy Systems

In recent years, two major attempts have been made to identify housing policy systems that have been adopted in the advanced capitalist countries of the world:

(1) Kemeny (1981, 1992, 1995) drew a distinction between *home-owning* and *cost-rental* societies – the former consisting of, for example, Australia, Canada, New Zealand, the UK and the USA, and the latter comprising, in particular, Austria, Germany, the Netherlands, Sweden and Switzerland. He suggested that there had been a divergence between those countries with private forms of social structure and those that favoured collectivist structures.

(2) Barlow and Duncan (1994) – following closely an analysis of welfare-state regimes by Esping-Andersen (1990) – suggested that there were three principal housing policy systems: *liberal*, consisting of, for example, Ireland, the UK, the USA, Australia and New Zealand; *corporatist*, consisting of mainly Austria, France, (northern) Italy and Germany; and *social democratic*, comprising, for example, Denmark, the Netherlands, Norway and Sweden.

BOX 4.2: WELFARE REGIMES OF WESTERN EUROPE AND HOUSING TENURE

In the liberal welfare regimes of the United Kingdom and Ireland, owner-occupation had become the dominant tenure by the last quarter of the twentieth century. Owner-occupation has been vigorously promoted by government through the provision of subsidies – which increasingly were designed to stimulate demand rather than supply. At the same time, there was generally less and less support for social housing. Apart from reducing public funding and the increase in rents to market levels (necessitating housing allowances), the social rented sector has been disadvantaged by extensive programmes of privatization. There has thus been an increased degree of polarization between owner-occupation and social renting, and the problems of how to deal with the more deprived segments of the urban population remain largely unresolved. The private rented stock, meanwhile, has also decreased in scale – in part because of rent control but also through unfavourable tax treatment and low investment returns.

continued

The social rented housing stock is proportionately larger in the social democratic welfare regimes of the Netherlands and Sweden than in the EU on average, and – as a legacy of social democracy – the social rented sector is still substantial in the United Kingdom, while in France – with strong socio-democratic tendencies – social housing has expanded rapidly in recent years. The Netherlands was comparable only with Sweden in terms of the volume of subsidies it allocated to social housing, although Sweden alone attempted to secure tenure-neutrality in the distribution of subsidies and protect the private rented sector. In both countries, however, there was a recognition in the 1990s that a high level of public expenditure on housing might be incompatible with other macroeconomic objectives. In the Netherlands, the Heerma Commission thus proposed that housing corporation debt (the debt of 'not-for-profit' housing organizations) should be cancelled, and that object subsidies both to housing corporations and owner-occupiers should be abolished (Heerma, 1992). With the adoption of these proposals, subsidies were soon mainly confined to housing allowances and mortgage tax-relief (i.e. subject subsidies). In Sweden, curbs on housing expenditure and rising rents were implemented within the context of tenure neutrality, but this necessitated marked increases in housing allowances to ensure that the least-well-off were not disadvantaged. In contrast, in France where there was a very clear need to increase the rate of housebuilding to satisfy future demand, it was considered essential to provide more resources for the social rented sector so that it could undertake a major housebuilding programme and improve its existing stock (much of which is in poor condition); arrest the decline of the private rented sector by introducing more attractive fiscal arrangements comparable to those enjoyed by owner-occupiers; and ensure that assistance to lower-income owner-occupiers is at least maintained (McCrone and Stephens, 1995). Thus, whereas housing policy in the Netherlands and Sweden is broadly in line with the third stage of policy development in Western Europe, in France – by necessity – policy has progressed to the fourth stage of development.

In the corporatist welfare regimes of Germany, Austria and Switzerland, private rented tenure has been maintained as the dominant form of renting. Housing policy in Germany has worked largely with rather than against the grain of the market – in contrast with housing policy in most other countries in Western Europe (McCrone and Stephens, 1995). Notwithstanding a substantial programme of housebuilding in the social rented sector, particularly in the early-1970s (Emms, 1990), the dominance of the private rented sector contrasts with all other EU countries despite pressures to strengthen rent controls in the 1990s. The owner-occupied sector still remains small compared to the EU average, in large part because of the availability of good private rented accommodation and the recognition that other forms of investment are more attractive in terms of performance and as a hedge against inflation (McCrone and Stephens, 1995). However, since a united Germany has experienced a substantial inflow of migrants from East Central Europe in recent years, and the western länder have witnessed a very considerable in-migration from their eastern counterparts, the Federal government has had little alternative but to acknowledge that there is a need to address the problem of a major shortage of affordable housing – the principal characteristic of the fourth stage of policy development in Europe. In Austria, with similar shortages of affordable housing, the rented sector accounted for around 45 per cent of total housing stock in the 1990s and is very broadly comparable in size to the owner-occupied sector. The rented sector is subdivided into private and social sub-sectors in approximately equal parts. Reflecting the needs of different groups in society (including immigrants), the pattern of tenure is typically corporatist, although subsidies tend to be directed at social housing and owner-occupation. In Switzerland, however, in the absence of major housing shortages, recent policy has concentrated on constraining the market for private rented housing by means of rent control while promoting the increase in the supply of, and demand for, owner-occupied housing. This has resulted in the need to reduce the cost of housebuilding in this sector and to facilitate demand by permitting the release of equity in occupational pension schemes. There remains the need to increase competitive pressures in the housebuilding and related industries and to liberalize the Swiss system of land-use control to ensure an adequate supply of sites for development (OECD, 1994). If, however, the private sector is to be maintained as a dominant tenure, rent controls may also need to be liberalized.

In the liberal system, 'welfare' support is minimal – with governments being willing to leave the provision of housing to the market. While owner-occupation is the principal tenure and buyers are assisted by demand-side subsidies, public-sector housing is provided only to supply a 'safety net' for those most in need. In the corporatist system, the social sector housing is substantially assisted by the state – as an 'enabler' rather than a provider, but the state is willing to act as a provider where the capacity of the family to address the problems of housing need is inadequate. In the social democratic system, the state intervenes to promote equality. Although there is a considerable degree of state intervention in many areas of housing (for example, in Sweden, by means of ensuring land supply, facilitating the provision of social housing, and providing state housing loans to all sectors), market forces are employed to keep down prices and promote diversity in forms of housing tenure and types of housing.

Barlow and Duncan add to Esping-Andersen's classification of welfare regimes by including a *rudimentary* category in their analysis. In such countries and regions as Greece, Portugal, Spain and southern Italy, where traditions of self-help and family support are evident, there is no strong right to welfare, although as social and cultural changes occur, and economic development continues, these areas could adopt any one of the aforementioned welfare regimes.

Since the late 1970s, both because of the need to constrain public expenditure and because of political change in many advanced capitalist countries, production subsidies have been brought under scrutiny or abolished, while more emphasis has been placed on subsidising demand through rent allowances and tax relief. In many countries, housing policies therefore moved from 'supply to enablement'. This has tended to strengthen liberal welfare regimes while weakening corporate and liberal democratic systems.

In the transition economies of East Central Europe and the former Soviet Union, there has been a recent decline in state housing since a high proportion of the stock has been transferred to private ownership, and it is evident that governments in this region have tended to embrace the liberal system of housing enablement, rather than either the corporatist or social democratic systems of provision.

With economic growth, housing policy systems in the newly-industrializing and developing countries might gradually emerge or become consolidated during the early twenty-first century. However, in the 1980s–1990s, there was a clear retreat from state provision in these countries – partly because of economic recession and severe constraints on public expenditure, and partly because of political ideology.

HOUSING SUPPLY IN THE DEVELOPED WORLD

The Housing Provision Process

Except for the provision of informal housing in newly-industrializing and developing countries, there are four main stages in the housing provision process (figure 4.1). First, the development stage in which an individual, private firm or public agency initiates the conditions that can support the construction stage (i.e. by ensuring that there is an adequate supply of land, capital, labour and organizational skill to facilitate construction). At the next stage, the builder brings together the factors of production in the construction process in order that housing is produced, and at the subsequent stage completed housing is allocated to public and private landlords and co-operatives, or to prospective owner-occupiers. The final stage of the process involves repair and maintenance to the dwelling over its lifetime (see Doling, 1997).

There is a need at all four stages for an adequate supply of finance and, to a varying extent, for an availability of subsidies.

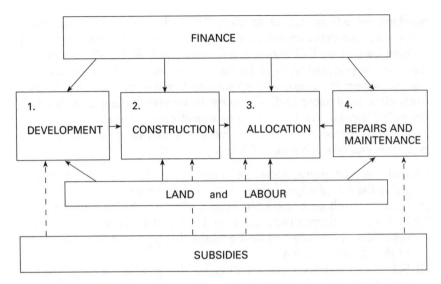

Figure 4.1 *The housing provision process (adapted from Doling, 1997)*

The Provision of Housing and Profitability

The provision of housing differs substantially from the provision of other goods (Short *et al.*, 1986). In the developed world, these differences are as follows. First, since land is used in the construction of housing, the relationship between developers, landowners and planning authorities is important. Second, there is a lengthy period from initiation to completion and sale. Builders are often dependent on loan finance throughout the construction process. Third, compared with household incomes, dwellings are expensive and therefore long-term loans are normally required, and fourth, the provision of infrastructure is required at the consumption phase and this will add to costs (see Doling, 1997).

Because of these attributes of development and construction, developers are faced with the problems of securing adequate profitability. However, they may be able to widen the gap between costs and prices through realizing land development profits (i.e. buying land when prices are low, and selling it developed when prices are high), and using more efficient processes of construction (to lower unit-costs).

The Housing Development Industry

Development is undertaken by a range of entrepreneurs across the private and public sectors, and it is often difficult to distinguish between development activity and construction. Although profit is the normal motivating force for development in most advanced capitalist countries, development for non-profit objectives is very common. Folin (1985) suggests that there are six principal types of developers: private individuals; private companies; non-profit companies (for example, housing associations, societies, trusts etc.); semi-public bodies – similar to non-profit companies but state controlled; local authorities; and government departments.

The construction process in any country is influenced by state intervention. This can take a number of forms:

(1) States can attempt to reduce production costs, for example, by encouraging the use of improved methods of construction.
(2) States can influence user-costs by providing supply-side subsidies.
(3) States can influence the location and siting of development – and can determine the amount of land available for housebuilding – by means of the planning system.
(4) States can influence consumption by the provision of demand-side subsidies.

The degree to which states intervene in construction is determined by the type of welfare regime which exists in the country under consideration. Barlow and Duncan (1994), in referring to Western Europe, explain that construction in *liberal regimes* is disproportionately undertaken by large private-sector companies in pursuit of speculative profits from land development gain; in *corporatist regimes*, private construction and non-profit construction are more in balance, as are the proportions of construction undertaken by small and large firms, but land supply tends to be speculative; and in *social democratic regimes*, large private firms compete over profits derived solely from the building process since land supply and its price are controlled by the state. In *rudimentary regimes*, land speculation does take place and profits can be made from development gain, but construction is undertaken by a balance of small private and non-profit organizations.

Although, in theory, the profit-seeking sector in each country could be given a free hand to supply housing, in practice the state intervenes to a greater or lesser extent in development and construction in every country – relying upon such methods as taxation in liberal regimes; taxation and subsidies in corporatist regimes; and taxation, subsidies and public land ownership in social democratic regimes.

Housing Rehabilitation

Since the 1960s, and to a varying extent, housing rehabilitation has supplemented new housebuilding as a means of satisfying housing needs.

In the advanced capitalist countries, it was often recognized that the most cost-effective way to improve the minimum standard of housing with the available resources was to concentrate upon rehabilitation, and it was also understood that rehabilitation rather than redevelopment (i.e. slum clearance followed by new building) would be the most likely way of maximizing capital values.

Needleman (1965) suggested that the comparative economics of redevelopment and rehabilitation depends on the rate of interest, the future life of the rehabilitated dwelling, and the difference between the running costs of the new and rehabilitated dwellings. Normally, rehabilitation would be worthwhile if the present cost of clearance and rebuilding exceeds the sum of the cost of rehabilitation, the present value of the cost of rebuilding and the present value of the difference in annual funding costs. In algebraic terms, rehabilitation would be more economic than redevelopment if:

$$b > m + b(1+i)^{-\lambda} + \frac{r}{i}\left[1-(1+i)^{-\lambda}\right]$$

where b = cost of demolition and redevelopment;
$\quad\quad m$ = cost of rehabilitation;
$\quad\quad i$ = the rate of interest;
$\quad\quad \lambda$ = useful life of the rehabilitated property in years;
$\quad\quad r$ = difference in annual repair costs.

Needleman extended his hypothesis by taking into account two additional variables: the comparative quality and comparative density of redeveloped and rehabilitated housing (normally redeveloped housing would be of higher quality and lower density than rehabilitated property). As Merrett (1979) explains, rehabilitation would be worthwhile if:

$$b > m + b(1+i)^{-\lambda} + \frac{r+p+a}{i}\left[1-(1+i)^{-\lambda}\right]$$

where b = cost of demolition and redevelopment;
$\quad\quad m$ = cost of rehabilitation;
$\quad\quad i$ = the rate of interest;
$\quad\quad \lambda$ = useful life of the rehabilitated property in years;
$\quad\quad r$ = difference in annual repair costs;
$\quad\quad p$ = excess of rent on (higher quality) redeveloped housing;
$\quad\quad a$ = annual cost of 'decanting' surplus households from areas of (lower density) redeveloped property.

Clearly if the cost of demolition and redevelopment falls below the sum of the other variables, or if the sum of the other variables rose above the cost of demolition and redevelopment, it would be more cost-effective to demolish old housing and redevelop sites for new housing.

Although more detailed versions of Needleman's formulae have been employed by both public and private-sector decision-makers, the Needleman approach has often been found by planners and developers to be too complex and time-consuming in practice. Lean (1971), possibly appreciating that less sophisticated models were necessary to determine the most appropriate process of renewal, devised the capital value method to compare redevelopment and rehabilitation. This involves a comparison of the costs of redevelopment and the differences in capital values before and after redevelopment with the costs of rehabilitation and the difference in capital values before and after rehabilitation. If, for example, £180,000 spent on redevelopment increased unit values by £210,000 and £60,000 spent on rehabilitation raised values by £90,000, then clearly £180,000 spent on rehabilitation would renew three times as many houses as the number supplied by redevelopment (and values would rise by £270,000 rather than £210,000).

In the 1960s and 1970s, empirical evidence in the USA and the UK seemed to suggest that rehabilitation was less costly than redevelopment (see Grigsby, 1963; Bagby, 1973; Listokin, 1973; National Community Development Project, 1975), though it was by no means conclusive since, for example, it was difficult to compare the clearance and redevelopment of a whole area with the rehabilitation of a relatively small number of (often scattered) properties. Nevertheless, governments in many countries saw rehabilitation as a major housing priority.

HOUSING SUPPLY IN THE DEVELOPING WORLD

Housing Aid

In newly-industrializing and developing countries, private financial institutions – because of low per capita incomes and job insecurity – are unwilling and unable to provide long-term credit to facilitate the development of an urban owner-occupied sector, while governments usually lack the resources to provide large-scale public-sector housing schemes to satisfy the needs of low-income households. Furthermore, in many countries in the developing world, a large proportion of the urban poor would find such accommodation beyond their means.

However, resources are sometimes available to assist those in need to help themselves. Since the 1980s, international aid agencies, such as the United States Agency for International Aid (USAID) and the World Bank, have provided the governments of over 50 newly-industrializing and developing countries with loans to facilitate the development of *aided self-help housing* (ASH) – the World Bank alone participating in 116 projects from

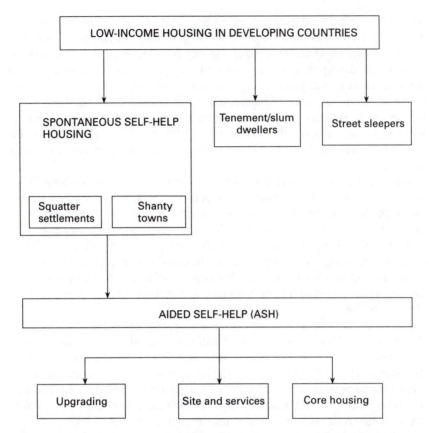

Figure 4.2 *Low-income and aided self-help housing in developing countries (adapted from Potter, 1992)*

1972 to 1990, involving an average of US$ 26 million per project (Pugh, 1995).

Stemming from spontaneous self-help housing, there are three types of ASH schemes: first, the upgrading of existing squatter settlements and shanty towns through the provision of basic services; second, the improvement of the physical layout of the area and establishment of security of tenure by means of either ownership rights or long-term leases; and third, the provision of sites and services for the development of core housing schemes – in which the first stages in the construction of a house (for example, a unit containing a bathroom and a toilet) are eligible for aid, but the subsequent stages are the responsibility of the household (figure 4.2).

Apart from ASH, there are housing programmes in many parts of the developing world – all aimed at providing new housing as well as upgrading existing urban settlements. These programmes provide some solution to the housing problems that are facing city governments, although housing need is escalating at a faster rate than supply. There has also been a need to address the problem of environmental degradation – in relation to housing, for example in Manila there has been a clear need to review the sewerage services available to the majority of urban households – who are obliged to rely on the septic tank. Effluents from these tanks are allowed to run into street drains and the river, thereby contributing to water pollution.

One of the most successful public housing programmes in South East Asia is in the city-state of Singapore. The programme – involving the selling-off of public housing to its tenants – is state-driven and state-sponsored, closely linked to the government's financial planning and savings system, and has relieved the government of a large proportion of its housing development and estate management debts. In parallel, the government – in its housing programme – has been able to address the health and environment problems associated with poor and inadequate urban housing, and has taken effective action.

Another successful housing programme is the Slum Improvement Programme in Thailand – which was implemented by the National Housing Authority. Some 26,000 dwellings were included in the programme during the period 1978–92 (Yeung, 1991). There was a similar Zone Improvement Programme in Metro Manila, which aimed at providing land tenure and services to over 1.8 million people in 300 areas over 12 years. Action was also taken to remove sewage from the streets (Pugh, 1989).

In Jakarta, the Kampung Improvement Programme – introduced in 1969 – was expanded under the Third Plan for the period 1980 to 1984, to cover some 200 cities and an urban population of 3.5 million people. The programme was to provide water supply and facilitate drainage in areas of poor housing (Soegijoko, 1985). In Malaysia, the Kuala Lumpur urban authority adopted a similar approach to improving housing conditions in squatter settlements. Public services were improved – from the provision of standpipes to the introduction of comprehensive health care (Lim, 1988).

Housing Provision and Urban Development

Undoubtedly, housing development has a marked effect upon urban economic growth – although the extent to which this is the case varies from country to country. Whereas in the developed world, urban population growth occurred in parallel with economic development, enabling housing needs to be very broadly satisfied, in most newly-industrializing and developing countries uncontrolled population in-migration – and a low level of economic development – have resulted in the proliferation of squatter settlements in the larger cities, and an 'anti-urban' bias among development planners.

However, in examining housing systems in both advanced capitalist and advanced socialist countries, Pugh (1989) observed that an overriding problem was the difficulty in balancing rents (or instalments in home purchase) with subsidies and the capacity to pay among low- and moderate-income households. Pugh recognized that in order to maintain an adequate provision of housing, it was therefore necessary to design forms of subsidy which would be robust enough to withstand fluctuations in the rate of economic growth and flexible enough to ensure that housing remained affordable throughout.

Pugh (1989) – drawing on the work of sociologists, and economists such as Myrdal (1968) – recognized that housing provision was a cumulative process in development since construction added to the GDP and employment, reinforced simultaneous improvement in health and education in the community, and assisted in modernizing attitudes to work and even to life if it could be associated with an enhanced work and home environment. Housing thus contributed to change and had various economic and social benefits.

In arguing that housing, health, labour, productivity and modernization were all closely related to one another, Pugh cited proponents such as Abrams (1964) and Frankenhof (1966) who held the view that housing investment should be well co-ordinated with the wider economy. It was also suggested that there was a positive relationship between accessible modern housing (with all its attributes) and the availability and standards of schools, medical care and shopping centres in an urban area (Wilkinson, 1973; Richardson, 1971).

The relationship between housing and developmental issues appears to have been the focus of much research. While it has been recognized for generations that housing and health care are closely linked, there is a need to consider the nature of this relationship and the impact on the environment in cities. Clearly if policy-makers focus attention solely on the cost of housing provision, there is a danger that the social benefits gained from provision – such as better health levels and environmental standards – might be overlooked.

HOUSING DEMAND IN THE DEVELOPED WORLD

Housing Finance

In both the private and public sectors, the development and purchase of housing require large sums of money derived from many different sources (a requirement much easier to fulfil in most advanced capitalist countries than in countries in a state of political and economic transition or in the newly-industrializing or less developed world). Developers and house buyers find it necessary to fund their activities from their own accumulated resources, the issue of share capital, loans provided by financial institutions, and loans provided by local and central government. It is also fairly common for developers to rely on more than one source of funding for a single project.

Since house purchase represents a very large capital outlay for the consumer, which can rarely be financed out of income, borrowing is necessary and the availability of long-term credit is of critical importance in making demand for owner-occupation effective. Although some house buyers may be able to obtain a long-term loan from a friend or a relative, an effective housing finance system is dependent upon institutions' ability to broadly match people's willingness to save with people's desire to borrow. This, according to Boleat (1985), is achieved by means of: *a contractual system* whereby potential buyers make regular savings over an agreed period of time at a low rate of interest, and then receive a loan equal to the difference between the full purchase price of a house and the value of their savings; *a deposit-taking system* whereby institutions such as commercial banks, savings banks and specialist housing banks attract savings from one group of people and lend them to another group of people who wish to buy; and *a mortgage bank system* in which financial institutions sell bonds on the capital market (at the prevailing rate of interest) to insurance companies and pension funds, and use the money to lend to house buyers (see also Doling, 1997).

As financial institutions have become deregulated throughout most advanced capitalist countries, and with the creation of the Single European Market, there has been a considerable convergence in national systems of finance. Nevertheless there still remains a blurred distinction 'between an Anglo-Saxon model based on savings banks and a European model based on mortgage banks' (Doling, 1997: 13).

Housing Subsidies

In advanced capitalist countries there are two principal forms of housing subsidy: supply-side subsidies – sometimes referred to as 'bricks and mortar' or object subsidies, and demand-side subsidies – sometimes referred to as subject subsidies. Governments subsidize the supply of housing if they provide land free or at a reduced cost, or provide finance at a sub-market rate of interest. Grants can also be made available to offset the cost of renovation or new housebuilding, and tax allowances may be provided to help builders purchase construction materials. Assuming that these subsidies will not be retained by the developer, they will reduce the cost-of-use incurred by the ultimate consumer.

In subsidizing housing demand, governments can provide social security payments as a means of supporting income and thereby facilitating expenditure in general, but since payments might not be directly linked to the cost of accommodation they cannot strictly be regarded as a housing subsidy. Housing allowances, however, are more specifically related to the cost of housing and are therefore a housing subsidy. Payments might also be in the form of loans at sub-market rates of interest or income tax relief on loan interest. In contrast to supply-side subsidies which reduce the user cost, demand subsidies increase the ability to pay.

Figure 4.3(a) shows that when a supply-side subsidy is introduced, supply is increased from SS to S_1S_1 and the price or rent of the housing is reduced from p or r to p_1 or r_1. Figure 4.3(b) shows that when a demand-side subsidy in introduced, demand is increased from DD to D_1D_1 and the price or rent of the housing is increased from p or r to p_1 or r_1.

The subsidization of the owner-occupied sector

The supply of owner-occupied housing is subsidised when governments provide: either free land or land at below market price for private development; low or tax-deductable interest loans; non-repayment grants; infrastructure at zero or sub-market cost.

The form in which demand subsidies are provided depends upon whether owner-occupied housing is deemed a consumer good or an investment good. If housing is regarded as a consumer good, the subsidy equals the extent to which the interest on a housing loan is tax-deductable, but if housing is deemed an investment good, the subsidy is the failure to tax the imputed rent income of the dwelling (an income broadly equivalent to an investment return from a business or shares, which is normally taxed). If, as in some countries, housing is seen as both a consumer good and an investment good, interest on loans is tax deductable, while imputed rent income is exempt from tax.

More fully, the relationship between tax deductions, taxation and subsidization is as follows:

(1) Where tax deductions against housing loans are permitted, and where taxes are imposed on imputed rent income, housing is treated as an investment good (as in the Netherlands, Sweden, Denmark, Norway and Spain).
(2) Where neither tax deductions against loans are permitted, nor taxes are imposed on imputed rent income, housing is treated as a consumer good (as in Australia, Canada and New Zealand).

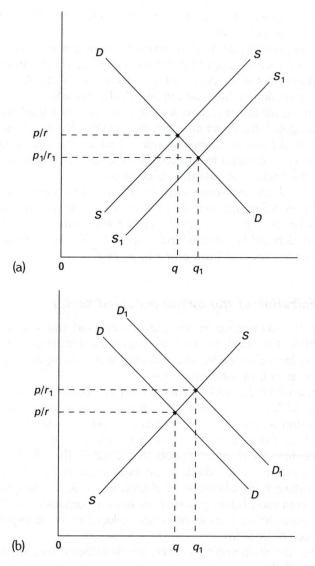

Figure 4.3 *The effects of subsidies on housing supply and demand*

(3) Where tax deductions against housing loans are permitted, and where taxes are not imposed on imputed rent income, housing is treated both as a consumer and investment good (as in the UK, the USA, France, Germany and Japan). This is the most favourable situation for house buyers since they are subsidised twice-over.

There are of course other housing subsidies. In some countries where housing might be deemed a consumer good, housing allowances are paid to low-income buyers, while in many other countries where housing might be deemed an investment good, a household's principal residence is exempt from capital gains tax.

In recent years, there has been a general shift of emphasis from investment subsidies to consumption subsidies – a shift consistent with a similar shift of emphasis from supply-side (or 'bricks and mortar') subsidies to demand subsidies. This has been intended to slow down the rate of new construction and to facilitate the consumption of the housing stock which already exists.

The subsidization of the social housing sector

The supply of social housing has been subsidized in a large number of countries, particularly from the 1950s to the 1970s. A variety of means were employed to increase the rate of new housebuilding: non-repayable grants, low-interest loans, tax deductions and cheap land, and to a lesser extent these are still available. To ensure that landlords pass on supply-side subsidies to tenants, governments normally place some restriction on the level of rents that are charged in the social sector. Demand subsidies, in the form of housing allowances, have increased in recent years as a result of cuts in supply subsidies and consequential rent increases.

The subsidization of the private rented sector

The supply of private rented housing can be maintained or increased if landlords are exempt from capital gains tax and are permitted to claim tax allowances on the cost of mortgage interest payments, repairs and maintenance, management expenses and insurance. However, only if such tax breaks are higher than those allowed on other business incomes can they be regarded as a supply-side subsidy.

In many countries, governments have imposed regulations preventing landlords from charging market rents, particularly during times of housing shortage. As a result of this form of state intervention, it is the landlord who – in effect – provides the tenant with subsidy, an amount representing the difference between the market rent and the controlled rent.

Demand subsidies are often considered necessary in the absence of rent control. As with social housing, these take the form of housing allowances.

Recent developments in subsidization in the advanced capitalist world

In many countries since the 1970s there has been a shift from supply-side to demand subsidies because: housing shortages have been reduced; governments have assumed that a reduction in supply-side subsidies would help to reduce the overall level of public expenditure and hence help curb inflation, and it was assumed – by many governments – that an emphasis on demand subsidies (rather than on supply-side assistance) would be more compatible with the free market ideal, particularly if they were confined mainly or solely to low-income households.

HOUSING TENURE IN THE DEVELOPED WORLD

Owner-occupation

In most advanced capitalist countries, owner-occupation, as a proportion of the total housing stock, has increased significantly in recent years, and has become statistically the dominant tenure (table 4.1). The same trend is also evident in some of the former centrally-planned economies of the Eastern bloc, while in many newly-industrializing and developing countries increased owner-occupation has been an outcome of rising incomes, government support, and the lower cost of provision resulting from illegal land subdivision and illegal land occupation (HABITAT, 1996).

BOX 4.3: HOUSING POLICY IN AUSTRALASIA

As in many other areas of the developed world, home ownership – with its significant financial benefits – is the preferred or 'natural' tenure in Australia and New Zealand, while – among tenants – those housed in the public sector have (until recently) been less disadvantaged, have paid lower rents and have had greater security than those accommodated by private landlords (Robinson *et al.*, 2000). But during the 1990s, the adoption of neo-liberal policies in both countries has weakened the role of public housing. By means of targeting, municipal housing authorities have attempted to transform public housing, from a sector with responsibilities to workers and their families to a provider of 'welfare housing' for those in serious housing need (Forster, 1995; Murphy, 1997).

In the early decades of the twentieth century, although Australian governments concentrated on expanding the owner-occupied sector, state housing authorities were established in the late-1930s and early-1940s to promote the development of public sector housing, and in 1945 the first Commonwealth State Housing Agreement (CSHA) committed the Federal administration to 'provide financial support for public housing, and to raise the quality of housing, particularly for low-income households' (Robinson *et al.*, 2000: 204). However, as in much of Western Europe, budgetary considerations in the latter quarter of the twentieth century encouraged the Federal government to reduce its support for public housing, perhaps most notably by changes in the 1995 CSHA. Simultaneously – as in Western Europe – there was a shift of emphasis away from 'bricks and mortar' support to income-based subsidies paid directly to tenants, and more reliance on the private sector (Hayward, 1996; Yates, 1997). Within the public sector, rents escalated to market levels to encourage wealthier tenants to satisfy their housing needs in the owner-occupied market, and security of tenure was reduced, yet – paradoxically – waiting lists for public housing are more likely to rise than fall since the level of public spending on affordable rented housing fell to a very low level in the late-1990s, creating a substantial shortage of affordable housing (Robinson *et al.*, 2000).

Public housing in New Zealand also shifted to a market-based system in the 1990s, where tenants were forced to pay dramatic increases in rents (up to private-sector levels) and where the only form of housing assistance was an accommodation supplement (available to all low-income households irrespective of tenure). However, the eligibility-ceiling for support was reduced, resulting in most low-income households having to pay a substantially increased proportion of their income on accommodation costs – thereby exacerbating housing poverty and spatial polarization (Robinson *et al.*, 2000). Since market rents are usually lower in outer suburban locations than in more central areas, low-income households tend to be concentrated around the periphery of New Zealand cities or to have migrated to even cheaper rural areas (Waldegrave and Stuart, 1997), while – in central areas – the better public-sector housing is being sold off, and – with the proceeds – private housing is being bought in low-rent areas and transferred to the public sector (Morrison, 1995). As a result of these processes, the urban periphery is thus 'increasingly being occupied by the most disdavantaged groups, including single parents, unemployed and Maori and Pacific Islanders' (Robinson *et al.*, 2000: 203).

There are, however, substantial variations in the size of the tenure across countries. Whereas Bulgaria, Ireland and Hungary had levels of owner-occupation of 80 per cent or above in 1989–90, less than two-fifths of the stock in West Germany, Switzerland, the Czech Republic and Russia was owner-occupied around the same time.

It is of note that the size of the owner-occupied sector is not necessarily related to the level of a country's prosperity, as measured by gross domestic product (GNP) per capita (table 4.1). In Switzerland and West

Table 4.1 *The growth in owner-occupation, 1945–50, 1970 and 1990, and gross national product per capita 1990*

	1945–50	1970	1990	GNP per capita 1990 (US$)
Bulgaria	–	–	87	2,270
Ireland	–	71	81	10,970
Hungary	–	–	80	2,870
Norway	–	–	78	26,340
Greece	–	–	77	6,020
Spain	–	64	76	11,180
New Zealand	–	–	72 (1991)	12,900
Australia	53	67	70 (1985)	16,960
UK	29	49	68	16,220
Finland	–	59	67	19,750
Italy	40	50	67	17,170
USA	57	65	64	23,340
Canada	66	60	64	20,600
Belgium	39	55	63	17,790
Japan	–	59	61	26,090
Norway	–	53	59	23,130
Portugal	–	–	59	5,360
Austria	36	41	55	19,290
France	–	45	54	19,750
Denmark	–	49	51	22,610
Netherlands	28	35	44	18,110
Sweden	38	35	42	24,360
Poland	–	–	41	1,700
West Germany	–	36	38	22,350[1]
Switzerland	–	28	30	32,760
Former Czechoslovakia	–	–	26 (1988)	3,470[2]
Russia	–	–	26	4,100

Notes: (1) GNP per capita for Germany in 1990.
(2) GNP for Czech Republic 1990.

Source: Oxley (1993); Hägred (1994); HABITAT (1996).

Germany, for example, where GNPs per capita are high, there is a fairly low level of owner-occupation, whereas in Bulgaria and Hungary (where per capita GNPs are low) the level of owner-occupation is very high. It is, however, not surprising that two of the former centrally-planned economies (Russia and the Czechoslovak Republic) had the lowest proportion of housing that was owner-occupied, while two other members of the bloc

(Bulgaria and Hungary) had very high proportions of owner-occupation (HABITAT, 1996).

It can be argued that, in general, the greater the extent to which countries are willing to accept constraints on the allocation of resources to welfare provision in such forms as unemployment support, sickness benefit, pensions and family allowances, the more they are willing to facilitate the expansion of owner-occupation, with the corollary that the stronger the general welfare orientation of the state, the greater the emphasis on social housing (Schmidt, 1989). However, it is important not to confuse correlation with causality. It is just as likely that high levels of owner-occupation lead to downward pressures on taxation and welfare provision as reduced levels of taxation and welfare spending lead to an increase in owner-occupation (Kemeny, 1992).

BOX 4.4: HOUSING POLICY IN THE UNITED STATES

As in much of Europe, the cessation of housebuilding in the United States during the Second World War led to a considerable housing shortage in the post-war period and a backlog of repairs and maintenance. The government responded by enabling both the Federal Housing Administration and the Veterans Administration (established by the Serviceman's Readjustment Act of 1944) to broaden the provision of mortgage guarantees, and under the Housing Act of 1949 local government was empowered to compulsorily purchase property, and to sell it to private developers to undertake slum clearance and redevelopment for residential purposes (Macionis and Parrillo, 1998). However, since developers were interested only in profitable schemes, newly supplied housing was invariably beyond the means of low-income households, while many of the displaced poor had little choice but to crowd into other low-grade housing – hastening the process of slum creation. Housing shortages were further exacerbated by redevelopment producing fewer homes than the number destroyed by slum clearance (Macionis and Parrillo, 1998). Meanwhile, the Federal government did little to increase the supply of low-income public housing, the stock increasing from as little as 1.2 million units in 1970 to only 1.3 million in 1980, the public stock remaining at this level thereafter (US Bureau of the Census, 1996; Macionis and Parrillo, 1998).

As part of the 'Great Society' initiative, the Federal government aimed to ensure 'a decent home for every American'. The Housing Act of 1968 thus set out to: promote the construction or rehabilitation of 26 million housing units, of which 6 million would be intended for low- or low–middle income families; and – as an alternative to providing public housing – it extended homeownership to the less-well-off through loan guarantees and subject

continued

subsidies of up to 80 per cent of the cost of house purchase (Macionis and Parrillo, 1998). An undesirable outcome was that the extra demand for homeownership inflated house prices and benefited speculators, while many households bought houses they could not afford to maintain and became victims of foreclosure. As an alternative to assisting low-income owner-occupation or the provision of public housing, developers – as from 1974 – became eligible for subsidies to build or rehabilitate private rental housing, and rent subsidies were introduced to reduce the cost of renting in the private sector.

However, it was clear that 'federally supervised urban housing programs fell well short of their lofty goals' (Macionis and Parrillo, 1998: 272). It proved difficult to: simultaneously promote housing renewal and satisfy the demands of the urban poor; extend low-income homeownership without serious knock-on effects; and provide sufficient funds to adequately support the rental assistance programme.

An entirely different explanation for varying degrees of owner-occupation is based on the notion that high-inflation environments provide an incentive for households to invest in real property. Clearly, where purchase is undertaken with the aid of a loan, inflation reduces the burden of repayments and makes buying more attractive than renting (*Economist*, 1992–93).

Recent policies

In the 1980s–1990s, many advanced industrial countries experienced, at best, slow economic growth, high levels of unemployment, difficulties in raising money to meet public expenditure and a political shift to right-of-centre governments. This led to a decreased level of state intervention in the market, and, in respect to housing, was reflected in: an attempt by governments to sell-off varying proportions of the public housing stock to the owner-occupied sector (in, for example, the UK, Ireland, Belgium and the USA); and a reduction in tax subsidies to owner-occupiers (such as in the UK, Sweden, Finland, Denmark and the USA).

Less government fiscal support for owner-occupation might have exacerbated slumps in housing markets in the 1980s–1990s. High levels of repayment arrears have been evident in the USA market since the early 1980s, and arrears increased rapidly in the UK, West Germany, Sweden, Finland, Denmark and Norway in the 1990s. In many industrial economies, problems of repayment have been made worse by high levels of unemployment, greater flexibility in working practices, more part-time working and a general reduction in job security.

Social Housing

Although there are many forms of social housing, the sector is distinguishable from other tenures in the following ways:

(1) The supply of social housing is strongly influenced by the level of social demand as indicated by the willingness and ability of government to provide affordable, good-quality rented housing.
(2) Dwellings are allocated according to need rather than the ability to pay.
(3) Rather than aiming to maximize profit, social landlords provide housing on a limited-profit or not-for-profit basis.

The provision of social housing

Before the First World War in the early years of industrialization, social housing was provided almost exclusively by the voluntary sector, but after 1918 there was increased intervention by the state to provide an alternative to the private rented sector, which was arguably unable to satisfy housing needs at a reasonable rent. Whereas in Sweden and the Netherlands, governments promoted both the voluntary and local authority sub-sectors, in the UK the state placed an emphasis on local-authority housing.

After the Second World War, large housing shortages and the need for economic reconstruction led to a further expansion of social housing in Western Europe, yet while UK governments continued to promote local-authority housing, elsewhere the growth of other non-profit organizations was increasingly encouraged. Within the Eastern bloc, state housing was seen as a means of avoiding exploitive landlordism and building an egalitarian society, while in Latin America the introduction of a social sector was a response to rapid population growth. In Africa and Asia social housing was favoured by many independent governments – although often the sector was rooted in the colonial past (HABITAT, 1996).

In the 1960s–early 1970s, most governments in the newly-industrializing and developing world either launched large social housing programmes or greatly enlarged existing programmes – often aided by financial institutions from abroad (for example, the US government-funded Inter-American Development Bank) or by indigenous banks (for example, the National Housing Bank of Brazil). In both Western Europe and the Eastern bloc, the sector was consolidated by major housing programmes.

Harloe (1995) suggests that – worldwide – there are two models of social housing provision: the 'residual' model and the 'mass model'. Under the residual model, small-scale housebuilding programmes are targeted at the poor and other disadvantaged households, including those dispossessed as a result of slum-clearance activity. Although residual social housing was first developed in Europe before the First World War, it is still regarded as the 'normal' form of social housing in many countries of the world, and is the only form of social housing in the USA. Subsidies tend to be directed at households rather than at the housing, i.e. are demand-side rather than supply-side.

The 'mass model', however, targets large-scale building programmes at a comparatively wide cross-section of income groups. In many countries, with the notable exception of the USA, mass social housing development occurred in the aftermaths of the First and Second World Wars – coming to an end in the mid-1970s. In contrast to residual housing, subsidies were directed at the housing rather than at the household, i.e. were supply-side rather than demand-side.

Table 4.2 shows that, in total, the social housing stock was extensively developed in Russia, the former Czechoslovakia, the Netherlands, Poland, the UK and Sweden; but in the USA, Italy, Spain and Greece it is of negligible size or non-existent. However, as is evident, the social rented stock has been in decline in a number of countries in recent years. During the 1980s–1990s, this was attributable to privatization and the promotion of owner-occupation, and to a decrease in housebuilding in the social sector.

BOX 4.5: HOUSING POLICY IN THE FORMER EASTERN BLOC

Because of economic and political pressures, market economies emerged in the countries of East Central Europe and the former Soviet Union in the 1980s and early-1990s, and gradually brought about the demise of the system of centrally planned command economies which had been set up under socialism in earlier decades. Under pressure from the International Monetary Fund and Western governments, 'shock therapy' began to bring about the liberalization, stabilization and privatization of the economies of the region (Gowan, 1995).

However, within the context of rapid political change, emerging housing policies in, for example, Hungary, the Czech Republic and Poland needed to take account of the legacy of previous policies before introducing new solutions to often old problems. Within East Central Europe there had been three common features of housing provision during the communist period of government (Turner, 1992). First, there was almost a complete absence of the private rented sector – private investment property being nationalized after the Second World War. Second, because of wartime destruction and the lack of building during the war, there was a substantial shortage of dwellings in the 1950s and 1960s which necessitated the large-scale construction of state or state-sponsored housing in high-rise estates. Third, although there were large home-owning sectors throughout most of East Central Europe (mainly because there were comparatively large rural populations), when communist governments took over in the 1940s it was not considered appropriate to nationalize this sector of housing – for both political and managerial reasons. However, after thirty years of little support from the state, the sector began to expand in the 1970s partly as a result of the unpopularity of high-rise estates and partly because of an increasingly overt demand for owner-occupation among the more privileged groups in society (Turner, 1992).

During the 1990s, with the substantial reductions in state-funded housing investment, with rents rising to market levels, with housing management being transferred from central government to private agencies, with an increased reliance on private finance to expand owner-occupation, and with massive programmes of privatization depleting the social housing stock, it was very evident that a liberal welfare regime was being created.

However, although housing privatization was undoubtedly 'the single most distinguishing feature of the transformation of the housing sector from the Soviet, centrally planned model to a more market-oriented system' (Struyk, 1996: 192), its effects were very variable and economically contentious. While programmes of housing privatization were introduced extensively throughout the former Soviet bloc, involving a large number of sales at discounted prices and enabling individual units in multi-household buildings to be privatized, quite a high proportion of state housing in some countries was not claimed by its tenants because of concerns relating to the costs of maintenance, repairs and rehabilitation, and fears about future property taxes. In the Russian Federation, with 100 per cent discounts, a total of 11 million units were sold between 1988 and 1994, but this represented only 36 per cent of the state housing stock at the start of privatization and in Hungary, with 50–85 per cent discounts, only 39 per cent of its stock of 306,000 dwellings had been sold from the mid-1980s to 1994. In Estonia, however, 85–90 per cent of its stock of state housing was sold between 1993 and 1995 with the aid of 90 per cent vouchers, and in Bulgaria over 90 per cent was sold between 1958 and 1994, with 90 per cent discounts (Struyk, 1996).

Critics of privatization often point out that without deep discounts, revenue from sales could be substantial and support the development of replacement social housing for the less privileged, and either fund the renewal of the remaining social stock, keep rent increases in check, or provide housing allowances if rents increase to cover costs of repairs and building work. A second controversy arises since it is often claimed that the best units in the best locations are bought by their occupants – the former apparatchiks and nomenklatura (favoured state employees and party members), and that there is also inequality between households on the waiting list for state housing, and those already in possession (Struyk, 1996).

Table 4.2 The decline in social housing, 1960–90

	Percentage of total housing stock	
	1960	1990
Russia	–	67
Former Czechoslovakia	–	45 (1988)
Netherlands	50	44
Poland	–	31
UK	44	25
Sweden	61	22
Hungary	–	20
Austria	40	20
Denmark	32	18
France	–	17
Finland	45	15
West Germany	33	15
Ireland	34	11
Bulgaria	–	9
Japan	–	8
New Zealand	–	8 (1991)
Australia	–	7
Belgium	–	7
New Zealand	–	6
Canada	–	5
Norway	30	4
Portugal	–	4
Switzerland	13	4
USA	–	3
Italy	–	3
Spain	–	1
Greece	–	0

Source: Doling (1994); Hedman (1994).

In Western Europe and the former Eastern bloc, governments have sold off a substantial proportion of their housing stocks to realize capital receipts and reduce the costs of management, repairs and maintenance, while simultaneously increasing the private rented sector and/or owner-occupation (depending upon whether sales have been to private landlords or to social housing tenants). A simultaneous reduction in the rate of housebuilding in this sector and a decrease in the size of the stock are also intended to reduce the level of public expenditure and public sector borrowing, and to further 'roll back the frontiers of the state'. This process has been particularly dramatic in East Central Europe, where 'the privatisation of the state housing stock may be the single most distinguishing feature of the transition of these countries' (HABITAT, 1996: 219). In many newly-industrializing and developing countries, recession, debt crises, cuts in public expenditure and structural adjustments have resulted in the discontinuation of large-scale social housing programmes, and the selling-off of much of the stock (HABITAT, 1996).

Private Renting

During the process of industrial development and associated urbanization, private rented housing emerged as the largest tenure. As a market commodity, both its rent and its availability were determined by demand and supply. On the demand-side, wages were low and irregular, but on the supply-side rented housing provided an attractive medium for small investors. However, since the nineteenth century, governments have intervened in the private rental market by regulating standards, imposing rent control and ensuring security of tenure.

At first, the maintenance or improvement in environmental health was the principal concern of governments, but this was later accompanied by regulations concerning construction materials, minimum space standards, maximum densities and infrastructural requirements. Rent control was introduced in a number of countries during the First World War since it was anticipated that housing shortages would inflate market rents. After much decontrol in the 1920s–1930s, rent control was reintroduced extensively during the Second World War and has tended to remain to a greater or lesser extent in most advanced industrial countries, although market rents have often been reintroduced for newly rented property. The same reason that led governments to introduce rent control (i.e. shortages and potentially rising rents) also led to the introduction of legal measures to provide security of tenure.

Since rent control, in effect, brings about a transfer of income from the landlord to the tenant, it is argued that sub-market rents have been the principal cause for the decline of the sector throughout most of the twentieth century. Figure 4.4(a) shows that with additional household formation, demand increases from D to D_1, but whereas under short-term free market conditions demand would equate with a fixed supply of dwellings (S) at r, under rent control (where the rent is fixed at r_1), demand is now in excess of supply by an amount equal to $q_1 - q$. Figure 4.4(b)

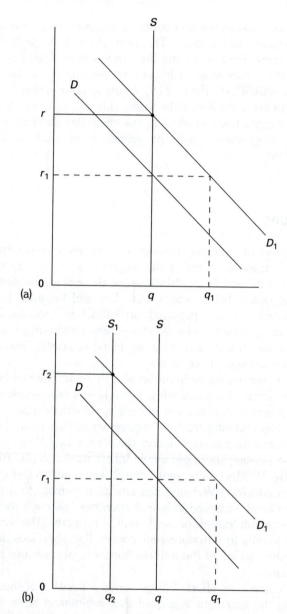

Figure 4.4 *The effects of rent control on the supply and demand of private rented housing*

shows that, in the long-term and, because of unsatisfactory returns, land-lords will withdraw their dwellings from the private rental market, decreasing supply from S to S_1. The shortage of private rented housing thus increases to $q_1 - q_2$.

Dwellings which are withdrawn from the private rented market will either be sold off for owner-occupation, occupied exclusively by the landlord or left empty. Households unable to obtain private rented accommodation will either become owner-occupiers or seek housing in the social rented sector.

In spite of the theoretical explanation for the decrease in the supply of private rented housing, Harloe (1985) has found that there has been a general tendency for the sector to decline in most countries regardless of whether or not rent control is in force. Doling (1997: 198) suggests that the decline 'can be attributed as much to increases in overall prosperity and national policies resulting in inducements to households to become owners or tenants of social landlords, as it can to policies that have restricted rents'. Nevertheless, although the sector has shrunk to a very small size in Finland, Ireland and the UK (as well as in Poland and Bulgaria for different reasons), it remains comparatively large in Switzerland, Germany and the USA (table 4.3).

To a varying extent, private rented housing co-exists with the social rented sector. Because of the maturation of social rented housing (an inflation-induced decline in the outstanding debt on the existing stock of dwellings compared to the outstanding debt on newly built, acquired or renovated dwellings), Kemeny (1995) suggests that there are two rental systems – 'unitary' and 'dualist'. Under the unitary system, private and social renting are integrated into a single market – as in Germany, Austria, Switzerland, the Netherlands, Sweden and Denmark. The state encourages the social sector to compete directly with the private rented sector to dampen rents and ensure a supply of good-quality housing on secure terms. Clearly the private rented sector will need to be a recipient of equivalent subsidies to those allocated to the social sector and be subject to the same form of rent regulation. Under the 'dualist' system, however, the state controls and residualizes the social rented sector to protect private renting from competition, as for example in the UK, Ireland, the USA, Canada, Australia and New Zealand.

It is of note that whereas the combined rented sector in the unitary system accounts for an average of 51 per cent of total housing in the relevant countries, in the dualist system the combined sector amounts to an average of only 30 per cent of the total – indicating the comparative strength of the former system (table 4.3). It is also notable that whereas the unitary system occurs in 'corporatist' and 'social democratic' welfare regimes, the dualist system occurs in 'liberal' regimes – as defined by Esping-Andersen (1990).

Table 4.3 Rented housing, 1990

	Private rental sector (percentage of total stock)	Combined rented sectors (percentage of total stock)	Type of system
Switzerland	66	70	Unitary
Germany	43	58	Unitary
USA	33	38	Dualist
Portugal	32	36	
Belgium	31	38	
Canada	31	36	Dualist
Denmark	26	44	Unitary
Austria	25	45	Unitary
Japan	24	32	
France	23	40	
Greece	23	23	
Italy	23	26	
New Zealand	23	29	Dualist
Australia	19	26	Dualist
Sweden	19	41	Unitary
Norway	18	22	
Spain	17	18	
Finland	9	24	
Ireland	8	19	Dualist
UK	7	32	Dualist
Poland	4	59	
Bulgaria	3	4	

Source: Doling (1994); Hedman (1994); Kemeny (1995).

HOUSING DEMAND IN NEWLY-INDUSTRIALIZING AND DEVELOPING COUNTRIES

The Informal Sector

In the developing world in the second half of the twentieth century, the surge of population from rural areas to cities invariably led to the pre-emption of urban land by the landless and homeless. The formation of squatter settlements and shanty towns not only prevented the creation of owner-occupied and rented tenures, but impeded the orderly development and expansion of the built environment, deterred investment in greatly needed urban enterprises, and was often associated with delays in establishing political stability (Abrams, 1977). In many countries – by the 1980s – over half of all city dwellers lived in informal housing, for example 90 per cent in Addis Ababa, 70 per cent in Casablanca, 61 per cent in Caracas, and 60 per cent in Bogota and Mexico City (Potter and Lloyd-Evans, 1998), while in Manila – by 1987 – the Presidential Commission on Urban Poor (PCUP) had estimated that 38 per cent of the city's total population lived in slum and squatter settlements. In Singapore – as early as the 1950s – some 130,000 people lived in squalor in *attap kampongs* (squatter settlements) – posing a threat to the general health of the whole city, despite the efforts of the municipality to provide standpipes and adequate drainage, and minimize the risk of disease (Fraser, 1952). Since the supply of land was severely limited in Singapore, the price of sites unoccupied by squatters was often three-times as expensive as land that contained squatter settlements (Abrams, 1977). Therefore, when fire displaced 16,000 persons from a squatter area, the government – in order to facilitate subsequential development – introduced legislation which enabled it to acquire land at only one-third of its cleared site value, with compensation paid to squatters for their loss of settlement rights. However, in Vietnam – with the emergence of a new market economy – land prices in the larger cities escalated dramatically (Nguyen, 1994), and the urban poor had little alternative but to establish larger and larger settlements on illegally occupied land, for example along canals and rivers, lacking piped water supply, drainage or sewerage.

Clearly, squatter settlements provide only rudimentary accommodation for their inhabitants: they are built to low standards and are poorly constructed; they offer very cramped conditions and accommodate populations at very high densities with serious risks to health; many are located on high-risk sites and are particularly vulnerable to floods, landslides and hazards associated with transport and industry; they are susceptible to fire and often infested by disease-transmitted rodents and insects; and they are often an embarrassment to municipal authorities and high-income elites (Clark, 1996).

However, although planners and politicians in developing and newly-industrializing countries initially viewed squatter settlements and shanty towns as a problem and often advocated demolition and clearance, it was soon recognized that dispossessed households would either become homeless or be rehoused in government housing schemes where they would find rents unaffordable. Since the 1960s and 1970s, therefore, squatter settlements have often been regarded as 'slums of hope' rather than 'slums of despair'. In, for example, the *colonias proletarias* of Mexico City, the *favelas* of Rio de Janeiro, the *barriados* of Lima, the *bustees* of Kolkata (Calcutta) or the *bidonvilles* of Dakar there is evidence that the condition of housing improves progressively over time as the real income of successive generations gradually increases and as modern standards of amenity are considered more important than location and ownership (Potter, 1992; Clark, 1996). Because of these favourable attributes, some governments and international aid agencies actively help to improve the condition of housing in squatter settlements through the process of *aided self-help* (ASH) – by which legal titles to land, low interest rates, building materials, technical assistance and essential communal services encourage people to build for themselves and improve their residential environment (HABITAT, 1987; Clark, 1996).

Despite their obvious disadvantages, squatter settlements are often an important first-destination for in-migrants and help them to assimilate with an urban way of life; they provide accommodation for those who would otherwise be homeless; they involve the reuse of a wide range of materials; and they provide a source of cheap and accessible labour for urban industries (HABITAT, 1987; Clark, 1996). Because of these recently acknowledged attributes, official attitudes to squatter settlements have progressed from opposition to illegal occupation and building, to an official recognition of the merits of informal housings, to a formal incorporation of squatter settlements into the wider city (Clark, 1996).

Housing and Urbanization in South East Asia

There is broad agreement that the rapid pace of urbanization in South East Asia – as in the rest of the developing world – has put tremendous pressure on the ability of cities and city governments to cope with, and manage, the large increase in urban population. In Thailand, for example, the National Housing Authority could build only 6,000–7,000 units annually in the 1980s against an estimated demand for 300,000 urban housing units. Equivalent shortfalls occurred in the Philippines where the level of urbanization rose from 30 per cent in 1960 to 49 per cent in 1990 (De Recio, 1994).

However, whereas population growth in South East Asia was the issue in the 1970s, population distribution and mobility became the issues of the 1990s (Findley, 1993). Rural–urban migration no longer dominates city development since international migration is proliferating. Governments therefore appear to be reviewing the measures that are taken in the past to discourage rural–urban migration. If estimates are correct, by the year 2000, 50 per cent of the world's population were living in cities, although in South East Asia the proportion was slightly less than half because of the slow-down in the rate of urbanization during the 1990s. Nevertheless there is the expectation that much of the growth in the urban population will be concentrated in the larger metropolises or 'mega-cities'.

While national governments have been reviewing development plans concerning urbanization programmes and how these programmes fit into national development strategies, they also need to consider global trends in order to manage the pace of rapid urbanization more effectively. Few cities are likely to empathize with the 'anti-urban' thinking of the 1970s which characterized development planning in Asian cities at that time (Ginsburg, 1994).

Development planners were more likely to agree with the traditional view that – through the concentration and specialization of labour – the city promotes the accumulation and distribution of capital (see Agency for International Development, 1968). Cities are identified with the growth of financial institutions and the development of entrepreneurial and managerial expertise. In addition to their crucial roles in facilitating national economic development, cities in newly developing countries – as in the developed world – perform important social functions both for their inhabitants and for the nation. Civilization flourishes in the cities. The city is a theatre of change and the centre of modernization of every aspect of life. The process of city development encourages innovation in all fields. Since the origins of urban life, cities have been the repository and generator of major expressions of human creativity.

In short, national governments – in developing countries – have recognized that they need to design ways of managing the pace of urbanization, particularly at a time when rapid growth seems inevitable. While it is evident that the housing stock and infrastructure of the major cities of the developing world are under severe stress because of the influx of migrants, it is equally clear that much of the investment from abroad, industrialization and economic growth are concentrated in these cities. Both national and city governments therefore have to face the challenge of introducing innovative solutions and strategies to cope with the effects of economic growth and the need for housing and a healthy urban environment.

BOX 4.6: HOUSING IN HONG KONG

Hong Kong has perhaps the most comprehensive housing stock of any newly-industrializing region. In the mid-1990s, very broadly the stock was divided equally between rented and owner-occupied housing, and equally between the public and private sectors (table 4.4), but it should not be assumed that the rented sector was entirely publicly owned or that the owner-occupied sector comprised only private housing since both sectors contained sub-sectors of both private and public housing.

continued

Table 4.4 Housing tenure in Hong Kong, 1995

	Rented		Owner-occupied	
	Publicly owned	*Privately owned*	*Publicly owned*	*Privately owned*
Percentage of total stock	37	11	11	41
Number	689,000	201,200	208,000	749,000

Source: Census and Statistics Department, *Annual Digest of Statistics*, Hong Kong.

As a consequence of large-scale immigration in the aftermath of the Second World War, and as the outcome of a fire in an area of squatter housing at Skek Kip Mei in 1953 – in which 58,000 people became homeless, a Department of Resettlement was established in 1954 to clear and resettle squatters in high-rise blocks (the scarcity of land preventing lower-density development). But although 100,000 resettlement units were built for squatters, the standard of the housing was poor – necessitating redevelopment and rehousing twenty or thirty years later. A Housing Authority was also established in 1954 with the responsibility of using public funds to provide housing for low-income and middle-income households living in poor accommodation. With means-tested access, rents were set at an affordable level but were sufficient only to cover administrative costs and the repayment of capital costs. Although the housing was superior in quality to that in the resettlement estates, it was nevertheless cramped and suffered from poor amenities. Densities were the highest in the world.

A reconstituted Housing Authority (served by a new Housing Department) was formed in 1973 to plan, build and manage all public housing estates in Hong Kong. At 7 per cent of household incomes in 1983, and 9 per cent in 1996, rents were set at affordable levels since management and maintenance costs were paid by the government, and rents were credited to government funds. Although there were no cash subsidies as such, Crown land was acquired cheaply and loans from the government's Development Loan Fund were at low rates of interest. By 1995, the Hong Kong government was the largest landlord in the world, owning 689,000 dwellings or 37 per cent of all units in the Crown Colony, although proportionately publicly rented housing has been in decline since the 1970s (when it accounted for around 41 per cent of the stock) owing to the growth in owner-occupation.

The private rented sector, comprising only 201,200 dwellings in 1995, or 11 per cent of the total stock, has been in decline in recent years – the sector accounting for as much as 39 per cent of the stock in 1972. Its supply has long been constrained by rent control – introduced in 1921 and revised in 1947 by the Landlord and Tenant Ordinance. Although a Committee of

Review in 1981 recommended that rent control should be phased-out when circumstances permit, decontrol was postponed at least until the late 1990s. While not a preferred tenure, private rented housing fulfils a useful role in Hong Kong since it provides accommodation for new immigrants waiting for housing in the public rented sector, educated young workers waiting to buy, and expatriates and professionals from abroad on short- or medium-term stays.

Since 1976, the public owner-occupied sector has been developed by the Hong Kong Housing Authority to provide an opportunity for low-income households to become owner-occupiers, since it is not normal for public-sector tenants to buy their own rented flats. Initially through the medium of its home ownership scheme (HOS), the Housing Authority enables tenants who wish to become owner-occupiers to buy new low-cost housing developed by the Housing Authority itself. Over 50 banks and deposit-taking companies provide special mortgages at subsidised rates of interest over 15 years, although in the event of discontinued payment the property can be sold back to the Housing Authority. A further public-sector initiative was the introduction of private-sector partnership schemes (PSPS) in 1978, but although broadly similar to the HOS, private developers are invited to tender for sites and fully participate in the scheme. Since the Hong Kong government acts as a mortgage guarantor both in the case of the HOS and PSPS, there is little risk involved in development at the lower end of the market.

URBAN HOUSING IN CHINA

Introduction

Housing in China has proved problematic for many years. Since economic reforms started in the 1980s, urbanization has become a token of modernization and, consequently, housing provision in urban areas has been a major social and economic issue. Virtually all urban housing is the state's property and is public-owned. It is allocated to the urban population either by the work-units or housing bureaux in each city. The fundamental problems of China's urban housing provision have been scarcity of supply, a low standard and under-maintenance. These problems have also affected the country's economy in that the land has not been valued correctly because of the neglect of site values in the allocation of land among competing urban uses, and fixed housing arrangements in each city have reduced labour mobility in the economy. The government has borne the costs of housing construction and maintenance and made fewer financial resources available for economic development. However, it is housing scarcity which remains the worst and the most urgent problem to be solved.

China has made many efforts to build houses. It is estimated that housing production in Chinese cities has reached 200 million m² per year since the early 1980s (Department of the Environment, 1995). However, the housing problem is still serious and it is believed that the major housing problem is in urban areas. Although there is a lack of detailed statistics on rural housing, there are apparently fewer major complaints from people living in rural areas about their housing. Families in rural areas usually provide their own housing, including the finance. The economic reforms have meant that many rural families have more disposable capital and building costs in rural areas are lower.

For many years, scarcity of housing has been a major problem for urban people. In 1980 the floor space per capita was only 3.1 m². By the end of 1994, this figure was around 4 m². It was still the case that almost 25 per cent of families had too few rooms. The usual form of urban dwelling is a flat. By Western standards, much housing in Chinese cities lacks basic facilities. In the early 1990s only 60 per cent of flats had a kitchen. Further, the sizes of flats and their rooms (often a small number of multi-functional rooms) are very small. It is anticipated that 150 cities and 2,000 organic towns will be set up by the year 2000 and 20 per cent of the market towns will be modernized (Department of the Environment, 1994). This is in addition to about 30 million m² of old and unsafe housing in big cities such as Shanghai, Beijing and Tianjin, which requires major maintenance work (Department of the Environment, 1995). The demand is unlikely to be met by the prevailing Chinese resources and, thus, foreign investment was planned to be introduced in the late 1990s.

In urban areas, the major responsibility for providing housing rests with work-units and housing bureaux. The work-units include the state-owned enterprises (SOEs) and other public-sector organizations that are responsible for providing housing for their employees. The housing bureaux are responsible for providing and allocating housing – mainly for those households who do not have work-units to ask for housing or whose work-units do not have housing stock to provide. These work-units and housing bureaux provide more than 80 per cent of urban housing in each local city council (Barlow, 1988).

Traditionally, housing in China has been viewed as a non-productive cost of production that must be borne to produce a 'truly' value-added output, which mainly consists of manufactured goods. Effective housing reform involves not only finding a way to pass the responsibility for housing from public to private ownership but, more importantly, finding a way constructively to alter the traditional socialist treatment of housing. The major objective of housing reforms is to move gradually from a complete socialist-planned housing system towards a market-based housing system. The socialist-planned housing system is a rent mode which is marked by subsidized housing, low rent, and works-units and housing bureaux being responsible for providing housing which is, essentially, free of charge. Housing has been treated as an in-kind element of benefit for employees. The market for housing has not existed and houses have not had a commercial value. A market-based housing system is, basically, a buy mode, which is marked by private ownership and market rent of housing. Housing can be traded freely according to its market value. The reforms involve introducing market mechanisms in what has been an administratively managed urban housing system. This step is particularly dramatic in a socialist country where ownership of property has been considered anathema for decades.

Housing reforms in the 1980s–early 1990s were concerned with firstly establishing a rental market and secondly introducing a process of housing privatization. However, both reforms were proved to be unsatisfactory, mainly because of the prevailing low rents, the lack of a housing finance system and the infancy of property law and regulations.

In 1993, the central government decided to modify the housing reform plan and put the housing system reform programme into effect in 1994 (called phase 2 reforms). The central issue in the design of the reforms has been how to privatize the housing stock, now in the hands of work-units and housing bureaux. The first major step is to privatize and transfer the houses provided by the SOEs to their workforce. The SOE workforce, with a total number around 100 million, accounts for 70 per cent of the workforce in urban China and, along with their dependants, represents most of the urban population (Economist Intelligence Unit, 1995). The housing burden of the SOEs has been one of the fundamental reasons for their inefficiency and their incurred production losses. The World Bank has provided assistance in promoting this move from the socialist-planned housing system to a market-based housing system.

At present, the phase 2 reforms have still focused on setting up the rental market, which was not realized in the phase I reforms. It is hoped that, gradually, rents will be increased to market prices. Therefore, the wages of the workforce need to be increased as a prerequisite for paying the market rents. The first major measure is the setting up of Housing Management Companies (HMCs) in the experimental cities in order to free the SOEs of their obligation to provide housing for their employees. Only then will the

SOEs have the money to increase the wages of their employees so that they can afford the market prices of housing.

Initial Housing Reforms Prior to 1994 – Phase 1

The initial phase 1 housing reforms (1984–93) focused on setting up a rental market for housing plus selling public-owned dwellings by providing large government subsidies. Furthermore, the reforms were seen as a way to ease inflationary problems. The hope was that saving for housing ownership would dampen consumption and divert demand away from consumer durables. The reforms were also seen as a means of raising funds to build new housing.

Reform programme

The reforms were announced in 1984. Since then, housing has been regarded as a commodity and, therefore, should have a market value. The 14 cities were selected to carry out housing reform in line with the central government policy. The local work-units and housing bureaux increased the rent from 1 per cent of monthly income for a standard family to 3 per cent of their monthly income. The housing bureaux also set housing prices to encourage people to buy their own houses. However, since the housing market had not yet been established, market rents, the usual focus of analysis in considering the demand and supply of rental housing, had not been observed in China and the housing prices set by the housing bureaux might not reflect even the construction cost. There were neither carefully planned steps nor detailed regulations to implement the reforms. In order to encourage people to buy their houses and, therefore, to ease the burdens on SOEs for supplying housing and, at the same time, meet demand for new housing, both of which were growing rapidly in the 1980s, a large number of municipal governments adopted programmes in the mid-1980s to promote individual home ownership by providing subsidies to those individuals who were willing to buy houses – of up to 70 per cent of the purchase price (Wang, 1989).

It soon became apparent that the 1984 programmes were unable to generate significant housing sales. This is because, although rents were still very low and subsidized pricing had been provided, it appeared that most people still could not afford to buy houses. There was also no financial support system, such as mortgages, available. In view of the worsening problems, in 1988 the central government decided to stop promotion of the subsidy on housing sales and to encourage an experiment towards establishing a market-based system of housing provision. Privatization of housing was announced, with the aim of introducing market mechanisms in what had so far been an administratively managed urban housing system. For a specific model, two small cities, Yantai and Bengbu, were selected in 1987 to experiment with substantial but restricted rent and wage increases. In addition, these two cities were encouraged to provide a financial support system to assist with house purchase. In 1992 the central government extended this initiative to make it applicable to all cities and set more gradual targets for rent and wage increases to substitute cash for in-kind payments.

The central government also encouraged the creation of housing funds, partly to support individual home ownership and, more generally, to augment the resources for housing construction. To manage the housing funds, local specialized institutions were established in Yantai and Bengbu as part of the 1988 reform experiment. Beginning in 1991, the newly created housing funds had been supplemented with provident funds, contributed equally by individuals and their employers and kept in employees' accounts. Essentially, this amounted to creating a trust for earmarked funds with rates for both deposits and loans lower than other prevailing rates. However, in most cities, both the housing funds and the provident funds were handled by the Real Estate Credit Departments belonging to local branches of the People's Construction Bank of China or the Industrial and Commercial Bank of China. Most of the funds were deposited by SOEs as part of their welfare reserves.

Experience of phase 1 reforms

Progress of the phase 1 reforms has proved disappointing without any substantial solutions towards the housing problems. The government strategy of rent increase and promotion of home ownership has fallen short of the modest target. Even the combination of low prices for housing and low interest rates has failed to generate significant housing sales to the general public, mainly because of low levels of income and savings and the disincentives to buy, created by low rents. The indication is that price adjustment, if not accompanied by other reforms, could end up making very little contribution to solving China's fundamental housing problems.

First, the rent increase did not result in the emergence of a truly effective rental market. This is because the increases in rents were insufficient. The housing stock in the experimental cities appeared to remain as seriously mis-allocated as ever, with doubled-up families facing waits of up to half a lifetime for apartments. The scarcity of housing has not been improved substantially.

Second, offering housing sales with large subsidies, although officially banned by the central government in 1988, was still common in many municipalities. This has occurred in the hope of reducing the burdens of the SOEs. However, this hope is somewhat unrealistic. Although SOEs rid themselves of the necessity to provide in-kind rent subsidies in the future, they will probably not recover even the construction cost of apartments sold in view of the reduced bids of buyers. Thus the demand for housing will increase further.

Third, some aspects of the efforts to provide financial instruments for housing loan repayments remained rudimentary. For instance, low-interest-rate loans could be provided to encourage purchase of housing, however these could lead to inflationary pressures if the interest subsidies are not financed by explicit taxes on others. In contrast, the short repayment schedules, normally required with these types of loans, implied unrealistically high household saving rates which discouraged ownership. Furthermore, the housing funds had not achieved their objective of promoting individual home ownership. Because the demand for individual loans was insignificant, most of the housing funds were used as short-term loans to SOEs for housing construction or purchase approved by the local government.

Fourth, much of the housing stock was seriously under-maintained which made old housing of low quality. Most housing still remains the responsibility of work-units and housing bureaux. Meanwhile, few signs existed of preparing prospective owners to assume responsibility for maintenance.

A critical shortcoming of the central government strategy up to 1993 was its inability to bring an end to the work-units and the housing bureaux, especially the direct obligations of the SOEs for employee housing. Given that current rents will have to be increased 10 to 30 times in real terms to reach commercially viable levels, it is doubtful whether such a target can realistically be achieved, in even gradual steps, and remain acceptable to consumers. As is apparent from the lack of progress so far, consumers are likely to resist even gradual rent increases if these are not fully compensated by income growth. This is because raising the proportion of income spent on rent, as envisaged in the central government strategy, represents real income reduction.

The affordability analysis that underlies the approaches in the phase 1 reforms is fundamentally flawed as it ignores expenditure incurred by SOEs for providing housing to their employees and, thus, is unavailable for compensating wage adjustments when rents are restructured. In effect, the strategy was geared less towards establishing a market-based housing system than to mobilizing more resources for housing. There is a growing discussion among the central government and SOE managers aimed at identifying an effective and feasible alternative strategy. There is a need for bolder reforms. However, the phase 1 reforms could not be expanded for lack of support and follow-up actions by the central government.

The picture that emerges is of a permanently distorted rental market in which the benefits of market allocation are lacking with losses on housing sales extending into the indefinite future and with chronic tension between the rationed markets (state-allocated housing) and unrationed markets (commercial housing).

The Housing System Reforms Since 1994 – Phase 2

Since 1994, drawing lessons from the failure of the phase 1 reforms, the central government has announced essential housing system reforms. These are associated with the whole country's economic reform progress.

Having succeeded in facilitating fast economic growth through the introduction of new management arrangements and market mechanisms, the central government has begun fundamental reforms in fiscal, financial and macroeconomic management, and enterprise and labour systems in order to move towards the next stage of economic development. Central to these reforms is SOE reform, as the problems of SOEs lie at the root of many difficulties in other areas. To improve SOE management, the current strategy to develop a 'socialist market economy', officially adopted in 1992, calls for more aggressive measures to increase accountability and efficiency of the SOE sector as a whole.

As noted earlier, the SOE workforce and their dependants represent most of the urban population (Economist Intelligence Unit, 1995). It has become apparent that housing is one of the major burdens of most SOEs and many of them have claimed that having to provide housing has led to loss of profits or loss of production. Consequently, it is widely recognized that establishing sustainable housing and social security systems is a crucial prerequisite to broad economic restructuring.

New reform programme

The new housing reform programme announced in 1994 by the central government includes:

- raising rents by a big margin: from 0.13 to 1.00 yuan/m^2, about 10 per cent of monthly income of a standard family (which was 3 per cent of monthly income during phase 1 reforms) and, in 2000, to 3.25 yuan/m^2, 17 per cent of monthly income, at current prices; the employees of the SOEs would be fully compensated by wage adjustments and gain more freedom of choice;

- selling public-owned dwellings in the cities to their tenants at three kinds of prices: standard price for high-income families, low-profit price for middle-income families and preferential price for low-income families; the preferential price is 350 yuan/m^2 which means that, for a standard family, a flat of average floor space will cost three times its annual income;
- offering mortgage loans over 25 years;
- allowing buyers to sell their houses in the real estate market after 5 years of ownership.

This programme aims to commercialize housing by establishing a market-based housing system. The central issue is how to implement the programme, and what measures and in which order they should be taken. The central government set up a Leading Housing Reform Office under the State Council to take charge of the implementation of the housing reforms. With consultancy aid from the World Bank, a new approach is being developed to pioneer this new programme which will focus on converting the in-kind housing benefits into cash wages and setting rents and sale prices at levels which cover at least the full cost.

A market-based housing system

There is general agreement on the desirability of a market-based housing system in which end-users select housing solutions from a wide range of options offered by independent commercial providers. In such a system, SOEs would not have any direct responsibility for their employees' housing other than providing full, competitive wages. Figure 4.5 illustrates a market-based housing system and figure 4.6 shows the current housing system in typical Chinese cities. Supply and financing of housing – functions now performed mainly by employers in China – would instead be carried out by independent housing consumers, suppliers and financial intermediaries in the market system. In order for commercial suppliers to sell or rent housing without subsidies, sales prices would have to recover all costs over the economic life of the housing. Consumers would deal directly with suppliers to choose housing according to their needs and affordability.

As costs of housing assets are large compared to the homeowner's income or to rental receipts, long-term credit is an essential ingredient of

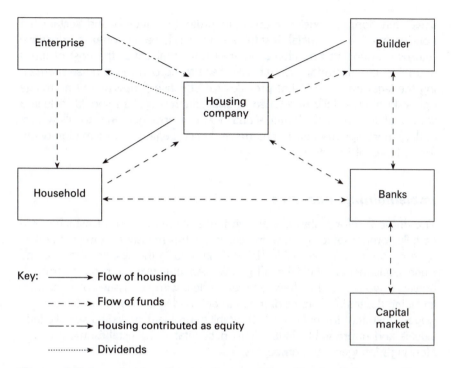

Figure 4.5 *A market-based system (source:* Urban Housing Reforms in China, *World Bank staff report, World Bank, Washington DC)*

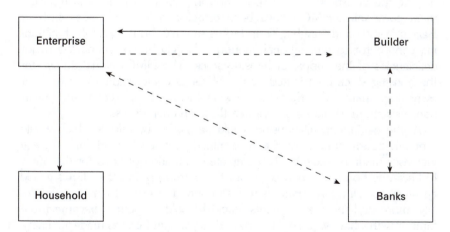

Figure 4.6 *Current housing system in China (source:* Urban Housing Reforms in China, *World Bank staff report, World Bank, Washington DC)*

a well-functioning housing market. In order to establish and sustain the housing market, financial institutions would have to offer competitive returns on deposits and charge interest rates that cover the cost of funds and their administration. Credit risks need to be controlled by strengthening the legal framework that provides for effective property and mortgage rights. Further, a fully developed housing finance system should include a variety of institutional channels and financial arrangements to allow secondary mortgage markets to emerge and encourage the participation of different types of investors.

Implementing measures

The phase 2 reform started with substantial increases of rent, which would be fully compensated by wage increases. As this measure redirects the flow of resources that are available already and used in the system, the rent and wage adjustments would be affordable. An effective alternative strategy, however, would need to have devices to deal with key issues of transition, including the initial absence of the market-based system of housing, finance, wage-adjustment formulae and affordability problems faced by specific individuals and unprofitable SOEs. This necessitates the establishment of the Housing Management Companies.

Housing management companies (HMCs)

As an alternative strategy for initiating a market-based housing system and helping the divestiture of enterprise housing, joint-stock housing management companies (HMCs) have been established in some cities such as Beijing, Yantai and Ningbo. Their task is to make housing a fully functioning contributor to the national economy, largely by correcting the major deficiencies of the supply of housing stock. The HMCs would administer the housing stock contributed by the SOEs as equity capital in return for ownership shares. Clearly defined ownership rights and corporate governance structure would help reinforce these characteristics.

At the beginning, all housing would be owned by HMCs which would rent out apartments at market-determined rent levels paid for by wage increases made possible by the complete elimination of need for the SOEs to bear any housing expenses. From this starting point, the HMCs would be ready to sell apartments, as well as continue to rent them out. Gradually, more and more apartments would be sold as people became more familiar with what ownership means and as younger families made life financial plans including housing saving during their earning years.

Over time, some occupants would choose to sell their accommodations to others and become renters if they liked, which would be allowed as part of a policy of freedom of choice. The resources presently devoted by the SOEs and housing bureaux to upkeep might be transferred to the new owners in the form of wage increases. Since there appears to have been chronic under-maintenance, the individuals, as owners, might undertake more maintenance than is covered by the wage adjustment, which would be anti-inflationary in taking expenditures away from other things. Transferring ownership to occupants would be a small price to pay for relieving the SOEs and housing bureaux of the burden of supplying housing and for achieving the long-term goals of efficient housing arrangements.

Initially, HMC customers would primarily consist of the employees of SOEs that originally owned the stock – because it is not only likely that the SOEs, which would be the share holders, would want to give priority to their own employees, but also commercial rents and prices would not be affordable by employees of other entities whose wages had not been adjusted. There are other types of companies, such as profitable private and joint-venture companies, which usually have cash capital but no housing stock because both the central and local planning authorities restrict them to building new residential houses for their employees. It is hoped that successful access to the housing market would induce these companies to invest in HMCs by making cash equity contributions. It would also be necessary to encourage more HMCs and other housing suppliers to enter the housing market and compete in order to prevent a few HMCs from monopolizing the market.

Wages

Compensating for higher costs of renting or buying housing, the SOEs would provide cash wage supplements to allow workers to pay higher rents or mortgage payments. The supplements would be financed from savings on housing expenditures, which would no longer be necessary. Since the housing stocks of SOEs were contributed by the SOEs, as their equity shares to the HMCs, the dividend profits on these shares would help to increase the wage supplements for the SOEs' workforce. The supplement should be determined on the basis of typical housing occupied by workers holding comparable jobs, not the specific housing unit occupied by a particular individual; and it would be made a part of the comprehensive wage and subject to adjustment as a whole, not according to changes in housing consumption in the future.

Finance

Commercial levels of housing rents and increased cash wages of individuals would make commercially priced housing loans for HMCs and individuals feasible. Financial projections have been prepared for all HMCs established by the end of 1993, reflecting current operational plans. A World Bank study showed that HMCs would be able to generate considerable cash flow and dividends even if they increased the standards of operation and maintenance to much higher levels than current ones (World Bank, 1995). The World Bank sensitivity analysis also showed that the levels of interest rate and capital investments had the most significant effect on the financial viability of an HMC; and the debt–service ratio (ratio between cash flow from operation and debt service) tended to be very sensitive to such key parameters.

Problems associated with the phase 2 reforms

This section addresses several major problems associated with the new approach and highlights the need for further work.

Non-equity SOEs and non-equity work-units

According to the plan for establishing HMCs as a solution to the housing problems, equity SOEs can contribute their housing stock to the HMCs. However, for those SOEs and work-units that cannot offer housing stock as a contribution to join HMCs, they have the problem of increasing their employees' wages to meet the increasing rent or to buy their accommodation.

There are two typical types of family in China as far as housing is concerned. In the first there is at least one member of the family belonging to an equity SOE which has housing stock to contribute to the HMC or, at least, one who works for a profitable joint venture or a private company which can pay a comparatively high salary in comparison with local standards. This kind of family appears to be able to afford the increasing rents. However, in the other type of family nobody works for an equity enterprise which has housing stock, or perhaps all members of the family are unemployed. Therefore, this kind of family would be unable to afford the rent increase. In this case, what would the government do? Should central or local government provide subsidies for their living? Then the burden would be added to the social security system. This would contradict one of the major objectives of the enterprise reform. However, should the central or local government not make any effort on this matter, consequent social problems would arise. Therefore, measures will need to be considered to help this type of family.

Possibility of monopoly

Because only a limited number of HMCs are being established, and these are supported by the central government, they may begin to monopolize the housing market. They would take advantage of the reform and so manipulate the housing market. This would, in fact, create more market distortions and consequent corruption. Monopoly and corruption would also be likely in the housing finance market because only a limited number of banks are authorized by the central government to deal with housing finance. There is no effective securities market in China. The banks which have the right to deal with housing finance could easily monopolize the housing finance market and, therefore, create more corruption. Policies and regulations to prevent monopoly and to establish more companies to function as HMCs, more financial institutions and a security market to deal with housing finance should, therefore, be considered by the central government.

Lack of knowledge of housing economics and expertise

There has been little attention paid to the need for better knowledge of housing economics and management that would make it possible to devise more effective selling terms to estimate how much housing can be sold and to help housing reforms contribute to the economy of China. Reforms devised in the absence of this knowledge run the danger of tinkering counterproductively, unleashing unanticipated effects. There is a severe shortage of skilled housing personnel in China who are able to understand and implement the reforms. Therefore professional training is needed urgently.

Weakness of regulatory framework

The proposed new housing reform programme requires the strengthening of a number of legal and regulatory instruments in China, including those governing registration and valuation of property, property rights, landlord–tenant relationships, foreclosure, eviction, condominiums and financial regulations. At present, contracts are used to overcome specific deficiencies in the national legal framework. However, further development of the regulatory framework will become increasingly important as the housing market develops.

Urban Housing in China: Conclusions

The establishment of a market-based housing system to privatize housing is the ultimate objective of China's housing reforms. Increasing rents has been the major step adopted so far since the housing reforms started in 1984. There is relatively little experience with the sort of system envisaged under the reforms. Houses have been sold below cost with many, if not most, families continuing to live as tenants, paying below-market rents. Therefore, it is not surprising that the housing reforms so far, whilst having moved away from a complete socialist housing system, have gone only a small part of the way to a market-based housing system.

The phase 1 reforms have proved disappointing. On the economics side, failure to follow cost-based guides in setting rents and housing sales prices contributed to the lack of success. Rents were set below costs and the link between the value that people place on housing and the cost to the country's economy failed to be appreciated. On the management side, the critical shortcoming of the strategy was its inability to bring an end to the enterprises' direct obligations for employee housing.

At present, the phase 2 reforms are focused on the setting-up of a rental market. However, the strategy would establish commercial levels of rents, higher cash wages and long-term mortgage financing which would lead to viability of ownership options. Therefore provisions must be made to allow households who wish to buy units and can accumulate the necessary down payment to obtain mortgage loans. The success of HMCs would create a viable rental market, which would attract further investment from private sources and insurance funds. However, as home ownership spreads, it would present a more important area of private investment. Because new housing would increasingly reflect consumers' tastes and budget constraints, the intrusive regulations and guidelines governing housing unit size and other related aspects would lose much of their justification, and would need to be replaced with a set of ordinances to safeguard health, safety and environmental considerations. It is hoped that, with rents and housing prices allowed to find market levels and with housing divorced from the SOEs and other public sector organizations, the fundamental gains from the housing reforms will be realized fully.

Several major problems associated with the phase 2 reforms have been identified. More attention should be paid to and more effective measures should be adopted towards the problems, especially on the legal side. Otherwise, the reforms could end up making very little contribution to solving China's housing problems, with the danger of worsening the situation.

THE QUALITY OF HOUSING AND ITS SURROUNDING ENVIRONMENT

As might be expected, housing in countries with high incomes per capita are larger and are more likely to consist of permanent structures and have more amenities than countries with low incomes per capita (table 4.5).

There are, however, substantial differences in quality among countries with broadly similar per capita incomes because of disparities in land and construction costs, and variations in government housing policy – particularly in relation to land, materials, infrastructure, subsidies and taxation. In, for example, Hong Kong, Toronto and Melbourne, the average floor areas per person were respectively 7, 42 and 53 m^2 in 1991 – even though all three cities had per capita incomes within the US\$ 15,000–\$20,000 range, whereas in Bogota and Athens, average floor areas per person were respectively 9 and 25 m^2 – despite both cities sharing the US\$ 5,000–10,000 per capita income band (HABITAT, 1996).

However, in terms of the physical environment, most urban housing in the developing world is far from satisfactory. Most cities experience problems relating to air and water pollution, sewerage, solid waste collection and environmental management. The nature and seriousness of these problems

Table 4.5 Housing quality in relation to per capita incomes, 1991

Per capita income per country	Floor area per person (m^2)	Persons per room	Percentage of permanent structures	Percentage of dwelling units with water connected to their plots
High	35.0	0.66	100	100
Middle–high	22.0	1.03	99	99
Middle	15.1	1.69	94	94
Low–middle	8.8	2.24	86	74
Low	6.1	2.47	67	56

Source: HABITAT (1996).

vary from city to city, for example – in Asian cities – air pollution is a serious problem in Manila and Beijing (Richardson, 1993), whereas water quality is a major problem in Jakarta, Manila and Bangkok. Sewerage problems are similarly a cause for concern in Bangkok and Manila, while solid waste collection and management is highly inadequate in Jakarta and Beijing. Only 2 per cent of Bangkok's population was connected to city sewers, and – since the early 1970s – dissolved oxygen levels in the Chao Phraya River diminished dramatically without much remedial action having taken place (Phantumvanit and Liengcharernsit, 1989).

In the Philippines, slums and squatter settlements along the banks of rivers and waterways of Manila have caused drainage problems, water pollution and flooding (Carino, 1994) – a consequence of the virtual absence of local facilities for sanitation and the disposal of solid waste. Together with the lack of government services, unhealthy living conditions in areas of informal housing have inevitably resulted in a high incidence of disease, particularly among children. Urban health statistics, however, often underestimate the seriousness of disease and malnutrition in poor neighbourhoods. In Manila, the infant mortality rates were three times higher in the slums and squatter settlements than in the rest of the city; tuberculosis rates were nine times higher; diarrhoea and anaemia were twice as common, and three times as many people suffered from malnutrition. Even in Singapore, it was found that the incidence of hookworm, ascaris and trichuris among squatters was more than twice that for the incidence of flat dwellers (United Nations Development Programme, 1990).

In Indonesia, there has been growing concern about the management of resources such as provision of potable water supplies in cities. In Jakarta, residential and industrial demand for water was forecast to quadruple during the last quarter of the twentieth century (Douglass, 1991). The concern was very great since the pollution levels of lowland rivers and water courses were dangerously high – particularly in respect of non-degradable organic chemical compounds and heavy metals. Alternative water supplies were severely inadequate. In 1980, only 26 per cent of Jakarta's population was served by piped water, but to increase this figure significantly posed a severe problem since – by the year 2000 – Jakarta was forecast to absorb 70 per cent of the total urban growth of Indonesia (Douglass, 1991).

The principal reasons for the lack of effective action to improve the environment of urban areas is not hard to find. Environmental quality is an income-elastic good and thus not a high priority for poor, or even middle-income nations (Richardson, 1993). The question is how long can environmental degregation continue before low- and middle-income nations realize that there is a need to manage urban environmental problems, especially if these are generated by an unco-ordinated provision of housing and related infrastructure?

The relationship between housing, environment and health in the cities of the developing world clearly poses an emerging and growing problem that needs to be fully addressed by city and national governments. To an extent, there has been a belated and growing recognition of the link between meeting housing needs and the environmental and health priorities of government – judging from recent housing programmes that have been put in place (see pages 159–60). But most of the current programmes need to be expanded and applied more widely in order to meet increasing housing need derived from the rapid pace of industrialization and urbanization. The programmes that have already been introduced reflect the wide diversity of needs and solutions – in respect of housing, environment and health, and they also demonstrate the role of international agencies as well as local institutions. It is also likely that, in the future, with growing needs and ever-more limited resources for urban housing (particularly land), more initiatives and greater creativity will have to be incorporated into future programmes to provide more effective solutions to the problems of housing need and environmental quality.

THE LOCATION OF HOUSING

Housing constitutes the largest urban land use (in some towns over 50 per cent of the total area) and may account for over 25 per cent of personal expenditure. There is a great variety of types of housing but most residential land is fixed in area and location. Forced out of areas of good business accessibility, housing land is less frequently redeveloped compared with other uses, but marginal changes may have important economic and social ramifications. Although there is a relationship between personal income, place of employment and place of residence, this relationship is subject to different and conflicting interpretations. There are basically three explanations of the rationale of private-sector housing location.

Travel cost minimization theory

It has been argued that if travel costs to work are nil or very low, householders will be prepared to pay the highest rents or prices for accommodation. Through the working of the price mechanism this would imply that the rich live very close to the central business district and the poor live in less expensive outer areas. But the converse is generally true. Low-income earners live close to their work (usually within the inner areas of cities) to minimize their travelling costs, rents are mainly regulated, and housing densities are high. As incomes rise, there has been a tendency for people to live further away from their work in areas of lower density and more expensive housing. Moreover, the outward spread of cities would only be compatible with travel cost minimization if employment was simultaneously decentralized and this usually does not take place.

But the theory is valid to some extent. Although house prices may be very high in the commuter belt, residential values per m^2 tend to diminish outwards from the central area as competition from business uses becomes less. Both in the cases of the unregulated furnished tenancies in the 'twilight' areas in inner London (up to 1974) and the exclusive leasehold properties in Belgravia and Mayfair, values could only be as high as they are because of the very large demand from persons unable or unwilling to incur high travel costs to gain access to employment and the other facilities of inner and central London.

Travel cost and housing cost trade-off theory

A perfect trade-off assumes that households of the same income group are prepared to pay, over a period, the same real aggregate cost of travel and housing – regardless of distance from a city centre (figure 4.7(a)). But often there is not a perfect trade-off and therefore it is assumed that households will attempt to minimize aggregate costs. Thus in the context of commuting into the city centre, there will be a migration of households inwards if travel costs rise, but a migration outwards if travel costs fall (figure 4.7(b)). If, on the other hand, housing costs rise, there will be an out-migration, but if housing costs fall there will be an in-migration (figure 4.7(c)).

Although there is an inverse correlation between site values and travel costs around many cities (for example, London), the same is not true of house prices and travel costs. High-income commuters do not have to trade off travel costs and housing costs – they can afford both; the rich may prefer to live in the commuter belt where they can benefit from a better environment and open space and where they can segregate themselves from lower socio-economic groups; and it may only be within the outer areas of cities that sites are available for the construction of new and expensive houses. Motorways, moreover, may make outer locations more accessible than many inner suburban locations from the central business district.

Even if there were an inverse correlation between house prices and travel costs, however, it is unlikely that householders would trade off. Housing expenditure (including rates as well as mortgage interest payments) and travel costs change frequently but households may only alter their location at intervals of five or more years. There is usually a long time-lag before householders react to changing costs, and there is a high degree of immo-

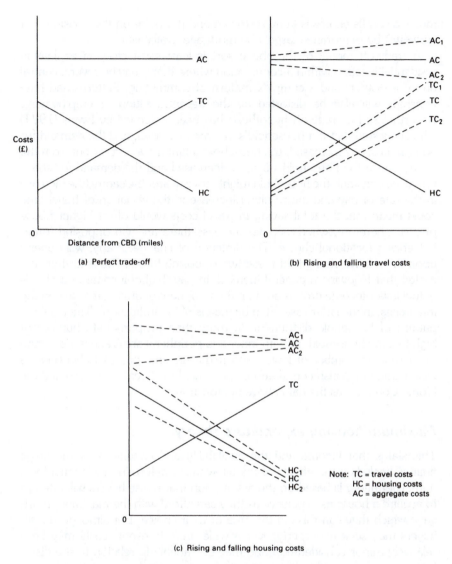

Figure 4.7 *The trade-off theory of residential location*

bility as non-economic reasons may outweigh economic considerations in determining locational choice. The main reasons why householders change residence may be due more to a change of job, marriage or a change in the size of family than to a changing relationship between travel costs and house prices. It is completely unrealistic to assume that a householder is free to locate anywhere from the central business district to the outer commuter belt. His choice is fairly restricted and the point on the housing cost curve will be determined largely by mortgage availability.

A trade-off model of the above sort is least satisfactory in explaining residential location within a conurbation where there may be several central business districts and a complex pattern of commuting. Patterns and relationships will also be distorted by the decentralization of employment. Nevertheless the trade-off hypothesis has been extended by Evans (1971) who suggested that if a household's income increased, and the demand for household space increased, the household might move further out from the centre; but if the household's income increased and the demand for space remained constant, the household might move nearer the centre (the increase in the rate of pay and the resulting increase in the valuation of travel time could mean that the total saving in travel costs would offset higher house prices). Therefore, when incomes increase there are two opposing forces influencing locational choice. The direction of change, if any, will depend upon the relative strength of these two opposing forces. Evans further suggested that following a general increase in pay, higher-income households outbid lower-income groups both on the periphery of urban areas and in the inner cites, in the latter case often by means of 'gentrification'. The resulting pattern of household distribution (a more than proportionate number of high-income households in both inner and peripheral areas and a more than proportionate number of lower- and middle-income groups in-between) is well marked in British conurbations, particularly in Greater London and the Home Counties, as the data above demonstrate.

Maximum housing expenditure theory

This states that income and the availability and conditions of mortgage finance (including the effects of tax allowances) determine residential location. The theory is based on the assumption that house-buyers will attempt to acquire a house as expensive as they can afford with the maximum mortgage which they can raise in the area of their choice. But although house-buyers may seek a property over a wide area, transport costs may be a relatively minor consideration and may be variable in relation to the distribution of houses within a specific price range. Environmental and social factors (and the prospects of capital appreciation) are likely to be a much greater influence over choice. This hypothesis, evolved by Ellis (1967) and Stegman (1969), implies that there is no overall relationship between income, travel cost/time and place of work, and that there is no effective trade-off.

In formulating policies, central and local government need to know why people live in a certain area, what types of houses should be constructed and in which locations, how significant are journey-to-work considerations, how far it is desirable to decentralize employment, how investment in either improved transport (to the central and inner areas) or in residential environmental improvement should be decided, and – if regional growth points are likely to provide a preferable environment and facilitate a more efficient transport system – how investment decisions should be made. Richardson (1971) suggests that if it is thought that there is a trade-off between housing expenditure and travelling costs then policy should concentrate on reducing travelling costs to work and/or developing high-density housing in the inner areas of cities. Alternatively, a policy of decentralizing employment would benefit particularly low-income householders in the outer suburbs. But if it is found that environmental conditions influence householders more than travelling costs, policies would need to concentrate on providing satisfactory residential environments rather than on reducing the cost of the journey to work.

In these circumstances, high-income buyers or renters wishing to locate as close as possible to the CBD – for their own environmental, social and economic reasons – will outbid low-income households and thus create areas of disproportionately high-income housing in the urban core (figure 4.7(a)) with low-income households being squeezed into high-density private rented housing or heavily subsidized social housing (or into squatter settlements, in the case of cities in the developing world). Alternatively – and for different environmental, social and economic reasons – high-income households might wish to locate in the outer suburbs, and will consequently outbid low-income households for space in the urban periphery (figure 4.7(b)). Only in the inner and middle suburbs in the developed world will low-income households be able to bid among themselves for housing, unimpeded by competition from high-income households (figure 4.7(c)), although in the developing world squatter settlements are likely to continue to occupy sites on the periphery of many cities for some time to come.

REFERENCES

Abrams, C. (1964) *Housing in the Modern World: Man's Struggle for Shelter in an Urbanizing World*, London: Faber & Faber.

Abrams, C. (1977) 'Squatting and squatters', in Abu Lughod, J. (ed.), *Third World Urbanisation*, London: Methuen.

Agency for International Development (1968) *The New Urban Debate*, Conference Report, Washington DC: AID.

Bagby, D.G. (1973) *Housing Rehabilitation Costs*, New York: Lexington Books.

Balchin, P. (ed.) (1996) *Housing Policy in Europe*, London: Routledge.

Barlow, M. (1988) *Urban Housing Reform in China: A First Overview*, Washington DC: Urban Development Division of the Policy, Planning and Research Department, World Bank.

Barlow, J. and Duncan, S. (1994) *Success and Failure in Housing Provision: European Systems Compared*, Oxford: Pergamon.

Boelhouwer, P. (1991) 'Convergence or divergence in the general housing policy in seven European countries', Paper presented at the conference on *Housing Policy as a Strategy for Change*, European Network for Housing Research, Oslo, 24–27 June 1991.

Boleat, M. (1985) *National Housing Finance Systems*, London: Croom Helm.

Burns, L. and Grebler, L. (1977) *The Housing of Nations: Analysis and Policy in a Comparative Framework*, London: Macmillan.

Carino, B.V. (1994) 'Urban environmental problems of Metro Manila', in Awang, A. (ed.), *Environmental and Urban Management in Southeast Asia*, Johor Bharu: Urban Habitat and Highrise Monographs, Institute Sultan Iskandar of Urban Habitat and Highrise.

Clark, D. (1996) *Urban World/Global City*, London: Routledge.

De Recio, A. (1994) 'The role of housing in environmental and urban management in Southeast Asia', in Awang, A. (ed.), *Environmental and Urban Management in Southeast Asia*, Johor Bharu: Urban Habitat and Highrise Monographs, Institute Sultan Iskandar of Urban Habitat and Highrise.

Department of the Environment (1994) *Second Report on Opportunities for UK Construction Companies in China*, prepared by He, J., London: HMSO.

Department of the Environment (1995) *Fourth Report on Opportunities for UK Construction Companies in China*, prepared by He, J., London, HMSO.

Doling, J. (1994) 'The privatisation of social housing in European welfare states', *Environment and Planning C, Government and Policy*, 12: 243–55.

Doling, J. (1997) *Comparative Housing Policy*, London: Macmillan.

Douglass, M. (1991) 'Planning for environmental sustainability in the extended metropolitan region', in Ginsburg, N. (ed.), *The Extended Metropolis: The Settlement Transition in Asia*, Honolulu: University of Hawaii Press.

Economist (1992–93) 'I own, I owe, so off to work I go', 26 December–8 January: 95–7.

Economist Intelligence Unit (1995) 'China's state enterprises', June.

Ellis, R.H. (1967) 'Modelling of household location – a statistical approach', *Highway Research Record*, 207.

Emms, P. (1990) *Social Housing: a European dilemma?*, Bristol: School for Advanced Urban Studies.

Esping-Andersen, G. (1990) *The Three Worlds of Welfare Capitalism*, Princeton MA: Princeton University Press.

Evans, A.W. (1971) *The Economics of Residential Location*, London: Macmillan.

Findley, S.E. (1993) 'The third world', in Kasarda, J.D. (ed.), *Third World Cities: Problems, Policies and Prospects*, London: Sage.

Folin, M. (1985) 'Housing development processes in Europe: some hypotheses from a comparative analysis', in Ball, M., Bentivegna, V., Edwards, M. and Folin, M. (eds), *Land Rent, Housing and Urban Planning: A European Perspective*, London: Croom Helm.

Forster, C. (1995) *Australian Cities: Continuity and Change*, Melbourne: Oxford University Press.

Frankenhof, C.A. (1966) *The Economic Role of Housing in a Developing Economy*, Rio Piedras: Housing Policy Seminar, University of Puerto Rico.

Fraser, J.M. (1952) 'Housing and planning in Singapore', *Town Planning Review*, 23.

Ginsburg, N. (1994) 'Planning the future of the Asian city – a twenty-five year retrospective', *Occasional Paper No. 36*, Hong Kong: Hong Hong Institute of Asia-Pacific Studies, The Chinese University of Hong Kong.

Gowan, P. (1995) 'Neo-liberal theory and practice for Eastern Europe', *New Left Review*, 213, September/October.

Grigsby, W.G. (1963) *Housing Markets and Public Policy*, Philadelphia: University of Pennsylvania Press.

HABITAT (1987) *Global Report on Human Settlements*, Oxford: United Nations Centre for Urban Settlements and Oxford University Press.

HABITAT (1996) *An Urbanizing World: Global Report on Human Settlements 1996*, Oxford: United Nations Centre for Human Settlements and Oxford University Press.

Hägred, U. (1994) 'The housing stock – age, quality and forms of tenure', in Hedman, E. (ed.), *Housing in Sweden in an International Perspective*, Karlskrona: Boverket.

Harloe, M. (1985) *Private Rented Housing in the United States and Europe*, London: Croom Helm.

Harloe, M. (1995) *The People's Home: Social Rented in Europe and America*, Oxford: Blackwell.

Hayward, D. (1996) 'The reluctant landlords: a history of public housing in Australia', *Urban Policy and Research*, 14(1).

Hedman, E. (1994) *Housing in Sweden in an International Perspective*, Karlskrona: Boverket.

Heerma, E. (1992) *Beleid voor stadsvernieuwing in de toekomst* [Policy for Urban Renewal in the Future], The Hague: Tweede Kamer 1991–92, 22396, 3, Staatsuitgeverij.

Kemeny, J. (1981) *The Myth of Home Ownership: Private versus Public Choices in Housing Tenure*, London: Routledge.

Kemeny, J. (1992) *Housing and Social Theory*, London: Routledge.

Kemeny, J. (1995) *From Public Housing to Social Market: Rental Policy Strategy in Comparative Perspective*, London: Routledge.

Lean, W. (1971) 'Housing rehabilitation or redevelopment? The economic assessment', *Journal of the Town Planning Institute*, 57.

Lim, H.H. (1988) 'Urban service provision in a plural society: approaches in Malaysia', in Rondinelli, D.A. and Cheema, G.S. (eds), *Urban Services in Developing Countries*, London: Macmillan.

Listokin, D. (1973) *The Dynamics of Housing Rehabilitation: macro and micro analysis*, Centre for Urban Policy Research, Rutgers University.

Macionis, J.J. and Parrillo, V.N. (1998) *Cities and Urban Life*, Upper Saddle River NY: Prentice Hall.

McCrone, G. and Stephens, M. (1995) *Housing Policy in Britain and Europe*, London: UCL Press.

Merrett, S. (1979) *State Housing in Britain*, London: Routledge & Kegan Paul.

Morrison, P.S. (1995) 'The geography of rental housing and the restructuring of housing assistance in New Zealand', *Urban Studies*, 10(1).

Murphy, L. (1997) 'The New Zealand experience of public housing reform', in Coles, R. (ed.), *The End of Public Housing: A Discussion Forum organized by the Urban Research Program*, Canberra: Australian National University.

Myrdal, G. (1968) *Asian Drama*, Harmondsworth: Penguin.

National Community Development Project (1975) *The Poverty of the Improvement Programme*, London: CDP Information and Intelligence Unit.

Needleman, L. (1965) *The Economics of Housing*, London: Staples Press.

Nguyen, D.K. (1994) 'Vulnerability of cities in a new market economy', Paper presented at the *Second Leadership Seminar Towards a Sustainable Urban Environment in Southeast Asia*, Johor Bharu: Institute Sultan Iskandar of Urban Habitat and Highrise.

OECD (1994) *OECD Economic Surveys 1993–1994, Switzerland*, Paris: OECD.

Oxley, M. (1993) *Social Housing in the European Community*, European Housing Research Working Paper Series Number 2, de Montfort University, Leicester.

Phantumvanit, D. and Liengcharernsit, W. (1989) 'Coming to terms with Bangkok's environmental problems', *Environment and Urbanisation*, 1.

Potter, R. (1992) *Urbanisation in the Third World*, Oxford: Oxford University Press.

Potter, R.B. and Lloyd-Evans, S. (1998) *The City in the Developing World*, Harlow: Longman.

Pugh, C. (1989) 'The political economy of public housing', in Sandhu, K.S. and Wheatley, P. (eds), *Management of Success: The Moulding of Modern Singapore*, Singapore: Institute of Southeast Asian Studies.

Pugh, C. (1995) 'Urbanization in developing countries: an overview of the economic and policy issues in the 1990s', *Cities*, 6.

Richardson, H.W. (1971) *Urban Economics*, Harmondsworth: Penguin.

Richardson, H.W. (1993) 'Efficiency and welfare in LDC mega-cities', in Kasarda, J.D. and Parnell, A.M. (eds), *Third World Cities: Problems, Policies and Prospects*, London: Sage.

Robinson, G.M., Loughran, R.J. and Tranter, P.J. (2000) *Australia and New Zealand: Economy, Society and Environment*, London: Edward Arnold.

Schmidt, S. (1989) 'Convergence theory, labour movements and corporatism: the case for housing', *Scandinavian Housing and Planning Research*, 6(2): 83–111.

Short, J., Fleming, S. and Witt, S. (1986) *Housebuilding, Planning and Community Action: The Production and the Negotiation of the Built Environment*, London: Routledge and Kegan Paul.

Soegijoko, S. (1985) 'Managing the delivery of urban services for the poor in Indonesia: case study of KIP in Bandung', *Regional Development Dialogue*, 6(2).

Stegman, M.A. (1969) 'Accessibility models and residential location', *Journal of the American Institute of Planners*, 35.

Struyk, R.J. (1996) 'Housing privatization in the former Soviet bloc to 1995', in Andrusz, G., Harloe, M. and Szelenyi, I. (eds), *Cities after Socialism*, Oxford: Blackwell.

Turner, B. (1992) 'Housing reforms in Eastern Europe', in Turner, B., Hegedüs, J. and Tosics, I. (eds), *The Reform of Housing in Eastern Europe and the Soviet Union*, London: Routledge.

United Nations Development Programme (1990) *Human Development Report, 1990*, New York: UNDP and Oxford University Press.

US Bureau of the Census (1996) *Statistical Abstract of the United States 1996*, Washington DC: US Government Printing Office.

Waldegrave, C. and Stuart, S. (1997) 'Out of the rat race: the migration of low income urban families to small town Wairarapa', *New Zealand Geographer*, 53(1).

Wang, Y. (1989) *Housing Commercialisation and Inflation*, Beijing: The State Council of China.

Wilkinson, R.K. (1973) 'House prices and the measurement of externalities', *Economic Journal*, 83.

World Bank (1995) *Urban Housing Reforms in China*, World Bank staff report, Washington DC: World Bank.

Yates, J. (1997) 'Changing directions in Australian housing policies: the end of muddling through', *Housing Studies*, 12(2).

Yeung, Y.M. (1991) 'The urban poor and basic infrastructure services in Asia: past approaches and emerging challenges', *Occasional Paper No. 7*, Hong Kong: Institute of Asia-Pacific Studies, The Chinese University of Hong Kong.

5

The Location and Globalization of Urban Economic Activity

INTRODUCTION

Regardless of the geographical location, origin or size of an urban area, a rational pattern of land use evolves. Normally after an assessment of various advantages and disadvantages, the location of any activity is determined either by the desire to maximize (or realize satisfactory) profits in respect of business users of land, or to maximize (or obtain acceptable) utility in the case of residential and other non-business users. The urban land-use pattern is determined mainly by activities competing for sites through the forces of demand and supply – demand being the quantity of property required at given prices or rents, and supply being the amount of property available at those prices and rents.

The demand for land is a reflection of the profitability or utility derived from its use by current or potential users. The greater the benefit to be obtained from using a site for any particular purpose, the higher the rent or price the would-be user is willing to pay. Since capital values are derived from annual rental values, so the higher the levels of rents the greater will be the capital values. As with any other form of investment, the prices of property interests rise in anticipation of future increases in rent incomes. Property investors may therefore be prepared to accept low yields or returns in relation to current property income in order to obtain the future benefit of an increased income and the possibility of additional capital gains.

The total supply of land in any country is fixed, except in cases of territorial gains and losses or reclamation and dereliction. But the supply of land for different uses can be either increased or decreased. Change in supply occurs when, for example, land transfers from one agricultural use to another, from farming to urban use, from residential to office or retailing use, and from private to public use.

The supply of land for specific uses is comparatively static in the short term. The underlying conditions of supply (the state of construction technology, sources of materials and other factors of production, number and type of public utilities, and the transport system) remain fairly constant. Because supply is slow to react to increases or decreases in demand, it is demand which is the major determinant of rental values, and consequently of capital values. In Britain, for example, from the 1950s until the late-1980s there was a substantial increase in property values because of the effect of increased demand for urban property upon a more slowly changing pattern of supply. The increased demand was the product of four distinct factors: inflation, credit availability, population growth and increased affluence.

(1) Until the late-1980s inflation not only increased property values in step with the rise in the general level of prices, but because property was regarded as a 'hedge' against inflation, and because of its scarcity in relation to demand, values increased ahead of general price levels. Property therefore became very attractive to developers and speculators.
(2) The availability of finance from institutional investors, not least from building societies, compounded the rate of increase in the level of effective demand. Interest rates on mortgages barely kept pace with the increased prices of property. After tax allowances on interest payments were taken into account the real financial cost of purchasing property was either very small or nil.
(3) The population increased over the period mainly as a result of changes in birth- and death-rates, by 1994 being over 14 per cent greater than in 1951 (table 5.1).
(4) An increase in population by itself would have had little effect upon the level of property values. But this increase occurred simultaneously with an increase in real incomes. These two factors led to an increase in the quantity of demand for property, and to qualitative changes, the result of changing social, economic and cultural characteristics. Changes included the earlier age of marriage and the dispersal of the family unit into separate dwellings, with young people leaving home at an earlier age, the demand for improved quality and higher standards of both new and older properties and the demand for second homes – the latter decentralizing increased values throughout the country – especially where there was an increase in accessibility resulting from motorway development.

Influenced by changes in the underlying conditions of demand, land within the market transfers to the user who is prepared to pay the highest price or rent (demand and supply forever moving towards an equilibrium

Table 5.1 United Kingdom population 1951–94

Year	Population (millions)	Birth-rate (per 1,000)	Death-rate (per 1,000)
1951	50.2	15.8	13.4
1956	51.2	16.0	12.5
1961	52.8	17.8	12.6
1966	54.4	17.9	11.8
1971	55.6	16.2	11.6
1981	56.3	13.0	11.8
1986	56.3	13.3	11.8
1994	58.4	12.9	10.7

situation). This monetary value will reflect utility in the case of house-holders, and profit levels in respect of commercial and industrial users.

Although the property market can be described as an economic mechanism rationing land between competing and occasionally conflicting users, it is one of the most imperfect markets and one of the most susceptible to change in underlying conditions.

The Inefficiency of the Market

The property market is one of the least efficient markets of all. The imperfect knowledge of buyers and sellers, the 'uniqueness' of each site and building, the strong preference of establishments for existing sites, the unwillingness of some owners to sell despite the certainty of monetary gain, the absence of easily recoverable investment in costly and specific developments, the immobility of resources once they are committed, the possible loss on initial investment, the time-absorbing and costly process of seeking and acquiring new locations, the expense and legal complexity of transferring property, the length and legal rights of property interests, the influence of conservationists, the slowness of the construction industry to respond to changing demand, the monopoly power of planning authorities, property companies, mortgage institutions, sellers of property and the design professions – these are some of the factors which prevent land from transferring smoothly to its most profitable use. The pattern of land use changes only slowly over a long period and at no time is the market in a state of equilibrium with all resources being optimally used.

Even where market prices (as determined by comparable valuation) are offered, a transaction may not take place as the owner may weigh non-monetary factors more heavily than monetary considerations.

Despite these imperfections the market still attempts to assert itself, albeit inefficiently. While there is a perpetual state of disequilibrium between demand and supply resulting in either the scarcity or overabundance of different land uses, a change in the demand for a specific use will ultimately have an effect on prices and rents and subsequently will produce a change in supply.

URBAN LOCATION THEORY

Location theory not only explains the pattern of land use, but by indicating a solution to the problem of what is the most rational use of land, it suggests ways in which the current pattern can be improved. Very rarely is an activity's location determined by a single locational requirement; a mixture of interacting influences usually explains each locational decision. A location may be selected only after an appraisal has been made of the advantages and disadvantages of alternative locations for the particular activity.

As the price mechanism largely decides the profitability or utility of goods and services, it determines subsequently the location of activity and the spatial structure of the urban area supplying those goods and services. But although land is developed to its highest and best use, the process is lengthy and is frustrated by changes in underlying market conditions and by severe market imperfections.

Factor inputs may be equally important in determining location. High levels of accessibility within the central business district are reflected in low transport costs, thus attracting the greatest demand for sites, especially from commercial users. Conversely, low overall accessibility and high transport costs within the suburban areas and the rural–urban fringe will attract a much lower level of demand, especially from commercial users.

There may be some general reduction in the cost of factor inputs because of internal and external economies of scale being realized within a city. Up to a certain population size the economies will become greater. Richardson (1971) argued that these will increase at a rate more than proportionate to an increase in population, but it is difficult both to quantify these agglomeration economies and to ascertain the optimum size of a city. He suggested that it would be useful to measure the per capita cost of retail and office services and of urban transport facilities, social services and entertainment at different levels of population, and to estimate at what level of population agglomeration diseconomies take over from the agglomeration economies, and when net social costs replace net social benefits.

It has been difficult to devise a location theory about urban land use in general, or commercial and industrial land use in particular. Inertia, stability in the occupation of land and the pre-empting of sites result in most urban land being used suboptimally. Land-use models are usually very simplistic as changes in population, technology and transportation continually exert an influence on the built environment. Further pressures come from central area redevelopment, and local and central government policy. Often similar types of use are seen to be feasible in different locations within the urban area. For these reasons it is difficult to suggest where optimal locations should be. It is probable that there may be several optima for the same use and that these locations are continually changing.

Notwithstanding these difficulties, neo-classical rent theory became concerned with rent as a determinant of optimum location. Derived from Ricardian rent theory, which suggested that the productivity of land determines rent – and given that rents diminish in unison with productivity as distance from the optimum location increases, neo-classical theory was based on the principle that rents diminish outward from the centre of a city to offset both lower revenue and higher operating costs, not least transport costs (Alonso, 1960, 1964, 1967). A rent gradient would emerge consisting of a series of 'bid-rents' which would exactly compensate for falling revenue and higher operating costs. Different land uses would have different rent gradients (figure 5.1), the use with the highest rent prevailing. Thus competitive bidding between perfectly informed developers and users of land would determine the pattern of rents throughout the urban area, and would allocate specific sites between users so as to ensure that the 'highest and best' use obtained – that is, land would be used in the most appropriate way to ensure the maximization of profit.

In figure 5.1 use *a* prevails up to a distance of two kilometres from the central business district, from two to five kilometres use *b* is dominant, and beyond five kilometres use *c* prevails. A change of use could be expected to take place through the price mechanism when one gradient falls below another. Although the Alonso model does not specify the type of land use associated with each bid-rent gradient, it must be assumed that on the edge of the urban area there is a separate agricultural rent gradient. It has been suggested (Sinclair, 1967; Goodchild and Munton, 1985) that outwards from the built-up area the proportion of the total value of land attributable to agriculture rises – until agricultural values exceed urban values and so dictate the predominant land use (figure 5.2). Inwards, speculative values increase as urban development becomes imminent and agricultural values become blighted.

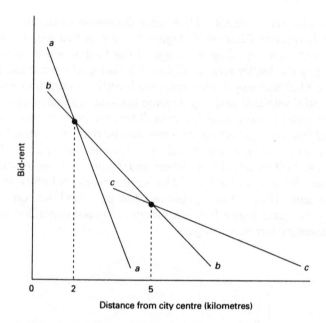

Figure 5.1 *Alonso's bid-rent–distance relationship*

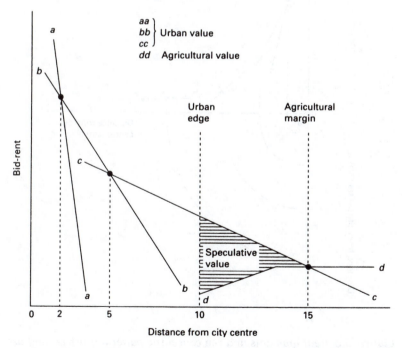

Figure 5.2 *Urban, speculative and agricultural values*

Alonso's bid-rent concept adds a value dimension to Burgess's concentric zone theory (see Chapter 3). Figure 5.3 shows that where rent gradients intersect there would be a change of use to that activity which could afford to pay the higher rent. In Figure 5.3 rent gradient *a* could coincide with the central business district, category *b* with the transition zone, categories *c* and *d* with low- and high-income housing, and category *e* with the commuter zone. In the central business district the gradient would be steep because of intense competition for a very limited number of sites, but would be very slight in the outer zones with a comparative abundance of land.
With an increase in urban population and/or an increase in total urban income, the demand for land would increase – raising bid-rents throughout the urban area. This, in turn, would result in each land use zone invading the next outer zone (figure 5.4) – a process of urban expansion explained in non-monetary terms by Burgess.

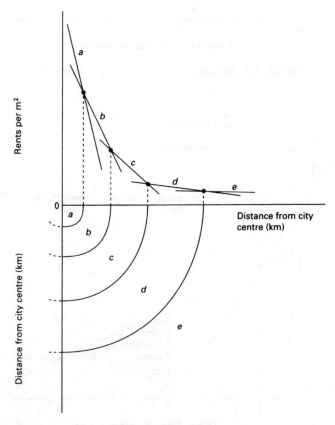

Figure 5.3 *Rent gradients and the concentric pattern of urban land use*

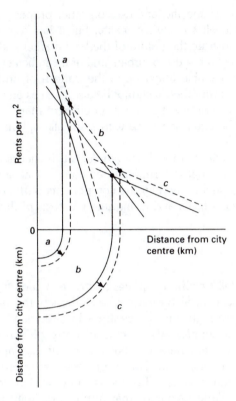

Figure 5.4 *The effect of rising rents on the concentric pattern of urban land use*

The Alonso theory has been subject to much criticism. First, it can be argued that the information available to the developers and users of land is incomplete and this alone produces an imperfect market. The theory fails to take account of the very distinctive nature of buildings and their uses. For example, once offices, shops and factories have been built they cannot be moved or easily converted for other uses – there is considerable inertia resulting in suboptimal use over time. Similarly, many large properties may not be suitable for subdivision or sub-letting at current use when demand for the complete property decreases (Fothergill *et al.*, 1987). It is also argued that since commercial, industrial and residential property is not homogeneous, varying in age, size, design, layout and location, each parcel of land is unique. This often provides the owner with a considerable degree of monopoly power which can be particularly exploited in urban areas. Alonso fails to take account of public sector land and ignores the external or spillover effects of specific land uses on other property. Alonso's theory is clearly a very idealized view of reality, but it has some merit in that it attempts to demonstrate the nature of the land market and emphasizes the notion of efficiency in the use of urban land. If it can be assumed that public policy has a very variable effect upon the pattern of urban land use and values, then the bid-rent theory cannot be dismissed as an irrelevance – particularly if it is also assumed that even an efficient market in private urban property cannot be equated *per se* with a socially optimal pattern of land use (Keogh, 1985).

Because the Alonso model is general, it is necessary to consider separately the locational determinants of commercial and industrial use. To do so it is essential to identify the components of the cost and revenue gradients of business firms and to indicate the basis of their profitability.

Costs

In advanced capitalist countries, prices and rents of land fall with increased distance from the central business district though the gradient is rarely smooth. Wages are higher in the centre – local demand for labour being greater than local supply. Also, personal costs of commuting need to be offset by higher remuneration, but this might also apply to travelling to decentralized employment. Transport costs are more of a reflection of accessibility than distance. Locations close to junctions, nodes and termini are particularly favoured, maximizing proximity to suppliers and markets. Although retailing is still generally attracted to the lowest overall transport cost location of the central business district, decentralized shopping centres are being developed following road improvements and increased car ownership. Modern manufacturing industry relies increasingly on heavy road vehicles for long-distance transportation and incurs lower transport costs on the fringes of cities than at more central locations. Capital costs (interest charges) are generally uniform and have little effect on location.

Revenue

Retailing revenue is determined by the size of the shopping catchment area or hinterland, not just in terms of population but also in terms of purchasing power. The distribution of the daytime population and points of maximum transit (where people cluster together) are also important. In the case of offices the spatial distribution, number and size of client establishments determine revenue.

In general, revenue is greatest within the central business district and so are aggregate costs. But as the distance from the centre increases, while revenue falls, aggregate costs (after falling initially) rise in suburban locations and beyond. This is mainly because of the upward pull of transport costs, which are no longer offset sufficiently by economies in the use of land and labour. Only within fairly short distances from the central business district are commercial users able to realize high profitability.

Costs, Revenue and Decentralization

So far in this discussion it has been assumed that rents generally diminish outwards from the centre of an urban area, and in a Ricardian sense reflect a centrifugal reduction in population density and the level of economic activity. However, since the late nineteenth century, both the population density and employment gradients have been flattening out as a result of decentralization (Hall, 1985) – in Western Europe population out-migration preceding employment change, and in the United States employment change pre-dating population out-migration. Rent gradients have also flattened out, but not always to the same extent, because of imperfections in the property market. The monopolistic ownership of central area land and restrictive planning policies have kept rents at a high level in the urban core long after the process of decentralization was begun. An implication of decentralization is therefore that costs do not necessarily fall continuously from the central business district and neither does revenue. Indeed, both costs and revenue may begin to rise when evolving outwards as increasing numbers of firms decentralize to exploit spatially expanding markets.

Profitability

To maximize profits firms need to locate where they can benefit from both the greatest revenue and from the lowest costs. But there is no single location where this can be achieved in absolute terms. Nevertheless, in an attempt to realize maximum revenue, specialized functions and activities serving the urban market as a whole might continue to locate centrally; firms requiring large sites and those attempting to reduce costs of over-concentration will be attracted to the suburbs. Firms locating close together to benefit from complementarity will incur lower costs because of external economies and enjoy higher revenue because of joint demand. Outlying business districts may be at least as attractive as the central business district in terms of profitability and more attractive than the relatively high-cost and low-revenue locations of the suburban belt in general.

But there is a high degree of inertia, most firms not operating at maximum profit locations. As with the level of output, firms find it difficult to adjust their locations to the optimum. A satisfactory rather than an ideal location is usually the best that can be achieved. The pattern of location, moreover, is stabilized by zoning and land-use controls.

INDUSTRIAL LOCATION

Within a national or international context, there are three main approaches to industrial location theory: the *least cost approach*, *market area analysis* and the *profit maximization approach*. The least cost approach is illustrated in figure 5.5(a). Average cost (*AC*) varies according to location, but average revenue (*AR*) is assumed to be constant. The optimum location is *O*, where the average costs are at their minimum and profit is at its maximum. The market area approach is illustrated in figure 5.5(b), where average revenue (*AR*) varies with location, but (*AC*) is assumed to be constant. Optimum location is at *O*, where average revenue and profit are at their maximum. The profit maximization approach is illustrated in figure 5.5(c). This shows that the optimum or profit-maximizing location may not necessarily be at the least cost or at the maximum revenue location but at a point in-between.

The least cost approach was advanced by Weber (1909), who suggested that there were three principal factors that determined location: transport costs, labour costs and agglomeration or deglomeration economies, and that in each situation the optimum output would be where costs fell below revenue by the greatest amount (figure 5.5(a)). In each situation, his approach was based on the assumptions that the spatial area for consideration is a single isolated country with an homogeneous climate, consumers are concentrated in given centres, perfect competition prevails, some natural resources (for example, water and building materials such as sand, gravel and clay) are ubiquitous, other resources (such as mineral fuels and ores) are localized, and labour is confined to a number of fixed locations and is immobile.

With these assumptions, Weber first considered the impact of transport costs. He suggested that if transport costs accounted for a high proportion of total production costs and were identical per tonne/km for both a sporadically located material and for the products manufactured from that material, then the optimum location would be at a source of the material rather than at the market if there was a loss of weight incurred in manufacture. Conversely, if materials were ubiquitous or the weight of the products was greater than the weight of the material required for their production (for example, through the addition of water, packaging or

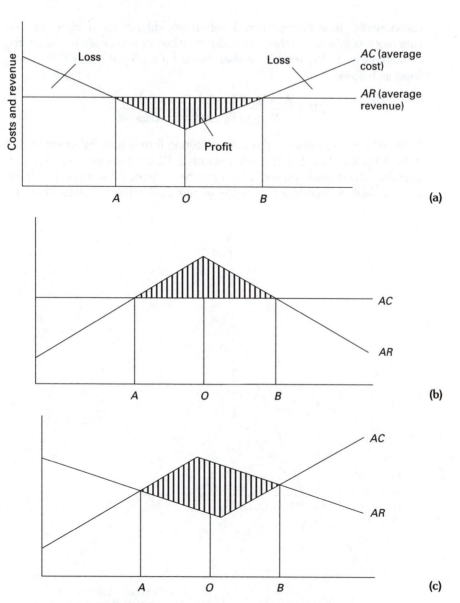

Figure 5.5 *Optimum locations for industry in different cost-revenue situations (adapted from Glasson, 1974)*

components), then the optimum location would be at the market. To indicate more precisely whether the optimum location was closer to the source of material or to the market, Weber devised a *material index (MI)*, calculated as follows:

$$MI = \frac{\text{Weight of localized material input}}{\text{Weight of the final products}}$$

If the *MI* is greater than 1, the manufacturing firm is material oriented, but if the *MI* is less than 1, it is market oriented. Weber took into account that, in reality, there would probably be a number of material sources. He therefore devised a *locational triangle* (figure 5.6) which showed that the

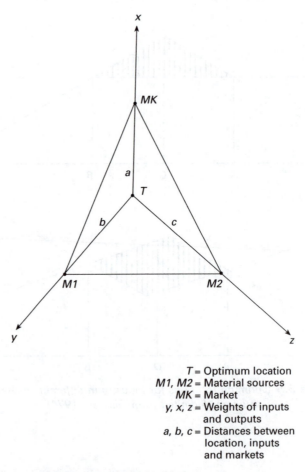

T = Optimum location
M1, M2 = Material sources
MK = Market
y, x, z = Weights of inputs
and outputs
a, b, c = Distances between
location, inputs
and markets

Figure 5.6 *Weber's locational triangle*

optimum location (*T*) is a balance between the forces exerted by the material sources (*M1* and *M2*) and the market (*MK*), suggesting that the point of least transport costs is where the total weight of procuring materials and distributing products is at the minimum.

Weber's loss of weight hypothesis was subject to constructive criticism. Hoover (1948) suggested that it should have recognized that transport costs per tonne/km are very rarely the same for both materials and products. Hoover pointed out that since transport companies normally charge 'what the traffic will bear', the transportation of products was likely to be far more costly than the transport of materials over any given distance. If, for example, there was an *MI* of 4, but the cost of transporting products per tonne/km was five times as great as the cost of transporting the material, there would be a tendency for the firm to locate at the market rather than at the source of material supply. He also analyzed material-procurement and product-distribution costs in a more detailed and realistic way than Weber, and suggested that 'break-of-bulk' locations such as seaports often offer greater cost advantages than either material locations or markets (figure 5.7) – a possible reason why some of the world's largest industrial areas are centred on ports such as New York, London and Buenos Aires (see also Alonso, 1968: 346–7).

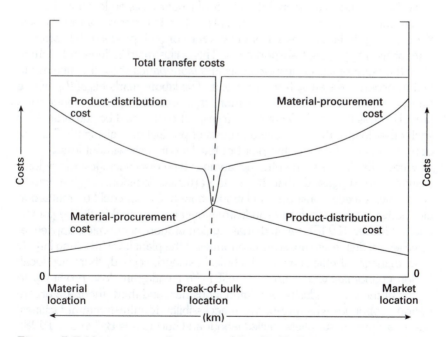

Figure 5.7 *Minimum transfer costs and break-of-bulk location (adapted from Hoover, 1948)*

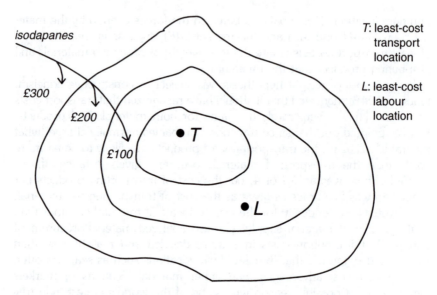

Figure 5.8 *The Weber 'least-cost', approach*

Weber secondly considered the effect of labour costs on location. Labour supply can attract a firm to a suboptimal location in terms of transport costs, if any savings in labour costs (from low wages or high productivity) compensate for high aggregate transport costs. This is illustrated in figure 5.8, where (*T*) is the point of least transport costs and *isodapanes* show the increase in unit transport costs away from this point. The labour market is at (*L*), where transport costs are £100 per unit more than that at (*T*), but if labour costs are £100 less than at *T*, labour and transport costs could be substituted for each other to give the same average costs of production – giving the firm the opportunity to relocate to the point of low labour costs without loss.

Weber, thirdly, examined the advantages (and disadvantages) of agglomeration. He suggested that if, in a particular location, agglomeration economies exceed transport and labour economies that could be realized in alternative locations, a firm or industry would be attracted to the agglomeration. Hoover (1948) claimed that agglomeration economies applied at three levels: first, there are scale economies at the plant level (resulting largely from managerial efficiency and technical savings); second, there are localization economies where firms benefit from locating in close proximity to others in the same industry or related industries; and third, there are urbanization economies which result from accessibility to infrastructural facilities, business services, suppliers, skilled labour and buyers (see Ball *et al.*, 1998). If, however, there were diseconomies of agglomeration (such as traffic

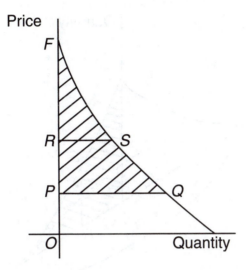

Figure 5.9 *Löschian demand curve*

congestion and high land and labour costs) these might encourage deglomeration.

A fundamental weakness of Weberian location theory is that, by focusing on the least-cost approach, a firm's revenue or profit is largely ignored as a locational consideration. Lösch (1954), however, suggested that the optimum location is where revenue exceeds costs by the greatest amount (figure 5.5(b)). Based on the assumptions that there were no spatial variations in the distribution of raw materials, labour and capital factor over an homogeneous plane, that there were uniform population densities and constant consumer preferences, and that there was no locational interdependency between firms, he constructed a simple demand curve and from this a 'demand cone' to determine the market area and revenue of a hypothetical producer (see Glasson, 1974). Figure 5.9 shows that at the centre of the market area near to a brewery (P), the unit price of beer is OP and the demand is PQ. At some distance from the centre (R), extra distribution costs result in a higher price (OR), and demand contracts to RS. At the outer edge of the market area, extra distribution costs are prohibitive, inflating the price to OF, and demand is zero.

If the hatched area FPQ is rotated around its axis, PQ, a demand cone is produced (figure 5.10). The centre of the market is the brewery at P, the market area is represented by the base of the cone, the quantity sold at any one point is indicated by the height of the cone, and the total revenue is represented by the volume of the cone. In due course, if the level of prof-

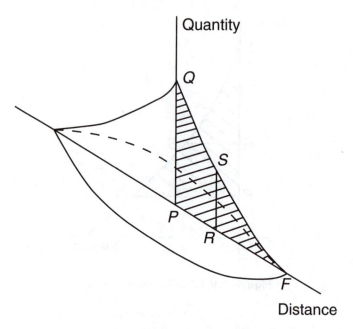

Figure 5.10 *Löschian cone*

itability permits, other breweries will develop their own market areas which in time will adjust from a series of circular areas to a network of hexagonal areas occupying the whole plane. In practice, each industry would have its own network of hexagonal market areas, the size of each area being determined by the revenue required by individual producers to maximize profits.

Clearly, Lösch's theory can be undermined if his assumptions are not generally applicable, for example, demand will vary markedly from place to place since uniform population densities are rarely found over a wide area – being normally much higher in towns and cities than in rural areas (see Richardson, 1969), while consumer preferences may also vary spatially.

While Isard (1956) and Greenhut (1956) both attempted to utilize Löschian theory in developing a profit-maximizing approach, it was recognized there were numerous problems that needed to be addressed before the credibility of this approach could be secured. First, because of the dominant role of oligopolies in the production process, any single major firm will often need to base its location decision on the location and markets of its competitors. Second, because of the difficulties of evaluating the relevant cost and revenue variables at different locations, most locations are suboptimal (although firms might be able to evaluate costs with a greater degree of certainty than revenue, and thus show a predilection for the

Weberian approach). Third, it is difficult to consider the optimum location (or locations) of large transnational corporations when they have a large variety of plants, often producing a wide range of products in a considerable number of different countries. Fourth, Löschian theory is, to an extent, irrelevant to the locational considerations of public-sector firms where profit-maximization might have to take second-place to social costs and benefits. It might also be of little importance to 'satisficers' – firms that are content to operate in suboptimal locations and make adequate profits in the long-term rather than attempt to maximize profits at all times. Finally, profit-maximizing theory ignores behaviourial factors, such as an industrialist's desire to locate in a socially-attractive city, or in a leisurely rural or coastal environment rather than in an area chosen as a result of a rigorous consideration of cost and revenue variables.

Towards the end of the twentieth century, and particularly in advanced capitalist countries, it was becoming clear that technological progress had reduced the importance of transport costs and resource-input considerations in location decision-making. Instead firms and industries – in an attempt to optimize location – were focusing increasingly on an amalgam of market potential, agglomeration economies, labour factors, resource and energy inputs, communication and transport infrastructure, taxation and government incentives, and the physical and social environment, and they increasingly recognized that globalization often meant that the optimal location for some or all of their activities would be in a different country or continent from the current location of their head office (see Ball *et al.*, 1998). At a domestic level, optimum locations for many operations have shifted geographically from the traditional manufacturing areas and older metropolitan areas to peripheral regions, for example, in the United States from the 'rustbelt' of the North-East to the South and West (Martin and Rowthorn, 1986; Dicken, 1992), or away from the North and North-West and inner cities of England to the M3/M4 and M11 motorway corridors of the South-East, South-West and East Anglia (Balchin, 1990).

BOX 5.1: INDUSTRIAL LOCATION AND INTER-REGIONAL POLICY IN GREAT BRITAIN

From the 1930s to the late-1970s, regional policy in Great Britain was based on three premises: that the problem of economic depression in parts of the north and west was due to localized deficiencies in demand associated with the collapse of basic and staple industries; that intervention was necessary on social grounds to reduce regional imbalances in employment opportunities, and on economic grounds to utilize unemployed labour and thus facilitate a

continued

higher rate of non-inflationary growth; and that it was necessary – through a 'carrot and stick' policy of incentives and controls – to attract industry away from growth regions with low unemployment to areas of high unemployment (Martin and Tyler, 1992).

Following the designation of a small number of Special Areas in the 1930s in areas of high unemployment, the old industrial districts of West Cumberland, the North-East, South Wales and Central Scotland were redesignated and extended as Development Areas under the Distribution of Industries Act 1945, and by the mid-1960s, even larger areas of high unemployment – containing 17 per cent of the working population of Britain – were designated as Assisted Areas of one form or another. In 1966, the whole of the Northern Region, Merseyside, the South-West, large parts of Wales and all of Scotland were thus designated as Development Areas (or Special Development Areas where there were particularly high levels of unemployment), and from 1973 to 1982 the boundaries of the Assisted Areas expanded with the inclusion of new Intermediate Areas – the Assisted Areas, as a whole, now containing about 50 per cent of Britain's working population (Martin and Tyler, 1992).

In the post-war years, industrial development certificate (IDC) controls – restricting new factory building in the South-East and the Midlands – were accompanied by government advanced factories and the reclamation of derelict land in the Development Areas. In the 1960s to 1970s, further policy instruments were introduced, such as the regional development grant (RDG), the regional employment premium (available from the mid-1960s to the mid-1970s) and regional selective assistance (RSA).

However, in the 1980s, the economic case for inter-regional policy was rejected by a Conservative right-of-centre government both in an attempt to reduce public expenditure (as a counter-inflationary measure) and in the ideological belief that a free market economy was more likely to stimulate growth than a planned economy. The White Paper *Regional Industrial Development* (Department of Trade and Industry, 1983) thus articulated the view that the case for continuing with regional policy was 'principally a social one with the aim of reducing, on a stable long-term basis, regional imbalances in employment opportunities' (para. 16). Wedded, however, to the neo-liberal view that too much government intervention and a lack of enterprise were largely responsible for the predicament of the depressed regions, the government was already embarked upon a policy of rolling back the map of Assisted Areas and attempting to alleviate supply-side weaknesses. From 1979 to 1982, Assisted Area coverage was reduced from 44 to 26 per cent of Britain's working population, and in 1984, with the aim of simplifying regional policy and making it more selective, the government abolished the Special Development Areas, and tightened the boundaries of the Development Areas in order that they would contain only 15 per cent of the working population – largely concentrated in the older conurbations, though the Intermediate Areas were expanded to cover approximately 20 per cent of the working population. In 1993, there were further revisions to the Assisted

Areas map, but population coverage fell only slightly from 35 to 34 per cent. In addition to reducing the size of areas eligible for assistance, IDC controls were discontinued (as early as 1982) to remove any disincentive to develop in the South-East and the Midlands, while demand-side subsidies were increasingly reduced or discontinued. RDGs were lowered from 20 per cent to a uniform rate of 15 per cent in the Development Areas, with a cost limit of £10,000 for each new job created, or alternatively firms could claim employment grants of £3,000 per job. In 1988, RDGs were completely abolished, with regional aid being confined to the construction of government advanced factories, and the provision of small regional selective grants (RSAs), regional enterprise grants (REGs) and regionally-differentiated business consultancy initiatives targeted at small firms.

In the early 1990s, the same right-of-centre government saw the need for a reinforced regional level of public administration. It consequently established nine 'integrated regional offices' (IROs) in England to co-ordinate the activities of government departments at a regional level. The principal function of each office was to handle bids for assistance from a new single regeneration budget (SRB) and from the EU Structural Fund.

Following the establishment of a Labour government, the degree of intervention over industrial location – to an extent – increased. The Regional Development Agencies Act 1998 established development agencies in each of the nine English regions and in Greater London – bodies similar to the Scottish Development Agency and Welsh Development Agency created (by an earlier Labour government) in 1976 in order to promote inward investment, help small businesses and co-ordinate regional economic development. In 1999, it was announced that while boundary changes to the Asssisted Areas would (from the following year) cover only 29 per cent of the population – a fifth less than the previous system – firms in Tier 1 areas (South Yorkshire, Merseyside, West and South Wales, and Cornwall) would be eligible for 40 per cent investment grants, while firms in Tier 2 areas (comprising much of Scotland, the North-East, and parts of West Cumberland, the North-West, the West and East Midlands, and much of the Kent coastline and Isle of Wight) would be eligible for 20 per cent grants. These would be paid from an allocation of £785 million over three years, through the medium of the SRB. Since the Tier 1 areas have per capita GDPs less than 75 per cent of the EU average, they would also be eligible for a large part of the £2.6 billion of structural funds allocated to the UK for the period 2000–2006, while Tier 2 areas would be eligible for a smaller share. It was also announced by government in 1999 that a Regional Venture Capital Fund would be established to attract new businesses away from the overheated South-East to the peripheral regions of Britain by enabling the marriage of state assistance and private investment. However, despite these cash injections, some forecasters warned that the 'North–South divide' was more likely to widen rather than narrow in the long term.

Optimum locations have also shifted in response to the transition from 'Fordist' to 'Post-Fordist' production technologies. Whereas the former technology was concerned at all stages of production with the manufacture of a standardized product over long runs, and required large-scale factory space – normally on a single site – and access to an abundant supply of semi-skilled labour, the latter technology is characterized by the breakdown of vertical integration, out-sourcing, flexible specialization, the utilization of smaller-scale manufacturing plant – often on several sites – and the employment of mainly skilled labour. Thus, although most manufacturing industry in the advanced capitalist world still remains within traditional urban areas, there has been increasingly a marked urban–suburban or urban–rural shift in location and employment, and in some areas, such as the Veneto region of Italy or in Baden-Württemberg in Germany, new industries and high-tech processes have encouraged the growth of new urban areas (Piore and Sabel, 1984).

BOX 5.2: INDUSTRIAL LOCATION AND INTER-REGIONAL POLICY IN EAST CENTRAL EUROPE

In socialist East Central Europe in the post-war period, national economic planning involved the allocation of investment funds to new industries in an attempt to generate agglomeration economies and create a spatially balanced distribution of productive capacity. New industrial plants were located in newly-established industrial towns, in single-company towns and in existing industrial centres (Balchin *et al.*, 1999).

With the adoption of the free market, post-1989, many areas of industrial development nurtured under socialism were disadvantaged by private investment being attracted to other, more profitable, locations in the region. Economic disparities increased with the decline in traditional industrial regions, and foreign direct investment (FDI) was targeted at capital cities, western border regions and selected regional centres (Balchin *et al.*, 1999). Although socialist institutions collapsed 'overnight', new planning machinery was developed only very slowly and with a great deal of uncertainty and sometimes confusion.

Within the region, the concept of regional balance was pursued more actively by former Czechoslovakia than by any other state. In the post-war years, the government aimed to industrialize Slovakia through the direction of new investment to the province and by the relocation of factories from the western frontier zone, and also to generate industrial development in the economically weak areas of southern Bohemia by a further flow of investment (Balchin *et al.*, 1999). Throughout the 1950s and 1960s, the industrialization of Slovakia – situated in the middle of the COMECON

continued

countries and away from the eastern borders of NATO – remained a priority, together with the concentration of new investment in heavy industries in existing centres (Pavlínek, 1992). However, since the mid-1950s, the older industrial regions of North Bohemia and North Moravia were preferred to the less-developed areas in the distribution of investment funds (Balchin *et al.*, 1999). Reforms of policy in the late-1960s brought forth selectivity in the regional distribution of investment grants and increased depreciation allowances, and by the early-1970s the strengthening of the centrally organized system of resource distribution led to the border zone and selected industrial districts being prioritized in respect of investment and the allocation of grants (Blažek and Kára, 1992). The implementation of a new system of regional planning – aimed at achieving a spatially rational and equal distribution of resources and a more effective use of factors of production – was hindered by political change in 1989.

The consequential adoption of the market system immediately led to an increase in regional economic disparities (Blažek, 1996), both between the Czech and the Slovak parts of the former federal state and in the new Czech Republic after 1982. Unemployment in the Czech Republic escalated to over 10 per cent in some of the older industrial regions and backward areas in the second-half of the 1990s, while entrepreneurship developed apace in the western part of the country and FDI was increasingly attracted to Prague and other selected cities and towns of the republic including some in the western border zone (Balchin *et al.*, 1999).

As in much of Western Europe in the 1990s, it was soon recognized that market-induced regional disparities in the Czech Republic needed to be contained or reversed – if only for social or political reasons. In 1991, it was declared that regional policy – along with general economic and social policy – would aim to reduce disparities in the working and living conditions of the population of all regions of the Czech Republic (Blažek and Kára, 1992). To this end, private enterprises – in regions adversely affected by structural change, in backward frontier regions and in regions with neglected infrastructure – were eligible for two-year tax holidays, grants for infrastructural improvement and support for employment generation (Kára, 1994). However, support was limited to small and medium-sized enterprises (SMEs) in areas defined annually according to unemployment rates, but which in total normally contained 20–25 per cent of the population of the republic. Further assistance was provided by means of loans and interest subsidies from the Czech and Moravian Guarantee and Development Bank.

The European Commission has also been important in industrial restructuring in the Czech Republic. In Ostrava and Northern Bohemia, for example, PHARE sponsored a regional development programme and also co-financed the establishment of regional development agencies in these areas, and clearly the commission will play a more important role in industrial restructuring when the Czech Republic becomes a member of the EU and hence eligible for Structural Funds.

A consideration of agglomeration economies is becoming more rather than less important in location decision-making. With smaller size, firms are unable to internalize specialist services and must locate in close proximity to those services, while demand uncertainties necessitate maximum access to the market to ensure that it can respond to financial markets, product innovation and customer demand. There is also a tendency towards a spatial division of labour (Massey, 1984), for example, head offices, and research and development activities tend to be located in the centres of agglomerations to gain full access to skilled labour markets, while production plant and 'back office functions' are located on the edge to benefit from lower land and labour costs (Ball *et al.*, 1998).

Within an urban context, the most recent trend in industrial location in advanced capitalist countries has been the urban–rural shift in manufacturing employment. This – according to Keeble (1987) – can be explained by any one of the following theories.

First, the constrained location theory postulates that since site dimensions affect both *in situ* changes (expansions and contractions) and unit turnovers (openings and closures), cramped sites inevitably account for a high rate of loss from both contractions and closures, especially in Inner London and the inner cities of the North (Dennis, 1981; Fothergill and Gudgin, 1982). Manufacturers, moreover, are unable or unwilling to match the rents paid by competing land users (such as office firms, retailers and warehouse operators) to secure the space necessary for survival in the inner city. It is notable that in periods of relatively fast economic growth (for example, 1967–75, and 1986–89) the decentralization of manufacturing was most marked, while in times of recession the pace of decentralization was much slower (such as in the periods 1976–83 and 1990–93) – the degree of competition for urban sites and the attraction of alternative locations being greater at a time of growth than at a time of recession.

Second, the production cost explanation suggests that higher operation costs in urban areas (directly – the higher cost of land and labour, and indirectly – the cost of congestion and inconvenience) have adverse effects on profitability investment, competition and employment, particularly *vis-à-vis* small firms (Lever, 1982; Moore *et al.*, 1984; Wood, 1987). Such firms would need to decentralize or risk closure.

Third, the capital restructuring theory maintains that in order to apply new techniques and to counter competition, large multiplant and often multinational corporations shift their operations from cities to rural areas to exploit less skilled, less unionized and less costly labour (Massey and Meegan, 1978).

Of these three explanations, the first might be considered to be the most credible, while the second approach is still subject to research. The third explanation is sometimes criticized on the grounds that spatial differences in union strength and labour costs are too small to be significant attractions *per se*.

Two further reasons could be offered to explain the decentralization of manufacturing industry. First, the out-migration of population (especially the professional, managerial and skilled manual classes) has been an important factor in attracting decentralized employment; and, second, planning policies played a major part in the decentralization of employment, particularly from London. Through the medium of new towns, expanded towns, industrial development certificates and office development permits, 'the coordinated decentralization of population and employment from London [became] . . . a central element in strategic planning for the South East in the first thirty years or so after the war' (Buck *et al.*, 1986). However, most decentralization has been independent of public policy and almost certainly would have occurred in the complete absence of regional planning.

Industrial inertia nevertheless exists. Some firms may have a traditional preference for central sites, or economies of agglomeration may compensate for the internal diseconomies of cramped sites and often obsolete and multistorey factory premises. Once a firm is located in a particular place it may eventually find difficulty in disposing of its old factory building, it might be reluctant to establish additional space elsewhere because of technical difficulties of splitting production, and it may be unwilling to incur the disruption of a move.

BOX 5.3: THE LOCATION OF INDUSTRY IN NEWLY-INDUSTRIALIZING AND DEVELOPING COUNTRIES

In the post-colonial era, most developing countries believed that the cure for underdevelopment was industrialization. Soon after independence, and in embryonic market locations, industrialization took the form of import-substitution, particularly with regard to the manufacture of textiles and clothing, and the processing of food, drink and tobacco. Very few developing countries industrialized beyond this – lacking resources to develop heavy industries such as steel, chemicals and petrochemicals (Dickenson *et al.*, 1996; Potter and Lloyd-Evans, 1998). Worldwide, these industries were increasingly market-oriented, but effective demand in the poorer areas of the world militated against development – India being a notable exception (Potter and Lloyd-Evans, 1998). Since the 1960s, many developing countries have industrialized by 'invitation', using fiscal incentives to encourage foreign firms to establish branch plants and to subsequently export manufactured goods back to the developed world. To facilitate this process, free trade zones (FTZs) and export

continued

processing zones (EPZs) were set up in many developing countries to exempt firms from duties and taxes, and some aspects of labour legislation (see Potter and Lloyd-Evans, 1998). Ports were often selected as locations for EPZs, notably in India, Taiwan, the Philippines and the Dominican Republic. By 1985, a total of 173 EPZs had been established around the world, employing nearly 2 milion workers (Hewitt *et al.*, 1992). However, while some developing countries approached or reached the stage of economic 'take-off' (i.e. the newly-industrializing countries) and increased their share of world industrial production, other developing countries experienced a decline in their share – creating a 'global shift' in economic activity (Dicken, 1992).

Latin America became a continent of newly-industrializing countries before any other developing region. Manufacturing output increased its share of GDP from 14 per cent in 1930 to 25 per cent in 1980, while, in the same period, manufactured imports fell from 20 to 15 per cent of the GDP (HABITAT, 1996). As was common in the developing world, industrialization was initially concerned with import-substitution, but in the recession of the 1980s and with reductions in domestic demand, many countries in Latin America attempted to develop export industries – with locational implications. In Mexico, for example, there was a shift from one market-oriented location to another as 250,000 jobs were lost and 6,000 firms were closed down in the capital (the country's dominant location for import-substituting industries), while in cities close to the United States' border there was a considerable growth in employment in export industries. There was also a shift throughout the continent of industrial development from national capitals to EPZs (HABITAT, 1996).

Apart from exporting a wide range of products to the rest of the world, the cities of Asia Pacific are also major markets for manufactured and processed goods – containing 32 of the world's largest urban centres in 1990. From as early as 1945, India achieved a high level of self-sufficiency in heavy industrial products – enabling the republic to become the 13th largest industrial producer in the world by the 1990s, and in South East Asia, injections of large flows of foreign investment enabled Singapore, Seoul, Kuala Lumpur, Taipei and Bangkok to become important industrial locations during the latter decades of the twentieth century. In Hong Kong, however, an emphasis on trade and financial services masked the failure – in the face of competition from Singapore and Taipei – to generate skills in developing IT and multimedia applications or in manufacturing silicon wafers, notwithstanding plans to develop mega-projects such as the Cyberport and Silicon Harbour. It is of concern that, in Hong Kong, only 0.2 per cent of the GDP was spent on research and development in 1995, compared with 1.2 per cent in Singapore and 1.4 per cent in Taiwan, and there were similar disparities in education expenditure.

Foreign investment also flowed into China in the late twentieth century, helping Guangzhou and the special economic zones (SEZs) of Shenzen, Shantou, Shekou, Xiamen and Hainan – with their seaport facilities – to become important locations for industrial development. In the early-1990s,

Shanghai – as one of China's 14 'open cities' – witnessed the introduction of a major programme of industrial and infrastructure development involving the creation of a high-tech metropolis on the estuarine land to the east of the city, referred to as Pudong – a development which will also compete with Hong Kong.

In Africa, import-substituting industries tend to be located in the major cities to gain maximum access to local markets, and in expectation that industrial development will trickle down to smaller urban areas. In Nigeria, for example, planning strategies since 1946 have tended to be 'top-down' and, as a result, by the early-1990s the country's 12 major cities contained 77 per cent of all industrial establishments and 87 per cent of total industrial employment; 76 per cent of total manufacturing employment was found along the coast in densely populated areas; and the capital – Lagos – contained 38 per cent of the country's industrial plants and 49 per cent of all industrial employment (Potter, 1992). Overall, there was very little or no trickle-down effects of industrial development to inland locations. The principal export commodity – oil – accounted for 90 per cent of total exports by 1982 (Potter, 1992), but refining tended to be market-oriented, and overwhelmingly in the developed world.

RETAIL LOCATION

Retail efficiency is highly dependent upon location, and within a location highly dependent upon site. Within short distances one site may be very superior to another. Often the selection of the right location and the right site means the difference between business success and failure. The willingness of retailers to pay rent to occupy a site, and the number of shops that can locate profitably in an urban area, are limited and dependent upon potential sales revenue, the degree of competition among retailers for a portion of that revenue, the availability of space for retail use, and planning rules and regulations. Retailers often recognize that they are unable to target the whole of a mass market, and instead respond to variations in the social class, age and lifestyle of consumers (*market segmentation*); and also undertake *niche-marketing* in an attempt to satisfy the very specialized needs of relatively high-income, credit-worthy and closely-defined groups of consumers (Carr, 1987).

Retail location theory is concerned with both the consumer's choice of store and the retailer's store-location decision. To an extent, Christaller's central place theory (see page 48) provides an explanation of how consumers decide where to shop and what sort of products to purchase. It suggests that whereas consumers would be willing to travel long distances to purchase expensive products at an upper-rank urban centre, they would travel only short distances to a lower-rank centre to purchase inexpensive products. The theory's weakness is that it is based on the assumption that consumers make only single-purpose shopping trips to the nearest centre supplying the product, but do not undertake multi-purpose trips to, for example, distant upper-rank centres to purchase an array of higher-order and lower-order goods, and thereby reduce total shopping travel costs.

In a development of the central place theory, Berry and Garrison (1958) suggested that the store-location decisions are influenced by the concepts of *range* and *threshold*. The range of a good or service is the maximum distance over which consumers are prepared to travel to obtain that product. Whereas low price, convenience and perishable goods have a short range and are purchased relatively frequently, more valuable goods have a long range and have a lower frequency of purchase. The threshold is the minimum amount of purchasing power necessary to ensure the profitability of the retailer and thereby support the supply of a good or service from a central place. The range of a product is limited at the upper level by the degree of competition from other central places supplying the same product, and at the lower level by the threshold necessary to permit it to function. As more specialized products require a larger threshold they usually need a more extensive range, therefore it is logical for an urban hierarchy to evolve based on the degree of specialization of central places and for hexagonal trade areas to emerge.

A principal weakness of central place theory is that it fails to consider how two neighbouring shopping centres of different sizes compete with each other, and the power of a new shopping centre to attract customers from a rival centre. Reilly's (1929) 'law of retail gravitation' suggests that a city attracts trade from a town in its hinterland in proportion to the size of the city and inversely to the square of the distance between a city x and town y. Accordingly:

$$Tx = \frac{Px}{d(xy)^2}$$

where Tx = the trade pull of the city;
         Px = the city's population;
         $d(xy)$ = the distance between the city and town.

Where there are two competing centres, the market area boundary between them would be determined where the relative pull of the two centres is equal. Clearly, if there is a small city with a population of Px and a larger city with a population of Pz, there would be some point between them where a consumer would be indifferent whether he or she shopped in Px or Pz. According to Reilly's law, the location of such a point is determined by the formula:

$$d = \frac{d(xz)}{\left[1 + \sqrt{\left(\dfrac{Px}{Pz}\right)}\right]}$$

where d = the point of consumer indifference;
  $d(xz)$ = the distance between the two cities;
  Px = the population of city x;
  Pz = the population of city z.

Thus, if city x has a population of 500,000 and city z has a population of 1 million and the distance between them is 240 km, then the point of consumer indifference will be:

$$\frac{240}{\left[1 + \sqrt{\left(\dfrac{500,000}{1,000,000}\right)}\right]}$$

or around 140 km from city z.

Clearly, the size of the population *per se* is an inadequate indication of a city's consumer demand. Consideration must also be given to its composition (age and sex structure; occupational and income distribution); purchasing power and consumer preferences; and some allowance must be made for future population change. Demand might also be influenced by the quantity and accessibility of retail floorspace, the mix of retail outlets and non-retail factors, and by advertising. Also, there may be many competing centres and many overlapping catchment areas in a state of flux, and thus the task of identifying boundaries becomes more complex.

A further problem arises in establishing a credible theory of retail location. Empirical evidence suggests that clusters of homogeneous and heterogeneous shops have emerged in the same locations – the former consisting of similar shops and the latter containing different types of retail outlets. In an attempt to maximize sales turnovers, and as a response to consumer-uncertainty and fairly infrequent buying, homogeneous retailers specializing in, for example, clothing, footwear and jewellery cluster together to enable consumers to compare product-differentiated goods and to benefit from price competition between adjacent outlets. Heterogeneous clustering, however, is a response to multi-purpose shopping trips and thus enables consumers to benefit from reduced travel costs. Small retailers gain external benefits from the drawing power of upper-order stores, while in planned shopping centres, 'anchor' stores (i.e. department stores and prestige retailers) normally produce a general increase in sales turnovers.

Models of the location of retail property normally focus on the relationship between the type of shop, the frequency at which consumers purchase goods, the level of their spending in relation to their incomes, sales turnovers and retail rents. A hierarchy of shops thus emerges which – from lower to upper orders – comprises convenience shops; shopping shops; speciality shops; and department and multiple stores.

RETAIL LOCATION AND DEVELOPMENT IN THE UNITED KINGDOM

Convenience shops

Customers purchase goods from these shops fairly regularly at short intervals, spending only a very small proportion of their net weekly incomes. Although retail turnovers and rents per m^2 are low, convenience shops are viable with only a small catchment area, a low consumer purchasing power and a small floorspace – say less than 280 m^2. Newsagents, tobacconists and confectioners, grocers, bakers and greengrocers are examples of shops in this category.

Over the past two decades, convenience shops have been unable generally to withstand competition from larger retailers; for example, the number of independent grocer shops in the United Kingdom fell from over 56,000 in 1971 to less than 40,000 in 1991 and their share of grocery turnover nationally plummeted from 42 to under 20 per cent. There has, however, been a renewed interest in the development of local convenience retailing (Jones, 1986). Small shops are proving viable if they remain open up to ten (or more) hours a day, seven days a week, are located close to the focal point of residential areas (particularly in the outer suburbs of Greater London and elsewhere in high-income areas of the South-East) and cater particularly for pedestrian and impulse shoppers. Development (and refurbishment) has recently been undertaken by specialist companies (for example, Cullens and Misselbrook & Weston), voluntary groups (such as Spar and Mace), the Co-operative Wholesale Society and petrol stations (notably those operated by BP) – rather than by independent traders. It is anticipated that up to 6,000 convenience stores of this type will be trading by the mid-1990s.

Shopping shops

Goods are purchased from these shops less regularly and at longer intervals, with shoppers spending a higher proportion of their net weekly incomes. Turnovers and rents per m^2 will be higher than in the case of convenience shops, but larger catchment areas and a greater purchasing power will be necessary. Examples of shops in this category include clothes shops, ironmongers, hairdressers and some soft furnishing stores.

Speciality shops

Customers buy goods at very irregular and lengthy intervals and may spend a multiple of their net weekly incomes. The turnover and rent per m^2 of this category of shop can be very high and profitability may be dependent upon a very large catchment area and a high purchasing power. Jewellers, furriers and furniture, antique and musical instrument shops fall into this category of retailing.

Department and multiple stores

In one building a department store will be concerned with convenience, shopping and speciality activity. Increasingly key traders (Marks & Spencer, Boots, W.H. Smith and Woolworth) are extending their range of merchandise and assuming many of the functions of department stores.

Service shops

These shops are often workshops and sometimes partly wholesale premises. Turnovers and rents per m^2 are usually small. Even though customers may spend a multiple of their net weekly incomes, they do so at very irregular intervals thus making a service shop dependent upon a large catchment area with a high purchasing power. Examples of shops of this type include furniture renovators and retread tyre dealers.

This classification of shops can be incorporated into the hierarchy of shopping centres, the structure of the hierarchy being as follows.

The central shopping area

This coincides approximately with the central business district except where there is exclusively office use. Generally shops co-locate with offices. Office employees are often the principal customers, and retailers may specialize in supplying offices with stationery, machinery, fittings and furniture. Moreover, as shops very rarely utilize space above the ground floor (except in the case of department and multiple stores), office use at higher levels ensures that valuable sites can be developed to their maximum.

Some large cities may have more than one central shopping area. It may be linear or nuclear in form. Except for service shops, all the other categories of retailing are well represented. Department stores and key traders may locate solely in the central shopping area because of this area having the maximum accessibility to the largest catchment area and greatest purchasing power. Customers may be attracted from all regions of the country and from abroad.

Within the central shopping area the relationship between retail turnovers and rents per m^2 is particularly pronounced. There is little inertia and, with the exception of the major retailers, shops are continually changing use as increasing demand raises rent levels. The 'turnover–rent gradient' may slope steeply or gradually away from the key or '100 per cent' sites, but in general as distance from the key sites increases, shops change in use from being department or multiple stores to women's clothing, jewellery, furniture and grocery shops. Corner sites are especially favoured where window display is important, for example in the case of footwear and menswear (figure 5.11). Throughout the central shopping area turnovers and rents are usually higher on the side of the street which receives the most sunshine, this being the northern (south-facing) side in the northern hemisphere.

With the redevelopment of bombed city centres after the Second World War, the central shopping area became increasingly important in the 1950s and 1960s, mainly because of the economies of scale associated with the growth of multiple stores, the wider range and larger stocks of goods that can be carried when turnovers are high, the rise in rents forcing out small

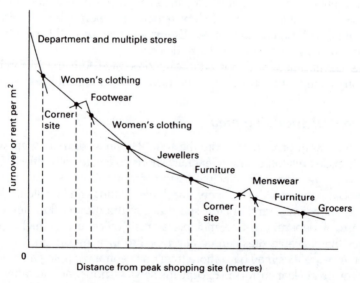

Figure 5.11 *Hypothetical turnover or rent gradient within a major shopping centre*

independent retailers, and the effective end of resale price maintenance after the Resale Prices Act 1964. In the 1970s planning authorities continued to concentrate new retail investments in city centres rather than on the periphery. Either in the form of large regional shopping centres of more than $40,000\,m^2$, or smaller centres of $5,000–40,000\,m^2$, these developments could blight not only other shops within the same city if central positions suddenly became off-centre locations but also other shopping centres in the regional or sub-regional hierarchy. By the 1980s, however, the average size of town centre schemes was decreasing and was significantly less than that of out-of-town development. In 1986, the *average* floorspace of town centre schemes under construction, with planning consent and proposed, ranged from only $11,600\,m^2$ to $13,200\,m^2$, whereas the average floorspace of out-of-town shopping centres at all stages of development ranged from $22,500\,m^2$ to $40,700\,m^2$.

Central shopping areas are currently posing considerable problems for investors and retailers. The purpose-built centre – first developed in the 1960s to consolidate urban shopping – is in danger of being forsaken by the major national retailers who increasingly favour decentralized locations. Institutional investors in town-centre shops, experiencing a decline in the value of their investments, are thus attempting to redesign, remodel and refurbish their properties to raise standards to those demanded by major retailers and their customers – an important objective being to secure the location of 'anchor tenants' such as the John Lewis Partnership and Marks & Spencer.

Anchor tenants and other national multiples undertake or commission increasingly sophisticated market research in determining retail location. *Local expenditure zone analyses* (defining consumer expenditure and preference within a system of non-overlapping retail zones), *geodemographic analyses* (classifying neighbourhoods by socio-economic indicators) and *isochronic maps* (showing access to shopping centres in terms of time rather than distance) are each used in this process (Hillier Parker, 1993).

City-centre investment is usually at the expense of small independent shops which cannot compete effectively with the multiples for trade or sites. The decline of shop numbers in the United Kingdom from 542,000 in 1960 to about 350,000 in 1991 indicates the vulnerability of the small shop. In view of the fact that most major shopping development schemes are undertaken by a partnership of a local authority and a property company, it is remarkable how little the proposals are subject to public scrutiny. The United Kingdom is, however, still overprovided with retail space, though much of it is in the wrong place. It is clear that the traditional high street has become increasingly obsolescent and unappealing because of a confusion of architectural styles, the inappropriate floorspace and layout of shops,

Table 5.2 The largest town-centre and out-of-town shopping schemes, Great Britain, 1992

Location	Town	Scheme	Floorspace (m^2)
Town centre	Manchester	Arndale Centre	128,000
	Milton Keynes	Central Milton Keynes	114,000
	Newcastle upon Tyne	Eldon Square	84,000
	Redditch	Kingfisher Centre	83,960
	Telford	Telford Shopping Centre	83,420
Out-of-town	Dudley	Merry Hill Centre	192,670
	Gateshead	Metrocentre	175,800
	Thurrock	Lakeside	123,800
	Sheffield	Meadowhall	118,400
	Hendon	Brent Cross	81,806

Source: Hillier Parker. *British Shopping Centre Development Master List,* 1993.

and the problems of traffic congestion, parking and shelter. It has been suggested that national multiples may soon no longer be satisfied with their town-centre shops – redesigned and refurbished every two to three years – and instead employ, once and for all, the easier option – decentralization (Carr, 1987). It is important, however, not to exaggerate the scale of the problem. Of the 748 shopping centres in excess of 4,645 m^2 (50,000 ft^2) developed between 1965 and 1992, 682 were located in town centres and only 66 centres (excluding retail warehouses) were located out of town, respectively accounting for a total of 10.2 million m^2 and 1.3 million m^2 (Cheeseright, 1987a, 1987b). The larger town-centre schemes, moreover, are broadly comparable in size to the out-of-town centres (table 5.2) indicating that, in terms of scale, they are similarly viable.

Ribbon shopping

This extends along the main radial roads towards or beyond the suburban shopping centres. There will be the greatest concentration of shops in the direction of the most densely populated or highest-income areas. Generally, department and multiple stores are absent and the only speciality retailers are motor traders – convenience and shopping shops predominate. From central areas outwards, accessibility, turnovers and rents diminish, although gradients are not smooth and small peaks occur near suburban centres.

Ribbon shopping development is faced with numerous problems. The distribution of shops may be overextended for convenient shopping, motorists may face parking restrictions, there may be no recognizable shopping centre (though key traders may be located in 'hot spots'), traffic or even physical barriers might divide shopping frontages, and there may be many redundant shops occupied by non-retail uses.

Suburban centres

These are usually of recent growth, although their origins may be old, in some cases dating from medieval times. The larger suburban centres may be part of an outlying business district with shops relating to offices in the same way as in the central business district. There are signs of substantial expansion where access to the central shopping area is poor, and where the suburban population and its purchasing power are high. In many cases car parking and servicing facilities are comparatively good. The same types of shop as are found in the central shopping area will be located in the suburban centre, although turnovers and rents per m^2 will not be as high.

Neighbourhood centres

These will either be in the form of small parades of shops or small shopping precincts dependent on a restricted catchment area and a fairly low purchasing power. Turnovers and rents per m^2 are relatively low. Convenience shops will be profitable, though shopping or speciality shops will be less viable. Yet even in neighbourhood centres, compound trading is ousting the small independent retailer.

Local corner shops

Though tending to disappear, the corner shop will remain if it can truly retain its convenience function. The catchment area is small and the required purchasing power is very low. In consequence, turnovers and rents per m^2 are also very low.

Decentralized shopping centres

In recent years, the applicability of central place theory has been severely weakened. With increased suburbanization, car ownership, traffic congestion and the difficulties and expense of car parking, the dominance of the CBD has been reduced. Simultaneously, the attraction of out-of-town shopping has increased. Greater accessibility, comparatively low-rent land, ample space for retail development and car parking, the demands for one-stop shopping, the extensive use of refrigerators and freezers reducing the need for frequent shopping trips to ensure fresh produce, and the absence of prohibited planning regulations in many countries have enabled out-of-town retailers to compete very successfully with their city-centre counterparts.

These consist of the activities of most types of shops – convenience, shopping, speciality – perhaps in a number of different buildings under different leases, and possibly with one retailer dominating; alternatively, the activities may be concentrated in one building operated by one firm. Out-of-town shopping centres were first developed in the United States – where there were 2,000 centres in 1956 (increasing to 28,500 by 1985) – but in recent years decentralized shopping has expanded in Europe, especially in France and the former West Germany, but less so in the United Kingdom.

Increased congestion and reduced accessibility have rendered retailing less and less profitable in the central areas of many cities in the United States, motivating the development of shopping centres in out-of-town locations. In Europe it is improbable that central shopping areas have reached the same level of congestion and subsequent decline, yet the viability of decentralized centres and stores has been recognized in spite of the continuing (and often increasing) profitability of central area locations.

There are six types of decentralized shopping facility:

(1) Out-of-town shopping centres – complexes of shops dominated by department stores with catchment areas of at least 250,000 people. In the United Kingdom by 1980, despite a number of applications, only the Brent Cross development had been permitted – a centre of $71,257\,m^2$. (It is often argued, however, that Brent Cross is not an out-of-town development at all, but rather a strategic suburban shopping centre.) Similar restrictions were placed on developments of this scale in France and the former West Germany. By 1986 only the Metro-centre in Gateshead had been added to the list of major out-of-town developments, but by 1992 a number of large-scale developments had been completed, notably Meadowhall in Sheffield, Merry Hill in Dudley and Lakeside in Thurrock (see table 5.2). Many other major out-of-town schemes proposed during the consumer boom of the late 1980s were shelved during the recession of the early 1990s or failed to obtain planning permission, but in 1999 a major scheme of $150,000\,m^2$ was opened at Bluewater Park in north-west Kent.

(2) Edge-of-town centres – complexes of shops dominated by supermarkets or variety stores with catchment areas up to 100,000 people. Planning permission has been more readily forthcoming than in the case of out-of-town centres.

(3) District shopping centres – smaller complexes of shops dominated by convenience trades, with catchment areas rarely in excess of 10,000 people.

(4) Hypermarkets – large free-standing stores of up to $23,000\,m^2$ combining food trades with the sale of a variety of cheaper household goods. They may contain banks, restaurants, hairdressers and other service trades. Although hypermarkets have proliferated in France (which had over 1000 in 1993) and in Germany, only a small number have been permitted in Britain (for example in Caerphilly, Eastleigh, Irlam, Telford and Merton).

(5) Superstores – also large, free-standing stores but with up to only $10,000\,m^2$ of floor area. Similar to giant supermarkets, they concentrate on food and household goods. In contrast to hypermarkets, a large number of superstores have been developed in the United Kingdom in recent years, often as nuclei of redeveloped town shopping centres or on inner city sites. Retailers such as the Argyll Group (Safeway), Asda, Sainsbury and Tesco have been notable in this field, and the number of superstores has increased (almost to the point of saturation in the major urban areas) from about 200 in 1980 to over 800 in 1993 – taking nearly 60 per cent of the retail food market. The growth in the number of superstores has been particularly rapid in London. Whereas in 1980 there were only 5 superstores in the capital, by 1993 the number had increased to 49, each in excess of $2,500\,m^2$. Since every store provides about 350 new full-time and part-time jobs, local authorities have been reluctant to withhold planning permission, despite protests from small shopkeepers. Outside urban areas, however, applications for planning approval have often been rejected (largely on environmental grounds, not least within the green belt), although as many as 50 per cent of superstore appeals have been successful – compared with an average success rate of appeal of only 35 per cent.

(6) Retail warehouses – are normally large, single-storey buildings of up to $6,500\,m^2$ (although there are plans for units of over $9,000\,m^2$). There have been three stages in their development since the early 1970s. *First generation* units were relatively small converted warehouse buildings (rarely in excess of $2,300\,m^2$), often located in industrial estates, and mainly concerned with DIY, carpets and furniture. *Second generation* units occupied prominent main road locations and provided adequate car parking. *Third generation* development consisted of retail parks – planned and purpose-built sites for clusters of warehouse 'shops' with scale economies such as shared car parking and advertising. Since the 1970s, Sainsbury, W.H. Smith and Woolworth have absorbed some of the earlier warehouse operators, and together with other national multiples (such as B&Q, Comet, Halfords and Texas) have operated from

their own purpose-built warehouses – becoming more selective in their choice of sites. A *fourth generation* of store appeared in 1993–94, the discount warehouse. Firms such as Cargo Club in Croydon and Costco at Thurrock offered customers the opportunity to buy at 'knock down prices' on bulk purchases, thereby posing a competitive threat to other decentralized shopping centres as well as to town-centre shops. It was likely that there were about 1.5 million m^2 of retail warehouse floor-space in the United Kingdom in 1993, but further growth was dependent upon a continuing increase in consumer spending, a further growth in car and home ownership, a retained interest in this sector by the major retailers, and, of course, planning consent.

Decentralized shopping development made considerable strides in the 1980s. It benefited from a consumer boom of unusual length and magnitude – starting in 1983 and continuing for at least six years (in 1987 alone, consumer spending in real terms rose by 5.8 per cent – the largest rise since 1972). There were significant reductions in direct taxation, there was large-scale credit expansion and wages rose significantly faster than inflation. Shop rents similarly increased ahead of inflation, reflecting soaring retail profitability (particularly in 1986 and 1987). Apart from a favourable macroeconomic climate, however, decentralized shopping also requires the following conditions: a high car-owning population and ideally a high proportion of families owning at least two cars; a large proportion of married women employed, making it necessary for shopping to take place mainly once a week and at one point; a high proportion of households owning deep-freezers; a highly developed ring-road system making adjacent locations as accessible to as large a catchment area and as high a purchasing power as is enjoyed in the central shopping area; the availability of large and inexpensive sites for the development of shopping facilities and spacious car parks; and the availability of finance and development expertise.

Like central shopping areas, decentralized facilities generally benefit from high accessibility, but unlike central areas, rents per m^2 are initially low. Although turnovers per m^2 may also at first be low, the very large retail floor areas result in a high level of total profitability. Consumers also benefit because internal economies of scale are passed on in relatively low prices, and lower travel costs might be incurred on shopping journeys.

But there are a number of obstacles in the way of decentralized shopping development. In Britain land values in outer urban locations may not be very much cheaper than in the central shopping area or existing suburban centres, ring roads are far less developed in Britain than in, say, the United States or the former West Germany – central areas retaining the highest level of accessibility in the urban area; two-car families still account for a very small proportion of shoppers, urban land (even on the fringe of the built-up area) is scarce and out-of-town shopping may be considered wasteful of land, especially if there are already large-scale supermarkets in suburban areas, and government policy may be opposed to the further development of out-of-town centres. Under the Town and Country Planning (Shopping Development) Direction 1986, moreover, local authorities are obliged to consult with the Secretary of State for the Environment before granting planning permission for developments in excess of $23,325\,m^2$, although in 1993 the government revised its *Planning Policy Guidance Note 6* which stressed the need for a balance between in-town and out-of-town development. Despite opposition from retailers in established shopping centres, however, there was little evidence by 1987 that decentralized retailing development had had a harmful effect on the viability of traditional shopping locations. But with the rapid opening of new out-of-town centres and superstores in the late 1980s, decentralized shopping increasingly accounted for a greatly increased share of the retail market to the detriment of retailing elsewhere. The Merry Hill centre, for example, attracted about 70 per cent of local shopping away from Dudley, its nearest town. It thus seemed that the government needed to do more to vet schemes in excess of $23,325\,m^2$.

Local authorities normally pursued a cautious approach to out-of-town proposals. Developers are often obliged to undertake *impact assessments* (IAs) in support of their planning applications, but invariably IAs show that the potential effect on town centres will be minimal. While the Secretary of State had not defined what was an acceptable impact, the 1986 Direction stated that in assessing the impact of a scheme, 'the vitality and viability of a nearby shopping centre as a whole' should be considered. The impact could, in reality, be enormous. In 1997–98, the government – in an attempt to focus on urban regeneration – imposed a virtual ban on further out-of-town shopping development.

In justifying new out-of-town proposals, developers argue that there is enough – and growing – demand to support both town-centre and out-of-town shopping provision. While research has shown that the majority of consumers have a preference for out-of-town rather than in-town shopping (McGoldrick and Thompson, 1992), this does not contradict the view that there is still an important role for town centres. Developers therefore point out that whereas out-of-town centres facilitate bulk-buying by car-borne shoppers, town centres accommodate a wide range of specialist shops and are more accessible to pedestrians – and as such are complementary rather than competitive. In historic cities, out-of-town centres can usually divert traffic away from the centre, easing congestion and parking problems, and as such could be welcomed by city-centre retailers.

Impact assessments, however, are not only very unreliable (different assessments could, for example, show a 10, 25 or 40 per cent impact on trade) but are very narrow. They do not take into account broader considerations such as the impact on the utilization of energy. It might be pertinent, for example, to question whether at a time when future supplies of cheap oil are unpredictable it is rational to develop a new kind of shopping dependent very greatly on the extensive use of the private motor car, and to bear in mind that such developments are highly regressive, in so far as the low-income consumer will probably not own a car and will be disadvantaged by a diminishing number of accessible shops.

The rise of the shopping centre

The distinction between individual shops and shopping centres is diminishing. This is because of the growth of compound trading, the tendency towards one-stop shopping and the increased use of franchises within stores. These trends have been brought about by economies of scale, changing shopping habits due to more married women being in employment, improved storage of food (by refrigeration) and the increased use of private cars. In assessing the value of a shop location it is essential to consider the centre in which it is situated. The relevance of the centre to a specific shop depends on whether the trade is receptive (that is, it receives trade from incidental or impulse shoppers) or self-generative (it attracts intending shoppers). The former group may be situated anywhere in the centre where it can tap trade, but self-generative trades are often gregarious for competitive or complementary reasons.

Shopping centres are footloose. In London, for example, the centre of shopping moved westward from St Paul's Churchyard in the seventeenth century, to the Strand in the eighteenth century, to Piccadilly and Regent Street in the early nineteenth century, and to Oxford Street by 1900. In each period the centre was the point of maximum accessibility, and as the means of transport changed there was a relocation of the transport node. As in the past, the future pattern of shopping will be determined largely by the pattern of transportation, and there is likely to be a continuation of current trends – the decline of small businesses and the falling number and increased size of shops. The pace at which this takes place will not only be dependent upon the rate of economic growth but also upon government policy concerning monopolies and consumer protection, and upon planning policy at a local and central level. Alternatively, with the increased decentralization of population, electronic shopping from home could evolve or there might be a re-emergence of the small independent shop in the small country town or village. This would reflect a changing demand and a reaction against the ever-increasing scale of both central and out-of-town shopping centres.

The recession of the early 1990s and its impact on shopping centre development

The consumer boom of the mid-1980s was characterized by falling interest rates, and a substantial increase in new construction orders and construction output in respect of retail property development. The subsequent slump was associated with a marked increase in interest rates (aimed at correcting a deteriorating balance of payments and the exchange value of the pound), and a decrease in new construction orders and construction output (table 5.3).

Although there was a squeeze of real profits and an increase in vacant shop units in the early 1990s, it soon became clear that town centres were more resilient to competition from out-of-town retailing than was previously estimated. Although edge-of-town and out-of-town shopping centres increased their share of retail spending from 4 per cent in 1980 to about 20 per cent in 1993, town-centre shops only experienced a very minor reduction in their share, from 56 to 53 per cent (Laurance, 1992). It was the relatively uncompetitive neighbourhood shop that suffered the greatest loss of trade – from 40 to 27 per cent of retail spending between 1980 and 1993.

Because of the impact of diminishing retail profits and consequential reductions in rents on new lettings, there was a general reduction in retail development. But whereas the amount of newly completed out-of-town shopping floorspace plummeted in 1991 and 1992 (the large retailers being more concerned with consolidating their position and cost-cutting than with expanding their activities out of town), the amount of newly completed town-centre floorspace, in contrast, decreased by a relatively small amount (table 5.4). The downturn in the development of out-of-town shopping centres was also much greater than the decrease in the rate of new floorspace added to retail warehouses – which (like the town centres) continued to attract developers and investors well into the recession. At the end of the recession, however, a new boom in the development of out-of-town centres – in general – failed to materialize owing to the constraints of public policy.

By the late 1990s, the retail market had recovered. In parts of the West End of London, for example, rents were as high as £5,000 per m^2 in 1999 – reflecting the renewed demand for refurbished or redeveloped properties from both transnational and UK retailers.

OFFICE LOCATION

In general the location of offices is fairly flexible, and a wide choice of locations may be appropriate – depending upon function. In the case of inter-

Table 5.3 The consumer boom and slump

	Growth in retail sales (per cent per annum)	Interest rates (per cent)[1]	Balance of payments (current account) as a percentage of GDP	£ exchange rate[2]	New construction orders (£m at 1985 prices)	Construction output (£m at 1985 prices)
1985	4.7	11.5	0.8	100	1,022	738
1986	5.3	11.0	0.0	92	1,066	938
1987	5.1	8.5	-1.0	90	1,482	1,207
1988	6.3	13.0	-3.3	96	1,664	1,255
1989	1.9	15.0	-4.0	93	1,586	1,418
1990	0.4	14.0	-3.1	91	1,078	1,313
1991	-0.7	10.5	-1.1	92	1,086	1,121
1992	0.7	7.0	-2.0	88	979	1,047

Notes: 1. Retail bank base rate, end of year.
2. Trade weighted index, average for year.

Source: Central Statistical Office: Department of the Environment.

Table 5.4 The impact of the recession of the early 1990s on the development of shopping centres in Great Britain

| | Town-centre schemes | | | Out-of-town schemes | | |
| | Annual openings | | Change in floorspace (per cent) | Annual openings | | Change in floorspace (per cent) |
	Centres	Floorspace (m²)		Centres	Floorspace (m²)	
1989	30	494,800		5	183,427	
1990	31	520,005	+5.1	55	303,542	+65.5
1991	29	538,950	+3.6	3	71,580	−76.4
1992	18	488,790	−9.3	–	21,528*	−69.9

Note: * Addition to the floorspace of existing centres.

Source: Hillier Parker, *British Shopping Centre Development Master List*, 1993.

national financial and business service firms – the command centres of an increasingly global economy – there is a tendency to locate in a relatively small number of global cities, where maximum agglomeration economies can be realized (Friedmann, 1986; Sassen, 1991; Clark, 1996); whereas the headquarters of other large firms, geared mainly to national markets, tend to cluster in major cities generally – the upper level of the domestic urban hierarchy, while offices serving regional or local markets have a more dispersed location pattern and are often located in lower levels of the urban hierarchy.

With regard to the head offices of major commercial and industrial firms, the general factors determining location are broadly the same as those influencing the location of manufacturing, for example, factor costs (such as rent and labour), transport and communication costs, agglomeration economies and revenue considerations. With regard to international offices in particular, location decision-making tends to be dominated in general by market and labour-force considerations, and specifically by the availability of suitable office space; the ease and quality of transport and communications; government attitude to new firms; language and cultural factors; the availability and quality of executive and professional staff; housing and health care for senior staff; and the overall cost of living (Dunning and Norman, 1983, 1987; see also Ball *et al.*, 1998).

The CBD, the favoured location for most head offices, provides maximum accessibility to a diverse labour market, communication technology infrastructure and market information – reflecting both 'inertia forces and the economies of agglomeration' (Ball *et al.*, 1998: 98–9), and – very importantly – face-to-face contacts, essential for the preservation of competitive advantage (Goddard, 1973; Archer, 1981).

OFFICE LOCATION AND DEVELOPMENT IN THE UNITED KINGDOM

Offices are of two kinds – those attached to factories and those which are independently sited. In the case of the former, location will be dependent upon the factors responsible for the location of factories (these will be considered later in this chapter), but in the latter, location is dependent upon general accessibility and in particular upon special accessibility to complementary firms and the offices of clients. Even so, location may be fairly flexible and the site might not be as important as in retailing. Office functions, moreover, do not have to be tied to the ground floor or lower floors of a building.

Independently located offices (with a total floorspace in the UK of over 50 million m^2 in 1993) can be classified into the following groups.

The Head Offices of Major Commercial and Industrial Firms

To benefit from accessibility and from a 'prestige' address, firms have demanded more and more office space within the central areas of cities and are attracted more to large rather than small cities – London being of foremost importance. In 1938 there were 8.8 million m^2 of office space in Central London, in 1966 the figure had increased to 16.7 million m^2, and by 1993 the area exceeded 22 million m^2. In the United Kingdom, office jobs as a percentage of the total workforce increased from 24 to 38 per cent between 1960 and 1990, and the percentage growth in office employment was five times the increase in employment generally – an increase much greater than in most other countries, including those with higher gross national products (GNPs) per capita. Office rents increased simultaneously, rising from about £15 per m^2 in the 1950s to £165 per m^2 in the City of London in 1973. This contrasted with rents of up to £45 per m^2 in other cities. By 1987, during the property boom, rents reached nearly £470 per m^2 and £420 per m^2 in the City and West End respectively. Taking occupancy costs (rent, local property tax and service charges), only Tokyo had higher outgoings than the City of London in 1987 – £720 per m^2 compared to £650 per m^2. Costs in downtown New York were £440 per m^2; in Paris £430 per m^2; and £230 per m^2 in Frankfurt. Suburban London and the South-East continued to increase in appeal with, for example, Windsor and Slough (adjacent to the M4) attracting rents of over £162 and £153 per m² respectively, and Redhill/Reigate and Crawley (close to the M25 and M23) commanding rents of over £125 and £102 per m². In other regions rents were much lower. For example, £79 per m² in Bristol and Birmingham, £69 in Manchester, £56 in Liverpool, £51 in Sheffield, and £44 in Newcastle upon Tyne and Plymouth. With such enormous regional disparities in rent, it was not surprising that 10 per cent of all new office investment in the United Kingdom in 1986 was in London.

By affording high rents and rates, office users usually push out alternative uses, except perhaps ground-floor retailing and in prestige retail districts such as parts of London's West End. High rents and rates are paid because of the intensive use of the floor area and because of substantial external economies of scale (such as access to labour, materials and service inputs, and where offices collectively provide a large market for advertising, accounting and legal services – each consequently supplied at low unit cost). Where earning capacity is dependent upon being sited in a specific area, users are simply willing to incur the expense. Firms place a premium on locations providing the maximum opportunity for face-to-face contact and maximum degree of access to information. As it is practicable to construct multistorey offices (in contrast to shops), those sites occupied by offices will be the most intensively developed and most valuable sites within the urban area.

But eventually the central business district becomes saturated. Further vertical development is too costly and, except for minor instances of infilling and redevelopment, horizontal expansion is impossible because of the lack of sites. Decentralization thus offers the only possibility for an expansion in office space and the process has been adopted in most capitalist countries. In the United States, for example, 87 per cent of major firms were located in the central business district in 1956, but this proportion decreased to 71 per cent by 1974 (Alexander, 1979) and continued to decline into the 1980s. In the United Kingdom, following the Control of Offices and Industrial Development Act 1965, office development became strictly controlled. Office Development Permits (ODPs) were required for all office development in the South-East and Midlands when the proposed floorspace exceeded 3,000 ft² (279 m²), and in Central London there was a complete ban on office development. Although ODP limits were subsequently raised in 1967 to 10,000 ft² (929 m²) outside the Metropolitan Area, to 10,000 ft² within the region (exclusive of Greater London) in 1969, and to 10,000 ft² in London in 1970, the effect in these years was to raise office rents substantially because of the inadequate supply of new development. Between 1965 and 1970 rents of new and old offices in central London increased by five and fourfold, respectively (in contrast to increases of 39 and 23 per cent in the respective rents of new and old offices in Manchester and Liverpool). Were it not for economic uncertainty and financial stringency, the Greater London Council's policy of restricting office development in Central London in the mid-1970s would have produced a similar soaring of office rents.

Encouraged by the Location of Offices Bureau (established in 1963), and influenced by expiring leases, premises due for demolition and the need for more space (and to a lesser extent by rising rents and rates, higher wages, labour scarcity and travel inconvenience), many firms have moved all or most of their office requirements out of London. General administration, routine accounts, records and technical departments have been decentralized since it has been recognized that the need for face-to-face contact had been exaggerated, but small reception departments usually remained (and many firms doubled up on their use of office space) within the central area. Between 1963 and 1977 over 2,000 office-using firms left Central and Inner London, accounting for about 145,000 jobs, yet suburban areas or towns within the South-East were usually preferred to other locations in Britain. Concentrated decentralization in the South-East made possible the retention of contacts between firms without their needing to incur the high direct costs of locating in London.

The pattern of decentralization has clearly been at the expense of provincial locations. Whereas, for example, the outer South-East increased its share of company headquarters from 7 to 15 per cent of the national total between 1968 and 1983 (a gain of 114 per cent), the North-West decreased its share from 8 to 5 per cent, Scotland from 5 to 4 per cent and the North from 4 to 2 per cent. The concentration of company headquarters in one region (the South-East) is in complete contrast with many other capitalist countries such as the United States and the former West Germany, where head-offices are widely distributed.

Within the Assisted Areas of the North and West, decentralized offices were induced not only by the absence of the need to obtain an ODP, but after 1973 by government grants paid to employees who moved with their work, and rent grants for periods of three to five years. Loans were also available at concessionary rates for normal capital needs, interest relief grants could be claimed, removal grants up to 80 per cent of cost were provided, and the government offset up to 80 per cent of the redundancy pay commitment of relocating firms. Under the White Paper *Regional Industrial Development* (1983), some service sectors previously excluded from regional development grants (RDGs) (for example, advertising agencies, credit-card companies, cable television and football pools) now qualified for assistance. Regional aid was to be allocated largely in the form of RDGs (which were limited to a cost of £10,000 per job) or as job grants (of £3,000 per job).

By 1977 the economic plight of the inner cities (not least Inner London) had been recognized. The Department of the Environment therefore altered the terms of reference of the Location of Offices Bureau to attract office development to the inner cities rather than exclusively to decentralized locations. The Inner Urban Areas Act 1978 further emphasized the importance of offices to the inner cities. But decentralization was finally rejected in July 1979 when the incoming Conservative Government (favouring a *laissez-faire* approach) abolished ODPs and closed down the Location of Offices Bureau. An office boom in Central London was anticipated. Despite some major developments in the early 1980s, by the middle of the decade big increases in demand pushed up rents in Central London ahead of the rate of inflation – a trend dramatically boosted by the deregulation of the City's financial markets in 1986 (the 'Big Bang'). Deregulation created an intensified demand for office space from conglomerates, solo firms, companies with futures determined by the Financial Services Act of 1986, and from spin-off accountancy and legal services. Most important was the strong demand for offices (such as those developed in Broadgate and redeveloped in London Wall) built to sophisticated specifications to house the electronics of the Big Bang. By mid-1987, rents in the City were already exceeding £465 per m^2 and had increased by over £90 per m^2 since December 1986. Even small office suites were now commanding £370 per m^2.

There were substantial fears of shortages of office space in Central London. Normally, the vacancy rate in the United Kingdom is never much higher than 8 per cent (in the United States it often exceeds 30 per cent), but by the mid-1980s this was drastically reduced. Whereas in January 1983 there were 4.1 years of new office supply in Central London, by January 1986 this had plummeted to only two years, and in 1987 it was estimated that while supply amounted to 240,000 m^2, demand had soared to 353,000 m^2. This shortage was exacerbated by older offices being taken out of use for redevelopment or refurbishment. The immediate effects of this inadequacy of space were: the increased degree of pre-letting, particularly to the banking and financial sector (by 1987 over 70 per cent of total floorspace under construction in the City was pre-let); the increased extent to which firms acquired the freehold of their offices (this was particularly the case among foreign operators, not least Japanese companies); and an inflationary impact on the West End office market where rents rose to £418 per m^2 in Mayfair in 1987.

The recession of the early 1990s and its impact on office development

The growth in the output of financial and business services in the mid-1980s was associated with falling interest rates and a substantial increase in new

construction orders and construction output in respect of office development. Subsequently, high interest rates and the associated slump had a
detrimental effect on new construction orders and construction output
(table 5.5).

In 1993, during the property slump, average rents on new lettings in the
West End of London plummeted to £430 per m^2 (from £756 per m^2 in
1988) and in the City of London fell to £323 per m^2, but were fairly stable
at £226 per m^2 in Manchester and £182 per m^2 in Glasgow – regional
divergence in the 1980s giving way to convergence in the early 1990s.
Taking occupancy costs, however, only Tokyo's central business district had
higher average outgoings than the West End of London (£1,612 per m^2
compared to £732 per m^2), while costs in the City of London were
£649 per m^2, and £545 per m^2 in Hong Kong, £431 per m^2 in Paris,
£409 per m^2 in Berlin, £397 per m^2 in Frankfurt and £362 per m^2 in
mid-town New York.

The property slump in London can be attributed largely to an excess
supply of new development in the City as a result of a substantial amount
of speculative office development in the late 1980s (for example, 1.1 million
m^2 of new office space was completed in the City in 1989, nearly four
times as much as in 1986), and a deficiency of demand in the West End.

A number of very large developments were completed in the City,
notably the later phases of Broadgate and all of London Wall, and up to
930,000 m^2 of office space at Canary Wharf in the London docklands
became available. By 1992, there were 3.7 million m^2 of unoccupied office
space in London, about 20 per cent of the capital's stock and equivalent
to two and a half years' supply of new office space.

By 1999, office development in London had recovered. West End rents
had risen to almost £600 per m^2 and vacancy rates were at their lowest
since the late 1980s at only 4.5 per cent, while, in the City, rents now
ranged from £470 to £500 per m^2 and at Canary Wharf were nearly £300
per m^2 – reflecting a significant reduction in vacant supply.

In both the United Kingdom and the United States, however, there is
evidence of a relocation of corporate headquarters from major cities to suburban areas or beyond as a result of: structural changes in the size of the
firm (for example, through merger where the need for centrally-located
office space is rationalized), changes in the firm's economic activities (from
manufacturing to services) and the diseconomies of city-centre locations
(congestion costs, higher property costs and higher labour costs). To satisfy
some of the demand for out-of-town locations, a large number of business
parks have been developed – on comparatively low-cost land, where firms
can benefit from lower rents and labour costs, more suitable premises, a
more attractive (and possibly landscaped) environment and often good road
accessibility. But there is also the tendency for some office employment to

Table 5.5 The office development boom and slump

	Growth in financial and business service (per cent per annum)	Interest rates (per cent)[1]	Balance of payments (current account) as a percentage of GDP	£ exchange rate[2]	New construction orders (£m at 1985 prices)	Construction output (£m at 1985 prices)
1985	6.4	11.5	0.8	100	1,775	1,635
1986	11.0	11.0	0.0	92	2,183	1,839
1987	10.1	8.5	-1.0	90	2,852	2,112
1988	7.6	13.0	-3.3	96	3,725	2,513
1989	4.8	15.0	-4.0	93	4,008	3,472
1990	2.7	14.0	-3.1	91	3,379	4,112
1991	-2.5	10.5	-1.1	92	1,969	3,347
1992	-2.7	7.0	-2.0	88	1,597	2,072

Notes: 1. Retail bank base rate, end of year.
2. Trade weighted index, average for year.

Source: Central Statistical Office; Department of the Environment.

235

remain in the CBD – 'non-routine, decision-making and research jobs, relying upon direct information transfers and contacts, are pulled towards large, diversified, service oriented CBDs at the top of the urban hierarchy' (Ball *et al.*, 1998: 99; also see Hepworth, 1989; Malecki, 1991). In contrast, other firms, employing less specialized labour, seek a suburban location. Within the same firm, a spatial division of labour emerges, whereby higher-level decision-making tasks remain in the CBD, but 'back office' functions – such as administration, routine clerical work and data processing tasks – are relocated in lower-rent, lower-labour cost areas.

In recent years, developers have consequently provided business parks on comparatively low-cost land in edge-of-town or out-of-town locations, to satisfy a demand among office firms for relatively low rents and labour costs, more suitable premises and a more attractive (and possibly landscaped) environment, with good communications and often good road accessibility. New developments, such as 'hot-desking' and 'office hotelling' (whereby workers do not have their own desks or offices but share space in a central office), and telecommuting and homeworking (where workers work at home but remain connected to their office via telephones, faxes and commuter modems) have also reduced the amount of office space per worker in the CBD, and encouraged the further dispersal of office functions.

THE GLOBALIZATION OF LOCATION

The Emergence of World Cities

In the late twentieth century, there was a tendency for an increasing number of firms in the manufacturing and service sectors to 'globalize' the location of many of their activities – selecting a small number of 'world cities' as control and command points within an expanding global economy. As described by Hall (1966), world cities (such as London, Paris, Randstad, Rhine-Ruhr, New York and Tokyo) are: major cities of political power, centres of industry, trade and finance; great ports and/or the focus of road and rail networks; and centres of higher education, research, medicine, and culture and the arts. As decision-making points for the global economy, they have more in common with each other than with most other urban centres in their own countries.

According to Friedmann (1986), a city is only eligible for world status if it is a major centre for manufacturing, finance and transportation; contains the headquarters of transnational corporations (TNCs) and a number of international institutions; experiences a rapid growth in the provision of business services; and has a substantial population. As a result of the quantification of these attributes, Friedmann suggests that there is a total of 18 world cities in core countries and 12 in semi-peripheral countries, and that these can be divided into primary and secondary centres (table 5.6), whereas Thrift (1989) argues that world cities can be classified as global, zonal and regional centres depending on the breadth of their control and command activities and the spatial extent of their influence: for example, New York, London and Tokyo are undoubtedly global centres; Paris, Singapore, Hong Kong and Los Angeles act as zonal centres; and Sydney, Chicago, Dallas, Miami, Honolulu and San Francisco are of regional significance. Sassen (1991) similarly claims that world cities serve as important nodes in the global network linking together investment, human, industrial and commercial capital; and, through instant communications, electronic cash transfers and rapid transportation they are not only locked together in a reciprocal relationship but also stand at the apex of the global urban hierarchy dominating the world economy. Clark (1996), however, suggests that despite their many similarities, individual world cities tended to specialize in those activities in which they reflected 'their history, location and the size and character of their national economies' (Clark, 1996: 141); for example,

Table 5.6 Hierarchy of world cities

Continent	Core countries		Semi-peripheral countries	
	Primary	*Secondary*	*Primary*	*Secondary*
Europe	London Paris Rotterdam Frankfurt Zurich	Brussels Milan Vienna Madrid		
North America	New York Chicago Los Angeles	Toronto Miami Houston San Francisco		Mexico City
South America			São Paulo	Buenos Aires Rio de Janeiro Caracas
Asia and Oceania	Tokyo	Sydney	Singapore	Hong Kong Taipeh Manila Bangkok Seoul
Africa				Johannesburg

Source: Friedmann (1986).

New York is unquestionably the principal centre of global corporate power, London is the principal supplier of financial and producer services to global markets, and Paris attracts most of the headquarters of international organizations and conventions.

In recent years, globalization has greatly increased. The command and control functions of firms, the creation of a network of global business linkage and the emergence of world cities as centres of the global economy have been facilitated by developments in telecommunications (such as the Internet and use of e-commerce), a consequential and unprecedented access to business information, and improved transportation. There has also been a rapid growth in the number and scale of TNCs, banking and foreign exchange markets, stock market transactions and the marketing of commodities; and a similar rate of growth in producer services such as management consultancy, accountancy, law, real estate, insurance, advertising, research and development, and public relations – all supported by the expansion of hotel accommodation, car hire, and the provision of credit and chargecards (Clark, 1996: 147).

Smith and Feagin (1987) revealed that as few as ten cities contained the headquarters of around half of the world's largest 500 transnational manufacturing corporations, but, as might be suggested from table 5.7, it was not population size but corporate control that distinguished world cities. Similarly, Reed (1984) showed – by means of 16 criteria – that financial institutions were concentrated into a comparatively small number of global

Table 5.7 Headquarters of the largest transnational firms (excluding banks), 1984

City	Metropolitan population (000s)	Number of firms
1. New York	17,083	59
2. London	11,100	37
3. Tokyo	26,200	34
4. Paris	9,500	26
5. Chicago	7,865	18
6. Essen	5,050	18
7. Osaka	15,900	15
8. Los Angeles	10,519	14
9. Houston	3,109	11
10. Pittsburg	2,171	10

Source: Smith and Feagin (1987).

	Table 5.8 Global financial centres in 1980		
Rank	*Type of centre*	*Centres*	
1.	Supranational: first order	London	New York
2.	Supranational: second order	Amsterdam	Frankfurt
		Frankfurt	Paris
3.	International: first order	Basel	Mexico City
		Bombay	Rio de Janeiro
		Brussels	Rome
		Chicago	San Francisco
		Dusseldorf	São Paulo
		Hamburg	Singapore
		Hong Kong	Sydney
		Madrid	Toronto
		Melbourne	Vienna
4.	International: second order	Bahrain	Montreal
		Buenos Aires	Osaka
		Kobe	Panama
		Los Angeles	Seoul
		Luxembourg	Taipei
		Milan	

Source: Reed (1984).

centres, which in turn were ranked into first and second order supranational and international centres (table 5.8).

World cities can also be ranked according to stock market comparisons (table 5.9), London Stock Exchange data again indicating the dominance of New York, London, Tokyo, Osaka and Frankfurt in the global economy.

Globalization and the Cities of Developing Countries

Despite the command and control powers of the TNCs, there is little indication that 'new production, innovations, capital and social surplus. . . [are] . . . trickling down the urban hierarchy in a step-by-step manner, from the top to the bottom' of the urban hierarchy (Potter and Lloyd-Evans, 1998: 67). Instead, production is becoming increasingly concentrated in a comparatively few centres. The decision to base production in one city in the developing world rather than in another will have a 'considerable impact on the geography of development and change, especially when it is remem-

Table 5.9 City-based stock markets (31 December 1992)

Exchange		Market value (fixed interest and equities) (£m)	Turnover (£m)	Companies quoted
1.	New York	3,963,428	1,160,561	2,089
2.	London	2,579,339	1,044,712	2,392
3.	Tokyo	2,462,682	393,267	1,768
4.	Osaka	2,460,181	95,682	1,168
5.	Frankfurt	1,136,303	891,017	665
6.	Luxembourg	937,188	736	221
7.	Toronto	733,801	41,491	1,119
8.	Paris	597,760	582,147	732
9.	Milan	493,979	867,519	229
10.	Brussels	287,493	6,834	318

Source: The Stock Exchange, London.

bered that many TNCs have annual turnovers which greatly exceed the gross national products of many small and impoverished developing nations' (Potter and Lloyd-Evans, 1998: 67).

Developing countries, facing spatial difficulties, therefore have a choice between allowing TNCs and other international organizations the freedom to operate in their major urban centres before previously-adopted strategies have an impact on their rate of national and urban economic growth, or holding back the activities of TNCs etc. at the top of the urban system until the filtering-down (or filtering-up) of previous growth-induced changes have occurred. Whereas the former choice could increase the rate of economic growth, it might also produce greater spatial inequalities, whereas the latter choice would produce the opposite effects. Since growth has been seen as a greater priority than equality, most developing countries have chosen the former approach (Potter and Lloyd-Evans, 1998).

Similarly, on a global scale, uneven urban development in the late twentieth century suggested that the market forces of divergence are greater than those of convergence – specifically in respect to patterns of ownership, capital accumulation and production. TNCs, for example, have increasingly dispersed manufacturing industry to low labour-cost locations (by establishing Fordist production line systems in the newly-industrializing countries), while increasing their control and command powers in world cities. In this respect, newly-industrializing Taiwan, Hong Kong and South Korea can be contrasted with the developing countries of Bangladesh (an agricultural exporter) and Nigeria (a raw material supplier). Many commentators, however, argue that there might be a convergence in patterns of economic and urban growth, not least through the homogenization of urban lifestyles and patterns of consumption (witness the transnational spread of such retailers as McDonalds, Burger King, Ikea, Gap, Marks and Spencer, Benetton and Body Shop, and products such as Levi jeans, Coca-Cola and Fuji films). However, it is the elite and upper income groups that tend to follow North American or European tastes and fashion, and thus convergence internationally might widen the differences in living standards between local populations. Simultaneous convergence and divergence therefore exist in many cities of the developing world, for example in Hong Kong and cities in Malaysia and Ecuador (see Armstrong and McGee, 1985).

It can be suggested, therefore, that in terms of patterns of Western consumption, convergence is occurring within the global urban system – with demand being spread in a hierarchical manner from world cities to regional prime cities, and down through the urban system; while in terms of production and ownership, divergence is occurring – with entrepreneurial activity being concentrated in the world's largest cities (Potter and Lloyd-Evans, 1998).

REFERENCES

Alexander, I. (1979) *Office Location and Public Policy*, Harlow: Longman.

Alonso, W. (1960) 'A theory of the urban land market', *Papers and Proceedings of the Regional Science Association*, 6.

Alonso, W. (1964) *Location and Land Use*, Cambridge MA: Harvard University Press.

Alonso, W. (1967) 'A reformulation of classical location theory and its relation to rent theory', *Papers and Proceedings of the Regional Science Association*, 19.

Alonso, W. (1968) *Industrial Location and Regional Policy in Economic Development*, Institute of Urban and Regional Development, University of California, Berkeley.

Archer, W. (1981) 'Determinants of location for general purpose office firms within medium-sized cities', *Journal of the American Real Estate and Urban Economics Association*, 9.

Armstong, W. and McGee, T.G. (1985) *Theatres of Accumulation: Studies in Asian and Latin American Urbanisation*, London: Methuen.

Balchin, P. (1990) *Regional Policy in Britain: The North–South Divide*, London: Paul Chapman Publishing.

Balchin, P. and Sýkora, L. with Bull, G. (1999) *Regional Policy and Planning in Europe*, London: Routledge.

Ball, M., Lizeiri, C. and MacGregor, B.D. (1998) *The Economics of Commercial Property Markets*, London: Routledge.

Berry, B.J.L. and Garrison, W.L. (1958) 'Recent development of central place theory', *Papers and Proceedings of the Regional Science Association*, 4.

Blažek, J. (1996) 'Regional patterns of adaptability to global and transformation processes in the Czech Republic', *Acta Facultatis Rereum Naturalium Universitatis Comenianae – Geographica*, 37: 61–70.

Blažek, J. and Kára, J. (1992) 'Regional policy in the Czech Republic in the period of transition', in Gorzelak, G. and Kukliński, A. (eds), *Dilemmas of Regional Policies in Eastern and Central Europe*, Warsaw: University of Warsaw.

Buck, N., Gordon, I. and Young, K. with Ermisch, J. and Mills, L. (1986) *The London Employment Problem*, Oxford: Oxford University Press.

Carr, J. (1987) 'Malls laugh as the high street dies', *Observer*, 28 June.

Cheeseright, P. (1987a) 'An awful lot of shopping in Manchester', *Financial Times*, 6 March.

Cheeseright, P. (1987b) 'A shop-around for the West Midlands planners', *Financial Times*, 20 March.

Clark, D. (1996) *Urban World/Global City*, London: Routledge.

Dennis, R.D. (1981) *Changes in Manufacturing Employment in the South East Region between 1976 and 1980*, London: Department of Trade and Industry.

Department of Trade and Industry (1983) *Regional Industrial Development*, cmnd 9111, London: Routledge.

Dicken, P. (1992) *Global Shift: The Internationalization of Economic Activity*, London: Paul Chapman Publishing.

Dickenson, J., Gould, B., Clarke, C., Mather, S., Prothero, M., Siddle, D., Smith, C. and Thomas-Hope, E. (1996) *Geography of the Third World*, London: Routledge.

Dunning, J. and Norman, G. (1983) 'The theory of the multinational enterprise', *Environment and Planning A*, 15.

Dunning, J. and Norman, G. (1987) 'The locational choice of offices in international firms', *Environment and Planning A*, 19.

Fothergill, S. and Gudgin, G. (1982) *Unequal Growth: Urban and Regional Employment Change in the United Kingdom*, London: Heinemann.

Fothergill, S., Kitson, M. and Monk, S. (1987) *Property and Industrial Development*, London: Hutchinson.

Friedmann, J. (1986) 'The world city hypothesis', *Development and Change*, 17.

Glasson, J. (1974) *An Introduction to Regional Planning*, London: Hutchinson.

Goddard, J. (1973) *Office Linkages and Location*, Oxford: Pergamon.

Goodchild, R. and Munton, R. (1985) *Development and the Landowner. An Analysis of the British Experience*, London: George Allen and Unwin.

Greenhut, M.L. (1956) *Plant Location in Theory and Practice*, Charlotte NC: North Carolina University Press.

HABITAT (1996) *An Urbanizing World: Global Report on Human Settlements 1996*, Oxford: United Nations Centre for Human Settlements and Oxford University Press.

Hall, P. (1966) (3rd edn, 1984) *The World Cities*, London: Weidenfeld & Nicholson.

Hall, P. (1985) 'A problem with its roots in the distant past', *Town and Country Planning*, 54: 2.

Hepworth, M. (1989) *Geography of the Information Economy*, London: Belhaven Press.

Hewitt, T., Johnson, H. and Wield, D. (eds) (1992) *Industrialization and Development*, Oxford: Oxford University Press in association with the Open University.

Hillier Parker (1993) *British Shopping Centre Development Master List*, London: Hillier Parker.

Hoover, E. (1948) *The Location of Economic Activity*, New York: McGraw-Hill.

Isard, W. (1956) *Location and Space Economy*, Cambridge MA: MIT Press.

Jones, P. (1986) 'Small shops, big implications', *Town and Country Planning*, 6.

Kára, J. (1994) 'New Czech regional policy', in Barlow, M., Dostál, P. and Hampl, M. (eds), *Territory, Society and Administration: The Czech Republic and the Industrial Region of Liberec*, Amsterdam: Universiteit van Amsterdam.

Keeble, D. (1987) 'Industrial change in the United Kingdom', in Lever, W.F. (ed.), *Industrial Change in the United Kingdom*, Harlow: Longman.

Keogh, G. (1985) 'The economics of planning gain', in Barrett, S. and Healey, P. (eds), *Land Policy: Problems and Alternatives*, Farnborough: Gower.

Laurance, B. (1992) 'High street shopping not yet dead', *Guardian*, 3 October.

Lever, W.F. (1982) 'Urban scale as a determinant of employment growth or decline', in Collins, L. (ed.), *Industrial Decline and Regeneration*, Department of Geography, University of Edinburgh.

Lösch, A. (1954) *The Economics of Location*, Newhaven CT: Yale University Press.

Malecki, E. (1991) *Technology and Economic Development*, Harlow: Longman.

Martin, R. and Rowthorn, B. (1986) *The Geography of De-industrialisation*, London: Macmillan.

Martin, R. and Tyler, P. (1992) 'The regional legacy', in Michie, J. (ed.), *The Economic Legacy 1979–1992*, London: Academic Press.

Massey, D. (1984) *Spatial Divisions of Labour*, London: Macmillan.

Massey, C. and Meegan, R.A. (1978) 'Industrial restructuring versus the cities', *Urban Studies*, 15.

McGoldrick, P.J. and Thompson, M.G. (1992) *Regional Shopping Centres: Out-of-Town versus In-town*, London: Avebury.

Moore, B., Rhodes, J. and Tyler, P. (1984) 'Geographical variations in industrial costs', *Discussion Paper 12*, Department of Land Economy, University of Cambridge.

Pavlínek, P. (1992) 'Regional transformation in Czechoslovakia: towards a market economy', *TESG – Tijdschrift voor economische en sociale geografie*, 83: 5.

Piore, M. and Sabel, C. (1984) *The Second Industrial Divide: Possibilities for Prosperity*, New York: Basic Books.

Potter, R. (1992) *Urbanisation in the Third World*, Oxford: Oxford University Press.

Potter, R. and Lloyd-Evans, S. (1998) *The City in the Developing World*, Harlow: Longman.

Reed, H.C. (1984) 'Appraising corporate investment policy: a financial center theory of foreign direct investment', in Kindleberger, C.P. and Audretsch, D.B. (eds), *The Multinational Corporation in the 1980s*, London: MIT Press, 219–43.

Reilly, W. (1929) *Methods of the Study of Retail Relationships*, Bulletin 2944, University of Texas, Austin TX.

Richardson, H.W. (1969) *Regional Economics: Location Theory, Urban Structure and Regional Change*, London: Weidenfeld & Nicolson.

Richardson, H.W. (1971) *Urban Economics*, Harmondsworth: Penguin.

Sassen, S. (1991) *The Global City*, Princeton NJ: Princeton University Press.

Sinclair, R. (1967) 'Von Thünen and urban sprawl', *Annals of the American Association of Geographers*, 57.

Smith, M.P. and Feagin, J.R. (1987) *The Capitalist City*, Oxford: Blackwell.

Thrift, N.J. (1989) 'The geography of international economic disorder', in Johnson, R.J. and Taylor, P.J. (eds), *A World in Crisis*, Oxford: Blackwell, 16–79.

Weber, A. (1909) *Über der Standort den Industrien*, translated by Freidrich, C. (1929) as 'Theory of the Location of Industry', Chicago: University of Chicago Press.

Wood, P.A. (1987) 'The South East', in Damesick, P.J. and Wood, P.A. (eds), *Regional Problems, Problem Regions and Public Policy in the United Kingdom*, Oxford: Clarendon Press.

6

Urban Development and Renewal

INTRODUCTION

Urban development takes place in the context of continual urban change as cities pass through different stages of growth and decline – and sometimes resurgence – during their life. According to the stages theory of urban growth (Van den Berg et al., 1982; Vanhove and Klassen, 1980), as economic development proceeds urban areas will move slowly from one stage to the next (figure 6.1).

THE STAGES THEORY OF URBAN GROWTH

A more detailed picture of urban change can be obtained from various cross-national studies which have based their analyses on specially defined 'functional urban regions'. Such regions, based on recognized urban centres, also include their surrounding commuter belts. They generally cover a wider area than would national urban statistics, and this has the obvious advantage of encompassing more extended forms of suburban development. Indeed, these studies tend to place more emphasis on the relationship between population trends in inner (core) areas and those in outer (ring) areas, than on population change overall. The assumption is that urban areas undergo various stages of urban development, exhibiting particular characteristics at each stage. The stages model, initially suggested by Hall, was subsequently developed by Vanhove and Klassen (1980) and Van den Berg et al. (1982).

Initially at least, the urbanization process is invariably associated with growing industrialization. As this process gathers pace urban areas move slowly from one stage to the next (figure 6.1). In the first early stage of urbanization agricultural labourers are drawn from the surrounding rural areas to the fast-growing industrial sectors located in the cities. Such changes began to occur more than 100 years ago in Britain, but only

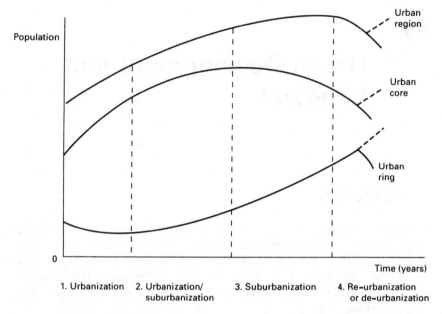

Figure 6.1 *Population size at stages of urban development*

towards the end of the nineteenth century or in the early twentieth century in most of Western Europe, and even later in much of Eastern Europe. At this stage, population growth in the urban 'core' is fast, while population in the surrounding 'ring' may actually decline as resources and population are drawn to towns and cities.

In the second stage, extensive transport facilities are created, as well as public amenities and better housing. The role of services expands, and manufacturing industries are moved further away from the centre. With better public transport, and especially growing car ownership, an increasing proportion of households may take advantage of suburban residence to achieve lower-density housing in a quieter environment while still maintaining reasonable access to the city. Planning authorities rarely resist these tendencies and eventually population growth in the surrounding 'ring' comes to exceed that of the core area itself.

By the third stage, the population continues to suburbanize but with falling population at the core, since residential uses there are increasingly coming into conflict with other uses, especially offices, which achieve higher land values. Overall, however, the urban region continues to grow, albeit more slowly. It is during this stage that the problems caused by excessive suburbanization become acute; the existing road network in particular can

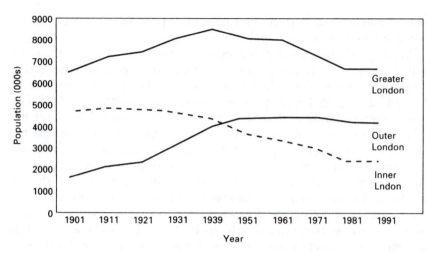

Figure 6.2 *London's population 1901–91*

no longer cope with growing numbers of commuters and congestion reduces the accessibility of workplaces near the city centre.

During the final stage(s) these effects may also spread to the suburban areas, which then cease to expand. At this point. Van den Berg *et al.* suggest that satellite towns 50–100 km from the 'core' city – themselves at an earlier stage in the urban lifecycle – will benefit from decentralization, thus encouraging job losses in the original urban system. As a means of reversing the decline of urban cores, these authors suggest measures to reduce congestion (in particular, by reducing traffic demand), to restrain suburbanization and to support the residential function of central cities. Although the theory recognizes the possibility of urban resurgence, this is not assumed to be a natural phenomenon but rather the result of concerted efforts on the part of central and local government to encourage urban renewal and introduce policies to deal more specifically with the problems mentioned above.

Figure 6.2 illustrates how population change in London since the beginning of the twentieth century has followed the pattern predicted by the stages theory. In spite of the recent stabilization of population it is too early to say whether de-urbanization has turned to re-urbanization. Moreover, unless economic development and employment can match any population upturn the term 're-urbanization' itself is perhaps rather meaningless. Up to now, urban population decline has tended to be matched (or more than matched) by employment decline and decentralization, so the prospect of a resumption of urban population growth in the absence of any accompanying improvement in urban employment opportunities must be one of particular concern to public policy-makers.

In newly-industrializing and developing countries, suburbanization and de-urbanization – as considered above – are far less prominent, especially in Africa and most of Asia. Daily commuting on any scale is impracticable because of relatively low levels of car ownership and limited-capacity feeder road networks (Clark, 1996). Also, in an attempt to maintain political and administrative power at the centre, few governments have controlled the growth of large cities and particularly the primate city, or have decentralized people and economic activity from congested core regions to the periphery or beyond. However, although urbanization tended to advance quickly under free-market and capitalist conditions, under socialism – for ideological, strategic or social motives – 'anti-urban policies' were often adopted, for example in China between 1959 and 1975 where zero urban growth measures were employed, or in Tanzania between 1969 and 1978 and in Vietnam between 1975 and 1980 where policies of planned de-urbanization were promoted (Potter and Lloyd-Evans, 1998).

Richardson (1981) suggested that if a policy of planned de-urbanization is employed, this could lead to the creation of one or more of the following: development corridors, growth poles, counter-magnets, secondary cities, provincial capitals, regional centres (with an associated hierarchy of urban settlements) and dispersed small service centres. But, if a policy of concentrated urbanization is in force, this could result in the adoption of a free-market 'do-nothing' approach, or the promotion of polycentric development, or the dispersal of new development from the congested urban core to the urban–rural fringe.

However, if – for ideological or economic reasons – *anti-urban* policies are adopted and result in the development of growth poles and other decentralized settlements, this might do little to weaken the power and influence of transnational capital (Friedmann and Weaver, 1979). Instead, the promotion of 'agropolitan' development would lead to the growth of cities based on the skills and resources of an agriculture population, and not on external aid and capital, although the latter would not necessarily be ruled out at a later stage (Potter and Lloyd-Evans, 1998). In due course, large cities would consequently lose their dominant position in the urban hierarchy, while development planning would focus on medium-sized or small settlements in a predominantly rural environment (Friedmann and Weaver, 1979; Lowder, 1991; Drakakis-Smith, 1996). The agropolitan mode of planned de-urbanization has been implemented – with varying degrees of success – in both socialist and capitalist countries, for example in China, Vietnam, Tanzania, Sri Lanka, Bangladesh, Pakistan and the Republic of Korea.

A more detailed consideration of urban development in advanced capitalist regions, in regions in the process of political and economic transition such as East Central Europe, and in the newly-industrializing and developing world will illustrate how and why there are differences in the stages of urban growth.

URBAN DEVELOPMENT IN ADVANCED CAPITALIST REGIONS

Western Europe

The pattern of urban development in Europe from 1950 to the 1970s clearly illustrates the validity of the stages theory. Dividing the period into three sub-periods, Van den Berg *et al.* (1982) found that, in Western Europe, all the countries studied moved up one or two stages (in contrast to East Central Europe where, for example, Yugoslavia, Poland and Hungary remained at broadly the same stage of urban development throughout the whole period). These findings, shown in table 6.1, illustrate, first, the evolutionary nature of the European urban system and, second,

---

Table 6.1 Changes in the classification of countries by dominant stage of urban development, Europe, 1950–75

Dominant stage	1950–60	1960–70	1970–75
1. Urbanization	Bulgaria, Hungary, Denmark, Sweden, Italy	Bulgaria, Hungary	Bulgaria
Urbanization with some suburbanization	Yugoslavia, Poland, Austria, Netherlands, West Germany	Yugoslavia, Poland, Sweden, Italy, Austria, Denmark	Yugoslavia, Poland, Hungary
2. Suburbanization	Switzerland, Great Britain, Belgium	France, Switzerland, West Germany, Netherlands, Great Britain	Austria, France, Italy, Denmark, Sweden
Suburbanization with some de-urbanization	–	Belgium	Great Britain, West Germany, Netherlands, Switzerland
3. De-urbanization	–	–	Belgium

Source: Van den Berg *et al.* (1982).

that it is not individual cities but the urban system as a whole that is affected by similar structural changes. The table, however, fails to show how the sequence developed during the last quarter of the twentieth century. It is probable that most countries (with the possible exception of those in East Central Europe) moved up a stage, while in several countries a further stage might have emerged – that of reurbanization. In western Germany, this, in part, would have been the result of an inflow of migrants from East and Central Europe as well as from the eastern *länder*.

In the 1970s–1980s, urban geographers began to recognize that the population growth of metropolitan areas could not proceed indefinitely. Census data for most advanced capitalist countries were beginning to show signs of population relocation towards non-metropolitan areas. In Western, Northern and Central Europe (although not in Mediterranean Europe), a process of counterurbanization was commencing. This was a result of several economic and demographic factors unique to the decade: economic recession and industrial disinvestment following the oil price rise of 1973/74; the run-down of the guestworker movement in north-west European cities; the expansion of higher education away from major existing population centres; the upgrading of public sector infrastructure and private services in rural areas; and the development of oil and natural gas exploitation, and defence and research industries in peripheral areas (HABITAT, 1996; see also Hall and Hay, 1978; Fielding, 1982; Champion, 1989; Cross, 1990).

During the 1980s, de-urbanization waned because of the impact of global recession on economic growth and employment; the slump in the price of agricultural prices which reduced the level of income and economic activity in rural areas; the restructuring of manufacturing operations designed to increase efficiency and replace Fordist models of production; the apparent demise of Keynesian approaches to the management of the economy; an ideological cutback in public sector infrastructure investment, regional aid and subsidies to declining industries; a shift of emphasis to inner-city regeneration; and large-scale immigration into Western Europe as a result of major political changes in East Central Europe (HABITAT, 1996).

Recent data indicate that by the late 1980s, de-urbanization was confined to Italy, Switzerland and parts of Great Britain and France, while some of the older metropolitan areas of northern Europe had experienced a significant economic resurgence (CEC, 1991). In Great Britain, for example, although there was a loss of 500,000 jobs from 20 of its major cities between 1981 and 1996, and a gain of 1.7 million jobs elsewhere in the country (Turock and Edge, 1999), employment growth in Greater London – particularly in international financial services – produced a high rate of in-migration (particularly of young people) and – in turn – a greater natural increase in its population. The capital's population therefore increased (from a low of under 7 million in 1981) to 7.2 million in 1999 and was projected to rise to 8.1 million by 2016. Strengthened by urban regeneration policies, a number of other large cities in the European Union – particularly in France, Germany and the Netherlands – also increased in population for the first time since their decline in the 1970s. This was often accompanied by the process of gentrification and environmental enhancement (CEC, 1991). By the late 1990s, half of the functional urban regions of the European Union were growing, often with stable or increasing populations in their cores.

Within the urban core and inner urban ring, gentrification is a problematic aspect of reurbanization. Suburbanization in the past was associated with the out-migration of younger and economically active households, with older and less mobile households remaining behind in the core. Although disinvestment and neglect produced a 'rent gap' in many inner-city housing areas, making the rehabilitation of old housing profitable, it also meant that low-income residents would be replaced by more affluent tenants who were able to afford higher rents (Wegener, 1995). In Great Britain this process was often compounded by the provision of improvement grants, where in London in the early 1970s landlords and developers received around 75 per cent of all grants awarded (Balchin, 1971).

In London, Paris, Brussels, Frankfurt, Milan and Munich, reurbanization is highly inflationary, since large-scale real estate speculation and exorbitant increases in commercial rents make housing in the core unaffordable to all except the most affluent. The same is also true of Budapest and Prague, where the inflow of transnational companies has resulted in soaring office rents and the displacement of housing in core areas (see page 254).

Wegener (1995) suggests that if reurbanization continues apace, the modern European metropolis might become three cities in one:

(1) the 'international' or global city with airports, hotels, banks, offices, luxury flats and a prospering central shopping area;
(2) the 'normal' city for indigenous middle-income households – hidden behind the international city in low-density suburbs or in high-rise housing areas on the urban periphery;
(3) the 'marginalized' city for the poor, the elderly, the unemployed and the migrant worker in parts of the urban core but also in degraded peripheral areas.

Gentrification is likely to hasten division. If gentrification takes place within the international city, the poor will be pushed out into low-quality high-rise housing of the 1950s and 1960s within the marginalized city (Wegener, 1995).

Although the two stages of de-urbanization and reurbanization tend to vary in their relative strength over time, they are capable of producing an outcome which will reinforce or counter the effects of other developmental factors at any one time. For example, an improvement in transportation and communications, an increased preference for owner-occupation and the development of outdoor recreation might over the long term well be reinforced by the forces of de-urbanization but countered by the forces of reurbanization; whereas the growth of business services and corporate headquarters, other activities requiring a high level of national and international accessibility, and a large supply of highly qualified personnel will be reinforced by the forces of reurbanization but countered by the forces of de-urbanization. However, there is no direct relationship – either positive or negative – between the later stages of urban development and short-term business cycles of between 3 and 5 years (associated with fluctuations in rates of interest, levels of employment, and labour and housing markets), long-term development cycles of (say) 10 years (linked to commercial property), or the 50–60 year Kondratieff cycle (associated with major phases of innovation and technological development) (HABITAT, 1996).

United States and Canada

Passing through the urbanization and suburbanization stages of urban development earlier in the twentieth century, metropolitan areas as a group experienced net out-migration for the first time during the 1970s (see Berry, 1976; Berry and Gillard, 1976), and while in cities such as New York, Chicago and Detroit, the rate of population growth diminished, in Pittsburg, Buffalo and Cleveland population declined in absolute terms (HABITAT, 1996).

In the United States, de-urbanization was the overall outcome of declining rates of natural increase, an ageing population and slower growth (if not a decline) in the older manufacturing regions due to economic restructuring and international competition; together with faster rates of growth in the non-manufacturing regions such as Texas and the mountain states because of the oil price shock and higher resource prices; and the increase in retirement and lifestyle migrations to Florida, California, Nevada and Arizona. Although it might seem that de-urbanization is heralding the death of the large industrial metropolis, it must be borne in mind that it is instrumental in creating a new generation of metropolises such as Phoenix and Orlando which have increased in population ninefold since 1950, and Dallas-Fort Worth, Houston, Las Vegas and San Diego which have increased fivefold over the same period.

During the 1980s–1990s, reurbanization superseded de-urbanization. The average growth rates of the largest metropolitan areas exceeded those of the smaller metropolitan areas and the non-metropolitan regions, with economic growth being mainly attributable to the service sector and, to an extent, high-tech industry. New York and Los Angeles experienced boom conditions since they were closely linked to the new service economy and the global economic system, Seattle benefited as a leader in niche industries, and Washington DC thrived as a centre of government. Some of the declining metropolitan areas had few traditional industrial jobs left to lose, and were set to exploit their own comparative advantages such as reduced traffic and congestion levels, less environmental pollution, lower housing and labour costs, new recreation and leisure facilities, and in some instances lower taxation. It remains to be seen, however, what effects the slump and boom conditions of the 1990s will have on the metropolitan growth and the development of non-metropolitan areas across the United States (HABITAT, 1996).

Canadian cities broadly followed US cities in terms of growth or decline during the latter decades of the twentieth century. During the period of de-urbanization, Alberta benefited from the oil shock of 1973/74, while the population of British Colombia escalated because of retirement and lifestyle migrations from the Canadian industrial heartlands. Reurbanization in the 1980s was associated with a reduction in the rate of growth of peripheral resourced-based regions such as Alberta, whereas central Canada accounted for half of the country's growth – the Toronto region not only being a thriving manufacturing and service centre, but also a provincial capital and a command centre for many national and cultural industries (HABITAT, 1996).

Japan

Since 1945, there has been a continuous period of urbanization and sub-urbanization in the three major metropolitan regions of Tokyo, Keihanshin (Kyoto–Osaka–Kobe) and Nagoya. However, it is probable that the de-urbanization stage of development is about to emerge.

The three metropolitan regions – increasing their share of the total population from 38 per cent in 1950 to around 50 per cent in 1990 – experienced their most rapid population growth in the early 1960s, and grew fairly rapidly until 1975 (largely because of substantial in-migration), but their rate of growth has since dropped dramatically. Although the growth of smaller urban areas was slow or negative from 1955 to 1970, it has increased substantially in recent years – partly as an outcome of migration from the metropolitan regions. It remains to be seen whether Tokyo, as one of the pre-eminent global cities, with be able to continue to absorb economic activity on a substantial scale and further delay the onset of de-urbanization.

URBAN DEVELOPMENT IN EAST CENTRAL EUROPE

Since 1989, the transformation of the economies of East Central Europe towards more market-oriented growth has brought changes in the scale, nature and distribution of economic activity which has had a marked effect on urban development. In Budapest, despite spectacular office development in the early 1990s, supply did not match demand, and rents soared to DM 45–55 per m^2 (in 1993) – as high as in Vienna and higher than in Amsterdam and Brussels (Kovács, 1993). Increasingly, the unsatisfied demand for offices was met by the rehabilitation and conversion of low-rent residential buildings into commercial use. Although the inner city had experienced population loss since the 1960s, its diminishing supply of low-rent housing in the 1990s inflated residential rents and property values and compounded the rate of out-migration of poorer families. Meanwhile, practically no public housing was built, and the municipal housing stock (transferred from the State in 1991) was severely depleted by the privatization of the better-quality dwellings at heavily discounted prices (Elter and Baross, 1993).

In Prague – where, unlike Budapest, new office development was restricted – the demand for offices and apartments in the urban core (often from transnational corporations and their employees) could only be met by the rehabilitation and conversion of low-rent residential buildings into either commercial use or luxury apartments as a means of closing the functional, rent and capital gaps that emerged with the adoption of capitalism (Sýkora, 1993).

Although it is evident that both Budapest and Prague are at an intermediate stage of urban development between urbanization and de-urbanization, the progression towards de-urbanization was reinforced in Budapest in the 1990s by the expansion of (largely unsupported and uncontrolled) 'self-help' housing districts on the periphery of Budapest – equivalent in concept to the 'informal sector' in the developing world, but in Prague it was countered by the lack of any provision for rehousing the dispossessed inhabitants of the inner city – the development of large-scale housing estates on the periphery being terminated in 1993 (Sýkora, 1993).

URBAN DEVELOPMENT IN NEWLY-INDUSTRIALIZING AND DEVELOPING REGIONS

Latin America

In some cities of Latin America, industrial and commercial development has continued to grow more rapidly within the urban core than outside it – indicating that, as yet, urbanization has not been superseded by suburbanization. Around Bogota, for example, while manufacturing establishments have been developed since the 1950s, the growth of such establishments has been much slower than in the city itself. In most cities, however, industrial and commercial development within the urban core has been overtaken by development on the periphery or beyond. In terms of population growth, core cities are growing more slowly than their suburban rings; 'commuting towns' are growing more rapidly than the inner suburbs and urban cores, and free-standing cities beyond the commuter range of the larger centres are sustaining population growth rates higher than those of metropolitan areas such as Mexico City, São Paulo and Buenos Aires, all suggesting that there has been a transition from the urbanization stage of development to exurbanization (HABITAT, 1996). It is notable that, despite the dominance of Mexico, São Paulo and Buenos Aires, a considerable proportion of the urban population of Latin America lives in cities with populations of only 20,000–300,000, many of which are prosperous, experiencing rapid population growth and deflecting migration away from the larger metropolitan areas.

The major example of de-urbanization in Latin America is that of Havana. Before the 1959 revolution and under free-market conditions, Greater Havana – with 21 per cent of Cuba's population – accommodated 75 per cent of the nation's industry, accounted for 80 per cent of its exports, and contained most of Cuba's health care, educational and cultural facilities. As a classic primate city, Havana not only dominated the Cuban economy, but attracted high rates of rural–urban migration, resulting in the rapid growth of insanitary and inadequate housing – about a third of which was self-build (Stretton, 1978; Potter, 1992; Potter and Lloyd-Evans, 1998). Because Havana historically had represented overseas capitalist interests and was regarded by the leaders of the socialist revolution as privileged and corrupt, policies were adopted to decentralize people, economic activity and social capital, from the city, and reduce the striking differences between the urban and rural areas in terms of income per capita. Thus although the population of Havana has increased from 1.2 million people in 1953 to around 2 million in the late 1990s (largely an outcome of natural increase), it has diminished to 18 per cent of the national total, while the growth of provincial towns with populations in the range of 20,000–200,000 has been encouraged (Potter, 1992).

South East Asia

Available data suggest that in some of the countries of South East Asia there has been a deconcentration of population within most of the larger metropolitan centres (which have experienced either slow or negative growth rates in recent years) and a substantial growth of population in the peripheral areas. In the larger cities, a process of suburbanization/de-urbanization has been set in motion by the expulsion of low/middle-income populations from core areas as a result of the development of offices, convention centres, hotels and a diverse range of service enterprises – together with the development of transport and communications. Apart from producing spatially-differentiated rates of population growth (for example, by 3.1 per cent per annum in central Jakarta throughout the 1980s, compared to 11.7, 20.9 and 19.8 per cent per annum in its three neighbouring districts), deconcentration led to either urban sprawl (for instance, by the creation of an extended metropolitan planning region of $100\,km^2$ around Bangkok), or to the formation of growth corridors away from the metropolitan areas (for example, between Jakarta and Bundung, and linking the Malaysian state of Johor with Singapore and Batam Island in Indonesia).

In Malaysia, the deconcentration of population is associated with its government's attempt to compete successfully with Singapore in the field of information technology. To counter Singapore's IT 2000 programme (which was intended to develop fully an information-based society on the island), the Seventh Malaysian Plan (1996–2000) aimed to utilize funds – equivalent to 11.5 per cent of the country's GDP – to bring the country up to developed nation status by the year 2020. It was intended that this will be achieved largely by facilitating 'a fundamental shift in the Malaysian economy away from a primary and manufacturing base toward information technology' (Marshall, 1998: 273) and by promoting massive investment in infrastructure and other development projects. To realize this objective, the Plan involved the creation of a $50 \times 15\,km$ Multimedia Super Corridor (MSC) south of Kuala Lumpur 'to provide total access to a digital fibre optic network' (Marshall, 1998: 273); to contain the new Federal administrative capital of Putrjaya – intended to accommodate 76,000 government employees; and to accommodate the new Kuala Lumpur international airport – a transportation node of South East Asia to rival that of Singapore. A further plan – 'Vision 2020' – involved the development of the Kuala Lumpur Linear City along the Klang River. Stretching over $12\,km$, the linear city will – if completed – comprise eight major developments along its route (consisting of apartments, offices, restaurants, hotels, retail use and entertainment) linked together by a rapid transit system. Both of these major developments are not only associated with a process of suburbanization, but – perhaps ironically – with attempts to convert Kuala Lumpur into a 'World City'.

China

Since the establishment of the People's Republic of China in 1949, the country has passed through three main phases of economic and urban development. Until 1959, despite Mao Zedong's ideological preference for Chinese citizens 'to remain in their villages and transform the country from there' (Macionis and Parrillo, 1998: 353), urbanization continued apace; but between 1959 and 1978 policies were adopted that were anti-urban and pro-rural – with several million urban youths and bureaucrats being re-employed in the countryside, sometimes permanently, and with 'every effort being made to promote the self-sufficiency of rural communities' (Potter and Lloyd-Evans, 1998: 84). From 1978 to the present, largely under Deng Xiaoping, an attempt has been made to reform the rural economy while acknowledging that the forces of urban growth are probably irresistible. Although the level of urbanization in China (at around 30 per cent) is still low, even by developing world standards, a number of cities have grown dramatically – Shanghai, for example, witnessing an increase in its population from 5.8 million in 1950 to over 10 million by the 1990s.

In recent years, therefore, policies have been employed which, on the one hand, have encouraged urbanization but, on the other hand, have promoted suburbanization/de-urbanization. Since the 1980s, largely as a result of the introduction of market forces, the quantity, quality and variety of consumer goods and services have improved, and many large Hong Kong and Japanese retailers have major outlets in the larger cities (Starr, 1999). Similarly there were more telephones, public buses, roads and green areas on a population basis in 1991 than in 1984, more residential floor space per capita, and a better provision of higher education and medical services – particularly in the larger cities (Chen and Parish, 1996). As an outcome of urban development, the total population of towns and cities grew to around 300 million by the mid-1990s, while the workforce expanded to 170 million (of which 65 per cent were employed in the state sector). In addition, as many as 100 million 'floating workers' have migrated from the countryside to the cities in search of work – normally in the informal sector. Until the mid-1980s, rural–urban migration was restricted by a rationing system (introduced in 1959) which allocated grain, cooking oil and cotton cloth only to persons with an officially registered residence. However, when these items subsequently became available on the free market, in-migration escalated and a labour market emerged (Starr, 1999).

During the 1980s, special economic zones (SEZs) were established along the coast to harness urban population growth and accelerate the development of economic relations with the outside world. They were designated (figure 6.3) in:

Shenzen	Shekou
Zhuhai	Xiamen
Shantou	Hainan

SEZs were to become show-places of high technology, modern manage-ment and efficiency, with production linked almost entirely to export markets – with the aim of earning foreign currency. It was envisaged that economic activity would be generated in the hinterland, warranting a pro-liferation of advanced industrial estates. To enable SEZs to perform their role, they received substantial state funding for infrastructure projects, and were exempt from the administrative interference of local authorities, while foreign investors were exempt from taxes for a maximum of five years, with permanantly lower taxes thereafter (Van Kemenade, 1997). However, although SEZs led the economic development of China, their viability was problematic. Western investment in high technology was not readily forth-coming, and SEZs were ideologically anathema to orthodox Marxists in China who regarded them 'as capitalist bases from which to undermine socialism' (Van Kemenade, 1997: 201).

Rather than add to the numbers of SEZs, the Chinese leadership decided to open 14 coastal cities to foreign investment (figure 6.3), namely:

Shanghai	Lianyungang
Tianjin	Nantong
Dalien	Ningbo
Guangzhou	Wenzhou
Qinhuangdao	Fuzhou
Yantai	Zhanjiang
Qingdao	Beihai

Since most of these cities had been treaty ports prior to the Second World War, it is possible that they 'had much better prospects of becoming centres of high technology than other cities' (Van Kemenade 1997: 204), but – unlike the SEZs – they remained part of the state economy and could not attract investment above ceilings of US$30 million (in Shanghai and Tianjin), $10 million (in Dalian) and $5 million (in the other open cities) without governmental approval.

Notwithstanding this constraint, Shanghai has experienced a speculative boom in real estate activity, in part related to an inflow of foreign banks into the Bund (the old commercial sector of the city), but also as a conse-quence of the government's plans to turn the city into an international stronghold of heavy industry and light and high-tech industries under state domination. The built-up area of the city, however, is being extended by the development of Pudong as a new centre for banking, commercial and high-tech activity, which in the new millennium will enhance the role of Shanghai in the global economy. Located on an estuarine site of $520 \, km^2$ (nearly as large as Singapore), Pudong offers enormous opportunities for investors, and by late 1990s had attracted a total of US$12 billion of foreign

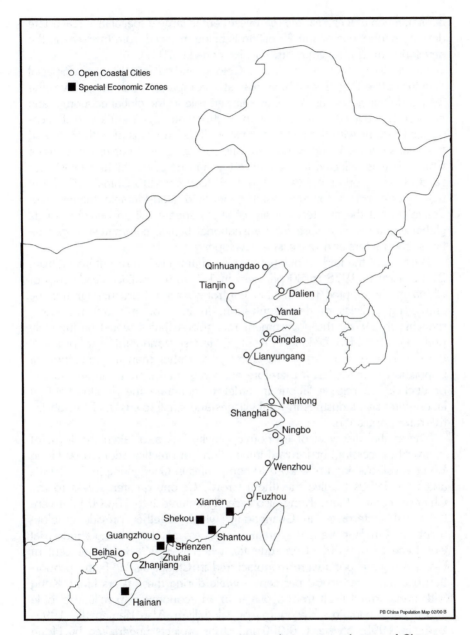

Figure 6.3 *The special economic zones and open coastal cities of China,
1998*

capital, much of it earmarked for investment in largely speculative real estate development, while nearly $5 billion is being invested from overseas in the development of a new airport (Van Kemenade, 1997).

Hong Kong, both as a Crown Colony and after 1997 as a Special Administrative Region of China, was at a comparative advantage over the 14 coastal cities because of its established role in the global economy, and because it provided a open door through which China enhanced its economic relations with the rest of the world. Thus in terms of both trade and financial services, Hong Kong currently surpasses all other urban areas of China. This is reflected in the region having one of the highest GDPs per capita in the world (US$24,760 in 1995 compared to China's US$750), the highest prices for real estate and land (considerable higher than Tokyo's), and the greatest density of skyscrapers – all an outcome of its global functions as a base for transnational banks, commercial organizations, contractors and real-estate developers.

Because of the fairly rapid increase in urbanization in recent years (from 21 per cent in 1978 to 30 per cent in 1995), the political leadership of China has attempted to maintain control over rural–urban migration by employing policies of deconcentration. In its economic reforms (commencing in 1978), the government recognized that it would be infinitely preferable for Mao Zedong – from a Marxist standpoint – to promote the diversion of industry to the countryside rather than the migration of population to the cities. It therefore encouraged an increase in agricultural productivity to release labour in order to generate the development of labour-intensive industries in rural villages and small towns, and to stabilize the rural population.

The spatial dispersal of economic activity has also taken the form of 'outward processing' or forward integration – a practice adopted by Hong Kong in establishing up to 20,000 companies in Guangdong in the 1980s and early-1990s to give the (then) Crown Colony greater access to the Chinese market. Hong Kong also recently entered into 10,000 joint ventures with enterprises in Guangdong, which together provide employment for 4 million people – greatly in excess of Hong Kong's industrial workforce of 680,000. Consequently, whereas in 1988, 35 per cent of Hong Kong's exports were manufactured in China, by 1995 the proportion had increased to 60 per cent – while during these years Hong Kong had 'transformed itself from a player in an economy of 6 million people into a participant in an economy of 1.2 billion' (Van Kemenade, 1997: 214). In 1995, of the 120,000 industrial projects undertaken by Hong Kong firms in China, around 80 per cent were in the Pearl River delta – in close proximity to the Crown Colony. The associated investment from Hong Kong (a sum of HK$63 billion) amounted to 62.5 per cent of all external investment in China in 1995. Clearly, the deconcentration of new

economic activity from Hong Kong could not be equated with suburbanization or de-urbanization since it was not paralleled by a corresponding
out-migration of population from the Crown Colony. It also contributed
to the formation of an enormous polycentred agglomeration based on
Shenzen–Zhuhai–Hong Kong, which in aggregate experienced a net inflow
of population rather than an outflow. Nevertheless, by dispersing a substantial amount of its potential economic activity (albeit to neighbouring
cities), Hong Kong has ensured that its population will be more easily
stabilized close to its optimum (notwithstanding vagaries in the number of
new arrivals from the rest of China), and that the process of urbanization
will be kept in check.

India

There are very few detailed studies of Indian cities to ascertain whether –
in aggregate – urban populations are concentrating or deconcentrating.
However, the dispersal of population and industry can be seen within and
around many of the largest metropolitan areas. Whereas population growth
within the built-up area of cities is often slow, new towns have emerged
and there has been a rapid growth in the population of small towns within
the metropolitan region. In the 1991 census, there were as many as 856
new urban centres – many of which were located in the more urbanized
states centred on the metropolitan cities of Delhi, Kolkata (Calcutta),
Mumbai (Bombay), Chennai (Madras), Bangladore, Ahmadabad, Hyder-
abad, Pune, Nagpur and Vishakhapatnam (HABITAT, 1996).

OPTIMAL DEVELOPMENT

Since a positive relationship exists between the size and quality of a building and the price or rent it can command, we need to examine more closely
the question of whether it is worth spending more on a building if, as a
result, it will sell for a higher price.

With any given site there comes a point when the addition of further
units of development capital produces successively smaller increases in the
expected value of the development on completion. This situation is shown
graphically in figure 6.4(a). With the addition of successive units of development capital (each unit representing, say, £10,000) to a particular site,
total returns (TR, or GDV) will continue to increase, but at a diminishing
rate. Finally, in the example shown, addition of the ninth unit of capital
adds nothing to the expected GDV of the project, and adding a tenth unit
of capital conceivably could start to reduce total returns. This could occur

in the case of, for example, a housing development, where at higher density, properties would eventually be built too close together which would negatively affect the selling price of all units and the GDV of the development as a whole. In the case of industrial property, values would be affected adversely if site coverage became excessive; and in the case of retailing, multistorey development might add little if anything to the GDV, apart perhaps from special cases such as shopping malls.

In the example shown in figure 6.4(a) it would not generally be advisable for the developer to maximize the GDV or total returns. This can be seen by looking at the contribution to the GDV of the last few units of capital applied to the site; clearly no developer would add the ninth unit of capital which would add nothing to the GDV but the same would also apply to preceding units if these added less to the GDV than it would cost the developer to employ them.

Figure 6.4(b) illustrates this point by showing the additions to the GDV of each successive unit of capital (otherwise known as the marginal returns or marginal revenue product of capital). From this graph we can see, for example, that the marginal returns to the eighth unit of capital amount to only £5,000. In other words, adding the eighth unit of capital adds only £5,000 to the overall GDV – considerably less than it would cost to employ it in construction.

In order to answer the question of how many units of capital the developer should apply to the given site, we also need to know how much it would cost the developer to employ a unit of capital (defined as £10,000 of development costs including normal profit and professional fees). This will itself depend upon such factors as the rate of interest on borrowing and the length of time that money is tied up in the development process. Let us assume for simplicity that this would add 10 per cent to the cost of a unit of capital, then the cost of additional units of capital (or the marginal cost of capital) would total £11,000. We can see from figure 6.4(b) that the first few units of capital employed on the project, up to and including the fifth unit, would produce marginal returns in excess of their marginal cost. However, the sixth and successive units of capital would each add more to the cost of development that they would increase the GDV. In other words, the marginal costs of employing these units of capital would exceed the marginal returns on so doing.

To maximize site-bid, development of a site should continue as long as the addition of an extra unit of capital increases the GDV by a greater amount than it adds to the total cost of development. This situation is analyzed graphically in figure 6.5. The figure assumes a given use (such as offices) and standard of construction. The horizontal axis measures – in units of £1,000 – the quantity of capital in the form of all construction and development expenditure applied to the site, including an allowance for normal

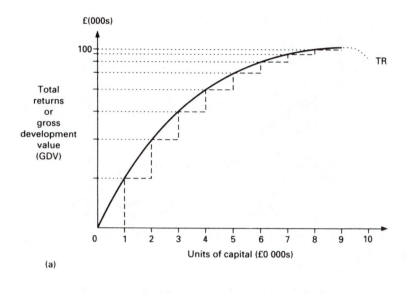

(a)

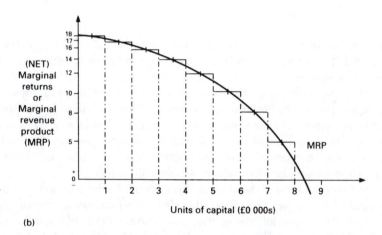

(b)

Figure 6.4 *Changes in gross development value (GDV) as successive units of capital are applied to a given site*

profit. The cost of a unit of capital is measured on the vertical axis. We assume for simplicity that the cost of an additional unit remains constant, hence the marginal cost (MC) curve forms a horizontal straight line. The MC curve will be higher the greater the level of interest charges and the longer the capital is tied up in the development.

The marginal revenue product (MRP) curve shows the amount by which

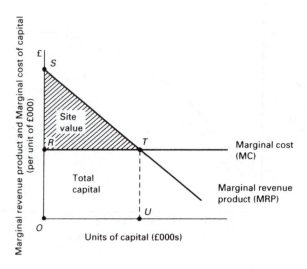

Figure 6.5 *Optimal site development and site-bid*

total returns (that is, GDV) are increased by the addition of one extra unit of capital. This estimate, as we saw earlier, could be based either on annual rental less outgoings or anticipated selling price on completion. MRP is shown to be declining as total capital applied to the site increases, illustrating the process of diminishing marginal returns to a fixed factor (that is, land). This may occur for several reasons: greater height may involve substantial additional expenditure on foundations; or car parking, lifts and fire escapes may be required; and construction costs may also rise. Rents on higher floors may also diminish, especially with retailing.

The optimum level of development is at point *T* where *U* units of capital are applied to the site and where the MRP of an additional unit of capital just equals the marginal cost of that unit. The total cost of capital is given by *ORTU* (that is, £*OR* per unit × *OU* units), whereas total returns or the GDV is given by *OSTU*. The difference between the two is *RST*, representing the surplus or maximum amount remaining once costs are deducted. It is also the maximum sum the developer can bid for the site – at a higher or lower level of capital investment, maximum site-bid would fall below *RST*.

Factors Influencing Site-bid

Maximum site-bid will rise if either the MRP curve rises or the MC curve falls (and vice versa). A rise in the MRP curve could occur if: (1) the value of the finished product rose; (2) capital productivity rose, for example, through technological advance; or (3) there was a fall in the price of any inputs, such that a unit of expenditure on capital results in a higher level of output (and higher MRP, given a constant price for output). A fall in the marginal cost curve could arise if: (1) the interest rate falls; (2) there is a reduction in the construction time so that capital is tied up for a shorter period; or (3) with reduced risk, a loan on more favourable terms can be achieved. In practice, changes influencing any of the above factors are likely to affect different types of development in rather different ways, perhaps favouring some land uses relative to others.

Different land uses (such as offices, retailing or housing) will result in different site-bids because of differences in capital intensity (for example, offices may use more floors than retailing) and differences in the occupier's profitability from use of floorspace – for example, high street retailing as opposed to residential uses. If there were no controls over land use, then competition would ensure that a particular site would go to its highest and best use – that is, the use providing the highest possible site-bid. Although the developer would clearly like to pay less than this, competition between developers should ensure that each puts in a maximum bid in an effort to obtain the site. However, even among similar development schemes (for example, housing) different site-bids may result; while this may be due to differences in efficiency as between developers, it is important to recognize that it may also result from qualitative differences in layout, density levels or even construction standards.

In practice, the planning process may restrict the type of use to which land may be put, or limits may be placed on the maximum permissible height of buildings – thus restricting the amount of capital that may be applied to the site. Also, location will affect the profitability of any particular land use significantly.

Finally, MRP will decline at different rates in different land uses; for example, while office users may be largely indifferent to high-rise buildings, housing developers may find that as total capital and housing densities increase, so this may reduce the anticipated selling prices of *all* (and not just additional) units. Where units of capital are large and indivisible (for example, successive floors in office blocks) MRP declines in a stepwise fashion. This is shown in figure 6.6 and table 6.2, which also illustrate the point that rising costs result in higher capital outlays for successive floors.

Where several uses are considered together, the analysis becomes more complex. For example, increased site-value may result from the addition of ground-floor shops to a residential block of flats (see figure 6.7). In the case shown, the optimal capital outlay remains unchanged at *OU* units.

On a larger scale, city-centre or out-of-town shopping and leisure developments will require very careful consideration in order to obtain the

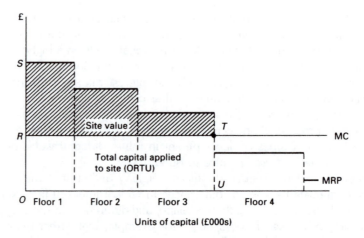

Figure 6.6 *Multistorey development*

*Table 6.2 The cost, revenue and site value of a hypothetical office development**

Floor	Capital outlay per floor (marginal cost) (£)	Capital value per floor (marginal revenue product) (£)	Residual (site) value per floor (£)
4	85,000	70,000	–15,000
3	75,000	80,000	5,000
2	60,000	90,000	30,000
1	50,000	100,000	50,000
Totals to third floor	Cost 185,000	GDV 270,000	Site value 85,000

* Present values.

correct mix and location of activities and facilities (for example, adequate parking and access to public transport) to achieve a maximum value for the available site.

URBAN RENEWAL

To set urban renewal into context, it is necessary – as a preliminary – to consider the characteristics of counterurbanization, and to examine the changing structure of the city.

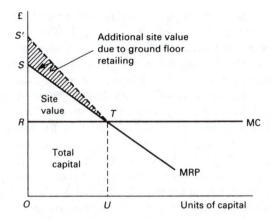

Figure 6.7 *Maximization of site-value for given capital investment*

Counterurbanization

One of the key questions posed by those studying recent population trends in Europe, the United States and Japan is whether the share of national population in the largest urban areas of these countries has in fact peaked and whether further growth will in future be confined to smaller towns and rural areas. We have already seen evidence for the United Kingdom to suggest that the largest cities were not growing as fast as the country as a whole in the 1950s and that smaller settlements had already made some recovery by the 1960s. However, the more important consideration is clearly whether such changes form part of a more widespread process, affecting advanced industrialized countries in general. While some studies have investigated overall population changes, others have placed more emphasis on migration patterns. Migration flows have often been more important than natural change in explaining spatial population changes and they more clearly reflect the place preferences of individuals. In all cases it is important to define settlements as being relatively self-contained units in terms of jobs and populations in order to exclude the effects of suburbanization and local metropolitan decentralization. This is desirable since these clearly represent extensions of existing urban settlements, rather than counterurbanization as such.

In Britain urban population changes occurred only slowly at first, and although unexpected in terms of its eventual scope, some decentralization was generally seen as being desirable to facilitate clearance of some of the worst slum areas (often in association with the New Towns programme). Elsewhere, however the decline of the largest metropolitan areas came as an even greater surprise. Indeed, in 1975, a report of the International

Geographical Union went so far as to state that urbanization had become a 'really worldwide phenomenon' (Campion, 1989). In contrast, Berry (1976) pointed out that since 1970, the United States metropolitan areas had grown more slowly than the nation as a whole and that this decline was mainly accounted for by the eight largest metropolitan areas, which had lost over a quarter of a million residents. Migration flows between these areas and the outlying non-metropolitan counties had also been reversed; while the largest metropolitan areas in the United States had gained (net) migrants over the 1960s, they lost them over the 1970s. Although much of this growth took place in smaller metropolitan areas and in counties with substantial daily commuting to metropolitan areas, it also appeared that remoter rural areas had recorded a large upturn in population change. Taking a broader view of counterurbanization (including all types of deconcentration) than might be used today, Berry attributed these changes to the residential preferences of individuals for low-density living. Housing and job markets would then adjust to these preferences to produce decentralization of both population and employment. Economic, technological and transportation factors would play a role in influencing the speed at which counterurbanization occurred. Berry clearly emphasizes the role of 'values' in residential decision-making; this approach has, however, been given some support by later studies showing negative correlations between city size and respondents' assessment of their standard of living and neighbourhood ratings (Hoch, 1987). The drawbacks with this argument are, first, that not everyone has a true choice of residential location; and, secondly, that employment decentralization is possibly at least as important in explaining population shifts as vice versa. For example in South-East England over the 1970s and 1980s, counties with the highest levels of employment growth were largely dependent on in-migration of workers, so that employment growth and population relocation were interdependent. If residential location had occurred independently of employment relocation, in-migration of population would have been associated with increased out-commuting (to London), which was not generally the case (Congdon and Batey, 1989).

More recent statistics, shown in table 6.3, appear to show that counterurbanization has gone into reverse in the United States, with metropolitan areas achieving higher population growth rates than non-metropolitan areas over the 1980s.

To what extent this is attributable to a fundamental reversal or merely a partial lapse in counterurbanization is unclear. As in the United Kingdom, service sector growth and financial deregulation coupled with an urban property boom may have had some influence, particularly given their impact on the United States housing market (Case, 1992).

In Europe, in addition to Great Britain, the process of counterurbaniza-

Table 6.3 Population changes in the United States, 1960–90, by
metropolitan type (percentages)

Period	Large metropolitan area	Other metropolitan area	Non-metropolitan area
Ten-year change			
1960–70	18.5	14.6	2.2
1970–80	8.1	15.5	14.3
Five-year change			
1980–85	6.0	6.1	3.6
1985–90	5.8	4.4	0.3

Note: Metropolitan areas are defined according to constant boundaries as of 1990. Large metropolitan areas include 39 CMSAs and MSAs with 1990 populations of 1 million and over.

Source: Adapted from Champion (1992: 3/4).

tion – defined in terms of net migration patterns – appears to have generally held up in France, Belgium, Denmark and the Federal Republic of Germany (FRG) over the 1970s and 1980s (and Switzerland, based on population change). Sweden, however, appears to have experienced a shift back towards urbanization over the 1980s, as has the Netherlands. In southern Europe, Portugal appears to exhibit an increasing tendency towards urbanization, possibly due to declining agricultural employment in rural areas and growing industrialization (Illeris, 1992).

Recent evidence suggests that counterurbanization has now become a feature of Italian population change, with metropolitan areas of Turin, Milan and Genoa in decline over the period 1981–85. In the FRG functional urban regions with over one million population experienced absolute population decline for the first time during 1980–85 (Champion, 1989). With unification, however, it is possible that these changes will be reversed because of in-migration. There are also signs of renewed acceleration in the United Kingdom and Denmark following a period of slower deconcentration in the 1980s (Champion, 1992). For France, however, the 1990 census results suggest that the Paris conurbation in particular has recovered markedly from its losses during 1975–82, partly because of a strong natural rate of increase in the population and what appears to be a halt in the long-term decline of average household size (in contrast to London). In Japan, rapid urbanization took place in the 1950s and 1960s, with massive population movements into the metropolitan regions. Urbanization there appears to have reached a plateau after about 1975. While Tokyo continues to see net out-migration, its population is not in decline and overall a process of coun-terurbanizations cannot be clearly identified. In fact, a net migration outflow from non-metropolitan to metropolitan regions, although small, appears to have resumed since the early 1980s (Champion, 1989).

Clearly, despite the general tendency for countries to have experienced population deconcentration at some point in the recent past, there are considerable differences between countries in terms of the timing and severity of this process. Some interesting generalizations can nevertheless be made, although many factors are obviously specific to certain countries or cities. One approach suggested by Frey (1989) is to highlight two separate processes, the first being population deconcentration – a shift from heavily urbanized to less densely populated areas. The second is the 'regional restructuring process' – referring to the spatial effects of changes in the locational requirements of firms in the production and service sectors.

Population movements can in reality be considerably more complex than Berry's initial hypothesis envisaged. Movements away from large urban areas can be increased by improvements in transport infrastructure and the consequent expansion of commuting fields around large cities. In some countries this trend has been associated with a strong desire for different types of housing (especially houses rather than flats). In France, for example, as many as a third of new dwellings built after 1975 were for households setting up home in rural areas. To a large extent this may simply reflect a form of extended suburbanization or peri-urban development with an asso-ciated increase in commuting (Champion, 1989). Yet it also reflects the fact that relatively little new development of individual housing now occurs in many European cities.

Increasing international migration flows may be a factor tending to reinforce recent urban growth in the South and West regions of the United States, and may also have been important in London in the early 1980s. The increase in retirement migration towards areas such as the south coast and the South-West in Britain has had the opposite effect. Changes in the composition of households may also influence migration trends – one-parent families with limited means are likely to be less mobile and will try to minimize travel-to-work time/distance; similar considerations apply to part-time workers and two-income households where one job is part-time. On the other hand, households composed of divorced adults appear to be much more mobile over longer distances (Moore and Clark, 1990). Particularly in the United Kingdom, the increase in part-time female work over the 1980s, and the subsequent increase in two-income households, together with the continuing rise in single-parent families, are likely to have been important in reducing net out-migration from London during the early to mid-1980s. Finally, although cities such as London exhibit net migration outflows overall, in younger age groups (18–24) the net migration flows are often positive, thus an upturn in the proportion of the national population in younger age groups may help to reduce the migratory outflow.

It has been suggested by Bourne (1993) that together, the effects of recession, reductions in employment in finance and related business services, a downturn in younger age groups and household formation, and an upturn in those of retirement age, would combine to bring an end to the gentrification (residential upgrading) of many inner city areas over the 1990s. Others have argued that changes in the workforce and the composition of households have widened permanently the social base for inner-city resettlement. They point out that in some countries (for example, Australia) the gentrification process is already extensive and is therefore unlikely to be reversed (Badcock, 1993).

Turning to the employment effects of the 'regional restructuring process', we can contrast, on the one hand, the decentralizing forces resulting from the urban–rural shift in manufacturing with, on the other, the centralizing forces brought about by the growth of financial and producer services over the 1980s. The processes involved have been examined in more depth by Fielding (1989), who describes how there has emerged a new spatial division of labour (NSDL), involving the increasing separation of command functions (for example, senior management, headquarters functions, and research and development) from production, and of white-collar employees from blue-collar. In large part this can be traced back to the growth of mass-market consumer industries from the 1960s; the rise of large industrial conglomerates and multinationals; and the boom in investment in branch plant operations – all from about the same time. More recently, corporate restructuring and the search for low-cost locations for routine production processes have contributed to the de-industrialization of major cities. To a lesser degree, this has also influenced the dispersal of office workers to areas lying outside the main metropolitan centres (Champion, 1989). One result is that relatively successful regions, seen as low-cost production locations with access to United Kingdom and EU markets, have been able to attract higher-than-average shares of inward foreign direct investment (for example, Wales, the West Midlands and the North) (Hill and Munday, 1992). On the other hand, the 'hi-tech' industries have tended to become polarized in the South and East of England (excluding London, however) (Massey *et al.*, 1991).

The full implications of the NSDL are not yet clear. However, one result could be further concentration of service functions in a small number of major (especially capital) cities with prestige environments. Manufacturing losses in these areas would continue at much the same rate as in the past, with consequent upward effects on unemployment and social polarization. Manufacturing employment growth would continue to gravitate towards the less urbanized areas; in the United Kingdom this would increasingly involve areas outside the South-East. Urban areas and regions will come to be characterized by the functions they perform, rather than the goods they produce or industries they host. Inter-industry linkages in an area may thus decline in importance and growth centre strategies may consequently become less effective (Glasson, 1992).

Finally, comparative studies, such as those by Cheshire (1990) have pointed to a growing polarization between 'successful' and 'unsuccessful' cities. National or regional factors were shown to be important in explaining why cities performed better or worse than expected, as were the effects of local urban policies. For example, cities in south-western France, and south and south-eastern Germany (FRG) appear to have improved compared with their predicted performance. Also, European economic integration appears to be of greater benefit to cities in the more central (core) regions than to those more peripheral ones (including Southern Europe, the Republic of Ireland, Western Scotland and North-West England). In particular, there is some evidence to suggest that the problems of Southern European regions are becoming concentrated in urban as opposed to rural areas as low-skilled workers from the latter continue to move to the cities in search of work (for example, in Naples and Andalucia). Other studies have identified stagnating cities linked to old industrial areas, ports or mining activities (respective examples being Birmingham or Turin, Genoa, and South Wales or the Ruhr), and dynamic towns or cities linked to tourist regions (for example, Spain) or dynamic rural areas with small/medium-sized towns (for example, north-east Italy) (Illeris, 1992).

A recent study of urban development in Germany (FRG) showed clearly how the north–south divide in that country – because of the relative concentration of declining industries in the north and hi-tech industries in the south – was especially evident in the performance of the agglomerations, influencing income and employment growth, unemployment and migratory balance (see table 6.4).

THE CHANGING INTERNAL STRUCTURE OF THE CITY

The process of urban renewal can be seen first as a reaction to changing requirements and demands being placed on the large conurbations, and secondly as part of the inevitable process of obsolescence and reconstruction. Redevelopment, rehabilitation and the relocation of activities are all part of the process of urban growth and renewal. As the economic life of buildings

Table 6.4 Indicators of change in selected agglomerations
in Germany (FRG)

	(North) Ruhr-North	(South) München
Percentage change in population 1970–85	–6.3	+10.1
Percentage change in dependent employment 1970–85	–20.1	+47.5
Percentage change in tax income per inhabitant 1979–85	+32.0	+46.4
Unemployment rate (1986)	13.7	5.4

Source: F.J. Bade, *Regionale Beschäftigungs entwicklung and Produktionsorientierte Dienstleistungen*, Deutsches Institut für Wirtschaftsforschung Sonderheft 143, Duncker & Humblot (1987).

comes to an end, so the existing stock must eventually adjust to new demands.

Theories put forward to help explain changes in the internal structure of the city over time must therefore address themselves to these questions. As the city expands, however, and especially at later stages of urban growth, new development on the urban fringe may become an increasingly attractive alternative to redeveloping the existing central area. This outward movement of development and construction activity is invariably associated with the outward movement of population and population densities. Blumenfeld (1954) was the first to point out the wavelike characteristics of urban expansion.

By examining population change over fifty years in fifteen concentric zones extending outwards from Philadelphia, he found a similar undulatory pattern within each zone. Relative to the average density for a particular period and starting from the centre, each zone in succession reached a peak density, from which it gradually declined. However, as one moved outwards so this peak density itself became much lower and the variations in density over time became less pronounced. Boyce (1966) noted that the fifty-year period required for an upward and downward movement corresponded roughly to the economic life of buildings, and went on to suggest that the (then) current redevelopment of the central-city area could represent a new 'wave' and a repeat of the whole process (as illustrated by the dashed lines in figure 6.8).

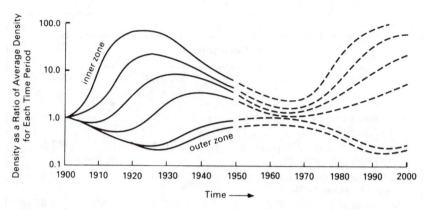

Figure 6.8 *Schematic presentation of zonal undulations over time in an expanding metropolitan area (adapted from Blumenfeld, 1954 and Boyce, 1966)*

According to Blumenfeld (1954), at any point in time there is a particular zone of maximum growth. As illustrated by the already mentioned Philadelphia study, this zone would initially move outwards over time, representing a 'tidal wave of metropolitan expansion' at the rural–urban fringe of the metropolitan area. Boyce (1966) argues that urban renewal and redevelopment are largely dependent on the ability to slow down or reverse the outward spread of this wave. In this sense, redevelopment at the centre can be seen as an alternative to further new development at the urban fringe.

Bourne (1967) examines these processes in more detail, paying particular attention to the alternatives of development and redevelopment. Figure 6.9 illustrates a hypothetical view of development activity as we move outwards from the central business district (CBD). In the city centre, where accessibility is highest, the economic life of buildings may be relatively short, since new building generally requires redevelopment of the existing stock, and changes in demand affecting this stock are relatively frequent (for example, new shopping malls, hi-tech offices and dealing rooms, and so on). Given that land values peak near the CBD, there is economic pressure to develop at high densities. Another peak in development activity may be expected near the suburban fringe, generally on greenfield sites, with lower costs permitting lower-density construction. Such development would tend to follow outward population movements, itself generating further demand. Accessibility may nevertheless be quite good in such locations, particularly given recent and prospective motorway programmes

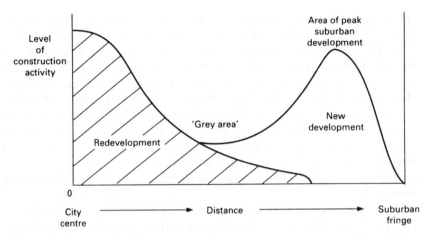

Figure 6.9 *Cross-sectional view of urban development activity (adapted from Blumenfeld, 1954 and Boyce, 1966)*

(such as the M25 orbital motorway which itself generated considerable development pressures outside the green belt fringe surrounding London). As a result, a wide range of development projects may be contemplated in such areas.

Over time, the central and suburban peaks of activity may gradually move outwards. However, physical expansion of the CBD will inevitably be much more restricted than that of the suburban fringe; indeed, in the case of London, many existing parts of the urban area were at some point in the nineteenth century villages at or beyond the rural–urban fringe. In-between these two peaks available sites will already have been developed to varying degrees. Some redevelopment will occur in better locations, otherwise new development will generally consist of infilling. Available sites may be small, with mixed uses more common, and frequently, accessibility may be impeded by congestion and difficulty of improving the transport infrastructure.

Particularly around the transitional zone, these problems may be compounded by high demolition and site preparation costs (for example, old power stations or the effects of toxic land contamination on former industrial sites), making redevelopment more costly. The overall atmosphere of decay in areas containing many redundant buildings and where improvement has failed to occur, may lead to even further decline; new investment may be considered to be too much of a risk, and owners of existing buildings may decide to neglect even essential repair and maintenance activity. This neglect may produce a short-term increase in returns but in the longer-term buildings will tend to decay more quickly. Although it could be in the interest of all owners to invest in improvement works if capital values are sure to rise subsequently, such investment may nevertheless fail to occur. This is often due to the fact that, taken individually, any single investment would probably have little overall impact on property values in an area. As a result, it is likely that no owners will invest since they cannot be sure others will do the same. Furthermore, the external costs and dereliction generated by such decisions may spill over, blighting surrounding areas where property values and the incentive for improvement may also become depressed.

In the case of housing, slum formation is the ultimate result (Walker, 1987). Here, a 'filtering' process may occur, through which older dwellings vacated by higher-income households become available to (larger numbers) of lower-income households. This filtering may permit considerable change of use from single-family habitation to multiple tenancy before redevelopment or rehabilitation takes place. While this process, which increases the supply of low-cost housing, is generally regarded as being socially and economically useful, there may come a stage at which the pressure of demand from low-income groups in inner urban areas places considerable pressures on this stock. As a result, overcrowding becomes more common, rents soar, housing becomes increasingly adapted to temporary requirements and the pace of housing renewal grinds to a halt, since landlords find no shortage of tenants and owners have little incentive to undertake major improvements in a decaying environment.

Although development peaks, and even an outward wave motion, may be discerned, the pace of development activity from area to area may be very uneven. As we have seen, in residential areas the filtering process may delay the timing of redevelopment or improvement substantially. In other areas, urban decay may lead to a process of cumulative decline which eventually spills over into neighbouring areas. One further body of research suggests that since the intensity of site development at the suburban fringe is influenced by the stage of the development cycle in which it occurs, redevelopment in subsequent waves will tend to concentrate first of all on the less intensive land use (Whitehand, 1987). For example, individual late Victorian villas (low-intensity, early-slump) are likely to be redeveloped sooner than early 1930s blocks of flats (high-intensity, early-boom) even where these happen to be in similar locations.

Finally, in addition to the influences discussed above, problems associated with the land market are also important. High land values will generally reflect high demand for a restricted number of sites, particularly within the CBD. However, especially in more outlying areas of the transitional zone, gross development values will often be depressed by uncertainty and locational constraints (for example, poor accessibility), and (re)development costs may be inflated by high site clearance and site preparation costs, and high reparcellation costs in trying to obtain sites of sufficient size for new uses. Consequently, the developer's (residual) valuation of available sites may often be below the values at which land owners may be willing to sell. Landowners must therefore be prepared to take a realistic view of urban site values if development is to proceed.

In conclusion, the above theories are all useful in helping us to understand the process of adaptation to change in urban areas. While the needs and requirements of various activities – retailing, industrial, offices and residential – may change at a fairly rapid pace with changes in technology and as fashions change, existing buildings are usually fairly fixed in terms of the services they offer. This problem of mismatch or 'functional obsolescence' can elicit a variety of responses. In some cases existing buildings can be adapted, but more frequently there is a call for new buildings. In the latter case, the alternative to redeveloping existing buildings within the urban area is often greenfield site development at the rural–urban fringe. In this context it is sometimes suggested that the existence of controls over the outward development of the city (such as green belts) will help to turn back these waves of urban expansion – thus in theory encouraging redevelopment rather than continuous urban sprawl. By raising capital values for new uses in urban areas, redevelopment may well be encouraged, but other problems may be created. Rising land values would affect some uses (for example, housing) more than others which could easily build at higher densities (for example, offices), and the cost of providing some types of social infrastructure (for example, roads) would also rise. Higher costs of living resulting from more expensive housing could well translate into higher wage demands. Moreover, some activities could decide to leapfrog the barrier entirely rather than move back towards the city – possibly resulting in urban job losses occurring at a faster rate than population decentralization. On the other hand, the unrestricted growth of urban areas would cause urban sprawl and increased congestion, and thereby reduce the incentive for inner city renewal.

As a consequence of the out-migration of people and economic activity, the inner cities became characterized by declining populations, a faster-than-average reduction in manufacturing activity, the lack of new high-tech industries and a growing dependency on low-paid service employment. Poor housing conditions were exemplified by a higher-than-average share of the older housing stock and large concentrations of poor-quality, high-rise dwellings – developed in the 1960s and 1970s.

Although these characteristics of urban decay were largely recognized as early as the 1960s, by the 1980s it had become clear that decay was not just confined to pockets of deprivation, but to whole areas of the largest agglomerations. However, it could be eliminated by massive investment in urban renewal (by the public or private sectors, or both), and other substantial benefits could accrue:

First, there would result a superior pattern of resource allocation. There would be less wastage of land (in otherwise high-cost areas) since densities would be transformed towards an optimum level. Derelict areas would be developed for housing and employment, and overcrowded areas decongested. Some decayed residential areas would be converted into commercial and industrial uses and vice versa. There would also be less wastage of manpower. Reduced unemployment would raise income levels and, together with an inflow of middle- and higher-income households (with the development of owner-occupied housing and co-ownership) many inner urban areas would be 'transformed', both economically and socially. Property values would, on aggregate, rise and spill over into peripheral areas. Secondly, there would be considerable social benefits. An improved residential and work environment (and higher incomes) would result in less ill-health, fire damage and crime, reducing the cost of health and fire services and the police. A healthier, higher-paid labour force might increase the level of productivity and lower the rate of absenteeism, and less deprivation would reduce the cost of welfare services and payments. Finally, an improved environment and higher property values would widen the tax base and enable the local authority to provide better services where required. Ironically, areas with poor environments requiring the greatest amount of public expenditures are least able to raise revenue to facilitate this process.

But to realize the above benefits, considerable costs would have to be incurred. These include research, survey and planning costs; administrative expenditure; the cost of acquiring decayed property; demolition costs; the cost of public and private developments; relocation costs (both economic and non-economic); and possibly the cost of land value write-down if sites are released for development at below their market value.

By identifying and quantifying the above advantages and costs of renewal investment carefully, cost–benefit analyses could be undertaken to a limited extent, and renewal projects ranked in order of greatest net benefit as a guide to decision-making. Full account would have to be taken of the urban economic base and the effects of the multiplier (Chapter 2).

The Processes of Urban Renewal

The term 'urban renewal' has three different meanings: *redevelopment* – the demolition, clearance and reconstruction of a whole area; *rehabilita-*

tion – bringing buildings of poor condition up to a prescribed standard; and *conservation* – involving partial clearance and appropriate rehabilitation in order to physically enhance an area (Richardson, 1971).

THE ECONOMICS OF REDEVELOPMENT AND REHABILITATION

Redevelopment and rehabilitation are often seen as alternative solutions to adapting buildings and sites to new demands and economic uses. Whereas rehabilitation involves maintenance, repair and adaptation in order to ensure a sound structure and some functional adjustment of the building, redevelopment implies the total replacement of existing buildings. Redevelopment therefore offers wider possible advantages in modifying land use, site coverage and density as well as introducing new building techniques and standards of construction, specification, design and layout. At the extreme, comprehensive redevelopment involving numerous buildings and activities may extend to large parts of an urban area, examples being found in many city-centre schemes in Britain during the 1950s and 1960s. Bourne (1967) suggested that for an individual building, the process of change and adaptation falls into a number of stages. We start from a situation where the building is occupied by the use for which it was designed. In the second stage the original use is replaced by another use representing a higher-order activity, or a more intensive use in the same activity (for example, splitting up of large, formerly owner-occupied dwellings into smaller units for private renting); at this stage there is little modification of the building. In the third stage there is partial conversion or modification of the building to better accommodate new uses and new occupants (for example, change of use of city-centre residential properties to offices). To be worthwhile, this generally requires a good location and accessibility. Finally, buildings are demolished and replaced, either by a more intensive use (for example, retailing to offices) or by a more intensive form of the existing use such as high-rise office space, business parks, shopping malls or high-density residential flats. Bourne recognized that not all buildings fulfil this sequence, nor do similar buildings always appear at the same stage at the same time (for example, because of locational differences). Yet the sequence usefully describes the process of adaptation of the built environment to accommodate changing demands. Moreover, Bourne emphasizes the fact that adaptation and replacement of buildings stem primarily from economic pressure rather than physical deterioration. This is particularly true in and around the Central Business District, where pressure for change and adaptation is often greatest and where buildings may become obsolete over a relatively short period of time. Whereas the physical ageing of buildings depends on their initial construction and subsequent maintenance and repair, obsolescence depends on other factors:

(1) the rate of technical innovation and the adaptability of existing buildings (for example, to the increasing demands of office users for information technology);
(2) problems caused by the changing pattern of urban growth and changes in the location of activities and population;
(3) negative external or neighbourhood effects on particular buildings or groups of buildings.

Common examples include the effects of urban road schemes, planning blight brought about by expected change of use, and the impact of urban decay on surrounding areas as residents and firms come to fear risking capital outlays on improving or even on maintaining their own properties.

Whereas many modern buildings are usually designed for life-spans of sixty years or slightly less (Larkham, 1992), the redevelopment of many types of building often occurs over a much shorter time period. Equally, the life-span of other buildings may be extended through major refurbishment and/or rebuilding, particularly in the historic cores of many cities. Yet other buildings may suffer the fate of abandonment and dereliction due to a combination of obsolescence, rising repair or running costs, and the lack of new activities finding them a profitable source of investment. It is to the further examination of these activities and alternatives that we shall now turn.

Redevelopment

In order for redevelopment to be profitable, the value of the cleared site for the new development (effectively the developer's maximum site-bid) must exceed the value of the site and building in its existing use. We will consider the determination of cleared site value in more detail shortly, because this differs from site-bid theory, as discussed earlier, mainly due to the existence of sometimes substantial demolition and site preparation costs entailed by redevelopment. For the moment we need to start by examining changes over time in the capital value of the site and building in its existing use.

Over time, buildings tend to become increasingly unsuited for the demands placed upon them by the market, thus influencing achievable rents. As they age, more expensive repairs become necessary as materials weather or decay. In addition, periodic updating (which could involve anything from meeting new fire regulations to changing shop frontages or

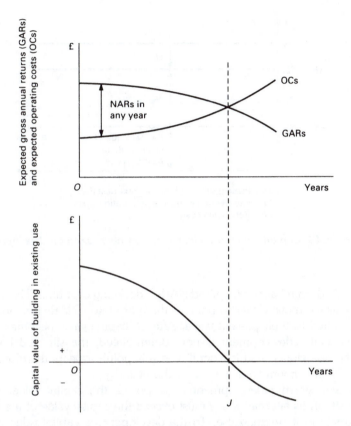

Figure 6.10 *Net annual returns (NARs) and capital value of a building in current use over time (price stability assumed)*

installing new heating or ventilation) often becomes more difficult and more costly.

This is illustrated in figure 6.10. In the upper diagram, expected operating costs (OCs) are shown as rising over time because outgoings on repairs and maintenance increase in later years. By contrast, expected gross annual returns (GARs) – based on estimates of total annual rent – may eventually fall in real terms as competition with other developments increases or as the initial building becomes increasingly obsolete relative to changing user demands. Net annual returns (NARs) for any year are given by the difference between GARs and OCs for that year. After *J* years, NARs fall to zero.

The lower diagram in figure 6.10 shows the capital value of the build-

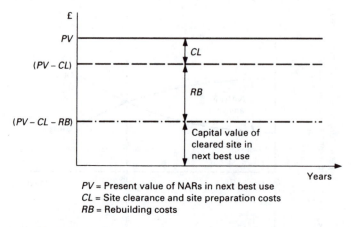

Figure 6.11 *Capital value of a cleared site in new use upon development*

ing – derived from future capitalized NARs – declining over time. This occurs because as we move closer to point *J*, there are fewer NARs remaining to be discounted to their present value. After *J*, capital value becomes negative, hence if redevelopment is not contemplated, the site and building would be abandoned and left derelict at this point; *J* years therefore represents the maximum technical life of the building.

However, when redevelopment is proposed, the capital value of the cleared site in its alternative use must exceed the capital value of the building and site in its existing use. To the developer, the capital value of the cleared site is determined by the present value of the site in its new use less the cost of clearing the site, any land preparation costs (for example, drainage) and the cost of rebuilding. This is illustrated in figure 6.11. It can also be seen that any increase (decrease) in clearance and preparation costs (*CL*) or rebuilding costs (*RB*) will push down (up) the capital value of the cleared site – other things (such as rent) being equal. Although the capital value of the cleared site is shown as remaining constant at whatever point in time the redevelopment is contemplated, in practice shifts may occur over time because of changes in demand or supply factors; for example, technological change may lower the cost of rebuilding, or changes in demand (such as towards out-of-town retailing) could influence expected rents, or, again, public subsidy could reduce site clearance costs.

As shown in the following diagrams, redevelopment may occur (at point *X*) when the capital value of the cleared site in its next best use comes to exceed the capital value of the building in its current use. This point is known as the economic life of the existing building. Two examples

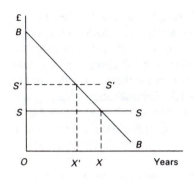

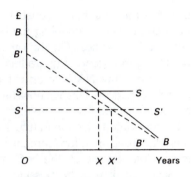

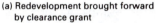

(a) Redevelopment brought forward
by clearance grant

(b) Redevelopment delayed by
rise in cost of borrowing
(rate of interest)

BB = Capital value of building (and site) in existing use
SS = Capital value of cleared site in best alternative use

Figure 6.12 *Factors influencing timing of redevelopment*

of economic changes which may influence the timing of redevelopment are given in figure 6.12. In 6.12(a) a clearance grant is shown as raising the capital value of the cleared site and bringing forward redevelopment from X to X' years. In 6.12(b) a rise in the rate of interest lowers both the capital value of the existing building (since future net earnings are capitalized at a higher rate) and the capital value of the cleared site – to B'B' and S'S' respectively. However, the current use is marginally favoured by this change, putting off redevelopment from X to X' years. This occurs for several reasons:

(1) the higher interest rate is applied to fewer net annual returns in the case of the existing building (this is why BB and B'B' converge towards later years of project life);

(2) the next best alternative use will, in addition, incur higher development costs because of the higher cost of borrowing, and, conversely, a fall in interest rates will tend to bring forward the pace of redevelopment.

Rehabilitation

Unlike redevelopment, rehabilitation involves improvement of the existing building, either in the same use or, not infrequently, in a more intensive use. On the one hand, rehabilitation may simply involve the reversal of neglect and decay, enabling the building to continue to provide an accept-able level of service. On the other, it may involve major refurbishment or rebuilding in a general upgrading of the building. In all cases the objective is to raise future NARs to an extent which will more than offset the outlay on rehabilitation. This is shown in figure 6.13. Rehabilitation taking place at point r in time produces higher attainable rents, thus raising GARs. In addition, some reduction in future operating costs is likely since, first, newer materials used in refurbishment will tend to age more slowly and require less maintenance than the ones they replace.

Secondly, it may be possible at the same time to undertake improve-ments that would reduce energy consumption; for example, by providing better standards of insulation. The combination of raised GARs and lower OCs improves net annual returns from point r onwards, as shown in figure 6.13(a).

Whether expenditure on rehabilitation is worthwhile therefore depends upon whether the present value of the rise in NARs (shown as the hatched area in figure 6.13(b)) exceeds the present value of the cost of work under-taken. Alternatively, since the rise in NARs will produce a higher capital value for the rehabilitated building at point r, this increase in capital values can be compared directly with the cost of rehabilitation.

Shops frequently undergo refurbishment to keep up with new trends, and offices occasionally undergo major rebuilding for similar reasons. Large residential properties can often produce higher capital values by conversion into smaller units, and even old industrial buildings or warehouses can some-times be converted economically to better uses. Increasingly, however, with commercial properties, the decision whether to undertake major refurbish-ment has become complicated by the possibility of redevelopment in the not-too-distant future (Pugh, 1992). Prime examples are certain 1960s office blocks and shopping centres which, because the possibility of rede-velopment is not far distant, may find that refurbishment would only extend their economic lives by perhaps another fifteen years. This problem can be illustrated as in figure 6.14 which also includes the cleared site value in the next best alternative use. Refurbishment of the existing building in year r would extend the economic life of the building from year x to y, but after this point is reached the value of the existing building becomes largely irrel-evant if redevelopment is contemplated, since the cleared site value (CSV) is in excess of the value of the building and site in its existing use. Clearly, as y moves left towards point r (that is, if CSV rises) so the advantages of rehabilitation become less clear and the more likely it becomes that prop-erty owners will 'sit it out' and await redevelopment, avoiding as much ex-penditure as possible on the existing building.

In the 1970s, a limited amount of empirical evidence in the United States

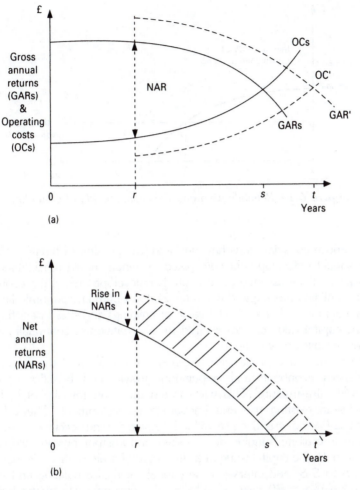

Figure 6.13 *Rehabilitation and net annual returns (NARs)*

(Bagby, 1973; Listokin, 1973) and in Britain (National Community Development Project, 1975) seemed to suggest that rehabilitation was cheaper than redevelopment, although in Britain the evidence was by no means conclusive since it was difficult to compare the clearance and redevelopment of a whole area with the rehabilitation of a relatively small number of (often scattered) properties. Nevertheless, in Britain (particularly after the Housing Act 1969) rehabilitation became a major housing priority (Chapter 4).

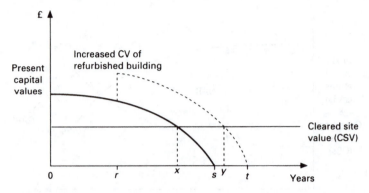

Figure 6.14 *Rehabilitation and the economic life of a building*

The above considerations have ignored the question of timing – that is, when should redevelopment take place, or when should rehabilitation be undertaken? Even assuming that a site is redeveloped when the economic life of a building has expired (Chapter 2), the optimum economic life of a building is not fixed. The capital value of buildings and sites in existing use and the capital value of sites cleared for alternative use continually fluctuate and establish new optima.

The capital value of sites for alternative use will rise if the urban area experiences economic and population growth and benefits from an improved infrastructure. This will shorten the economic life of buildings and sites in existing use and encourage redevelopment. The value of cleared sites for alternative use will fall if reverse trends occur – a decaying infrastructure alone bringing down values and postponing redevelopment. In figure 6.15 the capital value of a site cleared for alternative use increases from SS to S_1S_1 and intersects the capital value of a building and site in its existing use at 80 years – reducing the economic life of the building from the original optimum of 100 years. Conversely, a decrease in the capital value of the cleared site could extend the economic life of the building.

The capital value of a building and site might, however, also change. It could be expected to rise as a result of rehabilitation and/or conversion from, for example, a single-family dwelling house into bedsitters, flats or bed-and-breakfast accommodation. Recently, deconversions of flats and bedsitters into single-family freehold or leasehold properties have also increased the capital value of buildings and their sites. If rehabilitation and/or conversion (or deconversion) occurred when the age of the building was 80 years, the economic life of the building could be extended to 120

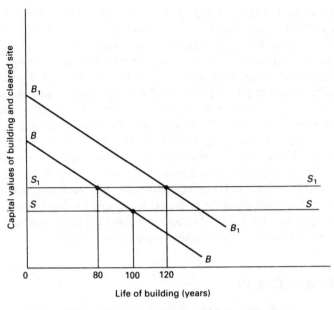

BB = Initial capital value of building and site in existing use
SS = Initial capital value of cleared site for its best alternative use
B_1B_1 = Increased capital value of building and site after rehabilitation etc.
S_1S_1 = Increased capital value of cleared site for its best alternative use

Figure 6.15 *Changes in the maximum economic life of a building (assuming general price stability)*

years, where values would again be in equilibrium. Conversely, if the capital value of the property is decreased (perhaps because of the building falling into serious disrepair), there would be a downward shift in the *BB* curve and the economic life of the building would be reduced.

The relationship of the capital value of the cleared site (for alternative use) to the capital value of the building and site (in existing use) is particularly relevant to the problems of the inner city. The inner city contains a high proportion of old dwellings – most of which have been modified over the years. Generally, the capital value of these buildings and their sites has increased to keep pace with the increase in the capital value of sites for alternative uses. Were it not for the conversion of houses into multi-occupied dwellings and other forms of accommodation, their demolition would have occurred many decades ago. The inner cities therefore often retain their nineteenth-century image which, except for a minority of buildings of architectural or historic interest, is one of gloom and decay. Yet it is not just the extended life of buildings (brought about by increases in their capital values) that is responsible for much of the inner city being a twilight area. In many cases, the capital value of sites cleared for alternative use is much greater than the current or potential capital values of the buildings, but the latter values have been kept artificially low by the effects of legislation. In the UK the Rent Acts of 1915, 1939, 1965 and 1974 subjected private land-lords to rent control or regulation, while tenants were granted increasing protection (Chapter 4). Although these measures should be viewed in the light of problems of housing need and affordability, the direct effect was that buildings which could neither be readily redeveloped nor maintained or repaired for want of an adequate return on investment were kept out of use. But after the Housing Act 1969, improvement grants became available increasingly for modernization and these have raised the capital value of properties. Grants have thus had the effect of retaining in use the older housing stock of the inner city until such a time as redevelopment is feasible.

HISTORIC BUILDINGS

Economic analysis of the problems facing historic buildings can be undertaken largely within the framework of the preceding sections. In many cases such buildings require substantial rehabilitation, without which further decay and dereliction would eventually occur. Unfortunately, it is often the case that financial returns from continued use may not justify the outlays required on improvement works. In other cases historic buildings, while remaining economically viable, may nevertheless be under threat from redevelopment – particularly in expanding CBDs and where they do not represent an intensive use of their existing site (compared to high-rise offices, for example). As such, the CSV of the site they occupy may well be in excess of the value of the historic building itself. These alternative positions are analyzed in figure 6.16(a) which shows the present capital values of the existing historic building as well as the cleared site value in the highest alternative use (for example, offices). The capital value of the historic building declines so that at year x redevelopment would be economically feasible, although if redevelopment was not contemplated, the building would be abandoned and left to decay after year y. Figure 6.16(b) shows how this may occur in practice. Although GARs may continue to rise as the historic building acquires a scarcity value over time, it is likely that OCs will tend to rise with structural wear and tear. If periodic major expenditure is required (for example, recasting of lead roofs) then OCs may increase in a stepwise fashion, falling off later. However, in many cases the situation may be even worse than that depicted. First, many historic buildings or monuments produce no direct revenue whatsoever, their public interest being entirely historical, social or

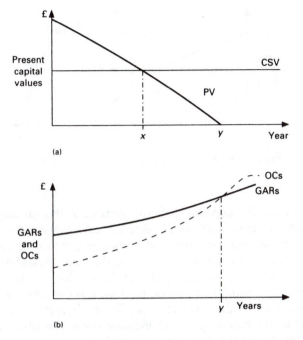

Figure 6.16 *Historic buildings – rising repair and maintenance costs offset higher gross annual returns*

architectural. Secondly, with monuments that are openly accessible to the public, such as Hadrian's Wall, for example, it may not be practicable to try to enforce charges for visiting the facility. As a result, for many such buildings and monuments, GARs are frequently zero or at best negligible, and without public or charitable funding the costs of maintenance and repair could not be met.

But even where individuals or firms are prepared to place a value on living or working in, or simply visiting historic buildings, the market tends to ignore the wider valuation society as a whole places on them. This occurs for several main reasons:

(1) GARs measure only the private benefits accruing to those owning or renting such buildings. In addition to this are the external benefits derived by passers-by or other activities in the vicinity (for example, tourism, shops).

(2) Particularly if the consequences of decay are irreversible, individuals might be prepared to pay something just to keep open the option of visiting the building at a later date ('option' demand). For very important historic buildings or monuments people may feel there is some

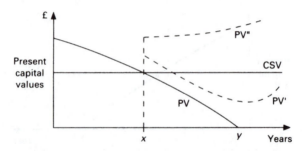

Figure 6.17 *Policy options for historic buildings*

intrinsic value in maintaining these assets even though they may not personally be able to visit them ('existence' value). Although for any individual, 'option' and 'existence' values may be quite small, many people might be willing to contribute something: thus, overall, such values could become very substantial. Some idea of these values can be observed in the voluntary contributions made by a growing number of individuals to bodies such as the UK's National Trusts. Rising real incomes and growing leisure time may further increase the appreciation of architectural heritage and the desire to preserve it.

(3) Because of their often unique character, the scarcity value of such buildings is likely to rise over time, but it is unlikely that present-day markets will fully reflect such future benefits (which may in any case be largely external in character).

Even where market solutions are sought (for example, opening up stately homes to the public), the results may not always be successful, particularly since, for reasons mentioned above, the revenue raised is unlikely to reflect fully the value of the facility to society.

Figure 6.17 illustrates policy options open to governments in the UK to help conserve historic buildings. First, designated buildings of architectural and/or historical interest can be 'listed', which prevents demolition or alteration without the consent of the local planning authority. Under the 1967 Civic Amenities Act such considerations were extended to the wider urban setting of conservation areas (of which there are now 8,000). While listing may prevent redevelopment from occurring at point x in figure 6.17 it will not necessarily prevent decay and dereliction by neglect (point y). Local authorities, even where this is permitted, only rarely take actions involving expense, such as restoration, since little finance is made available to them for these purposes. However, the powers of local authorities in this field have recently been increased, and under Section 54 of the Planning (Listed Buildings and Conservation Areas) Act 1990 they are able to execute urgent

repairs for the preservation of unoccupied or partly unoccupied listed buildings (following the issuing of an urgent repairs notice). Local authority
expenses can then be recovered from owners under Section 55 of the Act.
Owners have a right of appeal but this is unlikely to be successful unless
hardship can be proved. Following direction from the Secretary of State for
National Heritage, urgent repairs powers can also be applied to unlisted
buildings of importance in conservation areas. The full repairs procedure
under Section 48 of the Act is more significant as it can be used on occupied buildings. The works specified in a full repairs notice should not,
however, exceed those which are reasonably necessary for a building's
'preservation' – as opposed to its 'restoration'. Local authorities can now
recover from owners through the County Courts the cost of works required
by a relevant enforcement notice under the Planning and Compensation
Act (1991). Failure to carry out the terms of a full repairs notice within two
months can also lead to a compulsory purchase order (CPO) being made
by the local authority. In practice it would appear that full repairs notice
procedures only rarely end in local authorities having to undertake CPO
action. This is presumably helped by the knowledge of owners that, first,
(under the Historic Buildings and Ancient Monuments Act, 1953) local
authorities may be able to defray the expenses they incurred, and secondly,
if 'deliberate neglect' can be shown, then the local authority may request
an order for 'minimum compensation' under the Planning (LBCA) Act
1990. Thirdly, it is also possible that a low value would be determined in
any case as a result of a high cost of repairs – particularly since any development potential of the building would generally be ignored in calculating
the basis for compensation (Picard, 1992). Nevertheless, the comparatively
low level of full repairs notices issued (in relation to the 36,700 listed buildings thought by English Heritage to be 'at risk') (English Heritage, 1992)
would appear to reflect the financial worries of local authorities, as mentioned earlier.

The availability of grants (or, as has been suggested, tax incentives)
towards repair and restoration costs at x could in theory raise NARs and
capital values sufficiently (for example to PV' in figure 6.17) to prevent dereliction from occurring in year y. While GARs may then rise if the building
gains subsequently in value (as shown by the upturn in PV'), this would not,
on its own, be sufficient to prevent redevelopment at point x. While a combination of listing and grants might prove successful, the amount of cash
available from central government in the form of grants is, in practice,
limited and tends to be restricted to around 6 per cent of the total of just
over 441,000 listed buildings (that is, those classified as Grade I and Grade
II – although such classification does not in itself guarantee a grant).

Finally, the granting of permission for the building to be adapted to a
more intensive use (for example, industrial or residential to offices) may

sometimes provide a level of future NARs sufficient to cover not only the costs of repair and renovation, but also to prevent redevelopment from taking place (as shown by PV″ in figure 6.17), thus safeguarding the building in the long term. Unfortunately, only a small proportion of historic buildings are likely to be conserved in this way and, even where alternative uses are found, their demands (especially offices) may require major alterations to many interior features (for example, floor-to-ceiling height).

In conclusion, the conservation of historic buildings will only occasionally be resolved by market forces (Harvey, 1992) and, overall, greater financial support is required. Many historic buildings – provided they are not left to decay – have the potential not only to provide good service and tax revenues in the future, but also to enhance the national and architectural heritage for future generations. Yet nearly a quarter of listed buildings are at risk from neglect or in need of repair to prevent them becoming at risk. English Heritage alone has a £56 million backlog of conservation work for over 400 national monuments and historic buildings in its care (English Heritage, 1993).

URBAN RENEWAL POLICIES

With specific regard to redevelopment and rehabilitation in the United Kingdom, the European Union, the United States and Hong Kong, an examination of public policy will illustrate the differences in the aims, objectives and outcomes of governmental priorities, and highlight the differences in approach not only between different countries in the advanced capitalist world but also between these countries and an example of a newly-industrializing country.

The United Kingdom

Since the Second World War, there have been two broad approaches to urban renewal in the United Kingdom. The first was concerned with the redevelopment or rehabilitation of the built environment of the inner cities and the regeneration of their economic base (and involved – over time – the application of six different strategies), and the second focused on the alleviation of social deprivation (first in the 1960s and early 1970s, and more latterly from the 1990s into the new millennium).

The renewal of the built environment and economic regeneration

From 1946 to the late 1960s, a *filtration* strategy was employed and was based on the out-migration of households and employment prior to the clearance and redevelopment of urban sites. Out-migration resulted from both planned decentralization and market forces. Over the period 1946–66 under the New Towns Acts of 1946 and 1959, 21 Mark 1 new towns were designated in Britain to provide – through the medium of development corporations – overspill housing and employment for ex-city dwellers, and between 1967 and 1970 a further seven (Mark 2) new towns were designated, to act as 'counter-magnets' of economic activity and housing development. Under the Town Development Act 1972, a total of 70 town expansion schemes were initiated, whereby overspill provision would be provided through the framework of local government. During the years of planned decentralization, slum clearance schemes and massive public-sector housebuilding programmes were undertaken in the inner cities. In the period 1945–76, 1.24 million houses were demolished in England and Wales, but in the inner cities clearance was often followed by the development of subsidized high-rise housing at lower overall density. Clearance often had an adverse effect on local employment – factories, workshops, shops and so on being sacrificed on the altar of housing development and infrastructural improvement.

With specific regard to housing, a *boot-strap* strategy was introduced in the late-1960s and early-1970s and remained in place until at least the 1990s. The strategy, based on the rehabilitation of poor-quality housing, does not necessarily involve the displacement of occupants – unlike the filtration process – and in economic terms is thought less costly than redevelopment, although the evidence is conflicting. Under the Housing Acts of 1969, 1974 and 1980, improvement grants were therefore awarded to owner-occupiers, landlords, developers (and eventually tenants) to help them meet the cost of rehabilitation. However, the grant system was subject to some criticism since money was often awarded to persons quite able to fund the cost of rehabilitation from their own sources, and grant-aided rehabilitation – in London, for example – was associated with gentrification and the displacement of low-income households. The Local Government and Housing Act 1989 and the Housing (Grants, Reconstruction and Regeneration) Act 1996 therefore awarded only 'means-tested' grants – in effect, targeting relatively low-income owners and tenants, rather than poor housing. It is not surprising, therefore, that the rehabilitation of private-sector housing diminished quite significantly in the 1990s. In the public sector, however, while capital expenditure on new housebuilding plummeted in England, from £2.9 billion in 1979/80 to only £69 million in 1994/95, the amount invested in stock renovation fell slightly from £1.8 billion to £1.6 billion over the same period (DoE, 1995).

In respect of urban renewal in general, a *replacement* strategy was introduced in the late-1970s to ensure that in the wake of clearance, sound redevelopment schemes would be undertaken *in situ* without the need to undertake further overspill development or encourage people and economic activity to migrate to existing country towns. As an outcome of the Inner Areas Studies of Birmingham (Small Heath), Liverpool 8 and London (Southwark), and the subsequent White Paper *Policy for the Inner Cities* (DoE, 1977), the Inner Urban Areas Act 1978 funded a package of construction work in selected inner cities, targeting initially £100 million per annum for a total of 41 designated Urban Programme authorities in the inner urban areas of England and Wales. Each authority had powers to: provide the private sector with 90 per cent loans for the acquisition of land or site preparation; provide loans or grants towards the cost of setting up co-operatives or common ownership enterprises; and declare (industrial) improvement areas – where grants and loans would be available for the improvement and conversion of old industrial or commercial property, and for the improvement of the environment. Under the 1978 Act – and unlike earlier procedures – the promotion and control of urban renewal was a tripartite process, involving not only central government and the private sector, but also local communities (as represented by local authorities) through the medium of inner-city partnership programmes and inner-area programmes.

In the 1980s, with a government wedded to neo-liberal economics, local authorities (and their communities) were increasingly excluded from participation and decision-making in the urban renewal process. Where there was a partnership, it was a partnership between government and the private sector, and it is within this context that an *enterprise* (or property-led) strategy was developed and applied. Urban Development Corporations (UDCs) were designated under the Local Government, Planning and Land Act 1980. Appointed by the Environment Secretary rather than elected, 11 UDCs in England and Wales replaced the role of local authorities as planning authorities within selected inner-city areas, and were empowered – within their boundaries – to provide over a period of about 10 years an adequate infrastructure including road development, to reclaim and service land, and to develop new buildings and rehabilitate old factories with the aim of attracting private commercial and industrial development. The UDCs received 'leverage' (pump-priming) finance from the government amounting to over £500 million per annum by the early 1990s, and this in turn attracted up to five times as much private sector development. Despite this achievement, UDCs have been criticized since they are often remote from their local community, and there is little evidence to suggest that they have helped to reduce unemployment in the areas (most new jobs have evidently been filled by commuters), or reduced local shortages of affordable housing.

Private capital was also attracted to the inner city (and other deprived areas) by the designation of enterprise zones (EZs). Under the Finance Act

1980, a total of 27 EZs were established in England, Wales and Scotland – in which firms would be exempt from rates (local property taxes) on commercial and industrial buildings for 10 years, receive other tax breaks, and be generally exempt from local-authority development control. However EZs soon drew criticism. They attracted little new employment (most development was in the form of warehouses and superstores), shifted land values from adjacent locations – thereby causing blight, encouraged commercial and industrial landlords to raise rents to cream-off rate concessions, and cost the government around £860 million by 1988/89 (mainly through compensating local authorities for rate revenue foregone). After their 10-year life had expired, no further EZs were designated.

Further leverage funding in the 1980s took the form of derelict land grants (DLGs), urban development grants (UDGs), urban regeneration grants (URGs) and city grants (the latter replacing UDGs and URGs, and necessitating a forecast public/private leverage ratio of 1:4). Each form of grant was intended – in principle – to bridge the gap between the cost of development and its value on completion, or to provide temporary finance before any income was received from the development, and thereby provide an incentive to the private sector to undertake development in an area which it might not otherwise consider. However, it is possible that the above grants (together with UDC and EZ expenditure) were translated directly into the profits of developers and thereby distorted the market.

In housing, the enterprise ideology was extended to further reduce the role of local authorities. To accompany the selling-off of municipal housing to their tenants under 'right to buy' legislation, the government embarked upon a policy of rehabilitating and privatizating whole estates. It thus set up the Urban Housing Renewal Unit (UHRU) in 1985 – renamed Estates Action in 1986 – to provide assistance to local authorities, to draw in new private-sector funds and URGs, and to supplement existing Housing Investment Programme (HIP) allocations from the Department of the Environment – which increased from £75 million in 1987/88 to £364 million in 1992/93. After rehabilitation, housing would be either sold to trusts, sold off to owner-occupiers as low-cost housing, or retained by the local authority. Under the Housing Act 1988, the government launched a further initiative to privatize municipal housing, and was given powers to establish Housing Action Trusts (HATs) to repair or rehabilitate municipal housing, prior to transferring it to housing associations or selling it off to private landlords.

In 1992, the enterprise strategy was reinforced by involving local government in urban renewal in general. A new initiative was introduced – 'City Challenge' – which required programme authorities to bid for the funds that they required to undertake urban renewal projects. In making bids, authorities had to demonstrate that their programmes emphasized four key points:

(1) a comprehensive and ambitious vision for the area selected; (2) full and effective partnerships with the private sector; (3) participation and involvement of the local community; and (4) effective partnership arrangements for implementation and delivery – at first the most important criterion. Despite funds of up to £37 million per annum being available to each winning authority, it was unfortunate that a significant number of eligible authorities were unsuccessful in their bids – regardless of levels of unemployment and housing need in their area.

As an alternative to the 'top-down' property-led approach of central government, a *local government strategy* came into existence in the early-1980s. Many inner-city local authorities recognized that their electorates were not well-served by macroeconomic policy which limited the amount of central-government expenditure on renewal schemes during disinflation, or rendered inner-city locations uncompetitive with suburban or rural locations during boom conditions. It was also apparent to local government that it was being excluded from most of the new urban renewal initiatives currently being introduced. Local government therefore saw the need for 'bottom up' rather than 'top-down' solutions to the problems of renewal, and introduced a number of local enterprise boards (LEBs) or their equivalent. LEBs were initially funded by a 2 per cent levy on local property tax, and provided equity and loan guarantees, delayed repayment loans and 'seed money' to local ventures in order to attract consequential institutional investment. The main advantage of LEBs is that they were able to create or protect jobs at a much lower cost than that incurred, for example, by enterprise zones, but the main disadvantage is that they were probably underfunded from the beginning, and as an outcome of the Local Government and Housing Act 1989 were prevented from raising funds from local property tax.

Since central government considered it inefficient to continue to provide a wide range of initiatives designed to promote urban renewal, a *co-ordinated* strategy evolved throughout the 1990s. Under the Leasehold Reform, Housing and Urban Development Act 1993 – and in respect specifically to urban renewal – the government established English Partnerships to:

(1) take-over policy decision-making from the Department of the Environment, Department of Employment and Department of Trade and Industry;
(2) buy and develop inner-city sites, assume the responsibility of the Department of the Environment's role in awarding city grants and DLGs, and eventually be responsible for a large slice of the Department of the Environment's budget;
(3) administer City Challenge (until its demise in 1998).

With the creation of the Single Regeneration Budget in 1994, even more co-ordination was possible – for example, the Department of the Environment's City Challenge, English Partnerships and UDCs; programmes of the Department of Employment, the Home Office and the Department of Education, as well as the Department of Trade and Industry's regional spending, were all brought together under a single budget. With administration devolved to ten new integrated regional offices, it was intended that public expenditure on urban renewal would be substantially rationalized and possibly reduced. To this end, there is a rolling programme of bidding rounds for local partnerships to secure resources for up to seven years for a mix of economic, social and physical regeneration schemes – targeted in 1999 at the most deprived local-authority areas. To enable the government to focus on urban regeneration and regional development within an appropriate spatial context, ten Regional Development Agencies were set up in England in 1999 to take over the role and £400 million per annum budget of English Partnerships.

The alleviation of social deprivation

Social planning was introduced in the late-1960s to focus on people rather than on urban space or property, and initially involved an analysis of the basic causes of deprivation prior to the application of needs-related policies. Although central government – under the Local Government Grant (Social Need) Act 1969 – was empowered to award 75 per cent grants towards the cost of 'approved' projects bid for by local authorities and voluntary organizations (in England and Wales) in 'areas of special social need', it recognized that more information was required about the causes of deprivation. In the early-1970s, therefore, it established twelve Community Development Projects (CDPs) to undertake detailed analyses of inner-city problems in specific geographic areas and to identify solutions which would require implementation at a higher level. But prior to their demise in 1967, CDPs were claiming that urban deprivation was not the result of social malaise, but the effect of unemployment, inadequate income support, poor housing and a decayed urban environment – and called for more government intervention in the economy of the inner cities.

In 1974, the Comprehensive Community Programme (CCP) was initiated to tackle urban deprivation by means of a comprehensive Whitehall approach to urban problems and a new partnership between central and local government. However, because of conflict of interest between ministries, and between the ministries and the Treasury, little was achieved. At this stage, the weight of opinion favoured downgrading social planning and shifting the emphasis to strategies of redevelopment and rehabilitation, heralding the way to the 1978 Inner Urban Areas Act and 1979 Housing Act (see above).

After a gap of over twenty years, the government made a further attempt to improve neighbourhoods and increase the economic opportunities for the residents. Under the 'New Deal for the Communities', the government allocated £800 million in 1998 to be spent on housing and regeneration in 17 deprived local-authority estates over the following three years, with the deal being extended to up to 100 more neighbourhoods by the year 2000. In their bids for funding, local people, community and voluntary organizations, public agencies, local authorities and businesses would be brought together in order to demolish eyesores and build new social housing estates, raise educational standards and prioritize healthy living, crime prevention and job-creation. By supporting an holistic approach to regeneration with adequate funding, 'New Deal for the Communities' might prove to be a more successful approach to social planning than previous attempts in the 1970s.

An urban renaissance?

In its report, *Towards an Urban Renaissance* (DETR, 1999), a government-commissioned urban task force – chaired by Lord Rogers – signalled a new approach to urban regeneration – and its corollary, the control of development in the countryside. The report proposed that:

(1) greenfield land for housing should be used to accommodate only 40 per cent of the 3.8 million extra households that will form Britain by 2021 (large areas of the countryside could also be saved if densities were increased from typically 20 dwellings/ha to 40 or 60/ha);

(2) countryside developers should be faced with environmental impact fees (relating to loss of landscape, harm to wildlife, soil erosion, pressure on waste and water management systems, impacts on 'historic and cultural resources', increases in energy consumption and increased air pollution caused by greater road traffic use);

(3) public bodies and utilities should release redundant rural land and buildings, every council should have an empty property strategy and all contaminated land should be brought back into use by 2030;

(4) VAT should be harmonized on new housebuilding and residential conversions (in 1999 it was zero on housebuilding but 17.5 per cent on the conversion of old houses – clearly discriminating against the inner cities);

(5) a national campaign should be launched to improve urban design in association with local architecture centres;

(6) 65 per cent of transport expenditure should be targeted at projects to benefit pedestrians, cyclists and public transport users;

(7) 'Home Zones' should be created that put pedestrians first;

(8) 'Urban Priority Areas' (UPAs) should be introduced where special companies would promote urban regeneration using public and private
funds;

(9) lower council tax, tax relief on home contents and car insurance, and
lower or zero stamp duty on house purchase should be introduced
within the UPAs;

(10) a 'Renaissance Fund' of £500 million over 10 years should be available to help local groups to improve their own neighbourhoods.

The report was inspired by approaches to regeneration adopted elsewhere in Europe, for example, high-density housing development – of up
to 400 dwellings/ha – has been central to regeneration in Barcelona, while
environmental impact fees have recently been introduced in Germany. At
the time of writing, the report required legislation and fiscal assistance
before its proposals – in full or in part – could be implemented.

BOX 6.1: URBAN RENEWAL IN THE EUROPEAN UNION

Over the period 1994–99 it was recognized that the success of urban areas
was central to the overall growth and development of Objective 1 regions
(those in which development is lagging behind), while the highly urban character of Objective 2 regions (those with declining industrial areas) resulted in
constituent urban development projects taking a large share of European
Regional Development Fund (ERDF) assistance. Of the total ERDF budget of
60 billion ECU, around 21 billion ECU were being spent on development
within urban areas of at least 100,000 inhabitants (the EU definition of a city)
(CEC, 1997).

In the Objective 1 regions (table 6.5), the urban component of ERDF
allocations in the period 1994–99 ranged from as little as 19 per cent of the
total allocation in Northern Ireland to as much as 100 per cent in East Berlin,
or from 80 million ECU in the Netherlands to 5,984 million ECU in Spain.

A significant proportion of ERDF assistance was targeted at urban renewal
projects. In Portugal, the ERDF allocation was, in part, invested in the
improvement of living conditions in the *barracas* of Lisbon and Oporto. In
Italy, funds were targeted particularly at a range of economic and environmental regeneration projects in the cities of Naples, Bari and Palermo, but
also at cities in Abruzzo, Calabria, Campania, Puglia, Sardinia and Sicily; and
in Ireland, apart from investment in the Temple Bar area of Dublin, there was
support in other urban areas for local enterprise initiatives, employment,
physical renewal and economic regeneration. Objective 1 funding also assisted
the economic regeneration of the urban areas of French Hainault, as well as
the Belgian cities of Charleroi, Mons and Louvière – all centres of industrial
decline. In Northern Ireland, support was given to the development of the

continued

Table 6.5 The urban component of ERDF allocations in Objective 1 regions, 1994–99

Country	Million ECUs	Total Objective 1 funding (per cent)
Germany (East Berlin)	530	100
Belgium	515	90
UK (Merseyside)	271 [1]	90
France	750	56
Portugal	4,082	40
Spain	5,984	38
Netherlands	80	37
Ireland	900	35
Greece	3,207	34
Italy	1,000	30
Germany (Eastern länder excluding East Berlin)	1,140	20–25
UK (Northern Ireland)	126	19

Source: CEC (1997).
Note:
[1] Total ERDF support for Community Economic Development programmes in Merseyside and UK Objective 2 regions.

Belfast Docks, while in Merseyside and the Objective 2 regions of the UK, funding – amounting to 272 million ECU – was used to facilitate 'Community Economic Development' (CED) in specific areas of exceptional deprivation. By focusing on pockets of social exclusion and long-term unemployment, CED was intended to involve local communities and businesses in the process of regeneration, and by re-introducing the most vulnerable groups in society into the regular economy, CED made a positive contribution to the broader aims of urban economic development (CEC, 1997).

Jointly financed by the ERDF and local government, and with operations commencing in 1989, Urban Pilot Projects were designed to test new ideas in the application of urban policy – for example, in relation to the economic development in areas with social problems such as inner-city estates with high unemployment, or the economic and commercial revitalization of decayed historic centres. A total of 31 projects were supported throughout the EU, with the greatest number being located in the decayed urban areas of cities in France, Germany and the UK (see Balchin *et al.*, 1999). By the mid-1990s it was clear that ERDF funding enabled enterprises to be set up, employment to be generated, and land and buildings to be brought into beneficial use (Williams, 1996).

In 1994, the European Commission launched the Community Initiative URBAN to improve and extend the co-ordination of EU measures directed at urban problems and specifically to focus on the problems of spatial segregation in cities. The Commission was concerned that the unemployed and other socially vulnerable groups were becoming increasingly concentrated in specific neighbourhoods to worrying proportions in recent years (CEC, 1997). With programmes implemented in approximately 115 cities, URBAN had a budget of around 850 million ECU for the period 1994–99. URBAN aid specifically facilitated development programmes in the deprived areas of cities and was targeted at economic, social and environmental problems in areas with decaying infrastructure, poor housing and a lack of social amenities (CEC, 1994), and apart from funding new business initiatives, training schemes and health care facilities, it promoted the improvement of the infrastructure and the environment through the renovation of buildings and the rehabilitation of public places (CEC, 1994).

United States

Urban renewal in the United States dates back to the immediate post-Second World War years when it was seen as a means of pump-priming the economy. It was also welcomed by municipal governments and the private sector as a means of respectively raising the tax base and increasing sales and property values. Urban renewal was probably more necessary in the United States than elsewhere since suburbanization and the consequential decline of the urban core began earlier than in most other countries (Richardson, 1971).

It is remarkable that in one of the most capitalist countries, governments are able to exercise powers of eminent domain (i.e. rights of compulsory purchase) that are far more extensive than elsewhere and – after 1954 – were permitted to acquire land for private as well as public use (Richardson, 1971). As a consequence, municipal urban renewal schemes were often undertaken in a way that destroyed – rather than preserved – the character of small neighbourhoods (Jacobs, 1961), with the development of commercial uses or luxury apartments invariably replacing low-income rental housing. Although government had an obligation to relocate households displaced by a renewal scheme, this was often not fulfilled, and many households – particularly among the ethnic minorities – were forced into very poor and often densely occupied accommodation elsewhere in the inner city. Thus, slums were being shifted about from one part of the inner city to another, and – in net terms – not being removed (Richardson, 1971).

It was paradoxical that in a largely free-market economy, a municipal scheme – once it was complete – was sold at a discount to private interests, and most of the city's loss was subsidized by the federal government. It was also paradoxical that there were no shortages of powers and funds to acquire and redevelop areas, but a deficiency of will and resources to adequately compensate those disadvantaged by renewal (Richardson, 1971).

Although urban renewal projects – of which there were 1700 in 800 cities by 1965 – had received federal grants of only US$8 billion and accounted for only 0.2 per cent of total construction turnover in the period, they had resulted in the relocation or closure of 50,000 businesses and the eviction of around three-quarters of a million people (Richardson, 1971). After 1965, however, the magnitude of renewal programmes significantly increased – although governments preserved their powers of eminent domain and redevelopment.

A strategy of 'replacement' was introduced by the Kennedy and Johnson administrations as one of their 'Great Society' initiatives following ghetto riots in the 1960s. The federal government set up a Department of Housing and Urban Development in 1965, which in turn introduced the 'Model Cities Program' in 1966. The programme aimed to concentrate and co-ordinate the provision of federal resources allocated to the urban areas and to involve local communities in the improvement of their physical environment. Development programmes, however, soon came to depend upon private-sector initiative – for example, the successful Bedford–Stuyvesant scheme in Brooklyn which, while being managed by a community-based organization, was partly funded by Wall Street institutions.

In contrast, an 'enterprise' strategy was subsequently introduced by the Nixon and Ford administrations in the period 1968–76. It involved direct co-operation between the federal government and private investors – sidestepping community representation. Under a newly introduced 'New Towns Intown Program' the federal government used its community development block grant to fund urban development in anticipation of complementary private investment, and later the Housing and Community Development Act 1977 (of the Carter administration) introduced urban development action grants (UDAGs) to 'lever' funds from the private sector for joint public/private schemes. Under the 1977 Act, city authorities could only obtain UDAGs (for joint schemes with the private sector) if their areas suffered from a high level of deprivation, but a fundamental characteristic of the UDAG was that it would have had to enable private developers and investors to enjoy a level of return at least equivalent to that obtainable elsewhere. In addition to the above provisions, the federal government – under the 1977 Act – provide mortgage guarantees to encourage financial institutions to use mortgage-fund capital to finance urban development projects.

None of these (post-1965) initiatives, however, dealt satisfactorily with the problem of re-accommodating and compensating those displaced by renewal.

Much earlier than in the UK, urban authorities since the 1970s had been involved in joint private/public-sector development schemes. In Boston, Massachusetts for example, the Economic Development and Industrial Corporation not only helped the city retain and create industrial employment but also undertook joint enterprises with the Boston Redevelopment Authority – the city's planning, housing and commercial development agency.

However, both the redevelopment and rehabilitation of the built environment have become associated with 'gentrification' in US cities – as well as elsewhere in the capitalist world such as London and Paris. The gentrifiers are often relatively high-income, young couples without children who move into the decaying areas of the inner city – replacing low-income communities, since increased demand causes rents and therefore local property taxes to rise to uncompetitive levels (Macionis and Parrillo, 1998: 280). Whereas in the nineteenth and early twentieth century, middle-class people migrated to the expanding suburbs in search of a more congenial environment, they are now choosing to return to inner-city neighbourhoods since they feel that a more central location provides: shorter and lower-cost journeys to work; an increasing number of administrative and professional jobs; greater opportunities for women in the workforce; a greater amount of variety and stimulation in terms of retailing and entertaining; and a wider choice of housing in terms of prices, rents and quality – much 'central city housing built from about 1880 to 1910 [having] a level of craftmanship and quality rarely found in today's suburbs' (Macionis and Parrillo, 1998: 280).

Although earlier in the twentieth century, investment capital was injected into suburban housing, where profitability was higher, by the 1970s and 1980s a 'rent gap' emerged in the inner city and heralded the return of capital. Investment in housing renewal increased apace as the value of residential real estate in the central locations escalated. Clearly the inward 'invasion' of the city by the more affluent 'contradicts the predictions of an ever-outward migration of the affluent made by . . . Burgess in the 1920s' (Macionis and Parrillo, 1998: 280) (see page 88).

BOX 6.2: URBAN RENEWAL IN AUSTRALIA

In an attempt to reduce the negative aspects of urban growth such as urban sprawl, traffic congestion, long journeys to work and air pollution, and to make cities more ecologically sustainable, planners in Australia and New Zealand – over many years – have adopted strategies of decentralization,

continued

multi-centralization and urban consolidation (Forster, 1995; Robinson *et al.*, 2000). However, neither decentralization nor multi-centralization strategies were particularly successful. The former – which attempted to reduce the rate of growth of large cities by decanting population to smaller urban areas – was undertaken on such a small scale that the increase in population in regional growth centres in New South Wales (for example, Albury-Wodonga) and Victoria (such as Bathurst and Orange) was dwarfed by the continuing growth of Sydney and Melbourne. The latter stragegy – which encouraged the development of district sub-centres of employment and retailing – was similarly on an insufficient scale to be effective. Although the Melbourne metropolitan strategic plan for the 1980s identified 14 suburban 'district centres' as locations for new retailing and employment, only one has been successfully completed, although in Sydney multi-centralization was marginally more successful since, unlike Melbourne, the state government was willing to underpin commercial relocation by simultaneously relocating its offices.

By comparison, urban consolidation has been considerably more successful. It involves increasing urban densities through infill, the redevelopment of low-density areas, or the building of medium- or high-density housing in new areas. The argument for the strategy is that 'high densities will reduce urban sprawl as well as energy use and pollution, especially for transport, because public transport, walking and cycling would be encouraged' (Robinson *et al.*, 2000: 291; see also Newman and Kenworthy, 1989, 1992; Kenworthy, 1995). While it is questionable whether housing densities could be increased sufficiently to have any significant effect on suburban sprawl (Stretton, 1994; Troy, 1996; Maher, 1997), and whether a large proportion of households would choose to reside in high-density accommodation in preference to conventional suburban owner-occupied housing (Archer, 1996), the development of housing in the central business districts (CBDs) of cities has proved viable. In Australian cities, and particularly in Sydney, large numbers of city-centre residents help to reduce transport pressures and sustain a broad range of retailing and entertaining, while, in Auckland, planning controls were relaxed in the early-1990s to permit residential development throughout the city centre, and the city council offered tax relief to developers for converting office space into residential blocks (Lees and Berg, 1995). As a result, more than 4,000 people live in the CBD – creating 'a new vibrancy for the inner city, with street cafés, nightclubs and casinos' (Robinson *et al.*, 2000: 219).

In addition to housing development in the CBD, there has also been the process of gentrification in the inner suburbs, for example in Glebe and Paddington in Sydney, and Ponsonby and Kingsland in Auckland (Robinson *et al.*, 2000). Motivated by lifestyle opportunities, facilitated by an inflow of capital from abroad and a relaxation of lending restrictions by banks and building societies, and (in the case of Glebe) encouraged by public-sector involvement, rehabilitation schemes have significantly raised property prices, and – like elsewhere in the developed world – have resulted in an inflow of middle-income households and an outflow of the less-well-off who have sought cheaper housing in the suburbs.

BOX 6.3: URBAN RENEWAL IN HONG KONG

Whereas urban renewal schemes in the United Kingdom and United States are sometimes designed and managed by a three-way partnership between government, the private sector and the community, urban renewal in Hong Kong (as in many NICs and developing countries) is mainly the concern of the government and the private sector only, with the voice of the community seldom heard (Ng and Cook, 1999).

The severity of the renewal problem is substantial. It was estimated by the Hong Kong Planning Department in 1992 that there were 950 ha of comparatively old, cramped, deteriorating and very high-density housing in need of redevelopment or rehabilitation, but in 1998 the government identified only 76 ha requiring redevelopment or rehabilitation (Ng and Cook, 1999).

In the past, the Hong Kong government attempted on several occasions to upgrade the physical environment, but success was limited and progress slow. Although it made a commitment in 1997 to set up an Urban Development Authority, by 1999 no such boidy had been established.

Since about two-thirds of housing in need of renewal is private, it is not surprising that historically most urban renewal has been undertaken by the private sector – with redevelopment accounting for about a half of all new private dwellings in 1996, albeit with a small reduction in the stock (Ng and Cook, 1999). Most redevelopment in recent years has taken place on Hong Kong Island, where property prices (and returns from redevelopment) are highest, with less taking place in Kowloon where residential values are lower, and the rate of redevelopment fluctuates in relation to the house price cycle.

Until the establishment of the Land Development Corporation (LDC) in 1988, the government was reluctant to facilitate the renewal of private buildings. However, although the LDC has powers to identify and acquire sites for redevelopment, and prepare outline schemes for redevelopment in advance of selling the land and the proposal to the private sector, it might be questioned whether the redevelopment process is any more efficient or socially equitable than if it was left entirely to the private sector. Although the LDC has powers to undertake a comprehensive rather than an *ad hoc* approach to renewal – unlike the private sector – and is non-profit making, progress has been very slow. By 1999, only 2.76 ha had been renewed, equal to only 0.4 per cent of the area officially identified in 1992 (Ng and Cook, 1999). This is attributable, very largely, to housing development being unable to compete for resources with commercial development; for example, of the total amount of redevelopment presided over by the LDC from 1988 to 1998, 84 per cent was commercial and only 16 per cent was residential.

With regard to public housing, the role of the LDC is constrained by

continued

the Housing Authority being unwilling – because of its long waiting list – to rehouse tenants adversely affected by clearance and redevelopment schemes. Yet the interests of those communities experiencing or anticipating displacement is unlikely to be recognized since, for the time being, redevelopment is seen solely as a means of upgrading the built environment rather than a means of re-establishing a community (Cookson-Smith, 1998).

It remains to be seen whether the government's new Urban Renewal Strategy and Urban Renewal Authority will meet the needs of local communities as well as the requirements of the private-property sector.

REFERENCES

Archer, J. (1996) *The Great Australian Dream: The History of the Australian House*, Sydney: Harper Collins.

Badcock, B. (1993) 'Notwithstanding the exaggerated claims, residential revitalization really is changing the form of some western cities: a response to Bourne', *Urban Studies*, 30.

Bagby, D.G. (1973) *Housing Rehabilitation Costs*, New York: Lexington Books.

Balchin, P. (1971) *Housing Improvement and Social Inequality*, Farnborough: Saxon House.

Balchin, P. and Sýkora, L. with Bull, G. (1999) *Regional Policy and Planning*, London: Routledge.

Berry, B.J.L. (1976) *Urbanization and Counterurbanization*, London: Sage.

Berry, B.J.L. and Gillard, Q. (1976) *The Changing Shape of Metropolitan America: Commuting Patterns, Urban Fields and Decentralization Processes, 1960–70*, Cambridge MA: Ballinger.

Blumenfeld, H. (1954) 'The tidal wave of metropolitan expansion', *Journal of the American Institute of Planners*, Winter.

Bourne, L.S. (1967) *Private Redevelopment of the Central City*, Chicago: University of Chicago Press.

Bourne, L.S. (1993) 'The myth and reality of gentrification: a commentary on emerging urban forms', *Urban Studies*, 30.

Boyce, R.R. (1966) 'The edge of the metropolis: the wave theory analog approach', *British Colombia Geographical Series*, 7.

Case, K.E. (1992) 'The real estate cycle and the economy', *Urban Studies*, 29.

CEC (1991) *Europe 2000*, Brussels: Commission of the EC.

CEC (1994) *Europe 2000+: Cooperation for European Territorial Development*, Brussels: DG XVI.

CEC (1997) *Towards an Urban Agenda in the EU* (com(97) 197), Brussels: Commission of the EC.

Champion, A.G. (ed.) (1989) *Counterurbanisation*, London: Edward Arnold.

Champion, A.G. (1992) 'Urban and regional demographic trends in the developed world', *Urban Studies*, 29.

Chen, X. and Parish, W.L. (1996) 'Urbanization in China: reassessing an evolving model', in Gugler, J. (ed.), *The Urban Transformation of the Developing World*, Oxford: Oxford University Press.

Cheshire, P. (1990) 'Explaining the recent performance of the European Community's major urban regions', *Urban Studies*, 27.

Clark, D. (1996) *Urban World/Global City*, London: Routledge.

Congdon, P. and Batey, P. (eds) (1989) *Advances in Regional Demography*, London: Belhaven.

Cookson-Smith, P. (1998) 'Urban renewal and regeneration: an urban design process', *HKIA Journal*, 18: 4.

Cross, D.F.W. (1990) *Counterurbanisation in England and Wales*, London: Avebury.

DETR (1999) *Towards an Urban Renaissance: Final Report of the Urban Task Force Chaired by Lord Rogers of Riverside*, London: E. & F.N. Spon.

DoE (1977) *Policy for the Inner Cities*, Cmnd 6845, London: Department of the Environment, HMSO.

DoE (1995) *Annual Report*, London: Department of the Environment, HMSO.

Drakakis-Smith, D. (1996) 'Third world countries: sustainable development II, population, labour and poverty', *Urban Studies*, 33.

Elter, I. and Baross, P. (1993) 'Budapest', in *City Profile*, London: Butterworth-Heinemann.

English Heritage (1992) *Buildings at Risk: A Sample Survey*, London: English Heritage.

English Heritage (1993) *Annual Report and Accounts*, London: English Heritage.

Fielding, A.J. (1982) 'Counterurbanization in Western Europe', *Progress in Planning*, 17: 1–52.

Fielding, A.J. (1989) 'Migration and urbanisation in western Europe since 1950', *The Geographical Journal*, 155.

Forster, C. (1995) *Australian Cities: Continuity and Change*, Melbourne: Oxford University Press.

Frey, W.H. (1989) 'United States: counterurbanisation and metropolis depopulation', in Champion, A.G. (ed.), *Counterurbanisation*, London: Edward Arnold.

Friedmann, J. and Weaver, C. (1979) *Territory and Function: The Evolution of Regional Planning*, London: Edward Arnold.

Glasson, J. (1992) 'The fall and rise of regional planning in the economically advanced nations', *Urban Studies*, 29.

HABITAT (1996) *An Urbanizing World: Global Report on Human Settlements 1996*, Oxford: United Nations Centre for Human Settlements and Oxford University Press.

Hall, P. and Hay, D. (1978) *Growth Centres in the European Urban System*, London: Heinemann.

Harvey, J. (1992) *Urban Land Economics*, 3rd edn, London: Macmillan.

Hill, S. and Munday, M. (1992) 'The UK regional distribution of foreign direct investment', *Regional Studies*, 26: 6.

Hoch, I. (1987) 'City size and US urban policy', *Urban Studies*, 24.

Illeris, S. (1992) 'Urban and regional development in west Europe in the 1990s', *Scandinavian Housing and Planning Research*, 9.

Jacobs, J. (1961) *The Death and Life of Great American Cities*, New York: Random House.

Kenworthy, J. (1995) 'Automobile dependence in Bangkok: an international comparison with implications for planning policies', *World Transport Policy and Practice*, 1: 3.

Kovács, Z. (1993) 'Social and economic transition', Paper presented at the *ENHR Conference, Budapest*, 7–10 September 1993.

Larkham, P. (1992) 'Conservation and the changing urban landscape', *Property Management*, 10.

Lees, L. and Berg, L.D. (1995) 'Ponga, glass and concrete: a vision for the urban socio-cultural geography in Aoteoroa/New Zealand', *New Zealand Geographer*, 51: 2.

Listokin, D. (1973) *The Dynamics of Housing Rehabilitation. Macro and Micro Analysis*, Centre for Urban Policy Research, Rutgers University.

Lowder, S. (1991) 'The context of urban planning in secondary cities', *Cities*, 8: 54–65.

Macionis, J.J. and Parrillo, V.N. (1998) *Cities and Urban Life*, Upper Saddle River NJ: Prentice Hall.

Maher, C. (1997) 'Urban consolidation in the context of contemporary development trends', *Historic Environment*, 13: 1.

Marshall, R. (1998) 'Kuala Lumpur: competition and the quest for world city status', *Built Environment*, 24(4).

Massey, D., Quintas, P. and Wield, D. (1991) *High-Tech Fantasies, Science Parks in Society, Science and Space*, London: Routledge.

Moore, E. and Clark, W. (1990) 'Housing and households in American cities: structure and change in population mobility', in Myers, D. (ed.), *Housing Demography*, Madison: University of Wisconsin Press.

National Community Development Project (1975) *The Poverty of the Improvement Programme*, CDP Information and Intelligence Unit.

Newman, P. and Kenworthy, J. (1989) *Cities and Automobile Dependence: An International Sourcebook*, Aldershot: Gower.

Newman, P. and Kenworthy, J. (1992) *Winning Back the Cities*, Sydney: Australian Consumers Association and Pluto Press.

Ng, M.K. and Cook, A. (1999) 'Urban regeneration in Hong Kong – questions of partnership', *Town and Country Planning*, 68: 7.

Picard, R. (1992) 'Listed buildings: strengthening the powers of protection and prevention', *Property Management*, 11.

Potter, R.B. (1992) *Urbanisation in the Third World*, Oxford: Oxford University Press.

Potter, R.B. and Lloyd-Evans, S. (1998) *The City in the Developing World*, Harlow: Longman.

Pugh, C. (1992) 'The refurbishment of shopping centres', *Property Management*, 10.

Richardson, H.W. (1971) *Urban Economics*, Harmondsworth: Penguin.

Richardson, H.W. (1981) 'National urban development strategies in developing countries', *Urban Studies*, 18: 267–83.

Robinson, G.M., Loughran, R.J. and Tranter, P.J. (2000) *Australia and New Zealand: Economy, Society and the Environment*, London: Edward Arnold.

Starr, J.B. (1999) *Understanding China*, London: Profile Books.

Stretton, H. (1978) *Urban Planning in Rich and Poor Countries*, Oxford: Oxford University Press.

Stretton, H. (1994) 'Transport and the structure of Australian cities', *Australian Planner*, 31: 3.

Sýkora, L. (1993) 'City in transition: the role of rent gaps in Prague's revitalization', *Tijdschrift voor Econ. en Soc. Geografie*, 84: 4.

Troy, P.N. (1996) *The Perils of Urban Consolidation: A Discussion of Australian Housing and Urban Development Policies*, Sydney: The Federation Press.

Turock, I. and Edge, N. (1999) *The Jobs Gap in Britain's Cities: Employment Loss and Labour Market Consequences*, Bristol: The Policy Press.

Van den Berg, L., Drewett, R., Klassen, L.H., Rossi, A. and Vijverberg, C.H.T. (1982) *Urban Europe: A Study of Growth and Decline*, London: Pergamon.

Van Kemenade, W. (1997) *China, Hong Kong, Taiwan, Inc.*, London: Abacus.

Vanhove, N. and Klassen, L.H. (1980) *Regional Policy: A European Approach*, Farnborough: Saxon House.

Walker, B. (1987) *Welfare Economics and Urban Problems*, London: Hutchinson.

Wegener, M. (1995) 'The changing urban hierarchy in Europe', in Brochie, J., Batty, M., Blakely, E., Hall, P. and Newton, P. (eds), *Cities in Competition: Production and Sustainability for the 21st Century*, Melbourne: Longman.

Whitehand, J.W.R. (1987) *The Changing Face of Cities: A Study of Development Cycles and Urban Form*, Oxford: Blackwell.

Williams, R.H. (1996) *European Union Spatial Policy and Planning*, London: Paul Chapman Publishing.

7

Property Development

PROPERTY DEVELOPMENT IN THE UK

Property development is the process by which buildings are erected for occupation or for sale/investment. Owners may build premises for their own occupation, for example major retailers may erect supermarkets, alternatively, property developers may construct the same type of buildings for lease or sale. The process may be the same although some aspects of the financial appraisal may be different. A building offered for sale or investment is driven by a profit motive, a building for owner-occupation may be related to the profitability of the enterprise within the building and thus profit motivation may be redirected or constrained.

The owner-occupier sector has tended to be overlooked in property development texts, except for those of a macroeconomic nature. The problem lies with the fact that there is a substantial investment market in the UK where properties are developed for lease and sale, and it is this activity that is the most traditional approach for property developers in the property markets. This is unlike the situation in the European markets where development is more likely to be for the purpose of owner-occupation.

Property development is much like any other economic activity, satisfying wants with the application of scarce resources. In the case of property development, the wants are for space to work in, sell from, live in and enjoy recreational activities in. The process by which buildings are erected to provide space employs the key factors of production: land for the site, capital for purchase of the land and materials, labour to erect a building and manage the process, and the entrepreneurial talent of the property developer to initiate the process and bring the pieces together.

A simplified approach to property development from inception to completion would involve a number of stages. In the first case there would have to be a need for the space, either a direct demand from a potential owner-occupier or indirect demand as assessed in market conditions (demand outstripping supply and driving the price of space upwards). If a developer intends to develop a site then there would need to be a situation where the sale price or completed value exceeds the costs of development involved for the process to be initiated. This surplus profit arising from the profit in the development and also the size of the profit will need to reflect the efforts and risk of the developer as entrepreneur. If market research carried out on a proposed development shows sufficient demand exists, then the developer can produce sketch plans for the proposals as these will need to be discussed with the planning authority. In the UK, as in most countries, development of land is subject to restriction under the planning regulations and this is the first hurdle in the development process. Generally an informed consultant will be invaluable at this stage by knowing the type and scale of development which may be acceptable to the local authority, and the consultant may be able to negotiate the most advantageous bargaining position. In parallel with these sketch plans, an initial development appraisal is drawn up. On the basis of the scale and type of development, a value can be assessed and rough costs calculated; this would indicate a level of profit and whether it is worth continuing further.

This calculation is called a residual valuation. The costs of construction are usually assessed by comparison. There are databases and source books that analyze recent building contracts in different locations for different types of buildings. A cost per square metre can thus be calculated and applied to the gross internal floor area of the building (measured between the internal faces of external walls).

Further informal discussion with the planning authority will lead to a formal application to the planning authority. This application may be for outline permission (a permission indicating the type and density of the development) and subsequently for detailed permission. Once the detail of the scheme is known, then a detailed appraisal can be carried out. The planning application would require detailed drawings and these would now be complemented by additional drawings from the architect. In a traditional approach the drawings are costed in a bill of quantities by the quantity surveyor. In the early stages of the design process, the quantity surveyor will prepare a preliminary estimate, probably using one of the methods described by Seeley (1995) (these methods include unit, floor area, cube, approximate quantities, elemental comparative or interpolation). The valuer will provide updated values and rents, and funds will be raised to purchase the site (if not in ownership) and also for the costs of construction and ancillary costs.

With the finance, a building contract can be entered into and the building erected. At the same time, the valuer or agent will be advising on a marketing strategy and seeking possible purchasers or occupiers so that, once the building is completed, there will be a minimal period when the property is empty and not providing a return. The return will be an income if the property is let and retained as an investment, or as a capital sum if the building is sold. If the building is built and occupied by the owner as developer then a notional rent can be assumed to be passing.

Development Value

Development value exists where land or buildings can increase in value by the application of capital. It may be that this arises from a change of use of the land permitted by planning permission, but the property development process usually implies the application of capital in the form of works to the land. The residual valuation, one of a number of techniques of property appraisal which assess the profitability of the proposals, calculates the increased capital value of the land because of the proposals and deducts the costs of works and the original value of the land and buildings. In an economic sense, costs should include a 'normal' profit that reflects the risk and commitment of the developer; however, depending on the price paid for the land, an 'abnormal' profit may arise because of the particular circumstances.

The analysis can be summarized thus:

Basically   value − cost = profit

However, the residual valuation differentiates between the cost of construction and the cost of the existing land/building − the existing use value (EUV). The value of the completed development is termed the gross development value (GDV). Thus:

$$GDV - (building\ costs + EUV) = profit$$

If the land value is known because it has been agreed as a purchase price then this equation provides the calculation of the profit. However the general case is that the land cost is not known and thus the equation is rearranged:

$$GDV - (building\ costs + profit) = EUV$$

The EUV, being the existing value of land and buildings on the site, will thus determine whether or not a normal profit is earned. For instance, if the actual land cost negotiated is lower that the EUV determined by the above calculation then the profit increases, assuming the other costs to be static, and an abnormal profit is achieved.

The need to use a residual valuation approach arises because of the uniqueness of land and property as an asset class. This is reinforced by the uniqueness, in most situations, of development proposals for each site. If equal-sized plots were being sold in the same location with the same density and type of development then a form of comparative analysis could be applied, a price per hectare for instance. In these cases, adjustments would need to be made in the comparison and these adjustments, depending on their scale and complexity, could easily undermine the use of comparable valuation. The residual method has been criticized by the Lands Tribunal (the highest court for dealing with property valuation and compensation issues in the UK) because of the number of variables in the calculation and the assumptions and variances underlying the calculations used as inputs to the valuation. The residual valuation needs to be used in practice in most cases because the components of the development value and the profitability of each project will differ dramatically depending of the type and scale of the development proposals. The main variables in the calculation are:

Value of the site

depends on location, use (under planning law), topography, legal constraints, ground conditions, services and access (for example).

Value of the proposed development

depends on demand, use, density, design, layout and infrastructure.

Cost of construction

depends on size, shape and height, design, type of buildings, planning constraints on buildings and landscaping, site conditions, provision of services and access.

The extent of the variations in these factors means that each site may be unique and thus the calculation for the site value is a residual based on what can be achieved as development on the site. To summarize, there are two approaches to valuing the development potential of a site:

(1) A comparative approach

This is useful if there are direct comparables of sales but this is unlikely in a complex development situation where each development and thus the potential of each site will be unique.

(2) A residual valuation

Here the gross development value is assessed either by a capital comparison approach or by the investment method (the capitalization of an estimated future income flow using an appropriate multiplier). The net value from the site is calculated by deducting the costs of building and a profit figure from the gross development value, and this is thus a residual.

To clarify the valuation approach, it is important to distinguish between property appraisal, property valuation and property analysis. Recent debates have combined with criticism of traditional approaches of property valuation over the last 20 years or so, to assert that, in what has previously been termed property valuation, more extensive property analysis needs to be provided. Generally the approach that should be taken (Baum and Crosby, 1995) is that the overall property appraisal should be clearly divided between property valuation for purchase (valuation for market price) and the subsequent analysis of performance. In the first case, this is defined as *valuation* and in the second case it is defined as *analysis*, the overall process being termed *property appraisal*. Thus the valuation of a property (the calculation of the exchange value of property) is different from the subsequent analysis of the performance of the property as an investment (the appraisal of its actual worth). Calculations before and after purchase will not agree because of the lack of perfect knowledge in the market at the time of the transaction and the inability to predict future changes in the cash flow and the risk profile of the investment accurately. Thus the techniques discussed in this book can be used to anticipate the market value or else to record and analyze the progress of the investment subsequent to purchase. It is critical to understand the difference between these two approaches in the property appraisal process.

Having considered the above, the traditional methods used in valuation are traditionally called the five methods, these are:

- the investment method;
- the comparative method;
- the contractor's test (a cost-based method);
- the profits method; and
- the residual valuation.

The residual valuation, as we have already seen, is used in development situations but, in fact, the residual valuation may rely heavily on the other methods. It may use the investment method to determine the gross development value of the proposed development. It may use the comparative method to compare capital values or site values calculated with examples from the market. The costs calculated for building works are a form of the contractor's test approach. Depending on the type of property, the profits method may also be used to determine the gross development value.

A final point to be made about the valuation of the site is that the value of land is determined by its use and the intensity of that use. Land may have development potential but it will require planning permission for any form of development except for some minor works and some changes of use. The Town and Country Planning Acts determine this process of granting permission to develop. The Town and Country Planning Act 1990 basically defines development as:

> the carrying out of building and other operations on, under or over land.

Investment in Property

Property plays an important part in investment and commerce both as an investment in its own right and as a security for various forms of lending. For the individual investor, shares in a quoted property company are usually the most attractive way of investing in commercial property. The traditional property investment company has a number of characteristics that differentiate it from firms in the manufacturing or service sectors. Usually, it shows a relatively low current yield and the shares are bought mainly for long-term capital and income growth. The property company may finance itself to a greater extent on borrowed money than most manufacturing concerns and it is likely to pay out a higher proportion of its earnings by way of dividend.

Though the property company's shares will be valued partly according to their yield, the asset backing is also important, thus it is not just profitability but the asset base on which the profits are generated (from rents or disposals) which are important. If the liabilities of the company are deducted from the value of the properties and any other assets it owns, the resultant sum is what belongs to the shareholders. This sum, divided by the number of shares, gives a figure for the net asset value per share. The market value of the shares will normally stand somewhat below this figure and this is referred to as a discount to net asset value. Shares in a property company are described as giving a yield of so much per cent and standing at a discount of say 30 per cent to net assets. This does not mean that the company necessarily has any intention of selling its properties, or that the shareholders would necessarily receive as much as the net asset value for the shares if it did, as capital gains tax on disposal of the properties might have to be paid. Rather, this approach is more of a yardstick for comparing the assets of one company with another and can also serve as indicator of income growth in the future (which is presumed to be based on the income-generating ability of the assets). The relationship between share price and net asset value can fluctuate within wide limits and in the analysis it is important to distinguish between property investment and trading companies. Property investment companies get their income from rents; trading companies get their income from sale of completed developments. The idea of a *development* company on the other hand is not a useful concept, as it does not help in distinguishing the two principal objectives of the company to develop either for investment or for trade. The major developers, in terms of the scale of development activity, will tend to be the investment companies rather than the trading companies, in terms of the scale of development activity, although development activity may be carried out in a separate subsidiary.

The majority of quoted property companies invest mainly in commercial and industrial property; in other words, in office buildings, shops, warehouses and factories. Residential property has become increasingly unpopular as an income-yielding investment because of rent controls and other restrictions imposed by successive governments. Most property companies will have a fair mix of different types of commercial property though some will tend to specialize in one type: shops as a name applies in the case of Capital Shopping, or factory and warehouse buildings in the case of Slough Estates. Companies may also specialize by geographical area. The biggest of them all, Land Securities Investment Trust, has a spread of different types of top-quality commercial and industrial property throughout the United Kingdom, but is probably best known for its portfolio of office properties in Central London.

Some companies hold a fair proportion of their properties overseas, particularly in Continental Europe with some investment in North America. Often, however, these overseas ventures have met with disappointing returns and the US market is a particularly specialist and difficult area to operate in. Property companies differ, not only by geographical location and by the type of property they own. The nature of the operation they undertake will also differ. The commercial property investment company, to which we have referred earlier on, does much of what its name suggests: it owns properties and sees its income and the value of its assets rise as inflation and shortages of space force rent upwards in a good market. Many reaped, during the 1980s, the rewards from properties constructed twenty years before. If the income of the property company comes entirely from rents from well-located companies, this income is of very high quality. Up to the end of the 1980s, the rental income could be predicted to a degree but since then rental values have fallen, the incidence of overrenting is now very apparent and it is far more difficult to assess the expectations of rental income at the next rent review. The forecasting of the cash flow stream to the investment has thus become very difficult.

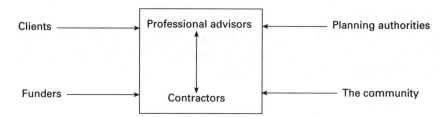

Figure 7.1 *The parties in the development process*

The Parties in the Development Process

The main parties involved in the development process (see figure 7.1) are:

The professional advisors

The architect, quantity surveyor, valuer, planning consultant and possibly consulting engineer, construction manager and project manager.

The clients

The developer and the landowner, who could be an occupier or an investor/trader in development property. The client could be a private or public-sector client. The client could be the owner of extensive estates such as a statutory undertaker or the heir to historic landed estates; it could be a major investor like a financial institution such as a pension fund or insurance company.

The planning authority

The planning authority would deal with planning and highway matters and may have policies to encourage development for employment purposes, for instance.

The contractor

The contractor is employed on the construction of the building and may in turn employ sub-contractors. The nature of the building contract or method of building procurement, as it is now more commonly termed, will determine the relationship of the contractor with the client.

The community

Local residents may have views on the proposed development in addition to the planning authority; as may pressure groups or specific interest groups affected by the development proposals.

The funders

These are the providers of short-term funds for the development and the providers of long-term funds in the event of a buyout or partnership arrangement at the end of the development. The development may be initially funded by the client who may also be an owner-occupier or financial institution.

THE ECONOMIC CONTEXT OF DEVELOPMENT IN THE UK

Introduction

The activity of property development in a macroeconomic sense can be considered to assist in:

(1) regenerating the local economy;
(2) using assets available in the production process more efficiently to obtain greater economic growth;
(3) achieving profitability, from an investor/developer's point of view.

Government policies in the UK, post-Second World War, creating the environment for property development, are examined in Box 7.1. There is a need to see the development process in the context of an economic and financial framework. The basic role of property development from a macroeconomic point of view is the need to revitalize the economy, to use assets that are available in the production process to obtain greater economic growth.

BOX 7.1: PROPERTY DEVELOPMENT IN THE ECONOMY

The role of property development in the economy:

1. To revitalize the economy by encouraging investment.
2. To use the assets available in the production process to obtain greater economic growth and added value.

> **The need for efficient property development is driven by government policy:**
>
> The post-war policy of demand management led to:
>
> - adjustments in government spending and taxation;
> - deflation and reflation of the economy;
> - problems of inflation.
>
> To solve inflation:
>
> - economists looked at the supply side of the economy;
> - saw the need to encourage efficiency and competitiveness in world markets;
> - hence the need for efficient space;
> - hence the need for effective property development.

Government policies until the 1970s relied on a Keynesian approach to 'demand management' which made adjustments of government spending and the amount collected in taxes to deflate or reflate the economy. Some economists rejected this simple approach and suggested that the subsequent rise in unemployment could not be countered by reflation and that this would lead only to inflation in the economy. Reflation has two main effects: the increased consumption causes prices to rise and imports to increase, and this leads to subsequent wage demands and an adverse position on the balance of payments. Limitations on the use of reflationary strategies have encouraged economists to look at the 'supply side' of macroeconomics rather than demand, and to this end they have attempted to improve the competitiveness of British industry. By producing more competitive goods, less of the spending encouraged by inflation will lead to increased imports because it is hoped that better designed goods will be available at competitive prices.

'Supply side' policies have a number of approaches. The Conservative Government in the 1980s endeavoured to take the public sector out of the economy so that market forces could operate unhindered. In a situation like this, if unemployment and lack of growth still exist, then they are blamed on the problems of market adjustments. However one does need to understand how market forces operate and sometimes fail. The supply of property is one aspect of the supply side of the British economy but there is generally some ignorance about the role of land and property in the overall production process and how their supply affects firms' activities.

Business and industry require land and premises in the same way that they require labour, machinery and financial capital. The problem is whether business gets the buildings that it needs within the required criteria of cost, design quality and time, with cost considerations covering the life of the building. The growth of the economy can be badly affected by the short-comings in supply.

Property developers tend to approach property from a different view from economists. They are likely to focus on a narrow band of the property market, more concerned with marketability and profitability of potential developments. The concentration is more on new space in speculative or investment schemes rather than on the larger stock of older owner-occupied properties. Economists are basically interested in the influence of property on economic growth and efficiency, and the effect of location on firms and jobs. Property development encompasses economics and geography, economics because property is an integral part of the process of wealth creation, and distribution and geography because all property has a unique location within urban and regional systems. Most theories of economics ignore the supply of land and property and assume that there is an automatic adjustment of supply to meet demand. Traditionally, economics failed to incorporate land and property into its analysis in a satisfactory manner. Neo-classical economics says that the price adjustments of rent and land values will regulate the demand for and the supply of physical space, but in a mixed economy the workings of the price mechanism are conditioned and controlled by public policy to the extent that the forces of the free market and intervention become interdependent. The level and pattern of urban land values are as much related to prevailing land use planning policy as they are to the market.

A major complication of economic theory is that it cannot accommodate the physical nature of property. Once a factory has been built, it cannot be moved even if its original user deserts it. Buildings vary in age, layout, size, construction and design, so it is difficult to find close substitutes. Other problems of the property market relate to time lags – the time spent on building the project. Finally, the property market is dominated by second-hand stock prices because the amount of new property coming onto the market is small compared to the total stock.

To summarize, there is a basic economic fallacy – that the supply of property adjusts quickly and smoothly to meet the needs of firms. Thus the supply of property exerts an influence on the firm's performance and on the national economy.

Development Activity

Although the stock of second-hand property dominates the market, the supply of new property must also affect price to a degree. Development is a land conversion process by change of use, construction, reconstruction or renovation of land and buildings. The scale of change

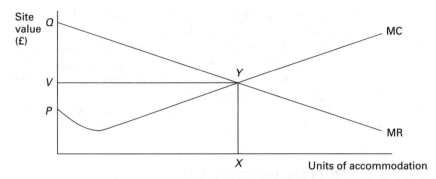

Figure 7.2 *The optimal size of a building*

differs, and the change is motivated, because of client needs. If the client's needs are profit oriented then this conversion process is generally stimulated by the need to achieve higher profitability from land use or a business enterprise.

If we assume that developers and property owners seek to maximize profits then there are two necessary pre-conditions before a development project will be initiated:

(1) the expected value of the completed development must exceed the cost of the site and all development costs, including a sufficient level of profit for the developer;
(2) the value of the site for development purposes must match (or exceed) its value for existing use.

The property developer is faced with a range of resource–use decisions on each project to enable a profit maximization position to be achieved. The principle underlying such decisions is that of discounted returns. The developer will neither strive to minimize total cost nor maximize the value of the completed property but to maximize the (discounted) difference between them. This principle will also dictate whether a developer should refurbish or develop.

The optimal size of building to erect on a cleared urban site can be depicted as shown in figure 7.2.

In figure 7.2, the optimal size of the building is shown by X units of accommodation, because Y is the profit maximization point where marginal cost (MC) = marginal revenue (MR), and at this point the site value is V. Profit is the area between the two curves shown by area PQY.

MR =   the extra revenue to be earned from the addition of each successive unit of accommodation to a fixed area of land. The extra accommodation is at higher, less-accessible levels and thus value falls (decreasing marginal productivity).

MC =   the additional costs of each extra unit of accommodation. Initially this falls (i.e. in building a second storey) but then it increases (extra lifts, more expensive foundations and the need for a structural frame, so project period lengthens).

PQY =   the profit the developer will make from the site (the difference between the total revenue and cost) (Fraser, 1993).

Cyclical Trends in Development Activity

Changes in the level of private-sector development activity are caused by changes in the availability of viable development opportunities and the expected profitability and risk of development. Thus the opportunity and the motive for development need to be apparent.

Rental values of commercial property vary according to changes in economic activity. In a reflationary phase of the economic cycle, rental and capital values will tend to rise with occupational demand, while supply will be relatively low, and construction and finance costs relatively stable. As values rise so there are more opportunities for development and competition between developers falls. Thus profit should rise at the same time that risk is falling (i.e. risk of rent voids). The opposite will happen in a deflationary period.

The Property Companies

Property companies have had a significant influence on the property market for most of the post-war period. The development 'boom' of the late-1940s and early-1950s, based on rental growth, low building costs relative to value and low interest rates, enabled property companies to increase their own internal funds. Thus the original growth in property companies was financed almost entirely by borrowed money. A ready source of funding was to be found through insurance companies and pension funds as the financial institutions began increasingly to dominate the savings market. Initially, the funds provided fixed-interest finance through mortgages and debentures. Subsequently, as the funds recognized the benefits of participation in the rental growth of property, they began to engage in sale and leaseback arrangements, partnerships and direct development. These developments meant that by the late-1970s the financial institutions came to be the dominant influence on the commercial property markets through their financial control. The tax status of the funds gave them a considerable advantage in direct development over the property companies.

In recent years there has been a decline in institutional interest in property investment and in direct development as the returns from other investments such as equities have risen and the rate of inflation has abated. This had led to increased opportunities for property companies to become more innovative in raising funds and attention being focused on corporate funding as a key source of property finance. Fixed-interest securities and discounted bond issues are recent examples of these developments. The problem of raising finance on the stock market is that the market discounts the property valuation of the assets. The share prices of property-investment companies tend to stand at an average discount of approximately 20 per cent to the net asset values of the companies when examined over a longer period.

The share price discount to net asset value dissuades property companies from raising money in the form of equity and thus encourages them to borrow money and increase their gearing. This is because, if the company buys £100 of assets in the market at that property valuation, the stock market will only finance them to the value of say £80. High gearing, which means a high percentage of borrowed funds in relation to equity capital, is advantageous during periods of rapid rental growth as rental profits can outstrip interest payments to shareholders. However, high debt payments encourage the chances of insolvency during period of declining profitability. Thus high gearing encourages investors to regard property companies as more risky investments.

Property Development for Owner-occupiers

Fothergill *et al.* (1987) offer insights into the wider economic context of property development. They provide a different approach from the one already taken in this chapter, concentrating on the economic aspects of location and use of buildings. The main argument of this text is that property is an important asset in the national economy. It maintains that if there is to be growth of the economy and further industrialization, then premises or space must be available to cater for this expansion. The text sets out to examine the roles of industrial property in revitalizing the economy. In terms of the significance of property, however, Fothergill *et al.* maintain that the most important contributor to economic growth is demand management, that is reflation or deflation in the UK and world economies. The authors consider the lack of skills and training of manpower, combined with the reluctance of financial institutions to provide long-term industrial finance, to be the important aspects affecting the supply of property. Fothergill *et al.* state that there is considerable ignorance about the role that land and property play in the overall process and how these elements affect the location of a firm's activities. This postulates the question: 'does manufacturing activity obtain buildings in locations where it needs them?' The approach of this text is accepted as being different from that of the approach of general practice surveyors, property developers and financial analysts, the latter grouping of professionals being more concerned with new-build speculative or investment space rather than the total stock of property:

> *for purely commercial reasons, the property world needs to know about yields and rates of return . . . our concern is with the industrial buildings as an input to production and a tool of economic development.* (Fothergill *et al.*, 1987: 10)

The trouble is that commercial reasons are often those that underpin the problems of providing space, and factors relating to return and investment need to be considered to adequately develop an effective strategy for space provision.

Property represents a substantial financial involvement in terms of assets held by commercial firms but there are significant problems of obsolescence in buildings, the existence of a stock of large, old buildings, often multi-storey, which are available for sale rather than for rent. These buildings have usually been made available by closure or relocation of businesses. These premises may never find an occupier and thus the only alternative would be to demolish, subdivide or convert them. There exist problems of mismatch where premises, once suitable for occupants become inappropriate. The problems of mismatch relate to the quantity of space and to problems of design and layout which constrain output and efficiency respectively. Property and location decision-making is critical to the firm; the supply of land and buildings exerts an important influence on location but the influence operates, not so much through the price mechanism, as through physical constraints and availability. There is a role for the public sector in the provision of industrial space because, although private developers would move in once the price is right, this could involve substantial problems in delays. The prejudices of private financial institutions against certain investment and the fact that private enterprise is not always quick to identify gaps in the property market exacerbate the problem (Isaac, 1988).

Fothergill *et al.* suggest that an appropriate strategy for the supply of industrial property space to facilitate the re-industrialization of the economy requires that:

- no firm should find expansion delayed through lack of space;
- efficiency should be improved by promoting transfers between premises;
- the industrial property market should promote a more equitable distribution of job opportunities.

Fothergill *et al.* calculated that to achieve a growth rate in output of 3.5 per cent per annum, new space is required nationally at a rate of 12.5 million square metres per annum compared to 5 million square metres per annum built between 1974 and 1985 in England and Wales. Market forces alone are unlikely to be able to cope with this level of supply.

DEVELOPMENT ACTIVITY IN THE UK

Over the last decade there has been a government relaxation in the area of property development, reflecting the general *laissez-faire* attitude in the economy. Funding of projects has been restricted, and institution funding has reduced and has been superseded by international funds from Europe and Asia Pacific especially, but recently these funds have also dried up.

Changes in the nature of property development because of the scale of building already carried out, demands for conservation of areas and single buildings, and existing constraints of infrastructure and neighbouring building have led to a change in emphasis from new building to rehabilitation. Local-authority and government-funded intervention has encouraged some urban regeneration and the overhauling of obsolete infrastructure. Local-authority partnerships of the most imaginative kind have been developed, although by the early-1990s financial restrictions had limited activity.

Limitations on the growth of the economy have restricted the need for planning intervention at a high level, although problems with national infrastructure and NIMBYism (the tendency to protest at developments which have an effect on the protestors' local area, usually of residence, but rather a protest relating to an ideal or political/social viewpoint; hence the term: *not in my back yard*) have affected strategic planning. New planning legislation puts more reliance on local plans and there has been a call for the re-establishment of a strategic authority for London.

Trends in the property market include attempts to obtain relaxation of green-belt policies to encourage new residential settlements and the private provision of social infrastructure. In the 1990s, in the commercial sectors of the property market all sectors were depressed, with industrial looking the most promising in terms of possible expansion. Lack of retail sales and a glut of office space have hit the respective sectors. Retail warehouses are also less in demand. The provision of large banking floors in the City of London in the 1990s following deregularization of the stock exchange (Big Bang) has led to a significant oversupply and demand is for smaller cellar office space for professional firms. B1 class property (arising from a change in the use classes order and reflecting a mixed office/industrial use) led to high-tech industrial development on new estates and again to an oversupply of this type of property.

The Development Process: A Summary

Cadman and Austin-Crowe (1976: 3) suggest that there were four key phases in the development process: evaluation, preparation, implementation and disposal. The most important phase was evaluation. They state:

> *Evaluation encompasses both the analysis of the marketplace in general and in particular – market research – and the financial assessment of the project. It should be carried out before any commitment is undertaken and while the developer retains flexibility . . . Evaluation involves the combined advice of the development team but in the end the responsibility for interpreting that advice rests with the developer, who has to decide whether or not to bear the risk of the project.*

The development process can be introduced here as a summary of the main stages:

- choosing a location;
- identifying a site and carrying out a detailed site survey;
- providing an outline scheme and appraisal;
- negotiating for site acquisition;
- design;
- planning consent;
- finance;
- site acquisition;
- detailed plans;
- tender documents for construction;
- construction;
- occupation or marketing and management.

One of the major problems facing property development is the supply of land and building in appropriate location for development. By providing urban land, rather than looking for greenfield sites with the associated environmental consequences, problems of development would be lessened.

There is however a shortage of available urban land, and Balchin and Bull (1987: 193) identify four causes of urban land shortage. These causes are:

(1) The slowness of planning procedures; the development process is hamstrung by delays at the planning application stage, however these may be necessary if the local community is to be given adequate time for consultation.
(2) In recent decades the government has attempted to contain urban growth by metropolitan and provincial green belts. At the same time, outer suburban local authorities have been reluctant to release land to accommodate the housing and employment needs of the inner-city population.
(3) During the boom periods, commercial development has squeezed out housing development from central and inner urban areas and thus, at these times, housing development has been unable to compete for sites.
(4) A large amount of urban land has been withheld from the market and much is in a derelict state.

Property Development

In practice, many property investment companies started out as property development companies in the higher-risk, higher-reward side of the property business, and some still undertake developments as well as their investment activities. In the UK development boom of the 1950s and early-1960s the approach was to raise long-term finance in the form of mortgage of two-thirds of the value of a completed development at a fixed interest rate. The mortgages came from insurance companies who were far less conscious in those days of the effects of inflation. Provided the development was valued at 50 per cent or more above the costs of acquisition and development, then the whole outlay could be recouped, and the profit surplus and any subsequent rise in the capital value of the building were added to the wealth of the developer. Many property companies still have cheap borrowings dating back to those days. Nowadays, rates for fixed-interest money are too high; inflation-conscious insurance companies want a share in any growth from the building and current developments are more likely to be financed by some form of partnership arrangement between the property company and the financial institution.

Some property companies develop buildings to sell at a capital profit on completion rather than to retain them for their rents, and still others make a trade of buying and selling properties without undertaking development. Profit from these sources is not as stable or as certain as income from rents and thus may be a less valuable contribution to the company's cash flow, although a useful addition. Thus the analysis of property companies should be undertaken with a view as to where the income comes from and of what quality it is. Investment in the property sector requires expert advice; it is a specialist sector of the market in which very few firms of stockbrokers, for instance, have particular expertise. Bricks and mortar are a sound investment but not in any condition at any price. The virtue of commercial properties, in the past, was that financial institutions invested directly in them on a large scale and there were thus ready buyers for a property company's assets, but this has become less likely and will not be so in the future. The UK market in property has had a number of ups and downs; the market in investment properties almost dried up in the financial crash of 1974–75 and values slumped drastically. Property companies which had undertaken too many developments on the back of borrowed short-term money found themselves unable to borrow more to pay the interest and unable to sell the properties to pay the debt. A number went bust; others had drastically cut their development programmes. In the early-1980s most property shares were relatively indifferent investments and comparatively few new developments took place. There was a revival in the mid-1980s when there was evidence of shortages. During this period, companies with good existing properties and good developments did well in a period before inflation began to decrease. By the end of the 1980s, property development companies were viewed in a much poorer light by investors and, although there was a resurgence of investment at the beginning of the 1990s, there is still generally a sceptical view of property investment in property company shares.

Property development is part of the property market which includes a user market, an investment market and a development market; a simple model of the overall property market is suggested by Keogh (1994) and discussed further in Chapter 8.

BOX 7.2: THE UK CONSTRUCTION INDUSTRY

The UK construction industry is inextricably linked to the property development process. As well as controlling the construction phase of development, construction firms may act as property developers in their own right and also project managers and financiers of property development projects. There are a number of specialist texts on the construction industry in the UK and thus this box will provide a brief overview.

The construction industry is characterized by the nature of the product, the structure of the industry and the organization of the construction process, the determinants of demand and the method of price determination. These aspects set the construction industry apart from other sectors. The nature of demand in the construction industry is for investment goods for which the ultimate use is:

(1) as a means to further production, e.g. factory building;
(2) as an addition or an improvement to the infrastructure of the economy, e.g. roads;
(3) as a social investment, e.g. hospitals;
(4) as an investment good for direct enjoyment, e.g. housing (Hillebrandt, 1985).

The demand is influenced directly by central or local government and, even where there is no direct influence, the public sector will have indirect influence. The extent of government influence and the investment nature of the demand mentioned earlier means that demand fluctuates in the sector, driven by the state of the economy and the government's socio-economic policies. Fluctuations are marked and rapid, a situation shared with the corresponding construction sector in most West European countries. Large variations in output lead to fluctuations in turnover and, because profit margins tend to be low in the sector, the profitability of firms is unstable (Briscoe, 1988). Company insolvency statistics show the rise in insolvency in the construction industry from 15.8 per cent of total insolvencies in 1981 to 23.4 per cent in 1993 (Wright, 1994). The importance of construction in the economy is related to the size of the sector, the fact that the sector is producing mainly investment goods and finally the fact that government is the client for a large part of the output (Hillebrandt, 1985). The role of government in this respect has, however, steadily reduced since 1985.

The Construction Sector of the UK Economic System

In any economy, construction is a key activity; it has an effect on the goods and services provided in the space in which the extractive, manufacturing and service industries are active. The flow of goods and services in the economy are thus directly driven by the construction process. With the construction industry contributing 9.1 per cent of the GDP in 1991, its role in the economy is vital. It thus remains an important sector in the UK economy despite a decline in recent years.

Variations in the gross national product of the UK will influence the demand for construction work and thus the associated level of employment. The output from the construction sector is a response to a demand for buildings which in turn is a derived demand in other areas, for instance the buildings material sector (Briscoe, 1988).

£ billion (at 1995 prices)

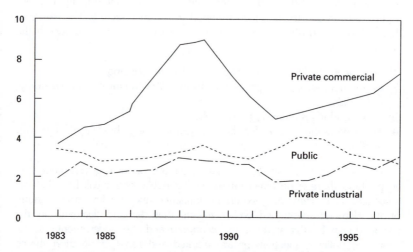

Figure 7.3 New non-housing orders (excluding infrastructure),
1983–97 (DoE, 1998: 9)

Figures 7.3 to 7.5 give some indication of the value of construction output in the UK. Figure 7.3 shows the value of non-housing work, excluding infrastructure, over the period 1983–97 at 1995 prices. It can be seen that private commercial work peaked in 1989, and – after decreasing to 1992 – recovered to a significant extent by 1997. Figure 7.4 provides a comparison of the types of new work in 1987 and 1997, again measured at 1995 prices. The only area of substantial difference was private housing, although there was some increase in private industrial work. Figure 7.5 shows how new work is shared between the various sectors in 1997 at 1995 prices.

Construction output derives from a number of distinct types of work. The recent decline in new work of the public sector is manifest in the downward trend in new housing and other work in this sector, which incorporates civil engineering and the construction of all public buildings. Since the early-1970s, the decline has also occurred in two categories of new private-sector work: new housing and industrial and commercial new work. Generally, the reduction in new work in the private sector has been less pronounced than that experienced in the public sector. The reduced activity levels in new output were mirrored in repair and maintenance output in the early-1990s.

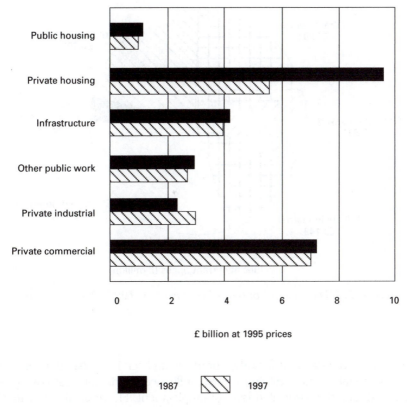

Figure 7.4 *Comparison of the value of new work for 1987 and 1997 (DoE, 1998: 10)*

It is not only in terms of output that construction makes a significant impact on the UK economy, for the industry also exerts associated influence on national employment. Throughout the 1970s the construction sector was responsible for about 6.8 per cent of the jobs in the economy. Since 1980 this proportion has fallen but construction remains a major provider of employment opportunities. In particular, by the mid-1980s almost one-fifth of all self-employed workers were active in the construction industry (Briscoe, 1988). By the early-1990s this proportion has reduced significantly with the spate of insolvencies.

The construction sector is greatly dependent on changes in the UK economy, in particular those which are the direct result of government policy. Construction output is a response to the demand for buildings and

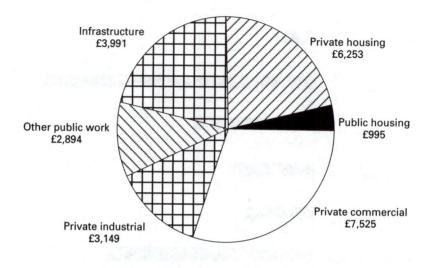

Values at current prices (£ million)

Figure 7.5 *The value of output of new work in 1997 (DoE, 1998: 10)*

this is a derived demand for other products and services. Variations in the gross national product will, in this way, influence the demand for construction work and the associated level of employment. However, the construction sector itself will determine the demand for products from other parts of the economy, especially the material supplies sector.

THE DEVELOPMENT OF REAL ESTATE IN EAST CENTRAL EUROPE

Much of the development in the main centres of East Central Europe is dependent on foreign investment, especially the impetus provided by foreign firms looking to develop assets for their own use and for investment. Foreign capital has been a key factor in liberating the controlled markets of the prime cities of the region – Warsaw, Budapest and Prague. Adair *et al.* (1999), together with information provided by Jones Lang Wooton (1997), have investigated the development of real estate in these three centres, and these cities provide interesting and slightly contrasting approaches, although the main issues are those of foreign capital liberating controlled real estate markets.

In Prague, the main negative barrier for the development of real estate was the lack of finance from domestic sources and thus foreign capital played a major role in stimulating development. Most new construction has been financed and developed by Austrian, German and French firms, and mainly traded by agencies from a UK background. The majority of new users of space are international firms or joint-venture companies.

In Budapest, the financial problems are slightly different. Hungary has attracted around US$13 billion of direct foreign investment since 1989, a greater share than other Central European countries. But short-term interest rates and the cost of borrowing are high. There has been a shortage of domestic finance so most real estate finance has been raised externally. The demand for space is largely from foreign companies and a few large indigenous firms mainly in insurance, banking and financial services and the professional services sector.

In Warsaw, the property market emerged later than those in Budapest and Prague; this was because of the uncertain political situation there. However the market is considered to have better long-term growth prospects, as it is the capital of a much larger country than the other competing East Central European cities. Foreign investors have been particularly active in the development of large office and retail projects. In contrast to Budapest and Prague, there is significant development space in central Warsaw, though strict procedures for building permits and unresolved property rights have inhibited the construction and planning phases for new development. This restriction has thus encouraged the refurbishment of existing space and the development of an out-of-town market (Adair *et al.*, 1999). In 1997 the office sector was booming because of high demand from international financial enterprises and domestic enterprises. In 1993 a number of business centres had been constructed, followed by a further phase of construction in 1995. The development of these major projects has been made possible by the involvement of foreign investors and developers. The European Bank for Reconstruction and Development (EBRD) has had a major influence on new development in the city.

BOX 7.3: THE CONSTRUCTION INDUSTRY IN EAST CENTRAL EUROPE

Throughout East Central Europe, the construction industry underwent a process of privatization in the aftermath of major political change in 1989–90 and during the consequential reintroduction of a free market economy. The privatization of construction resources in Poland (as in other countries in the region) was intended not only to lead to changes in ownership, but also to increase efficiency, while the restructuring of the industry aimed to increase

continued

the number and proportion of small and medium-sized companies, facilitate changes in construction technology, introduce new technologies and facilitate competition between companies (Hajduk, 1996). In the region as a whole, construction was almost entirely state controlled under communism, but by 1996 in the Czech Republic as much as 99 per cent of enterprises were in the private sector, in Hungary over two-thirds of construction firms were individual entrepreneurs, and in Poland the private construction sector accounted for 87 per cent of production as early as 1993 (Economist Intelligence Unit, various).

The construction industry in East Central Europe is of major importance to the economy of the region, but since privatization and the introduction of a free market its role has diminished proportionately in recent years. In the Czech Republic, whereas the construction industry accounted for 10.8 per cent of the GDP in 1990, its share fell to 6.8 per cent in 1998. In Hungary, it accounted for 5.8 per cent of GDP in 1991, but fell to 4.1 per cent in 1997; and in Poland, its share of the GDP fell from 9.3 per cent in 1990 to 5.7 per cent in 1997 (Economist Intelligence Unit, various).

The industry's performance, as in other regions of the world, is substantially associated with general economic trends and is closely affected by government economic policy. In the early-1990s, construction activity slumped across the region. It is of note that whereas the state sector was particularly depressed because of cuts in government capital expenditure and structural changes in the industry, the emerging private sector showed signs of growth. Construction output subsequently recovered in most sectors of the industry (except for housebuilding), with work in the Czech Republic increasing by 17 per cent in 1993, in Hungary by 27 per cent in 1992, and in Poland by 4 per cent in 1993 (Economist Intelligence Unit, various). By the late-1990s, however, the construction industry, like most other industries in the region, suffered a decrease in output, the vulnerable economy of the region being adversely affected by recession in many parts of the global economy including Russia.

Clearly, only time will tell whether the restructuring of the construction industry in East Central Europe will enable local firms – in the face of foreign competition – to play a full part in the development and redevelopment of the region's cities.

THE DEVELOPMENT OF URBAN LAND POLICY IN CHINA

Historical Background

The ownership of land in China is basically of two types. Firstly, there is state-owned land, mainly in cities and towns although the state also owns large forests and some farmland. The second type of land ownership is that by rural collectives, which is land in rural areas and towns not owned by the state (Li Ling and Isaac, 1994).

The state-owned land system has been established in a series of distinct phases since 1945. Between 1945 and 1949, the Chinese Communist Government nationalized land owned by the Nationalist Government. In this phase, land was also recovered from landowners who had supported the nationalists. From 1949, the Chinese government and its associated administration and organizations obtained land by buying and renting at market levels from private land owners, and this continued until 1953. On 5 December 1953, the State Council of the People's Republic of China passed laws that provided for the requisitioning of land for state construction purposes. Under these laws, all government organizations and state-owned enterprises were provided with land that was requisitioned by the government. The land then became state owned and returned to the state when the use finished. However, during the period from 1949 to 1956, private land continued to exist and could be sold, leased and given away. From 1956 onward, the government of the People's Republic of China proceeded with the nationalization of land, a process that was completed around 1982. On 4 December 1982, the Fifth Session of the National People's Congress passed the 'Constitution of the People's Republic of China'. Clause 4 article 10 of the Constitution stipulated:

'No organization or individual may appropriate, buy, sell or lease or unlawfully transfer land in other ways'

Thus, until recently, the land system which was established has meant that urban land was owned by the state, land being allocated by the state to users without charge or limitation on the length of use, and any private land transaction was prohibited. This system of land allocation is now referred to as the 'old land system' or 'old land use system'. The old land system was basically a product of China's economy during this period.

In the 1960s and 1970s the economy was a planned economy; there was a planned allocation of resources, so markets in factors of production did not exist. There were only two types of economic enterprise: state-owned and collective-owned enterprises. The financial interests of the managers and workers in the enterprises were divorced from the performance of the enterprise. There was no incentive to compete with other enterprises. Factors of production, including land, raw materials and machinery, were allocated by government. The price of these factors was fixed by the state as accounting measures and did not bear any relationship to market price, and there were no private-property rights. Managers and workers in state-owned enterprises lived in the houses provided by the enterprise. Some had private houses, but with no land attached and no transfer of ownership of these houses was allowed. The state-owned enterprises and collectives basically continued the production of the same type of goods for which they had been established and losses were subsidised by the state. There was no need to maximize the efficient use of the factors of production under this economy and, under these circumstances, a land market was considered irrelevant and the private market would 'wither away'.

Recent Legislation

From 1979 on, the People's Republic of China (PRC) began to institute policies of economic reform – its 'open-door' policies which have included reforms in agrarian production, foreign capital investment, incentives for production, reforms of the financial system and the introduction of free markets. In detail, these have consisted of:

- *Rural production reform.* Since 1979, the PRC began to popularize the rural contractual system that delegated the responsibility for determining output to producers. This resulted in a higher crop yield and in a crop surplus. Because of the increase in production and productivity, fewer workers were required on the land and this has released surplus manpower who have moved into urban areas to find work or set up township enterprises in the countryside.
- Also from 1979 on, the PRC began to establish *foreign investment ventures*, either equity joint ventures, co-operative ventures or wholly foreign-owned ventures.
- The analogous system to establish responsibility for agrarian production is a similar system applied to *urban indigenous enterprises*, and these enterprises now have an incentive-based system which has also allowed the establishment of individual property rights.
- There has been reform of the *financial system* instead of profits being taken by local and central government; a tax is now levied on profit and this tax is shared between local and central government.
- There has been reform of the *price system*; central-government price control on commodities and raw materials has lessened and the price determined in the markets has now become the important factor in the distribution of goods and raw materials.

A new economic system has now been established and is referred to as a 'socialist market' economy, differing from the previous planned economy in a number of critical aspects. In the market-driven economy, incentive-based competition between enterprises has arisen, and managers and workers now have interest and returns more closely allied to profitability.

The 'old land system' is now inappropriate for the changes which have taken place in the economy, and this system now particularly needs to change because the lack of a land market is depriving both central and local governments of the chance of raising finance through land sales for infra-structure development in urban areas. The lack of a land market leads to an inefficient allocation of land resources and lack of flexibility in the relo-cation of business uses. The 'old land system' does not attract foreign invest-ment, as there are no clear ownership rights. Finally, the burden of housing under the old system was left with the state or state-owned enterprises, and this was a problem because an obligation to provide housing existed, yet there was an inability to recoup a reasonable return from it. In order for managers and workers to be encouraged to purchase their own houses, a coherent property and land market has to exist.

Urban land-use reform began in 1979 when the PRC law on 'Co-operative Ventures' allowed indigenous enterprises to use their land as capital to co-operate with foreign investors. Between 1982 and 1987, pilot schemes in various cities were set up to collect land-use fees. The level of fee related to the land use, amount of supply and infrastructure, and the level of fees is shown in table 7.1.

From 1987, Shenzhen began to grant land-use rights and the three initial negotiations concerned rights granted to domestic enterprises. These rights are summarized in table 7.2.

Table 7.1 Pilot land-use fee schemes (12.8 yuan = £1 (August 1999))

Date of introduction	Area	Fee rate (yuan/m²/pa)	Amount collected in first year
1982	Shenzhen Special Economic Zone	1–4	10m yuan (1982)
1984	Hushuen City (in Lia Ning Province, north-east China)	0.2–0.6	13m yuan (1984)
1984	Guangzhou (only the Economic and Technological Development Districts, new construction projects, foreign investments)	0.5–4.0	20m yuan (1984)

Table 7.2 Initial land-use rights granted in Shenzhen

Date	Grantee	Terms
8 September 1987	Shenzhen Industrial Import and Export Corporation of China, National Aero-Technology Import and Export Corporation	By negotiation: 1,322 m² residential use 200 yuan/m² 50 years' rights
15 September 1987	Shenzhen Engineering Development Co.	By tender: 46,355 m² residential use 368 yuan/m² 50 years' rights
1 December 1987	Shenzhen SEZ Real Estate Co.	By auction: 8,588 m² residential use 610 yuan/m² 50 years' rights

In July 1988, Shanghai granted rights over a piece of land in the Hong Qiao Economic and Technological Development District to a Japanese company through international open tender, the premium for this being paid in US dollars.

Between 1988 and 1990, three major pieces of legislation were passed which consolidated the moves to reform the land market. In April 1988, the Seventh National People's Congress passed a significant amendment to the PRC Constitution that revised article 10, clause 4 of the Constitution to include the right of transfer of land use.

On the 27 September 1988, the State Council promulgated the 'Tentative Regulations of Land-Use Taxation in Cities and Towns of the People's Republic of China'. These taxes are levied on all indigenous profit-making enterprises and organizations. The bands of land-use tax are:

Large cities (>1 million population)   0.5–10 yuan/m² pa
Medium-sized cities (0.5–1 m)   0.4–8 yuan/m² pa
Small cities (0.2–0.5 m)   0.3–6 yuan/m² pa
Towns (<0.2 m), industrial and/or mineral regions   0.2–4 yuan/m² pa

Land is classified into different grades in the various cities and towns, and the taxes levied within the bands indicated above according to the grade. To date, the highest tax band of 8 yuan/m² pa has been levied in

Shanghai. This tax is for indigenous enterprises only; for foreign enterprises a system of land-use fees is levied which is separate and different. For indigenous enterprises the land-use taxes replace the land-use fees mentioned earlier. However in some cities, like Shenzhen, land-use fees are still collected for indigenous land users because the level of the fees is higher than the tax. The fees are shared with the central government on the same basis as the land-use tax.

The third piece of legislation was passed in December 1988 when the 5th session of the Standing Committee of the National People's Congress amended the Land Administration Law of the PRC. The significant changes are indicated below:

- the land-use rights of state- or collective-owned land may be transferred through legal procedures – the detailed methods for land-use right transfers will be regulated by the State Council;
- the state will practise a pay-for-use land system for state-owned land, whereby users will pay for the right to use the land under the regulation of the State Council;
- there will be prohibition of any occupation of state land or land belonging to a commune, or sale or letting, except in accordance with the law;
- there will be prohibition of use other than the permitted use;
- there will be forfeiture of monetary gain from illegal letting or illegal transfer of land, together with fines;
- the use of land by joining venture or foreign companies will be regulated by rules to be made at a later date by the State Council.

The purposes of these changes in the law was to prevent a collapse into anarchy in the land markets by ensuring that changes of use and occupation would have to be approved and registered. Also the state would retain the right to recover land required for public works or the needs of state-owned enterprises.

On 19 May 1990, the State Council promulgated two significant decrees that affected land use and the land market. Decree 55 was the 'Provisional regulations on the granting and transferring of land-use rights over state-owned land in cities and towns'. Decree 56 was the 'Provisional measures for the administration of foreign investors to develop and operate plots of land'.

Decree 56 is based on decree 55 but is used to grant large plots of land to foreign developers and encourage them to invest in infrastructure. These areas of land would be more than $1\,km^2$ and the developers could assign rights of parts of the land when the infrastructure was completed. The main conditions of decree 55 are set out in a table forming part of the decree. Decree 55 has popularized the land-lease system in China (Li Ling and Isaac, 1994).

BOX 7.4: THE CONSTRUCTION INDUSTRY IN CHINA

As in most developing and newly-industrializing countries, the construction industry plays a major role in China's economic development. Although the industry was instrumental in establishing a heavy industrial base during the thirty years after 1949, large-scale projects such as hydroelectricity and water control, bridge building and the construction of factory plant in heavy industry took precedence over housing development and small-scale ventures. However, as a result of calls from the Sixth National People's Congress in Beijing in 1984, the industry has been reformed through the liberalization of investment (for example, by the authorization of extra-budgetary investment in housing, offices and housing), attracting FDI in joint ventures, and introducing a system of public tendering (see Chen, 1999: 78–9).

The share of construction output has consequently increased from 13.9 per cent of the GNP in 1988 to as much as 23.7 per cent in 1994 (compared to less than half this proportion in, for example, East Central Europe and the UK in the mid-1990s). The number of enterprises in the construction industry, however, diminished slightly from 87,224 in 1988 to 77,857 in 1992, whereas the workforce increased marginally from 19.0 million to 19.6 million over the same period – suggesting a small increase in the scale of activity. However, although rural and urban collectively-owned enterprises accounted respectively for 81 and 12 per cent of all construction enterprises in 1992 and state-owned enterprises accounted for only 6.4 per cent of the total, state-owned enterprises (with 35 per cent of the industry's workforce) contributed as much as 43 per cent to the total construction output of the country (Chen, 1999: 79).

Despite (or because of) reforms, civil engineering remains the largest construction sector – accounting for 87.5 per cent of the industry's output in 1993, of which the southern province of Guangdong contributed the largest share, 15 per cent (Chen, 1999: 86). This was associated with the development of the SEZ of Shenzhen and the coastal city of Guangzhou in the region. New work in the industrial, commercial and residental sectors accounted for only 10.4 per cent of total output, of which Liaoning province in Northern China was by far the largest contributor.

Although in the past, most construction companies in China were state- or collectively-owned, other types of enterprises are rapidly emerging (as in East Central Europe). These comprise individually-owned units, units owned jointly by domestic and foreign companies, and wholly-owned foreign companies. Shareholding has been introduced, although the number of enterprises dependent upon share capital remained comparatively small in the 1990s – even though their shares are available in share markets such as Shanghai and Shenzhen as well as overseas.

While China's construction industry has made rapid strides in recent years, the industry is faced with a number of serious constraints, for example severe distortions in the price mechanism – resulting from problems relating to tendering, payment, contract management amd performance – might limit the extent to which the industry can continue to contribute to economic development; the co-existence of a centrally-planned economy and market economy leads – in some degree – to a general state of economic disorder in the construction market; and there is arguably a lack of initiative in the larger and medium-sized state-owned companies. In these respects, the construction industry in China differs substantially from that of East Central Europe, where privatization has been the dominant feature of reform within a free market economy.

REFERENCES

Adair, A., Berry, J., McGreal, S., Sykora, L., Ghanbari Parsa, A. and Redding, B. (1999) 'Globalisation of real estate markets in Central Europe', *European Planning Studies*, 7(3): 295–305.

Balchin, P. and Bull, G. (1987) *Regional and Urban Economics*, London: Harper & Row.

Baum, A. and Crosby, N. (1995) *Property Investment Appraisal*, London: Routledge.

Briscoe, G. (1988) *The Economics of the Construction Industry*, London: Mitchell.

Cadman, D. and Austin-Crowe, L. (1976) *Property Development*, London: E. & F.N. Spon.

Chen, J. (1999) 'The impact of China's economic reforms upon the construction industry', in Chen, J. and Wills, D. (eds), *The Impact of China's Economic Reforms upon Land, Property and Construction*, Aldershot: Ashgate.

DoE (Department of the Environment) (1998) *Housing and Construction Statistics (Great Britain)*, London: HMSO.

Economist Intelligence Unit (various dates) *Country Reports: Czech Republic*, 1st quarter 1994; *Hungary*, 2nd quarter 1992; *Poland*, 2nd quarter 1993. *Country Profiles: Czech Republic*, 1999–2000; *Hungary*, 1998–99; *Poland*, 1995–96.

Fothergill, S., Monk, S. and Perry, M. (1987) *Property and Industrial Development*, London: Hutchison.

Fraser, W.D. (1993) *Principles of Property Investment and Pricing*, Basingstoke: Macmillan.

Hajduk, H. (1996) 'Poland', in Balchin, P. (ed.), *The Impact of China's Economic Reforms upon Land, Property and Construction*, London: Routledge.

Hillebrandt, P.M. (1985) *Economic Theory and the Construction Industry*, London: Macmillan.

Isaac, D. (1988) ' "Property and industrial development", a review of *Property and Industrial Development* by S. Fothergill, S. Monk and M. Perry', *Journal of Local Economy*, 3(1): 56–8.

Jones Lang Wooton (1997) *City Profiles: Prague; Budapest; Warsaw*, London: JLW.

Keogh, G. (1994) 'Use & investment markets in UK real estate', *Journal of Property Valuation and Investment*, 12(4): 58–72.

Li Ling and Isaac, D. (1994) 'The development of urban land policy in China', *Journal of Property Management*, 12(4): 12–17.

Seeley, I.H. (1995) *Building Economics*, London: Macmillan.

State Council of China (various dates) Laws and Decrees as mentioned in the text.

Wright, K. (1994) 'Company profitability and finance', *Bank of England: Quarterly Bulletin*, 34(3), August.

8

Property Investment

RATIONALE OF INVESTMENT

Introduction

A property or building can be owner-occupied or rented, the latter being an investment property. It may of course be vacant, resulting from being surplus to the owner's requirements or a poor investment! A large proportion of property is owner-occupied but most of the conventional texts and theories in property are applied to the investment market. The investment market for property cannot be seen in isolation from other investment markets. The application of funds to property has to reflect competition from other forms of investment. The decision to invest in a particular area will be a comparison of return and security, and thus knowledge of alternative investments and their analysis could be very important. The application of financial techniques to property investment can also be important and this can clearly be seen in the securitization and unitization of property, which is a key area of development in property investment. Another important point to be made concerns the nature of the lender and the property to which finance is applied. At its simplest, the financial arrangement may deal with an individual purchasing a single property with a single loan, but it is usually more complex. Finance is generally raised by corporate entities, such as property companies, using existing property and other assets as collateral for the purchase of a portfolio of assets which may include property assets but not exclusively. Finally, it is important to realize the significance of property and property investment to the economy; the importance can be shown in three different ways: as a factor of production, as a corporate asset and as an investment medium. As a factor of production, property provides the space in which economic activity and production take place, and the efficiency and costs of such space will affect the cost of goods and services produced. As a corporate asset, property forms the major part of asset values in companies' balance sheets and the majority of corporate debt is secured against it. As an investment, it is one of the major types of investment held by individual investors and the financial institutions on which pensions and assurance benefits depend (Fraser, 1993).

The Structure of the Investment Market

There are three major areas of traditional investment opportunity (ignoring gold, commodities and works of art): fixed-interest securities, company stocks and shares, and real property. The London Stock Exchange, for example, provides a market for listed shares and certain fixed-interest securities such as those issued by the government, local authorities and public bodies. The market in real property contrasts with that of company shares and other securities. The property market is fragmented and dispersed while that of shares and other securities is highly centralized. The London Stock Market is an example of this centralization. The centralization of markets assists the transferability of investments, as does the fact that stocks and shares can be traded in small units thereby assisting transferability. Compared with other traditional investment opportunities, real property investment has the distinguishing features of being heterogeneous, generally indivisible and having inherent problems of management. The problems of managing property assets may include collecting rents, dealing with repairs and renewals, and lease negotiation; these problems may mean that real property is likely to be an unattractive proposition for the small investor. A decentralized market, such as exists for property, will tend to have high costs of transfer of investments and there will be an imperfect knowledge of transactions in the market.

The factors discussed above, which affect the real property market, make property difficult to value. There is no centralized market price to rely on and the value may be too difficult to assess unless a comparable transaction has recently taken place. The problems of valuation relate to difficulties of trying to relate comparable transactions to properties being valued or even trying to assess what transactions could be considered comparable. Because of the nature of the real property market, individual investors have tended to withdraw from the market and this has been reinforced by the channelling of savings into collective organizations, such as pension funds and insurance companies. This has meant that few individuals use their savings for direct investment in the property market.

Qualities of an Investment

An investment essentially involves an initial money outlay to recoup a future income stream or future capital repayment. The approach to the analysis of what is required of an investment is best done as a checklist of questions and answers. The major question is what an investor expects from the investment, to which the answers might be:

(1) security of capital and also liquidity so that the interest can be disposed of easily;
(2) security of income from the capital invested;
(3) regularity of income;
(4) low cost of purchase and sale of the investment;
(5) ease of purchase and sale of the investment;
(6) divisibility of the investment – is it possible to sell off parts of it?
(7) the security of the investment in real terms – is the value of the investment increasing in line with inflation?
(8) the opportunities for growth in value – is this growth more than the rate of inflation, i.e. is it real growth? (Isaac, 1998).

The type of investment chosen is related to a number of factors, and these factors will differ according to the investor. There may be a particular or peculiar arrangement – tax arrangements, for instance, or ethical considerations which may affect investment choice. The quality of an investment from an economic point of view must be a comparison of the return to the risk; the return is not just the cash flow arising but needs to be considered in relation to the original outlay and return on possible sale. So the cash flow needs to be considered relative to the original outlay, ongoing costs and risks involved in future income and capital revenues. A more detailed analysis would look at three prime areas: economic influences, psychic influences and aspects relating to social responsibility (see table 8.1). The major influence is the economic one and this relates to the risk/return profile of the investment. There are a number of aspects to this relating to risk and return of capital and income, and the associated area of external injections and taxation of income and capital. These matters are essentially financial. Other aspects which affect the risk and return are time matters relating to the incidence of inflows and outflows of income and capital; the life of the asset is associated with this, as is the concept of depreciation in value of the asset. Finally, risk and return are related to the liquidity of the asset and problems of management. There are psychic and social responsibility dimensions to the investment also. To summarize, there are three main qualities related to the property investment medium:

Economic

These relate to financial risk/return and cash flows and are looked at in detail later in this section.

Table 8.1 General and economic qualities of an investment

General qualities of an investment		
Economic	Psychic	Social responsibility
Specific economic qualities of an investment		
	Specific qualities	Influence of other general qualities
Economic qualities: risk/return	Overall risk/growth	
	Capital risk/growth	Psychic
	Income risk/growth	
	External capital injection/ leakage (subsidies, grants, taxes)	Social responsibility
	Time issues, the timing of cash flow receipts, costs repayments	Psychic
	Lifecycle of the investment	Social responsibility
	Depreciation and obsolescence	Social responsibility
	Transferability and divisibility	
	Management problems	Social responsibility

Psychic

The psychic effect relates to the 'feel-good factor' associated with land and property, the ability to see 'something concrete' in one's investment, such as bricks and mortar. The ownership of something tangible is also important – a basic factor of production that is in short supply and valued for its own sake, especially in heavily populated areas or in areas of natural beauty. There are status and prestige in the ownership of buildings and this may apply in terms of landmark buildings; large corporations may require flagship buildings for public relations and corporate image reasons.

Social responsibility

The ownership of land is linked with a social responsibility – an ethical consideration of investing in property; often the landscapes of property are attractive and treasured by individuals and the community. Development and management proposals can affect flora, fauna and the surrounding environment and buildings. There may be a responsibility in ownership related to the local community and its activities and viewpoints. Thus there are social consequences of the ownership of land; there is status but also social responsibility.

These economic considerations are now looked at in more detail. Overall risk and growth can be divided into two elements: capital risk and growth, and income risk and growth.

Capital Risk and Growth

Capital security is important to an investor; accounts at the bank will not be at risk unless the bank collapses, and this is unlikely. As we have seen in recent years, there may still be some form of insurance policy with the government, the Central Bank or a consortium of banks available to provide a life-raft. However, in the 1990s alone, in the UK, the collapses of Barings, the merchant bank, and BICC (Bank of Industrial Commerce and Credit) show that even large financial institutions may be at risk. In general terms, however, the capital invested in such institutions as banks and building societies as account monies are unlikely to be at risk, whereas alternative places to put money such as shares or works of art may lead to a partial or complete loss. When the concept of security is being examined the relationship between security in real terms and in money terms needs to be considered. Money terms ignore inflation whereas in real terms the purchasing power of money is considered. The purchasing power will need to be discounted. by the rate of inflation to find the security in real terms, and this discount may be offset by interest received on such deposits, and this interest may compensate. Real capital growth in property would require the growth in the capital of the asset to outstrip the rate of inflation. However, such an analysis while concentrating on inflation ignores those other elements which make up interest rates. Besides compensation for inflation, an interest rate will also need to compensate for delayed consumption and risk. The components of the return on the investment number three: an element that provides compensation for the time preference of money, a second element related to inflation that exists to maintain the real value of the return, and finally an element for a risk premium.

Income Risk and Growth

Most investments involve an initial purchase and a stream of income that provides a return, perhaps culminating in a capital receipt on resale. This is a simplification, as investments should generate a return but some may only do so at the end of the holding period, for instance a vintage car is likely to generate a loss of income up until the period of resale. In the property world, investment property companies will receive income periodically from rents as well as capital appreciation, but a trading company is likely to rely on the sale of the completed project alone. Income is at risk in many investments, not just because of absolute changes of income declared by the managers of the investment, for instance a reduction in the dividend, but also because the rate of return for the individual is related to the price paid. In the latter case, using a UK example, if a government stock issue price is £100 and the declared nominal rate is 10 per cent then £10 per annum is received. If the stock is purchased at a price higher than the issue price then, as the £10 income is still paid, the yield is higher. Consider the example in Isaac and Steley (2000):

Example: Yield on government stock

10 per cent 2004 Treasury Stock in May 1990
This stock was quoted as:

Purchase price	£89.625
Interest only yield	11.16 per cent
Gross redemption yield	11.54 per cent

The gross redemption yield includes the receipt of a capital sum at the end of the life of the investment; this yield can be calculated by using an internal rate of return approach. In this case the stock is purchased in £100 bonds on which £10 will be received annually and the investment will be subsequently bought back by the Treasury at face value in 2004.

$$\text{Initial yield on an interest only basis} = \frac{\text{income}}{\text{purchase price}} \times 100 \text{ per cent}$$

$$= \frac{£10}{£89.625} \times 100 \text{ per cent}$$

$$= 11.16 \text{ per cent}$$

Thus the nominal rate was 10 per cent but the existing interest only rate is now 11.16 per cent because of the change in price that will alter to reflect the market structure of interest rates.

Exchange risk can also have an effect on the income flows of a project funded with foreign currency.

Capital Injections and Taxation

Net-of-tax or after-tax returns are those which are of interest to investors. Gross funds (pension funds and other investment funds that may not pay tax) would not want to take on income taxed at source, as this reduces their return. Where a differential exists between the treatment of capital and income taxes, investors may opt for a low-income return but large capital growth; high taxpayers would opt for this alternative, for instance. Tax rate differentials between income and capital taxation have now been brought into line but tax allowances may alter actual individual tax rates. Tax shelters from capital allowances in construction or tax relief in certain locations (such as enterprise zones) are important; tax treatment of losses in offsetting profit elsewhere may create a tax shelter and improve returns to a portfolio of investments. Beside enterprise zone tax incentives, there may exist inducements to develop and invest in certain areas and certain industries, and these inducements may not only decrease the cost of occupation for an owner-occupier but may also increase investment returns.

Time Issues

The timing of receipts is very important, especially if an investor is dependent on one or two investments. For a larger investor, a portfolio of investments may balance out the timing of cash flows. Property income is usually paid quarterly in advance and is thus available on a more regular basis than dividend or gilt returns, which may be paid half yearly. The importance of timing in investment is to match income with liabilities.

Lifecycle of Investment

The lifecycle of an investment is important. Gilts (government stock) will have a higher price at the end of their lifecycle, all other things being equal, as the day nears for repayment of the original sum; however, there is a difference between gilts with a term and those without (such as undated Consols), in the same way as for leasehold and freehold property. A lease will incur great cost at review of the rent or when a lease comes to an end, and reinstatement works may have to be carried out under the lease. Freeholders with leases which are not prime property will, in particular, encounter disruption to their income flows as tenancies end and voids increase while awaiting reletting.

Depreciation and Obsolescence

Depreciation is the wearing out of an asset over time; this wearing out leads to a loss in income as the asset is less attractive to occupiers, and also to a loss in capital value as it is of less interest to investors. Depreciation may require redevelopment or refurbishment of the asset, a solution requiring capital outlay and loss of income during the reconstruction process. Depreciation can be economical (relating to changes in economic demand), physical (deterioration of the fabric of the building) or functional (relating to the use of the building), or a combination of all three. Land will need to be distinguished from buildings in this analysis, as the former will not depreciate generally (unless contaminated or affected by misuse or bad neighbours), but the latter will. Depreciation can be divided into curable and incurable depreciation. Curable depreciation relates to maintenance but incurable relates to obsolescence. Depreciation includes obsolescence, which can be further divided into internal obsolescence, such as the outdated design or facilities of a building (the technical and technological changes which render space useless), and external obsolescence which relates to the decay of the environment and economic changes such as changes in the location of industry (Isaac and Steley, 2000).

Transferability and Divisibility

There are higher transfer charges related to the sale and purchase of property assets than in other competing assets classes. There is a time element involved in land transactions also; as well as being costly in terms of accrued interest charged during the period of the transaction, time can also have an adverse effect in situations requiring a forced sale. If the property market is collapsing in a particular sector or location, it may be difficult to dispose of the property and the investor may well be left holding an undesirable asset. The complexity of transfer may involve mistakes being made in the conveyance of rights and liabilities over the land, and legal searches not being done appropriately. Competing investments like gilts and equities can be sold on day-to-day markets and if markets fall, computer programs can be triggered at certain points to ensure that the shares are disposed of before the price falls too far. There is a central market in these share assets with publicized prices, so there is knowledge of the net income that will be received. The delay in property transactions and the nature of offers made in property contracts may often lead to terms being renegotiated up to exchange of contracts. In a good market this may lead to a higher return to the vendor, as with gazumping in the residential owner occupier markets (where the vendor increases the price after initial agreement with the producer), but generally these situations build in additional risk and uncertainty and lead to abortive costs. Transfer costs on competing investments often amount to only 1 per cent of the price being paid, whereas with property transactions it is often 3–4 per cent. The divisibility of property is difficult and this has led to a move in property unitization to break down the equity investment into smaller parts more acceptable to the purchasing power and risk profiles of a wider range of investors. Stocks and shares can be purchased in small unit sizes and it is easy to build a portfolio of such assets that incorporates greater diversification and risk avoidance.

Management Problems

Even with a full repairing and insuring (FRI) lease, property requires informed and skilled management to deal with the technical and legal aspects, complex buildings and demanding tenants. There are numerous pieces of legislation to be considered that require professional advice, and the social aspects of ownership, noted earlier, can add to the problems of management. Maintenance and management problems can be numerous, especially when there is not an FRI lease. The problems include risks relating to voids, accidents and liabilities, deleterious substances (such as asbestos, which may have been used in the construction of the buildings), dangerous structures, nuisance generated by the building and so on.

CHARACTERISTICS OF REAL ESTATE INVESTMENT IN THE UK

An investment is an asset that produces income or capital growth which will convert to income during, or at the end of, the life of the asset. The investment market is often considered peculiar to the UK, a situation where investors in property construct buildings and others occupy and pay rent. Such a situation may be a product of the development of the landed estates, where historically the landed gentry as a class were divorced from those organizing and engaged in manufacturing and commerce. Such a debate is beyond the objectives of this book but certainly the landlord/tenant relationship appears peculiar to the UK and the countries of the old commonwealth (even in the territory of Hong Kong, the land was generally owned by the government). This is not to say that there is little owner-occupation in the UK but considerations of space allocation here relate more to economic factors such as production, labour and profit rather than investment returns arising from property and land.

Darlow (1983) has suggested three major reasons for this situation:

(1) a high percentage of the savings of individuals (the collectivization of savings, discussed elsewhere in this book) being channelled through a small number of private-sector financial institutions which have to find investment for their resulting cash flows;

(2) the tendency among many manufacturers and retailers in the UK to rent rather than own the properties they occupy, thus creating an income-producing investment for a potential landlord;

(3) the planning climate in the UK, which for most of the post-war period has kept the supply of good-quality commercial property below demand, thus rents have offered protection against inflation because of shortages, and capital values have appreciated.

Principles of Real Estate Investment

As an introduction to real estate investment it is useful to make comparisons with, for instance, investment in shares. Such a comparison is often applied to the respective returns but the mechanism and structure of investment in the two media is radically different. These initial differences were summarized by Brett (1989) and are shown in Box 8.1.

**BOX 8.1: THE CHARACTERISTICS OF PROPERTY –
A COMPARISON WITH COMPANY SHARES**
(adapted from Brett, 1989)

1. Commercial properties are of high value, whereas shares can be broken down to smaller sizes of ownership. Property ownership thus tends to be in the hands of large financial institutions rather than individuals.

2. Property is not a standardized investment – one share in a particular company is the same as another, but properties are not identical.

3. Property is not a pre-packaged investment – with a share you buy the management. With property you will need to manage it yourself or pay someone to do this for you.

4. Property is an investment that can be improved by active management. You cannot do this with shares. Property investment may require additional new money to restructure leases and refurbish or redevelop buildings, however.

5. Property investment can be created by finding sites, erecting buildings and finding tenants.

6. Points 3–5 show that some expertise is required in investing in and managing property.

---

7. There is no single market for commercial property – it is a localized market. The time spent in buying and selling is greater than with shares.
8. Market information is often imperfect and the data surrounding transactions are often not available or kept confidential.
9. The income stream from property is often geared to rent reviews in leases, and income increases will not be available until the next review, whereas the income stream from share dividends may change half-yearly.
10. Property investment can literally wear out (depreciation of buildings) or be made worthless by external activities (as with land).
11. There are a variety of ownerships in land from freehold to leases and licences which affect the value of the interest and level of risk of the income arising.
12. Different interests will be of concern to different types of investor depending on their tax status or investment requirements for income, capital growth or risk avoidance.
13. Different types of property (different sectors like retailing, industrial and offices) generate different returns and have different risk profiles, so may be chosen by differing investors.
14. Properties also have various risk profiles depending on whether they are prime (best quality), secondary or tertiary.
15. Property is presented as a long-term investment but may not necessarily be so. Most owners do retain their properties for long periods of time.

Property valuation is a means of providing an assessment of the capital value of, or the income arising from, a property investment. There is a range of possible investment opportunities from works of art through oil futures and gold to shares, government stocks and property. The point of investment is that it provides the investor with an income, growth in capital value of the investment or both.

Principles of Real Estate Ownership

Property investment is different from other types of investment in that ownership of physical assets like land and buildings is far more complex than the ownership of a share certificate. It also involves the owner in more responsibility and obligations than other forms of investment.

As mentioned above (see pages 343–4), it is important to recognize that property and property investment performs a vital role in the economy. This is manifested in three different ways:

- as a factor of production, property provides the space in which economic activity takes place, and the efficiency of using this space – and its cost – affect the cost of goods and services produced;

- as a corporate asset, property constitutes the major part of asset values in companies' balance sheets and substantial proportion of corporate debt is secured against it;
- as an investment, property is held by individuals as a form of personal wealth, and by financial institutions as a source of pensions and assurance benefits.

Characteristics of Real Estate as an Investment

Property investment is a long-term commitment of funds. Transfer costs and purchase time (up to six months) restrict opportunities for short-term dealings. Investors in property are looking for growth of income and capital. Note that these two aspects are interrelated. In the UK, the tradition in the commercial market is for occupiers to lease premises, thus ownership and occupation are split and an investment market in property is opened up. In the United States and Europe, there is more owner-occupation. In considering the characteristics of property investment it is necessary to look at a number of factors: the property investment market, the nature of income, the rate of return and the level of income.

DIRECT INVESTMENT IN REAL ESTATE IN THE UK

Property investment involves a long-term investment and a commitment because of the nature of the returns and the costs of transferability. Many property investors are also property developers but they may well keep property development in their portfolio rather than dispose of it, as would property traders. Well-selected properties can offer income growth and capital growth over the longer period. Property investment in the UK is strong because of the nature of the investment market, with occupiers taking leases for occupation rather than buying themselves. In many European countries, for instance, this would not be the norm and owner-occupation would predominate. The main considerations for investment are:

- the nature of the legal interest being acquired;
- the location of the investment and surrounding environment;
- the nature and design of the property itself;
- planning proposals for the area;
- terms of existing leases;
- expectation of income and capital growth from the property investment;
- the level of future demand, both for renting the accommodation and selling the investment at some future date;

- possible future changes in fashion, technology, demography and transportation infrastructure;
- underlying national economic trends;
- structural changes within the industry or sector from where tenant demand originates;
- current and future level of available competitive accommodation;
- government intervention, new legislation and taxes (Darlow, 1983).

The Acquisition Sequence

The sequence of acquisition is shown in figure 8.1, which gives details of the procedures carried out in the acquisition process.

Property Investment Markets

The market for commercial property is an established investment market but, because there is no central marketplace for property and because investment properties are unique, there is a difficulty in understanding how the market works. This is compounded by the fact that information on the product in the market and the nature of transactions is restricted, information being passed verbally rather than properly documented in the press or reports. The actual detail of the transaction in the market, the details of rents passing, the nature of the lease terms agreed and the yield used in any capital transaction may remain confidential. The property market is thus a dangerous place for the lay person to invest in.

The characteristics of property markets have been summarized by Darlow (1983):

- the market is fragmented, poorly recorded, secretive and generally unregulated;
- there is no central agency or institution such as Lloyds insurance for the insurance industry;
- there is no physical focal point such as a Stock Exchange for the transaction of stocks and shares;
- it is difficult to abstract an aggregation of property transactions;
- the market is diverse and complex in nature;
- there are national, regional and local dimensions to the market – property markets tend to be parochial, disorganized and vary in classification, such a geographical location, type of property, quality of property, value and size of investment;
- there is an imperfect knowledge of the market and within the market there is no central price or listing;

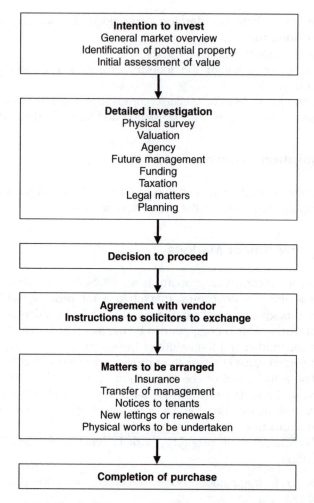

Figure 8.1 *Acquisition sequence (adapted from Darlow, 1983)*

- there is no central registry of transactions that is complete;
- the market is monopolistic, because of the inelastic supply of land;
- there is no freedom of entry and exit from the market because of locational, legal, finance, taxation and other constraints.

The late-1970s was a critical period for property investment since its performance was outperforming inflation. By the early-1980s, average rental growth was underperforming since inflation and returns from the capital markets were falling in certain sectors. According to the Richard Ellis Monthly Indices, only since 1986 has property begun to show significant real returns. In the early-1990s, wider performance measures, matched by increasingly sophisticated market research and analysis as property returns fell, produced a much keener understanding of the components of property investment by means of the yield, rent and valuations methods, and by the mid-1980s property was being measured relatively as well as absolutely. In the late-1970s, capital growth was driven by falling yields but in 1987–88, capital growth was generated by rental growth. In 1988 Richard Ellis tested the hypothesis that the property market moves counter-cyclically to equities and gilts and is thus a good prospect for the diversification of a portfolio. This study found:

(1) *very limited similarity* between property returns and equities (0.10 correlation coefficient);
(2) *no similarity* between property returns and gilts (0.03 correlation coefficient);
(3) gilts and equity returns were *more in line* (0.44 correlation) (Barter, 1988).

The comparative performance of property against other assets over the period 1980–96 and forecast for the period 1996–2000 is shown in figure 8.2 (Lennox, 1996).

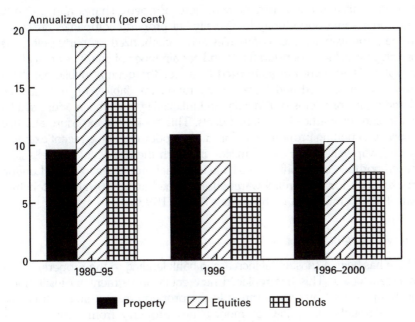

Figure 8.2 *Comparative performance*

If one takes away the sentiment of land and building, then a property investment is basically a flow of income arising from a property asset which can be distributed in many different ways to offer investors differing degrees of risk and thus differing yields and capital values. This is the basis of property securitization and the innovative forms of property finance which have been developed, and these new financial techniques attempt to overcome property's inherent illiquidity and inflexibility. But according to Barter (1988), the key concerns about property as an investment medium remain:

Illiquidity

Properties take three months to buy and sell. There is no certainty of price and terms until contracts are exchanged. This problem is acute for properties with capital values above £20 million because of the relatively small supply of potential single purchasers in the market, especially when there are no international purchasers. There are problems in appraising and financing the more substantial developments.

Inflexibility

There is a high unit cost with property purchases and little flexibility in the purchase because one needs to buy the whole. There are problems in portfolio diversification and management here. Property shares and property units offer some opportunity to diversify but property companies are taxed in the same way as other companies and unauthorized property unit trusts are only available to pension funds and certain types of charities and cannot be listed. Now there are authorized trusts for the general public but these may remain unlisted and have a corporation tax liability on the income. Some of the problems of illiquidity and inflexibility have been addressed by 'swapping' properties in matched deals. This avoids the exposure and bad publicity of putting properties up for sale in a poor market; a recent example was a swap valued at £34.35 million in which the Provident Mutual sold a mixed portfolio of six office, retail and industrial properties to Allied London in exchange for eight retail warehouses, valued at £21.6 million, together with £12.75 million in cash (Estates Times, 1993).

Growth of debt finance

There has been a substantial increase in bank lending to the property sector in recent years. This has replaced new equity investment by institutions. Such a process may pose a threat to the property market and is discussed later, although the inflow of money into property from banks is now decreasing.

Valuation methodology and precision

Conventional valuation methods are inflexible. The all risk approach of traditional valuation methods is difficult to apply to more illiquid properties such as major shopping centres and substantial office buildings. A number of cases reflecting errors in the valuation of hotels and restaurants also confirm this. Conventional valuations also have difficulty in the valuation of over-rented property where rents are expected to fall on review.

The future role of the property profession

The liberalization of the financial markets and the increased importance of debt in property funding require new competencies for chartered surveyors. The demands of the Financial Services Act for those providing information on finance and funding will require different and greater competence in the financial area. In this area and others, the professional institutions are reorientating themselves to the market.

Short-termism

Property is a long-term investment and cannot compete on similar terms with investments that pay off on a much shorter time horizon. Recent attitudes of funders and managers of companies in the UK indicate a short-term approach to investment and performance which may in most cases be a reflection of the recent difficult times in which these companies have had to operate. Companies may in some cases have opted for very short-term investment appraisals and rapid payback. The pressure to perform well has not only led fund managers to increase their activity in managing funds but also to a short-term perspective for investment. This strategy focuses on the short-term performance of companies in arriving at the valuation of a company's worth, with emphasis on current profit performance and dividend payments. This perspective, suggested by Pike and Neale (1993), has many consequences across the spectrum of companies, including:

(1) the neglect of the long-term by management, leading to a failure to undertake important long-term investments in resources and research and development;
(2) the volatility of short-term corporate results becoming exaggerated in securities markets, producing unacceptable fluctuations in share prices.

Because of its long-term production cycle, these consequences are likely to be very damaging to property and construction. A survey carried out by the Department of Industry's Innovation Advisory Board in 1990 concluded that City influence on corporate activity led to companies prioritizing short-term profits and dividends at the expense of research and development and other innovative investment, and that practices of key financial institutions sustained these priorities. Researchers in the United States have concluded that the increasing shareholder power of institutional investors has had a damaging effect on research and development expenditure among US firms. The financiers of the City of London reject this criticism by saying that much of the responsibility for the lack of long-term innovation investment is attributable to managers – to their preference for growth by acquisition, their poor record of commercial development and their reward systems based on short-term targets (Pike and Neale, 1993). The implications for property in this respect are very clear: property development and the development of its associated transport, social and services infrastructure are a long-term project. Development and refurbishment underpin the property investment market. Projects on difficult town-centre sites or involving major infrastructure works encounter problems of risk and uncertainty as they extend into the future. Then there are the problems of high transfer cost and illiquidity in property; to force the sale of a development or investment property at an inappropriate time, for instance half-way through a building contract, could cause a collapse in the price of the asset. This effect is accentuated because of the location attributes of property – markets are localized and imperfect. The problem of short-termism is that such an attitude is inappropriate to property finance where long-term strategy and returns are the key to successful projects (Isaac, 1996).

PROPERTY CYCLES IN THE UK

The property industry shows a cycle of activity which reflects the general business cycle. This problem, relating to changes in the returns in the market and having a dramatic effect on investment and development activity in the market, is especially evident in the office sector. Research by the Royal Institution of Chartered Surveyors (1994) provided some insights into the operation of this cycle. The research looked at the structure of the property industry and found that there were a number of interest groups operating in the market – occupiers, investors and developers. For occupiers the property was an input to their production process, a factor of production for their goods and services; for investors it provided an asset on which returns would be generated and compared to other asset classes; and for developers property was the output of their production process. The interaction between these groupings gives the indications of how the market operates. In the research, property cycles were defined as recurrent but irregular fluctuations in the rate of all-property total returns. Aggregate property returns were chosen to show the cyclical patterns, while rental performance, yield movements and development activities are linked to the property cycle but these linkages are elastic and flexible. Property cycles were found to be of 4–5 years' duration and these cycles matched the general business cycle in the economy. The causes of the cycle could be grouped into two areas:

(1) causes external to the property industry;
(2) those produced in the operation of the property industry.

External influences in the occupier markets, cyclical demand factors, GDP, consumer spending, financial and business services, and manufacturing demand act as the prime influence on rental values; interest rates and inflation also influence rent values in some markets. In the investment markets the external drivers are bond yields and inflation, which have a significant influence on property yields and property investment by UK financial institutions. The internal influences or drivers are the development cycle, the development lag (caused by the inflexibility in the building stock) and rent. Development activity showed internal cyclical supply patterns without even considering the external demand factors.

The formal findings of the survey were that:

(1) the UK property industry shows a recurrent cycle which meets the qualitative definition applied to economic cycles but cannot be described definitively by statistical techniques;
(2) the property cycle is the compounded result of cyclical influences from the wider economy, which are coupled with cyclical tendencies which are inherent in the property market;
(3) the critical linkages between property cycles and economic cycles can be captured in simple models.

Further research is thus required into the external and internal drivers to discover whether this impact can be smoothed, thus taking away the excesses of the cycle. The property market has integrated with the financial sector and there are wider implications to a market collapse in the sector; in the 1974 collapse it was secondary banks which were involved, but now there is much greater bank involvement. The damage that can be done to the financial system in the event of a collapse will be more general – the so-called contagion effect. The property cycle is related to the business cycle and this can be seen as series of fluctuations in activity which proceed in an irregular way: depression (low level of consumer demand and economic activity), recovery, boom (industry fully productive), recession and so on (Estates Gazette, 1995). A simplistic property cycle is shown in figure 8.3.

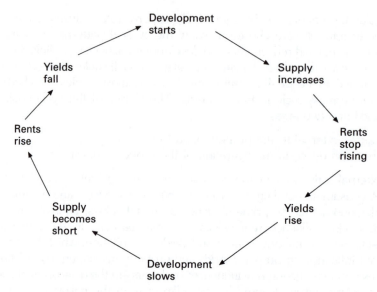

Figure 8.3 *The property cycle (London, 1996)*

Barras (1994) has suggested that there are four cycles identified in economic literature and has linked them to the property cycle. These are:

(1) The classical business cycle of 4–5 years' duration acting on all aspects of economic activity and operating on the property market through occupier demand.

(2) Long cycles of 9–10 years' duration which are generated by the exceptionally long production lags involved in property development, creating a tendency for supply to outstrip demand in every other business cycle.

(3) Long swings with a period up to 20 years are associated with major building booms: these may occur in every other long cycle of development; they are typically speculative in nature and of a scale sufficient to generate distinctive new phases of urban development.

(4) Long waves lasting up to 50 years have been proposed to explain alternating phases of high and low growth in the industrialized world economy, with each new wave being initiated by the adoption of a universal new technology (Estates Gazette, 1995). A conceptual model proposed by Barras is shown in figure 8.4.

Thus the property slump may last through the next business cycle, and because of the surplus in property there is no shortage in the next upturn.

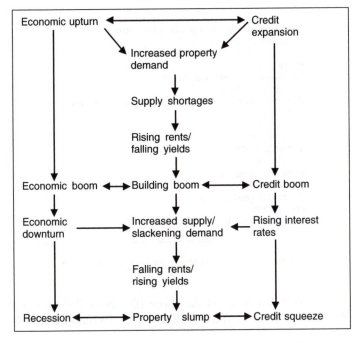

Figure 8.4 *The building cycle (Barras, 1994)*

When the next long cycle of development picks up, it will tend to be demand-driven with minimal speculative development because the banking system still has debts outstanding from the previous boom. Thus another long cycle will need to proceed before the necessary pre-conditions will be in place for another speculative boom. Barras suggests that this is why the property booms occur in every second long cycle of development and in every fourth short cycle of business activity.

Some original research was carried out by Barber White Property Economics (CSW – The Property Week, 1993); they concluded that their research dispelled a number of commonly held views about the nature of the property market. Firstly, although the retail market is the first to recover from recession, it is not the first to fall into recession – a collapse in office rents heralds a recession. Secondly, the property market lags the economy, with economic events causing the property cycle. Finally, it is wrong to criticize valuers for not paying enough regard to future rental growth prospects; capital value cycles and rental cycles do not coincide, and capital value cycles are more frequent than rental cycles. A property cycle route planner conceived by Barber White is shown in figure 8.5.

1.	**Shock moves economy into downturn**
	Office rents collapse
	Construction output declines
	Retail rents fall
	Office and industrial values fall
	Industrial rents fall
2.	**Around 2 years later - economy begins recovery**
	Construction output grows
	Office rental fall slows down
	Retail values rise
3.	**3–4 years later**
	Retail rents rise
	Industrial values rise
	Office values rise
4.	**Beyond 5 years**
	Office rents rise
	Industrial rents rise

Figure 8.5 *The property cycle route planner*

The RICS research explained the three phases of the cycle they perceived. Related to the London development cycle (Whitmore, 1994), these phases were:

- In the early stages of an economic upturn, rental growth is likely to be dampened by the surplus of space from the recession and the previous development boom.
- In the second phase, continued economic expansion faces a shortage of space; rents begin to rise rapidly and trigger-developments start. Since these will not reach the market for a year or more, the second phase of rapid rental growth is likely to be as long as a typical economic upswing. Shortage of space will often worsen, and rental growth will accelerate to the peak in the economy. Developers, reacting purely to current market conditions, will be encouraged to start more development.
- The third phase is likely to begin with weakening or falling demand, as the recession begins: buildings triggered in the early part of phase two will be completed. The consequent fall in rental values puts a sharp stop to development schemes in the pipeline, although the surplus of newly-completed space continues to rise, as the schemes started at the peak of the boom fall into recession.

The research concluded that, if the property industry has lacked foresight, it is because property cycles are built into the workings of the economy and property directly – they can never be smoothed out but with a better understanding their impact can be appreciated (McGregor *et al.*, 1994).

Property cycles are international in their effect. The nature and significance of cycles vary substantially, with exceptional cycles occurring internationally only occasionally. The increased significance of the cyclicality has been attributed by Pugh and Dehesh (1995) to the decreases in stability afforded by macroeconomic management since the 1970s, and they suggest that destabilization is at the root of many cyclical problems requiring the re-regulation of banking and finance. The effect of property cycles influences more than just property decisions taken in the market by individual investors, as Gibson and Carter (1995) suggest. The property cycle imposes a barrier to economic efficiency or represents a wasted investment depending on the point in the cycle. If understanding of the cycle is only just emerging in the UK, then how can senior managers in major corporations be expected to incorporate property into their strategic plans?

PROPERTY MARKETS IN THE UK

The post-war property market can be divided into a number of periods (Brett, 1989). These are the post-war development boom, the financial boom of 1967–73, the investment boom of the late-1970s, and the finance-led development boom of the late-1980s with the subsequent collapse into the 1990s. Differences between the boom periods reflect the different finance sources and methods available during each period.

The Post-War Boom Period

In the post-war boom period immediately after the Second World War there was a shortage of space. This was especially so in the office sector where the shortage of office accommodation was fuelled by the destruction of approximately 750,000 square metres of office space in the war. The economy was growing at a respectable rate against a background of low interest rates and low inflation. Property had been destroyed during the war, and space was scarce, so this led to a growth in rentals. At the beginning of the 1950s the Conservative government of the time recognized the need for a 'dash for growth' and encouraged a period of rapid economic expansion. Interest rates were low at this time and thus the yields on property investments were higher than long-term borrowing rates. Fixed-interest institutional money was available and readily used by the property companies. Financial partnerships between institutions and property companies were frequently established. Financing of property investments could be carried out using long-term mortgage funds at low rates which were fixed. Typically these funds would be provided by an insurance company. Short-term finance for the construction period usually came from bank sources or else from the building contractor. There was an overall attempt by the developer to raise the total funds necessary for the development from lending sources, thus not committing any of its own money. Property developments were thus intended to be 100 per cent debt financed with no equity involvement. Developers held onto their completed developments rather than selling them, partially as a response to the tax system, since tax was payable on the trading profit but there was no tax on the surplus created by the developer until the property was sold. Some new funding was achieved by the floating of the property companies on the Stock Exchange in the late-1950s and early-1960s. These flotations achieved cash for new development without the developers having to sell the properties. Developers at this time let their buildings on leases without review and were not concerned with the effects of inflation on their income stream but instead concentrated on income from development profits. Fixed-interest financing by financial institutions was standard practice by the 1960s and linked to shareholdings, options and conversion rights taken up in development companies by the institutions. Inflation rose in the early-1960s and the institutions providing finance as mortgages or debentures began to take a share of equity, initially by conversion rights and then eventually by establishing joint companies with the developers. The insurance companies were especially active. Developers who wanted to retain properties had to give away some equity to ensure finance at lower rates. Sale and leaseback, where the developer offered to sell the proposed building subject to the investor leasing the building back, became the dominant form of funding arrangement. This approach had many advantages, including not falling under the Government's credit control measures of the time (Savills, 1989). By the early-1960s, recession affected demand and credit squeezes made short-term financing difficult. The office development boom in London was eventually brought to an end by the Labour Government in 1964 with the Control of Office and Industrial Development Act 1965. This so-called 'Brown Ban', named after George Brown who initiated the legislation, in fact artificially restricted the supply and sowed the seeds of the next boom in the 1970s (Fraser, 1993).

The Financial Boom 1967–73

A renewed Stock Market boom commenced in 1967 and lasted until the crash in 1974. Institutional finance was being provided to the property companies in the form of leasebacks. Pension funds in this period joined the insurance companies in buying out completed developments and they dominated the investment market (Cadman and Catalano, 1983: 12). New forms of indirect investment, such as property bonds and property unit trusts, were established. The market was characterized by a series of takeovers in the late-1960s and this activity continued on into the early-1970s. By March 1972 property shares had risen over five times from the low point of 1967 (Brett, 1983). The assets of existing property companies were becoming more and more valuable because of the effect of the shortage of investment properties. The value of property companies was thus increasing because of the scarcity of space rather that because of accumulated development profits. Owing to inflation in this period, rent reviews were introduced, initially on a 14-year basis, later reduced to 7-year reviews and then to 5-year reviews. Between 1964 and 1974 there was a reduction of 40 per cent in the number of quoted companies as a result of amalgamation and liquidation (Ratcliffe, 1978).

To summarize, in the post-war era in the 1950s and 1960s the modern property developer had emerged and property companies had established themselves. The stimulation to development was based on the shortage of property in a period of low inflation. This meant that the rental levels of developments increased dramatically during the period while building costs were static. The other major stimulants to the developers were the fixed-interest rates and the lack of equity input. The growth of the property developers was on the basis of refinancing the development on a fixed-interest mortgage for 20–30 years. The institutions were providing finance for the developments and there was some link-up between developers and institutions. Over this period the institutions, generally insurance companies, insisted on having a greater share in the equity returns available. They purchased shares in the property companies and then made mortgage debenture loans convertible to shares so that an increased equity stake could be obtained if the scheme were a success. However, the taxation structure in the late-1960s affected this arrangement – gross funds (not paying tax) suffered from the taxation of income and dividends, and new structures of finance emerged. In the late-1960s and early-1970s developers began using sale and leaseback; the property was financed in the development stage using bank finance and was sold on completion. As time wore on, a shortage of schemes became apparent and the institutions (the insurance companies and now pension funds) purchased development sites directly with a building agreement and agreement for lease with the developer. Developers borrowed short-term for their developments or to finance acquisitions, because they thought rising asset values would counterbalance the deficit finance. They ignored cash flow and borrowed against the increased value of their properties to meet the income shortfall between rental and interest payments. The crash of 1974–75 showed how the economic indications had changed since the 1950s and 1960s. High interest rates, lessened demand and inflation of costs meant that profit levels were not achieved because of increased capital costs and income voids during which interest arrears fluctuated. The highly geared property companies had been fuelled by debt finance provided under fairly lax lending criteria. In the aftermath of the oil crisis of 1973, interest rates were raised to a penal level; secondary banks were heavily committed to property and began to collapse. Accounting conventions of the time had disguised the sharply negative cash flow of most property companies with large development programmes. It thus became impossible to sell a property and it was not possible to borrow on it. Property shares collapsed, as did the direct market in property (Brett, 1989).

The Investment Boom (Late-1970s) and the Rental Boom (Late-1980s)

In the late-1970s the institutions were keen buyers of property and values rose sharply during this period. Large institutions were undertaking direct development or using developers as project managers. Larger companies were borrowing in the hope that the cash flow would be positive at the first rent review. In the 1980s and 1990s the usual approach to funding was that the fund was invited to purchase the site and provide funds for the building contract. Interest would be rolled up during the development period and added to the development costs. On completion and letting of the building, the profit on the development would be paid over. On this basis developers built up a large turnover, basically matching their site funding and project management skills with the institutional investors. Such approaches greatly reduced the risk exposure of the developer to the project. Forward funding meant that the project was financed in terms of the development at a keen rate but generally the capital sum at the end of the project was valued at a higher yield. In the early-1980s recession and rising unemployment had affected the demand for property and rental increases fell, while yields increased. Property lagged behind the rest of the economy in its recovery. There was not another boom until 1986–87. The institutions were now less important as providers of funds for property and their net purchases dropped as they re-weighted their portfolios towards equities and gilts, disappointed with the performance of their property assets. A development boom, funded by the banks, had begun. The banks were prepared to lend to individual developments and roll up the interest until the property was disposed of. Thus developers were traders rather than investment companies. By the beginning of the 1990s the rental growth had tailed off and the market was collapsing. There were no buyers for the completed developments. The banks had to extend their development loans beyond the development period because there were no institutional funders in the market. Development loans were thus converted to investment loans, committing banks to staying in the market. Innovative financial techniques in the absence of traditional institutional finance were the key developments of the 1980s.

The 1990s

The present players in the lending market include:

Banks	Clearing Banks
	Merchant Banks (also providing an advisory role)
Institutions	Insurance Companies
	Pension Funds
Investors	Private Individuals
	Overseas Investors

At the beginning of 1990 there were 140 banks lending to property companies and developers in the UK, 40 per cent of which were overseas banks. In terms of bank loans £30 billion were outstanding to property lending, which equates to 7.5 per cent of all bank lending. Lending had increased by 20 per cent per annum from 1981 to 1990 and the Bank of England had become concerned. The lending banks' response subsequently had been to reduce loan-to-value ratios from 75–80 per cent to 66–70 per cent, but they still lent as they had to make profits. Some comparison has been made between the lending crisis of the 1990s and the property crash in 1974, but they were very different. In the 1974 crash, banks were unable to deal with unpaid loans and they had a weaker capital base. There was a weaker tenant demand at the time. The strong investor demand in 1974 was pushing yields down and thus trading profits were based on investor reaction rather than rental growth. The developers had poor covenants. There was poor research by banks and property companies. Nowadays there are better financial controls and banks are taking security (notwithstanding non-recourse deals). The property sector has been driven by tenant demand. Yields have moved but not significantly.

Market Model and Sectors

A model of the investment market has been provided by Keogh and this shows that property investment is part of the property market, which includes a user market, an investment market and a development market. The simple model of the overall property market suggested by Keogh (1994) is shown in figure 8.6. A schematic model of the property market has also been put forward by Fraser (1996), who suggests that the usual models of the property market concentrate on the interrelationship of the market in the three principal sectors – the letting, user or occupational sector; the investment sector; and the development sector – this causing the property market to be known as the 'three ring circus'. Fraser's model has a single ring with three arcs for the principal market sectors. It provides

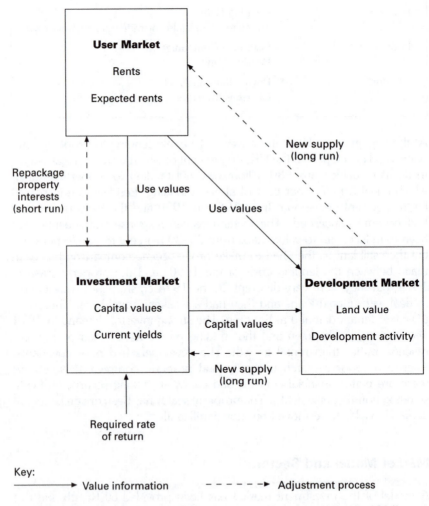

Figure 8.6 *A simple model of the property market (Keogh, 1994)*

a context of international, national and local economies to the setting of the market, and suggests that occupational demand drives the letting sector, investment demand drives the investment sector, and development costs the development sector – these three sectors in turn establish the property stock.

The other division of the investment market is to look at the types of property involved. The main sectors in the investment market are shops, offices, industrial premises and warehouses, residential, agricultural and leisure. This classification has been complicated by recent developments which include retail warehousing, class B1 developments and mixed developments. Retail warehousing is where the location and structure of the building relate to the warehouse sector, but the economic analysis and financial appraisal of such developments are related more to the retail sector than the warehouse sector. Class B1 use combines office use with light industrial use and also high-tech usage. Mixed developments are particularly workshop conversions that are developed from industrial space but may also include retail and residential space.

Registration of Land

Property markets in the UK suffer from lack of information because a Central Land Register did not exist in the UK before 1988; the only access to the register was in Scotland and Northern Ireland. The Land Registration Act 1988 made available to the public information on the registration of freehold and leasehold titles in land in England and Wales (Estates Gazette, 1996).

REAL ESTATE INVESTMENT MARKETS IN EAST CENTRAL EUROPE

Property markets and their development in East Central Europe are related to the transition from command to market economies. Case studies related to the major cities of the Czech Republic, Hungary and Poland show a background of rapid growth in the countries' economies. These countries have had significant growth in per capita GDP in the period since 1992, achieved against an economic environment of high inflation and high short-term interest rates (Adair *et al.*, 1999).

Socialist economies have an absence of land markets, along with fixed prices and state-controlled businesses. The development of major cities from this economic background by property developers has contributed both to the reorganization of land and its control and has also encouraged local economic regeneration. The capital cities of East Central Europe are the main points through which foreign companies enter a country. In the main cities of East Central Europe, Warsaw, Budapest and Prague, the property market was quickly established at the beginning of the economic transition with privatization programmes and policies that acted as a stimulus to the market by liberating prices and decontrolling rents. Further, the opening-up of trade also opened up the property markets to foreign demand for real estate assets.

Ghanbari Parsa (1997) has suggested that there are three distinct periods in the evolution of real estate markets in East Central Europe, as shown in table 8.2.

Political and economic reform have established the necessary legal and material conditions for the growth of property markets in Prague, Warsaw and Budapest, with demand from international firms expanding into the region and stimulating the growing domestic business sector. Lack of supply of prime-quality office space has encouraged development by international companies, who have both financed and traded the assets built.

By the mid-1990s there was a shift in demand from new companies providing the demand to expanding companies looking for space, reflecting a maturing of the market. There is little evidence, however, of a property

---

Table 8.2 Stages in the development of real estate markets in East Central Europe (adapted from Ghanbari Parsa, 1997)

Stage 1	Transformation period (1989–91)	Characterized by: • sharp rise in real estate prices; • liberalization of controlled prices and rents.
Stage 2	Entry of foreign firms (1992–94)	Characterized by: • shortage of internationally acceptable office property; • commencement of major developments; • high capital growth; • increase in demand.
Stage 3	Maturing period 1995–98	Characterized by: • substantial increase in supply of office property; • entry of domestic investment and development firms; • decreasing gap between supply and demand.

investment market emerging because of two reasons. One, there is only a small number of investment-quality grade buildings available and two, the risks, although yields are high, are perceived as too great.

REAL ESTATE INVESTMENT MARKETS IN CHINA: AN OVERVIEW (adapted from Dai *et al.*, 1999)

In the years since China has carried out the reforms of its economic systems and created its open-door policy, China's economic development has taken off. Of all the factors that have promoted economic growth, property investment and property markets have played important roles. Construction has become a key sector, more and more important in its impact. Consumer spending and investment demand have been rising rapidly, bringing an increased demand for offices, industrial space, warehouses, retail space and residential property, leading to a property boom. The reform of the economic system and the development of financial markets have also been important catalysts for the property market boom. Since the end of 1993, China's economic development has experienced serious problems; further economic reform has become more and more difficult, the financial markets have become full of speculative activity and fraud, while the property market has shrunk dramatically. From 1979 to the present, we can divide the property market development into four periods.

Period 1: The Primary Developing Period (1979–85)

The Cultural Revolution which lasted more than 10 years took China's economy to the edge of bankruptcy. The economy had to be rebuilt and previous economic development recovered. The Third Plenary Session of the Eleventh Central Committee of the Communist Party of China held in 1978 determined the general principles for reform and opening up of China. Since then the Chinese Communist Party, the exclusive party in power in China, has directed its attention to economic development, and not exclusively to a political agenda, as before. From 1979 to 1985 the main economic reforms were as follows:

- The decentralization of authority over saving and investment decisions devolved power of control of urban development to local authority, business enterprises and households.
- The setting-up of Special Economic Zones and fourteen Open Coastal Cities, giving them more free rights in economic policy, including preference taxes, and more freedom to import and export. They were pro-

vided with more state funds and more freedom to encourage investment from foreigners.

- The adoption of a policy giving preference and incentives for foreign direct investment.
- The setting up of a 'Responsibility System' for industrial production and operation, allowing firms the right to manage production and retain profits.

The economic system reform brought rapid economic development and led to a boom in construction investment. The construction investment boom primarily stemmed from a number of underlying factors. Firstly, sharply rising investment, commercial and service investments, outputs and productivity, while there was a scarcity of offices, industrial space, retail space, warehouses and residential property. Construction became the most important and most fundamental sector. Secondly, because of decentralization, municipal states and firms had more rights in saving and investment decisions, resulting in an unprecedented level of resources being allocated to construction, especially housing construction. At this time there was a very low standard of housing in China and the municipal governments and firms were seeking to solve this problem in respect of their own employees and residents. Thirdly, foreign direct investment became an important source of construction finance, especially in Special Economic Zones. Before 1985 more than half of foreign direct investment in property investment was in Shenzhen. In this period, property investment and property markets showed the following underlying characteristics:

- There was an imbalance of construction investment across different regions of China, from the hinterland to coastal cities, from nominal cities to the Special Economic Zones. In Special Economic Zones and Open Coastal Cities, construction investment was more important and boomed. In Shenzhen, construction composition as a proportion of local production was 19.4 per cent in 1979, 45.9 per cent in 1982 and 40.3 per cent in 1985 (State Statistical Bureau of People's Republic of China, 1992).
- The property market was at a very early stage in its development and a sophisticated modern property market had not come into being. Firstly, the allocation and use system of land had not been reformed, although there were intentions of transforming the system from centrally, state-planned to a market-oriented one. Secondly, housing had not been looked at as a commodity; it was provided as an in-kind benefit by the economic units who employed people in the commune or factory. Most households lived in public housing units allocated by their economic units and paid only nominal rents. The centrally planned housing system had not been reformed. Thirdly, and most importantly, private property rights

had not been completely removed. Following liberation, after the Second World War, the Chinese Communist Party abolished the private property-right system, setting up a state- and collective-ownership system. Urban land was nationalized and rural land was collectivized. In practice, it was a myth that land and property had become common property, as no-one held rights over the property, so it was open for appropriation by anyone 'according to needs'. No-one had the right to sell any property because no-one had ownership. So property transactions at this time were few, often they did not proceed to completion and they were not transparent. Most of these transactions were not carried out officially and thus there was no legal protection for them.

- Property finance was in a very early stage of development too. In fact, it is meaningless to talk about property finance at that time but rather about construction finance, as the activity related to new building. Construction finance was very conventional. State appropriation was the most important source of construction finance. Other sources were very limited, and in the process of development. Before 1984 China had no banking system and no financial market.

Period 2: The Reforming and Adjusting Period (1986–90)

Overheating investments, especially extra-budgetary investment in building investment, had brought out many problems in the economy. Firstly, and most importantly, a demand-push inflation became a problem for the government. The prices of those commodities produced in the planned-pricing system were rising. In some cities panic purchasing occurred in 1986 and 1988. These commodities were mainly consumer materials. The price rises of these commodities made people discontented with the government and this hindered further economic system reform. Secondly, there were shortages in the supplies of water, electricity, transportation and communications, especially in the Special Economic Zones and the Open Coastal Cities. Many factories could not continue nominal production because of shortages in the electricity and water supplies. This reflected the fact that investment in the infrastructure was at a very low level and needed to be improved. It could not meet the needs of a great deal of highly increased investment in production. Thirdly, there was an irrational and unbalanced capital construction investment structure, non-productive investment increased too quickly and extra-budgetary investment was out of control. Non-productive investments made up 20.9 per cent of the total construction investment in 1978 and by 1985 it had reached 43.1 per cent (State Statistical Bureau of People's Republic of China, 1991–1995). Foreign investment was concentrated too much in property, commerce and hotels, rather than in large-scale industrial investments, especially high-tech projects. This was regarded as not good for sustained economic growth and further economic system reform. In view of the above problems, the government created a policy of 'adjustment reform, re-regulation and improvement', carrying out new reforms which will now be discussed.

In 1986, the Law of the People's Republic of China on Foreign Capital Enterprises was adopted; this removed the preference given to certain sectors in respect of foreign direct investment. It strengthened management and guidance on foreign direct investment. In 1988 the government further clarified the strategy relating to foreign investments. The economy was divided into four parts for investment: encouraged sectors, agreed sectors, limited sectors and prohibited sectors. Property was in the agreed sector, which had no special preferential treatment.

From 1985 the government began a reform of the financial system. Up until 1984 economic system reform had made great progress and worked successfully, but the traditional financial system became an obstacle to further reform. The government had to reform the financial system to make progress. According to the reform principles adopted, the banks were to function fully as banks but supervised by a central bank, the People's Bank of China. Budgetary grants were replaced by loans with interest charges, enterprises could retain profits (subject to taxation), and individuals and enterprises could accumulate surpluses in bank accounts. Banks were to act as intermediaries for these funds, channelling them into profitable investments. Increasingly, competition between the specialized banks was permitted by allowing an overlap in the customer base, and thus China had begun to develop a deeper, more articulated financial system. Since 1985 the progress in the development of this system has been rapid.

Shareholding system experiments were boldly carried out in certain cities. This was a key development in the enterprise system reform. From then on, issuing company stocks and shares became an important source of finance.

The bond market began to be set up and developed. The government began to allow some firms to issue enterprise bonds as a source of raising funds. There was only a primary market – no secondary market – so bonds could not be transferred. The bond market was in a very early stage.

In 1988, the State Council printed and issued the 'Plan for the Implementation of Reform of the Housing System', to be carried out in stages and by various groups in the nation's cities and towns, thus beginning the housing system reform. Housing reform is closely related to the development of the property market. The global housing reform in China had four broad themes. First, there was a need to develop a strong central macroeconomic-management institution and a framework that encouraged rapid, non-inflationary growth. Second, sector policies were required to guide the provision of the physical infrastructure so as to lessen constraints on other economic agents, while promoting the wide use of beneficiary financing where equity objectives and the presence of externalities did not dictate otherwise. Third, an adequate 'safety net' financed by the widest possible revenue base had to be provided for the unemployed, the sick, the disabled, the retired and the poor. Fourth, economic transactions had to be shaped, as much as possible, by market signals generated by competitive markets devoid of barriers to trade. These goals suggested a new economic system where the roles of government, utilities, institutions, enterprises and households were more clearly delineated than before. Housing reform included some main underlying actions. First, raising rents and phasing out local-government control of housing rents while changing in-kind compensation to visible wages. Second, encouraging households to buy housing using lower prices with high government subsidies. Third, removing economic units from the activity of housing production, management and delivery, and encouraging rent companies and other property companies to develop, produce, manage and buy and sell housing units according to market signals. Fourth, clarifying housing property rights.

In 1987, Shenzhen made great moves in land reform by, firstly, starting to allocate land by means of public tender and, secondly, holding China's first auction in recent history in December 1987. Since then, a move to a market system and a mechanism of transferring land-use rights was widely introduced and adopted. In April 1988, to facilitate the working of the new system, the Seventh National People's Congress passed an amendment to the PRC Constitution which revised Clause 4 of Article 10 from 'No organization or individual may appropriate, buy, sell or lease or unlawfully transfer land in other ways' to 'No organization or individual may appropriate, buy, sell or lease or unlawfully transfer land in ways other than in accordance with the law'. In December 1988, following on from the amendment of Article 10, the Fifth Session of the Standing Committee of the Seventh National People's Congress subsequently amended the Land Administration Law of the People's Republic of China in a way which further clarified the legality of transferring land-use rights. The significant provision included, firstly, that land-use right of state- or collective-owned land could be transferred through legal procedures. Detailed methods for land-use right transfers would be re-regulated by the State Council. Second, the state would practise a paid land-use system for state-owned land; detailed methods of the paid land-use system of state-owned land would be regulated by the State Council. Third, there would be prohibition of any occupation of state land belonging to a commune or any sale or letting thereof, except in accordance with the provision of the law. This clause also empowered the resumption of use of land belonging to a commune. Fourth, the prohibition of the use of land other than in line with the permitted use. Fifth, the

forfeiture of any monetary gain from any illegal letting or any illegal transfer of land together with fines being imposed on the people responsible for
such transactions. Sixth, a provision that the use of land by joint venture
companies or foreign companies would be regulated by other rules to be
made by the State Council. Seventh, land-use fees would have different rates
for different uses and locations.

Land reform set the foundation of property market development.
According to the law, urban land is owned by the state, and rural land is
owned by the collectives. Land-use rights can be traded in the market. It is
the land-use right that is traded and not ownership. However, commonly,
ownership has three types of exclusive rights: rights to use, to derive
income, and to transfer. These rights are now legally valid in land use. So,
in practice, there is little difference between ownership and land-use rights.
The system of private-property rights, abolished after liberation, has now
been re-established. It has removed an important obstacle to property
market development. The economic reform and adjustment of this period
have brought Chinese economic reform to a new stage. There are break-
throughs in many fields, such as enterprise-system reform and land-system
reform. If there had been no 1989 democratic-movement incidents, economic reform and development would have been smoother and more
rational, based on the 1986–88 reforms. The 1989 incidents made foreign
investors stop their investment projects, especially some large-scale, high-
tech projects. Some Western countries imposed economic sanctions.
Chinese leaders began to be more conservative about further reform and
economic openness. The central government began tightening economic
policy, causing economic growth and economic reform to reach their lowest
points in 1989 and 1990.

The property market had developed gradually during the period of the
late-1980s, and it reflected certain characteristics:

- First, property investment in Special Economic Zones was more controlled, especially in Shenzhen. More and more foreign investors
  preferred industrial projects because of the state's preference policy, and
  more and more investments were outside the property sector.
- Second, more property transactions began to take place. In many big
  cities, especially in Beijing, Shanghai, Shenzhen, Guangzhou and Tianjin,
  more commercial buildings were being constructed and more households,
  especially those who were affluent, increased the demand for private
  housing. Meanwhile, land-use-right transactions were active (Peng Kun-
  Ten, 1995).
- Third, property prices increased a great deal after the 1988 housing and
  land reforms. Rents increased since the programme approved by
  the State Council in February 1988 directed local government to phase

out existing rent controls, and to increase rents and wage payments according to a one-time readjustment based on a scientific rent formula meant to mimic market rents. House prices increased dramatically (Li Zhen-Wei, 1994; State Statistical Bureau of People's Republic of China, 1994).

- Fourth, the property financial market was more active than before. The reform of the financial system gave commercial banks more freedom to provide credit. Some new banks were set up, such as the Transport Bank of China and the Investment Bank of China, and these banks channelled savings deposits into investments and began to compete with each other. They had some say in the decision of which investments to finance. Normally, banks were involved at an early stage in the project-approval process; they could raise issues and object to the financing mix, and their input could lead to a redesign of the project so as to improve the financial rate of return. Banks could refuse to sign the final assessment plans and, if banks strongly disagreed, sometimes the project would not be financed even though it was in the economic plan. Banks gave mortgages to property companies, usually short-term construction financing. Besides bank loans, there were several other sources of finance which developed during this period. Local bond and stock markets developed and the money market became active too.

Period 3: Boom Period (1991–93)

After the adjustment and rationalization of 1988–90, further acceleration of reform, and opening and speeding-up of economic development occurred from 1991. Firstly, Taiwan, South Korea, Malaysia, Singapore and other South East Asian countries broke the economic blockade set up by the Western World to China, setting up a new upsurge of investments. Since 1992, Taiwan has become one of the five largest investors in China. Secondly, and most importantly, Deng Shaoping, the reform designer, during his visit to South China in 1992, said that China should seize the opportunity, and quicken the pace of reform, opening-up and economic construction. His speech removed the obstacles to further reform on opening-up the economy created by the political left. After that, the Party Central Committee made a series of decisions on accelerating reform, opening-up and economic construction, and clearly put forward the goal of establishing the system of a social market economy at the Communist Party Congress that was of great historical significance. Since then, China's reform, opening-up and modernization drive have entered a new phase. Accompanied by deep and comprehensive reform, a great demand for investment and consumption has occurred, the high growth rate of GNP and increase in people's living standards attracting the attention of the world. Within the improving sectors, the property industry became the most obvious.

The growth in the Chinese property business stems primarily from the following underlying factors:

- Sharply rising industrial, commercial, and service output and productivity. In 1991, the real GNP growth rate was 7.0 per cent, much bigger than in 1989 and 1990. In 1992 it was 13.4 per cent, and increased to 13.4 per cent by 1993. There were rising standards of living – the annual average growth in urban national residents' consumption level in the Seventh Five-Year Plan was 3.6 per cent, but in 1992 it was 9.3 per cent. The index of per-capita income of urban families, compared to a base of 100 in 1978, was 209.5 in 1991, 228.3 in 1992 and 251.6 in 1993 (Wang Shiyuan, 1994).
- Sharply rising foreign investments and rising inflow of foreign personnel. The amount of foreign direct capital actually invested in the economy between 1979 and 1990 was US$22,219 million. In 1992 it was US$11,291 million and in 1993 it was US$27,771 million, bigger than the total amount between 1979 and 1990.
- A government that wants to perpetuate Communist Party control within the newly-developing socialist market economy through social and economic reforms, at a time of scarcity in quality office and industrial space and standard housing accommodation.
- The property financial market had developed and was very active. All the banks, especially the People's Construction Bank of China and the Industrial and Commercial Bank, made property investment easily fundable. Housing mortgages began to develop, an aspect that was discussed in Chapter 4.
- The enterprise reform provided enterprises with greater rights to invest, finance, manage and obtain more profits. Inter-firm money flows began to become active. Many enterprises put idle funds into high-risk and high-reward investment projects, such as securities investment and property. The share market, which was only experimental and had not spread widely, saw relatively rapid development. The share-ownership enterprises had rights to decide the investment projects, without the control of government, and many of them regarded property as a key area for investment projects.
- Many common investment funds have been set up, which were preferred especially by Zhu Rongji, who as Vice Premier was mainly responsible for financial markets and had been Chairman of the Central Bank. There were usually two types of investment for the common investment funds: the first is investment in securities, and the second is property investment.

Period 4: Period of Restraint (1994–96)

Overheated property investment and property trading brought many problems, which harmed China's sustained economic development. Property investment absorbed too much investment and funds were thus insufficient for industrial and agricultural investments. Secondly, overheated investment in property brought price rises in building materials and this encouraged inflation. Thus, after 1994, the government began to control property investment. At the same time the economic situation changed; after 1994 the high inflation rate become the key problem of economic development which led to people's general dissatisfaction with the government and to social disorder. The government was determined to cut the inflation rate as a first aim of macroeconomic management. So proposals were put forward by central government for tighter fiscal and financial policies. The tighter policies made the national capital investment go down and the demand for property, especially offices, shops and hotels, went down too. In view of the overheating of investment in non-productive projects, central government also took measures to discourage investment in those areas, especially property and securities investment. Real estate was listed as an area where foreign investment was restricted. Since 1992, central government restrained any new approvals for property projects; earlier approval projects that were still deemed necessary were however to be permitted along with the necessary financing. Beijing banned investment in luxury construction investment projects in 1995. Starting in July 1993, the People's Bank of China restrained the growth of land development and property business, by asking the state-owned financial institutions to call in outstanding property loans and cut off the money to unapproved property projects. The central government also took measures to cut speculation in the property market. By the end of 1994, a system of taxes was implemented, including a notorious property gains tax, introduced to force developers to pay taxes up to 50 per cent. In another attempt to limit speculation, a rule has been imposed which forbids the resale of premises within a period of five years. Whilst controlling property investment, the government concentrated also on the financial markets as another main area requiring adjustment. All illegal trading in the financial market was banned, including the illegal 'sale-back' government bonds exchange, the government bond future market, and some commodity futures exchanges. Many financial institutions faced serious financial problems because of limits on their operations introduced by the government. Influenced by financial peril and disorder in property investment, many commercial banks and financial institutions stopped financing property investment. Property investment projects cannot obtain loans as easily as previously. Because of all the above reasons, since 1994, property investment and the property market have experienced difficulties. Some of the difficulties encountered are outlined below:

- The growth rate of construction investment has gone down. In 1994 it was 45.4 per cent and in 1995 it fell to 18.9 per cent, which are all less than the growth rate in 1993 (State Statistical Bureau of People's Republic of China, 1991–1995, 1993–1995).
- The property price index has fallen (State Statistical Bureau of People's Republic of China, 1993–1995).
- Many property companies have faced serious financial problems. Some have gone into liquidation, others have just disappeared.
- Much construction that was uncompleted has had to be stopped. Investment companies have no sources from which to raise funds to continue construction.
- Structural problems in construction investment are very serious. On the one hand, the overheated investments in luxury hotels, shops, offices and villas have led to an oversupply of these kinds of property; on the other hand, there are insufficient ordinary offices and residences. There is over-speculation in the property market. There are more traders and dealers, fewer developers. A piece of land is often sold many times over before being developed.

Examining and analyzing the history of property investment and the property market, we can come to some conclusions about the Chinese property market. Firstly, since economic reform and the opening-up of the economy, property investment and the property market have developed rapidly. Economic reform and the policy of opening-up have stimulated production and high capital construction investments, making the construction industry more and more important in economic development. When economic reform went further, incorporating land-system and housing-system reforms, property investment rapidly increased, the property business became active and the property market developed. The rapid development of the property market is due greatly to the economic reform and the policy of opening-up. Secondly, property investment and property markets are very sensitive to government policy. China is in a transition stage from the old planning system to a new market system. Although it has made great progress in many fields and has many characteristics of the free market, the government still plays a major role in the economy. For the new and expanding sectors, such as the securities market and the property market, government policy is important. Government expansion policies in economic operations in the early-1980s stimulated a boom in construction investment all over China and a boom in property investment in the Special Economic Zones, especially Shenzhen. The government's reform and expansion policy led to a boom in the property market from 1991 to 1993. Meanwhile the conservative and tight economic policy at the end of the 1980s made property investment shrink and the economic squeeze since 1994 has made the property market look attractive to investors. Thirdly, foreign direct investment is an important factor that stimulates property investment and the property market. Foreign direct investment is both an important finance source in property investment and an important demand force. Foreign capital inflows brought great demands for property investment and especially foreign direct investment in the Special Economic Zones in the early stages of economic reform, and the opening-up has led to a boom in construction and property investments. A new upsurge in foreign direct investment after 1991 became an important factor in the property boom. Fourthly, and most importantly, the Chinese property market is still at a very elementary stage, far from mature, and needs to be developed.

The reasons for this lack of maturity in the property market can be seen from the following:

- There are few stable mature investors, developers, dealers and consumers in the property market. Many investors and developers are in the market for single transactions, aiming for speculative high profits. Most property dealers have no professional experience and knowledge and, if the property market is not active, they switch to other fields. Because China has relatively low income levels, construction costs are relatively high; there is a high ratio of average unit price to average annual urban household cash income – which is 20:1 in China, whereas in most market economies it varies between 2:1 and 6:1. Also, as the necessary finance instruments are not available, few Chinese people can afford to buy property.
- The property finance market is in a very early stage of development. Mortgages have not developed. There are few specialized financial institutions except for the state-owned Construction Bank. Investment and development loans are available only on very strict terms. This is discussed in more detail in Chapter 4.
- There is no legal system in place that protects and assists property transactions. Existing laws and regulations are far from complete and perfect; some of them are ambiguous and full of loopholes. In practice, many disputes cannot be resolved in accordance with existing laws.
- The property market is very speculative and this brings serious problems. Property prices are volatile and are usually at a high level. Capital flows in and out of the sector occur very frequently. Speculative profit-taking is the norm and, if returns fall, investors will move out of the market.

Conclusion

As a developing country, China has several restraints on its property market development. The first is *resources restraint* – land resources are the basis of property development. Land resources are scarce for a population the size of China's. The average amount of land per capita is 13.4 mu/person, much less than that for the rest of the world, which is 44.5 mu/person (15 mu = 1 ha). Moreover, of the land resources, there is much land that is difficult to develop and make use of, such as the Gobi Desert, and land subject to permafrost and firn, glacier and swamp. Arable land is also scarce comparably, arable land per capita being 1.38 mu, equal to 26.7 per cent of that generally available worldwide.

The second is *capital restraint*. China is a developing country that is seriously short of capital. All industries, especially basic industries such as agriculture, energy, transportation and communication, in the developing stage need capital urgently, demand outstripping supply. Since 1979, the growth rate of property investment has been more than that of total fixed capital investment each year. In the first half of 1995, total property investment increased by 26.3 per cent, although the growth rate decreased by 17.7 per cent. It was also higher than state-owned fixed capital investment of the same period. In order to sustain balanced development and a low inflation rate, property investment must not make up too high a proportion of national capital. In China, capital shortage will remain for a long time to come.

The third is *demand restraint*. Potential demand is big, but effective demand is less than supply. The effective demand for property is limited by the lower standard of living. In 1993, the average housing area per person was $7.3\,m^2$. Those people with less than $4\,m^2$ amount to more than 4,000,000, so the potential demand is very large but, because of the low living standards, purchasing power is limited. The current property market is characterized by high house prices and low annual household income. In Beijing and Shanghai, average house prices are more than $7,000\,yuan/m^2$. For an ordinary household it is impossible to buy a house. In Chongqing it is reported that housing of $50\,m^2$ costs 10–30 times the annual income of an ordinary household.

The fourth is *structural restraint*. China is in a transitional period from a centrally state-planned to a market-oriented economy. The economic system is characterized by duality, both central-planning and free-market decision-making existing side-by-side, which makes the system unclear and full of contradiction. Although land reform and housing reform have been carried out, reform in the property market is far from perfect and complete, many problems exist and these hamper its development.

The fifth is *financial restraint*. The financial market in China is far from mature and developed. The financial system is in a process of reform and transition. Property investment has been separated from the financial institutions, whereas property investment is closely linked with financial institutions in developed countries. Both housing finance and commercial development finance are in very early stages, undeveloped and controlled by government, and so are far from market-oriented. When the government carries out an economic squeeze, this kind of restraint becomes very serious.

REFERENCES

Adair, A., Berry, J., McGreal, S., Sýkora, L., Ghanbari Parsa, A. and Redding, B. (1999) 'Globalisation of real estate markets in Central Europe', *European Planning Studies*, 7(3): 295–305.

Barras, R. (1994) 'Property and the economic cycle: building cycles revisited', *Journal of Property Research*, 11(3), Winter: 183–97.

Barter, S.L. (1988) 'Introduction', in Barter, S.L. (ed.), *Real Estate Finance*, London: Butterworths.

Brett, M. (1983) 'Growth of financial institutions', in Darlow, C. (ed.), *Valuation and Investment Appraisal*, London: Estates Gazette.

Brett, M. (1989) 'Characteristics of property', *Estates Gazette*, 21 January: 14.

Cadman, D. and Catalano, A. (1983) *Property Development in the UK – Evolution and Change*, Reading: College of Estate Management.

CSW – The Property Week (1993) 'New research reveals market pattern', *CSW – The Property Week*, 28 October: 13.

Dai, J., Isaac, D. and Wills, D. (1999) *Real Estate Markets in China: An Overview*, London: University of Greenwich.

Darlow, C. (ed.) (1983) *Valuation and Investment Appraisal*, London: Estates Gazette.

Estates Gazette (1995) 'Property cycles explained', *Estates Gazette*, 25 November: 147–8.

Estates Gazette (1996) 'Tenants are lukewarm on new lease code of practice', *Estates Gazette*, 6 January: 40.

Estates Times (1993) 'Swaps not cash', *Estates Times*, 19 November: 24.

Fraser, W.D. (1993) *Principles of Property Investment and Pricing*, London: Macmillan.

Fraser, W. (1996) 'A schematic model of the commercial property market', *Chartered Surveyor Monthly*, January: 32–3.

Ghanbari Parsa, A.R. (1997) 'Impact of globalisation on urban development in Central Europe', Paper presented at the *International Conference on Land*, RICS, London.

Gibson, G. and Carter, C. (1995) 'Is property on the strategic agenda?', *Chartered Surveyor Monthly*, January: 34–5.

Isaac, D. (1996) *Property Finance*, London: Macmillan.

Isaac, D. (1998) *Property Investment*, London: Macmillan.

Isaac, D. and Steley, T. (2000) *Property Valuation Techniques*, 2nd edn, London: Macmillan.

Keogh, G. (1994) 'Use and investment markets in UK real estate', *Journal of Property Valuation and Investment*, 12(4): 58–72.

Lennox, K. (1996) 'Thumbs up for property: IPF/EG survey', *Estates Gazette*, 20 April: 41.

Li Zhen-Wei (1994) *An Empirical Analysis of Real Estate Demand in Guangzhou.*

London, S. (1996) '*Lore of the property market*', *Financial Times*, 23 September.

McGregor, B., Nanthakumuran, N., Key, T. and Zarkesh, F. (1994) 'Investigating property cycles', *Chartered Surveyor Monthly*, July/August: 38–9.

Peng Kun-Ten (1995) *An Analysis of New Supply of the Guangzhou Real Estate Market.*

Pike, R. and Neale, B. (1993) *Corporate Finance and Investment*, London: Prentice Hall.

Pugh, C. and Dehesh, A. (1995) 'International property cycles: the causes', *Chartered Surveyor Monthly*, January: 33.

Ratcliffe, J. (1978) *An Introduction to Urban Land Administration*, London: Estates Gazette.

Royal Institution of Chartered Surveyors (1994) *Understanding the Property Cycle: Economic Cycles and Property Cycles*, May, London: RICS.

Savills (1989) *Financing Property 1989*, London: Savills.

State Statistical Bureau of People's Republic of China (1991–1995) *China Statistics Abstract 1991–1995*, China Statistical Information and Consultancy Service Centre.

State Statistical Bureau of People's Republic of China (1992) *Shenzhen Statistics Yearbook 1992*, Shenzhen.

State Statistical Bureau of People's Republic of China (1993–1995) *China Statistics Yearbook 1993–1995*, China Statistical Information and Consultancy Service Centre.

State Statistical Bureau of People's Republic of China (1994) *Tianjin Statistics Yearbook 1994*, Tianjin.

Wang Shiyuan (ed.) (1994) *China Economic Systems Reform Yearbook 1994*, China Reform Publishing House.

Whitmore, J. (1994) 'RICS identifies the property cycle', *Property Week*, 12 May: 4.

9

Urban Planning, Land Policy and the Market

INTRODUCTION

In advanced capitalist countries – and to a varying extent over many decades – governments have intervened in the land market and thus influenced the pace and volume of property development and investment. It is clear that land values can be increased or decreased by spatial planning; market-determined values can frequently ignore social needs, and interests in land often yield monopoly or 'windfall' gains for the owner. Most governments, therefore, impose a system of land taxation to extract – for the benefit of society – a share of increased values resulting from planning or market forces, and sometimes – and for the same reason – take land into public ownership through various forms of land nationalization.

Although the real estate market is clearly an economic mechanism rationing land between competing uses, it is often subject to criticism for at least one of the following reasons:

(1) as a means of allocating land between different uses, the market suffers from imperfections – demand and supply being rarely in equilibrium;
(2) it disregards the needs of the less profitable, and often unprofitable yet socially desirable, uses of land for such purposes as schools, hospitals and public open spaces;
(3) it maintains and highlights national inequalities of income and wealth.

Thus, in many capitalist countries, governments modify the price mechanism within the contexts of planning objectives, social need and the distribution of incomes and wealth.

Urban Planning, Real Estate Values and Social Needs

Urban planning, in a *reactive* sense, can be seen as a means of increasing the value of private and profitable uses of land by establishing complementarity of land uses while keeping conflicting uses apart through such devices as zoning and density regulations. The zoning and density control aspects of urban planning eliminate some of the imperfections of the real estate market, and enable land to move more readily to its 'highest and best use'.

However, in a *proactive* sense, urban planning might ensure that when the market mechanism fails to provide socially desirable development, public authorities will become involved in the development process and might need to evaluate social considerations by means of cost–benefit analysis (see Chapter 10). This attempts to provide a method of evaluation and appraisal intended to indicate not only the private or direct costs and benefits of development, but also the social or indirect costs and benefits. Cost–benefit analysis is used mainly for assessing alternative proposals for development, and has been applied mainly to transport schemes and urban development projects.

Social considerations are further taken into account when local authorities attempt to secure planning gain from a private development project. In an eagerness to secure development consent, developers are often willing to forgo a proportion of their anticipated profits by either making a payment in cash to a local planning authority or by providing socially desirable facilities such as a library, leisure centre or low-cost housing in addition to their principal (profit-making) development.

GOVERNMENT INTERVENTION IN THE REAL ESTATE MARKET

A major criticism of the real estate market is that it perpetuates or widens the unequal distribution of incomes and wealth stemming from private 'unearned' windfall gains or 'undeserved' losses. Land values are not just reflections of their current uses but also of possible future uses. For example, farm output, production costs and prices determine agricultural land values. If, however, it is thought that farmland could be used more profitably for some other purpose, such as housing or industry, then the land will increase in value. The rise in value occurs before the land is transferred to a new and higher use – conferring windfall gains on the landowner. The value of a specific use of land, however, could fall if competing land uses experienced a decrease in value, but since inflation is more endemic in the capitalist world than a downward movement in the general level of prices, rising land values rather than falling land values are more common.

In all advanced capitalist countries, and irrespective of land use, speculation is thus the driving force behind private development and there is a related tendency for landowners to withhold sites from the market to push up values. Although windfall gains are enjoyed by the private owner, often little of the increased value is recouped for the benefit of the community. Less profitable uses of land are crowded out of the market and the public sector is unable to compete effectively to acquire land for essential needs. Recognizing these regressive aspects of the market economy, governments of many countries in recent years have attempted to constrain, harness or replace market forces by at least one of the following methods:

(1) controlling development value without taking land into public ownership;
(2) the taxation of windfall gains;
(3) controlling development by transferring private land to public ownership;
(4) ensuring that planning gain is realized.

Each of these processes is now examined in turn.

CONTROLLING DEVELOPMENT WITHOUT TAKING LAND INTO PUBLIC OWNERSHIP

It has been recognized for some time that planning authorities have powers to: increase or decrease the supply of land for development purposes by means of land-use zoning and through the granting or rejection of permission to develop; reparcel land ownership and land use to facilitate the implementation of a planning scheme; impose conditions on the granting of permission (for example, by restricting the height or floorspace of buildings); and exercise pre-emptive rights to acquire land free from the necessity to compete in the open market (see Darin-Drabkin, 1977; Lichfield and Darin-Drabkin, 1980).

If the supply of land for development increases as a result of planning policy (often in response to an increase in demand), land prices will either remain fairly stable or even fall, but if the supply of land decreases as a result of the action of planning authorities, land prices could be expected to rise.

Figure 9.1 shows that when supply is increased from SS to S_1S_1 in response to an increase in demand from DD to D_1D_1, land prices (p) remain stable; whereas figure 9.2 shows that if supply increases sufficiently, land prices fall from op to op_1. However, figure 9.3 shows that when supply is decreased from SS to S_2S_2, land prices rise to op_2.

A wide range of land-management policies have been in use in different countries in recent years, and a brief examination of these will indicate their principal attributes:

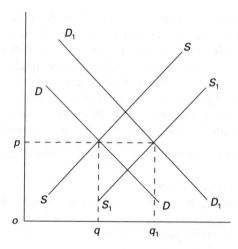

Figure 9.1 *Stable land prices – with demand and supply increasing*

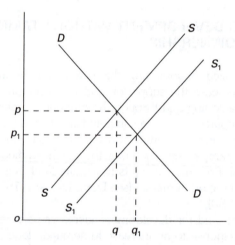

Figure 9.2 *Falling land prices – with supply increasing*

(1) Long-term national and sub-national land-use planning

Denmark has probably the most advanced land-use planning system in the world. By means of Comprehensive Macro-Zoning, zones for urban, rural and recreation use are declared, and, since urban zones contain areas for expansion, the release of rural land for urban purposes is normally prohibited. Plans, revised every four years, are binding on municipalities.

In the UK, controls date back to the early decades of the twentieth

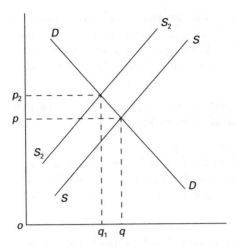

Figure 9.3 *Rising land prices – with supply decreasing*

century, but the current planning system derives mainly from the Town and Country Planning Acts of 1947 and 1968, and the Planning and Compensation Act of 1991. All development, as defined, requires consent from the local planning authority and – in terms of use and density – must broadly conform with local plans or unitary development plans prepared by lower-tier authorities, which in turn need to broadly conform with structure plans prepared by upper-tier authorities.

The Netherlands has a system whereby local plans are approved by the provincial planning authorities and co-ordinated when necessary. However, municipalities exercise development control in accordance with local plans.

In Sweden, four types of plan are prepared: a regional plan, a master plan, a town plan and a building plan. All detailed plans have to be ratified by regional and national authorities. Only if development conforms with the relevant detailed plan can a municipality grant a building permit.

In Japan, a city planning law was introduced in 1968. It provided for the designation of any area for which integrated development, improvement and construction within an urban area was necessary. Two types of area would thus be designated: 'urbanization promotion areas' and 'urbanization control areas'. The former areas were either built-up or due for development within 'say' 10 years and, within them, development in accordance with the city plan would be authorized, whereas in the latter areas premature urban development would be curbed.

In Latin America, with the possible exception of Brazil, Chile and Venezuela, there has been little effective urban land-use control despite

attempts to adopt 'European-style' planning systems. Even in these countries practical results are only partly successful because of the absence of
sufficient legislation. In Uruguay, however, urban development plans and
policies have ensured a relatively high degree of regulation.

(2) Readjustment schemes (compulsory reparcelling of land in an area of development)

In France, both compulsory and voluntary reparcellation of sites (*lotisse-
ment*) is undertaken, the former by private urban renewal companies and
the latter by owners, but municipalities may attach conditions to the *lotisse-
ment* scheme, for example in respect of the financing and/or the provision
of public services.

Largely because of its federal constitution and the comparative strength
of its free-market economy, West Germany did not develop a comprehensive planning system during the years to unification in 1989, nor has one
emerged subsequently. At most, municipalities are involved in reparcellation schemes to private owners, the latter having to execute infrastructure
works at their own expense and, if appropriate, dedicate space for public
uses (planning gain). Owners qualify for compensation if a change of site
results in loss, or they may be liable to a windfall tax if they are allocated
more valuable land.

In Japan, readjustment laws were first introduced in 1909, and throughout the rest of the century have been applied with a considerable degree of
success. In all, over 30 per cent of the country's total urban land area has
been subject to readjustment (*Tochi Kukaskusen*) – the main objectives of
which are to provide specific areas with adequate infrastructure, to establish more rational patterns of land use and to facilitate a reallocation of
housing sites. Readjustment has also been extensively employed with
success in South Korea.

(3) Special land-use controls in areas of development

In France, maximum building coefficients (plot ratios) were imposed at 1.5
in Paris and 1.0 elsewhere to deter intensive development. Above these
limits, intensive development – although permitted – was subject to tax.

Italy introduced its planning system only in the 1960s. In respect of the
preparation of all urban plans, legislation imposes standards on building
density and height, the ratio between industrial and residential uses, and the
provision of areas for public services. Building licences are required in each
local-authority area, and are granted only if the primary infrastructure exists
or the applicant agrees to develop it. All private plans to develop must be
approved at local, regional and national level and the developer must at

least contribute to the cost of infrastructural provision. Penalties are imposed on the defiance of control.

(4) Pre-emption rights

In France, *préfects* are empowered to declare ZADs (Zones d'Aménagement Déféré) where the future development of, for example, a new town is contemplated. No alternative new development is then permitted and public authorities are given pre-emptive rights ('first refusals' if land comes up for sale). ZADs were increasingly declared in urban areas in the 1970s–1980s to facilitate regeneration.

Conclusion

The above land-use control measures are mainly passive and any effect on land values usually benefits the owner rather than the wider community. The implementation of plans is largely dependent upon the private market which determines the course of development. Some governments, however, might wish to introduce tighter systems of planning control, as in Denmark, and in some countries, such as France, local authorities might wish to exercise pre-emptive acquisition rights. In both cases, social need is deemed to have a priority over private gain.

THE TAXATION OF WINDFALL GAINS

As has been recognized, the property market perpetuates the unequal distribution of incomes and wealth derived from private 'unearned' windfall gains and 'undeserved' losses. In capitalist countries, land ownership is very fragmented and, since many sites have very specific locational attributes, owners are often able to exercise monopoly power. A buyer anxious to acquire a site to develop the land to a 'higher and better use', might thus be obliged to pay a price to acquire land considerably in excess of its current use value.

Assuming a potential change of use to a more profitable activity, the difference between the anticipated market value and the current use value is known as the 'development value' (or 'floating value' if there are only expectations of a change to a higher use). In figure 9.4, the demand for agricultural land is indicated by the curve DD and the demand for housing land is shown by the curve D_1D_1. Where these curves intersect the supply line SS, the current use and market uses are determined and the difference between them is the development or floating value.

However, demand may decrease because of changes in its underlying

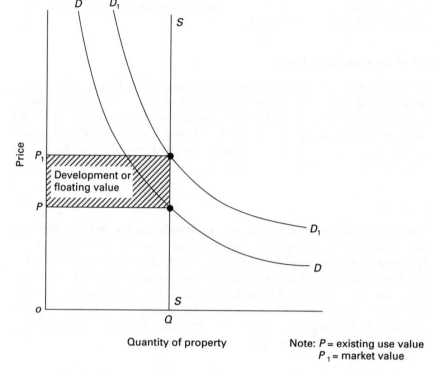

Note: P = existing use value
P_1 = market value

Figure 9.4 *The effects upon value of an increase in demand*

condition. Not only might development and floating values be eroded but current use value might also fall – in both cases through no action of the real estate owner. 'Betterment' and 'worsenment' are terms used to describe respective increases and decreases in the value of property. In the *narrow sense*, betterment is the increase in property values resulting from:

(1) an increase in real gross national product (GNP) per capita;
(2) the effect of an increase in the value of adjacent property;
(3) a general increase in prices.

Worsenment in this sense implies falling values resulting from a decrease in the real GNP per capita, the effect of a decrease in the value of adjacent property, or from a general slump in prices.

In a *broader* sense, betterment is any increase in the value of real estate resulting from:

(1) central- or local-government policy, for example, through improvement in the infrastructure (such as transport development);

(2) the exercise of planning power and most notably through the granting of permission to develop.

Worsenment in this sense might be an outcome of public works schemes having a detrimental value on real estate values, or the result of the failure to obtain permission to develop. Values can also diminish in advance of a planning scheme through the process of blighting.

BOX 9.1: THE POLITICAL ECONOMY OF BETTERMENT TAXATION

Both philosophical and pragmatic arguments have been presented for and against imposing taxes on betterment (and granting compensation for worsenment). In 1817, David Ricardo, a British political economist argued in his book *The Principles of Political Economy of Taxation* (Ricardo, 1971) that land was different from other factors of production (labour and capital) since it was fixed in supply and was a 'free' gift of Nature not capable of being created by humankind. Demand, rather than any action of its owner, determined the value of land, thus economic rent was entirely an 'unearned' increment and should (in the view of Ricardo) be taxed. In the 1870s, Henry George, in his book *Progress and Poverty* (George, 1979) argued that – since a substantial migration of population into California was pushing up rents and widening gaps between landowners and the landless – a 100 per cent tax on economic rent should be imposed. This, he suggested, would restrict the power of land monopoly, remove the incentive to keep land off the market, deter the tendency to speculate in property and eliminate inequalities arising from the ownership of property. Land taxation, moreover (in the opinion of George), would remove the necessity to impose taxes on labour and capital and thus widely generate income.

In figure 9.5, with a given quantity of land q and a rent of r, the landlord's net income would only be $rn \times q$ since tax revenue $(r - rn \times q)$ would be recouped for the benefit of the community. Since the tax cannot push up the market rent above its equilibrium level at r, the incidence of tax falls entirely on the landowner.

In the twentieth century, the introduction of spatial planning legislation has complicated the arguments for government intervention in the market pricing of property, but nevertheless it has been widely recognized that land taxation not only gives the community a fiscal share of the additional value of land created by community activity and the investment and planning decisions of central and local government, but also can facilitate the redistribution of income and wealth, and raise revenue to meet some of the costs of providing public services.

continued

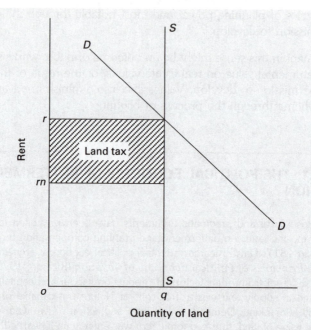

Figure 9.5 *Taxation and the supply of land*

The case against betterment taxation revolves around the arguments: that land profits are the result and not the cause of land scarcity and high values; that land is a commodity like anything else and should not be subject to any special form of taxation; and – like other commodities – that land can be withdrawn from the market if betterment taxation is too high, thereby necessitating compulsory purchase at inflated prices.

Systems of land taxation vary from country to country and are often subject to continual change – often for ideological reasons, but some of the systems that have been employed in the advanced capitalist world are briefly examined below.

In the UK, land taxation has taken two principal forms:

(1) Rising property values have been subject normally to capital gains tax, although most owner-occupied housing has been exempt.
(2) There have been three major attempts since the Second World War to develop a land policy that reconciles the aims of planning and the workings of the market. Under the Town and Country Planning Act 1947, a 100 per cent development charge was imposed on development values – a tax that was abolished by the Town and Country Planning

Act of 1953 since it deterred the private market from functioning (although, in the long-term, it would have enabled local authorities to acquire land at existing use value to build up large land banks for development). A betterment levy of 40–50 per cent was subsequently introduced under the Land Commission Act of 1965, but remained in existence only until 1971 owing to complexities in assessment and collection. The Development Land Tax Act of 1976 then introduced a 66–80 per cent tax on development values, but this was discontinued in 1984 since it was not only costly to collect but it proved to be 'a highly complex, heavy-handed instrument of central taxation which . . . [like the 1965 levy] . . . ended up with little relationship to local land policy considerations' (Grant, 1999: 66).

At the turn of the century, however, the absence of betterment taxation in Britain is considered a tragedy for two reasons. 'First, the issue will not go away: it permeates the planning system, and, secondly, it distorts planning policy and creates inequalities on a large scale . . . it gives huge prizes to the winners in the sweepstakes of planning applications; but the losers get nothing' (Cullingworth, 1999: 5). For these reasons, it is understandable that the Urban Task Force chaired by Lord Rogers – and possibly mindful of the failure of widely-based tax initiatives in the past – suggested that the government should consider imposing a 'greenfield tax' on real estate development, or an 'environmental impact tax' or fee on development in greenfield locations (DETR, 1999). Both would either produce hypothecated revenue for inner-city regeneration, or possibly steer development to brownfield areas – largely in the inner cities. Clearly 'a shift towards land policy would begin to redeem the balance between planning and the market, which, since 1953, has been firmly tipped towards the latter' (Evans, 1999: 274).

Denmark has had few such problems. Its planning system has been underpinned by a land value increment duty on the increase in value caused by a public-authority decision to permit a change of use. The duty has ranged from 40 to 60 per cent and has normally been paid at the time the public authority makes its decision, rather than on realized betterment value. Medium-term mortages (for example, for 12 years) help owners to pay if they cannot otherwise afford the tax.

In recent years, land profits in France have been taxed as income if the sale of land was made within five years of acquisition, but – after five years – sales were subject to capital gains tax at 60 per cent. In calculating the tax, the purchase price was increased by 25 per cent *plus* a cost of living escalator, *plus* a further 3 per cent per annum (to allow for maintenance). Betterment has also been intercepted by a tax of up to 100 per cent on the value of development in excess of the permitted building coefficient.

The Federal Republic of Germany – in the 1970s – imposed a 100 per cent levy on betterment resulting from urban renewal schemes, many of which included reparcellation. The differences between the new and old site values were entirely recouped for the benefit of the community, but the levy was paid only on the completion of a scheme in order not to financially frustrate development.

In the Netherlands, no special form of land tax is deemed necessary because the municipalities have a monopolistic power of acquisition and can thus ensure that private landowners are unable to realize betterment on their disposal of land.

Sweden, in recent years, has been a comparatively high tax country and land-related taxes were no exception:

(1) Land profits have been treated as income and provided a source of income tax. After two years, only 75 per cent of the profit was taxable, with inflation and the cost of improvements being taken into account, while in the case of owner-occupied residential property there was a further nominal allowance. For property that had been in ownership for many years, the purchase price was assumed to have been either 150 per cent of its 1940 assessment or the owner could have chosen the estimated value which it would have fetched 20 years before the sale.
(2) Land has been included in the annual graduated taxation of wealth at a basic rate of 0.2 per cent above a modest threshold.

Despite the possibility of using many different forms of taxation, very few of the above countries or cities have succeeded in collecting the major part of the additional value of land resulting from increased demand. With a few exceptions, planning authorities have been starved of the resources they require to comprehensively implement their development plans (even in partnership with the private sector), while municipalities have often been unable to finance the provision of an adequate supply of local services to satisfy essential needs.

SVR or LVT (as applied in Denmark and parts of Australia and the United States) might, however, provide the best means of collecting betterment for the benefit of the community, and, unlike development charges, would encourage owners to release land for development rather than withdraw it from the market (see also pages 408–10).

CONTROLLING DEVELOPMENT BY TRANSFERRING PRIVATE LAND TO PUBLIC OWNERSHIP

Land-use controls alone have often proved inadequate to ensure that planning schemes at the 'right time, of the right sort and in the right place' are implemented for the benefit of the community as a whole, whereas taxation – at best – has often not achieved its objectives and – at worst – has encouraged owners to withhold their land from the market. By means of acquisition, public authorities have therefore sometimes taken responsibility for ensuring that, when required, there is an adequate supply of land for appropriate development in the right location and at a reasonable price. In recent years, governments of a number of countries have, to a variable extent, exercised powers of land acquisition – a few of which are examined below.

In the UK, policy in respect of land acquisition has been severely affected by political change ('left of centre' governments generally favoured acquisition, 'right of centre' governments were usually opposed to it), whereas in all the above countries there was normally a consensus view about the role of government in the land market, and hence – in contrast to the UK – there was greater continuity of policy. In the UK, Labour governments introduced legislation in 1947, 1967 and 1975 to nationalize land – largely on a temporary basis – to hasten the pace of development for 'essential' purposes. Land was to be acquired at market values less tax on windfall gain (see above), and subsequently used either for public-sector needs or sold off for private development, normally at market values. As with the two previous attempts to nationalize land, the 1975 Act proved to be an administrative disaster since central government had been 'unable to provide local authorities with the necessary finance to implement it, or the loan sanctions necessary to acquire the land available' (Grant, 1999: 66). As had befallen the 1947 and 1967 Acts, the 1975 legislation was repealed by a subsequent Conservative government, and since 1979 local authorities in the UK have had to rely on their compulsory purchase powers if they wish to acquire land – with compensation being paid at full market value.

Denmark, in contrast, relies comparatively little on compulsory purchase powers to facilitate the implementation of planning schemes, but municipalities have pre-emption (first-refusal) rights over any land for sale in excess of a specific area (for example, $6,000\,m^2$).

France, however, has taken land into community ownership in recent years by a variety of methods:

(1) Expropriation (compulsory purchase) has been the most important legal power of local authorities for acquiring land for public purposes – notably infrastructure and housing. The needs of urban development were seen increasingly as a legitimate reason for expropriation.
(2) Within the ZADs (see above), public authorities exercised pre-emption rights – keeping land prices down. The cost of acquisition was minimized since compensation was based on prices prevailing one year before the zone's declaration.

(3) In the Paris Region, *L'Agence Foncière et Technique de la Région Parisienne* (AFTRP) purchased land required by public bodies for urban development projects (including new towns). It had expropriation powers and was financed by government loans provided by the National Fund for Real Estate.

(4) ZACs (Zones d'Aménagement Concerté) were declared in city regions wherein building regulations were suspended in order for comprehensive redevelopment to be carried out – usually by a public/private sector company. ZACs were particularly suitable for large-scale commercial and residential development but, in the case of the latter, development was undertaken by the public sector alone (see Couch, 1990).

Following acquisition by each of the four methods, land (other than that retained for public use) was normally sold at market value or the total value of the lease collected at once. Projects are therefore self-financing and profits are used for further acquisition.

Local authorities in Italy have powers to expropriate private-sector land for infrastructural development and housing – in accordance with approved development schemes. Compensation for expropriation amounted approximately to an average of market values (excluding the impact upon value of the intended development) and ten years' accumulated rent (or accessible value) declared for the purposes of taxation.

The Netherlands has relied on municipal acquisition schemes. Amsterdam, for example, has undertaken land acquisition in advance of development since the nineteenth century, and over the past half-century has expropriated nearly all the land it requires for development. The responsibility for planning, acquisition and development was vested in the city's Department of Planning and Public Works – facilitating positive rather than restrictive planning. Compensation for acquisition was at market value, but this was kept at a low level because of the monopoly buying power of the municipal authority. In the case of expropriated agricultural land, farmers received compensation based on the low market value of their land *plus* a payment equivalent to ten years' loss of agricultural income. Amsterdam leased all its publicly-owned land (while Rotterdam has tended to sell it off), and rents had to take into account the costly development of infrastructure and social housing in newly-developing areas.

Sweden has had an array of different methods for acquiring land and for its disposal:

(1) Municipalities had pre-emption rights in respect of land in excess of a defined area (for example, $3,000\,\text{m}^2$) or with a rental value above a specific amount (for example, 200,000 kroner).

(2) The central government encouraged municipal authorities to acquire

land in advance of development and to build up large land banks for the purpose of developing planned communities with integrated transport systems. STRADA – the municipal land-buying agency for Stockholm – consequently assembled large land reserves cheaply. It was prohibited by the Official Secrets Act to publish information about its proposed operations to prevent land speculation and, together with other municipalities, used its strong bargaining power to acquire each year up to 40 per cent of all land acquisitions.

(3) In the 1970s–1980s, local authorities no longer had to prove that the private sector was incapable of developing land for approved purposes before expropriating land. This speeded up the pace of acquisition since it could take place even before compensation payments were settled.

(4) From 1972 to 1980 inclusive, compensation for expropriation was set at values prevailing on 1 January 1971, but compensation after 1980 was set at values prevailing ten years before acquisition. Retrospective valuation was undertaken to prevent landowners benefiting from services provided by a local authority and to deter speculators from profiting from the effects of increasing population pressure on land values.

(5) Municipalities received government loans to acquire land and to build up a reserve of land for up to ten years ahead, and they could also borrow from a low-interest loan fund to invest in land disposed of with leasehold rights and developed with the assistance of government housing loans.

(6) Government policy encouraged the disposal of a large proportion of acquired land by means of leasehold, but leases were generally based not on the market value of land but on the economic cost of acquisition and infrastructure.

In Australia there have been many local acquisition schemes, for example the Metropolitan Perth Regional Planning Authority was able to compulsorily acquire suburban land at rural values and to develop it for a range of uses on a wide scale, while the South Australian Housing Trust became a monopolistic purchaser of land for public housing and infrastructure development – its market power keeping prices at a low level. In Canberra, all land has been publicly owned and leased to private developers – leases being offered at public auctions for specific uses.

In most capitalist countries, the public acquisition of land has been piecemeal or transitional. It is mainly the private market which determines the course of development and the condition of the built-environment. In recent years, only in Sweden (and to a lesser extent the Netherlands) has there been a fundamental and comprehensive policy of public land acquisition

---

BOX 9.2: STATE-OWNED LAND IN SINGAPORE AND HONG KONG

By the 1960s, one-third of all land in Singapore was state owned and used by the public sector, and a large part of the remainder was held by the private sector on 20–33 year leases from the government. A Land Acquisition Act in 1966, moreover, gave the government wide powers to acquire private land compulsorily, with compensation being based on the market value of land in its existing use. Land was acquired to facilitate large-scale housebuilding programmes and the development of industry and services, with land being released annually by the Ministry of National Development to meet – for example – an annual demand for about 5,000–6,000 private residential units in the 1990s.

In Hong Kong – both as a Crown Colony until 1997 and subsequently as a Special Administrative Region of the People's Republic of China – all land has been owned, and continues to be owned, by the public sector – initially by the Crown and now by the State. However, there is a private market in land rights since very long lease agreements (initially issued by the government) can be bought and sold. Land can revert to the public sector at any time, with compensation based on current market value (although payment has been often delayed). Acquisition can also be in the form of an exchange of real estate, while much undeveloped land has been acquired through coastal reclamation. Using these methods of acquisition, the government of Hong Kong has undertaken extensive housing development programmes in recent years, together with satellite neighbourhoods in the adjacent New Territories.

---

and ownership as a means of attempting to ensure that development is in the interest of the community as a whole.

THE REALIZATION OF PLANNING GAIN

For many years, taxes have often been imposed on private developers and users of land to help finance the provision of associated public-sector development.

Related proportionally to the volume of building planned for any site, *equipment* taxes in France have been imposed as a prior charge to facilitate the development of infrastructure – the tax being collected either when the owner has applied for a building permit or when he or she sells the property to a developer. If the owner has provided land for public road development, he or she has been exempt from the tax. In addition, to help fund the provision of infrastructure, taxes have been placed on the turnovers of commercial firms in the new towns around Paris, but, at least initially, taxation has been low or non-existent in order not to deter business enterprises from moving to these locations.

Italy also has a system of land taxation directly related to the provision of infrastructure. Since the introduction of legislation in 1967, the *Lege Ponte* (Bridge Act), the landowner is obliged to pay all the 'primary' development costs, but for 'secondary' development works the municipality can determine the proportion of costs to be incurred by the landowner.

The realization of planning gain serves much the same purpose as dedicated taxation. It is a benefit, either in cash or in kind, which can accrue to a local authority as a consequence of granting development consent to a private developer (see pages 389–93). In the past, planning gain was normally related solely to the approved development and consisted of negotiated payments towards the cost of access roads, water supply and sewage disposal necessary for the development to take place. Currently, planning gain often includes the private development of less profitable or unprofitable uses of land for the benefit of the community, such as social housing, a library or a leisure centre, in addition to the principal and profitable development for which approval is sought.

The realization of planning gain has evolved into an alternative means of intercepting betterment for the benefit of the local and wider community, although it must be accepted that there is a very thin line between negotiated payments and/or the provision of public services by a private developer, and outright bribery.

LOCAL PROPERTY TAXATION

In most advanced capitalist countries, a system of local taxation and user charges is in place to provide revenue to meet a proportion of the costs of supplying public services. On the assumption that land values or – more precisely – property values are communually-created, various forms of property taxation tax (including site-value rating) are common, and are an important means of raising revenue.

The Attributes of Local Property Taxation

Local property taxes have many advantages:

(1) They are normally simple in form, well-understood and generally accepted by local electorates. Local property taxes are often viewed as being equitable since they are normally related to the value of the real estate.

(2) The tax yield is easily forecast, and there is normally certainty of payment and yield since property is geographically immobile (unlike capital and labour) and real estate taxes cannot easily be evaded.

(3) The costs of collection are relatively small, for example, in the UK they are less than 2 per cent of yield. Normally, once taxable values have been assessed, the tax is easily calculated and can be readily increased or decreased in line with local government expenditure.

(4) Local property taxes being well-understood and broadly equitable, with certainty of payment and small cost of collection – clearly conform with the canons of taxation as set out by Adam Smith in 1776 in *An Inquiry into the Nature and Causes of the Wealth of Nations* (Smith, 1992).

(5) Although a local property tax is normally geared to the capital value of commercial and industrial buildings (as determined by the value of output), it is often a lump sum on residential real estate and thus penalises underoccupation. Where appropriate, this may encourage the owner to rent-out part of his or her dwelling.

(6) Last, but not least, local property taxes might promote accountability and autonomy. In setting the rate of tax, local government is answerable to the local electorate, while, in providing local government with its own source of revenue, property taxes enable it to enjoy a degree of financial independence from central government.

There are also disadvantages:

(1) Although not normally the case with regard to a commercial or industrial property, the value of a house or an apartment is not a reliable guide to the owner's capacity to pay, particularly for the elderly on limited incomes.

(2) Taxes on residential property are often regressive since they can take a higher percentage of the income of the poor than the income of the rich, although this can be remedied directly by a system of rate rebates or indirectly by welfare payments. In the case of non-residential property, there are often similar problems of equity; for example, whereas agricultural land and buildings might not be taxed, retail and industrial premises might be taxed regressively – small firms often finding the tax burden more onerous than large corporations with higher turnovers.

(3) Local property taxes suffer from a lack of buoyancy because they do not increase or decrease automatically with fluctuating property values. For the purposes of taxation, revaluations might take place only after intervals of, say, three or more years.

(4) The payment of local property taxes requires a more conscious effort compared with (for example) a sales tax or income tax paid on behalf

of an employee by an employer. Households may also be deterred from expanding or improving their dwellings since to do so might, in due course, involve a bigger tax liability.

(5) There is not necessarily any connection between the use a taxpayer makes of local services and his or her local property tax liability. Local services, moreover, can be enjoyed by firms and households that are neither based within the locality nor liable to its property tax.

(6) Areas in which the need for local welfare provision is greatest often have the lowest taxable values per head, and therefore the real estate tax as a percentage of taxable value would, through necessity, be high. But in areas where welfare needs are less, taxable values are often high and thus the tax – as a percentage of taxable value – would be low. Government grants might therefore be necessary to reduce the need of poorer authorities to impose high rates of local property taxation, or alternatively revenue could be redistributed from richer to poorer areas.

(7) Local property taxation clearly distorts market prices and thus, in the long-term, has distributional affects. In, for example, figure 9.6(a), the total rent initially paid for the use of a building is $r \times m$. However, in the short-term, the supply of property (line S) is inelastic, thus with the imposition of a local property tax, the demand for the building by the tenant (who is responsible for the payment of the tax) decreases from DD to D_iD_1. In consequence, the landlord will be obliged to lower the property's rent from $r \times m$ to $r_1 \times m$ (assuming that there is an absence of a long-term tenancy agreement). The tax, in effect, has thus been borne by the landlord.

Whereas, in the short-term, the supply of property is inelastic, in the long-term it becomes relatively elastic. Because of the impact of the local property tax on the net income of landlords, they might convert their property to other less burdensome uses, fail to replace them when they fall into serious disrepair, or divert their capital to other, more-profitable or lower-taxed forms of investment. In consequence of the relatively elastic supply, part of the tax burden is passed on to the tenant; for example, in figure 9.6(b), from r to r_2 while the remainder of the tax (rr_1) is incurred by the landlord, the total tax paid being $r_2 - r_1 \times m_1$, and the supply of rented property contracts from m to m_1.

If, however, the revenue from local property taxation finances the improvement in the local infrastructure or the provision of better services, an increase in the demand for property could be generated. With the demand curve shifting to the right, rents would rise and the supply of marketable real estate would expand to m or beyond.

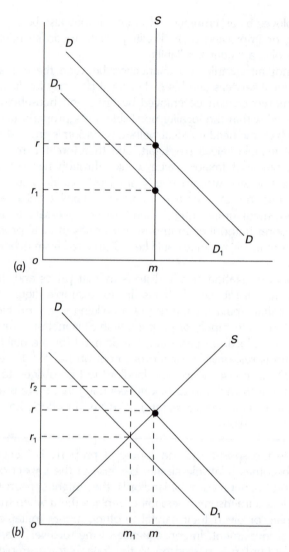

Figure 9.6 *The effects of local property taxation on rents*

NET ANNUAL VALUE AND CAPITAL VALUE AS THE BASIS FOR ASSESSMENT

Normally local property taxes are levied *ad valorem*, but the tax will be imposed in relation *either* to the real estate's net annual value (NAV) *or* its capital value *or* its site-value.

Net Annual Value

To determine NAV, it is initially necessary to estimate the gross annual value of the property (the yearly rent that the real estate might reasonably be expected to let for on a specific date), and then to deduct certain costs which are likely to be incurred by the owner, for example the cost of maintenance and insurance. The resulting NAV has certain advantages:

(1) It is comparatively easy to assess since, in a free market, rentals can be calculated on the basis of comparisons with similar real estate within the same location.
(2) Since both buildings and land are valued, it is probable that yields will be higher than if land alone is the basis of assessment, especially where the building cost of real estate is a high proportion of the total cost.

But there are also serious disadvantages in using NAV as the basis of assessment:

(1) If there is rent control, there is little or no evidence of free-market rents and therefore NAVs might bear little relationship to the value of the property if sold on the open market.
(2) Since the tax falls on buildings, as well as on land, it can be regressive, particularly in the case of residential property where lower-income households might find themselves paying proportionately more tax than that incurred by higher-income owners.
(3) Since repairs, maintenance and improvements might add to the value of the building, the NAV of the property might consequently rise and the owner, as a result, could incur an increased tax liability. A tax based on NAV might thus deter an owner from keeping his or her real estate in reasonable condition.
(4) Compared to urban land, agricultural land yields little or no revenue, to the detriment of rural authorities.

In the UK until 1990–91, local property taxes (*rates*) had been levied since the sixteenth century. Based on annual rental values, rate assessment was increasingly unsatisfactory since market rents had either been eliminated or distorted by rent regulation, and revaluation had not taken place since 1973. Rates were replaced by a poll tax (on the occupation of residential property) and a uniform business rate, but poll tax was superseded by a council tax in 1993 (see below).

In Sweden, local property taxes are levied on annual rental incomes of landlords or the imputed rent income of owner-occupiers, and no depreciation allowance is available to the latter households.

Capital Value

The capital value of property is the price at which it could be sold on an open market. If the capital value equals the NAV, capitalized at the relevant rate of interest, it should produce an equivalent base for taxation as NAV.

However, future-use value might be included in capital value (particularly if there is a highly speculative market) and therefore the capital value of underdeveloped or vacant sites might be higher that their respective NAVs, and the tax liability would be increased. As a result, there would be greater use of existing property and/or redevelopment would be encouraged. If, in the assessment of the capital value (of, for example, slum housing), allowances are made for the state of repair and length of life of the property and the risk of rental default, the capital value will be deflated and the tax base would be smaller. However, if little is spent on repairs and maintenance, net returns relative to gross yields will be high and there might be little financial gain in redeveloping the site.

The introduction of the council tax in the UK, payable by all households, was an attempt to combine a real estate tax based on banded capital values with a system of relief for households on low incomes to reduce the regressive attributes of the tax.

In France until the 1970s, local property taxes were collected on both built and unbuilt land on the basis of annual rental value. They varied, for example, from 0.3 to 0.7 per cent of the assessed value. More recently, capital value has become the basis for assessment, with upper rates of taxes set, for example, at 1–3 per cent.

SITE-VALUE RATING

The essence of SVR is that the site-value (the market selling price of the land alone, as distinct from the buildings and the land on which they stand) should be assessed for taxation on the assumption that it is available for the most profitable permissible development. In different forms, such as land value taxation (LVT) or site value taxation (SVT), SVR is both a betterment tax and a property tax, and has been adopted in several countries such as Denmark, the United States, Australia and New Zealand.

As the basis of a local property tax, SVR has numerous advantages:

(1) SVR is arguably relevant and fair since land values increase as a consequence largely of community development and growth, not through the actions of individual landowners.
(2) Since the site-value rate would be on the value of the site alone, it would not penalize improvements – in contrast to capital value rating.
(3) SVR would encourage development since buildings would not be rated,

and it would be disadvantageous to waste land on uses of low profitability or utility.

(4) Unlike betterment levies, SVR would deter the withholding of undeveloped land from the market.

(5) Research has indicated that SVR could be as remunerative as conventional local property estate taxation based on NAV or capital value, although a higher proportion of the tax yield would come from agricultural and recreational land, and a lower proportion from residential, commercial and industrial areas.

(6) Research has also suggested that it is easier to value the site alone, rather than the combined value of land and structures.

Nevertheless, SVR also has some disadvantages:

(1) The site-value can only be assessed when there is competition for a vacant site. At other times, comparative valuations will need to be undertaken but these might be unreliable.

(2) SVR might necessitate the use of comprehensive land-value maps to ensure precision in valuation over both urban and rural areas.

(3) There are often difficulties in isolating the site-value from the value of the whole property, particularly after improvements have taken place.

(4) Detailed land-use plans (determining permitted development) would need to be produced by planning authorities to deter undesirable piecemeal development.

(5) SVR could cause some hardship to owners/users of agricultural land and underdeveloped urban sites, particularly if potential site-values rather than current values are taken into account. Hardship would be increased if potential values were never realized owing to changing market conditions or changes in planning policy.

(6) Rating on an annual basis would be necessary to avoid inequitable treatment of site owners.

(7) SVR could be more costly to collect than other forms of property taxation.

(8) SVR might only be suitable where land is plentiful and not already developed.

(9) If the environment is constantly changing, the assessment of site-value can only be provisional, but it is unlikely that revaluations would occur as frequently as under the NAV method of assessment.

In spite of these disadvantages, a number of countries and cities have deemed it advantageous to employ SVR (or LVT or SVT) as a property tax.

In Denmark, for example, a site-value tax of between 0.5 and 8.5 per cent has been imposed in recent years on site-values, but, since this was deductable from income tax liability, land has sometimes been held for this purpose. Like its planning system, Denmark's system of valuation is among the most sophisticated in the world. Every four years, every site is revalued and the results are published on land-value maps. There are also revaluations when real estate undergoes a change in status

Australia similarly favoured the imposition of site-value taxation (SVT) on betterment. In Sydney, for example, there has been both a flat-rate city SVT and a progressive SVT levied by the state government of New South Wales – the combined rate having varied, for example, from 2.5 to 5.66 per cent on site-values. Revaluations have occurred every six years for the purpose of tax reassessment.

In the United Kingdom, Lord Roger's Urban Task Force briefly considered SVR as a means of speeding up the release of vacant land in brownfield areas (DETR, 1999), while specific proposals for LVT have been set out by Lichfield and Connellan (2000).

BOX 9.3: LAND-VALUE TAXATION IN THE UNITED STATES

In the United States, a number of cities in Pennsylvania (New Castle, Scranton, Pittsburgh, Harrisburg and McKeesport) pioneered the introduction of a graded land-value tax (LVT), shifting the incidence of tax from buildings to land. In Pittsburg, for example, whereas in 1978 2.4 per cent of the assessed value of a property derived from buildings and 4.9 per cent of the assessed value from land (a ratio of 1 : 2), by 1983 2.7 per cent derived from buildings and as much as 15.1 per cent from land (a ratio of 1 : 5.6) (Cord, 1983).

The equalized tax rates for the five cities in 1982 (soon after the introduction of the graded tax) are shown in table 9.1. In these cities there was a marked reduction in land withheld from the market and windfall gains were intercepted for the benefit of the community. Many other cities in the United States subsequently introduced variations of the graded tax as a general move towards LVT.

Table 9.1   *Graded tax rates, cities in Pennsylvania*

	Buildings (per cent)	Land (per cent)
McKeesport	0.5	2.3
Harrisburg	1.1	3.3
Pittsburgh	0.8	3.3
Scranton	0.9	3.4
New Castle	2.3	4.0

Source: Harrison (1982).

ALTERNATIVE SOURCES OF LOCAL REVENUE

If there are adequate and politically-acceptable alternative sources of local revenue to meet increasing public-sector commitments, particularly at a time of inflation, the level of local property taxation might be 'capped', although it is unlikely that a tax on property would cease to fulfil a role as it has many advantages.

In appraising alternative or concurrent methods of raising local-government revenue, certain fundamental criteria assist in the evaluation:

(1) the subject of the tax should be widely distributed throughout the country;
(2) the tax base should lend itself to variations throughout the country;
(3) the tax should not be disproportionately expensive to administer and collect;
(4) the tax base and its potential yield should be buoyant, both facilitating adjustment over time and providing increases in yield without increasing the rate at which it is levied.

Two forms of alternative local taxation are worthy of consideration.

Local Income Tax (LIT)

LIT is normally related to the ability to pay, it possibly provides a high yield, and is comprehensive and complementary to local property taxation. Those currently evading local property taxation would be required to pay, and LIT has built-in flexibility and buoyancy. But:

(1) Income tax is normally assessed according to the place of employment which, in respect of local revenue collection, would necessitate a complete restructuring.
(2) The physical allocation of income, particularly profits, may be an extremely difficult task geographically. Should the firm be assessed according to the location of its production or to its central management? In addition, prosperous areas would tend to become more attractive, as they would demand lower taxes. This would extend the disparities between areas.
(3) There is a potential time-lag between the assessment and collection of taxes which could bring problems for budgeting.

LIT is in use in many countries, usually alongside income tax levied by central government. In Denmark, for example, although central government collects income tax, a proportion of the revenue is redistributed to local authorities according to the place of residence of the taxpayer. This provides the main source of local-authority revenue for the funding of land acquisition and the provision of local services.

In Sweden, in addition to the central government imposing income tax, municipalities levy income tax at a progressive rate (in recent years at rates ranging from 10 to 18 per cent), while regional councils have tended to impose a flat rate of tax (for example, at 25 per cent). Local authorities have received approximately 50 per cent of all tax revenue, equivalent to about 20 per cent of Sweden's GNP. A large proportion of this revenue finances infrastructure development.

Local Sales Tax (LST)

Local sales taxes are simple and productive, as being related to economic activity they are both flexible and buoyant with automatic collection from the purchaser. However, the tax would tend to be regressive and involve considerable local disparities relating to the boundary at which it would be imposed.

User Charges

In addition to tax revenue, local-authority budgets might, to some extent, rely on service charges. In Germany and the United States, for example, substantial sums are raised from charges paid by users of public services. However, there is a limit to the imposition of user charges in the public sector:

(1) for egalitarian reasons, it might be inappropriate to impose high charges for education or social services;
(2) in the case of 'public goods' (such as street cleaning) it would be impossible to exclude non-payers from the consumption of the benefit.

Conclusions

In the advanced capitalist world – with varying degrees of success – market forces have been constrained, harnessed, replaced or manipulated in order to: control or encourage property development; tax or boost windfall values;

take private land into public ownership or privatize publicly-owned land; or generate and realize planning gain. Throughout much of the twentieth century, governments – according to their political nostrums – have thus regarded urban planning either as a means of helping the market to work more efficiently, or as a mechanism for redistributing land values and land uses more equitably and according to need. At a municipal level, however, it is generally recognized that a source of local revenue is essential for the provision of local services, and debates revolve around which source should be tapped, rather than whether or not local taxation is desirable.

In countries in political and economic transition, and in the newly-industrializing and developing world, planning systems are either in the process of transformation (from former systems of state planning) or in their infancy. But with economic growth, and particularly urban growth, it is a matter of urgency that modern systems of urban planning are introduced, and that means are found – other than a complete reliance on the market – to deal with problems of land scarcity in relation to essential needs, and the question of betterment value. With regard to local property taxation, the adoption of LVT might provide a useful means of not only financing urban services, but also of speeding-up the release of important sites for the development of the local infrastructure (see Vickers, 2000).

REFERENCES

Cord, S. (1983) 'LVT: six steps to meet objections', *Land and Liberty*, 90: 1068–9.
Couch, C. (1990) *Urban Renewal: Theory in Practice*, London: Macmillan.
Cullingworth, B. (1999) 'Introduction and overview', *British Planning: 50 Years of Urban and Regional Policy*, London: Athlone Press.
Darin-Drabkin, H. (1977) *Land Policy and Urban Growth*, Oxford: Pergamon.
DETR (1999) *Towards an Urban Renaissance: Final Report of the Urban Task Force Chaired by Lord Rogers of Riverside*, London: HMSO and E. & F.N. Spon.
Evans, B. (1999) 'Time for a new look at land and taxation', *Town and Country Planning*, 68: 8–9.
George, H. (1979 edition) *Progress and Poverty*, London: Hogarth.
Grant, M. (1999) 'Compensation and betterment', in Cullingworth, B. (ed.), *British Planning: 50 Years of Urban and Regional Policy*, London: Athlone Press.
Harrison, F. (1982) 'The Pennsylvanian tax raiders', *Land and Liberty*, 89: 1056–7.

Lichfield, N. and Connellan, O. (2000) *Land Value and Community Betterment Taxation in Britain: Proposals for Legislation and Practice*, Cambridge MA: Lincoln Institute for Land Policy.

Lichfield, N. and Darin-Drabkin, H. (1980) *Land Policy in Planning*, London: George Allen & Unwin.

Ricardo, D. (1971 edition) *Principles of Political Economy and Taxation*, Harmondsworth: Penguin.

Smith, A. (1992 edition) *The Nature and Causes of the Wealth of Nations*, Harmondsworth: Penguin.

Vickers, T. (2000) 'LVT – better than betterment levy', *Town and Country Planning*, 69: 5.

10

Welfare Economics, the Environment and Urban Congestion

INTRODUCTION

One only needs to cast a glance at urban activities to realize the degree to which actions are encouraged or constrained in some way in an attempt to bring about a more efficient allocation of resources: control of urban traffic flows, subsidies to public transport, planning controls and limits on permitted housing densities, to name but a few. In addition, public-sector infrastructure projects (such as roads, bridges and airports) will generally affect the well-being or welfare of a large number of individuals, and since many of these benefits (and costs) are of a non-monetary nature, economic theory must provide the means to assess such changes.

In the private sector, direct monetary costs and benefits (revenue) determine the profitability or otherwise of increased output and investment. In the public sector, all (not only monetary) costs and benefits for *all* individuals affected by an investment must in some way be evaluated. Welfare economics, then, is the study of how such economic changes can be assessed in terms of the welfare implications that affect individuals in society.

Welfare economics helps to address such problems as how to evaluate costs and benefits of a non-monetary nature, how to assess social benefit when no charge is made for a public facility (such as parks, open spaces and monuments) and how to adjust for market failure – for example, when decisions are made in the private sector or by private individuals which fail to reflect costs imposed on others (such as urban traffic).

First, it is necessary to consider how we can define and compare the welfare, utility or well-being of individuals in society. Secondly, the measurement and assessment of levels of welfare and changes therein must be addressed. Thirdly, the question of whether the free market can always be relied upon to maximize the well-being or welfare of society must be considered. Fourthly, the means by which the public sector evaluates the welfare implications of investment projects (cost–benefit analysis) must be looked at closely. Lastly, the case for public control over the urban environment must be examined, with reference to examples.

THE CONCEPT OF ECONOMIC WELFARE

Few people would argue with the observation that as an individual's consumption of goods and services increases, so his or her well-being, satisfaction or economic welfare might also be expected to increase. In practice, this could occur either because of a rise in the individual's income (with prices of goods and services unchanged) or because of a fall in the price of some goods and services consumed by that individual (assuming the individual's income remains unchanged). Of course, the individual's increased consumption of, say, cigarettes might conceivably do him or her some harm, but in general it must be assumed here that the individual knows best. In other words, his or her change in welfare must be measured as he himself or she herself values it – that is, in relation to what he or she is willing to pay to achieve a particular pattern of consumption. Problems arise, however, when we try to go further. For example, how is the welfare of different individuals to be compared? If it is realized that different individuals will generally have different capacities for deriving satisfaction from a unit of expenditure, the problem of making interpersonal comparisons of welfare becomes apparent.

To take a simple problem, how is a move from a situation where all the population have real incomes of £100 per week to one where half the population have £200 per week and the rest nothing, to be assessed? Both yield the same overall monetary value for society but with very different distributional consequences. While traditional measures of national output or consumption suffer from these (and other) problems of interpretation, we can for the moment fall back on another criterion for assessing economic changes which provides a more widely acceptable starting point.

In an attempt to remove the problem of interpersonal comparisons in assessing changes in social welfare, Vilfredo Pareto (1848–1923) suggested the following criterion: any economic change can be unambiguously said to improve social welfare only if at least one member's welfare increases while no other individual's welfare diminishes. Changes which satisfy this criterion are termed 'Pareto improvements' or 'gains'. This proposition is illustrated in figure 10.1.

The vertical and horizontal axes measure the level of satisfaction or utility of two individuals. A and B. At the initial position r the welfare levels of A and B can be seen by reading off the corresponding points on the two axes. Alternative situations s and t correspond to different bundles and distribu-

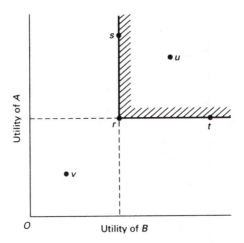

Figure 10.1 *Pareto gains and losses*

tion of goods between *A* and *B*. They yield situations where one individual is better off while the utility of the other individual is unchanged. However, at a position such as *u*, both individuals are better off. In contrast, at *v* both are worse off. Of all these changes, *s*, *t* and *u* all conform to the criterion for a Pareto improvement. In fact, any position between *s* and *t*, within the hatched area, also conforms to this criterion.

In practice, situations are likely to arise where although one or more individuals may suffer from a change, a great many others may, in fact, gain. Kaldor (1939) and Hicks (1940) suggested that as long as the gainers from such a change could fully compensate the losers while themselves remaining better off, the change could produce a net welfare gain for society in line with the Pareto criterion. Kaldor went on to suggest that the job of the economist was only to point out when such a gain was possible, the actual process of compensation being another matter – political, legal or interpersonal in nature. Such changes could then be termed *potential* Pareto improvements, and the concept is clearly more attractive and operational than one where no-one should lose out from any project.

Again, the point can be illustrated using the same diagram as previously, but assuming this time that output is fixed and corresponds to a particular bundle of goods which may in principle be distributed in a variety of ways between individuals *A* and *B*. Line *11* illustrates this proposition (figure 10.2) and combinations of welfare between the two consumers may occur anywhere along this utility possibility curve depending on the distribution of goods. Similarly, *22* represents possible outcomes resulting from alternative distributions at a higher level of output.

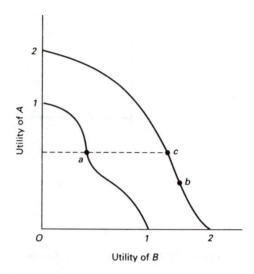

Figure 10.2 *Potential Pareto improvements*

The actual position of the individuals along any utility possibility curve or frontier such as *11* or *22* will be determined by the distribution of income between them. However, this will have been determined by the level of production itself, since the consumers are also the owners of factors of production within the economy. In sum, given the ownership of factors, any level of output automatically determines factor rewards and therefore the distribution of income. The latter in turn determines what goods the individuals may purchase and consequently their respective levels of welfare. If, for example, there is a move from *11* to *22*, it may be found that the two individuals move from a point such as *a* on *11* to one such as *b* on *22*. Individual *A* is clearly worse off at *b* since the income distribution and relative prices have moved against him. Nevertheless, a Pareto gain is possible: *B* could in principle take a cut in consumption along *22*, donate goods to *A* and thus raise *A*'s welfare back to his or her pre-change position at *c*. According to the Hicks–Kaldor criteria, the change from *a* to *b* would be approved as a potential Pareto gain.

Of course, in the absence of lump sum taxes on beneficiaries such as *B*, there is no way of actually compelling *B* to compensate *A* (unless *B* has in some way infringed *A*'s property rights). Clearly, it is no good relying on *B*'s altruism to solve this problem, but without payment of compensation a Pareto gain remains only a possibility rather than an established event.

The problem of how to measure costs and benefits of an intangible nature will be dealt with later. For the moment we need to look at how, in general, non-priced benefits and costs relate to the present notion of social welfare and changes within it.

WELFARE, EXTERNALITIES AND PUBLIC GOODS

In relating measures of welfare to output of goods and services in the economy, such as gross national product (GNP), we are assuming implicitly that the welfare of individuals and societies is dependent on the consumption of *marketed* as opposed to *non-marketed* output. Hence, such measures of economic welfare will largely avoid valuing the quality of, say, environmental services. In a broad sense these include aspects of both the physical and the social environment; for example, the quality of air and water, the countryside and access to it, and the right to peace and quiet.

First of all, however, a general model needs to be developed which will give a view of the components of the economic system as a whole. This model may then be adapted to include also non-marketed goods and services.

We shall start with a simple model which comprises two individuals, two marketed goods and two factors of production. Factor and good markets are assumed to be perfectly competitive. Combining the two factors (say, land and labour) in the production of different quantities of the two goods, the production frontier *PP* given in figure 10.3 can be derived.

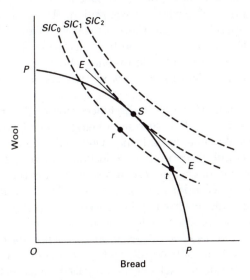

Figure 10.3 *Welfare maximization: a simple model*

Moving along *PP* it can be seen how many units of one good can be exchanged in production for one unit of the other good. This is known as the marginal rate of transformation. The concave shape of *PP* illustrates that factors are not equally efficient in each sector, so that when resources are transferred from, say, wool to bread production, although the latter increases, it does so at a diminishing rate. Combinations of the two goods (here bread and wool) which are to the left of *PP*, such as *r*, are clearly *possible* but also *inefficient* and correspond to suboptimal use of the two factors.

The two consumers' preferences for the two goods available are given by the series of social indifference curves, *SIC*. Higher curves denote higher levels of welfare for *both* consumers. Points along each curve denote bundles of the two goods between which the two individuals are indifferent (that is, yield identical levels of welfare).

For the two individuals to maximize welfare, production and consumption must occur at *S*, which corresponds to the highest attainable *SIC*. At this point, SIC_1 is at a tangent to the production frontier, and the slopes of both curves are therefore the same (*EE*). This indicates that the rate at which goods are exchanged in production along the production frontier (marginal rate of transformation) is equal to the rate at which the individuals wish to exchange the same goods in consumption (marginal rate of substitution). These rates are in turn equal to the market price ratio of the two goods *EE*, which can therefore be viewed as the price ratio under conditions of welfare maximization. A point such as *t*, while being *technically efficient* in the sense of being on the production frontier, is *economically inefficient* in terms of welfare maximization. This can be seen either because it corresponds to a lower level of social welfare, SIC_0, or because the marginal rates of substitution and transformation differ; specifically, at the margin, society would prefer to exchange bread for more wool in consumption even if the relative price of wool rises (as occurs when we move from *t* to *S*).

Unfortunately, imperfections in the functioning of the free market may in practice prevent a position such as *S* being reached. There are several potential sources of market imperfection which affect good or factor prices; they include monopolistic control of production, various distortions in factor markets and the non-pricing of certain resources. It is principally the latter which is of most concern for present purposes. The non-pricing of certain resources (for example, environmental services) is in practice quite common and results because production (or consumption) in one sector of the economy can have a negative influence on production (or consumption) in another sector, without any corresponding monetary (or other transfer) taking place. Such non-market effects are called 'externalities', and these will now be considered in more detail.

Externalities

Externalities can be defined as benefits or costs which accrue to an individual, group or firm as a direct result of *consumption* or *production* by another individual, group or firm for which no price is paid or no payment is received. In the following discussion we shall deal mainly with *negative* externalities that involve non-market costs between individuals/firms, individuals/individuals or firms/firms. *Positive* externalities involving non-market benefits also exist and their analysis is simply a mirror image of the former.

Let us assume that, still in the context of the previous model, we have a case of 'production on production' externality. Assume that two goods are produced (beer and leather), and that the factory producing leather dumps toxic waste products into the river, resulting in the beer factory downstream having to treat its water supply, which is required for brewing. The resultant increase in costs for the brewery may well be in excess of the cost if the waste had been treated initially at the tannery.

Let us assume this is the case and that for only a very small extra cost the leather firm could eliminate its waste – although quite clearly it will not do so unless there is some legal or financial constraint imposed. If the amount of labour available is fixed, we can illustrate the output possibilities in the two industries as in figure 10.4.

Lines *OL* and *OB* show the output possibilities for each industry considered *separately*. They show, for example, that if six units of labour are employed in each industry, a total of six units each of leather and beer may be produced. However, since we have assumed that leather production imposes a negative externality on beer production, we need to establish the

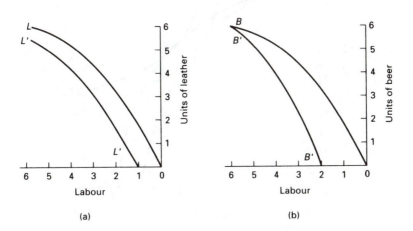

Figure 10.4 *'Production on production' externalities*

outcome when *both* industries are considered *together*. This situation is illustrated by B'B' and OL; leather production is unchanged (OL) but beer production is now lower for any number of labour units employed (assuming for simplicity that some units are employed in eliminating the source of the problem). As illustrated, OB and B'B' touch at a certain point. This is because we have assumed fixed resources (say six units of labour), so that the point of intersection of B'B' and OB corresponds to zero production of leather, where all units are employed in beer production.

The final line, L'L', illustrates the position in the leather firm where costs of removing the toxic waste are taken into account. For simplicity it has been assumed that this involves a fixed cost of diverting one unit of labour towards some alternative method of waste removal.

The production frontier facing this society for any combination of employment between the two industries can now be derived. In figure 10.5, SS illustrates the production frontier when leather production is uncontrolled, and S'S' illustrates the case when the leather firm undertakes waste removal. The latter represents the 'true' production frontier reflecting the *social* (as opposed to the *private*) marginal rate of transformation, but will clearly only be reached if the leather producer has some incentive (or duty) to control waste disposal. Only if this occurs is society able to reach a higher social indifference curve SIC_1 which in this case also results in higher

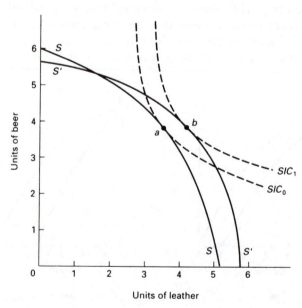

Figure 10.5 *Production frontiers and the internalization of external costs*

production levels of *both* goods (from *a* to *b*). In the presence of external-ities (as discussed previously) such a move can be achieved by setting an appropriate tax on the firm or group which generates the externalities (more details will be given later). This process is referred to as *'internalization'*, that is, the setting of a market price on otherwise non-priced cost (or ben-efits). In this case, only if the external cost is made internal to the leather firm will optimal decisions regarding output and pricing be made in the economy (Lipsey and Lancaster, 1957; Baumol, 1972). As a result, social welfare can be maximized at point *b*.

One final comment on this example is that we have not included any estimation of the possible benefits accruing to other users of the river (for example, from fishing, bathing etc.). If such benefits exist then the policy will clearly have resulted in both a greater production volume and an improved level of environmental quality. For other types of externality, such as those which impinge directly on the individuals' consumption of, say, environmental benefits, the analysis is complicated because such consump-tion does not generally rate in any standard monetary measure of national welfare. For example, while the construction of a new airport will bring measurable economic benefits, the disbenefits to nearby residents in terms of noise, congestion and pollution will not be included in measures of national welfare such as GNP. Nevertheless, it is clear that these external effects have a real impact on personal welfare.

The problem then is one of evaluating such non-monetary gains and losses and expressing them in monetary terms. This will be discussed, but before doing so there is another important category of goods, the pro-vision of which involves externalities. Such goods are known as *public goods*.

Public goods

The reference to 'public' implies anything from a group of individuals to a locality or region, country or group of countries. A pure *public* good has characteristics which are opposite to those of a pure *private* good. The latter are *rival* in the sense that consumption of the good (for example, a shirt) by one person precludes its consumption by another person or persons. Following from this, it is clear that the greater the demand by con-sumers, the more units of the good must be produced and the more resources must be devoted to the production of these units.

Private goods also have the characteristic of *excludability* – a unit or units of the good can be consumed by one person to the exclusion of others, and consumption of the good affects the welfare of no other individual. The latter condition implies an absence of externalities.

In contrast, 'pure' public goods are both *non-rival* and *non-excludable*.

They are non-rival in the sense that one unit can satisfy more than one consumer, implying that no additional resources are required as the number of consumers rises. Public goods are non-excludable in that once provided, it is impossible to exclude anyone from consuming them – in other words, the effects of providing a good are automatically extended to the whole community. As such, the good is associated with (positive) externalities (such as street lighting). Perhaps the most obvious example is national defence. The decision by governments to provide defence automatically extends the benefits to all, regardless of whether or not they have contributed to its expense (non-excludable). Also, the cost is essentially the same however many people are covered by defence (that is, non-rival). In practice, few goods are 'pure' public goods. Many goods, however, share certain public good characteristics.

One of the key points shared by public goods is that provision would either not occur or would be suboptimal if left to the free market. This problem arises because, since provision automatically benefits everyone, it is in the interest of the individual to understate his or her preferences and avoid payment. In other words, individuals would attempt to 'free-ride' (that is, avoid payment) while still enjoying the benefits of the good. If this is true for each individual, then, taken as a whole, society may not provide the good even if it is in everyone's interest to do so. Of course, it is possible that one or more individuals who rate the good very highly in their scale of preferences might be prepared to foot the bill. One problem here is that the good may then reflect only the preferences of these individuals and be underprovided relative to the preferences of the rest of the community.

Clearly, also, no producer would wish to undertake marketed production of the good, since it would be impossible to prevent individuals consuming the good without paying (non-rival).

In contrast, the state will often be in a better position to estimate the demand for public goods, undertake their provision and organize payment via taxation. Nevertheless, problems may remain – in particular, some individuals may be taxed too highly relative to their valuation of the good, while others may be taxed too lightly. However, in the context of a large number of public goods, individuals may find that excess taxation for some public goods may be offset by undertaxation relative to their preferences for others.

While the case for supply via public institutions may appear clear-cut for 'pure' public goods, it has been shown that many goods exhibit only *some* public good characteristics. Is there, then, a case for public supply of these goods? For example, while environmental resources such as air quality, water quality, peace and quiet, and open spaces are largely public goods in the sense that once provided they are widely available, they may nevertheless be rival and excludable in the sense that spatial opportunities for their consumption may differ. Facilities such as open spaces in urban areas may become congested so that additional users reduce the benefits to existing users. In particular, residential immobility may mean that different groups in society have unequal access to environmental resources. If income were evenly distributed and households perfectly mobile, spatial differences in access to environmental resources might not matter. Individuals with low environmental preferences could continue to live in, say, decaying inner cities, while those with high environmental preferences could choose to live in more peaceful locations with greater access to environmental resources. Other things being equal, substantial local differences in environmental services would eventually become capitalized in different property values. Since, however, assumptions relating to income distribution and housing mobility are probably not met, the likely result is that residents living in low environmental conditions are not so much those who place low values on such resources as those who cannot afford to move or who cannot find similar accommodation elsewhere.

Another important example of 'impure' public goods involves goods where, although it is possible to exclude consumers, it would be inefficient or suboptimal to do so. Examples of such goods are public roads, museums, bridges and parks, Here, as long as there is no congestion of the facility, there is no additional cost, either in provision or to other users, of adding one more consumer. In principle, a toll or other charge could be made, but such a charge (assuming no congestion) would lead to a lowering of welfare. This point can be illustrated by considering a major tunnel project.

Assume, first, that the welfare benefits of the project – that is, the sum total of the potential users' willingness to pay – can be measured accurately from the demand curve for the good in question (Pearce, 1983). It will also be assumed that the social (or opportunity) cost of the project is reflected accurately in the costs involved, measured in monetary terms, and that overall, the total benefits of the project outweigh the total costs.

In the present case, the demand curve for tunnel crossings could be estimated from analysis of existing traffic flows in the area plus some estimate of traffic likely to be generated by the new facility. A social cost–benefit analysis would also include indirect benefits (or costs) of the project such as reduction on congestion elsewhere, but for purposes of simplicity such effects will be ignored in the present ease.

The estimated demand curve is given by DD in figure 10.6. It shows that at a zero price per crossing C_1 crossings would be undertaken, while at a charge of P_1 no crossings at all would be undertaken. If the tunnel is provided publicly at zero user cost, then the total welfare gain (willingness to pay) is given by the area under the demand curve DD. If, however, the tunnel is provided and run by private individuals who charge a toll, the result

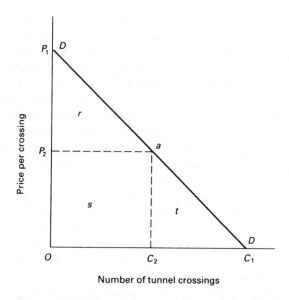

Figure 10.6 *Demand curve for tunnel crossings*

will be different. Assuming revenue maximization is desired, the private supplier will charge a toll such as P_2 per crossing. In this case only C_2 crossings will be undertaken, and $C_1 - C_2$ crossings will have been dissuaded by the toll. The benefit derived from C_2 crossings is given by the areas r and s, which represent the willingness to pay for these crossings. However, the actual revenue received is only area s (that is, $P_2 \times C_2$). The remaining area, known as the *consumer surplus* (area r), represents the difference between willingness to pay and the amount actually paid for the service.

It is immediately evident that the reduced number of crossings results in a lower level of consumer benefit – that is, area $r + s$ in contrast to area $r + s + t$, where no charge is made. Although revenue of area s is obtained by the tunnel operator, this is of no allocative importance; the tunnel would otherwise have been financed via taxation, and charging a toll merely constitutes another form of payment. Area t, however, is of allocative significance as it represents a lowering of welfare because fewer crossings are undertaken with a toll. A further feature is of note: if the total cost of the project had been estimated to be just above $r + s$ (which is still exceeded by total benefits of $r + s + t$, assuming zero user cost), then although the project would have produced a net welfare gain, no private supplier (charging a positive price) would have been able to provide the tunnel, assuming similar costs.

Are there ever circumstances under which even the public sector would be justified in charging a toll? In practice, such charges are observed on the Severn Bridge and the Dartford Tunnel in London, and are widely observed on motorways, bridges and tunnels throughout Europe.

Several explanations may be put forward. First, the facility may be largely specific to a particular area or group of users, and in practice it may be impossible to distinguish such groups in order to cover construction and ongoing costs through taxation. In practice, however, with increasing long-distance private travel and haulage it may become more difficult to view any particular facility as region- or area-specific, thereby increasing the case for deriving revenue from road taxation or even personal or indirect taxation. This is especially true if there are important non-monetary costs involved in actually charging a toll, such as long delays.

Secondly, it is possible that excessive use of the facility will itself result in non-monetary costs – for example, too many visitors may result in damage to historic monuments or may affect the enjoyment of other visitors. If the facility becomes congested, causing damage, delay or other forms of externality, then a charge in proportion to the damage and inconvenience caused becomes justified, since it is now no longer the case that the good can be enjoyed by everyone, irrespective of the number of users.

A final and important category of public goods involves goods which, although mainly rival and excludable, nevertheless exhibit important external benefits. Such goods (known as merit goods) include health, education, housing, public libraries and fire services.

In principle these goods could all be provided by the private sector but, because of externalities, private provision would result in suboptimal supply. Additionally, it may be felt that public provision at low or zero user cost is preferable to private provision, since even if the latter is subsidized, there may nevertheless be individuals who are too poor to afford even this. Moreover, the possible 'costs' of non-consumption by the individual may be high or so severe that public provision at zero user cost is considered indispensable (for example, the fire service).

There exist numerous types of activity which exhibit actual or potential externalities. While the case for direct public control does not extend equally to all such activities, indirect control in the form of taxes and subsidies can often achieve the desired result of optimal resource allocation.

HOUSING, EXTERNALITIES AND PUBLIC POLICY

Consider urban housing improvement where property-on-property type externalities exist. In such cases, properties are generally run-down and in need of renovation. This will involve substantial financial outlay for long-term improvements such as reroofing, rewiring, plumbing and glazing, as well as for shorter-term but more 'obvious' improvements such as redecorating. If all properties in the area were renovated then it is likely that property values would rise sufficiently to at least compensate owners for their expenditure on major maintenance items. However, if only one or a few owners undertake the investment, their property values alone might not increase sufficiently to compensate them if the area as a whole remains undesirable. Worse than this, if the area was already in a state of cumulative decline, house owners who invested might find they had done so in an asset that was actually declining in real value (Baumol, 1965). In this situation, nothing may persuade house owners to undertake major or even more minor repairs.

The problem, of course, is that while everyone may gain from joint action to improve an area, the benefits derived from housing renovation are substantially *non-excludable* in the sense that external benefits to other householders (who do nothing) occur in the form of an improved neighbourhood and, hence, higher property values. The 'residential environment' can be said, therefore, to have public good characteristics, and in consequence faces problems of suboptimal provision. Many households are likely to 'free-ride' and enjoy the benefits of an improved environment (and higher property values) without undertaking investment. Yet if everyone does the same, no renovation will occur, even though all may want it. This situation is referred to as the 'prisoner's dilemma' (Davis and Whinston, 1961).

One solution is for improvement grants to be concentrated on areas of greatest housing decay. This would provide confidence in an area and encourage owners to undertake improvements which they might not otherwise contemplate for the reasons just discussed. As long as the overall benefits to residents exceed costs to the state in subsidy and administration, plus the renovation costs paid by residents themselves, then the project will have produced a net improvement in social welfare.

Alternatively, or in addition, the state or local government could undertake selective compulsory purchase followed by renovation and eventual sale or letting on to the residential market. Lastly, with wider use of compulsory purchase powers, wholesale redevelopment of an area may be contemplated.

Whichever solution is chosen, some form of public intervention is required to ensure that existing residents do not lose out. They may suffer if, for example, excessive private redevelopment in more intensive uses (such as offices) occurs, or if overextensive housing redevelopment causes large-scale residential displacement. If housing improvement programmes simply push existing residents into even more precarious housing conditions, then the change can hardly be described as a 'Pareto improvement'.

Public intervention in housing supply provides a further example. The case for public provision of subsidised housing has traditionally rested on three main arguments. First is the argument for redistribution in kind, which assumes that certain groups in society, for a variety of reasons, are likely to underconsume housing and remain ill-housed in spite of quite high levels of public spending on income support. Secondly, and linked to the first argument, is the view that society must ensure that a minimum standard of housing consumption is established and maintained. Although other reasons may exist (for example, to avoid overcrowding), the principal one may be that poor housing standards represent an environmental health risk. Public supply of low-cost housing may thus be seen partly as an alternative to controlling standards at the lower end of the private housing (and rented) sector. Thirdly, since a system of income subsidies alone may be unable to tackle regional and local shortages of adequate housing for low-income families, it may be thought necessary to intervene on the supply side to provide sufficient housing of suitable standard directly, at an affordable and controlled cost to residents.

The problem associated with a 'pure' income subsidy to tenants can be illustrated by comparing income transfers with price subsidies, such as low-cost housing provision. In figure 10.7, point a on the budget line CC gives the initial position of the low-income household. At this point it is achieving its highest possible level of welfare, given its (non-subsidized) budget constraint. It is consuming H_0 housing and G_0 other goods at this point.

Assume that the government wishes to achieve a minimum standard of housing consumption equal to H_1. If it provides an income subsidy it will need to raise the household's income level to $C + S$ to achieve this ($C + S$ is parallel to CC but vertically above it by the level of subsidy). The household now maximizes welfare at point b on the new budget line $C + S$. Note that if the pattern of household indifference curves had shown less preference for housing as income rose, then the degree of subsidy S required to achieve H_1 would have been much greater.

Alternatively, the government could lower the relative price of housing to CC' (say via public provision) and could then enforce a minimum standard of housing H_1. Suppose this is what happens and compare this situation with the alternative of an income subsidy discussed earlier. By providing H_1 housing at a reduced cost to the household of CC', the total cost to the state is given by the vertical distance between CC and CC', that is, xc. The cost of the income subsidy which would be required to achieve the same objective is given by the vertical distance between C and $C + S$, and is equal to S or xb. It can be seen that xb clearly exceeds xc, illustrating the point that the least-cost method of achieving a target level of housing consumption is via direct provision/price subsidy.

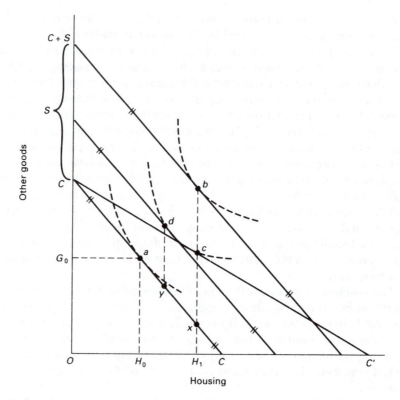

Figure 10.7 *Housing subsidies and the consumption of housing services*

In most European countries these aims have been achieved through the quasipublic sector – including co-operatives, housing associations and municipal housing corporations, which generally have received public subsidies in return for maintaining quality levels, a given proportion of low-income tenants and approved rents.

But what has happened to household welfare? It can be argued that since *b* lies on a higher indifference curve than *c*, the income subsidy has raised household welfare by a greater amount than the price subsidy. The point here, however, is whether society really wishes to achieve this degree of redistribution – if *xb* is judged to be excessive, then the price subsidy should be favoured instead. In practice, however, the state cannot even be sure that an income subsidy of *xb* will be sufficient to persuade all low-income households to consume a minimum of H_1 housing. Some may purchase considerably more and others less, yet it is impossible to vary the subsidy in line with individual preferences!

In conclusion, then, the view that income transfers are in some way optimal, in that they allow more individual choice than subsidies to housing provision, cannot be supported, assuming that the main reason for intervention is because of negative externalities (social costs) generated by low-standard housing. To make this point absolutely clear, a comparison can be made with an income support policy of the same budgetary cost as the price subsidy. This is shown by dy (equals cx) in figure 10.7. As shown, d corresponds to the same level of welfare as point c, but to a level of housing consumption well below the desired level of H_1. The situation could just as easily have involved both a lower level of welfare *and* lower housing consumption. A number of studies show that the income elasticity of demand for housing rarely exceeds unity, suggesting that rather large income transfers may be required to encourage housing consumption (Vipond and Walker, 1972; Ball and Kirwan, 1977).

In practice, local-authority housing and housing-association accommodation probably conform most to the idea of a 'pure' price subsidy (achieved through central-government grant). Mortgage interest relief (MIR) probably conforms less; although MIR no longer has a 'perverse' income effect (lowering the relative price of housing *more* for *higher* income groups because of relief at higher marginal tax rates), it still does nothing to help those on low or variable incomes who could not in any case obtain (sufficient) mortgage finance.

COST–BENEFIT ANALYSIS

In the private sector, investment decisions are made with reference to the market mechanism on the basis of estimated monetary costs and benefits. Cost–benefit analysis (CBA) is basically an extension of these investment appraisal methods with modifications to make them suitable for project appraisal in the public sector. The main distinction is that public-sector CBA attempts to account for all the costs and benefits which affect the welfare of individuals, including those of a non-monetary nature. To facilitate comparison and assessment it is usual for such non-monetary costs or benefits to be translated in some way into monetary terms.

From the 1960s onwards, the CBA technique was extended to cover a wide range of applications, including water resource management, motorways, nationalized industries, airport locations, forestry, recreational facilities and a wide range of urban investment projects. While individual projects may pose specific problems, there are a number of considerations which are common to most.

(1) The first of these concerns the notion that projects in the public sector should be capable of achieving a potential Pareto improvement in social welfare. That is, expected social benefits should *exceed* expected

social costs (all appropriately discounted to present values). Here social benefits involve any gain in welfare resulting from the project, including intangible – that is, non-market benefits (for example, investment in public transport may produce benefits in the form of lower congestion, accidents, noise and pollution). Furthermore, since many public facilities (such as parks) are provided free of charge to users, social benefit, determined by willingness to pay (WTP) criteria, may have to be estimated indirectly. Various methods exist and may involve one or more of the following:

(i)   Consideration of demand for similar facilities elsewhere for which charges are made (such as historic monuments).
(ii) Extensive questionnaire analysis of potential users. Although the problem here is that in the case of public goods where 'free-riding' occurs, individuals may deliberately understate their preferences.
(iii) By implication from observed behaviour – for example, with recreational facilities (for example, in the Lake District of England) demand may be seen to fall with increasing distance from the facility. Willingness to pay can be imputed from the additional travel costs (in time and money) that users are known to incur as distance increases.

Social costs will include any intangible costs (such as environmental damage, noise, nuisance and congestion) as well as the construction and ongoing cost of the project – reflecting the production forgone (that is, opportunity cost) when resources are moved to the public sector. Concerning the latter, two problems may arise. First, if there is imperfect competition in the supply of goods (or factors) used in production or construction, then market price may exceed marginal cost – that is, the true cost of the good to society. Seen in another way, if the project's purchase of input X increases the output of a monopolist supplier, the relevant opportunity cost relates to the marginal cost of extra resources hired and not to the observed (and higher price) charged by the monopolist. Similarly, if workers being employed on a project would otherwise have remained unemployed, then hiring them at the going wage will not result in a reduction of output elsewhere in the economy – hence the marginal cost to society is, in fact, less than the wage rate paid to the labourer (Price, 1977). It can be noted that the net cost to the Exchequer will also be lower than the wage rate in this case, since the government benefits from lower unemployment and social security payments and receives higher direct and indirect taxes.

Secondly, market prices may require adjustment to take account of indirect taxes (subtracted) or subsidies (added), or because market prices may not reflect social costs adequately (for example, farmers may be unaware that their farming techniques are impoverishing the soil). However, while consideration should always be given to the need for adjusting market prices, in practice it may not always be feasible to do so; in many cases it may be too difficult or too costly to obtain the necessary information with a good degree of accuracy.

(2) The second set of considerations concerns the evaluation of non-market gains and losses. Here it is useful to distinguish two categories of intangibles. The first is where, although no direct market exists, there is nevertheless an indirect (or surrogate) market in other goods which is in some way influenced by the intangibles in question. The process of defining such alternative markets is known as shadow pricing. For example, although there is no market for peace and quiet, if individuals buying and selling houses are observed to place higher or lower valuations on similar properties in quieter or noisier situations, then resulting differences in house values can be taken to represent the willingness to pay for peace and quiet. However, it is necessary to isolate all other factors influencing property prices; for example, although house prices may fall near motorways or airports, there may exist locational advantages which would tend to counteract the disadvantages. Hence, basing an analysis solely on observed price variations may tend to produce an underestimate of the willingness to pay for peace and quiet. Also, while individuals may be good judges of peace and quiet, they may be less likely to have full information about other environmental effects (such as lead pollution) – but even if they did, it is unlikely that the full effects would be reflected in the housing market, since many households may not have a real choice of relocating elsewhere. Overall, then, the presumption is that intangible costs of an environmental nature are likely to be partially, but not fully, reflected (or internalized) in the property market.

Another example is the valuation of travel time, widely applied in transport studies, where time savings may account for by far the largest category of benefit deriving from motorway or road schemes. A distinction is made between time savings in work-time and those in leisure-time. Concerning the former, hourly earnings (plus some savings on overheads) may be taken to represent production gained from the time saving of one hour (or *pro rata*), assuming that the wage rate is an adequate reflection of the workers' marginal product. One problem here is that, in practice, large rather than small time savings are more likely to result in productive work and, in reverse, longer travel times (for example, by train or aircraft) may not always result in lost production if, for example, businessmen are able to work while travelling. Time savings during leisure time could, theoretically, be valued at a similar rate, since if workers are able to choose their hours of work then, at the margin, they should be expected to value an hour's work at an equivalent rate to an hour's leisure. In practice such choice is rarely available, hence an alternative approach to the evaluation of leisure time must be sought. For example, if an individual is observed to choose a faster but more expensive means of travel in preference to a slower and cheaper alternative, then as long as no other factors (such as comfort) come into play, his or her willingness to pay for time saved on the faster route in terms of the cost difference can be measured. Using this method, various studies have suggested that leisure-time values are proportional to travellers' incomes, at around 25 per cent of the latter, although considerably higher or lower values cannot be ruled out (Pearce, 1971).

It is likely that, in practice, an individual's valuation of leisure time may vary from case to case and depend on many other factors, including frequency, length of trip and means of travel. Nevertheless, travel-time evaluation has played an important role in many studies, including the Roskill Report on the third London airport (Roskill Commission on the Third London Airport, 1970–1971), and the Victoria Line Study (Foster and Beesley, 1963; Layard, 1972). In the former, although the Foulness site produced the lowest estimates of noise-nuisance cost, the procedure adopted resulted in these benefits being vastly outweighed by its more distant location because of the high valuation placed on travel-time savings of relatively high-income air passengers. In the Victoria Line Study, the valuation of travel time proved less contentious. Since the new line would benefit passengers (over and above the revenue collected) it was reasonable to assume that users would have been willing to pay for the extra convenience (and time saving) of a direct line. Furthermore, since congestion would be reduced elsewhere in the transport system, some estimate of time savings here was essential.

A second category of intangibles involves those for which no efficient surrogate market exists. The Roskill Commission Study just mentioned, for example, placed no value on the loss of wildlife or preservation of countryside because of the difficulty of valuation. Yet even in these circumstances, a residual approach may be adopted. If a dam project, for example, is expected to produce an excess of measurable benefits over costs of £2 million, decision-makers can at least come to some conclusion as to whether they consider this figure to be sufficient to outweigh the loss of countryside and recreational amenities. The attractions of this approach may, however, be reduced if many intangibles exist.

(3) Distributional issues represent the third major consideration. Even if a project is expected to produce an excess of social benefit over social cost, there may still be some objection that the criterion of a potential Pareto improvement tells us nothing about *who* gains and *who* loses. In other words, as it stands, the criterion carries no distributional weight; it cannot, for example, help us to decide between, say, two projects where the first benefits everyone by £10 and the second benefits only the richest by £20 and all others suffer losses – since both could achieve a potential Pareto gain. It is worth stressing at this point that the distributional question does

not arise when compensation is actually made, since the welfare of any losers is maintained and, overall, there is still a net improvement in social welfare (in theory by transfers from gainers who still remain better off). In contrast, when compensation is not made – which is, in fact, common because of the impracticality of lump-sum transfers – the distributional question becomes a key issue.

Clearly, individual monetary assessments of gains or losses (in terms of WTP) are likely to be strongly dependent on the level of personal income. It follows that project assessment will therefore tend to place relatively greater weight on the demands (or costs) of those on high incomes, and relatively less weight on the demands (or costs) of those on low incomes. For example, strict adherence to WTP criteria might suggest that road projects in urban areas should be located nearer to low-income housing than high-income housing, since the latter's WTP assessment of noise nuisance (reflected in house values) could generally be expected to exceed the former's.

If no adjustment of the WTP evaluation of gains or losses is made, then projects are being assessed implicitly on criteria that reflect the existing distribution of income. As Pearce has suggested, this is tantamount to saying that those who have been rewarded once (via higher earnings) should be rewarded once again in the choice of public projects. In contrast, in the above example one might wish to argue that a more widely acceptable assessment of noise nuisance would tend to put rather more weight on the number of individuals involved and the level of noise in alternative schemes than on the higher WTP of high-earning groups. A move in this direction could be achieved by weighting WTP assessments of intangible costs. Hence, values obtained for higher-income groups could be 'scaled down', while values for lower-income groups could be 'scaled up'.

The arguments in favour of adopting weighting procedures are undoubtedly strong since the main aim is to integrate considerations involving both efficiency and distribution. Failure to do so could result in glaring inconsistencies (for example, it might suggest that environmentally damaging projects should be located in 'poor' rather than in 'rich' localities). While it is possible that a weighting procedure would still sanction projects which made the rich richer and the poor poorer, weighting at least ensures that efficiency criteria will have been balanced against distributional considerations.

Although, as we have seen, distributional issues are less important when compensation occurs, even here many problems remain. In particular, compensation may often understate the nuisance caused – for example, houses will be valued at market prices which totally neglect any element of consumer surplus (that is, benefit exists in excess of the market price which an owner will derive from a particular dwelling or location) (Pearce, 1975).

Additionally, compensation is paid not by the beneficiaries themselves but out of general taxation. Although the cost to an individual taxpayer is minute, when multiplied over numerous projects distributional effects may be significant, especially if costs must be met by taxpayers, many of whom may be on low incomes themselves.

In conclusion, given the choice between two alternative projects producing the same net welfare gain to society, the appeal is clearly greater for the one where fewer people are to be made worse off. In practice, such handy alternatives are rare; in assessing public projects, planners should, at the very least point out the size and allocation of gains and losses together with recommendations concerning the feasibility of compensation.

(4) The fourth major consideration concerns the discount rate, the choice of which involves investment, savings and consumption decisions over time. All saving decisions involve the 'sacrifice' of lower consumption today in exchange for the promise of consumption at a higher level tomorrow. This is achieved by means of investment which places today's resources into production, which will yield results only at some date in the future. The decision of just how much saving and investment should be undertaken today by society can be illustrated, as in figure 10.8.

Consider the simplest case of a single individual in a 'Robinson Crusoe' world who is faced with fixed material resources (Layard, 1972). His savings/investment decision over two time-periods (t_1 and t_2) concerns how much of his time and effort (in t_1) he should spend on projects (say farming) which will yield a return in the next period (t_2). Spending his time in this way, however, involves Crusoe in a form of 'saving', since he will have less time to spend on activities (such as, say, collecting fruit) which yield an immediate benefit. This choice is illustrated by CC' which is Crusoe's *production frontier* (or production possibility curve). At the limit, he could consume nothing in t_2 but OC in t_1, or consume nothing in t_1 but (provided he did not starve) OC' in t_2. In general OC' can be expected to exceed OC because of technical advance and the use of capital-intensive production techniques; in Crusoe's case, by developing irrigation in t_1 he may ensure higher food output in t_2 than if he had attempted non-irrigated planting for consumption in t_1.

While Crusoe could achieve any combination of consumption levels given by CC', he will in practice choose that combination which gives him most benefit. This in turn will depend upon his relative preference for consumption in t_2 as against consumption in t_1. Crusoe's indifference curves, three of which are shown on figure 10.8, each tell us the combinations of consumption in t_1 and in t_2 which provide him with identical levels of satisfaction. As usual, higher indifference curves represent higher levels of welfare. In this case, Crusoe would reach his highest indifference curve by being at point s on CC'. This corresponds to consumption of 100 units in t_1 and

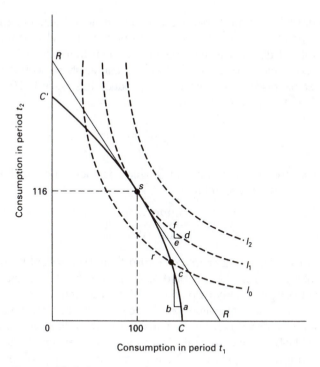

Figure 10.8 *Savings and investment decisions over time*

116 units in t_2. But in period t_1, if consumption accounts for only 100 units, this means that remaining resources $(C - 100)$ must have been invested for future consumption. In other words, $C - 100$ represents both the level of saving and investment that occurs in t_1.

Point s is unique in that it equates the *time preference* of the individual with the marginal profitability or efficiency of available investment opportunities. These two rates are identical only at point s, and this is shown because the two curves (CC' and I_1) have the same slope (they are tangential) at this point. To show the importance of this, consider the two small triangles abc and def; ab and de represent one unit less of consumption in t_1. Considering I_1, it can be seen that (at the margin) Crusoe is indifferent between losing de in t_1 as long as he is rewarded by ef in t_2. But looking at the corresponding segment of the production frontier, it can be seen that the investment opportunities facing him are so good that he can achieve cb (which is greater than fe) by forgoing a unit of consumption in t_1. The reader should convince himself or herself that the same conclusion applies to all units sacrificed in t_1 as Crusoe moves back from C to s. After this point the marginal efficiency of investment falls below Crusoe's rate of time preference. Only at s are these two rates identical and equal to RR. If RR represents points on the two axes of 200 units in t_1 and 220 units in t_2, then the rate of discount in the economy is such that 220 units in t_2 will have a present value (that is, in t_1) of 200. It can easily be seen that, in this case, the actual discount rate which will produce this result is 10 per cent. That is, given the discounting equation

$$PV = \frac{S}{(1+r)^n}$$

where PV = present value of a sum S which accrues n periods hence, if r = discount rate (fractional) then

$$PV = \frac{220}{(1+0.1)^1} = 200$$

Projects which yield a higher rate of return than 10 per cent (those to the right of s along CC') will be accepted, and those with rates of return below 10 per cent (left of and above points s) will be rejected.

There are a number of features of the real world which very much complicate the above description of the Crusoe economy. In reality, there exist many individuals making separate investment and savings decisions, and these may not always coincide. There are numerous types of investment, long-term and shorter-term, high-risk and low-risk, and in consequence a variety of interest rates also, depending on the credit risks involved and the degree of liquidity.

In view of these considerations, it may be asked whether decisions on savings and investment made by individuals will necessarily prove optimal for society as a whole. For example, while individuals may 'know best' about their own welfare, can they realistically be expected to take a longer-term view involving future generations? If not, then society as a whole – which has such responsibilities – may need to adjust the 'market'-derived discount rate in making its own decisions about whether to invest, and how much.

In order to investigate these issues, figure 10.8 can easily be transformed so that CC' now represents the production frontier facing society and I_1 represents the *social* indifference curve (that is, the consumption patterns between which society is indifferent). Once again, at s the *social rate of time preference* (STP) given by the slope I_1 equals the *marginal efficiency of capital* given by the slope of CC'. The latter is often referred to as the *social opportunity cost* (SOC) of capital, meaning the amount of current resources which has to be given up (or is displaced) to produce a unit of consumption in the future. In practice, it is taken to be represented by the rate of return on marginal projects in the private sector.

Clearly, the only point on the diagram where these two rates, SOC and STP, are equal is at *s*. Any other point will correspond to a sub-optimal level of investment and savings. The question facing the public sector, then, is how to determine the appropriate discount rate to apply to its own decisions regarding public investment. The problem here is that while the marginal efficiency of capital (MEC) or SOC rate is, in principle, observable, the social time preference rate is not – at least, not directly. This would not matter too much if there were no dispute concerning the equivalence of the SOC and STP rates. The general presumption, however, is that the observable 'market' rate is likely to exceed the STP rate at *s*, so that the economy is in fact at a position such as *r* on the figure, corresponding to lower levels of investment, savings and welfare.

First, market interest rates reflect the *private* rate of return on investment rather than the *social* rate. The latter is likely to be higher than the former because of spillover effects from one sector to another which raise the productivity of labour and other factors of production elsewhere. Yet only the private rate of return will enter into individual investment decisions. As a result, levels of investment and savings in the economy may be too low (that is, discount rate may be too high) (Sen, 1967).

By itself, company taxation would also cause the market rate to diverge from the STP rate at *s*, since for a firm to pay *RR* per cent to its creditors it must in fact earn a rate of return on its capital in excess of *RR* per cent (Baumol, 1972).

In addition, as Pigou (1920) has argued, market rates reflect the fact that individuals are 'myopic' and have an irrational preference for present consumption. If this is indeed that case, then use of market rates reflecting 'myopia' will tend to penalize the assessment of benefits which accrue at some distant point, perhaps to future generations.

For public-sector projects of a long-term nature, the choice of a 'market'-derived test discount rate may, for these reasons, prove particularly objectionable. Pearce (1983), for example, illustrates this problem in the context of evaluating risks associated with the storage of nuclear waste. Say it is known for certain that an event causing £10 billion in damage at current prices will occur 500 years ahead (that is, in year 500). Discounting at 10 per cent using the above formula gives a present value of only 25 pence to the incident! More generally, the implications of this 'scaling-down' effect stretch far and wide to virtually all aspects of longer-term environmental importance.

Finally, the 'market rate reflects the inability of the private sector to "pool" risks across many projects (and taxpayers) in the way the public sector is able to do. As such market rates will reflect a positive "risk premium" which will be higher the greater the lack of risk-pooling by institutions in the private sector' (Arrow and Lind, 1970).

In practice, however, the opportunity cost approach – based on commercial rates of return – appears to have dominated thinking on public-sector discounting. In 1969 the Treasury test discount rate for public-sector investment was set at 10 per cent. This was subsequently reduced and most projects are now required to achieve an 8 per cent rate of return. It should be noted, however, that this represents a real rate of return with costs and benefits being expressed in real (that is, inflation-adjusted) values.

In defence of the SOC approach it is sometimes argued that setting a lower discount rate (reflecting STP) would redirect resources from the private to the public sector, since the latter would only need to secure a lower rate of return. Against this it can be argued that the cost of borrowing for the government (that is, the yield on long-term government securities) is in fact lower than for the private sector, reflecting the fact that lending to the government involves no element of risk (that is, it is 'gilt-edged'). While public-sector projects are not themselves without risk, a slightly lower rate than for the private sector would be justified since, as has been seen, a lower element of risk is inherent in public-sector investment as a whole.

Perhaps the strongest argument for adopting an SOC approach is in the case where private-sector output and investment compete directly, and could be displaced by public-sector investment (for example, in haulage). In this event one might wish to ensure that the public sector does at least as well as any private-sector projects it displaces.

However, the assumption underlying the SOC approach – that because of increased competition for available savings, public-sector investment in some sense 'crowds-out' private-sector investment – is not entirely without criticism. First, since government revenue comes mainly from taxation (rather than from borrowing), it is not only savings but also consumption that is displaced. If individuals are not content with the rate of return on public investments financed in this way (perhaps reflecting STP), it is up to them to change it via the democratic process. Second, with growing capital mobility it is increasingly difficult to argue that domestic investment is restrained significantly by the level of domestic savings (the United Kingdom, for example, has traditionally been a net exporter of investment funds).

In contrast, the main argument in favour of the STP rate is that it more fully reflects the rate at which society as a whole is prepared to trade present for future consumption.

Thus there appears to be no clear-cut answer to the choice of discount rate and it has even been suggested that a compromise approach would be to choose a rate that reflects both SOC and STP. In practice, a variety of rates is often used in sensitivity testing. This is certainly a useful addition to CBA methods, given not only that STP and SOC rates are perceived to differ, but also that estimates of either can vary over time. For example, in the late 1970s real interest rates were, in fact, negative. Equally, estimates of the STP rate are sensitive (and positively related) to future expected growth rates. In the final analysis, it is important to recognize that the outcome of using a higher SOC-derived rate will affect not only the level of public investment but also its direction – penalizing public-sector projects where benefits are intrinsically long-term in nature.

CBA as a planning aid

While CBA raises many conceptual and operational problems – particularly regarding the valuation of benefits and costs and the choice of discount rate – it has nevertheless established itself as a useful technique. It may not be as exact a technique as might be wished but it does at least provide the decision-maker with a rational framework, and it allows systematic examination of all aspects of a scheme, including intangibles which would not be allowed for in any purely private appraisal. This is an essential part of public-sector investment; simply ignoring non-market effects does not make them go away, since even if CBA is not undertaken, any decision to go ahead or abandon a project carries an implicit statement about the present value of the social costs and benefits involved.

As Lichfield's planning balance sheet approach (PBS) (Lichfield, 1966; Lichfield and Chapman, 1970) has shown, the technique can be an important aid in the planning process, making clear the types of cost and benefit involved and the groups who are affected. In this approach the community is divided into categories (for example, producers and consumers) and the costs and benefits are calculated for each sector. The totals for the various sectors are then added to establish whether the scheme as a whole produces a net benefit or cost. Many of the items in the planning balance sheet relate to non-monetary costs and benefits; these may often be measured in physical or time units or, where they cannot be quantified in any way, are listed as intangibles. The PBS approach has the advantage of making clear not only the net social benefit of alternative projects but it can also point to their distributional consequences.

For the urban planner, while CBA is potentially a useful aid to planning decisions it does not avoid the need to make value judgements in the comparison of intangibles arising from alternative projects and in the overall conclusions to be drawn from the assessment of costs and benefits. However, as long as such value judgements (for example, relating to distributional effects) are made clear, the analysis cannot be accused of 'subjectivity'.

CBA is least useful where the benefits of a project are intrinsically difficult to value. For example, if security considerations, or perhaps the long-term development of an area, are of overriding importance, then decision-making becomes a political issue. Similarly, where projects may have major irreversible consequences it can be argued that no decision should be made which limits severely the opportunities or options available to future generations. In contrast, CBA is perhaps most useful where a single project or only a few alternative projects are involved and where the range of intangibles is not too wide as to make comparison difficult. In practice, it is often the case that once decisions are made in principle (for example, the Roskill Commission on the Third London Airport), CBA is then brought in to facilitate the choice between alternative projects.

APPLICATION OF COST–BENEFIT ANALYSIS IN DEVELOPING COUNTRIES

The application of cost–benefit analysis in developing countries has proved difficult over many years. The major difficulty lies in the estimation of shadow prices of 'primary' factors (Little and Mirrlees, 1974). Because of the degree of market factor distortions and the imperfection of market information, limited case studies have been conducted so far, particularly at the macroeconomic level.

Cost–Benefit Analysis of Public Investment in China

Introduction

Since embarking on economic reforms and the 'open-door' policy in 1979, China has been achieving rapid economic growth and development. The Chinese government has made substantial investments in the construction sector, especially in establishing the Special Economic Zones (SEZs), which bear a close resemblance in many respects to export processing zones (EPZs) in the rest of the world, as test-beds for development policies and bases for foreign investors. Stimulated by the improvement in the investment environment and the preferential treatment provided by the Chinese government, a significant amount of foreign direct investment (FDI) has been attracted, which has been viewed as a major source of technology and an instrument of export promotion (Chen, 1992).

The programme of establishing the SEZs, especially in the early-1980s, can be seen, essentially, as construction projects because they were built on the sites of either isolated agricultural or fishery areas. From the viewpoint of China, most of the construction investments are regarded as public investment. It is, therefore, of interest to examine the extent to which such investment benefits society. To what extent does the contribution of the investment to national economic welfare, particularly in the SEZs, justify the expenditure? Or could the resources have been better used elsewhere in the economy? This section investigates this type of investment by using cost–benefit techniques. Since a large proportion of these investments were spent in the SEZs before 1990, this study will concentrate on the SEZs. Among the SEZs, the Shenzhen SEZ is the most extensive and economically mature, and it is thus taken as the example.

As was demonstrated, the essence of cost–benefit analysis is to measure the net benefits from investment in a project to society rather than to private investors. In other words, cost–benefit analysis takes into account the true opportunity costs of resources to society. The resources used in a project and the output they generate should be valued at their true opportunity costs to society and not at ruling market prices. The basis for using opportunity costs, or so-called *social accounting prices* or *shadow prices*, is that they correspond more closely to economic scarcity, use of resources and social preferences rather than do market prices.

The approach used in this study derives originally from the Little–Mirrlees cost–benefit technique (Little and Mirrlees, 1974) as modified by Warr (1986). The Little–Mirrlees method is well known. Warr used this method to evaluate the Philippines' Bataan export processing zone. In his study, the zone was treated as an enclave, a bounded area outside the customs territory of the country. Emphasis was on the transfer of funds and resources between the zone and the rest of the country's economy. The aim was thus to study the net benefits and costs, as experienced by the rest of the country's economy, resulting from the existence of the zone, compared with the hypothetical case in which it was absent. Income distribution considerations within the country were disregarded in order to simplify the analysis. Changes in the income of foreigners received zero weighting and changes in the income of all national citizens were weighted equally.

Further modifications are required when this method is applied to China. Since the majority (more than 70 per cent) of the firms operating in the zone were joint ventures (JVs), all the firms in the zone are treated as if they were JVs. Technologies transferred to the zone are all considered as labour-intensive.

Economic Features of the Shenzhen SEZ

The Shenzhen SEZ covers a fenced area of $327.5\,km^2$ and shares a border with Hong Kong. The proximity to the Hong Kong market generates many obvious economic benefits for Shenzhen. The zone was set up with a substantial construction investment of over US$8 billion, on the site of a remote fishing village in 1979 (Chen, 1992). The objectives of establishment of the zone included promoting exports, attracting foreign capital, creating employment opportunities, obtaining Western technologies and promoting regional development. Investment incentives were provided by the government, including exemption from corporate tax for a fixed term, exemption from customs duties of machinery imported for production and export purposes, freedom to repatriate profits at a pre-specified rate and autonomy in many administrative aspects.

Since its establishment, the Shenzhen SEZ has become the fastest growing economy in the country, with an average annual growth rate of gross domestic product (GDP) of around 20 per cent and industrial output of around 50 per cent. More than 70 per cent of the companies operating in the zone involved joint-venture investment. The industries in the zone are export-oriented manufacturing with imported materials or materials from other parts of China. More than 80 per cent of their products have been exported. The zone's exports contributed about 15 per cent of the country's total exports by the end of 1993. The real estate development and service sector has received more than 50 per cent of the total FDI in the zone and has contributed most to foreign-exchange earnings (Economist Intelligence Unit, 1993; State Statistical Bureau of China, 1993; Chen, 1994).

Cost–benefit analysis of the construction investment

The benefits of the zone to China include: foreign exchange earnings, employment opportunities, technology transfer, tax revenues and insurance premiums, and Chinese partners' share of the net profits of JVs. The costs consist of: construction expenditure, administrative expenditure, and electricity and water provided by the Chinese government. The estimation of each parameter will now be discussed in detail.

Foreign exchange earnings

This benefit brought in by FDI consists of the foreign currency that the firms in the zone convert into Chinese currency to meet their domestic wage bill plus purchases of locally produced raw materials, less the value of their local sales of final products. The domestic wage paid by firms is included in the net employment gain. The products manufactured by the firms in the zone are mainly for export. Even if some of the products are sold in the domestic market, they are sold for foreign currency. Thus, only the purchases of domestic materials are taken into account in the estimation.

Conversion of foreign exchange into the Chinese currency *Renminbi* (RMB) is made at the official exchange rate. However, with exchange controls and domestic protection, the social value of foreign exchange in terms of the RMB received by China exceeds the value of the domestic currency that the firms are given in exchange. The RMB is overvalued. Therefore, the social value of the foreign exchange received from firms in the zone should be estimated at the shadow price. Estimation of the shadow price of foreign exchange for China has been made by the Shenzhen Foreign Exchange Adjustment Centre, and is referred to as the 'official adjusted exchange rate'.

The net gain of foreign-exchange earnings is estimated as the local raw-material purchases by the firms in the zone multiplied by the proportional difference between the shadow price of the foreign exchange and the official exchange rate. For example, in 1988, the shadow price of foreign exchange was 1.77 times as much as the official-exchange rate, giving a proportional difference between the shadow price of the foreign exchange and the official exchange rate of 77 per cent. This means that the net gain of foreign-exchange earnings was 77 per cent or US$34 million of local raw-material purchases. Thus, in this year, the net gain of foreign-exchange earnings to China was US$26 million (table 10.1).

Employment

The Chinese government's interest in the employment generated by the zone obviously reflects the view that the social benefits derived from generating an additional job outweigh the costs. In economic terms, this may be interpreted as meaning that the wage received by the worker in the zone exceeds the opportunity cost of his or her employment elsewhere. The problems associated with measuring the opportunity cost of labour are well known. In China, there are no minimum wage restrictions. Therefore, the market wage rate provides a good indication of the opportunity cost of labour, and the shadow wage is estimated as the market wage outside the zone.

The net gain from employment in the zone to China is thus estimated as the wage bill in the zone minus the estimated social opportunity cost of employing these workers. According to the State Statistical Bureau, the weighted average ratio of the shadow wage to the market wage in the zone is 0.44. That is the opportunity cost of employment in the zone is 44 per cent of the wage received in the zone. The net gain from employment is thus estimated as the actual wage bill multiplied by 0.56. This adjustment factor is applied to the wages paid by the zone each year.

Technology transfer

The Chinese government hopes that Chinese firms will benefit from the technological knowledge of foreign firms entering the zone. However, most

Table 10.1 Annual components of cost–benefit analysis of the Shenzhen SEZ (US$ millions)

	1979	1980	1981	1982	1983	1984	1985	1986	1987	1988
Foreign-exchange earnings	7.3	10.6	14.7	16.8	14.9	21.7	11.6	17.5	19.3	26.0
Employment	1.5	2.2	3.0	5.6	5.0	9.3	16.4	16.6	26.4	52.6
Technology transfer	0.1	0.1	0.1	0.3	0.2	0.6	1.7	2.8	4.8	7.2
Tax revenues and insurance premiums	0.0	0.0	2.5	2.5	9.1	15.9	29.5	34.5	40.9	55.1
Net profit share of Chinese JV partners	−5.9	−4.9	3.5	−9.5	−3.6	−3.3	−19.7	−17.3	32.2	1.32
Construction expenditure	−16.9	−23.4	−27.0	−49.5	−51.6	−84.7	−140.9	−96.2	−67.4	−92.8
Administrative expenditure	−0.1	−0.1	−0.1	−0.3	−0.3	−0.6	−1.2	−1.1	−1.7	−4.1
Net benefit	−14.0	−15.5	−3.2	−34.1	−26.3	−41.2	−102.6	−43.2	54.5	45.3

Sources: The Shenzhen Statistical Bureau, the Office for SEZs of the State Council of China and the State Statistical Bureau.

of them are involved in labour-intensive production and have little technological knowledge to offer that is not already widely available. Those firms
that do have unique technological advantages (electronics firms are the best
example) protect this knowledge carefully.

However, managerial techniques and methods of product quality control
are inevitably transferred to the local middle-level managers employed.
When these managers move to employment elsewhere in China, the training they have received confers a benefit on the domestic economy, which
is not captured in the wages they receive in the zone.

The net benefit to China from this transferring of skills can be calculated
in the following way. It is assumed that initially the firms in the zone employ
foreign skilled personnel, whose shadow price is their wage (W) (assuming
their consumption is entirely on imports and their savings are all repatri-
ated abroad), and the local middle-level managers that the firms employ are
paid a wage (C). As a result of training within the firms, the local managers
become skilled and replace the foreign skilled personnel, reflecting the
higher productivity due to the acquisition of skills. These local managers are
referred to as 'technical persons' in this study.

The wage they could receive in employment elsewhere in China can be
used as a shadow wage that reflects the opportunity cost of this category
of labour. This shadow wage is estimated as the wage received by the foreign
skilled personnel discussed above. Suppose that the real resource costs of
training the local managers to the same level (in the zone, the costs of training are assumed to be borne by the foreign firms) are K per year, then the
net benefit of technology transfer each year can be calculated as:

$$(W - C + K) \times N$$

where N denotes the number of technical personnel employed in the
zone.

Tax revenues and insurance premiums

The revenues raised from firms in the zone represent a clear source of economic benefit for the domestic economy. They consist mainly of taxes collected by the Chinese government and insurance premiums collected by the
Chinese insurance companies. This is a net benefit to China because they
would not be received if the firms were not operating in the zone. Firms
that transfer to the zone from elsewhere in China, or foreign firms that
would have entered China in any case, are exceptions, which can be
ignored.

The tax rate is usually stipulated at 15 per cent of profits. However,
because of favourable treatment for foreign firms in the zone, the State Statistical Bureau estimates the actual rate at around 10 per cent.

Net profit share of joint venture partners

This net benefit to China is the JVs' profit share minus the opportunity costs of the inputs provided by the Chinese partners.

The profit share of the JVs to China is estimated from the total JVs' equity owned by the Chinese partners multiplied by the private rate of return on the JV investment. When the life of the zone is assumed to be 25 years, a 24 per cent private rate of return is obtained (Chen, 1993).

As far as the opportunity costs of the inputs provided by the Chinese partners are concerned, most of the Chinese partners' contributions to the JVs relate to land, factory and residential buildings. The Chinese managerial contribution has been considered in the technology transfer from the zone to elsewhere in China. This is part of the government construction expenditure, which, if not spent in the zone, would be used elsewhere in the country. This benefit has been previously calculated (Chen, 1993).

Construction expenditure

The Chinese government public expenditure required to set up the zone represents a clear economic cost. Some of this might have been required in the absence of the zone, for example on local roads. However, since the zone was constructed largely on reclaimed land, construction work would not have taken place. The largest expenditure involved is specific to the zone. It includes construction of government-supplied land, construction of factory and residential buildings, provision of public utilities and communications and transportation facilities, levelling the site, seaport and airport construction, provision of international trade centres, research laboratories, hospitals and recreation grounds. The costs of government-supplied land, construction of factory and residential buildings have already been counted as inputs provided by the Chinese partners of JVs and are thus excluded here.

It should be noted that only the construction investment of the zone consisted of both Chinese government public expenditure and capital invested by foreign firms in the zone. Only the Chinese contribution is relevant to the cost–benefit calculation and, therefore, should be included.

Administrative expenditure

The administrative costs of the zone have two main components: the opportunity costs of administrative personnel and those of administrative buildings. The cost of administrative buildings is included in the construction expenditure and is thus excluded here.

Electricity and water supply

The prevailing shortage of electricity in China and the relatively high expenditure involved in setting up the electricity network necessitates the government providing subsidies for those using electricity. In practice, only part of the commercial demand for electricity is supplied at the standard rate (subsidized rate), the remainder being charged at an adjusted rate, which is estimated by the State Statistical Bureau as the marginal social cost of generating electricity in China and can be used as the shadow price of electricity.

Electricity supplied to the firms in the zone is charged at the adjusted rate. Since it would be charged at the same rate if supplied to other parts of China, it does not have a welfare effect on China and, thus, is irrelevant in the calculation of the net benefit from the zone. The same applies to water supply.

Discount rate

China is faced with shortages of foreign exchange and savings. The alternative to FDI is foreign loans. The international rates of interest on these loans are therefore usually regarded as the true opportunity costs of capital, which, being less distorted, are also supposed to reflect the marginal social productivity of capital. Real rates of interest on international borrowing are usually taken to be the appropriate real discount rates in this situation.

These real interest rates rose over the period 1979–88 in the range of 5–9 per cent for the various kinds of hard foreign currencies. A weighted average of the real interest rate calculated by the Bank of China amounts to approximately 7.5 per cent over the period.

Results of the cost–benefit calculation

Figure 10.9 presents the net benefit from the zone during the period 1979–88. The calculation is based on a discount rate of 7.5 per cent and an assumed life for the zone of 25 years, with a 56 per cent wage difference between the firms in the zone and the firms outside the zone. The streams of annual net benefit estimated for the period 1979–88 are assumed to remain at the 1988 value over the rest of the life of the zone. Therefore, a net present value of US$59 million and an internal rate of return of 10.7 per cent are obtained. This is a high rate of return by the standards of public projects. It is clear from figure 10.9 that the benefits of employment, revenues raised and foreign exchange earnings are responsible for this outcome.

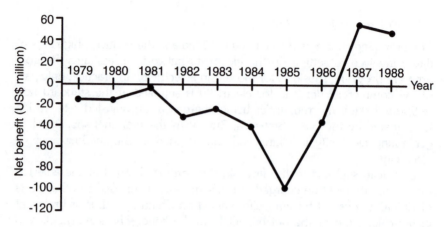

Figure 10.9 *Net benefit of the Shenzhen SEZ, 1979–88*

Omissions and biases

Simplifying assumptions have been necessary for the evaluation. Some of these may have biased the estimated social profitability of the zone upwards rather than downwards. These include the following:

- The firms that enter the zone would not be present in China if the zone did not exist; in fact, a few non-Hong Kong firms would presumably have invested elsewhere in China.
- An assumption of the majority of firms in the zone being JVs is also made, although about 25 per cent of the total of firms are either Chinese firms or wholly-owned foreign subsidiaries.
- The JVs discussed cover all the sectors; the calculation of net profit share of Chinese partners is based on a 24 per cent of JVs' rate of return; the Organization for Economic Co-operation and Development (OECD)'s survey on 103 JVs in the zone suggests that the highest profit-making firms in the zone were hotel and real estate development, with an average rate of return on investment of around 76 per cent (Osborne, 1986); the average rate of return on investment for the industrial firms in the zone was only 15 per cent (Osborne, 1986); a survey in 1989 also shows that real estate and construction companies earned more than a 50 per cent rate of return (Chen, 1992); this situation has not changed dramatically.
- The construction expenditure that the Chinese government spent in the zone may be underestimated; because the zone is located in Guangdong province, some of the construction expenditure allocated by central government to the province has been attributed to the zone; this may reduce,

although only slightly, the amount of infrastructure costs calculated for the zone.

- The government possibly overstates the taxes received from firms in the zone for political purposes.
- The data of the costs for establishing the SEZ are possibly understated by the Chinese authorities because they are presumably anxious about demonstrating that the zone is a great success; although the zone does seem to be a beneficial public investment, the social returns from it could be overestimated.

Sensitivity Tests

As far as the quality of data is concerned, most of the data used for the cost–benefit calculations were provided by the Office for SEZs of the State Council of China and the Shenzhen Statistical Bureau, and are considered to be of relatively high quality and reliable. This is also confirmed by most of the firms interviewed in the zone during a survey in 1989. Data errors seem likely to be small. Even so, it is of interest to see to what extent the results of the cost–benefit analysis would be affected by variability in the data by carrying out sensitivity tests.

The discount rate is an important issue in the evaluation, since net benefits follow the familiar pattern of negative values from 1979 to 1986, followed by positive values in 1987 and 1988. Therefore, the net present values of the benefits are calculated for a wide range of discount rates from 2.5 per cent to 12.5 per cent. The results are shown in figure 10.10.

The life of the zone is also an important variable, since the streams of annual net benefit estimated for the period 1979–88 are assumed to remain at the 1988 value over the rest of the life of the zone. Therefore, the net present values and the internal rates of return are also re-calculated under three alternative assumptions about the life of the zone: a 20-year life, a 25-year life and a 30-year life. Figures 10.11 and 10.12 present the results for the NPVs and the IRRs respectively.

The shadow wage of labour is estimated as the market wage outside the zone. This is because there are no minimum wage restrictions in China, which suggests that the market wage provides a good indication of the opportunity cost of labour. However, the shadow wage used in the calculation is a weighted average of different classes of workers and, furthermore, there are various kinds of government subsidies to workers besides their wages, such as housing and medical allowances. All these may differ between the zone and the area outside the zone, so it is of interest to see by how much the results of the cost–benefit analysis would change if the assumed wage differential varies. Therefore, the net present value and the

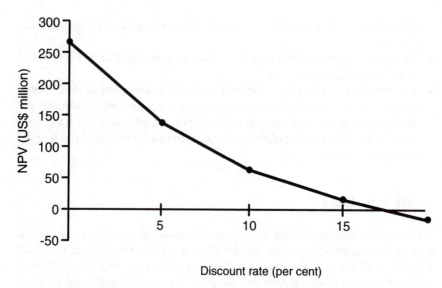

Figure 10.10 *Sensitivity test: NPV–discount rate variation*

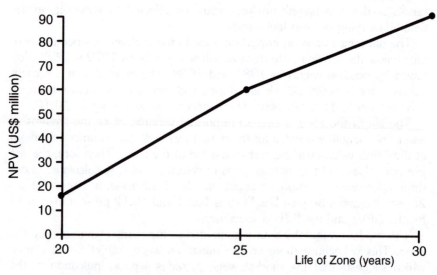

Figure 10.11 *Sensitivity test: NPV–life of Zone variation*

internal rate of return are re-calculated for a wage difference varying from 36 per cent to 76 per cent (figures 10.13 and 10.14).

Another variation in the data is construction expenditure of the zone. Since the zone is located in Guangdong province, some construction expen-

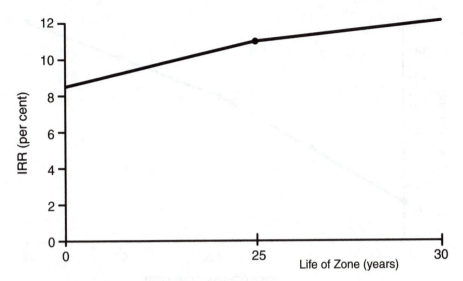

Figure 10.12 *Sensitivity test: IRR–life of Zone variation*

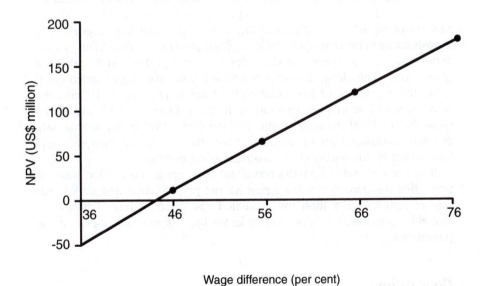

Figure 10.13 *Sensitivity test: NPV–wage difference variation*

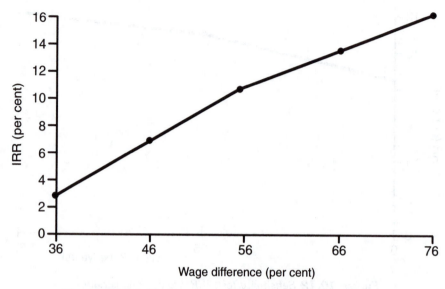

Figure 10.14 *Sensitivity test: IRR–wage difference variation*

diture allocated by central government to Guangdong province could be attributed to the zone. As Guangdong province has experienced rapid development of infrastructure construction, it is unlikely that the proportion of infrastructure expenditure which Guangdong province could attribute to the zone would not be spent elsewhere for the same purpose in the absence of the zone. Therefore, diversion of construction expenditure which could affect the calculation of the social costs of the zone seems to be unlikely, or at most only a small proportion of the total. Figures 10.15 and 10.16 show the results of the re-calculations of net present value and internal rate of return to demonstrate the extent to which the cost–benefit analysis would be affected by the variation of construction expenditure.

It can be concluded from the sensitivity tests, under most of the assumptions, that the zone generates a positive net present value and an internal rate of return higher than the estimated real discount rate. This means that the cost–benefit analysis can tolerate the assumed variations of the parameters.

Conclusion

The above cost–benefit analysis indicates that the Chinese government's construction investment, particularly in the case of the SEZs, is a beneficial public investment from the standpoint of China's economic welfare.

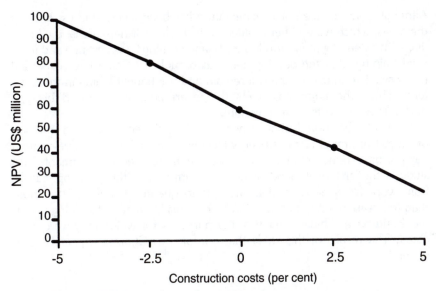

Figure 10.15 *Sensitivity test: NPV–construction costs variation*

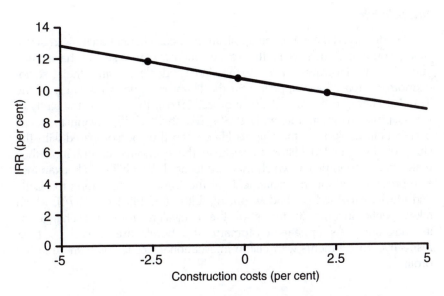

Figure 10.16 *Sensitivity test: IRR–construction costs variation*

Although considerable public expenditure has been incurred in establishing the areas, which were either isolated agricultural or fishery areas, the benefits, such as employment, foreign-exchange earnings, tax revenue and technical training, that the development has brought to China have exceeded the costs. The infrastructure will remain and will benefit China in the long-term. This is the major reason why the government has extended this type of development to the whole country.

It should be noted that, since cost–benefit analysis as a method of project appraisal has not been widely used in China, such a calculation has not been done as an *a priori assessment* for public investment. This study is the first of its kind. It does two important things: it provides a framework for analysis, and it attempts to quantify benefits. After more than ten years of operation, the SEZs are considered an outstanding investment and have achieved many of the purposes for which they were instigated. The results of this study thus conform to Chinese expectations in general.

Cost–Benefit Analysis of the Service Industry in Developing Countries

Introduction

Considering the difficulty of the application of cost–benefit analysis in developing countries, such as in the service industry, few studies have been carried out. However, two such studies dealing with their socio-economic impact have appeared in the literature: one is the study of the Trinidad Hilton in the late-1970s (Forbes, 1976), the other is the study of the Cyprus Hilton in the early-1980s (Wanhill, 1985). Wanhill's social cost–benefit analysis of the Cyprus Hilton can thus be compared with the study of the Trinidad Hilton to evaluate the economic contribution they make to the countries in which they are located. Wanhill's study examines a 'representative' income statement for the Cyprus Hilton using the Little and Mirrlees method of shadow pricing (Little and Mirrlees, 1974), which takes public income in terms of the equivalent foreign exchange as its maximum. As appears customary, the hotels are owned by their respective governments with Hilton International Co. taking a share in the profits.

Shadow prices

The Little–Mirrlees method of shadow pricing is designed to account for two kinds of market price distortions:

- Market factor distortions relating to the opportunity cost of labour and public funds in conditions of high unemployment and low investment.
- Protectionist trade policies in the trade sector working their way through to relative prices in all markets, including that for factors. Thus all prices are adjusted to foreign exchange equivalents, the shadow price of a unit of foreign exchange being 1.0.

Wanhill's shadow price estimates for Cyprus were constructed with the intention of aiding project selection in the post-1974 invasion situation, which created an urgent need for investment and foreign exchange, and a severe unemployment problem.

The essence of using shadow prices in project evaluation is to divide the basic inputs and outputs of the project into certain 'primary' factors. In this case-study, foreign exchange (imports and exports), taxes (transfers), skilled labour, unskilled male labour and unskilled female labour are designated as the primary factors. Once the shadow prices of these factors have been found, it is a simple matter to calculate the shadow price for all kinds of intermediate and final commodities and services. The most popular method of presenting shadow prices is in the form of accounting ratios, i.e. shadow price/market prices, which are simply conversion coefficients from market to social efficiency prices. The algebraic procedure is as follows.

Let p be a $k \times 1$ vector of primary factor accounting ratios; v an $m \times 1$ vector of required accounting ratios for the various intermediate and final goods and services; A an $m \times m$ matrix of input goods whose column elements represent the normalized coefficients to produce one unit of the output good or service; and B a $k \times n$ matrix whose column elements represent the normalized primary factor input coefficients. Then

$$v = A'v + B'p$$

which implies

$$v = (1 - A')^{-1} B'p$$

where $(1 - A')^{-1} B'$ is an $m \times k$ matrix of the direct and indirect primary factor input coefficients to produce one unit of the output goods.

For Cyprus, the value of m is set at 95. This number is made up of a range of 46 consumer goods and services, 36 intermediate goods which are chiefly to do with construction but also include office equipment, and a variety of non-traded services which have not already been included under the consumer section, such as business services, advertising and promotion, port-handling margin, transport margin and so on. It will be readily appreciated that this kind of exercise requires the same information sources as would be used to construct an input–output table.

The Cyprus Hilton

The use of these accounting ratios is shown in table 10.2, which presents the income statement of the Cyprus Hilton for the year 1973 – the last 'normal' operating year before the invasion. Being an international hotel, the revenue side is mainly foreign exchange earnings which are valued at 1.0. The accounting ratio of 0.83 for food sales to local guests is the mean of 24 food items. Beverages have a low accounting ratio of 0.55 because there is a large element of excise duty which takes an accounting ratio of 0.0 since taxes are simply transfers, and represent no real resource flow.

On the cost side, the accounting ratio for minor operated departments is a general one for local purchases of non-food items, while that for other departmental expenses is the mean ratio for the 46 consumer goods and services. The distribution of the latter accounting ratios (ARs) is shown in figure 10.17. It can be seen that the distribution is bi-modal which arises from the fact that some items undergo processing in Cyprus while others are directly imported and carry only port-handling, tariffs, transport and trade margins. The mean accounting ratio shown in figure 10.17 may be interpreted as the Standard Conversion Factor. The latter is a term ascribed by Little and Mirrlees to a generalized consumption commodity accounting ratio reflecting internal market price distortions. The accounting ratios for

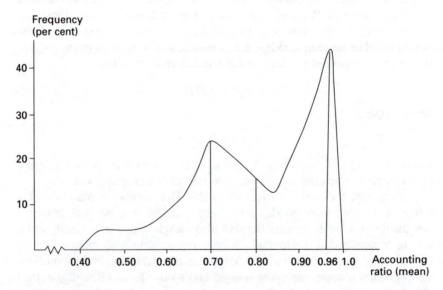

Figure 10.17 *Distribution of accounting ratios for consumer goods and services (Wanhill, 1985)*

Table 10.2 Hilton Cyprus Ltd: statement of income 1973 (A)

(1) Category	(2) Percentage of total revenue	(3) Accounting ratios	(4) (2) × (3) as a percentage of total revenue
Revenue			
Rooms	45.6	1.0	46.6
Food			
Tourist sales	23.8	1.0	24.3
Local sales	6.0	0.83	5.1
Beverages			
Tourist sales	10.2	1.0	10.4
Local sales	2.5	0.55	1.4
Minor operated departments and other income	<u>11.9</u>	1.0	<u>12.2</u>
Total revenue	100		100
Costs			
Cost of sales			
Food	7.2	0.83	6.1
Beverages	5.2	0.55	2.9
Minor operated departments	<u>6.5</u>	0.81	<u>5.7</u>
	18.9		14.7
Payroll and related expenses			
Skilled labour	18.2	0.80	14.9
Unskilled male labour	5.9	0.61	3.7
Unskilled female labour	<u>4.8</u>	0.70	<u>3.4</u>
	28.9		22.0
Departmental other expenses	13.4	0.80	10.9
Undistributed non-payroll expenses			
Administrative and general expenses	2.6	0.89	2.4
Marketing	3.4	0.93	3.2
Energy costs	7.0	0.62	4.4
Property operation and maintenance	<u>3.5</u>	0.76	<u>2.7</u>
	16.5		12.7
Total income before fixed charges	22.3		39.7

Source: Wanhill (1985).

459

the items making up undistributed non-payroll expenses are for office equipment, advertising and promotion, electricity, and general repairs and maintenance respectively.

Payroll costs constitute payments to primary factors and the accounting ratios are the expression of the shadow wage/market wage. The calculations of the shadow wage rates for unskilled labour are too lengthy to be discussed here, but are amply covered by Scott (1976). All we need to say here is that the shadow wage is composed of three items:

- the value in terms of foreign exchange of increased income to the average unskilled employee;
- the cost in terms of foreign exchange of the employee's extra consumption;
- the effort cost of working when moving from unemployment to employment.

The definition of skilled labour is any employee who can be regarded as fully employed in Cyprus. In practice, the best estimate of the relative percentage of skilled labour may be found by using the definitions and manpower surveys of the Ministry of Labour of Cyprus in relation to salaried and wage-earning employees. The shadow wage for this type of labour is the foreign exchange value of the forgone product elsewhere in the economy. The most applicable accounting ratio is the Standard Conversion Factor for consumer goods and services, which is 0.80 in this case. There is, however, one difficulty – the distribution of accounting ratios shown in figure 10.17 is derived using a known value for skilled labour. This can be solved by using a trial-and-error iterative procedure until convergence is achieved.

The effect of using socially efficient prices instead of market prices on the Cyprus Hilton's income statement can be found on the bottom line of table 10.2. Total income before fixed charges is raised from 22.3 per cent to 39.7 per cent of revenue. This latter figure may be interpreted as the gross social surplus in accordance with national income definitions. Fixed charges constitute rent, interest, depreciation and amortization, taxes, etc. Not all of these items are costs in social terms. After allowing for the consumption cost of interest payment, the resource cost of depreciation and the foreign exchange cost of payments to Hilton International (rent being a payment to the government), the social profit still comes to more than 25 per cent of revenue.

Comparisons with the Trinidad Hilton

Tables 10.3 and 10.4 compare the income statement for the Cyprus Hilton with that for the Trinidad Hilton (Forbes, 1976). The only difference

Table 10.3 Hilton Cyprus Ltd: statement of income 1973 (B)

(1) Revenue	(2) Percentage of total revenue	(3) Accounting ratio	(4) (2) × (3) as percentage of total revenue
Tradeables	96.3	1.0	98.4
Skilled labour	0.6	0.80	0.5
Unskilled male labour	1.3	0.61	0.8
Unskilled female labour	0.4	0.70	0.3
Taxes	1.4	0.0	0.0
	100.0		100.0

(1) Costs	(2) Percentage of total revenue	(3) Accounting ratio	(4) (2) × (3) as percentage of total revenue
Tradeables	30.4	1.0	31.1
Skilled labour	20.7	0.80	16.9
Unskilled male labour	11.9	0.61	7.4
Unskilled female labour	6.9	0.70	4.9
Taxes	7.8	0.0	0.0
Total income before fixed charges	22.3		39.7
	100.0		100.0

Source: Wanhill (1985).

461

Table 10.4 Hilton Trinidad Ltd: statement of income 1963

(1) Revenue	(2) Percentage of total revenue	(3) Accounting ratio	(4) (2) × (3) as percentage of total revenue	(1) Costs	(2) Percentage of total revenue	(3) Accounting ratio	(4) (2) × (3) as percentage of total revenue
Tradeables	100.0	1.0	100.0	Tradeables	29.5	1.0	29.5
				Skilled labour	6.1	0.82	5.0
				Unskilled labour	26.9	0.34	9.1
				Taxes	9.2	0.0	0.0
				Total income before fixed charges	28.3		56.4
					100.0		100.0

Source: Forbes (1976).

between table 10.2 and table 10.3 is that, in the latter, intermediate inputs have been decomposed into their respective primary factors. The labour percentages, for example, now constitute direct and indirect payments so that the various labour shares in table 10.3 expressed as a ratio of those in table 10.2 indicate the earnings multiplier effects arising from the operation of the hotel. Thus for every Cyprus pound spent on the direct employment of unskilled male labour, a further pound's worth of wages to this kind of labour is generated elsewhere in the economy through the hotel's purchasing operations. Consumption multiplier effects arising from the additional consumption benefits to newly employed labour are embodied in the shadow wage calculation.

When comparing the two hotels on the basis of their income statements, several features emerge. First, the higher gross social surplus for the Trinidad Hilton, after allowing for the differences in total income before fixed charges, is principally due to the lower shadow wage for unskilled labour. Second, there is a marked contrast in the relative shares of skilled labour. The reasons for this probably lie in the different definitions of skilled labour and the fact that the Trinidad Hilton was in its start-up period while this study was considering a fully operational concern. In an industry where there is a large element of on-the-job training, labour, which at the inception of the Cyprus Hilton would have been unskilled, would have certainly been trained by 1973. This is an important benefit of tourism projects that is sometimes overlooked. Finally, note that the import content in operating both hotels is relatively high. This is true of many multinational luxury hotels since they aim to provide the international traveller, particularly when on business, with familiar surroundings and so offer a fairly uniform standard of design and services. It has been suggested that developing countries would in many respects be better served by the construction of small hotel complexes which would share common facilities such as restaurants and recreation areas (Kaplan, 1979). It has also been argued that greater local benefits would accrue through the use of indigenous design, construction, fittings and furnishings, management and labour. This has been the policy of the Caribbean Development Bank for some time. However, surely the choice is not mutually exclusive; it depends on the market and the legitimate interests of the governments concerned. There is no economic evidence in the two studies considered that Hilton are not contributing to the welfare of the countries in which they are located, but rather the converse is true. By co-operating with a multinational chain, a government is gaining access to a worldwide marketing network and operational expertise which it cannot hope to match. History has shown that, when governments have become completely involved in revenue operating concerns, their track-record has not on the whole been good.

THE VALUATION OF ENVIRONMENTAL RESOURCES

Environmental resources such as clean air and water, peace and quiet, access to the countryside and recreational facilities are valued by the population at large. However, monetary evaluation of the benefits derived from such resources is often essential to support policies to control environmental pollution and the case for spending on projects which may secure environmental improvements. In these cases, the general principle of valuation is that monetary estimates should reflect *either* what people are willing to pay to gain a benefit (for example, travel cost to recreational facility) *or* the compensation required to accept a cost (for example, increased noise).

A number of methods for deriving such values (for example, travel-cost and hedonic pricing techniques) have already been discussed in the context of CBA. Increasingly, however, environmental resources are being valued using contingent valuation methods (CVM) which involve asking people, under controlled conditions and often indirectly, what they would be prepared to pay to achieve an environmental gain (for example, improvement in air quality) or to preserve an environmental asset (for example, a wildlife habitat) (*Journal of Environmental Planning and Management*, 1993). Finally, actual markets for environmental resources should not be overlooked. For example, soil erosion or atmospheric pollution can be largely or partially valued by assessing their respective impacts on the value of crop production in farming.

In the case of conservation, it is important to recognize the concept of total economic value (TEV). The TEV of an environmental resource comprises two main components: total use value and total non-use value (Pearce, 1991). Total use value itself has two components:

(1) The value to individuals of uses made of the conserved area (for example, recreational visits) and any indirect benefits or functions that the area provides (for example, ecological functions such as drainage).
(2) Option value, which refers to the value that individuals may place on retaining the facility for possible future use.

Non-use value comprises existence value which refers to the intrinsic value of the area or facility to individuals even though they do not intend to make use of it. Existence values are often associated with decisions to donate to causes involving, say, the protection of endangered species, rainforests, historic buildings and monuments and so on. Contingent valuation methods are particularly useful in encompassing both 'option' and 'existence' values, although one problem with using this method is that it is not generally possible to separate out the component parts of TEV (Pearce and Barde, 1991).

Lastly, concern for the future state of the environment underlies the recent philosophy of 'sustainable development', which suggests that current development should not take place at an unacceptable environmental cost to future generations. A 'constant natural assets' rule has also been advocated, which would seek to maintain the stock of environmental assets for future generations (Pearce, 1991). This is not generally taken to mean that no environmental damage should ever occur, but rather that whatever environmental damage is done by a development should be compensated for in similar terms, either through restoration or via alternative provision elsewhere. For example, woodland or wildlife habitats lost through a road-building programme could, in theory, be re-created nearby. Problems arise, however, with unique environments if these are to a large extent irreplaceable.

Several authors have argued that environmental quality should be included in national measures of welfare. There are formidable problems in adopting such an approach, but the main aspects of this line of argument can be shown simply as in figure 10.18. Since the analysis is essentially the same as in the previous diagrams, it will be discussed only briefly. Assuming that an improvement in environmental quality will generally result in a lower level of material consumption (since resources may need to be

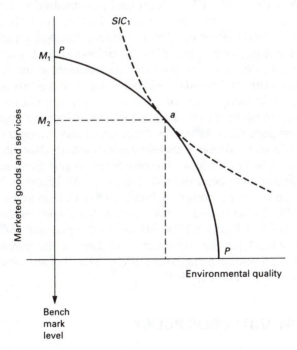

Figure 10.18 *Environmental quality and production frontiers*

diverted from the market sector) and vice versa, society's set of choices can be defined along the frontier *PP*. If environmental benefits are given no weight in this system, then it is likely that maximization of production of marketed goods and services would lead to an extreme position such as M_1. However, if individuals place value on environmental quality (which it is assumed they cannot express via the market), the point which maximizes society's welfare is in fact at a and SIC_1. At this point, however, measurable income has fallen to M_2!

In many cases, economic development proceeds at an unacceptable cost to the natural environment, to human health and, ultimately, to the economy itself through environmental degradation of natural resources. Economies in this position may not even remain on the production frontier shown in figure 10.18. As such, improvements in both environmental quality *and* marketed goods may be possible. Estimates of both non-marketed pollution costs (for example, loss of recreational uses) and marketed pollution costs (for example, forestry and materials damage) in the former Federal Republic of Germany amounted to some DM103 billion over the period 1983–85, equivalent to around 6 per cent of its gross national product (GNP) (Pearce and Kerry Turner, 1990). The direct effects of environmental degradation on GNP (that is, marketed costs alone) may be around 5 per cent of GNP in developed industrialized nations, around 5–10 per cent in East European nations, and as much as 15 per cent in the developing world (Pearce, 1991) – mainly through direct pollution damage, soil erosion, land degradation and deforestation. Improvements in environmental quality may thus lead to improvements in the economy as well as to environmental benefits. Although the solutions are not likely to be without cost, in many cases the costs of control may not involve major investments so much as simply changing the way things are done (see also figure 10.5 on page 422). Where evidence exists concerning the costs and benefits of reducing pollution, it usually suggests that the benefits of control outweigh the costs. For example, the benefits of air pollution regulations in the United States have been estimated at over \$37 billion in 1981 compared to the cost of regulations of between \$13–14 billion in the same year (Portney, 1990). In the United Kingdom, estimates of environmental expenditure came to £14 billion for 1990–91 (about 2.5 per cent of GNP). Over 60 per cent of this figure was on pollution abatement, the remainder being spent mainly on resource management, improvement of amenities and conservation (*Economic Trends*, 1992).

POLLUTION AND PUBLIC POLICY

The problem of controlling externalities caused by pollution is, if anything, more important and also more complex than has been the case in the past.

In the United Kingdom, central-government control dates back as far as 1863, when public outcry against emissions of hydrochloric acid gas from the alkali industry led to the Alkali Act of that year. Subsequently, control of industrial processes not covered by this act was granted to local authorities under the Public Health Acts; however, the emphasis was clearly not on prevention, since action could only be taken if nuisance could be proved.

Following the great London smog of 1952, the Clean Air Act 1956 gave local authorities positive powers to control smoke, dust and grit emissions from combustion processes. These and subsequent acts have ensured improvements in urban air quality and substantial reductions in both smoke and sulphur dioxide emissions into the air (Royal Commission on Environmental Pollution, 1984).

But while some of the old-fashioned environmental problems of smoke and dust appear now to be largely under control, scientific and public concern has shifted to the effects of toxic chemical pollutants, often at low levels of concentration. In particular, emissions of carbon monoxide and hydrocarbons have increased, while emissions of nitrogen oxides have not declined (Royal Commission on Environmental Pollution, 1984) (table 10.5). Other pollutants, especially photochemical oxidants such as ozone, have only been monitored more recently and at relatively few sites, but there is growing evidence to suggest that at elevated levels the effects may be injurious to humans and plant life.

In the urban context, primary atmospheric pollutants can produce secondary pollutants such as photochemical smog – seriously affecting major cities, particularly Los Angeles, São Paulo and Tokyo, and many other cities under certain atmospheric conditions. The smog is formed by the photochemical action of sunlight on pollutants, mainly nitrogen oxides, aldehydes and certain hydrocarbons (from motor vehicles and industrial sources) which react to produce elevated levels of photochemical oxidants and visibility-reducing haze. Chemical reactions of this type are very complex (ozone, for example, may interact with other pollutants) and may occur over long periods of time as air masses are transported over long distances. The effects of secondary pollution are not, therefore, restricted to urban or industrial areas but in many cases take a wider geographical dimension (Royal Commission on Environmental Pollution, 1984). A further problem generated by urban activities is that of acid deposition, which begins when sulphur dioxide and nitrogen oxide emissions – largely from power stations, industry and motor vehicles – are oxidized in the atmosphere to form sulphuric and nitric acids. The resulting acidic deposits are often transported across national frontiers, and are generally recognized as being a major cause of much of the recent damage to forests, lakes and rivers in much of Europe, including the United Kingdom. As many as one in five trees in the EU may have been severely affected.

Table 10.5 Emissions of selected gases and smoke, by emission source, 1990, United Kingdom (percentages and million tonnes)

	Carbon monoxide (CO)	Sulphur dioxide (SO₂)	Black smoke	Nitrogen oxides (NO$_x$)[1]	Carbon dioxide (CO₂)
Percentage from each emission source					
Domestic[2]	4	3	33	2	14
Commercial/public service[3]	–	2	1	2	5
Power stations	1	72	6	28	34
Refineries	–	3	–	1	3
Agriculture	–	–	–	–	–
Other industry	4	16	13	8	23
Railways	–	–	–	1	–
Road transport	90	2	46	51	19
Civil aircraft	–	–	–	1	–
Shipping	–	2	1	5	1
All emission sources (= 100 per cent)					
(million tonnes)	6.66	3.77	0.45	2.73	159.55

Notes: 1. Expressed as nitrogen dioxide equivalent.
 2. Includes sewage sludge disposal.
 3. Includes miscellaneous emission sources.

Source: Warren Spring Laboratory; Department of Trade and Industry.

The complexity of problems brought about by urban pollution can be further illustrated by reference to the findings of several surveys concerning spatial differences in health. In a study in the United States, the concentration of three measures of pollution (sulphur dioxide, nitrogen dioxide and suspended particles) was generally found to increase with city size. The study suggested that major health benefits relating to respiratory diseases and cardiovascular diseases (estimated at more than $1.5 billion annually in direct savings on earnings and medical costs) could be achieved from a 50 per cent reduction in air pollution in major urban areas (Hoch, 1972). While no such monetary estimates have been made for the United Kingdom, the results of studies examining (standardized) mortality rates from various diseases, particularly lung–bronchus cancer, show (for 1980–82) that these have tended to be considerably higher in large urban areas when compared to rural areas: large parts of the cities of West Central Scotland, Tyne and Wear, Cleveland, Humberside, Merseyside, Greater Manchester, West Midlands and Inner London appear to experience mortality rates more than

20 per cent above the United Kingdom average, rising in some cases to as much as 80 per cent (Howe, 1985). When compared with earlier studies (for example 1959–63) (Howe, 1970) the overall geographical pattern seems largely unchanged, except that there appears to have been a marked improvement in Greater London and the surrounding area, apart from Inner London.

Some types of pollution (such as mercury and cadmium) – when discharged into rivers or estuaries – pose special problems in that they are bioaccumulative and can become concentrated via the food chain, progressing, for example, through various forms of aquatic life as far as birds (as well as humans) feeding on poisoned fish. In such cases the effects of pollution are uncertain in magnitude and liable to occur at some distance or point in time from the initial emission. Moreover, since the effects are cumulative, reduction of emissions may not result swiftly in improved quality of the receiving environment. To achieve this, extensive clear-up of previous pollution may be needed. However, pollution problems do not always involve urban or industrial activities; for example, the overuse of nitrogen fertilizers by farmers in East Anglia and surrounding regions is blamed for the exceptionally high nitrate levels in drinking water that affect over a million people in that area (*Guardian*, 1986).

Finally, since some pollutants are considered to be very dangerous even in low concentrations, nothing short of a total ban on their import and use may be considered reasonable (for example, brown and blue asbestos, previously used in the building industry). For other types of pollutant where exposure costs could be high (such as radiation) the risk of exposure is fortunately minute if adequate precautions are taken. Nevertheless, the risk evaluation – derived from the probability of an incident occurring multiplied by the damage costs inflicted – may in fact be high if low risk is offset by high potential damage costs. Locating such activities away from densely populated areas would be sensible (that is, would lower the risk evaluation), but regular monitoring may nevertheless be required. Similarly, with the recently discovered problem of radioactive radon gas found in some homes, a reasonable suggested move would be to ensure that the problem is recognized when new housing is being sited and designed.

An example will illustrate the alternative policy approaches to pollution control (Turvey, 1963). Assume that A is a firm discharging its waste products into a river and that B is a town downstream of A through which the river passes. Figure 10.19(a) shows how A's marginal benefit curve, MB_A (that is, marginal revenue – marginal cost), falls as output rises. If A were under no constraints it would maximize profits by operating at output Qp. The figure also shows B's marginal external cost curve, MEC_B, resulting from the effects of the river pollution. This is seen to rise from left to right since, with higher output and pollution, the town may experience higher

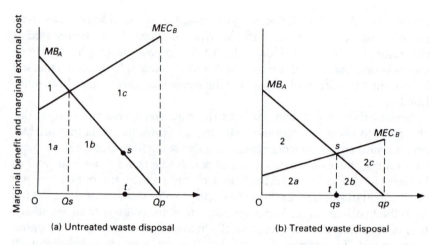

Figure 10.19 *Private benefits and social costs in production: the optimum level of pollution control*

water purification costs and may be unable to use the river for recreational purposes. If water quality deteriorates further, it may well become a nuisance for nearby residents. If A operates at output Qp, it can be seen that the total external cost inflicted upon B is given by the area under the MEC_B curve – that is, $1a + 1b + 1c$. Similarly, the total benefit to A is given by area $1 + 1a + 1b$.

Figure 10.19(b) illustrates the case where the firm has undertaken steps to treat or reduce its waste disposal into the river. This has the effect of reducing the firm's marginal benefit curve (since marginal costs are now higher), but since, for any level of output, pollution is now lower, there is a substantial reduction in the town's marginal external cost curve. Operating at its profit-maximizing output (qp) A's total benefit is now slightly lower at $2 + 2a + 2b$, but B's total external cost is greatly reduced at $2a + 2b + 2c$.

However, from the point of view of society, the optimal solution is for production to take place up to the point where the marginal benefit to the firm of an extra unit produced is equal to the marginal external cost to the town. Beyond this point, marginal external cost to A exceeds the marginal benefit to B. In figures 10.19(a) and (b), MEC_B equals MB_A at points Qs and qs respectively. However, point qs in figure 10.19(b) is clearly superior, since the net benefit to society is equal to area 2 (that is, $2 + 2a - 2a$) while in figure 10.19(a) the net benefit at Qs is only area 1 ($1 + 1a - 1a$).

There are essentially three ways in which the level of output qs could be achieved: (1) taxation, (2) bargaining and (3) regulation.

(1) Taxation involves the 'polluter pays' principle. It was first suggested

by Pigou, who showed how the optimal control of externalities could be achieved by charging the polluter a tax equal to the marginal external cost at the optimal level of production (*qs*). Since the tax would become part of the operating cost of the firm, the latter would need to take it into full account when determining the profit-maximizing level of output. In the case of figure 10.19(b), a Pigovian tax given by *st* (per unit of output) would have the effect of shifting *A*'s marginal benefit curve down, parallel to MB_A.

The problem with this approach is that where both the *nature* and *scale* of *A*'s activities vary, it will be necessary to adopt *two* controls rather than one. With reference to figure 10.19, it can be seen that *both* the level of output and the method of waste disposal (figure 10.19(b)) must be controlled to achieve *qs*. By itself, setting a tax equal to *st* will not achieve the desired result, since the firm would continue to produce (and discharge waste) as in figure 10.19(a) at a level of output slightly below *Qp*.

(2) If there is no impediment to negotiation between the parties involved, it can be shown that bargaining will always produce the optimal solution. In this case MB_A and MEC_B represent the bargaining curves of the two parties. If *A* is liable to pay compensation to *B* then the firm will choose to introduce waste treatment (figure 10.19(b)), will pay 2*a* in compensation to *B* and retain a net gain of 2 (note: this is greater than 1 in figure 10.19(a)). Although the distributional consequences would differ, it might be possible for *B* to compensate *A* to achieve the same result; *B* would be willing to pay up to 1*a* + 1*b* + 1*c* − 2*a* to secure a level of *qs* output, as in figure 10.19(b). Although this may seem unfair, there may nevertheless be circumstances under which it might appear reasonable – for example, *B* might represent a new housing development and the firm *A* may not see why it should incur additional costs if it had been operating for some time without causing externalities when there had previously been few residents in the area.

In practice, however, negotiation may be virtually impossible if there are many sufferers and polluters, or if the source of pollution is unclear.

(3) Regulation could operate if the firm were required first to undertake waste treatment (figure 10.19(b)), and secondly to reduce output (and corresponding pollution) to *qp*. As with the tax solution, this would require full knowledge of *A*'s marginal benefit and *B*'s marginal cost curve, with and without pollution control. The administrative costs of obtaining this information (as well as monitoring discharges) may themselves be quite high and could at worst outweigh any benefits from the scheme. Given the problems involved, a second-best solution may be appropriate; if only the total costs and benefits of production are known, then a total ban on waste disposal would be better than *Qp* output, in figure 10.19(a) (since total costs of 1*a* + 1*b* + 1*c* exceed total benefits of 1 + 1*a* + 1*b*). If more is known about

the alternatives, then a requirement that firms must undertake waste treatment (as in figure 10.19(b)) would be better still – giving a net gain of $2 - 2c$ at qp.

To sum up: first, if negotiation is possible, then a tax is unnecessary except where distributional considerations are involved; secondly, where alternative production methods exist then two controls rather than one may be required; and thirdly, if there are substantial costs in imposing a tax, some form of regulation may be preferable.

In many cases, however, the situation may call for discrete changes in practices or output, or the introduction of controls by firms rather than major changes in production processes. For example, in the previous example the firm or industry may be faced with a choice between different *levels* of waste treatment rather than a straight choice between untreated and treated waste disposal. In this case, it is generally more appropriate to view the cost to the firm in terms of the rising cost of abatement equipment rather than in terms of the value of lost output for a given technical process (that is, *MB* of the firm) (Pearce and Kerry Turner, 1990). This is shown in figure 10.20. The horizontal axis measures pollution, increasing from left to right. In the absence of controls, the firm(s) would be emitting p_1 units of pollution. Assuming that pollution abatement controls are available and can be brought in gradually, the marginal control costs facing the firm are likely to rise along the *MCC* curve from right to left. This illustrates the point that, while the first few units of pollution may be relatively easy and inexpensive to eliminate, at greater levels of control, marginal control or abatement costs often rise sharply, as more elaborate and more

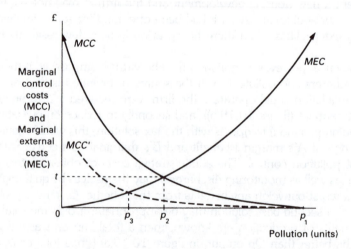

Figure 10.20 *Pollution control and abatement technology*

expensive techniques are called for. As in previous diagrams, marginal external costs (*MEC*), sometimes also known as marginal damage costs, are shown as rising with greater levels of pollution emission. The optimum level of pollution can be seen to occur at point p_2 where *MCC*s just equal *MEC*s. The marginal cost of controlling further units of pollution after p_2 is clearly less than the external costs that these units would cause.

In order to achieve this outcome, the authorities could, for example, impose an emission standard equivalent to Op_2 units of pollution. Generally, this would need to be backed up by substantial fines for firms violating emission limits, otherwise there would be little incentive to comply. Alternatively, a tax of Ot per unit of pollution could be set. Firms would then cut pollution from p_1 to p_2, since (from p_1) up to p_2 units controlled, the (marginal) costs of control are less than the tax they would have to pay. However, up to p_2 units of pollution, firms would clearly prefer to pay the tax (since Ot is less than the *MCC*s). With improvements in control technology over time, the *MCC* curve would fall, for example to *MCC'* in figure 10.20. We can see that this would imply a change in public policy – either reducing the tax to the new point of intersection of *MCC* and *MEC*, or tightening up the emission standard to p_3.

Taxes and emission standards would both require the authorities to have detailed information on the *MEC*s and *MCC*s, and they would both require precise knowledge regarding actual emission levels by firms. In the case of standards, legal sanctions would need to be applied in a consistent manner. Administrative costs and uncertainty could however be reduced by introducing emission standards in various stages. Further emission reductions might only be justified if the total control costs to firms were expected to be less than the reduction in external costs to society (that is, the benefits of pollution reduction). For example, in figure 10.21 a reduction in pollution from p_1 to p_2 would cost firms *ade* in control costs but would reduce external costs by *abcd*, and would thus produce net benefits of *bcde*. While there are likely to be considerable problems in estimating *MCC* and *MEC* functions, the estimation of total control costs and benefits for smaller reductions may prove more straightforward. In the United States, the so-called 'net benefits' criterion has been applied since 1981 to assess regulatory action (Pearce and Barde, 1991).

Compared to taxes, emission standards are often criticized as doing little to encourage firms to consider further possible reductions in pollution. This occurs since standards effectively treat the environment as a 'free good' up to the permitted pollution levels. By contrast, since under the 'polluter pays' principle firms would pay tax on all units of pollution, they have a permanent incentive to seek cheaper ways of controlling emissions and thereby reduce their total tax bills. Furthermore, where firms face very different control costs (perhaps because some plants are much older and more dif-

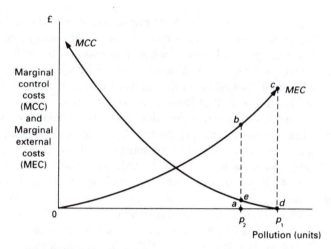

Figure 10.21 *Net benefits of pollution abatement*

ficult to adapt) a pollution tax is likely to be less costly overall than a policy of requiring each firm to undertake a given cut in pollution (Pearce, 1975). This occurs because, under a given tax, firms with relatively low control costs are likely to undertake proportionately more pollution reduction, whereas firms with high control costs would generally undertake less (and pay more tax instead).

It is sometimes argued that pollution taxes and emission standards do not always take account of the ability of the receiving environment to assimilate or disperse the pollution concerned. For example, smoke from domestic chimneys in rural areas may disperse easily and cause few, if any, problems, whereas in densely populated urban areas, this may not always be the case. One possible response to this problem – which is made more complex if many polluters and processes are involved – is to enforce environmental standards representing maximum allowable concentrations of the pollutant in air or water. Such standards are generally easier to administer since pollution is measured in air or water samples rather than at source where many polluters may be involved. However, by paying less attention to pollution at source, environmental standards can result in complex arguments about who or what is responsible (as with nitrate levels in drinking water) and it may be very unclear what the best method is to achieve compliance in cases where the standards are breached. Finally, as with emission standards, environmental standards also appear to provide a 'licence to pollute' up to the limits set.

Overall, the view of the Royal Commission on Environmental Pollution is that more traditional forms of regulation such as emission standards (sometimes known as consents) must remain in place. However, it also recognizes that (water) pollution charging schemes – in addition to discharge consents – have been successful in reducing pollution in countries such as Germany and the Netherlands. The worry, as some studies have suggested, is that pollution taxes alone might not guarantee achievement of the necessary standards (Silberston, 1993). As mentioned above, some combination of taxes *and* standards, or even a system of tradeable permits (which sets emission levels for certain pollutants and effectively auctions pollution rights up to these limits) may well be capable of producing a cost-effective and acceptable solution.

In practice, environmental control policies are generally developed around environmental or air quality standards (EQSs/AQSs) or emission standards (ESs). At present in the United Kingdom, EC directives set AQSs for lead, sulphur dioxide, smoke and nitrogen dioxide, while water quality standards exist for drinking water (nitrate levels) and bathing areas. Examples of ESs exist for classes of alkali and acid works and for cadmium and mercury discharges. To some extent, the advantages of EQSs and ESs can in practice be combined by introducing limit values (LVs) that require outer limits for both EQSs and ESs to be achieved. However, in setting standards, objectivity and scientific proof are not always easily achieved or obtained given the numerous issues and uncertainties involved; in the words of one specialist (on the problem of lead pollution) 'the things we would like to know may be unknowable, so there is some virtue in just getting rid of the problem' (Gowans, 1984).

BOX 10.1: POLLUTION CONTROL IN THE UNITED KINGDOM

Traditionally, the United Kingdom has favoured a case-by-case approach, with emission limits being set at varying levels depending on local environmental conditions, financial implications and so on. However, most European countries and the European Commission favour uniform effluent emission limits based on the best available control technology. By 1987 it became clear that the United Kingdom would accept a new approach more consistent with EC thinking. Policy was streamlined in the late 1980s, and in 1987 a central body, Her Majesty's Inspectorate of Pollution (HMIP), was established.

The current system of pollution control stems from the Environmental Protection Act 1990 (EPA) (Tromans and Clarkson, 1991; Harris, 1992; Layfield, 1992a, 1992b; Pugh-Smith, 1992). Industrial processes proscribed by regulations made under the Act may not be carried on without the prior grant of an authorization by an 'enforcing authority'. In the case of more complex

continued

and potentially more damaging processes and substances, HMIP is the relevant authority. It operates within the framework of 'integrated pollution control' (IPC) exercisable in respect of any environmental medium. This enables a cross-media approach to be taken towards emissions into air, water and land. A greater number of less complex and less potentially polluting processes require authorization from local authorities under the system of local authority air pollution control (LAAPC). IPC and LAAPC have common features regarding the regulatory framework, administrative provisions and standards and measures employed. In particular, one of the main statutory objectives to be achieved in every authorization set out in Section 7(2) of the Act, involves ensuring that, in carrying out a prescribed process, the 'best available techniques not entailing excessive cost' (BATNEEC) will be used. In practice, this involves not only the provision of appropriate technology, but also its effective use, which may include the number, qualifications and training of persons employed in the process, and the design, construction, layout and maintenance of the building in which it is carried on (Section 7(10) of the Act).

In order to achieve consistency of authorizations, the Chief Inspector publishes guidance notes stating HMIP's views as to achievable standards and methods of achieving them. Applications that do not conform with the relevant guidance note will probably only gain authorization if an applicant can establish that use of the best available techniques would entail excessive cost.

Overall, as technology evolves, it is generally anticipated that the application of the BATNEEC concept will mean that firms will be expected to meet higher control standards. Finally, the National Rivers Authority (NRA), established in 1989, provides consents for other non-prescribed discharges into watercourses, and is also responsible for monitoring water pollution. Further amalgamation of the NRA, HMIP and other regulatory bodies into a unified environmental protection agency seems likely to take place during the 1990s.

In the future, it is likely that economic incentives (taxes and subsidies) will increasingly become part of the European Union's (EU) environmental policy (Delbeke, 1991). Indeed, the 'polluter pays' principle was confirmed in the Single European Act, Article 130R(2), and is forming the basis for the design of economic instruments.

Finally, environmental considerations and national planning and development control policies have been brought closer by the EU's Environmental Impact Assessment Directive (see DoE, 1988, 1989), obliging member states to assess the environmental impact of major construction projects before they are implemented. Certain categories of project – crude oil refineries, thermal power stations, chemical installations, major roads and railways, large airports and trading ports – must be subjected to an impact assessment. Other categories of project may undergo an assessment at the discretion of the Member States. For example, other transport projects may require an assessment at the discretion of the competent authority (for example, highway or planning authority) if the project is likely to have significant environmental impact. Such projects could include other roads, harbours, other airfields, light rail schemes, pipelines and marinas (Ferrary, 1990). An environmental statement (ES) must accompany planning applications for projects which fall into the above categories. This must include a description and evaluation of the likely effects of the project on human beings; flora and fauna; soil, water, air, climate and landscape; the interaction of all these factors; and material assets and the cultural heritage. It should also suggest appropriate methods of mitigating such effects. Finally, the overall environmental assessment must take into account information and opinions received; and the public must be consulted and can propose alternatives (CEC, 1990).

AIR POLLUTION – GLOBAL ISSUES

Global pollution arises because the effects of many types of pollutant can cross national boundaries, affecting those Earth's resources that we all share such as the atmosphere and the world's oceans. Global warming, which we shall consider below, is one such problem, brought about by the recent and rapid increase in 'greenhouse gas' emissions.

Global Warming

Carbon dioxide is known to be the main contributor to the 'greenhouse effect'. This occurs as heat from the Sun becomes trapped, reducing the rate of heat loss and raising Earth's temperature (figure 10.22). The burning of fossil fuels and deforestation have increased the concentration of carbon dioxide by a quarter over the past 200 years and on present trends, atmospheric CO_2 may double by the year 2030 (figure 10.23) (Ferrary, 1990). However, even with increased energy efficiency and conservation measures, and use of alternative fuels, carbon dioxide concentrations will probably continue to rise over the next fifty years as aggregate world energy demand increases. The possible effects are not known for certain, but it is expected that in the long-term, global average temperatures could rise by between 1.5–4.5°C producing changes in sea levels, rainfall patterns and agricultural production. Given that around 3 billion people live in coastal regions, the effects of coastal erosion on infrastructure, housing and transport systems in these areas could be substantial. However, all countries would clearly be affected to some degree by changing climatic conditions.

It has been estimated that the capital cost for the United Kingdom of

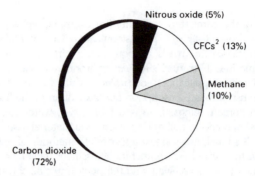

Notes: 1. Man-made emissions.
        2. Chlorofluorocarbons.
Source: Department of the Environment.

Figure 10.22 *Relative contribution to the greenhouse effect of various gases, 1990[1], percentages*

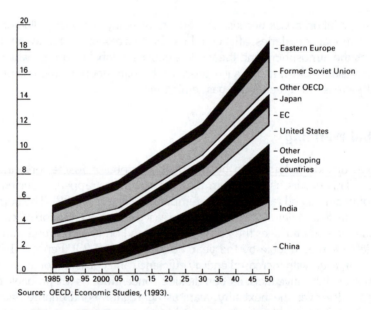

Source: OECD, Economic Studies, (1993).

Figure 10.23 *Projected carbon emissions (billion tonnes)*

improving sea defences to cope with a sea level rise of up to 1.65 m by the year 2050 would amount to at least £5 billion (Boorman *et al.*, 1989). The size of this figure suggests that some areas might have to be left unprotected because the works involved would not be justified on cost–benefit grounds. Overall, Organization for Economic Co-operation and Development (OECD) estimates put the cost of stabilizing CO_2 emissions to 1990 levels by the year 2050 at between 1 per cent and 3 per cent of world GDP.

In view of the potential seriousness of global warming, the EU encouraged Member States to make commitments to stabilize emissions of CO_2 at their 1990 levels by the year 2000. However, this objective proved difficult to achieve. This was partly because of the increase in the volume of transport, for example the share of total United Kingdom energy demand accounted for by all transport activities – currently about 30 per cent of total energy demand by final users – rose steadily throughout the 1990s (although transport accounted for less than a quarter of United Kingdom CO_2 emissions). In 1988, transport exceeded the energy demand of both industrial and domestic sectors for the first time (figure 10.24) (DoE, 1989). Of the four main transport sub-sectors (road, rail, air and water), roads now account for about 80 per cent (and car travel alone about 70 per cent) of energy used for transport. The DETR anticipates that road traffic volume may increase by around 125 per cent between 1988 and 2025. Without measures to moderate growth of car mileage or to improve fuel economy, CO_2 emissions from personal travel might increase by as much as a third as early as 2005 (Hughes, 1991). However, particularly in built-up areas, congestion is already a problem and this will get worse as traffic increases, further reducing fuel efficiency and increasing urban pollution. At the European level transport accounts for around 25 per cent of CO_2 emissions, with almost half of this due to urban traffic alone. Improved public transport, light rail schemes and so on, combined with traffic restraint measures such as road pricing, would certainly help reduce congestion and improve the urban environment (see table 10.6). Schemes such as the Tyne and

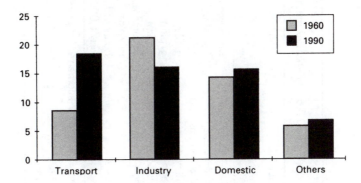

Source: *Digest of United Kingdom Energy Statistics* (HMSO, 1993). Crown copyright.

Figure 10.24 *Final users' energy consumption by sector, United Kingdom, 1960 and 1990 (billion therms)*

Table 10.6 Differential impact of transport modes on a number of environmental variables

Environmental variable	Unit	Car	Car with 3-way catalytic converter	Rail	Bus
Land use	m²/person	120	120	7	12
Primary energy use	g coal equivalent units/pkm	90	90	31	27
Carbon dioxide emissions	g/pkm	200	200	60	59
Nitrogen dioxide emissions	g/pkm	2.2	0.34	0.08	0.02
Hydrocarbons	g/pkm	1	0.15	0.02	0.08
Carbon monoxide emissions	g/pkm	8.7	1.3	0.05	0.15
Air pollution	polluted air m³/pkm	38,000	5,900	1,200	3,300
Accident risks	hours of life lost/1,000 pkm	11.5	11.5	0.4	1

Note: pkm = passenger kilometre. One passenger travelling one kilometre is 1 pkm; g = gramme.

Source: Based on Teutel, D. (1989) Die Zukunft des Autoverkehrs, Heidelberg, Report Nr 17 Umwelt- und Prognose Institut (UPI).

Wear Metro have undoubtedly been a success but in general (and outside London), bus patronage has been falling and in the late 1980s passenger kilometres declined steadily by 3–4 per cent a year (Hills, 1991). Nevertheless, the EU is keen to encourage such schemes: for example, in 1993 the European Investment Bank provided a £98 million loan to enable the Jubilee Line extension in London to go ahead.

About 30 per cent of Britain's CO_2 emissions originate from heating and lighting and so on in domestic dwellings. While studies (Department of Energy, 1989) suggest that considerable savings on space heating can be achieved without difficulty in 'new build', the rate of replacement of the existing stock is very slow. In existing dwellings, many of which are very old, the scope for cost-effective energy efficiency improvements (mainly through cavity fill and loft insulation, double glazing, improved boilers and controls, and improved lighting) is much more restricted. Domestic energy consumption may increase by as much as 20 per cent between 1985 and 2005. However, with increased application of energy efficiency measures, savings of around 5 million tonnes (as carbon) could be achieved representing around 11 per cent of 1985 CO_2 emissions from domestic sources.

One problem is that even if measures are cost-effective, it is well known that individuals may fail to undertake the necessary investment. This might arise for a number of reasons: first, for major works, the required expenditure may be high in relation to earnings, and credit may be expensive; secondly, home owners who move frequently may feel that such investment is not fully reflected in capital values on sale; thirdly, consumers may lack the necessary technical information on which to base their decisions; and finally, many groups, particularly the poor and the elderly, may have high implicit discount rates (possibly as high as 80 per cent), meaning that they would only invest in more expensive energy-saving work or equipment if the long-run cost savings were very high indeed. Although grants exist for energy-saving investment in the home, other policy approaches could include requiring houses for sale to undergo an energy audit (as in Denmark, for example) which would help to raise the sale price of more efficient homes.

In terms of electricity generation, the government worked towards achieving 1,500 megawatts (MW) of renewable energy by the year 2000 (which, of course, would have produced no direct CO_2 emissions). However, this still only accounted for a very small proportion (3 per cent) of the United Kingdom's total energy requirements – the equivalent of only three modern 500 MW power stations. In 1991, the House of Commons Select Committee subsequently recommended a higher target of between two to three times this level.

In 1991 the European Commission (EC) announced its intention to introduce a carbon tax. This would have been placed on fossil fuels (coal, oil and gas) in proportion to their carbon content, thus taxing CO_2 emissions at source. Similar taxes exist in Sweden and have been considered in the United States. The proposed tax, planned to be phased in gradually, would have had many beneficial effects. First, it would have reduced energy demand through direct reductions in use. Secondly, it would have encouraged higher levels of investment in energy efficiency measures; and thirdly, it would have promoted a switch to less energy-intensive forms of transport. Finally, it would have encouraged a shift in energy generation towards less environmentally damaging fuels (for example, renewable energy sources such as wind and tidal power), and more efficient means of deriving energy from fossil fuel sources, for example, combined heat and power. Tax revenues – possibly as much as £17 billion – could have been used to reduce taxation elsewhere, to offset some of the effects on poorer households, and to subsidize energy-efficient public transport systems. However, some industries, particularly those using large quantities of electricity (for example, iron and steel, chemicals, cement, clay and glass), would be greatly affected by such a tax (CEC, 1992). On the other hand, higher investment levels could result as firms would be likely to replace older, less efficient machinery and buildings at an earlier opportunity. The disadvantages lie primarily in the undoubted regressive nature of the tax and its probable dampening effect on travel in rural areas. Also, trade distortions could arise if other countries did not introduce similar taxes, since domestic industries would be penalized. Furthermore, if world oil prices fell as a result of EU actions, energy consumption in non-taxing countries would probably rise, thus reducing net gains at a global level.

At the Rio de Janeiro 'Earth Summit' in 1992, the UN Framework Convention on Climate Change was signed by delegates of 158 countries to slow global warming. However, the agreement was in principle only, and the United States (with only 4 per cent of the world's population but 25 per cent of the world's CO_2 emissions) signed only on condition that it lacked targets for improvement. As a development of the Rio summit, delegates from 166 countries participated in the Berlin Climate Conference of 1995 in an attempt to seek an agreement over the reduction of CO_2 emissions. Whereas the industrialized countries were willing to limit emissions to 1990 levels by the year 2000, opposition to this constraint came from members of the Organization of Petroleum-Exporting Countries, fearful of an adverse effect on their exports.

In an attempt to set targets and timetables for the reduction of greenhouse gases to the year 2020, delegates from 124 countries met in 1997 at the Kyoto summit. But whereas the UK (with its own target) aimed to reduce emissions of CO_2 by 20 per cent from 1990 levels by 2010, and the EU sought only a 15 per cent cut for its members, both Japan and the United

States opposed the EU's proposal on the grounds that 'the EU countries could do deals among themselves, allowing Germany and Britain to make larger, easier cuts, and other countries to do less, such as Portugal and Greece' (Lee, 1999: 247). At the conclusion of the summit, it was agreed that – under the Convention on Climate Change – Japan would reduce CO_2 emissions by 6 per cent, the United States by 7 per cent and the EU by 8 per cent, but since trading in emissions was permissible, the United States could 'buy notional reductions from a rundown Russia and cut by only 3.5 per cent' (Lee, 1999: 247). This was agreed by China as a *quid pro quo* for exempting developing countries entirely from emissions reduction – even though China 'will eventually overtake the USA as the world's largest CO_2 emitter, and the developing countries with their soaring populations will become the largest greenhouse source' (McCarthy, 1998: 3). However, without emissions trading, the United States would not have ratified the agreement, and many signatories thought the agreed 5.2 per cent cut by 38 countries had been too high. But even this cut – which is unlikely to be achieved by 2010 – is considered inadequate by United Nations' environmentalists in comparison to the 60 per cent required to counteract the impact of greenhouse gases on the world's climate (United Nations, 1999).

BOX 10.2: AIR AND WATER POLLUTION IN CHINA

With the enormous size of China's population, rapid economic development is threatening the natural environment. Substantial population growth, industrialization and highly subsidized water and energy – with no incentive to conserve their use – have all had a dire effect on the environment. 'Worse, the deficiencies in the quantity and quality of land, air, and water are escalating rather than improving' (Starr, 1999: 168–9).

Two-thirds of China's factories, with their obsolescent and inefficient equipment, are burning excessive quantities of soft coal – the principal cause of air pollution throughout much of the People's Republic, while in Hong Kong airborne particulates from vehicle emissions produce a level of air pollution nearly 50 per cent greater than that in New York (Gittings, 1999). With the development of the motor industry (with annual targets of 3 million new cars set for the early years of the new millennium), the effects on pollution will be severe. Already the air in 90 per cent of China's cities does not meet Chinese government clean-air standards (which are not as stringent as Western ones), and China has become the fourth largest source of greenhouse gases in the world (producing 10 per cent of the total) (Starr, 1999). At current rates of economic development, China will produce three times the present US level by 2025 (Starr, 1999).

The consumption of tap water in China's cities increased fivefold in the

continued

period 1980–95, but not only is the water supply inadequate, its quality is rapidly deteriorating. Factories and cities discharged 37.3 billion tons of sewage and industrial waste into waterways and coastal waterways in 1995 (Starr, 1999), while in Hong Kong 75 per cent of the SEZ's sewage is discharged into the harbour with only minimal screening (Gittings, 1999). Aside from Hong Kong, more than a quarter of China's freshwater supply is polluted, and 90 per cent of the water flowing through its major cities is undrinkable.

Severe air and water pollution has occurred 'not because of an absence of agencies, laws or regulations. On the contrary, China has a reasonably complete set of environmental protection laws and regulations and a fully articulated structure of government offices devoted to environmental matters' (Starr, 1999: 172).

In 1973 (five years before economic reforms began), a national conference addressed the problem of environmental pollution. In 1979, an Environmental Protection Law was passed by the National People's Congress, and in 1984 the National Environmental Protection Agency (NEPA) was set up. In 1989, the National People's Congress revised the Environmental Protection Law. Environmental impact studies were now required for all major construction projects, and stiff fines for violating the pollution limits were imposed. All this produced positive results. In the mid-1990s, China was spending about 1 per cent of GDP, or US$6.5 billlion on environmental protection annually (almost comparable with the international average level of expenditure, which stands between 1 and 2 per cent of GNP) (Starr, 1999: 172), while in Hong Kong as much as US$3.4 billion will be spent on constructing a new sewage disposal system during the first decade of the new millennium (Gittings, 1999).

Research in the environmental sciences has led to a new, clean-burning coal compound being introduced in the cities to replace the highly polluting soft coal, and natural gas is replacing coal (in, for example, Beijing) as a household and industrial fuel. Both coal and water are being brought into the price range that should encourage conserving their use (Starr, 1999: 172).

In China, environmental issues are particularly difficult to resolve since 'a clash of interests between the central government and regional authorities often ends in deadlock and inaction' (Starr, 1999: 173). When decisions are eventually taken, economic development takes precedence over environmental protection – as was demonstrated at the Kyoto summit when China negotiated an opt-out from the proposed cuts in CO_2 emissions. Also, there is undoubtedly insufficient funding for environmental concerns at the national level. As in Russia and Eastern Europe, China has a double burden: first, it must reduce the damage currently being done to the environment and, secondly, it must clean up the damage caused by past pollution. Far more than 1 per cent of the GNP might therefore have to be spent on environmental enhancement. It can only be hoped that in the new five-year plan, environmental protection and sustainable development will be very much on the agenda.

In the UK, however, policies have been put in place to cut CO_2 emissions to a much greater degree than that agreed at Kyota (20 per cent as opposed to 5.2 per cent by 2010). Since the financial year 1997–98, the government was committed to increase the tax on petrol by at least 5 per cent a year above the rate of inflation, and in the budget of March 1999 it was announced that an energy tax would be introduced in April 2001 applicable to all industrial and commercial energy users, including agriculture and the public sector, but not transport.

OTHER GLOBAL PROBLEMS

As with other aspects of global pollution, the reduction of greenhouse gas emissions presents certain *public good* characteristics and problems. Because it is shared by everyone, efforts to improve the global environment by one country will automatically be extended to others. There is thus an incentive not to implement costly environmental protection measures but to *free ride* on other countries' efforts to control emissions. Clearly, if everyone adopts this approach improvements will never occur, which is why binding international agreements are so essential.

Another of the major global environmental problems concerns damage to the ozone layer (see figure 10.25), caused largely by chlorofluorocarbons (CFCs), mainly of the type used in aerosols. Ozone depletion will increase

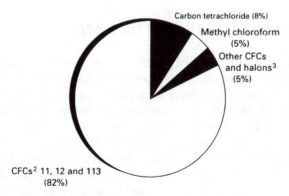

Carbon tetrachloride (8%)

Methyl chloroform (5%)

Other CFCs and halons[3] (5%)

CFCs[2] 11, 12 and 113 (82%)

Notes: 1. Based on 1985 gas emissions.
            2. Chlorofluorocarbons.
            3. CFCs 114 and 115, halons 1301, 1211 and 2402 and HCFC 22.
Source: UK Stratosphenc Ozone Review Group.

Figure 10.25 *Relative contribution of various gases to depletion of the ozone layer[1], percentages*

the amount of ultra-violet radiation reaching Earth, resulting in an increased incidence of skin cancer and serious effects on agricultural crops and marine life. In 1992, recorded concentrations of ozone in the atmosphere above Europe, Russia and Canada were at their lowest level in 35 years, and a 50 per cent destruction of the ozone layer above populated areas of southern Argentina and Chile was reported (World Meteorological Organization). In 1987, the Montreal Protocol, which was an attempt to reduce substances that deplete the ozone layer, was signed by all major CFC-producing countries. More recently, the EC has proposed to phase out CFCs by 1995.

On the international issue of acid rain referred to earlier, European agreement was reached leading to the Large Combustion Plant Directive in 1988. By 2003, emissions of sulphur dioxide will have been cut, in stages, by 60 per cent from their 1980 levels. Nitrogen oxides (NO_x) were also to be reduced by 30 per cent, ending in 1998. Other northern industrial countries would have preferred larger cuts, but levels and progress were reviewed again in 1995 and the United Kingdom could well be called upon to make greater reductions. However, since around 50 per cent of NO_x emissions are due to road transport, the requirement to fit all new cars with catalytic converters from January 1993 should greatly reduce these emissions, as well as improving the urban environment.

Finally, since some poorer European member states may find financial difficulty in adhering to EU environmental commitments, the Cohesion Fund proposed under the Maastricht Treaty will help to channel cash to environmental projects in Greece, Spain, Portugal and the Irish Republic.

SUSTAINABLE URBAN DEVELOPMENT

In addition to the problems of pollution in the developed world, around 600 million urban dwellers in the newly-industrializing and developing countries 'live in life-threatening environments with respect to overcrowded and inadequate shelter, sanitation and drainage, unsafe housing sites and working conditions, and the absence of primary health care' (Potter and Lloyd-Evans, 1998: 188; see also Hardoy et al., 1992; Kirkby et al., 1995). Clearly, in the developing world, it is normally the urban poor who are the principal sufferers when their habitats are subjected to environmental hazards such as earthquakes, floods, hurricanes and landslides – compounded by air and water pollution.

Economic Growth Versus Environmental Enhancement

Since it is widely recognized that developing countries invariably opt for short-term economic gains at the expense of the environment (Potter and Lloyd-Evans, 1998), at the Rio Summit the advanced industrial countries of the world insisted on greater efforts by the developing countries to conserve resources, but without giving due consideration to the poverty of many of these countries. While the Summit was clearly mindful of the Brundland Commission's definition of sustainable development, i.e. 'development which meets the needs of the present, without compromising the ability of future generations to meet their own needs' (WCED, 1987), it failed to acknowledge that the most effective way of encouraging developing countries to reduce the exploitation of their natural resources would have been through the reduction of their debt burden.

It is ironic that attempts by the World Bank, for example, to increase urban productivity and the adoption of Western technology, are producing less sustainable forms of development and, in consequence, increased poverty and environmental degregation (Potter and Lloyd-Evans, 1998: 91; see also Braidotti *et al.*, 1994). In contrast, *sustained development* within the context of continued growth could, arguably, ensure that an adequate use of natural resources would improve the quality of, and access to, basic services such as health, education and housing.

Whereas in advanced industrial countries, the concept of the 'sustainable city' is associated with high-density living and a movement of population back to the urban core in order to reduce travel-to-work times and energy consumption, and damage to the ozone layer, in the developing world the immediate concerns are water supply, sanitation, shelter and access to secure livelihoods (Potter and Lloyd-Evans, 1998).

While it is acknowledged that sustainable cities should not – through the medium of their production and consumption patterns – impose unsustainable demands on local or global natural resources and systems, there is a 'lack of consensus as to whether developing world cities should be seen as centres of economic productivity as proposed by the World Bank, or centres of environmental problems and concentrations of social deprivation (see United Nations, 1995), or whether they are locales from which to promote equitable and sustainable development' (Potter and Lloyd-Evans, 1998: 192–3). There is, however, little doubt that 'environmental problems become more serious when the urban population increases without the appropriate institutional framework' (Potter and Lloyd-Evans, 1998: 193) – as, for example, in many of the cities of Asia Pacific – and when rural–urban functions are blurred through the development of 'extended metropolitan regions' (McGee and Yeung, 1993). Nevertheless, cities – even in the developing world – should be better placed than rural regions to meet such sustainable goals as a healthy living and working environment, a safe water supply, the provision of sanitation, drainage and garbage treatment, paved roads, an adequate economic base and good governance (Hardoy *et al.*, 1992).

Urban Environmental Needs

Although the World Bank's *Brown Agenda* focused on population growth, basic needs and economic productivity, it emphasized the need for governments to control growth and enforce the relevant legislation in order to reduce the risk of environmental hazards (World Bank, 1991, 1993). However, the agenda failed to recognize that environmental degregation disproportionately disadvantaged the poor, who – as a result – suffer high rates of infant mortality, limited life expectancy, disability and work-related injury, disease, a poor quality of life and mental ill-health (Potter and Lloyd-Evans, 1998). Bearing in mind that more than 50 per cent of the world's population live in substandard housing, and that within Asia alone 60 per cent of the urban population is living in slums and squatter settlements, it can surely be argued that 'access to safe land, adequate shelter and basic services constitute fundamental human rights which must underlie any notion of sustainable development' (Potter and Lloyd-Evans, 1998: 96; see also Hardoy and Satterthwaite, 1989; Hardoe *et al.*, 1992; Satterthwaite, 1995).

With the unplanned expansion of cities in the developing world, there has been little or no increase in the provision of services, in controls over environmental degregation and in the development of an appropriate framework for urban governance. As a result, informal settlements have spread into marginal areas vulnerable to environmental hazards such as flooding and landslides, and – within these areas – a high incidence of biological pathogens and restricted access to safe water and sanitation increase the risk of serious illness and premature death (Potter and Lloyd-Evans, 1998; see also WHO, 1992).

Although organizations such as the World Bank (1991) and ILO (1995) suggest that the main way in which developing world cities can finance environmental improvements is by means of increased economic growth, this fails to take into account that within 'free market economies' such an approach might not only result in 'unregulated construction, the unsuitable location of industry, the exploitation of human resources and widespread pollution' (Potter and Lloyd-Evans, 1998: 198), but also in the widening of the gap between the rich and the poor within the developing countries, and in global trading arrangements which favour the advanced capitalist countries but reduce the ability of developing countries to sustain their own environments.

Uncontrolled industrial location in the poorer countries has been associated, in part, with the movement of hazardous industries from the developed to the developing world, and in part by the location decisions of nationalized industries. In India, for example, the explosion at the Union Carbide factory in Bhopal in 1984 led to much loss of life, and in Mexico

City the explosion at the nationalized PEMEX petroleum plant (also in 1984) similarly led to many fatalities, while in more recent years a number of industrial fires in the developing world have resulted in large losses of life (Potter and Lloyd-Evans, 1998). In addition, severe environmental abuse is inflicted on local communities by multinational and nationalized industries dumping toxic waste, discharging toxic effluent into rivers and releasing toxic gases into the atmosphere – practices which are generally banned or constrained within the developed world.

It is increasingly recognized that many of the problems of sustainability in the developing world are attributable to the failure to develop good governance. Although there is a need at a national level to consider equity, social justice and human rights, access to basic needs and greater environmental awareness, at a local level 'priority must be given to employment, shelter and poverty alleviation, as poverty undermines households' ability to control their own sustainable development' (Potter and Lloyd-Evans, 1998: 202).

URBAN CONGESTION

There can be little doubt that population increase and urban congestion rank among the world's biggest problems, but even if in some countries – notably within the developed world – population grows more slowly than in the recent past, or even falls, there is still a tendency towards urbanization. However, although urbanization is both a result and cause of an increase in GNP, economic growth is not without its price – a sum largely omitted from GNP statistics. It has caused appalling traffic congestion in most of the world's cities, it is associated with the decay of the inner urban areas since 'greenfield' locations have become either more attractive or the only economically feasible locations for residential populations and industry and commerce, and its effects have put increased pressure on local government or state finance.

Economics and the Traffic Congestion Problem

Transport – because of its demands on land – plays an important role in determining the scale, nature and form of urban areas. Whereas the proportion of land occupied by roads and parking is only 16 per cent in Greater London, in most other cities of the developed and newly-industrializing world it is considerably higher – rising to US levels, where, for example, it was as high as 40 per cent in Cincinnati, 50 per cent in Detroit and 60 per cent in Los Angeles even in the 1970s (Doxiadis, 1971). Together with roads and their ancillary uses, railway facilities, airports, docks and harbours make the total area of land devoted to transport in most of the world's cities, the largest single urban land use after housing. The efficiency of transport, and implicitly the efficiency of the use of land for transport, should greatly contribute to the level of productivity, growth and thus the standard of living, but ironically it is economic growth, together with changing consumer preferences and technical advance (permitting more convenient and personal travel over more extensive areas) that produce the problems of urban road transport.

BOX 10.3: TRAFFIC CONGESTION IN THE UNITED KINGDOM

Following a high level of public expenditure on road development in the late-1980s and early-1990s – based on the principle of 'predict and provide', a cost-cutting government in the five years from 1992/93 brought about a 25 per cent reduction in transport investment and left a legacy of severe congestion and an under-financed, under-planned and under-maintained transport system – in part an outcome of bus deregulation (from 1985), the axing of the Crossrail project in London (in 1993) and rail privatization (in 1996–97).

By the end of the 1990s, there were 28 million vehicles on Britain's roads, twice as many as in 1970, but more significantly the number had increased by a fifth since the late-1980s. The DETR (1998a, 1998b) moreover, forecast that traffic will increase between a third and three-quarters nationally by the year 2020 (and that over 80 per cent of the increased number will be private motor cars). Clearly, congestion – particularly in cities – will become increasingly serious unless radical measures are introduced to force people out of their cars and on to buses and trains.

In contrast to many other countries, the principal reason for congestion in Britain is not only inadequate investment, but also poorly-targeted funding. OECD research reveals that Britain not only invests less than 1 per cent of its GDP on roads, railways, bus and tram networks – equivalent to a per capita sum of only £110 (compared to £168 in France, £200 in Germany, £208 in Sweden and £420 in Switzerland), but also relies more on roads than any other EU member (Walters, 1999). Whereas in the UK 88.3 per cent of all passenger journeys were by car and 11.7 per cent by buses and trains, the EU average was 82.2 per cent by car and 15 per cent by public transport (Walters, 1999).

Arguably, financial carrots and sticks (in the form of extra public expenditure and congestion taxation) are required in the UK if the confict between the car and the environment is to be resolved. During the period of Labour government post-1997, an integrated transport policy gradually emerged based on the need to create more of a balance between the demand for public transport and the use of the private motor car.

In an attempt to satisfy or even boost the demand for public transport, the government in 1998 announced that – out of extra transport funding of £1.8 billion – £700 million would be available for the establishment of 150 new local transport systems to facilitate bus travel and restrain car use, £300 million would be allocated to help local bus services, and an extra £300 million or more would be invested in rail services. Subsequently, in July 2000, the government announced that £123 billion of public money would be allocated to transport over the following ten years. Like the 1998 provisions (which necessitated a supplementary injection of £3–5 billion of private funds), the new allocation is linked to plans to raise an extra £56 billion from the private sector through the medium of public/private partnerships.

However, a third source of funding might emanate from the private motorist, and to this end the Transport Bill of 1999 set out the conditions whereby local authorities – by 2005 – could tax congestion through toll and company car park charges, and divert the proceeds – predicted to be as much as £1 billion per annum – to public transport. This, however, was not exclusively a fiscal matter, since an underlying policy aim was to persuade one in ten car users to give up their vehicles, and the remainder to use public transport more frequently. Possible methods of implementing toll charges would include electronic systems administered by local authorities, who would also have the power to levy new workplace parking charges on businesses, but not on non-workplace parking at, for example, out-of-town retail and leisure sites – an omission criticized by environmental groups such as Friends of the Earth. In London, under the Government of London Act 1998, the mayor has the power to impose tolls on motorists using designated routes and levy fees from big employers with company car parks. As in the rest of the UK, the revenue will be used to improve public transport – which in London includes the underground as well as rail and bus services.

Whether or not the above carrot and stick policies will work, only time will tell, but it is a matter of some concern that most of the extra funding for public transport will only become available after congestion charges and workplace parking taxes are in place. Since motorists will thus be deprived of the option to switch over to an adequately subsidized and technically efficient form of public transport during the early years of direct road pricing, legislation will be unpopular and possibly – from a political point of view – unsustainable. Alternatively, during the period 2000–2010, the Chancellor might consider releasing further resources to fund (in partnership with the private sector) a modern and low-cost system of public transport until such time when congestion charges etc. provide most of the necessary funds.

Road Use and Development

In most countries of the world, the number of motor vehicles in use has increased at a faster rate than expenditure on highways. Road-building and improvements have consequently not kept pace with the growth of motor traffic – with the result that most urban areas in the developed and newly-industrializing world are suffering from varying degrees of congestion.

In Western Europe and the United States – although the total population has virtually stabilized – the rapid increase in the number of car-owning households and the increase in the number of families with more than one car have led to a substantial increase in car-ownership reaching, for example, 600 per 1,000 of the population in Italy in 1996, or 747 per 1,000 in the United States (*Economist*, 1998a). Facilitating an increase in separate social trips, separate shopping trips and separate journeys to work, economic activity – as a consequence – has become decentralized within the urban arena, and residential choice has become increasingly dissociated from the location of jobs, schools and shopping centres. In the United Kingdom, more than two-thirds of all journeys to work are now made by car (compared to about half in 1980), and nearly one-fifth of all morning peak traffic involves taking children to school; while in the United States, 73 per cent of workers commuted by car in 1990 compared to 64 per cent in 1980 (*Economist*, 1998a).

In the cities of the newly-industrializing world, traffic congestion is of rapidly increasing severity with around 400 cars per thousand population in Kuala Lumpur and Bangkok in the mid-1990s, 200 per thousand in Jakarta, 150 per thousand in Singapore and Seoul, and 100 per thousand in Manila (*Economist*, 1998a). However, in these burgeoning cities, traffic congestion is not an outcome of in-migration (and population growth) *per se*, since the poor – who constitute the majority of in-migrants – are rarely car-owners and even find public transport fares beyond their means. Instead, congestion is the result of rising incomes and high income elasticity of demand for car (or two-car) ownership. With steadily increasing urban incomes, car ownership in, for example, Mexico City increased by 30 per cent from 1991 to 1996, and in Seoul doubled over the same period (*Economist*, 1998a).

Traffic congestion, however, might be regarded as 'the price that has to be paid' to ensure economic growth and a higher material standard of living, and it might also be of less general concern than other urban problems such as poverty (often juxtaposed with great wealth), disease, poor education, crime and non-traffic pollution. Many commuters, moreover, experience relatively little congestion, and fairly short journey distances and journey times to work, and are willing to commute in order to experience a wider choice of housing, residential location, jobs, schools and social facilities.

However, since traffic congestion adds to the costs of production, is a major contributor to air and noise pollution, is a cause of accidents and results in an excessive dependence on oil, it is not only inflationary but also socially and environmentally unsustainable. For some time, this has been recognized and since the 1960s four possible solutions to congestion have been considered (see Roth, 1967):

(1) doing nothing, and allowing congestion to be its own deterrent;
(2) redeveloping cities to accommodate all the vehicles wishing to circulate within them (assuming public funds are available);
(3) restricting the use of motor vehicles in core areas so as to reduce total traffic volumes to the capacity of existing streets;
(4) imposing an economic solution by recognizing that road space is scarce and rationing it by a direct form of pricing.

The first approach – inevitably – would be long-term, it might not succeed unless there were accompanying and effective measures to decentralize households and economic activity, and even if this approach was eventually successful there would be intolerable cost burdens inflicted on the urban economy in the meanwhile.

In many cities of the world, therefore, the second approach seemed preferable and was – to an extent – applied in the 1960s–1970s. It involved the development of a hierachy of 'urban corridors' (for intra-urban traffic), primary and secondary distributor roads (for local traffic), and the creation of 'urban rooms' (for specific urban land uses) – all along the lines proposed in the UK by the *Buchanan Report* (Ministry of Transport, 1963). However, proposals were often found to be impracticable and uneconomic for the following reasons:

- They relied heavily on the depreciation and obsolescence of buildings and subsequent urban renewal brought about by massive investment. But given such opportunities for change, it would have become possible to have opted for a programme of comprehensive decentralization – the physical difficulties in accommodating the ultimate traffic level not then occurring.
- The approach might have been adopted in response to an over-forecast of the total number of vehicles likely to use urban roads at some future date. If, on the one hand, urban net residential densities increased, there would normally have been a reduction in the proportion of the car-owning population, regardless of income distribution. But, on the other hand, if substantial decentralization occurred, the *raison d'être* for major urban road-building programmes would cease to exist, regardless of any increase in the volume of car ownership.
- It was questionable whether financial resources would be available to fund

large-scale urban road-building programmes and the accompanying rede-velopment of the built-environment.

The third approach – that of traffic management by such means as bus-lanes, one-way streets, traffic-calming measures, pedestrianization etc. – has been widely adopted throughout the world, but might be of only temporary value because of the substantial increase in urban traffic that is forecast for the early years of the twenty-first century.

The fourth approach recognizes that motorists and the community in general incur both the direct and indirect costs of road use, and seeks to ensure that – through a system of direct road pricing – the motorists pays his or her full cost for the use of road space.

Direct Costs

These comprise the initial costs of highway construction, ancillary capital costs of road servicing equipment, loan charges on capital, and ancillary costs on such items as lighting, signs, research, administration and policing. It is argued that motorists should at least meet these costs, but in many countries taxes on fuel and on vehicles are regarded as part of general taxation and are not specifically earmarked for road expenditure.

Indirect Costs

Although individual motorists will tend to weigh only their personal costs of travel, their decision to drive will often impose additional costs in terms of money and/or time on other road users. It is, however, difficult to measure the consequences of such 'negative externalities' and many estimates have been made in recent years. In the United Kingdom it was estimated in the 1990s that congestion wasted 1.5 billion hours of motorists' time per annum, at a cost of £10 billion pounds each year, while the European Union's transport directorate in 1995 put the cost of congestion at around 2 per cent of the GDP in the union as a whole (*Economist*, 1998b). In the United States in 1994, research indicated that the cost of driving delays nationwide amounted to $48 million or 0.7 per cent of the GDP, and based on other estimates in the same year it was suggested that the annual costs of congestion to the urban driver amounted – on average – to $400, or $1,000 in Los Angeles (*Economist*, 1998b). In newly-industrializing countries, the indirect costs of road use are similarly sub-stantial, for example in 1990 it was calculated that Bangkok lost as much as one-third of its potential output because of traffic congestion (*Economist*, 1998b) – a loss broadly replicated in many other cities of the newly-industrializing world.

It must be borne in mind, however, that roads that are always uncongested would be economically wasteful, and that some congestion and relatively low (rather than high) average speeds may be necessary if the average total costs of road use are to be kept to the minimum. Also, there are indirect benefits to take into account as well as indirect costs, and many motorists are willing to trade off a residential location of their choice against the cost and inconvenience of congested journeys to their place of work, schools and shopping centres etc.

Nevertheless, in net terms, the economic costs of congestion are substantial. The costs of fuel and vehicle depreciation resulting from congestion are – as far as possible – passed on in higher product prices; working time lost in traffic delays is both costly and unproductive; and unpredictable delivery times compel factories to use capital unproductively by keeping reserve stocks of materials and components. Congestion also reduces accessibility to the urban core – often to such an extent that retailing and other commercial activities become less and less profitable and central area land values diminish (as is the case for many cities in the United States). The development of out-of-town shopping centres and office complexes might – in the short-term – offer a viable and less congested alternative, but very soon these too suffer from congestion with all its negative externalities.

Disequilibrium of Demand and Supply

The provision of road space, at a price to the motorist of substantially less than cost, results inevitably in excessive demand. Prior to an examination of possible solutions to the problems of excess use, the underlying features of demand and supply are considered.

Demand comprises journeys to work (the largest component of demand), travelling during work, and journeys for shopping or leisure purposes. More specifically there is peak demand – with longer-distance commuting becoming an increasingly important feature; revealed demand – the overall level of demand determined by population size and distribution, incomes and wealth, car-ownership preference and working hours; and suppressed demand – the traffic generated in response to the construction of new roads or the improvement of existing roads.

Supply consists of roads and railway track, and either private or public transport – private car, motorcycle, moped, bicycle or bus, train or underground railway. But although in mass-commuting the underground railway is four times more efficient than the bus, and the bus eight times more efficient than the car, the car is more flexible, convenient and comfortable and scores heavily over public transport over short journeys – all compensating the motorist's incurred cost of congestion.

Short-term solutions

Immediate reactions to the problem of disequilibrium have included the more intensive use of short-haul bus services, the adding of extra coaches to commuter rail services and the adoption of new traffic management schemes (such as one-way roads, linked signals and clearways), but the overall gain is usually minimal and at best stop-gap.

Long-term solutions

These have involved large-scale road development to allow for a freer traffic flow. This approach was used widely during the 1950s and 1960s, reinforced by the Buchanan proposals, and figured largely in the Greater London Development Plan 1969.

But new road development provides an unrealistic solution because:

(1) There would be an adverse environmental impact. The Crowther Steering Group to the Buchanan Report warned that cities in the United Kingdom could not accommodate the style of road patterns common in the United States.
(2) Despite higher speeds, real time-saving might not be reduced because greater distances would be involved. Suppressed demand would soon saturate capacity.
(3) Public transport would become uneconomic as diverted demand would reduce revenue, necessitating higher fares or reduced services.
(4) The cost of development would be enormous – over £19 million/km in inner areas, falling to £5 million in suburban areas in the 1960s. Investment in public transport would be much more cost-effective – for example, the initial 18km of the Victoria Line cost £60 million to develop in the 1960s and has a capacity of 40,000 passengers per hour; 18km of an urban motorway would have cost £132 million and carried only 10,000 persons per hour (at an average of 1.4 persons per car). Yet public transport usually operates at a loss and will continue to do so until the motorist pays the full costs of his or her road usage.

In the very long-term, excess demand could be eliminated by both strategic and detailed land-use planning. New linear settlements, out-of-town shopping and industrial and commercial relocation would extinguish inward and outward commuter traffic flows. The dilution of peak demand could also be brought about by a radical staggering of working, shopping and leisure hours.

Both in the short- and long-term, demand must be controlled so as to equate with the supply of transport facilities.

Road Pricing Theory

An economic system allocates factors of production and distributes goods and services so as to maximize social welfare. A traditional way of doing this is by means of the price mechanism, with competitive markets and prices determined competitively for each product, paid ultimately out of individual consumer incomes. With freedom to enter a market, suppliers produce on a maximum profit basis at a price equalling the cost of the last unit of output (marginal cost). Enough of each item is purchased by consumers to make the marginal benefits from spending an extra unit of income in all cases equal.

But in the case of roads, supply and demand considerations are entirely different. The motorist is influenced essentially by marginal private costs – those which he or she incurs directly and which expand as congestion increases. Motorists will continue to use road space, however congested, as long as their marginal private costs are less than the marginal private benefits (monetary and non-monetary) which they enjoy through using their vehicle. It must be assumed that their marginal private benefits equal the price they are willing to pay and therefore are equivalent to demand. Marginal social costs equal marginal private costs plus the cost that the vehicle imposes on the rest of the traffic – that is, congestion costs.

The demand for road space is the relationship between the price of a vehicle-kilometre (determined largely by fuel and vehicle taxation) and the quantity of vehicle-kilometres required at that price. As the price of a vehicle-kilometre falls the quantity demanded expands, and as the price rises the quantity demanded contracts. For essential journeys, demand is relatively insensitive to price changes and is inelastic, but in the case of less essential journeys demand is fairly sensitive to price changes and is relatively elastic.

In figure 10.26, marginal private costs (*MPC*) equal demand *D* at *t*, the maximum traffic flow an individual motorist is willing to join. But at this level of flow, marginal social costs (*MSC*) are considerably higher – the individual motorist clearly not paying the extra cost of congestion that he or she is imposing on other road users. If the traffic flow was reduced to t_1, then marginal social costs would equal demand. The imposition of a road tax equal to an estimation of the difference between marginal social costs

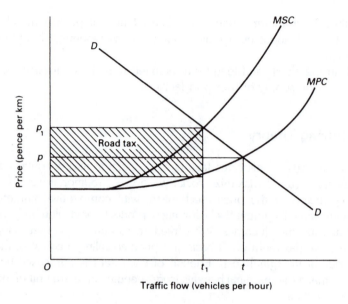

Figure 10.26 *Road tax and costs*

and marginal private costs at t_1 would lead to a contraction of demand from t to t_1 as the price the motorist would be obliged to pay would have risen from p to p_1.

Under such a direct road pricing system, the best use of existing roads would be realized, as each motorist would pay the marginal social cost resulting from his or her use. This would be equivalent to the optimum price and would be independent of the capital cost of the system. The major difficulty in applying this system is determining the optimum level of traffic. Ideally, the price imposed should reduce the level of traffic to where the revenue collected equals the costs imposed by the vehicle upon the community in general and other vehicles in particular, but trial and error would be inevitable in pricing and establishing the optimum flow. Despite these difficulties, direct road pricing was recommended by the Smeed Report in 1964 (Ministry of Transport, 1964). It suggested that variations from the optimum price might be made with little loss of benefit. If revenue exceeded total congestion costs, a self-financing road expansion or improvement programme would be feasible, but if revenue fell short of total congestion costs, road contraction might be necessary. Only in the long-term should revenue equal total congestion costs.

A system of road pricing would thus involve road users paying more directly for the consumption of road space. Road space would be subject broadly to the economic principles on which we rely for the allocation of most of our goods and services. The advantages of this is that it would lead to the more efficient use of existing roads because users would be deterred by higher charges from using congested roads, and encouraged by low charges to use uncongested roads; and there would be a built-in criterion for investment, namely profitability. Currently, vehicle and fuel taxation assume as given the existing costs of the road system, and total costs are allocated among users and non-users without there being any reliable guidance as to which sections of the road network should be expanded and which contracted.

Methods of Road Pricing

The current method of taxing motorists (involving vehicle licences, VAT and petrol tax) fails to cope with current traffic problems in the following ways. It does not discriminate between locations where congestion costs are high or low; it fails to discriminate between times when congestion costs rise or fall; and although more petrol tax is paid on heavy-fuel-consuming vehicles than on low-fuel-consuming vehicles this is completely independent of location, time of day, or day of week and the degree of congestion. However slight the effect of petrol taxes in restraining congestion, it is probable that vehicle excise duties have even less effect. Taxes *in toto* incurred by the motorist unequivocally fail to control traffic flows in the right places at the right times.

Alternative indirect methods of charging motorists have been proposed in recent years. Outlined by Roth (1967) these include:

(1) *Differential fuel taxes*. There would be different rates of taxation in different areas relating to the level of congestion.
(2) *Tyre taxes*. These could be seen as an alternative to petrol taxes.
(3) *Differential licences*. These could relate to zones of an urban area (for example, an expensive 'red' inner zone, and a less expensive 'blue' outer zone) and could be purchased for periods from a year to a day. Licence discs would need to be displayed on vehicles and there could be an exemption from licensing at night and at weekends. Because of its relative simplicity, differential licensing lends itself to experimentation, perhaps over a 5- to 8-year period. This system has been in use in Singapore for a number of years.

Whereas the above methods are indirect, relating to some product or requirement allied to road use, the optimal method may perhaps be a direct charge for road use. Direct charging could be by means of one or more of the following:

(1) *Toll gates.* Although these are the earliest and simplest method to have been used, in urban areas they can be costly and inefficient, can impede traffic flow and are impracticable where a large number of access points are required.

(2) *On-vehicle point pricing.* Meters attached to vehicles would pick up electrical impulses from cables laid across the road at selected pricing points. The meters would be read periodically by the pricing authority and accounts would be rendered.

(3) *On-vehicle continuous pricing.* Vehicles would be charged according to the time or distance travelled in a designated pricing zone. The meter would expire after a length of time or distance travelled in the pricing zone.

(4) *Electronic tolling. Either* a vehicle could be equipped with an identification tag which, on entering a pricing zone, could be registered by a roadside microwave beacon and the motorist's account debited, *or* vehicles could be equipped with meters which accepted rechargeable 'smart cards' (activated by roadside beacons) which displayed the remaining credit. Schemes are in use in an increasing number of countries (see page 502).

Some Economic Consequences of Direct Road Pricing

The disadvantages of direct road pricing are numerous:

(1) Many critics (Beesley, 1968; Lemon, 1972; Sharp, 1973) predict that urban motoring would become the privilege of the wealthy.

(2) As a high proportion of low-income motorists travel exclusively in towns and largely at peak hours, a road tax would be clearly regressive.

(3) It was argued by Richardson (1974), however, that middle-income motorists would suffer the most. The low-income non-motorist might benefit from cheaper and more reliable public transport, the wealthy could afford the road tax without hardship, but the middle-income car owner might wish to continue using his or her car and thus incur the burden of the tax.

(4) If the road tax revenue was entirely invested into new and improved roads, congestion might ultimately reappear. Sharp (1966) suggested that motorists would trade off the new tax initially against reduced travelling times.

(5) If a sufficient number of private motorists diverted their demand to public transport, overcrowded services and higher marginal costs of operation might result.

(6) Private traffic might be forced off congested routes by road pricing and begin to use less busy residential streets as 'short cuts' – thereby spreading environmental costs.

(7) Although it is technically possible to adopt a road pricing system by means of electronic devices, administrators and the police prefer a non-discriminatory system applicable to all sections of the community, and not one which is difficult to enforce or can be interpreted as being unfair.

(8) In the view of Munby (1971), continually changing conditions would make it necessary to adjust prices – the optimum price being difficult to estimate initially. It cannot be assumed that motorists (any more than non-motorists) always react rationally to changing economic circumstances. Road pricing would result inevitably in under-capacity or excess capacity of road space.

(9) A system of road pricing aimed at restricting the number of vehicles entering urban areas would necessitate the development of costly diversionary ring roads or bypasses for the use of through traffic. Often referred to as 'lorry routes', these roads might have no less of an impact on the environment than the existing full-capacity roads of the inner built-up area.

(10) Direct road pricing – like other means of reducing traffic congestion – of course has unpredictable effects (see *Economist*, 1998b). Traffic congestion clearly differs from most other activities that cause negative externalities since its root cause is human behaviour which is difficult to predict and hence difficult to control. Each motorist's precise preference – with regard to the route taken (for example, from home to work), the time of the day travelled and his or her reaction to charges – cannot be accurately predicted in advance. The motorist – see *Economist* (1998b) – might change his or her preference every day, and this could result in a range of outcomes, for example:

- if measures taken to reduce the volume of traffic on a given routeway at specific times are initially successful, they would either speed-up travel times on the routeway and quickly attract motorists from other routes, or encourage greater volumes of traffic to use the routeway at other (less expensive) times, or lead to an excessive demand for public transport;
- if – as an alternative – new roads are constructed, motorists might be inclined to undertake journeys that they would otherwise not have attempted; and
- if – as a further option – commuter rail services are expanded, bus services could become less competitive and reduced in number,

causing bus commuters (whose needs might not be served by rail) to travel to work by car.

If direct road pricing – or any other means of limiting the volume of traffic entering cities – is successful, it is far from certain that reduced traffic flows will reduce journey times. There is evidence from the United Kingdom and the United States that suggests that if, initially, reduced congestion cuts commuting times, daily distances to work increase (as households out-migrate) and average commuting times remain constant.

But the advantages of direct road pricing as seen by Walters (1961), Hewitt (1964), Roth (1967) and Lemon (1972) are no less substantial:

(1) The resulting reduction in traffic in congested areas would produce a freer flow of traffic.
(2) The subsequent increase in average speeds would reduce the costs of delay.
(3) There would be a considerable saving in paid working time of people travelling during employment, and a saving in fuel – of great importance at a time of high energy costs.
(4) There would be greater productivity from buses and commercial vehicles. In the case of buses there could either be fewer crews and stocks required for the same level of service, or existing crews and stocks could produce a higher level of service. It is unlikely that road pricing would lead to an increase in fares.
(5) Road tax revenue would provide local and central government with funds for the improvement of road networks, the subsidisation of public transport, or for general purposes.
(6) Provided traffic did not become diffused over the road network and continued using (but at less volume) traditional routes, there could be a net reduction in environmental affliction.

Clearly, in a number of countries, the advantages of direct road pricing have been considered to be greater than the disadvantages. Road pricing – by means of permits – was therefore adopted in Singapore, Norway and Canada in the 1980s, but subsequently – with improved technology – electronic pricing was introduced not only in these countries, but also in Germany, Austria, France, Italy, Spain and in parts of the United States.

In addition, direct road pricing – particularly if accompanied by improved public transport – could enhance property values. Better accessibility would increase both the efficiency of firms and the desirability of residential property. Depending upon the comparative costs and benefits of redevelopment and rehabilitation, *either* redevelopment would take place following an increase in the demand for sites and a consequential increase in site values, *or* rehabilitation would occur associated with the increase in the demand for buildings and their value. Figure 10.27(a) shows that with a rising site-value, redevelopment would bring about the foreshortening of the economic life of the original building, while figure 10.27(b) indicates that rehabilitation would maintain the building's economic life following an increase in site-value. In reality, the economic life of the building could be increased by more or fewer years than the number required to maintain the building's original economic life.

Road pricing has a number of other consequences. Motorists continuing to use road space would incur a higher cost, a cost previously passed on to other motorists. But they would probably attempt to minimize these costs whenever possible by travelling at cheaper times or by cheaper routes, by making fewer but longer shopping expeditions and by making greater use of vehicle passenger capacity. Road pricing might only be intended to reduce traffic flows by 10–12 per cent, and this reduction might only involve less-essential journeys, the 'second-car' trip-makers and those middle-income commuters ready to transfer from the motor car to public transport as soon as the former becomes more expensive and/or the latter becomes more attractive.

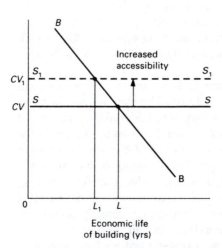

(a) Increase in the demand for a cleared site for the development of an alternative use.

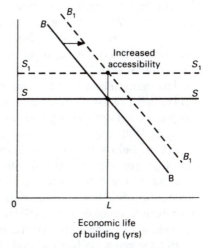

(b) Increase in the demand for a building (and site) in its existing use for the purpose of rehabilitation following an increase in the value of the cleared site.

Notes: BB = Capital value of building (and site) in existing use
         SS = Capital value of cleared site in best alternative use
         CV = Capital value of property

Figure 10.27 *The effects of increased accessibility upon the timing of redevelopment or rehabilitation*

Road pricing would probably not be difficult to enforce – certainly no more difficult than enforcing the 30 mph (48 km/h) speed limit, where it is estimated that only 10 per cent of offenders get caught. But rather than low fines and a low rate of enforcement, high fines could be imposed which would probably deter potential lawbreakers.

Investment

It is all too obvious that since urban roads are frequently congested, a solution to the problems of congestion would involve an increase in the supply of road space, at least on a selective basis, but sometimes extensively. In practice, investment techniques are not sophisticated enough to produce an optimum solution. Conventionally, the future unrestrained traffic flows over the urban road network are forecast, and there is then an attempt to allocate resources and provide facilities to meet this demand. Various *ad hoc* constraints may be proposed where flows would still be excessive.

Investment must take into account present costs and future needs. Although costs (at least direct costs) are predictable, benefits may not be. Information is required on how road development affects traffic speeds, delays, travelling costs, accidents, the environment, property values, commerce and industry – that is, how it affects vehicle operating costs and indirect costs. Road development is economically justifiable if total benefits exceed total costs.

The economist's role in road investment is to assess the relative costs and benefits of the alternative proposals advanced by planners and highway engineers. An approach pursued increasingly is to undertake a cost–benefit analysis. With regard to road investment, it was first used in Oregon in the 1930s to help select a route between two points. Although the costs of development were compared with the benefits of savings in fuel, time and tyre wear, there was no consideration of the indirect effects on local economies. Similarly, the London–Birmingham motorway was subject to a cost–benefit analysis in the 1950s (after a decision had already been taken to build it). This also ignored the more indirect benefits and costs.

But the main problem in undertaking a cost–benefit analysis, especially in urban areas, is to quantify and value all the many intangibles obtaining to the project. Since the pricing system is dominant, producers generally rely on the cost–profit criterion as a means of assessing investment priorities, but in the case of road development this simpler, less costly and possibly more effective approach requires the establishment of an efficient road pricing system before it can be applied.

Road pricing would result in highway authorities adopting the attitude of a competitive service industry, that is, expanding investment in the profitable sections and reducing expenditure in the less profitable or loss-making sections. In the former, costs borne by the authorities would increase, but congestion costs would diminish. Lower congestion costs might then justify a reduction in charges if the savings enjoyed were greater than the development, environmental and other costs. Although profits would be made on some roads and losses on others (the flexibility of road pricing not being perfect) road pricing would indicate the level of demand, identify the locations for development and be very useful in investment decision-making.

To date, no effective solutions have been applied to the problem of urban traffic congestion. Meanwhile, despite increasing energy prices, the shift from public to private transport continues. It is over thirty years since the Buchanan Report was published, but few technological answers have been introduced to solve satisfactorily the problems imposed on people by cars and highways. Architects, engineers and planners are unable to develop towns to accommodate traffic satisfactorily at present and future densities, even at unrealistically high costs. Restricting traffic from entering large areas of towns and re-routing it away are not entirely feasible because of the numbers of vehicles involved and the effect on populations elsewhere. Demand reverting to public transport as it exists today is unlikely to take place on a significant scale and there are few technological developments anticipated which would eliminate the attraction of the private car as a personal mode of transport.

Indirect methods of pricing currently ignore congestion as they do not relate to the price users have to pay for the costs of road use. Although direct road pricing systems seem complex, they would greatly simplify the overall problem of congestion by equating demand and supply. They would also assist in ordering the priorities of use and increasing the efficiency of roads, ensuring a more stable foundation for the operation of public transport services, improving the urban environment and providing a valid means by which public authorities would be able to allocate resources for both road development and related public activities.

There is no reliable evidence to suggest that road pricing reduces the attractiveness of town centres with regard to commerce or amenity. Road pricing is probably beneficial rather than detrimental to the economic and social life of a town or city.

Yet road pricing has not been widely introduced. There have been political reasons for this; the motorists' lobby is very strong and in the public sector there are wide-ranging implications (not just confined to transport) in the concept that the consumer should pay the full marginal social cost for goods and services received. But governments are increasingly coming around to accepting road pricing. In the UK, for example, an official publication (DoE, 1973) suggested that the government was thinking along these lines, and in its 1993 Green Paper *Paying for Motorways: Issues for Discussion* (Department of Transport, 1993), it was suggested that motorists would be directly charged for much of Britain's 2,000-mile motorway network – generating about £700 million per annum.

In 1999, legislation was finally drafted in the UK to give the go-ahead for congestion charges in urban areas (see p. 491).

PUBLIC TRANSPORT

Since the nineteenth century, public road transport has in many ways been regarded as an 'inferior good'. With the development of the motor car and rising real incomes, travellers have moved away from public to private transport. Congestion has largely been caused by the motor car. The London Transport Executive, referring to recent statistics, proclaimed that if 700 commuters travel to London they could fill 14 buses or 500 cars (that is, 1 bus for every 35 cars). One major effect of congestion has been that the efficiency and attractiveness of the bus have diminished.

There are no fundamental reasons why public transport should not be able to compete in speed, frequency or convenience with the private car if competition is on equal terms. Present conditions prevent this in the following ways:

(1) Private motorists are not being charged the full price (equal to their marginal social cost) for their use of roads.
(2) The increased congestion on roads and the subsequent rise in bus operating costs have necessitated ever-increasing fares.
(3) At off-peak hours and in outer suburban or rural areas, operators do not undertake marginal cost pricing as it is thought that fares would be intolerably high – cross-subsidization of unremunerative services being necessary.

But the comprehensive subsidization of public transport has its advantages:

(1) The present features of road transport tilt the balance in favour of the car and away from the bus. With road pricing applied to the private motorist the balance would be tilted the other way. Although the marginal costs of a car journey may only be, say, 20 per cent of a bus journey per traveller, it is in fact considerably more; for example, 50 motorists would take up more space and impose higher congestion than 50 passengers on a bus. But the pricing of private motoring might not by itself attract back to public transport more than a marginal

number of travellers. Bus services might have to operate at reduced fares, so that there is an absolute and not just a relative price advantage. This could be justified because whereas private motorists would be subject to a new road tax mainly on the basis of their marginal private costs being less than the marginal social costs they inflict on other motorists, buses incur higher marginal private costs (over long stretches of their cost curves) than the marginal social costs they impose on traffic in general. Therefore buses would be eligible for 'negative taxes' or subsidies.

(2) At a time of high oil prices, a rediversion of demand to public transport could have advantageous effects on the balance of payments.

(3) Subsidies would offset the regressive nature of road pricing by offering an alternative mode of transport.

(4) Generally, environmental costs are lower with public transport and a diversion to it would improve the situation.

(5) Reasonable mobility should be facilitated by local and central government for social reasons and the cost should be borne by the community as a whole.

(6) Highly subsidized or even free public transport would be warranted if the savings in travelling, congestion and administrative costs exceeded the extra rate poundage. By the early-1980 the Greater London Council (GLC) and most of the metropolitan counties were implementing cheap fare policies – for example, the GLC reduced London Transport fares by an average of 32 per cent in 1981. Even then only 46 per cent of the fares in London were subsidized, in contrast to 56, 61, 70, 71 and 72 per cent in Paris, Berlin, Brussels, Milan and New York respectively. Although in London, the cut in fares required a 6.1p in the pound increase to GLC ratepayers, the total increase would have been 11.9p in the pound because of a penalizing decrease in the central-government's block grant. Despite GLC policy reversing the trend of dwindling passengers for the first time in twenty years and cutting car commuting by 6 per cent, in December 1982 the House of Lords deemed cheap fares uneconomic and hence illegal under the Transport (London) Act 1969 – the Act not taking into account cost–benefit considerations. Because of the reform of fare zones, London Transport was legally able to reduce fares in 1983 (by as much as 25 per cent), but at the cost of a 32 per cent increase in rates. Again, there was a marked increase in the proportion of commuters travelling by public transport and a decrease in commuting by car.

Under the Transport Act 1983, however, the Ministry of Transport could impose strict limits on the power of the (then) metropolitan counties to subsidize public transport (with inevitable increases in fares), and under the Transport Act of 1985, all bus routes outside London were opened up for competition from 1 October 1986. Unprofitable services were put out to tender by local authorities, with the probability that the bidder requiring the lowest subsidy would be offered the relevant routes. Underlying the 1985 Act was the government's desire to cut public spending by eliminating subsidy as far as possible, but also to extend untrammelled market forces by privatization and deregulation. Within a year of the Act, 55–70 per cent of the formerly subsidized services were being run commercially, but with service cuts, lost routes, substantial fare increases, job losses and passenger confusion. Metropolitan areas were particularly badly hit. In London (after the abolition of the GLC and London Transport in 1986), the newly-established London Regional Transport Authority's initial subsidy of £190 million was reduced to £74 million in 1987–88 and to a targeted £59 million by 1988–89 – again with service cuts and lost jobs. Many of London's bus routes, moreover, were put out to tender and privatized, and it was planned to deregulate services in the capital by 1995. In the view of the all-party House of Commons Transport Committee, this plan would result in more congestion, unreliable services and a fall in the number of passengers – a forediction largely borne out by events.

The subsidization of public road transport (except in the case of the abolition of fares) should not be seen as contradicting the principles of road pricing, but as part of the road pricing system where the basic parameters are marginal private costs and marginal social costs, and where the means of bridging the gap between these costs are taxes or subsidies. Since buses inflict very low congestion, environmental and accident costs on society, the marginal social costs of this mode of transport are often lower than its marginal private costs – and generally decrease with the volume of services (assuming a reciprocal reduction in the volume of motor car traffic). Figure 10.28 shows that if a subsidy were to fill the gap between these costs, bus operators could cut fares from f to f_1 but increase services from b to b_1.

The subsidization of public road transport can also be examined in relation to marginal cost pricing. In many urban areas – because of high overhead or fixed costs – fares and the number of services determined by the equilibrium of demand and marginal cost (MC) will produce a loss equal to $abcf$ (in figure 10.29). In a market economy, and in an attempt to break even, operators will therefore tend to reduce the number of services from t to t_1 and raise fares to f_1. However, if the government is willing to subsidize public transport, fares and the number of services could remain at f and t respectively – the subsidy being worthwhile if size $abcf$ is offset by a reduction in congestion, environmental, accident and opportunity costs imposed on society by private motorists.

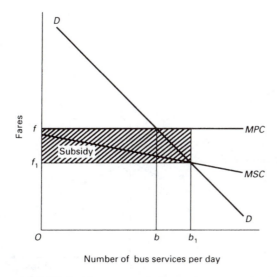

Figure 10.28 *Public transport demand, costs and subsidy*

Road pricing (involving both the taxing of private motorists and the subsidization of public transport) would thus reduce congestion, improve accessibility and eliminate the need for commercial firms to relocate. In short, road pricing would improve the efficiency of the urban economy.

To date, no effective solutions have been applied to the problem of urban traffic congestion. Meanwhile, despite relatively high energy prices, the shift from public to private transport continues. A general trend in public policy initially towards zonal (differential) licensing and ultimately towards comprehensive road pricing and more heavily subsidized public transport may be seen as a solution to the problem of traffic and the environment. But in addition, the very special needs of the elderly and disadvantaged might require additional measures. Access credits have been recommended by a number of organizations (Ardill, 1986) to enable the least mobile and less wealthy members of society to make use of the telephone or a home computer terminal to acquire information and to order goods for delivery, or to pay fares, road prices or hire taxis. Small, flexible-route minibuses would also increase accessibility and provide an economic substitute for the private motor car or taxi.

It is perhaps reassuring that in the *Planning Policy Guidance Note 13* of 1994, at last the Department of the Environment and Department of Transport recognized the need to plan for future employment, retailing and leisure facilities within the context of public transport networks, albeit a decreasingly subsidized network.

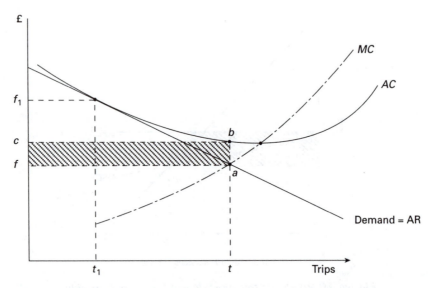

Figure 10.29 *Marginal cost pricing of public transport – with subsidization*

Fixed Transport Systems

Compared to the car, suburban and urban rail and tram services have similarly been regarded as 'inferior goods'. However, in an attempt to control
the level of car-created congestion, investment in fixed transport systems is
proceeding on a large scale throughout the world. In the 1990s, both Manchester and Sheffield (re)introduced trams; Athens started to build two more
underground lines (in addition to the one it already had); Rome extended
its underground lines; Seattle planned to develop a $3.9 billion tram and
commuter train system; Dallas-Forth Worth began to utilize its first commuter trains; and Bangkok commenced work on four different rapid transit
systems (*Economist*, 1998c). Also in the early-1990s, Hong Kong completed its mass transit railway (MTR) rail system, and similar systems were
well underway in China.

In some cities, fixed transport systems are, however, not the *panacea*
that planners often expected. In Vienna, for example, whereas highly subsidized public transport – accompanied by large parking fees and strict regulation of on-street parking – has minimized congestion within the central
city, peripheral autobahnen are highly congested as motorists are attracted
into the city as far as the boundary of the restricted area. In Toronto,
however, it has become increasingly recognized that fixed systems (developed in the 1980s) are inefficient since they are inappropriate to the needs

of areas of low population or employment density on the urban periphery, and that new networks are becoming obsolescent as commuting patterns change (*Economist*, 1998c).

The opportunity costs of wasteful investment have clearly plagued the development of many systems. In London, the Jubilee line extension to the underground absorbed billions of pounds (sterling), while other parts of the extensive tube system and most bus services remained seriously under-funded; and in Athens, the costly development of its new underground lines (which is 90 per cent financed by the European Union) can be contrasted with the lack of any expenditure on creating bus lanes in congested streets, or giving buses priority at traffic signals – possibly more effective solutions to the city's burgeoning congestion problem (*Economist*, 1998c). In the European Union as a whole – despite massive investment – passenger mileage on urban rail systems increased by only 9 per cent in the last three decades of the twentieth century, while in the United States – in the 12 cities in which rail transit systems have been built since the 1970s – the total number of passengers was no greater in 1995 than in the late-1970s (*Economist*, 1998c). Clearly, the majority of the commuting public are expressing a preference for car-borne transport and find that public transport of all kinds is relatively inconvenient, unpleasant and excessively time-consuming.

Despite the many pitfalls involved in attempting to curb the private motorist and in providing alternative means of travel within cities, a 'do-nothing approach' would undoubtedly be a recipe for disaster in terms of the unacceptable costs of congestion, environmental pollution and accidents which would be borne by society as a whole. Clearly the debate is not about whether *laissez-faire* or public intervention should prevail, but about which of a number of different forms of intervention should be relied upon to provide solutions to the problem of traffic congestion:

- one possible solution would be for governments to establish public–private partnerships for the purpose of owning, investing-in, developing and operating public transport;
- another solution would be for governments to enable public transport utilities to raise capital from the private sector (for example, through the issue of bonds); and
- a final approach would involve substantial subsidization funded by taxation – for example, by hypothecated road charges.

However, only through the use of extensive cost–benefit analyses would decision-makers be able to opt for the approach that produces the greatest benefits to the public as a whole. Short of this, decision-making would be based largely on political judgement alone.

URBAN TRANSPORTATION IN DEVELOPING COUNTRIES

Introduction

This section examines the dimensions of urban transportation in developing countries and evaluates the applicability of transportation system management (TSM) strategies in these countries. The broad requirements to meet urban transportation needs of developing countries are reviewed. The planning and management agenda that can be useful in meeting not only the transportation needs but also the broad social and economic goals are then discussed.

Urban Transportation Problems in Developing Countries

Not only the institutional arrangements are different, but the dimensions of transportation problems in developing countries greatly differ from those in many developed countries. Urban areas in developing countries, particularly the mega-cities, are experiencing population growth at a much faster rate than those in developed countries. In a period of 65 years, the developing world's urban population has increased tenfold, from about 100 million in 1920 to 1 billion in 1985. Though the expenditures on urban transportation of developing countries range from 15 per cent to 25 per cent of their total annual expenditures, they must increase their capability to supply and effectively manage by at least 75 per cent merely to maintain their current level of services, which is woefully inadequate (Khisty, 1993).

The urban congestion in many developing countries is primarily due to the mixed traffic flow with a high degree of pedestrian and bicycle traffic. The road network is greatly limited in these countries. In addition, a high proportion of the urban population in developing countries has low incomes and the density of urban areas is very high. Furthermore, the available funds for capital expenditure and maintenance and operation are very limited. Urban land use in many developing countries is mixed and some cities do not have any zoning policy. Increased car ownership in the urban areas of the developing countries is an additional problem to be tackled. The number of cars in the Bangkok metropolitan area and three other provinces in the vicinity was estimated to be 0.56 million in 1989 and was forecast to increase to 2.1 and 3.7 times the current figure by the years 1997 and 2006 (Miyamoyo and Udomsri, 1994). Often, it is very difficult to obtain the relevant data required by urban planning analysts. There are many other differences but the aspects discussed above are sufficient to illustrate the fact that urban transportation in developing countries cannot be managed with borrowed tools and strategies from developed countries. Instead, urban transportation planning and management in these countries require a decidedly different emphasis.

Applicability of transportation system management concepts in developing countries

The original intent of the Transportation System Management (TSM) concept, which was adopted in the United States in 1975, was to make more productive use of existing transportation facilities (Weiner, 1986). In the TSM concept, existing streets and motorways, railways, parking and pedestrian facilities and transportation vehicles – both private and public – are to be viewed as elements of a single urban transportation system; and these individual elements are to be organized with the help of various operating, regulatory and pricing policies into one efficient, productive and integrated transportation system (Orski, 1976). Over the years, a host of TSM strategies has been developed with emphasis on low-cost, high-pay-off options. Procedures to evaluate the effectiveness of various TSM strategies are also available (Abrams *et al.* 1981).

The TSM concept, as it is used in developed countries, does not have much significance in developing countries because the thrust of TSM regulations in developed countries has been on short-term and low-cost actions involving existing transportation facilities. An important implied assumption is that the transportation infrastructure is essentially in place and the increased travel demand needs to be accommodated primarily by increased efficiency of the existing system. However, in most developing countries, the existing urban transportation infrastructure is far from complete and long-range facility planning still remains the critical concern in urban areas. To rely primarily on short-term TSM-type actions would be nothing more than an attempt to rearrange the chaos.

This does not mean there is no room for TSM strategies in developing countries, because the primary objective of TSM regulations is appropriate for developing countries as it calls for better and more efficient use of existing facilities in order to conserve limited public resources available for new capital investments. Therefore, although the role of TSM in developing countries is not as significant as that in developed countries, many TSM actions can still be modified and implemented in developing countries. The critical issue is that the management of urban transportation systems in developing countries requires much more than simply adapting the TSM strategies used in developed countries.

A major emphasis of TSM strategies in developed countries has been on how to lure travellers from personal transportation and private cars to public transport. On the other hand, in developing countries, car trips may account for as little as 10–15 per cent of urban travel using public transport, and problems arise because of the excessively high demand for bus and other transport systems. The strategies for management of urban transportation systems in developing countries therefore need to be innovative, with particular emphasis on how to make the public transportation systems accommodate the astronomical demand. In addition, in most cities of the developing countries, a major problem arises from the conflict between motorized and non-motorized traffic. Pedestrians, bicycles and other slow-moving non-motorized vehicles compete for the limited road space with cars, buses, trolley-buses and tramcars, causing, in some cases, interminable traffic jams. Short-term, low-cost TSM options, such as providing exclusive zones for car operations, can provide only limited relief. Long-term solutions to these situations will come mainly through physical segregation of non-compatible traffic flows, and such solutions involve substantial commitment of financial resources.

Transportation system management requirements in developing countries

It must be recognized that the objective of an urban transportation system is to provide efficient movement of people and goods, not vehicles. Transportation needs change with time and an appropriate management approach is required to plan for both immediate and long-term needs in an integrated manner. Transportation planning and management should be made with a goal of achieving long-term sustainable development for society as a whole. Most importantly, transportation needs cannot be considered isolated from the broad social and economic environment.

Another important objective of TSM in developing countries must be to integrate transportation development into urban-growth guidance and land-use management. Since most of the urban population increase in the developing countries will take place in large cities, and the quantity of movement (person-miles travelled or ton-miles transported) grows geometrically as the city size increases, resulting in increased dependency on motorized travel, transportation planners have repeatedly suggested that economic activities be shifted from large agglomerations to small- and medium-sized cities.

The urban planning process in developing countries is much more complicated than in developed countries owing to economic uncertainty, changing policies and political instability. Hence, in developing countries, urban transportation system management must take a strategic approach in which the planning process should be able to identify major shifts in demographic, social and economic conditions, and should provide appropriate strategies for addressing changes in transportation that would follow from such alterations. Moreover, as there are many providers of urban transportation services, both public and private, it is necessary that the management of urban transportation services takes place in a co-ordinated and integrated manner. For a productive process, urban TSM must follow a structured organization, which will serve not only as a vehicle for co-ordination of efforts, but also as an authority to implement the actions. Furthermore, much greater attention should be given to the fiscal aspects of urban transportation management than is given at present. It is essential that all components of an urban transportation system be evaluated in terms of economic viability, in addition to their being effective in terms of system objectives. A sound fiscal management is necessary for both short- and long-term actions.

Planning and Management Agenda

The urban transportation infrastructure in a developing country should be viewed mainly as a network of public transportation facilities with complementary intermediate forms of transportation such as pedestrian, bicycle and other alternative transport systems. While the car has greatly increased personal mobility, it has also created many social, economic and mental problems including accidents, pollution, noise and blight, and escalating demands on land and other scarce natural resources. Furthermore, car-oriented transportation systems have seriously impaired the accessibility of those who do not own or drive cars. In addition to improving conventional public transportation systems, increased attention is needed in the provision of alternative transport services, such as that provided by group-riding rickshaws. Motorized alternative transport operation fills the gap between the car and public transport, and attracts commuters of the middle-income group who are neither willing to ride on public transport nor able to afford to run a car. Pedicabs or rickshaws are used predominantly in the lower-income countries, where labour costs are low (Hook, 1995). This type of transportation generates a substantial number of jobs in poor countries and also helps to create an unpolluted environment in residential areas. Bicycles often provide the only means of non-walking personal transportation affordable to low- and moderate-income groups for short and medium trips.

In many large cities in developing countries, the peak period lasts for several hours and congestion occurs even at hours that are supposed to be off-peak. This phenomenon is primarily due to the inadequate capacity of the existing transportation facilities. Actions such as reduction of peak-period travel demand through staggered working hours or staggered days of work may provide significant relief to already overburdened transportation systems. However, in order to achieve the required result, much effort will be needed to co-ordinate the schedules of government offices, institutions, and commercial and industrial establishments, which requires strong marketing and follow-up skills from transportation planners and managers. However, a strong political will combined with active participation of the enforcement authority are necessary if such measures are to succeed.

Improved traffic control and management programmes, including computerized traffic signals, use of one-way streets, routing of through-traffic away from city centres, street-parking prohibitions and car-free zones, are considered necessary to overcome congestion problems. However, the practicality and effectiveness of some of these measures in developing countries can be questioned. The overwhelming number of pedestrians and slow-moving vehicles make traffic signals and other control devices virtually ineffective, unless special measures are taken to separate motorized vehicles from non-motorized traffic. However, proper care should be taken to redesign these strategies so that they become appropriate for the local traffic conditions.

Consideration of urban transportation system management commonly involves service and demand management techniques. The importance of managing physical facilities is often ignored. However, the productivity of urban transportation systems is low in many cities because of the lack of maintenance of rolling stock and associated breakdown and downtimes. Hence, in most of the developing countries, the bus-systems have been fully or partially privatized to ensure an efficient service. Lack of maintenance of road and track facilities may also contribute to high use costs and added travel time. An urban transportation management programme must therefore include appropriate maintenance and rehabilitation programmes for urban streets, rail tracks, public transport vehicles and other physical elements. The approaches being used in pavement management systems can be effectively extended to develop a comprehensive facility management system.

The presence of mixed traffic with inadequate road spaces and rapid growth of automotive traffic have made safety a critical concern for transportation managers in developing countries. While a significant part of a safety programme would involve educational, enforcement and vehicle-inspection activities, a great deal of safety improvement can be achieved through proper planning and management of traffic flows and facilities.

Transportation planners and managers must also devote adequate attention to allocate the associated costs among appropriate users. Some parts of transportation costs may not be attributable to users, as they may be considered to have been accrued for the good of the entire community and these costs may then be borne by general tax revenue. User cost responsibilities, on the other hand, must be compared with revenue contributions to assess the associated equities. There are various road-pricing strategies that can be undertaken to make cars pay their share of costs for using road services. It is often argued that cars, in particular, are not paying the social costs of air pollution, accidents and other adverse effects. In addition, current car-user charges are uniform, regardless of where and when the car is used, therefore peak-hour users are being subsidized by off-peak drivers. Appropriate measures to remedy the pricing inequity may include differential parking fees and area licensing schemes.

There is a host of activities that can be explored for adoption in developing countries with private-sector participation. The major theme of these activities is private-sector participation in transportation financing which may range from a small contribution by local merchants to joint public–private ventures in the simultaneous development of large-scale, high-capital transportation systems and adjacent land development. Joint development is particularly suitable for rail transport, projects where railway stations and terminals can be planned in conjunction with residential and commercial development. In some cases, the cost of arterial improvements or extensions can be tied to a private developer's cost of urban development. Concession projects, such as build–operate–transfer, are one of the very popular mechanisms in vogue to get the co-operation of the private sector to cover shortage of public funds. Establishment of transportation co-operatives is another example of private-sector participation.

In many developing countries, transportation planning is carried out using methodologies that emerged in developed countries. Such applications have serious limitations because conditions in developing countries are very different, particularly with respect to financial and human resources, level of car ownership and the political context of decision-making. Moreover, the traditional urban transportation planning process has been criticized for its excessive data collection needs and its inability to respond quickly to policy changes. Furthermore, use can be made of emerging statistical and mathematical techniques, including various artificial intelligence tools, to develop focused sets of plan objectives and criteria as well as to provide appropriate evaluation tools.

To ensure that capable professionals are available to plan and manage transportation systems efficiently, programmes that have an appropriate multi-disciplinary approach towards education and training are essential. Moreover, a determined effort must be taken to make arrangements to create a central and rich databank that can be accessed by all the planning agencies. Absence of pertinent and necessary data often creates a hindrance in the development of planning tools.

Conclusions

Modern Transportation System Management (TSM) has been widely adopted in developed countries to solve urban transportation problems with low-cost, short-term actions. Although the basic concept is valid and many of the strategies are applicable to developing countries, the planning and management of urban transportation systems in developing countries require a different emphasis because transportation infrastructure is far from complete. Consequently, the role of TSM may not be as significant as that in developed countries because long-term facility planning still remains the critical concern in developing countries.

As only a small percentage of urban residents use cars in developing countries, emphasis should be placed on developing a system based on public transportation. To complement conventional public transportation services, increased attention is needed on the provision of alternative transport services. In addition, there is an urgent need for spatial segregation of pedestrians and slow-moving traffic from motorized traffic. The cost of developing networks of facilities for the exclusive use of slow-moving traffic networks may be high however, but the benefits in terms of reduced congestion and improved safety would be great enough to compensate for the costs.

As peak periods last for many hours and congestion occurs even at off-peak periods, demand management strategies involving staggered work hours may not have much impact in developing countries. Also, because of the presence of an overwhelming number of pedestrians and slow-moving vehicles, the effectiveness of traffic signals and other traffic control devices may be questionable. Nevertheless, some of these measures are worth pursuing, particularly in conjunction with other long-term solutions.

Transportation planners and managers must devote adequate attention to financing. The full costs of providing transportation services should be identified and efforts made to allocate these costs among appropriate users. The potential of private-sector participation in financing transportation improvements should also be explored.

An effective transportation management programme must include appropriate maintenance and rehabilitation programmes for urban streets, rail tracks, public transport vehicles and other physical elements. Also, appropriate planning tools which are applicable in the context of developing countries should be developed. In addition, to ensure the availability of capable professionals, efforts should be made to improve education and training programmes in transportation engineering and management.

The importance of considering transportation needs within the context of broad social, economic and environmental concerns is particularly critical in developing countries. As there exists a large population of urban poor, transportation programmes must be evaluated in terms of social equity. In addition, careful land-use management and growth-guidance strategies are essential in order to minimize the long-term demand for transportation and other services in the large cities of the developing countries.

REFERENCES

Abrams, C.M., DiRenzo, J.F., Smith, S.A. and Ferelis, R.A. (1981) 'Measures of effectiveness for TSM strategies', *Report No. FHWAçRD-81/177*, December, Washington DC: Federal Highways Administration.

Ardill, J. (1986) 'Transport must face up to the future', *Guardian*, 11 December.

Arrow, R. and Lind, R. (1970) 'Uncertainty and the evaluation of public investment decisions', *American Economic Review*, 60.

Ball, M. and Kirwan, R. (1977) 'Urban housing demand: some evidence from cross-sectional analysis', *Applied Economics*, 9.

Baumol, W.J. (1965) *Welfare Economics and the Theory of the State*, London: Bell.

Baumol, W.J. (1972) 'On taxation and control of externalities', *American Economic Review*, 62.

Beesley, M.E. (1968) 'Technical possibilities of special taxation in relation to congestion caused by private users', *Second International Symposium on Theory and Practice in Transport Economics* (OECD European Conference of Ministers of Transport, 1968).

Boorman, L., Goss-Custard, J. and McGrorty, S. (1989) *Climatic Change, Rising Sea Level and the British Coast*, Natural Environment Council, Institute of Terrestrial Ecology, London: HMSO.

Braidotti, R. *et al.* (1994), *Women, the Environment and Sustainable Development: Towards a Theoretical Synthesis*, London: Zed.

CEC (1990) 'Environmental policy in the European Community', *European Documentation*, 5.

CEC (1992) *European Economy*, No. 51, May.

Chen, J. (1992) *Foreign Direct Investment in China – Policies and Performance*, PhD thesis, Lancaster: Lancaster University.

Chen, J. (1993) 'Social cost–benefit analysis of China's Shenzhen Special Economic Zone', *Development Policy Review*, 11(3), London: Overseas Development Institute, Blackwell.

Chen, J. (1994) 'China: economic growth and construction activity', *Strategic Planning in Construction Companies*, Technion, Haifa: A.J. Etkin International Seminar on Strategic Planning in Construction Companies, June 8–9.

Davis, O.A. and Whinston, A.B. (1961) 'The economics of urban renewal', *Journal of Law and Contemporary Problems*, 16.

Delbeke, J. (1991) 'The prospects for the use of economic instruments in EC environment policy', *Royal Bank of Scotland Review*, December.

Department of Energy (1989) *An Evaluation of Energy Related Greenhouse Gas Emissions and Means to Ameliorate Them*, London: HMSO.

Department of Transport (1993) *Paying for Motorways: Issues for Discussion*, Cmnd 2200, London: HMSO.

DETR (1998a) *A New Deal for Transport*, London: HMSO.

DETR (1998b) *Breaking the Log-jam*, Consultative Paper, London: HMSO.

DoE (1973) *Urban Transport Planning*, Cmnd 5336, London: HMSO.

DoE (1988) *Environmental Assessment*, Circular 15/88, London: HMSO.

DoE (1989) *Environmental Assessment – A Guide to the Procedure*, London: HMSO.

Doxiadis, C. (1971) *Urban America and the Role of Industry*, United States National Association of Manufacturers.

Economic Trends (1992) No. 467, November.

Economist (1998a) 'All jammed up', September 5th–11th.

Economist (1998b) 'The unbridgeable gap', September 5th–11th.

Economist (1998c) 'Railroad job', September 5th–11th.

Economist Intelligence Unit (1993) *Country Profile: China and Mongolia (1993/94)*, London.

Ferrary, C. (1990) 'Environmental assessment and transport', *The Planner*, 9 November.

Forbes, A. (1976) 'A cost–benefit study of a luxury hotel', in Little, I.M.D. and Scott, M. (eds), *Using Shadow Prices*, London: Heinemann Educational Books.

Foster, C.D. and Beesley, M.E. (1963) 'Estimating the social benefit of constructing an underground railway in London', *Journal of the Royal Statistical Society*, Series A, 126.

Gittings, J. (1999) 'Kowtow command angers Hong Kong democrats', *Guardian*, October.

Gowans, Sir J. (1984) Quoted in Royal Commission on Environmental Pollution, *10th Report*, London: HMSO.

Guardian (1986) 16 December.

Hardoy, J.E. and Satterthwaite, D. (1989) *Squatter Citizen*, London: Earthscan.

Hardoy, J.E., Mitlin, D. and Satterthwaite, D. (1992) *Environmental Problems in Third World Cities*, London: Earthscan.

Harris, R. (1992) 'The Environmental Protection Act 1990 – penalising the polluter', *Journal of Planning and Environmental Law*, June.

Hewitt, J. (1964) 'The calculation of congestion taxes on roads', *Economica*.

Hicks, J. (1940) 'The valuation of social income', *Economica*, 7.

Hills, P. (1991) 'Private transport – what future for the private car in the city?', *The Planner*, 13 December.

Hoch, I. (1972) 'Urban scale and environmental quality', in Ridker, R.G. (ed.), *Pollution, Resources and the Environment*, US Commission on Population Growth and the Environment, Washington DC: USCPO.

Hook, W. (1995) 'Economic importance of non-motorized transportation', *Transportation Research Record*, 1487.

Howe, G.M. (1970) *National Atlas of Disease and Mortality in the UK*, London: Nelson.

Howe, G.M. (1985) 'Does it matter where I live?', *Transactions of British Geographers*.

Hughes, P. (1991) 'Exhausting the atmosphere', *Town and Country Planning*, October.

ILO (1995) *World Employment 1995*, Geneva: International Labour Office.

Journal of Environmental Planning and Management (1993) 36: 1.

Kaldor, N. (1939) 'Welfare propositions of economics and interpersonal comparisons of utility', *Economic Journal*, 49.

Kaplan, A. (1979) 'When less is more: a look at the long-term in building for tourism', *The Cornell Quarterly*, 20(2).

Khisty, J. (1993) 'Transportation in developing countries: obvious problems, possible solutions', *Transportation Research Record*, 1396.

Kirkby, J., O'Keefe, P. and Timberlake, L. (1995) *Sustainable Development: A Reader*, London: Earthscan.

Layard, R. (ed.) (1972) *Cost Benefit Analysis*, Harmondsworth: Penguin.

Layfield, Sir F. (1992a) 'The Environmental Protection Act 1990. The system of integrated pollution control', *Journal of Planning and Environmental Law*, January.

Layfield, Sir F. (1992b) 'Integrated pollution control in practice', *Journal of Planning and Environmental Law*, July.

Lee, G. (1999) 'Environmental policy: too little too late', in Jones, B. (ed.), *Political Issues in Britain Today*, Manchester: Manchester University Press.

Lemon, L.K. (1972) 'An economic examination of traffic congestion in towns', *Administration*.

Lichfield, N. (1966) 'Cost–benefit analysis in town planning: a case study, Swanley' *Urban Studies*, 3.

Lichfield, N. and Chapman, H. (1970) 'Cost–benefit in urban expansion: a case study, Ipswich', *Urban Studies*, 7.

Lipsey, R. and Lancaster, R. (1957) 'The general theory of the second best', *Review of Economic Studies*, 24.

Little, I.M.D. and Mirrlees, J.A. (1974) *Project Appraisal and Planning for Developing Countries*, London: Heinemann Educational Books.

McCarthy, M. (1998) 'Why hot air is stopping the world doing a deal on global warming', *The Independent*, 14 November.

McGee, T.G. and Yeung, Y.-M. (1993) *Urban Features in Pacific Asia: Towards the 21st Century*, Hong Kong: Chinese University Press.

Ministry of Transport (1963) *Traffic in Towns*, London: HMSO.

Ministry of Transport (1964) *Road Pricing: The Economic and Technical Possibilities*, London: HMSO.

Miyamoyo, K. and Udomsri, R. (1994) 'Present situations and issues of planning and implementation regarding land-use and transport in developing metropolises', *Infrastructure Planning and Management*, 482.

Munby, D.L. (1971) 'Management: the economist's viewpoint', *Symposium on Traffic and Towns* (Annual Meeting of the British Association for the Advancement of Science).

Orski, C.K. (1976) 'Transportation system arrangement in perspective', *Proceedings of ASCE Conference on Urban Transportation Efficiency*, New York: ASCE.

Osborne, M. (1986) *China's Special Economic Zones*, Paris: Development

Centre for the Organization for Economic Co-operation and Development, OECD.

Pearce, D.W. (1971) *Cost Benefit Analysis*, 1st edn, London: Macmillan.

Pearce, D.W. (1975) *Environmental Economics*, London: Macmillan.

Pearce, D.W. (1983) *Cost Benefit Analysis*, 2nd edn, London: Macmillan.

Pearce, D.W. (1991) 'Towards the sustainable economy', *Royal Bank of Scotland Review*, December.

Pearce, D.W. and Barde, J.P. (1991) *Valuing the Environment*, London: Earthscan.

Pearce, D.W. and Kerry Turner, R. (1990) *The Economics of Natural Resources and the Environment*, London: Harvester Wheatsheaf.

Pigou, A.C. (1920) *The Economics of Welfare*, London: Macmillan.

Portney, P. (1990) 'Public policies for environmental protection', *Resources for the Future*, Washington DC.

Potter, R.B. and Lloyd-Evans, S. (1998) *The City in the Developing World*, Harlow: Longman.

Price, C.M. (1977) *Welfare Economics in Theory and Practice*, London: Macmillan.

Pugh-Smith, J. (1992) 'The local authority as a regulator of pollution in the 1990s', *Journal of Planning and Environmental Law*, February.

Richardson, H.W. (1974) 'A note on the distributional effects of road pricing', *Journal of Transport Economics and Policy*.

(Roskill) Commission on the Third London Airport (1970–1971) *Report*, London: HMSO.

Roth, G.J. (1967) *Paying for Roads*, Harmondsworth: Penguin.

Royal Commission on Environmental Pollution (1984) *Tenth Report*, London: HMSO.

Satterthwaite, D. (1995) 'Viewpoint – the understanding of urban poverty and of its health consequences', *Third World Planning Review*, 17: iii–xii.

Scott, M. (1976) 'Shadow wage in Mauritius', in Little, I.M.D. and Scott, M. (eds). *Using Shadow Prices*, London: Heinemann Educational Books.

Sen, A. (1961) 'On optimising the rate of saving', *Economic Journal*, 71.

Sen, A. (1967) 'Isolation, assurance and the social rate of discount', *Quarterly Journal of Economics*, 81.

Sharp, C.H. (1966) 'Congestion and welfare: an examination of the case for a congestion tax', *Economic Journal*.

Sharp, C.H. (1973) *Transport Economics*, London: Macmillan.

Silberston, A. (1993) 'Economics and the Royal Commission on Environmental Pollution', *National Westminster Bank Review*, February.

Starr, J.B. (1999) *Understanding China*, London: Profile Books.

State Statistical Bureau of China (1993) *China Statistical Yearbook 1993*, Beijing: China Statistical Information and Consultancy Service Centre.

Tromans, S. and Clarkson, M. (1991) 'The Environmental Protection Act 1990: its relevance to planning controls', *Journal of Planning and Environmental Law*, June.

Turvey, R. (1963) 'On divergencies between social cost and private cost', *Economica*, August.

United Nations (1995) Preparatory Committee for the United Nations Conference on Human Settlements (Habitat II): draft statement of principles and commitments and global plan of action, *The Habitat Agenda*, October.

United Nations (1999) *Global Environmental Outlook, 2000*, New York: United Nations.

Vipond, J. and Walker, B. (1972) 'The determinants of housing expenditure and owner-occupation', *Bulletin of the Oxford Institute of Economics and Statistics*, 34.

Walters, A.A. (1961) 'Empirical evidence on optimal motor taxes for the United Kingdom', *Econometrica*.

Walters, J. (1999) 'UK loves to drive but hates to pay the cost', *The Observer*, 27 June.

Wanhill, S.R.C. (1985) 'On the social profitability of hotels', *Working Paper*, Guildford: Department of Hotel, Catering and Tourist Management, University of Surrey.

Warr, P.G. (1986) 'Export promotion via industrial enclaves: the Philippine's Bataan Export Processing Zone', *Working Paper*, Canberra: Department of Economics, Research School of Pacific Studies, Australian National University.

WCED (1987) *Our Common Future*, Oxford: World Commission on Environment and Development and Oxford University Press.

Weiner, E. (1986) 'Urban transportation planning in the United States: a historical overview', *Report No. DOT-1-86-09*, Washington DC: US Department of Transportation.

WHO (1992) *Our Planet, Our Health*, Report of the Commission on Health and Environment, Geneva: World Health Organisation Publications.

World Bank (1991) *Urban Policy and Economic Development: An Agenda for the 1990s*, Washington DC: World Bank.

World Bank (1993) *World Bank Development Report*, Oxford: Oxford University Press.

11
Conclusions

In the late twentieth century, urbanization increased on a global scale, the world's largest cities continued to grow apace, patterns of urban land use were converging rather than diverging, and residential, industrial and commercial development was increasingly determined by the ascendency of the free market and the retreat of government intervention. However, in most regions of the world, inequalities in urban living standards were increasing, housing need was far from satisfied, and there were serious concerns about urban transportation and the urban environment. It is probable that the urban economy of much of the world during the new millennium will develop in the same direction as that already established at the end of the twentieth century – i.e. within an increasingly global economy, rates of urban population growth and economic development will continue to be interdependent, while there will be an increased concentration of economic activity in locations offering the greatest economic advantages.

Although projections indicate that the world's population will continue to grow during the twenty-first century, fortuitously this will be at a decelerating rate. However, table 11.1 shows that the annual rate of population growth in the more-developed regions is significantly slower than that in the less-developed regions – where it is likely to continue to outpace economic development. Therefore, whereas the more-developed regions contained 19 per cent of the world's population in 2000 – with the less-developed regions accommodating 81 per cent of the total, by 2050 their respective shares of the world's population will be 12 and 88 per cent.

In comparing economic regions, it is notable that projected annual population growth rates in the advanced capitalist world and in countries in the process of political and economic transition are similarly low, ranging, in the period 2000–10, from a percentage decrease of –0.2 (in Italy and the Russian Federation) to a percentage increase of only 1.1 (in Australia). However, in the newly-industrializing and developing countries, projected rates of annual growth are generally much higher, ranging in percentages from 0.8 (in China) to as high as 2.9 (in Kenya), 3.0 (in Zaire) and 3.1 (in Saudi Arabia) in the same period. It is anticipated that annual rates of growth will generally diminish during the years 2010–50, but that established disparities will remain.

By the year 2025 (see table 11.2), the advanced capitalist countries and countries formerly in political and economic transition might be experiencing broadly similar levels of urbanization – with projected urban populations ranging from around 76 per cent of the total populations of the Czech Republic and Italy to respectively 85.7 and 93.3 per cent of the total populations of the Russian Federation and the United Kingdom. However, among the newly-industrializing and developing countries there could be wide disparities in urbanization – with projected urban populations ranging from 45.2 per cent in India and 48.3 per cent in Tanzania to 88.9 per cent in Brazil and 93.4 per cent in Argentina.

In general, the projected annual rate of growth in urbanization diminishes between the periods 1975–2000 and 2000–25. The advanced capitalist countries and countries formerly in political and economic transition experienced broadly similar trends in urbanization during both periods. Projected rates of growth, in 2000–25, ranged from –0.1 in Germany and 0.2 per cent in the Russian Federation to 0.9 per cent in Poland and 1.2 per cent in Australia. However, among the newly-industrializing and developing countries in the same period, there were wide disparities – with urbanization increasing by as little as 1.1 per cent in Argentina and 1.5 per cent in Brazil to as much as 4.6 in Tanzania and 4.8 per cent in Zaire.

In considering the projected annual growth rates of urban agglomerations (table 11.3), it is similarly evident that there are major disparities between the mega-cities of the advanced capitalist world and the large urban areas within newly-industrializing and developing countries. In the former group of cities, projected rates of growth range from 0.1 per cent and virtually zero in Paris in 1995–2005 and 2005–15, to 1.6 and 0.8 per cent in Toronto in the same periods. However, in the latter group of countries, projected rates of growth in the same periods range from 0.7 and 0.5 per cent in Buenos Aires to 5.16 and 4.31 per cent in Nairobi. Despite a general decrease in rates of urbanization, it is clear that the newly-industrializing and developing world will urbanize more rapidly than the developed world during at least the first half of the twenty-first century.

In the more developed regions, it is very probable that, at an urban level and in aggregate, economic development will at least keep pace with population growth and sometimes exceed it, but there will be distinct disparities from city to city and from region to region depending upon a range of different determining factors.

In Europe, urban development during the early twenty-first century will undoubtedly take place both within the context of new technology and the economic and political restructuring of the continent resulting from consolidation of the EU and the removal of the Iron Curtain. It is possible that

Table 11.1 The projected size and growth of the world's population, 2000–50: by economic region and selected countries

	Projections (000s)				Annual growth rate (per cent)		
	2000	2010	2025	2050	2000–10	2010–25	2025–50
WORLD TOTAL	**6,158,051**	**7,032,294**	**8,294,341**	**9,833,208**	**1.33**	**1.10**	**0.68**
More-developed regions*	**1,185,536**	**1,212,865**	**1,238,406**	**1,207,504**	**0.23**	**0.14**	**-0.10**
Less-developed regions⁺	**4,972,515**	**5,819,430**	**7,055,935**	**8,625,703**	**1.57**	**1.28**	**0.80**
Advanced capitalist countries							
United States	275,119	297,486	331,152	348,966	0.78	0.71	0.21
Japan	126,472	127,152	121,594	110,015	-0.05	-0.30	-0.40
Germany	81,700	80,466	76,442	64,244	-0.15	-0.34	-0.70
France	59,024	60,130	61,247	60,475	0.19	0.12	-0.05
United Kingdom	59,022	59,919	61,476	61,635	0.15	0.17	0.01
Italy	57,254	55,985	52,324	43,630	-0.22	-0.45	-0.73
Canada	31,029	33,946	38,266	39,870	0.90	0.80	0.16
Australia	19,222	21,367	24,667	26,060	1.06	0.96	0.22
Countries in political and economic transition							
Russian Federation	145,552	141,134	138,548	129,831	-0.17	-0.22	-0.26
Poland	38,786	39,938	41,542	43,154	0.29	0.26	0.15
Czech Republic	10,346	10,444	10,622	10,875	0.09	0.11	0.09
Hungary	9,940	9,678	9,397	9,223	0.85	0.62	0.32

Newly-industrializing and developing countries

Latin America							
Brazil	174,825	199,327	203,250	264,349	1.31	0.96	0.55
Mexico	102,410	177,651	136,594	161,450	1.39	1.00	0.67
Colombia	37,822	42,959	49,359	56,402	1.27	0.93	0.53
Argentina	36,648	40,755	46,133	53,121	1.06	0.83	0.56
Sub-Saharan Africa							
Nigeria	128,786	168,370	238,397	338,510	2.68	2.32	1.40
Zaire	51,136	68,876	104,639	164,433	2.98	2.79	1.81
Kenya	32,577	43,552	63,360	92,194	2.90	2.50	1.50
Tanzania	34,074	44,154	62,894	91,132	2.59	2.36	1.48
Arab World							
Egypt	69,146	81,490	97,301	117,398	1.64	1.18	0.75
Saudi Arabia	21,257	28,880	42,651	60,897	3.06	2.60	1.42
Iraq	23,753	31,097	42,656	57,691	2.69	2.11	1.12
Algeria	31,158	37,489	45,475	55,674	1.85	1.29	0.81
Asia Pacific							
China	1,284,597	1,388,474	1,526,106	1,605,991	0.78	0.63	0.20
India	1,022,021	1,189,082	1,392,086	1,639,863	1.51	1.05	0.66
Pakistan	161,827	210,104	284,827	381,488	2.61	2.03	1.17
Indonesia	212,731	239,601	275,598	318,802	1.19	0.93	0.58

* *More-developed regions* comprise all countries and areas of North America, Europe, Japan and Australasia.
+ *Less-developed regions* comprise all countries and areas of Latin America, Africa, Asia (excluding Japan) and Oceania (excluding Australasia).

Source: HABITAT (1996: Statistical Annex, Table 1).

Table 11.2 Projected urbanization and the growth of urban population, 2000–25: by economic region and selected countries

	Level of urbanization (per cent) (estimates and projections)			Annual growth rate (per cent) (estimates and projections)	
	1975	2000	2025	1975–2000	2000–25
Advanced capitalist countries					
United Kingdom	88.74	90.00	93.33	0.25	0.31
Germany	81.17	87.69	91.98	0.46	−0.08
Australia	85.92	84.69	88.59	1.24	1.18
United States	73.65	77.46	84.91	1.17	1.11
Japan	75.69	78.39	84.86	0.64	0.16
Canada	75.61	77.16	83.67	1.24	1.16
France	73.02	73.45	81.73	0.48	0.57
Italy	65.64	67.11	76.25	0.22	0.15
Countries in political and economic transition					
Russian Federation	66.43	77.93	85.68	0.96	0.18
Poland	55.40	67.11	78.39	1.29	0.90
Hungary	52.79	67.28	78.67	0.74	0.40
Czech Republic	57.82	66.37	76.22	0.69	0.66
Newly-industrializing and developing countries					
Latin America					
Argentina	80.73	89.40	93.39	1.77	1.10
Brazil	61.15	81.21	88.94	3.06	1.47
Mexico	62.76	77.71	85.82	3.07	1.55
Colombia	60.71	75.21	84.14	2.71	1.51
Sub-Saharan Africa					
Nigeria	23.38	43.29	61.64	5.34	3.88
Kenya	12.92	31.76	51.48	7.05	4.59
Zaire	29.50	31.03	49.82	3.35	4.76
Tanzania	10.08	28.20	48.25	7.17	4.60
Arab World					
Saudi Arabia	58.70	81.80	88.20	5.63	3.09
Iraq	61.39	77.08	85.42	3.98	2.75
Algeria	40.33	59.65	74.05	4.23	2.38
Egypt	43.45	46.36	62.20	2.57	2.54
Asia Pacific					
Indonesia	19.36	40.34	60.74	4.74	2.67
Pakistan	26.40	37.85	56.73	4.53	3.88
China	17.25	34.49	54.51	4.07	2.52
India	21.31	28.56	45.24	3.17	3.08

Source: HABITAT (1996: Annex, Table 3).

Table 11.3 Projected population and growth rates of urban agglomerations, 1995–2015: by economic region and selected countries

		Estimates and projections (000s)			Annual growth (per cent)	
		1995	2005	2015	1995–2005	2005–15
Advanced capitalist countries						
Japan	Tokyo	26,836	28,424	28,701	0.57	0.10
United States	New York	16,329	16,962	17,636	0.38	0.39
France	Paris	9,469	9,584	9,591	0.12	0.01
United Kingdom	London	7,335	7,335	7,335	–	–
Germany	Essen	6,481	6,526	6,526	0.07	–
Canada	Toronto	4,483	5,273	5,716	1.62	0.81
Italy	Milan	4,251	4,251	4,251	–	–
Australia	Sydney	3,590	3,771	4,031	0.49	0.67
Countries in political and economic transition						
Russian Federation	Moscow	9,233	9,302	9,306	0.07	–
Poland	Katowice	3,552	3,742	3,930	0.52	0.49
Hungary	Budapest	2,017	2,027	2,039	0.05	0.06
Czech Republic	Prague	1,225	1,253	1,297	0.23	0.35
Newly-industrializing and developing countries						
Latin America						
Brazil	São Paulo	16,417	19,030	20,783	1.48	0.88
Mexico	Mexico City	15,643	17,293	18,786	1.00	0.83
Argentina	Buenos Aires	10,990	11,772	12,376	0.69	0.50
Colombia	Bogota	5,614	6,904	7,677	2.07	1.16
Africa						
Nigeria	Lagos	10,287	17,037	24,437	5.05	3.61
Zaire	Kinshasa	4,214	6,317	9,855	4.04	4.45
Kenya	Nairobi	2,079	3,484	5,361	5.16	4.31
Tanzania	Dar es Salaam	1,734	2,577	3,965	3.96	4.31
Arab World						
Egypt	Cairo	9,656	11,901	14,494	2.09	1.97
Iraq	Baghdad	4,478	5,794	7,324	2.58	2.34
Algeria	Algiers	3,702	5,157	6,276	3.31	1.96
Saudi Arabia	Riyadh	2,576	3,865	5,117	4.06	2.81
Asia Pacific						
India	Mumbai (Bombay)	15,093	21,208	27,373	3.40	2.55
China	Shanghai	15,082	19,435	23,382	2.54	1.85
Indonesia	Jakarta	11,500	16,748	21,170	3.76	2.38
Pakistan	Karachi	9,863	14,644	20,616	3.95	3.42

Source: HABITAT (1996: Annex, Table 4).

Europe will experience a 25-year upturn in the Kondratieff long-wave cycle in the early years of the new century – based on the development of telecommunications and new industries such as biotechnology (HABITAT, 1996). However, the planned strengthening of the Economic and

Monetary Union and the probable inclusion of several of the countries of East Central Europe within the EU might mask or distort the impact of the cycle on the urban economy.

It is unclear whether these changes will lead to the further growth of cities and towns in the European core to the disadvantage of the continent's periphery, or whether they will produce forces that will counter centralization. Thus, future economic activity could *either* – on the one hand – be concentrated in the so-called 'Blue Banana' (comprising cities and towns in south-east England, Benelux, south-west Germany, Switzerland and north-west Italy) or in the Mediterranean sunbelt (containing urban areas in northern Italy, southern France and north-east Spain); *or* – on the other hand – be dispersed towards the periphery to counter the diseconomies of concentration (such as congestion and environmental costs), and to benefit from improved transportation and telecommunications, and from EU structural funds (HABITAT, 1996). Alternatively, there is evidence that individual cities and towns might benefit more from their inherent economic characteristics than from their location in relation to the core or periphery, while neighbouring places often develop very differently despite similar locations.

The extent to which retirement migration will have an impact on the pattern of urban development in the early twenty-first century is uncertain, and it is also unclear how economic change in East Central Europe will affect the distribution of population throughout the continent (HABITAT, 1996). It is likewise not possible to predict the degree to which employers might wish to reinforce the position of the largest cities or whether they will decentralize their factories, retail complexes and back office jobs to distant towns, and it is uncertain whether residential choice will be determined by centralizing or decentralizing forces.

HABITAT (1996) thus predicts that European economic integration, the development of a technopoles network and a much improved transport and telecommunications infrastructure will each have a major effect on the pattern of urban development in the early twenty-first century, and that stringent environmental policies might also have a major impact on urban areas since they could close down some industries while others would have to fundamentally change their methods of production to meet emission standards.

With regard to both the United States and Canada, it is unclear whether the trends and patterns evident throughout the 1990s will continue into the new century. The age structure of the population and migration are likely to remain significant factors in urban population growth. However, although it is estimated that the proportion of the population over 65 will rise from 12.5 per cent in 1989 to over 21 per cent by 2010, it is uncertain whether America's senior citizens will continue to migrate in large numbers from the metropolises to smaller cities and towns, and to environmentally attractive regions (HABITAT, 1996). It is also uncertain whether immigrants – whose numbers in the future are potentially large – will be principally attracted to areas of labour shortage (where their economic impact will be positive) or to other areas – where immigration might become a source of social tension over jobs, public resources and urban space.

HABITAT (1996) suggests that inter-urban trends evident in the 1980s and early-1990s are likely to continue. Whereas cities in the Great Lakes metropolitan regions and parts of the industrial North-East will continue to stagnate, the coastal regions – particularly in the South and West – are likely to continue to be recipients of considerable industrial investment, internal migration and immigration, particularly from Mexico and Puerto Rico.

Further influences over urban growth include heightened global competition through the revised GATT agreement of 1993, and economic integration as an outcome of the Canada–US Free Trade Agreement of 1988 and (with its extension to Mexico) the North American Free Trade Agreement (NAFTA) in 1993. It is probable that these developments will reinforce the locational attractions of cities in the South and West – including the west coast of Canada, as well as urban areas in many parts of the United States with high-tech industries or high-order service functions. However, urban areas already in decline – for example, rust-belt manufacturing centres (such as Cleveland, Buffalo and Detroit) – will be increasingly unlikely to compete with low-wage cities in Mexico and other low-wage countries.

Notwithstanding regional disparities in urban growth in Western Europe and North America, many inner cities across the devleoped world might be unable to secure adequate investment funds for urban regeneration well into the twenty-first century in the absence of appropriate policies. In consequence they will be characterized by high levels of unemployment, high rates of crime and the evolution of an educational underclass, whereas the affluent – except in small areas of gentrified housing – will continue to move out to more attractive areas (see Hall and Pfeiffer, 2000).

In the less-developed regions of the world, population growth in many cities is likely to continue to surge ahead of economic development. While urban areas are growing worldwide, Asian cities are exploding by 3 per cent per annum and African cities by approximately 4 per cent (table 11.3). People are clearly trading-off rural poverty and the lack of opportunities for appalling city conditions and dismal living standards. Infrastructure is often inadequate for the needs of modern industry and commerce, and its slow and piecemeal development will probably fail to keep pace with the demand for food. The urban poor in particular – whose numbers doubled in the 1990s to 1 billion – are thus likely to face continuing unemployment (or under-employment), poor housing, and severe malnutrition and food shortages unless there is substantial investment in the built-environment, including its infrastructure. It can only be hoped that the International Monetary Fund and the World Bank – through their heavily indebted poor country initiative (HIPC) – will reduce the debts of the world's 41 poorest nations and create the conditions necessary to facilitate an increased level of infrastructure investment as a prelude to sustained urban development. It is also to be hoped that conditions of world trade no longer discriminate against the poorer nations of the world and their burgeoning cities – notwithstanding the need to apply solutions sensitively to the problems of labour-exploitation and income distribution. Clearly it should be a matter of concern that, although trade liberalization stimulates urban growth, it also damages the poor and widens inequalities of income (Madeley, 2000). Based on a sample of 38 countries, research has revealed that between 1965 and 1992 trade agreements – while benefiting the wealthy – correlated negatively with income growth among the poorest 40 per cent of the population (Lunberg and Squire, 2000).

It is within this global context that an understanding of the economics of urbanization, urban growth, urban land use and values, urban housing, the location of non-residential urban land uses, urban development, property development and investment, urban planning, the environment, and urban congestion and transport – all examined in this book – might help decision-makers on the world stage to maximize the benefits and minimize the costs of an increasingly globalized urban economy in the twenty-first century. It remains to be seen, however, whether the governments and institutions of the world will be sufficiently and appropriately proactive to enable this to be achieved.

REFERENCES

HABITAT (1996) *An Urbanizing World: Global Report on Human Settlements 1996*, Oxford: United National Centre for Human Settlements and Oxford University Press.

Hall, P. and Pfeiffer, U. (2000) *Urban Future 21*, London: Spon.

Lunberg, M. and Squire, L. (2000) 'The simultaneous evolution of growth and inequality', Washington DC: World Bank.

Madeley, J. (2000) *Hungry for Trade*, London: Zed.

Index